THE EUROPEAN UNION AND SECURITY SECTOR REFORM

Also from John Harper Publishing in association with DCAF:

The European Union and Terrorism
edited by *David Spence (2007)*

"This book brings together key thinkers and is a welcome analysis of terrorism challenges. David Spence has succeeded in giving us a timely and thoughtful complement to the terrorism debate."

***Franco Frattini**, European Commissioner for Justice, Freedom and Security*

The European Union and Security Sector Reform

edited by

David Spence
and
Philipp Fluri

The European Union and Security Sector Reform

Published by John Harper Publishing
27 Palace Gates Road
London N22 7BW
United Kingdom
www.johnharperpublishing.co.uk

ISBN 978-0-9551144-9-6

Printed and Bound in Great Britain by Cromwell Press Ltd.

TABLE OF CONTENTS

ABOUT THE AUTHORS

Alyson Bailes was Director of the Stockholm International Peace Research Institute (SIPRI) from 2002 until autumn 2007, when she became a visiting professor at the University of Iceland. She spent most of her earlier career in the British Diplomatic Service, finally serving as Ambassador to Finland in 2000-2002, having previously been Political Director of the Western European Union. She writes mainly on European defence and security and on public-private sector relations.

Elmar Brok is a German Christian Democrat MEP, having been first elected to the European Parliament in 1980. From July 1999 to February 2007 he chaired the EP Committee on Foreign Affairs. He represented the EP in the intergovernmental conferences on the Amsterdam, Nice, Constitutional and Lisbon Treaties.

Inger Buxton is an administrator in the European Commission's Directorate General for External Relations on conflict prevention issues. She is a Swedish diplomat who has worked on conflict prevention and peace-building in different capacities in the Swedish Ministry for Foreign Affairs, at the Stockholm International Peace Research Institute (SIPRI), for Save the Children and for the London-based NGO Saferworld. Before joining the Commission, she worked as an Adviser on conflict management in the Swedish International Development Cooperation Agency (Sida). Ms Buxton is currently serving as co-chair of the OECD-DAC Network on Conflict, Peace and Development Co-operation (CPDC).

Patrick Doelle is an administrator at the European Commission. After several years as a criminal police officer in Germany, he worked at the European Institute of Public Administration for a research project on organisational reforms of police and prosecution services in the EU. His career in the Commission started at OLAF before joining EuropeAid where he is currently working in the unit 'Security and Migration'. He is (co-)author of several articles in the area of Justice and Home Affairs.

Alex Dowling is Coordinator of DCAF's Brussels Office, working on NATO and EU security sector reform issues. Previously, Mr Dowling spent one year at the NATO Parliamentary Assembly in Brussels. Before that he studied in London, completing a Master's degree in War Studies at King's College London as well working in the voluntary sector on human rights issues.

Dr Mark Downes currently works for the OECD Development Cooperation Directorate on conflict prevention, peace-building and security issues. He is an Administrator of the DAC Network on Conflict, Peace and Development Cooperation (CPDC) and co-led (with Graham Thompson) the multi-donor process to develop the *OECD DAC Handbook on SSR: Supporting Security and Justice*. Previously Mark worked as Head of the Strategic Development Unit (policing) of the Law Enforcement

Department of the OSCE Mission to Serbia and Montenegro. He has worked and published on a range of conflict and security related issues including post-conflict policing, governance reform and parliamentary oversight of the security sector.

Dr Magnus Ekengren is Senior Researcher and Director of the Programme for European Security Research at the Swedish National Defence College. He was previously Deputy Director at the Policy Planning Unit of the Swedish Ministry for Foreign Affairs. Recent publications include *The Time of European Governance* (Manchester University Press, 2002) and 'New Security Challenges and the Need for New Forms of EU Co-operation - the Solidarity Declaration and the Open Method of Co-ordination' (in *European Security*, 2006).

Dr Philipp Fluri is Deputy Director of the Geneva Centre for the Democratic Control of Armed Forces (DCAF) and Executive Director of DCAF Brussels. Dr Fluri joined the Swiss Department of Defence in 1991 as an international security expert. He served as a Democratisation and Human Rights expert on the OSCE AG to Chechnya in 1995/6 and as the Acting Personal Representative of the OSCE Chairman-in-Office on the Karabakh issue in 1996. Dr Fluri holds doctoral degrees from the Universities of Bern (1987) and Fribourg (1990). He has taught as a Visiting Professor at the University of Pecs/Hungary, and is an Honorary Professor of Taras Shevchenko Pedagogical University/Ukraine.

Catriona Gourlay is a European Commission-funded Marie Curie Research Fellow at the United Nations Institute for Disarmament Research (UNIDIR) in Geneva, where she conducts a research project on EU-UN cooperation in crisis management. Previously, from 1995 to 2005, she was the Executive Director of the International Security Information Service, a Brussels-based research organisation working on European Security and Defence Policy.

Antoine Gouzée de Harven is programme manager in Directorate-General EuropeAid of the European Commission. After a short career in the non-government sector, he joined the European administration where he held three different posts before taking up his current duties in the area of security. He has successively covered the fields of conflict management, resolution and prevention, as well as good governance and human rights. He is the co-author of several publications in the domains of security and human rights.

Duncan Hiscock is a researcher who has written extensively on security issues in the former Soviet Union. He has previously worked as International Consultant to the Director at the International Centre for Policy Studies in Kyiv, Ukraine, and as Project Coordinator for Eastern Europe at Saferworld. Recent publications include *Beyond the Reach of State Monopoly Controls: A Comparative Overview of Russian Controls on Arms Brokering* (PIR, 2007), 'The Commercialisation of Post-Soviet Private Security' in *Private Actors and Security Governance* (DCAF, 2006), and *Security Sector Reform in Armenia* (Saferworld, 2005).

Dr Rory Keane (European Commission, Brussels) works on SSR and DDR in the Democratic Republic of the Congo. He is a former Marie Curie Post-doctoral research fellow and has previously worked on peace building issues, mainly in the Balkans. His most recent publications include: 'EU Foreign Policy: A mix of human security and realist elements' in Sandra J. MacLean, David R. Black, and Timothy M. Shaw eds., *A Decade of Human Security* (Aldershot, UK: Ashgate, 2006); 'Police reform amidst transition: The Organization for Security and Co-operation in Europe' (co-author Mark Downes), *Journal of Civil Wars*, Vol. 8, No 2 (June 2006).

Sebastian Keil studied Political Science, Sociology and Peace & Conflict Studies at Philipps-University Marburg, Germany and at Missouri State University, USA and has written his Masters thesis on Post-Conflict Reconstruction in Afghanistan. During the summer of 2006 he was working as an intern at the Geneva Centre for Security Policy.

Suying Lai is a lobbyist working on conflicts and humanitarian response at Oxfam Novib in The Hague. She was previously a research assistant at DCAF and an intern at the Permanent Delegation of the European Commission to the UN in Geneva. She holds an MA in political science from the Free University Amsterdam.

David Law is a DCAF Senior Fellow and Coordinator of the SSR Working Group. Previously, David was a consultant for technical assistance projects sponsored by the EU and Canada, and lectured on security issues at universities in Europe and North America. From 1984-94, David was a member of NATO's international staff, where he was an advisor to three Secretaries-General. Before joining NATO, he was associated with non-governmental organisations active in inter-parliamentary cooperation, adult education, development, youth work and refugee resettlement.

Derek Lutterbeck is currently Deputy Director of the Mediterranean Academy of Diplomatic Studies in Malta (MEDAC). Prior to joining MEDAC, he worked as a Programme Coordinator at the Geneva Centre for Security Policy (GCSP). His research interests include migration policies and transnational organised crime, as well as security sector reform issues. He earned a PhD in political science from the Graduate Institute of International Studies in Geneva.

Jörg Monar is Professor at the Faculty of law and the Institut d'Etudes Politiques of the Robert Schuman University of Strasbourg where he holds an EU Marie Curie Chair of Excellence on EU internal security governance. He is also Director of the SECURINT project on internal security governance, a Professor and Member of the Academic Council of the College of Europe (Bruges) and a founding editor of the *European Foreign Affairs Review*.

Oksana Myshlovska is Research Assistant for the Security Sector Reform Working Group at the Geneva Centre for the Democratic Control of Armed Forces. She is currently a PhD candidate at the Graduate Institute of

International Studies (Switzerland). She holds a BA degree in Political Science from the Kyiv-Mohyla Academy (Ukraine), a Specialist Degree in International Relations from the Ivan Franko L'viv National University (Ukraine) and an MA in International Relations from the Graduate Institute of International Studies (Switzerland).

Dr Karl-Heinz Rambke has been a faculty member of the Geneva Centre for Security Policy (GCSP) since 2003. He is a general staff officer with the rank of Colonel serving in the German Armed Forces. Seconded by the Federal Ministry of Defence of Germany to the GCSP, he has been active as Co-Director of the European Training Course and as Co-Director of the International Training Course. Currently he is a visiting professor at the Swiss Federal Institute of Technology, Zurich, lecturing in strategic studies.

David Spence is Political Counsellor at the European Commission's Delegation to the international organisations in Geneva. He has been lecturer in politics at the Sorbonne, head of European training in the UK's Civil Service College and secretary of the Commission's task force for German unification. He has also worked in the Commission on ESDP and terrorism and was head of training for the Commission's external delegations. He has edited all three editions of *The European Commission* (John Harper Publishing, London, 3rd edition, 2006), edited *The European Union and Terrorism* (John Harper Publishing, 2007) and was co-editor (with Brian Hocking) of *Foreign Ministries in the EU: Integrating Diplomats* (Palgrave, 2005).

Dr Friedrich Tanner has been Director of the Geneva Centre for Security Policy (GCSP) since October 2006. Prior to this he was Deputy Director (Training and Academic Affairs) of the GCSP and Visiting Professor at the Graduate Institute of International Studies (IUHEI), Geneva. He was the Director of the Mediterranean Academy of Diplomatic Studies for four years, has taught at New Mexico State University and was a visiting scholar at Harvard (CFIA), Johns Hopkins (SAIS) and Princeton (CIS). Dr Tanner received his academic training at the IUHEI (licence, rel. int.) and the Fletcher School of Law and Diplomacy (MALD, PhD). He is the author of numerous publications in the subject areas of conflict resolution, peacekeeping and Mediterranean security.

Graham Thompson is the DFID Conflict Adviser in Sudan. He previously worked as the Security Sector Reform (SSR) Adviser for the Conflict, Humanitarian and Security Department (CHaSe) in the UK Department for International Development (DFID), where he was the lead adviser for the Global Conflict Prevention Pool Security Sector Reform strategy. He was also the Chair of the OECD Development Assistance Committee's SSR task team until January 2007 and has been centrally involved in developing the Implementation Framework for Security Sector Reform (IF-SSR). Graham has experience in supporting Security and Justice Sector Reform at a practitioner and policy level working both within DFID and across wider UK Government through the Africa and Global Conflict Prevention Pools. He has provided support to the design and delivery of Security and Justice

Development programmes in Sierra Leone, Ghana, Nigeria and South Africa. Through his work in the Security Sector Development Advisory Team, Graham provided the UK input to the UK/US/Canada supported National Security Strategy development process in Jamaica and led the design and delivery of an influential SSR programme in Guatemala as well as providing advice to initiatives in Indonesia, Sri Lanka and Afghanistan.

Dr Willem van Eekelen started his career as a member of the Netherlands Foreign Service. He was elected to Parliament in 1977 and served as State Secretary for Defence, for European Affairs, and as Minister of Defence. He was Secretary General of the Western European Union between 1989 and 1994 and subsequently was a Senator in the Netherlands Parliament. He is a member of the governing boards of the Stockholm International Peace Research Institute (SIPRI) and Centre for European Security Studies (CESS) and of the advisory board of DCAF.

Authors write in a personal capacity and the views they express do not necessarily reflect those of the institutions for which they work.

PREFACE

By David Spence and Philipp Fluri

Since its inception in 2000, the Geneva Centre for the Democratic Control of Armed Forces (DCAF) has cooperated with governments throughout the world and with the European Union to promote good governance and democratic reform of the security sector. As an International Foundation with 49 member governments it has researched and documented good practice, encouraged the development and promotion of relevant norms at national and international levels, made policy recommendations and provided in-country advice and practical assistance programmes, especially in the countries of Europe's 'New Neighbourhood'. DCAF's Brussels office is now a platform for deepening cooperation with the European Union and the Brussels international community.

This book is a contribution to the widespread discussion of the EU's increasing involvement in security issues. Although the threats of the Cold War need no longer concern us, Europe now faces a much more volatile and complicated security environment. New threats have emerged outside the EU, both within and between States, and the EU is concerned as much by the effects of these threats in terms of its own security as it is in terms of what it can do to assist its international partners to face the same threats. Indeed, threats are not limited to the traditional forms of intra- and inter-state conflict. The world is increasingly confronted by organised crime and the continuing threats of the post- 9/11 world. Here again a sound response integrates all components of the security sector.

Achieving good governance of the security sector is recognised by international actors and development donors as not only the key to improving the efficiency and effectiveness of conflict prevention, but also as an indispensable contribution to ensuring the rule of law, democratic principles, steady development and human security. The EU endeavours to help other countries face the challenges in the transition towards democracy by strengthening civilian and parliamentary oversight mechanisms with the aim of democratic control of the security sector and its component parts – the armed forces, paramilitary forces, police, border guards, intelligence agencies and state security structures in general.

Both the EU response to terrorism and its efforts in the field of security sector reform have been documented and analysed by DCAF over the years. The European Union's security sector governance policy has evolved quickly[1], and the need for a democratically justifiable response to the challenges of political terrorism remains paramount.[2] The objective of this book is to enable government and non-government experts to describe how they see the EU's security sector reform policy evolving. It gives a voice to those who work and analyse security issues in the European Union on a daily basis. The book includes both personal and institutional statements and observations. The reasoning behind these various policy approaches is simi-

1 Hanggi, Heiner and Tanner, Fred (2005) *Promoting security sector governance in the EU's neighbourhood.* EU-ISS Chaillot Paper No. 80, July 2005

2 Spence, David (Ed.), *The EU and Terrorism*, 2007 (John Harper Publishing)

lar, so we have left a degree of (we believe welcome) duplication in the texts. Our hope is that the book will carry the message of the crucial contribution of security sector reform both to those who work in this specialised area and those whose work may well rely for its effectiveness on the premise of sound security sector governance.

Acknowledgments

The editors would like to thank Ms Sue Lai without whose competent assistance and cooperation this book would not have been published. Further thanks go to Ambassador Alyson Bailes for her highly pertinent introduction and to Dr Magnus Ekengren and the Swedish Defence Academy for providing a conference framework for authors and other experts to share experience and analysis.

Geneva and Brussels, November 2007

Introduction: The EU and Security Sector Reform

by Alyson Bailes

Security sector reform has come full circle in the last fifteen years, which coincidentally cover the period of existence of the EU's Common Foreign and Security Policy. Before the fall of the Berlin Wall SSR was a concept most used in the field of development policy, evolving out of the concern to promote good governance in less developed countries so that aid would not be misapplied or wasted, *inter alia* through excessive military spending. From 1990 onwards it became a very important aspect of transformation, partnership, and enlargement policy in Europe, and the most prominent laboratories of SSR became the former Communist countries, which needed to adjust their defence and security policies in order to qualify for membership of NATO and – to a lesser extent – the EU. This gave a significant twist to the concept. Reform in the context of future Alliance membership clearly did not mean reducing the national defence effort, but in some cases actually increasing it, while making it less 'national' in the sense of shifting the focus increasingly towards readiness for multilateral operations abroad.

Nowadays, with NATO and the EU having enlarged to cover practically the whole territory of traditional non-Russian Europe, SSR experts are beginning to look back towards the wider world for their next set of tasks – but with some significant differences from the 1980s. One obvious difference is that the present targets for concerted international efforts at SSR are often *post-conflict* states or, in some cases, governments still struggling to put conflicts behind them in the sense of being able to control their whole territory: witness Afghanistan, Colombia, Georgia and Moldova, or in its own special way, Iraq. Two more subtle differences lie in the total geographical range of SSR, and in the range of those who are offering to help promote it. First, the continuing impact of the events of 1989-90 can be seen in the fact that Western states can offer to support defence reform in societies that used to be deeply under Soviet control, like the Central Asians, although these countries clearly pose much bigger problems than the Central Europeans. And there would be few people bold enough to attempt SSR activities in Russia itself.

Secondly, promoting and supporting SSR is not now, and in this author's view should not be, the monopoly of a few strong Western countries that happen also to be major aid donors. Nations who experienced SSR in the 1990s can pass on their experience to others in the 2000s, but we are also seeing processes that equate to SSR (even if they are not always called that) going on between countries in non-European regions, such as parts of Africa, Latin America and the Caribbean. Finally, in all regions and contexts there is stronger pressure than ever for states to run their SSR programmes not in isolation but within a properly coordinated institutional or at least multilateral framework, using standards that are as transparent and as universally accessible as possible.

Any policy field with such a complex history is liable to suffer from complications, ranging from identity confusion to contradictions between differing motives, methods and interests and perhaps even some questioning of legitimacy. In these introductory remarks to the substantive chapters of this book, challenges of this kind will be taken as a guide not for the sake of accentuating the negative, but because they raise questions that are truly interesting and may illuminate challenges of present-day security and politics ranging well beyond SSR itself. In logical order, the first question is: are we sure we know what SSR is and what it covers? The second question is: why are we so sure that we (i.e, the Europeans and other 'Westerners') are the right people to help with it and that we have the means to succeed? The third question concerns how to reconcile SSR with other aims and processes in security or governance that various people see as being in contradiction to it, or that have been found to cut across it in practice. Here such issues are pertinent as the distinctions between SSR and DDR (Disarmament, Demobilisation and Reintegration), or the broader issue of security and development, SSR and the post-9/11 slogan of democracy promotion, or for that matter SSR and the arms trade – all issues on which the EU has pronounced in no uncertain terms over the past four years.

What is SSR?

It is important to recall that SSR started as a tool of 'good governance' policies. Even if it has grown a long way since then, it will start to lose its distinctness and credibility if it ever loses contact with such fundamental goals and values as pluralistic democracy and democratic control (including the role of parliaments), transparency, honesty and humanity. More specifically, the World Bank's authoritative definition of what constitutes 'good governance' in general refers to a voice for the people and accountability for the government: political stability and non-violence; government effectiveness, regulatory quality and the rule of law; and last but not least, control of corruption. 'Good governance' in all of these senses can coincide with 'good defence'; so no-one should have any basic problem with SSR also promoting defence modernisation and efficiency, above all when the focus includes interoperability and thus creates new capacities for cooperative international peace missions. However, if we ever find ourselves promoting an efficient, modern defence (with or without exportable capacities) in a given country without doing anything to democratise the process, we are not only failing in the prime purpose of SSR but will also possibly be wasting our time: the progress made will not be strongly anchored at popular level and could be overthrown, if either the people get more power or the rulers change their minds. This objection can arguably be directed at much of the USA's security assistance since 9/11 (e.g. Azerbaijan, Kazakhstan and Uzbekistan until recently; Pakistan, Colombia…); and – without wanting to go further into that argument here – it can surely be concluded that the EU cannot afford to make the same mistake, if it wants both to use its limited resources productively and to keep its relatively 'clean', benign and peaceful international image.

In fact it is doubtful whether the relevant decision-makers and experts in Brussels would ever go down the road of building up a set of military satellites and collaborators for the EU without regard for their democratic record

– if only because consensus 'at 27' would not be achievable. But there is a reminder here that we may need to look carefully both at the interaction between an EU SSR programme and what EU nations may be doing *individually* in their defence or security-related assistance contacts with some of the same countries, and at what the planners of the European Security and Defence Policy (ESDP) might be planning with them for the purposes of purely military cooperation (bases, logistics etc). Europe, as a whole, may otherwise potentially end up sending mixed messages. Conversely, the image and coherence of the operational side of ESDP could be much helped by considering a possible SSR dimension and/or follow-on programme for every ESDP conflict management operation or, at least, making sure that any defence training and transformational services delivered by the EU in the process can be fitted into a larger, coherent, SSR network.

A different point on the *nature* of SSR concerns its functional scope and here it is hard to disagree with the interpretation held by the EU (and the OECD-DAC) that it covers more than traditional military organs and activities. What we might call the vertical expansion of the concept to cover everything from heads of government down to the roles of private companies, NGOs and individual citizens has been accompanied over the last decade by a horizontal expansion to cover (at the least) border guards, any other paramilitary forces, the police, the law and justice system, especially as it relates to public order, and the work of intelligence agencies. In this author's view there is a strong case for the concept also to take account of the 'defence economy', including not just armaments production but the handling of industries with dual-use nuclear, chemical or biomedical capacities that are important for non-proliferation policy; and the handling of critical infrastructure and civil emergency management. This set of aspects brings us squarely into the still rather under-analysed (and under-regulated) area of relationships between the public authorities and the private business sector in tackling security challenges.

Of course, no-one would think it realistic for current providers of SSR, including the EU, to offer detailed reform prescriptions for these last areas – and still less for other new and fashionable dimensions of security like energy and the environment – not least because not many of our own countries have got a proper grip on them yet. But when talking to the more central and traditional security authorities and helping them in the first phases of designing their overall security concepts, plans and coordination structures, donors surely need at least to ask them how they intend to handle these less traditional areas and, in particular, how hard they have thought about the proper distribution of resources and bureaucratic efforts between traditional defence – including external missions – and the other areas more relevant to internal, societal and individual human security. It is a cliché nowadays to recognise that defence forces as such are of very limited use in tackling even 'new threats' of human origin like terrorism or proliferation. Even the most perfect military reform is of very little help to a society facing mass deaths from bird 'flu, AIDS or starvation. Even more to the point in the normative framework of SSR, the rights and welfare of parliaments, of civil society and of individuals can be just as much damaged by misconduct of police, border and intelligence personnel, by private security companies or by companies that cause massive environmental pollution and careless accidents, as they can by the ravages of uncontrolled military forces.

SSR and other objectives

What of the broader interface between SSR and other tools and policies designed to build security and good governance? First, what is the relationship between DDR and SSR in post-conflict cases? Although SSR can also and should also be applied as a conflict prevention measure or in states that are not at risk of conflict at all, it clearly or even primarily has a place after conflict where it should not be seen as a rival or enemy to DDR, but rather as a complementary tool or even a guarantee of the correct wider framework in which DDR should be carried out. Although most conflicts have seen an over-large proportion of the population resorting to arms and thus require early action to disarm and reintegrate a large number of them, it is hard to think of a case where it is right or practical to leave a nation with no army at all. Redesigning that army and other crucial parts of the security sector then becomes a proper task for SSR and ought to start in parallel with DDR. Otherwise there is a risk of an unclear and inappropriate framework for any remaining armed forces on the one hand, and on the other the possibility of a security vacuum, exploitation by neighbours, and/or a demand for the indefinite presence of foreign forces, just as we have seen in Iraq.

A similar answer may be given on the broader issue of how to reconcile security and development policies. It has long been obvious that good, sustainable development is unlikely to work in countries that spend too much on the military, or where the military and other security actors have excessive rights compared with the rest of the population. But recent experience has made abundantly plain that unless you can give – or give back – lasting external and internal security to a weak and troubled state, it has no real hope of succeeding in peaceful development either. And it is more likely that all external aid poured into the country (including humanitarian aid) will end up wasted or having perverse effects. A very useful tool of policy in such cases – as recognised even by the latest version of the USA's National Security Strategy – may be to encourage the growth of regional communities with direct or indirect security agendas that can surround and support the suffering state and hopefully release it sooner from the need to depend for its security and welfare on intervening states from thousands of miles away. If Europe's own history teaches us anything it is, surely, that building good security and good SSR is much easier when you do it across a region as a whole than if you try to get good results from isolated protégé states still stuck in the middle of a backward and predominantly hostile environment.

This leads me to a short remark on SSR and the more ideological agenda of 'democracy promotion' that has been an important driver of US policies since 9/11 – even if a little less has been heard of it in President George W. Bush's second term. The states that the USA has singled out both as its favoured democratic partners and as its targets for regime change have often had one thing in common, namely that they are somewhat isolated in their regions and have unstable relations with the dominant local powers – Israel with the Arab states, Azerbaijan with Moscow, Taiwan with China and so on. Now, it is surely rather hard to teach a partner state SSR as part of democratic reform when you are at the same time giving it massive military aid, perhaps much more than it can sensibly and transparently use, to build it up against its neighbours as a kind of strategic proxy. You also do not create a very easy environment for SSR by forcibly invading a state and compelling it to change its regime. Our own unlawful use of force may be the problem in some such cases, by sending double messages; but more often the problem is that we are making it even harder for the affected state to live at peace with its neighbours, and thus creating a climate in which its future defence spending is likely to be either excessive or insufficient or both. This is one reason why I believe the EU could, paradoxically, be a rather good carrier of the SSR message: precisely because it is not (yet) playing its own military strategic game in most parts of the world, and would genuinely like to see local states getting on well with each other rather than picking up military proxies and protégés for itself.

Last and not least, should we see national arms sales as always a complication for SSR and as inevitably conveying double standards and mixed messages? Surely not, because in our own European efforts for military modernisation and interoperability we have urged each other explicitly to buy more state-of-the-art defence equipment of more compatible kinds. If it were wrong to rearm then, frankly, the whole of Central Europe's SSR experience would have no legitimacy at all! Through the European Defence Agency (EDA) the EU is now actively promoting the joint production and potentially joint marketing of such items, including outside the European area. On the other side, the EU has a state-of-the-art code of conduct to prevent the irresponsible export of conventional arms to the wrong people by any of its members: though it is widely, and correctly, felt that the code would be much more effective and convincing if it could be put in legally binding form. There is, therefore, a great deal to be said for bringing the question of equipment procurement explicitly into European SSR dialogues with other countries and – much as with the level of defence spending – arguing with them that it is not armaments as such that are wrong, but illogical, non-transparent and corrupt methods of choosing, acquiring and using them. We should of course also think about including adequate teaching and clear norms in our SSR packages covering the universal limitations on armaments that all good states should respect, and including not just WMD-related controls but also the various prohibitions and limitations on use laid out in humanitarian law.

Who should do SSR?

This brings us back to the core question of why the EU or European countries individually should think they are qualified to help other countries with security sector reform, using the definitions and against the background laid out above. In actuality, the very modern, typically broad and multifunctional European vision of security is both a major asset and a potential handicap. Generally speaking, European states that belong to the EU or NATO or both do not design their own defences today on the assumption of a military attack. We may keep some elements of territorial defence as it were in reserve, particularly in Northern Europe, but we more and more design, train and equip the cream of our forces to take part in multilateral military interventions far away from the homeland. In many countries we have also defined homeland security against the so-called 'new threats' as an important task of our forces, and we have looked at new ways that the military and police and various civilian actors could work together for those kinds of scenarios and also in natural disasters affecting their own territory. In Central Europe, where most Western states gained their main experience of promoting SSR in the 1990s, we basically imported those same concepts: we set out at the same time to make Central European forces more interoperable for EU- and NATO-led missions, and to encourage them to toughen up their civilian defences, particularly in terms of border control, which was a *sine qua non* of entry to the EU and to the Schengen system.

Now, this kind of modern or even post-modern, internationalised or 'sublimated' military profile may make perfect sense in the integrated European environment – even if a lot of Central Europeans as well as Nordic populations are not entirely happy with how far it has been pushed and how fast. But there are very few if any other regions of the world that enjoy a similar local and external strategic environment. Even the non-European countries that contribute the highest numbers of UN peacekeepers – Bangladesh, India and Pakistan – have very real military threats to contend with in their own region, mainly from each other. And the same goes for countries as close to the European Union as Georgia, Moldova and Azerbaijan, which find themselves in a quite different security world from our own, with barely frozen conflicts and/or serious internal insurgencies affecting their own territory. Even countries recovering from conflict in regions like Africa, where on the face of it Europe can make a real difference through multifunctional peace-building contributions, may need to be rebuilt first as 'strong states', with strong territorial defence policies, probably including a fair and universal system of conscription, in order to reaffirm the government's authority and unity and to guarantee control of the national territory before anyone can even start dreaming of going out to help with other people's crises or of 'professionalising' defence in general. SIPRI's study, over the last five years, of defence spending in a wide range of African states, including such tragic cases of conflict as the Congo and Sierra Leone, has rather unexpectedly shown that we often need to help such states spend more, not less, on defence as they start on the road to recovery.[1] As in other fields of public business, you often need an initial injection of resources to support a reform that will provide more security at hopefully decreasing cost in the longer term.

All this leads to a pretty simple conclusion, namely that our credentials for offering other people a model of SSR do not lie in the present-day European model of defence and security policy as such. Indeed, we could be making a big mistake by trying to impose that model on many of the countries outside Europe who need and want our help. But that just leads us back to the earlier point that SSR is about the defence process or the way of designing and running defence forces, rather than about precisely what size and sort of forces any given country should have. To return to the SIPRI

1 See Hutchful, E. and Omitoogun, W., *Budgeting for the Military Sector in Africa: The processes and mechanisms of control*, Oxford University Press: Oxford, 2006.

African study, we were able to conclude that certain techniques of rational threat assessment, defence prioritisation, transparency and honesty in the allocation and use of military funding would help all the countries that we looked at regardless of their widely varying substantial needs. And surely we Europeans are both qualified and justified to teach others this democratic way of defence?

Well, yes and no. Standards of defence and security governance in Europe as a whole are generally high, but our national practices are not at all consistent in terms of democratic process and control, any more than all European defence forces yet share the same national defence philosophy and force profile. The episode of the Iraq war shows how widely our national views can differ on basics like the legitimate use of force and the acceptability of pre-emption. It also reminds us that different countries' constitutions vary widely in terms of how far parliaments can control the act of going to war, how much information governments have to release to their parliaments and peoples, who controls the money-bags and so forth. If we look at broader aspects of the security sector we see a similar variety in the degree of democratic control over intelligence agencies, or over the rights of ethnic groups vis-à-vis military service and the police, or over the nature of police forces themselves – countries like Britain feeling that a permanent armed police force would be an offence to the constitution, whereas in Italy the armed Carabinieri are not only accepted but widely respected and admired. So even if we can reduce the hard core of a European SSR policy to the agenda of democratic process and democratic control, exactly what country's version of those things are we going to teach? Are we going to have to try to agree on some harmonised or average EU 'standard' in all these matters before the EU as an institution can go out and conduct SSR programmes? Or should we make a virtue precisely out of the fact that we have a wide range of acceptable national models to offer; but then how do we avoid making it too confusing and complicated for the countries receiving our help?

Last but not least, under the heading of European qualifications, we need to think hard and at an early stage about the resources and the leverage we have to succeed in the goal of SSR, which is nothing less than to persuade countries to make possibly sweeping changes in precisely the areas of government that are considered most vital for national security and most sensitive for national sovereignty. Again, our experience of reform in the Central European nations now belonging to the EU and NATO, or even in the Western Balkans, may not be a good guide because in Western Europe we frankly had it too easy in the last decade. We did provide some concepts, some training and some equipment, although usually at commercial prices for the larger items. But all the really hard choices and sacrifices were made by the countries themselves, under the pressure of their driving will to get into both NATO and the EU as soon as possible. That is not an incentive that we can currently offer with any confidence even to a country already in NATO like Turkey, let alone to our Eastern or Southern Mediterranean neighbours. And that particular kind of leverage is clearly irrelevant to cases in Africa or Latin America or even Central Asia.

We are thus standing on a weaker foundation than before, exactly when we have to start tackling cases that are tougher than before because the countries have less rational defence systems or fewer democratic approaches to governance in general, or both. How for instance do we propose to do SSR in a Central Asian or North African country where one man, the monarch or the president, ultimately makes all defence decisions? Even if we are skilful in adapting our concepts to such environments, where will we find the sticks and carrots to drive the lessons home? Are we proposing to make progress in SSR an actual condition for receiving other kinds of benefits from the EU, as we did with the 'non-proliferation clause' on Weapons of Mass Destruction (WMD) policy a couple of years ago? Can we tell countries that their SSR performance will, more specifically, determine the EU's treatment of them in terms of defence assistance, or the licensing of arms sales? But the EU does not actually have a defence assistance programme, and those particular carrots are still held in the hands of European nations who are not very likely – as hinted above – to let their bilateral assistance or arms supply relationships be steered *positively* from Brussels in the name of a collective SSR policy, even if they accept some collective judgements on whom we should *not* sell to. All these issues exist independently of the question of who in the EU's central mechanisms should fund and execute such a policy. And even if we could address that question for once without silly institutional jealousies, we would come up against the fact that a good SSR programme needs a combination of military, police, civilian, financial, hardware and development aid competences that at the moment are scattered between a number of different staffs and organs in Brussels, let alone in national capitals.

In closing, one final generalisation may be in place. The EU is in several ways one of the best potential agents to carry out a modern-day, wide-reaching SSR programme, but it is very far from being the easiest choice. This author would strongly contend that it is worth making the effort to overcome the many problems, and not only because SSR is a worthy and worthwhile goal in itself. As this introduction to the excellent detailed chapters in this book has attempted to show, getting our minds clear on what is needed to operate a European SSR programme coherently and professionally might also help us to get our minds clear on many of the larger and still unresolved issues of the European defence and security personality today.

I: SECURITY SECTOR GOVERNANCE AND SECURITY SECTOR REFORM: THE EU POLICY FRAMEWORK

1. The Evolution of the Concepts of Security Sector Reform and Security Sector Governance: the EU perspective

David Law and Oksana Myshlovska

Introduction: Sources and Content of the EU's Approach to SSR

The idea of security sector reform (SSR) originated in the 1990s from donors' concerns that many developing countries were failing to achieve sustainable development because of conflict and insecurity. The Minister for Development Cooperation of the Netherlands, Agnes van Ardenne, captured this connection between security and development when she observed that: '...There is no point investing in roads, schools and hospitals if they can be destroyed by war the next day'.[1] A similar preoccupation put SSR on the agenda of countries in transition in Central and Eastern Europe, which as a rule had inherited weak, corrupt, and unaccountable security sectors from the previous communist regimes. More recently, as the international community has intensified its support for peacebuilding in conflict and post-conflict settings, SSR has also become a central feature of crisis management and reconstruction strategies.

The EU has a great deal to offer in the area of SSR. Since its inception, the EU has been a significant player in the field of international development and is now the world's largest contributor of development aid. With the development of its Common Foreign and Security Policy (CFSP) and European Security and Defence Policy (ESDP) and in view of its growing experience in civilian and military crisis management operations, the EU has also emerged as a major security player on the international stage. To guide its many foreign, security and development policy activities – what the EU calls its 'external action' – it has also been a major innovator of programmes and methodologies, including SSR, arguably one of the most promising policy instruments that the EU has adopted to date. The EU boasts an immense cooperation network spanning national governments, intergovernmental and nongovernmental organisations. This is of particular importance for SSR, which more often than not is implemented by a consortium of different actors. In sum, the EU calls on considerable expertise in a broad range of development and governance programmes in various socio-economic contexts.

The EU has been involved in a number of SSR areas, including police and military operations, efforts aimed at strengthening the rule of law and reinforcing judicial and penitentiary systems, the civilian aspects of crisis management and civil emergency protection. It has, however, until very recently lacked a coherent approach towards the security sector. This began to change very rapidly as of 2003 when the EU adopted its first ever European Security Strategy (see Annex 1). The strategy provided a new framework for the EU's ambition to become a global security player. It also featured SSR as one of the EU's key external policy instruments. In 2005, the EU adopted its Strategy for Africa, and the Democratic Republic of Congo became the first recipient of an EU SSR mission. This was followed in November 2005, by agreement of the European Council of a *Concept for European Security and Defence Policy (ESDP) support to SSR* (Annex 3), outlining the EU role in civilian and military crisis management missions in the framework of the ESDP. This concept paper described SSR activities as a central feature of these missions, all of which have been undertaken under the EU's CFSP. In May 2006, the European Commission complemented the Council's SSR concept by developing a (first pillar) *Concept for European Community Support for SSR*. The Commission's document identified seven SSR-relevant policy areas, which fall under first pillar competence: Development Cooperation, Enlargement, the Stabilisation and Association Process, the European Neighbourhood Policy, Conflict Prevention and Crisis Management, Democracy and Human Rights and the External Dimension of the area of Freedom, Security and Justice. An overarching EU framework for SSR was then adopted in June 2006, defining the spheres of competence for EU institutions and spelling out the modalities for their common action.

The EU's approach to security issues has been influenced by a variety of sources; it has been shaped by the activities of its member states, the EU's participation in the work of other international organisations active in the security field and its own experience in implementing internal and external policies related to SSR. This chapter analyses these three strands of the EU's contribution to SSR. First, it sets out a conceptual framework for understanding the EU's engagement in SSR. The next section discusses how some EU member states, namely the UK and the Netherlands, have played a key role in shaping EU thinking about SSR. The chapter then looks at how the EU has drawn upon the work of other international organisations, namely, the OECD, the OSCE, NATO and the Council of Europe, and the nature of the SSR-related cooperation arrangements that have been established among these organisations. Following a review of the SSR activities managed and carried out respectively by the EU Council and Commission, the concluding section suggests how future EU presidencies might further develop the SSR agenda.

EU and SSR: Conceptual Considerations

The role and scope of the EU have grown substantially during the last decade. The EU has taken on twelve new member states and is set to take on several more as the Balkan states reach eligibility for membership. At the same time, the EU has become active in an increasing number of policy areas, both externally and internally. Notwithstanding the resistance of certain capitals, the supranational level has gained responsibility for more functions from member states than it has relinquished to them, though it has done so in a shared multi-pillar structure incorporating areas remaining under intergovernmental control. The structure is characterised by complex inter-relationships and an arguably untidy division of competences between the Council, the Commission, the European Parliament, and member states. As a result, there is frequently considerable overlap in the programme activities carried out by various EU actors in different country contexts. Not only is there consequent turf fighting between the rival bureaucracies involved, but decision-making mechanisms and budgeting timeframes vary across EU actors, often resulting in poor coordination.

The nature of the EU SSR concepts and activities reflects the nature of the EU itself. The Council and the Commission have developed their own SSR concepts to match their policy and operational needs. CFSP/ESDP activities fall under the second pillar, the reserve of intergovernmental action, while other external actions fall under the first pillar, or community action. These are managed in the supranational framework by the Commission. Responsibility for third pillar activities is divided between the Council and the Commission. Security issues have tended mainly to be a Council prerogative. However, with the emergence of the SSR policy framework and its broad approach to security, involving inter alia development, human rights, human security and good governance dimensions, security has become a cross-cutting issue for all EU institutions. SSR provides a unique opportunity to develop a unified EU approach to security across the various mandates and activities of its diverse decision makers and policy contexts. Table 1 provides an overview of what and who is at stake.

Table 1. *The EU involvement in SSR*

<table>
<tr><th>Actor</th><th>Commission</th><th>Council</th><th>EU and other international organisations (IOs)</th></tr>
<tr><td>Framework</td><td>supranational</td><td>intergovernmental</td><td>cooperation</td></tr>
<tr><td rowspan="2">Main areas of SSR and SSR-related activities</td><td>First pillar activities:
Development cooperation, Enlargement, the Stabilisation and Association Process, the European Neighbourhood Policy, Conflict Prevention and Crisis Management, Democracy and Human Rights, and the External Dimension of the area of Freedom, Security and Justice</td><td>Second pillar activities:
European Security and Defense Policy (ESDP), EU battle groups, European Rapid Reaction Force, PSOs</td><td rowspan="2">SSR guidelines, SSR Implementation Framework (OECD)
Peacekeeping, human rights, development (UN)
PSOs (NATO)
Democratic control of armed forces (OSCE)
Human rights (CoE)</td></tr>
<tr><td colspan="2">Third pillar activities (divided responsibility between the Council and the Commission):
Police and Judicial Co-operation in Criminal Matters (PJCC)): trafficking (drugs, weapons and human beings), terrorism, organised crime, border control, police cooperation</td></tr>
</table>

continued:

Actor	Commission	Council	EU and other international organisations (IOs)
Framework	**supranational**	**intergovernmental**	**cooperation**
SSR-related decision-making bodies	- Vice-President of the Commission for Justice, Freedom & Security - EU Commissioners for: Development and Humanitarian Aid, Enlargement, External Relations & European Neighbourhood Policy - Policy Directorate General (DG) for Justice, Freedom and Security - External Relations DGs for: Development, Enlargement, EuropeAid Co-Operation Office, External Relations, Humanitarian Aid	- European Council - Council of the EU - Presidency of the Council -High Representative for CFSP - General Affairs and External Relations Council - Justice and Home Affairs Council - Political and Security Committee (PSC) - European Union Military Committee (EUMC) - European Union Military Staff (EUMS) - Politico-Military Group - The Civilian Crisis Management Committee (CIVICOM)	OECD: OECD DAC UN: DPKO, Peacebuilding Commission UNDP: Bureau for Crisis Prevention & Recovery NATO: North Atlantic Council and partnership bodies OSCE: Forum for Security Cooperation, Conflict Prevention Center, Strategic Police Matters Unit, Action Against Terrorism Unit CoE: Committee of Ministers, Parliamentary Assembly
Cooperation patterns/ mechanisms	Article 3 of the Treaty on the European Union requires EU institutions to co-ordinate their actions closely Common actions of the Commission and the Council (and other EU institutions) in the CFSP framework are carried out through the following mechanisms: General guidelines Common strategies Joint actions Common positions		The EU plays the following roles vis-à-vis other IOs: - Complementing the lead organisations (UN, NATO) - Burden-sharing (UN, OSCE, NATO, CoE) - Provision of financial and political support for the UN and regional organisations (OSCE, ECOWAS, AU) - Creation of regional organisations (Stability Pact for South Eastern Europe) The EU has concluded cooperation agreements with the following IOs: NATO-EU Berlin Plus arrangements, Joint Declaration on EU-UN Co-operation in Crisis Management, EU-OSCE Cooperation in Conflict Prevention, Crisis Management and Post-Conflict Rehabilitation
Budget	Various thematic and geographic budgets, including: Instrument for Pre-accession Assistance, European Neighbourhood and Partnership Instrument, European Development Fund (EDF), European Investment Bank (EIB)	CFSP budget (general budget of the European Community for operations other than having military or defence implications) ATHENA mechanism (financing of the common costs of EU operations having military or defence implications)	EU member states contribute over two thirds of the NATO and OSCE budgets, over four fifths of the Council of Europe budget, about two fifths of the UN regular and peacekeeping operations budget and around half of the contributions to UN funds and programmes

The two SSR concepts developed by the Council and Commission have a number of features in common. Drawing heavily upon the Guidelines developed by the OECD DAC (the Development Assistance Committee of the Organisation for Economic Cooperation and Development), they use the same definitions of SSR and are oriented by the same SSR principles. The EU has adopted the OECD's broad definition of the security sector, which includes all groups in society that are capable of using force as well as the institutions that manage, direct, oversee and monitor them, and otherwise play a role in the development of a country's security policy and the provision of its security.

The main difference between the two concepts is functional. The activities carried out by the Commission are exclusively civilian in nature. Those of the Council, on the other hand, can be either civilian or military, or involve a combination of civilian and military means. The background to the involvement of the Commission and the Council in SSR activities also differs. Many activities that fall under the first pillar date back to the foundation of the European Community. ESDP, on the other hand, is a relatively new sphere of EU activity. ESDP is a post-Amsterdam Treaty (1997) extension to the Common Foreign and Security Policy, which only became part of the *acquis* in 1992. To date, 17 ESDP operations have been carried out, covering a wide range of SSR activities, from police and military missions to rule of law and peace monitoring missions.

The concepts were designed to complement each other. As mentioned in the *Concept for European Security and Defence Policy (ESDP) support to SSR*, its purpose is to develop SSR as a policy framework that helps ensure 'more coordinated and strategic approaches to Community activities falling under the different policy instruments'. The European Commission's Communication *A Concept for European Community Support for SSR* insists, as does the *Concept for ESDP Support to SSR*, that EU support to SSR needs to be coherent across the three pillars. The conclusions adopted by the European Council on 12 June 2006 bring the two concepts together under an overall EU policy framework for SSR. Table 2 below compares the Council's and Commission's concepts, looks at what the two documents have in common, how they differ and what the areas of convergence are.

Table 2. *Comparison of the Council's and Commission's SSR concepts*

	Council ***Concept for European Security and Defence Policy (ESDP) support to SSR***	**Commission** ***Concept for European Community Support for SSR***
General	The document contains a list of general SSR norms, principles and guidelines and enumerates generic SSR-relevant activities. CFSP is a recent area of EU activity, having been agreed in the 1992 Maastricht Treaty. ESDP was institutionalised in the 2000 Nice Treaty. ESDP's first activities were, however, only launched much later with the first police mission, to Bosnia-Herzegovina, and the first military operation, in FYROM, in 2003.	The document provides an overview of SSR-related activities in the following areas: Development Cooperation, Enlargement, the Stabilisation and Association Process, the European Neighbourhood Policy, Conflict Prevention and Crisis Management, Democracy and Human Rights, and the External Dimension of the area of Freedom, Security and Justice. Some Community actions go back to the foundation of the European Community.

continued:		
	Council ***Concept for European Security and Defence Policy (ESDP) support to SSR***	**Commission** ***Concept for European Community Support for SSR***
Similarities	Both concepts: - relate to the external action of the EU - take the OECD's definition of the security sector, SSR and SSR principles as their basis - take a broad approach to SSR - do not work out EU-specific SSR decision mechanisms and instruments - identify the same country contexts in which SSR can be carried out: relatively stable countries, countries in transition, and post-conflict countries - envision the integration of SSR into national development plans or broader multi-lateral frameworks - have as their objective to make EU support to SSR coherent across the three pillars	
Differences	The document is broad in nature; it contains only generic SSR principles. The document is not country specific; it refers to SSR for "EU partner countries". In the Council document, the main areas of SSR support cited are the following: reform of security forces, police reform, justice and rule of law enforcement, border and customs sector, financial and budgetary aspects of the security sector, DDR; SSR carried out in the form of advice and assistance to local authorities.	The document is more specific; it reviews various spheres of the EU's involvement in SSR. The document reviews SSR-related activities in over 70 countries in different regions (Eastern Europe, North and South Caucuses and Central Asia, Western Balkans, Africa, Caribbean and the Pacific, South Mediterranean and the Middle East, Latin America and Asia). In the Commission document, the main areas of SSR support cited are the following: reform of civil management bodies, civil oversight mechanisms, justice reform, law enforcement, armed forces, DDR, SALW and regional capacity building.
Convergences	To ensure convergence in their SSR activity, ESDP and Community action are to observe the following principles: - complementarity of actions, especially in crisis and post-crisis situations - division of responsibility - coherent approach to SSR - case-by-case analysis to define which mechanisms are most appropriate in a given situation (ESDP or Community)	

The achievement of coherence, harmonization and coordination in EU external action and between the EU internal and external policies has become an important issue on the EU's agenda. The Communication from the Commission to the European Council entitled *Europe in the World – Some Practical Proposals for Greater Coherence, Effectiveness and Visibility* (June 2006) stressed the need to use available internal and external policies more coherently and effectively to strengthen the EU's external action. This involves improving strategic planning, coherence between the Union's various external policy instruments, as well as cooperation between EU institutions and between the latter and the member states.[2] The Communication also calls for using 'the particular competences and strengths of the Member States and the institutions'.

In addition, action has been taken to simplify the EU's financial instruments. The new 'financial perspectives' for the period of 2007 to 2013[3], approved in 2005, had 'the aim of rationalising and simplifying the current legislative framework governing external actions of the Community'. Six new consolidated financial instruments are now operational: three thematic instruments – humanitarian aid, stability, and macro-financial assistance – and three geographical instruments – the instrument for pre-accession assistance (IPA), the European neighbourhood and partnership instrument (ENPI) and the development cooperation and economic cooperation instrument (DCECI). The previous fifteen thematic programmes have been consolidated into eight: democracy and human rights, human and social development, environment and sustainable management of natural resources, civil society and decentralised cooperation, food security, cooperation with industrialized countries, programmes transferred to geographic programmes (regional programmes) as well as migration and asylum.

As Table 1 suggests, achieving coherence in the SSR policy area can be a daunting task. At the moment, the Council and Commission concepts demonstrate that the EU commitment to SSR issues is more political than practical. Further progress will require top-down streamlining of the SSR approach across EU institutions and field missions, development of EU-specific SSR implementation guidelines and other SSR mechanisms. All this represents a tall order. Yet, progress in developing its SSR policy instruments will doubtless facilitate the EU's efforts to introduce greater coherence in its security activities.

Shaping the EU's SSR Agenda: the Role of EU Member States at the National Level and in other International Organisations (IOs)

EU member states not only set the SSR agenda in the EU Council, but pursue their own SSR policies and programmes in third countries. The idea of SSR was pioneered by an EU country almost a decade ago, the UK.[4] Furthermore, EU member states have played a central role in developing a coherent SSR methodology and they were among the first implementers of the concept on the ground. This section first looks at the activities of two countries that have been particularly active in the area of SSR, the UK and the Netherlands. It then examines the EU's contribution to the realisation of various SSR goals through its members' participation in the leading IOs involved in SSR: the OSCE, NATO, the OECD DAC, the Council of Europe and the UN.

SSR and EU Member States

Many EU member states have long been active in the areas of conflict management, post-conflict peacebuilding and development cooperation in developing countries. During the 1990s, a surge in intrastate conflicts and the phenomenon of 'failed' or 'collapsed' states made it clear that new policy frameworks and approaches would be needed to succeed in these areas. The UK and the Netherlands are particularly interesting examples of how EU members came to adopt a national SSR agenda in response to these new challenges.

The UK's work on the development of the SSR concept, its principles and practices has had a substantial impact on the emerging international consensus on SSR. In 1998, the UK government was the first to articulate the notion of an integral connection between security and development. It was also an early champion of the concept of defence diplomacy, which combines diplomatic and military tools with a view to preventing conflicts or managing crises. In 2000, in order to make its conflict prevention policies more effective, the UK integrated SSR into its International Development Strategies.[5] In 2002[6] it developed an interdepartmental strategy[7] on SSR. The UK's SSR Strategy relies on three areas of action: policy development and analysis, technical assistance, and capacity building. In 2002-03, the SSR strategy was funded for the first time with £2.8 million.[8] In 2003-04, funding increased to £5.05 million.[9] The funds supported the development of defence diplomacy education and other military training courses, as well as the establishment of two institutions that have come to play a leading role in UK SSR activities: the Defence Advisory Team (DAT) and the Global Facilitation Network for Security Sector Reform (GFN-SSR).

Recognizing the importance of SSR and defence diplomacy, in 2001 the United Kingdom established the Defence Advisory Team (DAT). It was renamed the Security Sector Development Advisory Team (SSDAT) in March 2005. The SSDAT currently consists of 15 experts. It provides in-country advice and assistance on security sector governance, security sector and defence reviews, effective planning of security forces, financial and human resource management, and development. GFN-SSR provides resources in the field of conflict prevention and security sector reform. Its main activities include information sharing, training and capacity-building, and networking and policy development.

The UK Government also set up a Global Conflict Prevention Pool and an Africa Conflict Prevention Pool.[10] These were interdepartmental funding tools designed to coordinate the use of resources as well as to provide policy advice and information on SSR. Much of the UK's security sector reform work is financed through these two pools, which receive both overseas development assistance (ODA) and non-ODA funds for programmes based on strategies agreed by the Ministry of Defence (MOD), the Department for International Development (DFID) and the Foreign and Commonwealth Office (FCO). In 2006, the UK was part of the European Commission's team contributing to the OECD DAC's work on the development of the *Implementation Framework for SSR (IF-SSR)*. The Framework is intended to be a guide for governments and their partners in conducting SSR assessments and designing, implementing, monitoring and evaluating SSR programmes.

The Netherlands has also been an active player in advancing the SSR agenda. The Foreign Policy Agenda, an annual statement of foreign policy goals, reflects the Netherlands' approach of mainstreaming conflict issues in development cooperation. The Policy Agenda emphasises that peace, security, and stability are prerequisites for poverty reduction. The Netherlands calls for an integrated approach in pre-conflict and post-conflict zones and in failing states 'to prevent conflict, create the right conditions for reconstruction, carry out reconstruction activities, set up operational administrative and security structures, promote sustainable development, and eliminate breeding grounds for radicalisation'.[11] In 2003, the government tasked the Clingendael Institute, a Dutch non-profit foundation partly funded by the government, to develop the SSR policy framework for its development work.[12] To help implement its SSR activities, the Dutch government also established a Stability Fund[13], which seeks to ensure greater programme coherence through pooled funding.

The EU has also paid increasing attention to the need to seek symmetries in the activities of member states and the EU institutions. The European Council decisions at Feira (June 2000) and Göteborg (June 2001) emphasised the need to deploy the member states' resources in the fields of police reform, rule of law, civil protection, and public administration. The Commission has recognised that in some instances member states can play an important role in facilitating SSR activities, for example in the reform of armed forces in transition or developing countries.[14] The EU SSR concepts also call for the EU to use member states' expertise in the field of SSR more effectively. In practice, however, the EU does not take full advantage of its member states' expertise. In many instances, coordination of SSR activities in the field is weak because mechanisms governing cooperation between EU institutions and member states remain underdeveloped.

The EU and IOs

Effective multilateral engagement in the area of SSR was first referred to as a strategic objective of the EU in the European Security Strategy (ESS) published in 2003.[15] Long before this, however, the EU and its member states had been exposed to various SSR activities through their membership in several international organisations active in the area of SSR.[16] Involvement in various SSR initiatives of IOs has been instrumental in the maturing of the EU's own SSR agenda.

The EU is represented in all key international institutions and fora by both member states and the European Community, represented by the European Commission. In addition to its involvement in the norm-setting activities of the OECD DAC, the EU has played a leading role in the efforts of the OSCE, NATO and the Council of Europe to develop norms and best practices for democratic security sector governance. The EU has also led the effort to introduce elements of SSR policy in the post-communist countries of Eastern Europe. Moreover, the EU member states and the Commission are the biggest contributors to the core budgets of these international organisations, as well as contributing additional funding to special projects initiated by them (see column 3 in table 1).

The EU has actively participated in shaping the post-Cold War security architecture on the European continent by supporting the work of the OSCE. The OSCE has developed a comprehensive security concept, which combines political, military, economic, environmental and human dimensions. The EU played a key role in the adoption of the OSCE Code of Conduct on Politico-Military Relations, agreed by the OSCE participating states in 1994. This calls for the democratic control of all security forces, not just the military, and establishes a number of other groundbreaking principles that are crucial for democratic governance of the security sector. The document sets benchmarks not only for countries in transition, but also for EU member states. The European Commission was among the signatories of the document agreed at the OSCE Istanbul Summit in November 1999 entitled *A Charter for European Security*.

The Charter set out a number of goals for the OSCE's involvement in field operations, including increased involvement in police-related activities. It committed the organisation's member states to the Platform for Co-operative Security in order 'to strengthen co-operation between the OSCE and other international organisations and institutions, thereby making better use of the resources of the international community'.[17] Over the last few years, the OSCE has also stepped up its involvement in dealing with new security challenges such as combating international terrorism, violent extremism, organised crime and drug trafficking. The EU and the OSCE meet regularly at ministerial level to discuss the areas of action and policies that intersect, namely the European Neighbourhood Policy, ESDP, and other activities in the Western Balkans, South Caucasus, Ukraine, Moldova, etc.

The EU has also supported SSR-related activities in the context of NATO, such as the development of democratic civil-military relations for post-Communist countries. *Berlin Plus* security agreements agreed between NATO and the EU between 2002 and 2003, based on the conclusions of the NATO Washington Summit, include three main elements: EU access to NATO planning capabilities, NATO European command options, and EU use of NATO assets and capabilities. *Berlin Plus* agreements have been put into practice on a number of occasions, for example, in the EU-led military operation Concordia in the former Yugoslav Republic of Macedonia in 2003, and in the military operation Althea in Bosnia-Herzegovina that was launched in 2004. Regular EU-NATO consultations and exchanges of information also take place concerning the ESDP operations conducted autonomously by the EU.

Fifteen EU member states and the European Commission sitting on the OECD DAC helped develop the latter's *Guidelines on Security Sector Reform and Governance: Policy and Good Practice*, adopted in 2004. This document became the basis for the EU's own SSR concepts and now serves as a key point of reference for all SSR practitioners. In 2006, the OECD DAC led a team of experts working on the development of the *Implementation Framework for SSR* mentioned above. The EU, which has not yet developed guidelines for SSR implementation in the field, may well end up using the Framework for designing its own field activities.

The resolutions of the Parliamentary Assembly of the Council of Europe (PACE) have established important norms for the democratic control of armed forces in Council of Europe (CoE) member states. PACE also adopted in 2005 a Recommendation on the *Democratic Oversight of the Security Sector in Member states*, an important norm-setting document of the CoE in the field of SSR.[18] The Third Summit of Heads of State and Government of the Council of Europe, which took place in Warsaw in May 2005, adopted a political declaration and an Action Plan[19] that included a statement on the need to create a new framework of enhanced cooperation and political dialogue between the CoE and the EU.

The EU has also provided substantial support to UN agencies, funds and programmes. Areas of collaboration between the two organisations include such SSR-relevant subjects as human rights, crisis management, post-crisis reconstruction and rehabilitation, conflict prevention and governance. In

2003, the UN and the EU signed a Co-operation Agreement in Crisis Management.[20] This agreement in the area of civilian and military crisis management established a 'joint consultative mechanism at the working level to examine ways and means to enhance mutual co-ordination and compatibility' in such areas as planning, training, communication and best practices. More recently, the EU has been very supportive of the newly-created UN Peacebuilding Commission.

In sum, to address the key issue of coordination and cooperation in the field, the EU has concluded different types of cooperation agreements with a range of international organisations and, as the EU gradually develops its expertise in SSR, it has substantial potential to play an increasingly important role in coordinating SSR programmes in the field.

The EU Council of Ministers and SSR

This section looks briefly at the accomplishments in the area of SSR, first, under the recent British, Austrian and Finnish Presidencies and, second, as a result of the Council's support to SSR in the CFSP/ESDP framework.

EU Presidencies and SSR

The Presidency plays a key role in setting the Union's agenda and priorities, and reviewing progress in various areas of external and internal action. It chairs EU meetings, represents the EU abroad, and speaks on its behalf at summit meetings and international conferences. The effectiveness of the Presidency depends on the commitment, experience and resources of the member state holding it. To ensure policy continuity between the Presidencies, a first Multiannual Strategic Programme of the Council, developed for 6 consecutive presidencies, was adopted in 2003.[21] The programme did not yet mention SSR among the Council's strategic goals. But, considerable progress in SSR was achieved under the British (second half of 2005), Austrian (first half of 2006) and Finnish (second half of 2006) Presidencies. The *Concept for ESDP support to SSR* was launched under the UK Presidency. *Community Support for SSR* was adopted under the Austrian Presidency. The Finnish Presidency furthered the operationalisation of the EU's approach to SSR in the Western Balkans, and worked on the elaboration of an EU approach to DDR. The three Presidencies' Programmes of Action[22], reports on ESDP[23], and annual reports on EU conflict prevention activities[24] all included references to SSR and reviewed progress in this area.

In addition, all the Presidencies took action to disseminate and deepen knowledge of SSR by organising seminars and training. The UK Presidency co-organised, in conjunction with the European Commission and the non-governmental organisations Saferworld and International Alert, a seminar on 'Developing a Security Sector Reform Concept/Strategy for the EU' in November 2005. The objective was to develop a shared understanding of security sector reform and review the EU's role in it. The Austrian Presidency organised and funded, in cooperation with the Geneva Centre for the Democratic Control of Armed Forces (DCAF), a Swiss-based foundation, and the EU Institute for Security Studies, an autonomous EU agency providing a think tank function for the Council, a seminar on 'Security

Sector Reform in the Western Balkans'. It took place in Vienna in February 2006.[25] Its aim was to build on the progress made under the British Presidency, in particular the ongoing work on an overarching EU approach to SSR, and to focus attention on the SSR needs of the Western Balkans. The Finnish Presidency and DCAF co-organised a conference on 'Enhancing security sector governance through security sector reform in the Western Balkans – the role of the European Union', which was held in Zagreb in December 2006.[26] This was designed as a contribution to the work underway at the EU to translate the policy framework agreed in 2006 '... into operational actions by the European Community and in the framework of ESDP', as decided by the General Affairs Council held in Luxembourg in June 2006.[27]

SSR and CFSP/ESDP: Crisis Management and Conflict Prevention

CFSP and ESDP have rapidly evolved. The 1997 Amsterdam Treaty's aim to 'strengthen the security of the Union in all ways' set the stage for greater EU involvement in the security field in third countries, and this had important implications for the way that EU member states' own approach to SSR at home has developed.

Although there is no agreement on their geographic scope and priority, the agreement on the so-called Petersberg tasks[28] in 1992 set the stage for a progressively growing EU role in civilian and military missions. Following the guidelines set out by the Cologne European Council (June 1999), the Helsinki European Council (December 1999) decided to create a civilian management mechanism[29] to coordinate and put to more effective use the various civilian means and resources at the disposal of the EU. At subsequent Council meetings, the targets for the civilian dimensions of crisis management were set. The Feira Council (June 2000) identified four priority areas in the development of civilian capabilities: police capabilities, the rule of law, civilian administration, and civil protection. The Civilian Headline Goal 2008 adopted by the Brussels European Council in December 2004 added monitoring missions, SSR and DDR programmes to the goals established at Feira. The Ministerial Civilian Crisis Management Capability conferences now regularly discuss ways of improving civilian capabilities.[30]

The European Council of Göteborg stated in its conclusions that 'conflict prevention is one of the main objectives of the Union's external relations and should be integrated in all its relevant aspects, including ESDP, development cooperation, and trade'.[31] The *Communication on Conflict Prevention*, adopted by the European Commission in April 2001, made a series of proposals on how to improve the integration of conflict prevention objectives into the EU's external action. The 2001 *EU Programme for the Prevention of Violent Conflict* identified 'administration of justice, improving police services, and human rights training for the whole security sector, as a means of contributing to conflict prevention'.[32]

In parallel to the development of its civilian capabilities, the EU also took steps to build a military capability. In 1999, it adopted the Helsinki Headline Goal, which set the target of deploying up to 60,000 troops (to carry out the Petersberg tasks), and decided on the creation of a European Rapid Reaction Force. In 2004, it adopted the Headline Goal 2010, which complemented the

Helsinki Headline Goal and envisaged the creation by 2007 of rapidly deployable battle groups that could be swiftly deployed anywhere in the world. It also decided to create a European Gendarmerie.

Since 2003, the EU has launched more than a dozen missions. There were military operations in FYROM, DRC and Bosnia-Herzegovina, a civilian-military supporting action in the Darfur region of Sudan, an SSR mission in the DRC, a monitoring mission in Aceh, rule of law missions in Georgia and Iraq, border assistance missions to Ukraine, Moldova and Rafah (Gaza Strip), police missions in Bosnia-Herzegovina, FYROM, the Palestinian Territories and the DRC. These missions have included the reform of various components of the security sector.

Table 3. *ESDP Operations*[33]

Country/ Mission	Dates	Description	Main SSR Focus	Number of personnel (approx)	Budget (in euros)
Bosnia and Herzegovina / European Union Police Mission (EUPM)	Jan 03 – present	1st ESDP mission, successor to the United Nations International Police Task Force (IPTF) in BiH Peace implementation	Police reform Fight against organised crime	530 police officers	38 million (2005) 12 million (2006)
FYROM / EU Military Operation (EUFOR Concordia)	March – Dec 03	1st military mission, successor to the NATO's operation Allied Harmony (implementation of the 2001 Ohrid Agreement)	Creation of an enabling environment for the local security forces	350 military personnel	6.2 million (2003)
Democratic Republic of the Congo / EU Military Operation (Artemis)	June–Sept 03	Improvement of the security situation and of humanitarian conditions, protection of IDPs	Creation of an enabling environment for the local security forces	1800 troops	7 million (2003)
FYROM / EU Police Mission (EUPOL Proxima)	Dec 03 – Dec 05	Training, advising local police Local policing and confidence building within the population	Fight against organised crime; enforcement of the rule of law; reform of the Ministry of Interior (including the police); creation of a border police	200 international personnel	15 million (2004)
Georgia / EU Rule of Law Mission (EUJUST-Themis)	July 04 – July 05	Assistance in development of a coordinated approach to the reform process in the rule of law field	Judicial system (in particular the criminal justice system)	10 international experts	2.3 million (2004-05)
Bosnia and Herzegovina / EU Military Operation (EUFOR Althea)	Dec 04 – present	Enforcement of the Dayton/Paris agreement; contribution to a safe and secure environment in BiH Successor to NATO's SFOR (carried out with recourse to NATO assets and capabilities); the largest EU-led military operation	Creation of an enabling environment for the local security forces	7000 EUFOR troops 500 personnel of the Integrated Police Unit (IPU)	71.7 million (2004-2007)

Country/ Mission	Dates	Description	Main SSR Focus	Number of personnel (approx)	Budget (in euros)
Kinshasa, DRC / EU Police Mission (EUPOL Kinshasa)	April 05 – present	Establishment of an integrated police unit (IPU) to protect state institutions and reinforce local security forces	Police reform	30 personnel	4.3 million (2005) 3.5 million (2006)
Democratic Republic of the Congo / EU Security Sector Reform Mission (EUSEC DR Congo)	June 05 – present	Advisory and assistance mission in SSR	Advice on a comprehensive SSR approach	8 experts	1.6 million (2005) 4.75 million (2006)
Iraq / EU Integrated Rule of Law Mission (Eujust Lex)	July 05 – present	Training of judges, magistrates, senior police and penitentiary officers	Support for the rule of law	20 international personnel	10.9 million (2005)
Darfur, Sudan / EU Support to the African Union Mission (AMIS II)	July 05 – present	Political, logistical and financial support to the African Union monitoring mission in Darfur	Advice on police reform	60 international personnel	1.1 million (2006)
Aceh, Indonesia/ EU Monitoring Mission (AMM)	Sept 05 – Dec 06	Monitoring peace agreement implementation	DDR	130 personnel (from the EU member states)	15 million (2005-06)
The Palestinian Territories / EU Police Mission (EUPOL COPPS)	Nov 05 – present	Implementation of the Palestinian Civil Police Development Plan; training of police and criminal justice officials	Police reform, criminal justice	30 personnel	6.1 million (2005)
Rafah Crossing Point in the Palestinian Territories / EU Border Assistance Mission (EU BAM Rafah)	Nov 05 – present	Compliance with the principles agreed for the Rafah crossing point between Israel and the Palestinian Authority	Training in border and customs controls	80 personnel	7.6 million (2005)
FYROM / EU Police Advisory Team (EUPAT)	Dec 05 – May 06	Training and advising local police	Police reform, training of border police, fight against corruption and organized crime	30 police advisors	1.5 million (2005)
Moldova-Ukraine / EU Border Assistance Mission (EUBAM)	Dec 05 - present	Training and advising border guards and customs officers	Border guard and customs reform, border surveillance	7 field offices 101 international staff	20.2 million (2006-07)
Kosovo / The EU Planning Team (EUPT Kosovo)	Apr 06 – present	Transition between selected tasks of the UN Interim Administration Mission in Kosovo (UNMIK) and a possible EU crisis management operation in the field of rule of law and other areas	Planning for police and justice system reforms	25 staff members	3 million (2006) 10 million 2007)
Democratic Republic of the Congo / EU military mission (EUFOR Congo)	Aug – Nov 06	Military operation in support of the UN Mission in the DRC (MONUC) for the election process	Provision of security Protection of civilians	2000 personnel	16.7 million (2006)

Efforts have been made to improve dialogue between the security and development communities within the context of the Civilian Crisis Management Committee (CivCom), created by the Council in May 2000. The Committee provides information, recommendations and opinions on civilian aspects of crisis management. A police unit, attached to the Council Secretariat, was created by the Nice European Council in December 2000 to enable the EU to plan and carry out policing operations. As a follow up to the Police Action Plan, adopted at the EU Council in Göteborg, efforts have been made to improve the management and coordination of the policing capacity within the ESDP framework. Two conferences for EU Chiefs of Police were organised on the initiative of EU Presidencies in 2001 and in 2004.[34]

EU Community Action

This section reviews the most important EU policy areas, managed by the European Commission, that have an SSR dimension, i.e. development, democratisation, human rights, enlargement and justice and home affairs (JHA).[35] All of these areas involve cross-cutting policies requiring coordination between the EU institutions and member states. The EU Commission makes an important contribution to crisis management through a wide range of policies such as humanitarian assistance, civil protection and reconstruction. These instruments complement ESDP operations in the overall crisis response of the EU. Development aid merits special attention since it is one of the most important sources of financial assistance to developing countries and provides an important framework for programmes designed to reform their security sectors.

Development Cooperation

From $24 billion in 1970, the overseas development assistance (ODA) provided by contributing countries rose to $54 billion in 1990, more than doubling in 20 years. By 2004, it had increased again by 33%, to $72 billion. Both the Community and EU member states have been active in external assistance for many years. The EU has become the most important actor in the field of development, with activities in developing and transition countries around the world. The EU is the world's largest ODA contributor, having increased its share of ODA from 44.1% in 1970 and 46.6% in 1990, to 55% in 2005.[36] EU member states also regularly rank among the leading bilateral donors.

Notwithstanding the ever greater availability of development aid, indicators for developing states, especially those in Sub-Saharan Africa, have remained weak.[37] Policy-makers and researchers started questioning the effectiveness of development aid decades ago.[38] A great deal of work has been done by governments[39] and international organisations[40] dealing with development of ways to make assistance more effective. Since 2003, the Center for Global Development has compiled the Commitment to Development Index (CDI), which measures the extent to which aid from rich to poor countries has had a positive impact on development.[41] Security is one of seven policy areas that are measured to obtain an overall score of development, since conflict has been shown to be one of the most important checks on development. According to the data provided by the UK's Department for International Development in its 2000 White Paper on International Development: 'Of the 40 poorest countries in the world, 24 are either in the midst of armed conflict or have only recently emerged from it. This problem is particularly acute in Africa where twenty per cent of the population lives in countries affected by armed conflict. Armed conflict also leads to population displacement. It is estimated that 10.6 million people in Africa are internally displaced – the majority of them uprooted by war'.[42]

Until 2004, the main categories of development assistance were education, health and population, production, debt relief, other social infrastructure, emergency aid, economic infrastructure, and programme assistance. Almost half of EU ODA spending was allocated to social programmes[43], which included education, health, population and reproductive health, water supply and sanitation, government and civil society, and other social infrastructure and services. In 2004, reflecting the emergence of the SSR concept, the OECD DAC decided to add to the list of ODA eligible actions such SSR-related activities as peacebuilding and conflict prevention, management of security expenditures, enhancing civil society's role in the security system, issues related to child soldiers, and controlling, preventing and reducing the proliferation of small arms and light weapons (SALW).[44] The new financial instruments (2007-2013) will make more funds available for SSR missions or missions with SSR elements.

The Cotonou Agreement, signed in June 2000 for a 20-year period, is the latest in a series of agreements between the EU and the countries of the African, Caribbean and Pacific region (ACP group). The agreement introduced new conditionalities for the ACP countries, namely, respect for human rights, democracy and the rule of law, which became 'essential elements' whose violation can lead to partial or total suspension of development aid. Although the agreement does not mention SSR directly, a number of SSR-related cooperation areas were mentioned and a comprehensive approach to programming was introduced. For example, the political dimension of cooperation identifies excessive military expenditure, drugs, and organised crime as areas for EU development action and stipulates that: 'Broadly based policies to promote peace and to prevent, manage and resolve violent conflicts shall play a prominent role in [the ACP] ... dialogue, as shall the need to take full account of the objective of peace and democratic stability in the definition of priority areas of cooperation'.[45]

The Commission's Communication on *Governance and Development* of 2003 argues that 'security is key to regional stability, poverty reduction and conflict prevention'.[46] It holds that SSR efforts aimed at the provision of effective management, transparency and accountability of the security sector make it an integral component of good governance. The new Financial Perspectives and the 10th European Development Fund[47] offer a range of financial instruments with specific provisions for governance, human rights, election observation missions, peacekeeping, and regional integration.

In the *EU Strategy for Africa* (December 2005), the first integrated European political framework to improve coordination as well as the coherence of EU and member states' policies and instruments in support of

Africa, SSR is mentioned among the tools used in post-conflict reconstruction efforts to 'secure lasting peace and development'.[48] The document states that: 'The EU should also develop a strategy and capacity to foster security sector reform (SSR) in Africa that will take into account the related institutions and capacity building programmes of the EC and Member states, whilst identifying the scope of action to be pursued within the European security and defence policy (ESDP) framework'.[49]

The European Consensus on Development, signed on 20 December 2005[50], provided a common framework of objectives, values and principles that the EU supports and promotes as a global player. This is a good example of a coordinated approach that provides for cooperation among various EU agencies, information sharing and cross-pillar activities. Although the *Consensus* does not make direct reference to SSR, the connection between security and development is at the heart of the document. It defines insecurity and violent conflict amongst 'the biggest obstacles to achieving the MDGs' (the UN Millennium Development Goals).[51]

Democratisation and Human Rights

The 1992 Treaty on European Union states that one of the main objectives of the CFSP is to develop and consolidate democracy and the rule of law, respect for human rights and fundamental freedoms. The EU has done a great deal to advance these objectives in its external policies by including[52] democratisation and human rights considerations in its conflict prevention strategies and development cooperation policies, as well as in association, partnership and other types of agreements governing the EU's relationships with third countries and potential members.

The 2001 Commission Communication on *The European Union's Role in Promoting Human Rights and Democratisation in Third Countries*[53] established targets focused on improving the EU's approach to human rights and democratisation. The document proposed to achieve coherence and consistency between various EU policies and mainstream human rights and democratisation policy into other EU policies and actions. The *Communication on Conflict Prevention* also mentions a possible Commission role in supporting human rights training for the entire security sector.[54] More recently, the 2006 *EU Annual Report on Human Rights* has highlighted the interdependencies between human rights, democracy, security and development: 'The EU regards human rights and democracy as fundamental pillars of enhancing peace and security as well as promoting development objectives'.[55] Integration of human rights considerations into crisis management activities has thus resulted in greater EU involvement in addressing issues such as women's rights and the security of children affected by armed conflict. The *Report on Human Rights* also welcomes the adoption of the OECD Risk Awareness Tool for Multinational Enterprises in Weak Governance Zones, which addresses, inter alia, the need to observe human rights related to the management of security forces.[56]

The European Initiative for Democracy and Human Rights (EIDHR)[57] was created by an initiative of the European Parliament in 1994. Projects funded by virtue of this initiative in the field of democratisation, governance and rule of law have supported some SSR-related projects, for example, strengthening of civil society, rule of law and governance, as well as conflict presentation and resolution. In 2007, the EIDHR was succeeded by a new thematic programme on democracy and human rights in accordance with the EU's Financial Perspectives for 2007-2013. Programmes in these areas will continue to be financed from the external assistance budgets and from the European Development Fund.

Enlargement, Stabilisation and Association Process, ENP

The Commission's SSR concept states that 'security sector reform is an integral part of EU enlargement, as regards pre-accession countries, and is an important part of development cooperation and external assistance to third countries'.[58] Some SSR elements were originally included in agreements with candidate and potential candidate countries (agreements on stabilisation and association) and were later regularly reviewed in country progress reports. These elements fall under the political Copenhagen criteria for membership (guaranteeing democracy, rule of law, human rights, respect and protection of minorities) and the third Copenhagen criteria (adoption and implementation of the *acquis communautaire*). Improvement of border control, accountability of police services, civilian oversight of the military, and parliamentary oversight of defence and security structures occupy a central place in both enlargement strategy and progress reports.[59]

A recent *EU Enlargement Strategy and Main Challenges 2006–2007*[60] emphasises the importance of implementing a number of SSR principles in candidate countries. For example, it makes the following assessment of Turkey under the political Copenhagen criterion: 'Civilian democratic control over the military needs to be asserted, and law enforcement and judicial practice further aligned with the spirit of the reforms.'[61] A similar assessment is made about Serbia: 'The reform of the *military* has continued but with difficulties and resistance from some elements within the army. Civilian oversight of the military, which is a key European Partnership priority, is still insufficient. The new Constitution and the revised parliamentary rules of procedures set out the bases for a more effective civilian oversight'.[62] The need for police reform is mentioned for Bosnia-Herzegovina and judicial reform for almost all candidate countries.

The EU encourages good governance of the security sector in its near abroad through the European Neighbourhood Policy (ENP), launched in May 2004. The European Neighbourhood and Partnership Instrument[63], which replaced MEDA (the principal financial instrument for the implementation of the Euro-Mediterranean Partnership) and TACIS (Technical Aid to the Commonwealth of Independent States) on 1 January 2007, takes a new approach to cross-border cooperation and can put more resources at the disposal of SSR programmes. The following SSR activities are mentioned under the Instrument: ensuring efficient and secure border management; promoting cooperation in the field of justice and home affairs; and the fight against, and prevention of, terrorism and organised crime. Thus, SSR is referred to in many agreements with candidate and partner countries and in reports on their progress in meeting EU conditionality, yet the EU still needs to develop a cohesive approach and devise a rigorous system of benchmarks for guiding and measuring implementation.

The EU Area of Freedom, Security and Justice

With changes in the nature of the strategic environment, coherence between internal and external dimensions of security and the coordination of the activities of key actors operating at home and abroad has grown in importance for the EU. This relatively new consensus has been particularly manifest in EU efforts to elaborate a more effective, joint approach to such transnational and cross-border challenges as illegal migration, trafficking and smuggling of human beings, terrorism and organised crime.

The progressive establishment of 'the area of freedom, security and justice' was a new objective set by the Treaty of Amsterdam in 1997. The Tampere Programme, adopted by the European Council in October 1999[64], and the Hague Programme for Freedom, Security and Justice agreed in November 2004[65] address the fight against terrorism and organised crime; civil and criminal justice; fundamental rights; information sharing; migration management; and a common asylum, border management and visa policy. A progress report on the implementation of the programmes is prepared by the Commission and submitted to the Council and Parliament every six months. In order to achieve the goals of the Tampere and Hague Programmes, comprehensive instruments have been adopted that address civil liberties, human rights and development issues in countries and regions of origin and transit. The Hague Programme underlines that freedom, justice, control at external borders, internal security and the prevention of terrorism should henceforth be considered indivisible within the Union as a whole: 'an optimal level of protection of the area of freedom, security and justice requires multidisciplinary and concerted action both at EU level and at national level between the competent law enforcement authorities, especially police, customs and border guards'.[66] *A Strategy for the External Dimension of JHA: Global Freedom, Security and Justice,*[67] adopted by the Council in November 2005, underlined the connection existing between JHA (Justice and Home Affairs), the CFSP, ESDP and development policies of the EU.

These efforts to develop a comprehensive approach to asylum, immigration and external border issues, in addition to strengthening cooperation among police, customs and judicial authorities, illustrate how the EU is applying SSR methodology in the JHA area.

Future Action

The recently elaborated Council and Commission SSR concepts provide highly useful statements of definitions, principles, and orientations for SSR-relevant EU actions. Yet, while the EU is now clearly committed to the SSR policy approach, the operationalisation of SSR in the EU's various policy areas is in its infancy. Mechanisms for mainstreaming SSR into the EU's development, human rights and democracy, conflict prevention and crisis management, and enlargement policies all need to be further developed. Furthermore, SSR needs to be better integrated into the Stabilisation and Association Process, European Neighbourhood Policy, and its programmes for establishing an area of freedom, security and justice. It will be incumbent on future EU Presidencies as well as the various Directorates General involved in SSR issues within the Commission to take this process forward.

The EU SSR concepts have borrowed a great deal from the thinking that has evolved in other international organisations. They therefore do not always reflect accurately the EU's specificities. As the concepts are integrated into the practical work of the Council and the Commission, EU objectives and policy instruments need to be given greater consideration. This can be facilitated by the organisation of intra-institutional training and seminars on SSR as well as mapping exercises to scan the range of EU activities and concerns in the area of SSR. Such efforts would doubtless help integrate SSR into the EU's broader policy framework.

The EU's SSR concepts acknowledge that the development of joint actions with other international organisations is necessary and that empowerment of regional organisations and actors is required if sustainable reform is to be achieved. Yet, how the EU is to manage efficiently this cooperation with international organisations and donors in the SSR field clearly needs further research and pragmatic policy-making.

In the EU context, SSR has been conceived as a concept running across three pillars. It is thus consistent with the 'whole-of-government' approach promoted by the OECD DAC. Yet, even the EU's overarching SSR framework is not very explicit on how the cooperation mechanisms are to operate between the Commission, the Council, and the member states. The SSR framework stipulates that SSR activities can be either carried out by the Council, the Commission or by both. But it is short on guidance about which EU institution takes the lead in which circumstances and how it may have to work with other parts of the EU in the process. It may be that this will have to be decided on a case-by-case basis, but it would surely be preferable for the EU to do some advance thinking on how it might proceed in different situations. This would certainly help the EU make more effective decisions in the inevitable ambiguity and confusion of future crisis situations.

There are signs that the EU is in the process of enhancing the coherence of its external activities and improving coordination across its three pillars. Inter-agency working groups and closer cooperation with the member states, both mentioned in the *Europe in the World* document cited above, will play a key role here. In addition, there is growing recognition that ESDP civilian and military missions need to be better integrated with Community programmes, and that the SSR expertise of such lead member states as the UK and the Netherlands needs to be leveraged more effectively.

Effective action on SSR will require that EU institutions and member states invest in training activities for civilian and military staff in SSR programme design and delivery, both at headquarters and in the field. Effective SSR action will also require appropriate and timely financing. The new Financial Instruments and the new ODA regulations show great promise, but again there is a divide between theory and practice that needs to be closed.

The *EU Enlargement Strategy and Main Challenges 2006–2007*, shows that the EU needs to develop a comprehensive and coherent approach to SSR for the candidate countries. On the one hand, the EU can argue that SSR, while a new approach, is consistent with the Copenhagen *acquis*. Yet, on the other, it needs to develop methodologies for achieving three key SSR-related tasks: first, to analyse the current state of national security sectors; second, to measure progress in making security sectors more professional and responsive to the needs of the population; and third to be able to compare EU assessments of progress and backsliding across countries. The EU has announced plans to devise benchmarks for candidate countries in its *EU Enlargement Strategy and Main Challenges 2006–2007*[68], which could be extremely helpful in enhancing SSR implementation. The EU will also need to customise its SSR involvement for each country and region in its respective country strategy papers. In doing so, the EU can use the methodology developed by the OECD's *Implementation Framework for SSR* or, for example, take as a model the Internal Security Sector Review recently carried out in Kosovo.

Last but certainly not least, the EU needs to foster a culture of security sector reform among its own members. It is well placed to do so. Its ranks include several countries that have carried out SSR programmes as part of their democratisation process and their quest for integration into European and Euro-Atlantic institutions. The EU also counts, as discussed above, several members that have played a leading role in the development of the SSR approach. Ultimately, the success of the EU's efforts in the area of SSR may well depend on how its own members cope with the process of rethinking and reorganising their security resources and relationships, and whether it can, therefore, convincingly lead others by example.

Endnotes

1 Dutch Ministry of Foreign Affairs, 'More Scope for Peace and Security Within Development Budget', Press release, 4 March 2005, available at:

www.minbuza.nl/en/news/pressreleases,2005/03/more_scope_for_peace_and_security_within_development_budget.html

2 Communication from the Commission to the European Council, *Europe in the World – Some Practical Proposals for Greater Coherence, Effectiveness and Visibility*, 8 June 2006, available at: http://ec.europa.eu/comm/external_relations/euw_com06_278_en.pdf

3 The European Commission, Communication From the Commission to the Council and the European Parliament, *External Actions through Thematic Programmes under the Future Financial Perspectives 2007-2013*, 3 August 2005, available at:

http://ec.europa.eu/comm/external_relations/human_rights/doc/2005com_0324_en.pdf

4 The term 'SSR' was coined in 1998 by the then British International Development Secretary Clare Short. See her speech 'Security, Development and Conflict Prevention' given at the Royal. College of Defence Studies (13 May 1998).

5 Department for International Development, United Kingdom. *Eliminating World Poverty: Making Globalization Work for the Poor*. White Paper on International Development, December 2000, available at: http://www.dfid.gov.uk/pubs/files/whitepaper2000.pdf; Department for International Development, United Kingdom. Eliminating World Poverty: Making Governance Work for the Poor. White Paper on International Development, July 2006, available at: http://www.dfid.gov.uk/wp2006/.

6 DFID/FCO/MOD, United Kingdom, *Strategy for Security Sector Reform*, 12 June 2002, available at: http://gsdrc.ids.ac.uk/docs/open/CON10.pdf

7 Between the Ministry of Defence (MOD), the Department for International Development (DFID) and the Foreign and Commonwealth Office (FCO).

8 DFID/FCO/MOD, United Kingdom, *The Global Conflict Prevention Pool: A Joint UK Government Approach to Reducing Conflict*, September 2003, p. 40.

9 Nicole Ball, *Evaluation of the Conflict Prevention Pools. The Security Sector Reform Strategy*, Evaluation Report EV 657, March 2004, p. 47, available at:

http://www.dfid.gov.uk/aboutdfid/performance/files/ev647ssr.pdf

10 DFID/FCO/MOD, United Kingdom, The Global Conflict Prevention Pool: A Joint UK Government Approach to Reducing Conflict, September 2003, available at: http://www.dfid.gov.uk/pubs/files/global-conflict-prevention-pool.pdf

11 Netherlands Ministry of Foreign Affairs, *Policy Agenda*, available at:

http://www.minbuza.nl/en/ministry,policy_and_budget/Policy-Agenda-2007.html

12 Clingendael Institute, *Enhancing Democratic Governance of the Security Sector: An Institutional Assessment Framework*, prepared for the Netherlands Ministry of Foreign Affairs, The Hague, 2003, available at: www.clingendael.nl/cru/pdf/2003_occasional_papers/SSGAF_publicatie.pdf; Clingendael Institute, *The Stability Assessment Framework – Designing Integrated Responses for Security, Governance and Development*, The Hague, 2005, available at: www.clingendael.nl/publications/2005/20050200_cru_paper_stability.pdf .

13 http://www.minbuza.nl/en/developmentcooperation/Themes/Development,stability-fund

14 European Commission, *Communication from the Commission on Conflict Prevention*, 11 April 2001, p. 14, available at: http://ec.europa.eu/comm/external_relations/cfsp/news/com2001_211_en.pdf

15 *European Security Strategy* (ESS), 12 December 2003, http://www.consilium.europa.eu/uedocs/cmsUpload/78367.pdf

16 An overview of SSR activities undertaken by various international organisations see the Background paper titled *Intergovernmental Approaches to SSR* prepared by DCAF for the workshop on "Developing a SSR Concept for the United Nations" held on 7 July 2006 in Bratislava and co-hosted by the Ministry of Foreign Affairs and the Ministry of Defence of the Slovak Republic, available at: http://www.dcaf.ch/_docs/ev_bratislava_060707_IGO_paper.pdf

17 OSCE, *Charter for European Security*, Istanbul, November 1999, available at: http://www.osce.org/documents/mcs/1999/11/4050_en.pdf

18 It is available at: http://assembly.coe.int/Documents/AdoptedText/TA05/EREC1713.htm

19 http://www.coe.int/t/dcr/summit/20050517_plan_action_en.asp

20 Joint Declaration on UN-EU Co-operation in Crisis Management, September 24, 2003, available at: http://www.europa-eu-un.org/articles/en/article_2768_en.htm

21 The Council of the European Union, *Multiannual strategic programme of the Council, 2004-2006*, Prepared by the Six Presidencies Ireland, Netherlands, Luxembourg, United Kingdom, Austria and Finland, 8 December 2003, available at: http://www.eu2006.at/includes/Download_Dokumente/MAPEN.pdf.

22 *Prospects for the EU in 2005. The EU Presidency of the European Union*. Presented to Parliament by the Secretary of State for Foreign and Commonwealth Affairs by Command of Her Majesty, June 2005, p. 21, available at: http://www.fco.gov.uk/Files/kfile/Prospects%20in%20the%20EU%202005_CM%206611,0.pdf; Federal Ministry of Foreign Affairs of Austria, *The Austrian EU Presidency 2006*, 23 November 2005, p. 33, available at: http://eu2006.bmbwk.gv.at/en/downloads/weissbuch_bmaa_engl.pdf; *The objective for Finland's EU Presidency: a transparent and effective Union*, 30 June 2006, available at: http://www.eu2006.fi/news_and_documents/press_releases/vko26_/en_GB/162650/#en

23 UK Presidency Report on ESDP, p.28, available at: http://register.consilium.eu.int/pdf/en/05/st15/st15891.en05.pdf; Austria Presidency report on ESDP, 12 June 2006, available at: http://www.eda.europa.eu/reference/060612%20-%20European%20Council%20-%20Presidency%20Report%20on%20ESDP%2010418-06.pdf

24 The Council of the European Union, *Presidency report to the European Council on EU activities in the framework of prevention, including implementation of the EU Programme for the Prevention of Violent Conflicts*, 13 June 2006.

25 The Food for Thought paper prepared by DCAF for the seminar is available at:

http://www.dcaf.ch/news/ev_vienna_061302_paper.pdf

26 *Enhancing security sector Governance through Security Sector Reform in the Western Balkans – the Role of the EU*, Discussion paper, Zagreb 8 December 2006, http://www.dcaf.ch/news/ev_zagreb_061207_paper.pdf

27 2736th Council Meeting General Affairs and External Relations General Affairs, Luxembourg, 12 June 2006, p.16, available at: http://europa.eu/rapid/pressReleases Action.do?reference=PRES/06/161&format=PDF&aged=1&language=EN&guiLanguage=en

28 The Petersberg tasks is a common name used to refer to the Petersberg Declaration adopted by the Western European Union in June 1992. The Petersberg tasks include: humanitarian and rescue, peacekeeping and combat tasks in crisis management, including peacekeeping.

29 On the use of civilian instruments in crisis management see: European Commission Conflict Prevention and Crisis Management Unit, *Civilian instruments for EU crisis management,* April 2003, available at: http://ec.europa.eu/comm/external_relations/cfsp/doc/cm03.pdf

30 For example, see Civilian Capabilities Improvement Conference 2006, *Ministerial Declaration*, Brussels, November 2006, available at: http://www.consilium.europa.eu/uedocs/cmsUpload/civilian_crisis_management_20.11.pdf

31 Presidency Conclusions, Göteborg European Council, 15 And 16 June 2001, p. 13, available at: http://www.eu2001.se/static/pdf/eusummit/conclusions_eng.pdf

32 *EU Programme for the Prevention of Violent Conflict*, Göteborg Programme, June 2001, p.4, available at: http://www.eu2001.se/static/eng/pdf/violent.PDF

33 This table has been complied on the basis of the EU Commission's website for the ESDP http://www.consilium.europa.eu/cms3_fo/showPage.asp?id=268&lang=EN&mode=g and the corresponding sites of the operations. The overall CFSP budget increased from €62.6 million in 2005 to €102.6 million in 2006.

34 *Declaration of EU chiefs of police following the meeting on police aspects in the ESDP – framework*, Warnsveld, the Netherlands, 25 October 2004, available at: http://www.consilium.europa.eu/uedocs/cmsUpload/Final%20Warnsveld%20CoP%20Declaration%2025%20Oct%202004.pdf

35 For an exhaustive overview of the EU SSR-related activities see Hanggi, Heiner and Fred Tanner. "Promoting Security Governance in the EU's. Neighbourhood", Chaillot Paper, No 80, July 2005, pp. 27-42.

36 These percentages combine both the European Community and EU member states contributions.

37 For example, the per capita income in Sub-Saharan Africa increased only from 330 to 350 USD between 1970 and 1990, reaching only 745 USD in 2005 (The first two figures are quoted from: Fuehrer, Helmut. *The Story of Official Development Assistance. A History of the Development Assistance Committee and the Development Co-operation Directorate in Dates, Names and Figures.* Paris: OECD, 1996, the last figure is from http://web.worldbank.org).

38 Cassen, Robert. *Does Aid Work?* Oxford: Oxford University Press, 1985; Hansen, Henrik and Finn Tarp. "Aid Effectiveness Disputed", *Journal of International Development*. April, Volume 12, Number 3, 2000, pp. 375-98; Easterly, William. "Can Foreign Aid Buy Growth?", *The Journal of Economic Perspectives*, Volume 17, Number 3, 1 August 2003, pp. 23-48; Sachs, Jeffrey. *The End of Poverty: Economic Possibilities for Our Time*, New York: Penguin Press, 2005; Easterly, William. *The White Man's Burden: Why the West's Efforts to Aid the Rest Have Done So Much Ill and So Little Good*, New York: Penguin Press, 2006; Calderisi, Robert. *The Trouble with Africa: Why Foreign Aid Isn't Working*, New York: Palgrave Macmillan, 2006.

39 *The Role of Foreign Aid in Development*. A CBO Study, The Congress of the United States, Congressional Budget Office, May 1997, available at: http://www.cbo.gov/ftpdocs/0xx/doc8/foraid.pdf; Department for International Development, United Kingdom. *Eliminating World Poverty: Making Governance Work for the Poor*. White Paper on International Development, July 2006, available at: http://www.dfid.gov.uk/wp2006/; Department for International Development, HM Treasury, United Kingdom. *The Case for Aid for the Poorest Countries*, 2002, available at: http://www.hm-treasury.gov.uk/media//93EF6/case_for_aid02.pdf; Canadian International Development Agency. *Canada Making a Difference in the World: A Policy Statement on Strengthening Aid Effectiveness*, September 2002, available at: www.acdi-cida.gc.ca/aideffectiveness.

40 OECD, Development Assistance Committee (DAC), *International Development Statistics –2006 Edition*, available at: www.oecd.org/dac/stats; World Bank, *Assessing Aid*, 1998, available at: http://www.worldbank.org/research/aid/aidtoc.htm; World Bank, *The Role and Effectiveness of Development Assistance. Lessons from World Bank Experience*, 2002, available at: http://wbln0018.worldbank.org/eurvp/web.nsf/Pages/Paper+by+Ian+Goldin/$File/GOLDIN.PDF

41 http://www.cgdev.org/section/initiatives/_active/cdi

42 Department for International Development, United Kingdom. *Eliminating World Poverty: Making Globalization Work for the Poor*. White Paper on International Development, December 2000, p.28.

43 44.3% by the EC, 39.8% by the World Bank, 45% by the Asian Development Bank, See OECD, *Development Aid at Glance. Statistics by Region*, 2006 Edition, p. 18.

44 OECD, *Conflict Prevention and Peace Building: What Counts as ODA?*, March 2005, available at: http://www.oecd.org/dataoecd/32/32/34535173.pdf.

45 *The Cotonou Agreement, Partnership Agreement Between the Members of the African, Caribbean and Pacific Group of States of the one part, and the European Community and its Member States, of the other Part*, p.14, available at: http:/ec.europa.eu/development/body/cotonou/pdf/agr01_en.pdf

46 Communication from the Commission to the Council, the European Parliament and the European Economic and Social Committee, *Governance and Development*, 20 October 2003, p.7, available at: http://www.oecd.org/dataoecd/1/26/20334754.pdf

47 2008-2013 European Development Fund (Revised Cotonou Agreement) is the main instrument for providing Community aid for development cooperation in the ACP states and overseas collectivities and territories (OCTs).

48 The Council of the European Union, *The EU and Africa: Towards a Strategic Partnership*, 19 December 2005, p.2, available at: http:/ec.europa.eu/development/body/communications/docs/the_eu_and_africa_towards_a_strategic_partnership_european_council_15_16_12_2005_en.pdf#zoom=100

49 The Commission of the European Communities, Communication from the Commission to the Council, the European Parliament and the European Economic and Social Committee: *EU Strategy for Africa: Towards a Euro-African pact to Accelerate Africa's development*, 12 October 2005, p.23, available at: http:/ec.europa.eu/development/body/communications/docs/eu_strategy_for_africa_12_10_2005_en.pdf

50 Joint Statement by the Council and the Representatives of the Governments of the Member States Meeting within the Council, the European Parliament and the Commissions, *The European Consensus on Development*, 20 December 2005, available at: http:/ec.europa.eu/development/body/development_policy_statement/docs/edp_declaration_signed_20_12_2005_en.pdf#zoom=125

51 Ibid, p.11.

52 The most important documents in this regard are: Commission Communication, *The External Dimension of the EU´s Human Rights Policy: From Rome to Maastricht and Beyond*, 22 November 1995, available at: http:/ec.europa.eu/comm/external_relations/human_rights/doc/comm95_567_en.pdf; European Commission, Communication from the Commission to the Council and the European Parliament, *The European Union's Role in Promoting Human Rights and Democratisation in Third Countries*, 8 May 2001, available at: http:/ec.europa.eu/comm/external_relations/human_rights/doc/com01_252_en.pdf; The European Commission, Communication From the Commission to the Council and the European Parliament, *Thematic Programme for the Promotion of Democracy and Human Rights Worldwide under the Future Financial Perspectives (2007-2013)*, 25 January 2006, available at: http:/ec.europa.eu/comm/external_relations/human_rights/doc/2006com_23_en.pdf .

53 European Commission, Communication from the Commission to the Council and the European Parliament, *The European Union's Role in Promoting Human Rights and Democratisation in Third Countries*, 8 May 2001, available at: http:/ec.europa.eu/comm/external_relations/human_rights/doc/com01_252_en.pdf

54 European Commission, Communication from the Commission on Conflict Prevention, 11 April 2001, p. 14, available at: http:/ec.europa.eu/comm/external_relations/cfsp/news/com2001_211_en.pdf

55 Council of Ministers and European Commission, *EU Annual Report on Human Rights 2006*, p.7, available at: http:/ec.europa.eu/comm/external_relations/human_rights/doc/report_06_en.pdf

56 Ibid, p.42.

57 http:/ec.europa.eu/europeaid/projects/eidhr/index_en.htm

58 Commission of the European Communities, Communication from the Commission to the Council and the European Parliament , *A Concept for Community Support for Security Sector Reform*, 24 May 2006, p.9, available at: http://eur-lex.europa.eu/LexUriServ/site/en/com/2006/com2006_0253en01.pdf

59 http://ec.europa.eu/enlargement/key_documents/reports_nov_2006_en.htm; on benchmarks for SSR implementation, see Heiner Hänggi, *The Role of Security Sector Governance in the EU's Democratic and Acquis Conditionality*, Paper prepared for the ECPR Panel 'SSG Conditionality in EU Accession Policy', Istanbul, 21-23 September 2006.

60 The European Commission, Communication From the Commission to the Council and the European Parliament, *EU Enlargement Strategy and Main Challenges 2006 – 2007*, 8 November 2006, available at: http://ec.europa.eu/enlargement/pdf/key_documents/2006/Nov/com_649_strategy_paper_en.pdf

61 Ibid, p. 11.

62 Ibid, p. 46.

63 *Regulation of the European Parliament and of the Council of laying down general provisions establishing a European Neighbourhood and Partnership Instrument*, 24 October 2006, available at: http://ec.europa.eu/world/enp/pdf/oj_l310_en.pdf

64 Presidency Conclusions, Tampere European Council, 15-16 October 1999, available at:

http://www.consilium.europa.eu/ueDocs/cms_Data/docs/pressData/en/ec/00200-r1.en9.htm

65 The Council of the European Union, *The Hague Programme : Strengthening Freedom, Security and Justice in the European Union*, 13 December 2004, available at : http://ec.europa.eu/justice_home/doc_centre/doc/hague_programme_en.pdf

66 Ibid.

67 Council of the European Union, *A Strategy for the External Dimension of JHA: Global Freedom, Security and Justice*, 30 November 2005, available at: http://register.consilium.europa.eu/pdf/en/05/st14/st14366-re03.en05.pdf

68 The European Commission, Communication From the Commission to the Council and the European Parliament, *EU Enlargement Strategy and Main Challenges 2006 – 2007*, 8 November 2006, available at: http://ec.europa.eu/enlargement/pdf/key_documents/2006/Nov/com_649_strategy_paper_en.pdf

2. The European Community Perspective on SSR: The Development of a Comprehensive EU Approach

Inger Buxton

Introduction

In May 2006 the European Commission (EC) put forward a first comprehensive approach to Security Sector Reform (SSR) as a first pillar contribution to the EU's external relations.[1] This followed the adoption of a (second pillar) European Security and Defence Policy concept for Security Sector Reform in 2005[2] and led to the subsequent endorsement of an overarching EU Policy Framework in June 2006.[3] These EU policy developments were the culmination of different individual member state initiatives, joint efforts at international level and the EU's own long experience in support of activities in different sub-sectors of the security system in various countries. For the Commission this had included the development of Operational Guidelines for Integrated Border Management for the Western Balkans and the inclusion of SSR in key policy documents, such as the EC *Communication on Conflict Prevention* of 2001[4] and the EC *Communication on Governance and Development* of 2003.[5] Cooperation with EU member states and other donors in the OECD's Development Assistance Committee (DAC) on SSR[6] also had significant impact on policy developments. The continued efforts to achieve commonly agreed standards and approaches by international actors were clearly of immense conceptual and operational importance in the emergence of this new policy framework. This chapter sets out the issues relevant to the European Community pillar of the European Union.

Where Security Sector Reform is Relevant – Development, Governance and Human Security

While there can be windows of opportunity to initiate SSR in an immediate post-conflict context, as far as EC support is concerned, more is provided in relatively stable environments where countries are undergoing transition towards a greater degree of democracy. Of the around 70 countries that received support between 2000 and 2005, more than half were not in a crisis or post-crisis phase.[7] The bulk of EC support thus went to countries in transition, in particular as part of the EU Enlargement and Stabilisation and Association Processes. Indeed, comprehensive reform processes generally require a more stable environment for the development of democratic institutions and culture.

As is the case with other multilateral and bilateral donors, the focus of EU development cooperation (both community and member states) has gradually shifted from growth related aspects to poverty reduction, including human rights and democratic governance. This is reflected in the European Consensus on Development adopted in 2005[8] and in the governance communication of 2003, *Governance and Development*.[9] The latter argues that a country's ability to eradicate poverty and promote sustainable development hinges on the quality of its governance, with SSR being an integral component of good governance. It also reflects on the importance of the more upstream aspects of reforming the security system, in terms of 'effective management, transparency and accountability of the security environment that upholds democratic principles and human rights'.[10]

This can be seen as an outcome of the changes that have taken place in the Commission's thinking on the inter-linkage between development and security. Security has increasingly come to be seen as a prerequisite for development, at the same time as development is necessary to address root causes of violent conflict and insecurity. As with other foreign policy and development cooperation actors and donors, the Commission subscribes to the notion of human security, which puts comprehensive security of people rather than the territory of the state or a particular regime at the heart of security policy. This broader EU security concept was reflected both in the European Security Strategy and in the EU Consensus on Development, as well as in a number of other key EC policy documents including the EC *Communication on Conflict Prevention* of 2001.

The EC *Communication on Security Sector Reform* outlines how the human security concept is useful not only in defining the relationship between its citizens' needs and the state's responsibilities (including the state's ability to maintain peace and guarantee the citizen's security of life, property, political, economic and social rights), but in understanding the inter-linkage and differences between external and internal security needs. It thereby helps clarify the separation of tasks between the different institutions and bodies constituting the security system. The human security concept has of course wider relevance to society and the functioning of institutions than what security sector reform encompasses. At the same time, the traditional view has ceded place to a view of SSR that includes other law enforcement institutions than the military and police, such as border guards and customs authorities. In the new approach to SSR, the security system also covers the wider justice system (the judiciary, prisons, prosecution services, human rights commissions and ombudsmen functions) as well as security management and oversight bodies (the legislature, executive, traditional authorities and civil society). The latter is especially important in order to ensure civilian control and democratic oversight. Thus, the Commission has defined its SSR concept as 'those aspects which are designed to contribute to peace, the protection of life and limb, and to ensure the upholding of the law and oversight through the justice system and democratic institutions of the relevant executive bodies'.[11]

Following the endorsement of the overarching SSR policy framework at the European Council in June 2006, the EU developed a joint EU concept for Disarmament, Demobilisation and Reintegration (DDR). This was endorsed by the European Commission and the Council of the EU in December 2006. The aim was to outline existing best practice and current international understanding and approaches to DDR, based on work already done by the UN and the World Bank, and to identify ways to strengthen EU support in the future. Given the close link between SSR and DDR in post-conflict settings, the development of the DDR concept was a natural next step in efforts to enhance EU conflict prevention and crisis management capacity. Apart from DDR, the links between the EU's activities in SSR and the areas of transitional justice, reconciliation, the promotion of human rights and efforts to strengthen good governance and democratisation have also been recognised.

EC Experience, EC Instruments and the Impact of Practice

To prepare for the EC Communication, the Commission conducted a survey in the summer of 2005 to map past and current EC support to SSR related programmes and projects over the past five years. This was compiled and summarised in a Commission staff working document, which formed part of the annexes to the Commission Communication.[12] The results showed that the EC is and has been engaged in over 70 countries around the world in support of SSR. This covers a large spectrum of activities. In the area of justice reform, it includes legal reforms and capacity building of interior or justice ministries, judicial and prosecution institutions, prison services, judicial and law faculties, legal aid, human rights commissions and ombudsman functions. Support is also extended to reforms of law enforcement institutions, including police, border management and customs services and support to relevant executive branches of government and democratic oversight mechanisms, including parliaments and civil society capacity building. In the area of border management it included capacity building of key ministries, border guards and customs institutions. Police reform has also been a relatively important area in the Western Balkans, Central America, Afghanistan, South Africa and the DRC. In a few cases it has included reform of armed forces, though limited to human rights and humanitarian law training and support to army integration centres and army families. This is not only because defence reform falls outside ODA eligibility for development cooperation assistance (on which more below), but also because member states consider military aspects to be a second pillar rather than Community competence.

EC support to justice reform and law enforcement has been especially significant. It has included capacity building of key institutions to promote access to justice and the rule of law. It is not only a priority in many of the developing countries with which the EU is cooperating, but part of the Community *acquis* itself. This makes security sector reform a cornerstone of EU integration and enlargement. EU support is generally implemented through the Stabilisation and Association process. It has thereby come to be incorporated into the external policy of the Union as part of the external dimension of EU policy on Freedom, Security and Justice. It covers a number of issues which fall under what is today defined as SSR, but without being necessarily labelled as such, including support in the areas of rule of law, good governance and institution building in sectors such as migration, border management, law enforcement, judicial cooperation, the fight against terrorism and organised crime. In addition, the EC's conflict prevention policy views SSR as a key area to address root causes that could contribute to violent conflict as well as to building sustainable peace in post-conflict settings. In its *Communication on Conflict Prevention*, the Commission stated its intention to play an increasingly active role in the security sector.

The EC mainstreams democracy and human rights in its development cooperation programmes and in the EU's political dialogue with partner countries. Human rights clauses now figure in all EC bilateral agreements. SSR related support in this area has been given under the European Initiative for Democracy and Human Rights, in support of the rule of law, access to justice and human rights institutions to countries in Eastern Europe, Latin America, Africa and Asia. In terms of geographical instruments and more long-term support, the EC has been especially active under the CARDS (Western Balkans), TACIS (Eastern Europe and Central Asia) and MEDA (Middle East) programmes and to a lesser extent through the ALA programme (Asia and Latin America) and the EDF (Africa, Pacific and Caribbean). In all of these the main focus has been on justice reform and border management.

Countries such as Bosnia, Ukraine, Albania and the DRC are especially interesting, given the multi-sector approach taken by the EC and made possible by the high priority given these countries by the EU and the absence of other actors taking a clear lead in the reform process. In Albania it includes EC support through CARDS to the Customs Assistance Mission in Albania (CAM-A), the Police Assistance Mission of the European Community to Albania (PAMECA) and the European Assistance Mission to the Albanian Judicial System (EURALIUS). While most programmes have been country specific, there was also some support at regional level, most notably in the areas of border management and law enforcement, where addressing cross-border organised crime was important, as in the case of the Commission's Border Management Programme in Central Asia (BOMCA) or the Border Assistance Mission to Moldova and Ukraine (EUBAM).

The new Instrument for Stability, which replaced the Rapid Reaction Mechanism on 1 January 2007, offers an enhanced capacity for the EC to provide short to long term support to promote peace and stability. Short term crisis response has been extended in terms of resources and scope. Now, activities can be supported for up to 18 months, with a possible extension by a further six months.[13] In addition, a long-term component has been included which enables the EC to support trans-regional cooperation, which includes SSR related activities to strengthen the capacity of law enforcement and judicial and civil authorities to address organised crime, terrorism, illicit trafficking of people, drugs, firearms and explosive materials and in the effective control of illegal trade and transit.[14]

With more flexible and rapid support under the Instrument for Stability the EC is able to kick-start Community support. This might be in relation to action under the European Security and Defence Policy (ESDP), as in the case of rule of law and institutional reform of the judiciary in Georgia and police reform and army integration in DRC. Or it might be instead of a second pillar ESDP action in the form of a crisis management mission, as with the EU border management mission for Moldova-Ukraine. It might also have no ESDP component, as in the case of Central Asia.

At the same time, there have been an increasing number of second pillar activities carried out in the framework of the ESDP. The separate action within the two EU pillars has highlighted the need to ensure greater coherence and coordination between the pillars and member states' bilateral support. This was a major aim of the joint EU policy framework in June 2006.

From ad-hoc EC Intervention to a Coordinated EU Approach

The broad range of activities under different EU policies and instruments and the large range of geographical locations overall has made it difficult to develop a comprehensive, coherent and unified SSR policy for community support. The EU does not re-label all activities that fall within the broad scope of SSR as 'SSR'; nor are the approaches taken the same in all geographical locations and under all the different instruments. So, the EC Security Sector Reform Communication and the EU policy framework are helpful steps in creating common definitions of what security sector reform is about and what principles should be guiding EU activities in the area. The potential to act clearly depends on the level of overall EU engagement and political weight in a country and the interest of EU member states and national stakeholders. The incentive to support reform has generally been greater in pre-accession countries where the EU has a specific driving role.

Understanding how the security system functions as a whole is vital. EU support to police reform for example needs to be coupled with reforms in other parts of the system, including the courts and prisons, border management and defence. This does not mean that the EC or EU should necessarily be directly engaged in all of these areas in any given country. Instead they need to engage with other international actors in supporting national stakeholders in assessing security needs and in implementing comprehensive reforms.

The recent efforts to strengthen EU capacities in SSR should also be seen as a part of wider efforts to strengthen the EU's overall role and capacity to promote peace, security and development. Coordinated assessment is one key to effective policy. A number of joint EU assessment missions in SSR have been conducted since June 2006. They have included staff from the Commission, the Council Secretariat and occasionally member states. In the case of the DRC, this led to the development of a joint Commission-Council SSR concept underlying a number of other steps taken to implement policy commitments. Discussions have taken place between the Commission and member states on common profiles and training standards for staff deployed to the field. In addition, training courses for Commission headquarters and field staff have been held and steps to strengthen support functions in the thematic units responsible for SSR within the Commission are under way.

The emergence of the concept of security system governance to describe an effectively functioning security system has been especially significant. The EU's new policy framework implies EU commitment to a set of principles based on international best practice and a human security perspective, enabling a whole-of-government or cross-pillar EU response in SSR. This facilitates common understanding of needs and approaches and should provide a sound basis for first and second pillar coordination and coherence.

Common Conceptual Approaches with other International Actors

In order to strengthen the EU's engagement further, the EC Communication identified a number of areas where steps could be taken to enhance both capacities and the comprehensive approach itself. One area is overall political dialogue as well as programming dialogue with partner countries, where regular discussions can take place on SSR standards and the principles that need to guide SSR reform, including respect for human rights, good governance and rule of law.

As a major provider of external assistance, the Commission has found it essential to work closely with other donors in these countries in the area of peace and security, and thus Security Sector Reform, including EU member states. This is an area which has seen rapid developments in both policy and operational terms in recent years. But it was long seen as 'non traditional' by many development actors, the traditional view of SSR being primarily concerned with reform of defence forces and civilian institutions with a right to use force (e.g. the police). The adoption of new concepts and the EU policy framework thus mark an important change from a concept with exclusively military and police relevance to a wider, comprehensive and system-wide approach to security sector reform.

The UN system and especially UNDP and IOM are important implementers of EU support to security sector reform. Common approaches and coordination with them and other international organisations such as NATO, the Council of Europe, OSCE, non-governmental organisations and other major donors of development assistance are central to a holistic approach in support of SSR. This ensures not only conceptual clarity but also avoidance of duplication of efforts in the same countries. Cooperation in the OECD's Development Assistance Committee led to the DAC Guidelines on Security System Reform and Governance[15] and the current joint donor work to develop an implementation framework in the form of an SSR Handbook. Efforts within the DAC reflect the role development cooperation has come to play in support of the civilian aspects of SSR, not only because of the financial resources it can bring to bear, but because of its direct link to overall development objectives. These include governance, human rights, democratisation and conflict prevention, which are seen as elements of the path to create or restore the appropriate environment for development and poverty reduction. SSR requires long-term engagement and a comprehensive approach, which development cooperation can provide. This implies presence on the ground and support provided through specific SSR projects and programmes or within a wider public sector reform package.

To reflect the role development cooperation has come to play in addressing insecurity and violent conflict, including through security sector reform, Official Development Assistance (ODA) has been extended over the last few years to include a number of security related activities that are eligible for financing through development aid. However, there are aspects of SSR in the defence and intelligence areas which fall outside ODA and where the primary actor on the assisting government side is not the development cooperation agency or responsible ministry, but the ministry of defence. At the same time, defence reform has to go hand in hand with reforms on the civilian side. It requires a whole-of-government approach by donor governments to ensure that policies and funding can match the different needs. ODA is not an activity *per se* but a reporting framework. Donor governments need to ensure funds available under different instruments are reported accurately in relation to ODA, in order to ensure that the whole spectrum of peace support and promotion of security aspects can be financed, without undermining the criteria for development assistance developed over the years. The European Community has funded non-ODA activities through the European Development Fund. This has included most of the activities under the Africa Peace Facility and in support of army integration in the Democratic Republic of the Congo.

Operational Coordination with other Actors

In addition to the conceptual work in the OECD-DAC, the EU has established operational coordination on conflict prevention and crisis management with the UN. The EU-UN desk-to-desk dialogue on conflict prevention takes place on a biannual basis and SSR issues also figure in meetings of the EU-UN Steering Committee on Crisis Management. The EU also works with international and regional actors, such as the Council of Europe, the North Atlantic Treaty Organisation (NATO), the Organisation for Security and Cooperation in Europe (OSCE) and the African Union (AU) in the area of SSR. In the case of the African Union and sub-regional organisations in Africa, this has included support to strengthen their capacity in crisis management and peacebuilding. For the EC as a major donor, UN agencies and non-governmental organisations are not only strategic partners but major implementing partners for EC funding of security sector reform. NGOs contribute to EU work, as implementers of EU assistance and in helping to define the terms of policy recommendations. In November 2005, the UK Presidency and the Commission organised an SSR seminar together with Saferworld and International Alert, which contributed to the final stages of the development of the EU comprehensive policy approach to SSR in 2006.

How productive are these relations between the EU and other actors? Common definitions of SSR used by international actors and exchange of best practice in operational terms have certainly made coordination between international actors easier, though cooperation at headquarters level does not always trickle down to the field. Likewise, operational cooperation in the field does not always result in better policy coordination at headquarters. This is probably as much due to lack of capacity and institutional bottlenecks within organisations as to a lack of will to coordinate with others. But good working relations are clearly necessary if effective assistance to partner countries is to be ensured. Generally, cooperation with regional, national and local actors in partner countries and regions still needs improved dialogue and an increase in shared perspectives and best practice.

The DAC work not only provided an important basis for Community policy developments, but also impacted on the efforts within the second pillar of the EU, the CFSP/ESDP. Both the Commission's Communication and the ESDP concept paper draw on definitions and principles established in the DAC guidelines and recognised that the essence of the impact of the new SSR concept is less the efficiency of individual services and more the holistic and system wide approach, where reforms in one sector must of necessity be linked to reforms in other sectors, based on their specific functions and their distinct tasks within the overall system. By taking a whole-of-government approach, cutting across the EU pillars, the DAC work has provided EU member states and the EU institutions with a policy basis as well as a useful implementation framework for operational coordination with other major actors.

Policy Developments in 2005-2006: from a Sub-Sector to Comprehensive Approach

The rapid development since the late 1990s, and especially after 2001, of strengthened EU capacity and objectives in the areas of conflict prevention and crisis management have had significant impact on the way the Union is currently approaching SSR, both in policy and operational terms. The ESDP missions and the Community's Rapid Reaction Mechanism and now the Instrument for Stability, have covered and cover a number of SSR related activities, especially in post-conflict settings. They complement SSR support under the long-term community instruments and included both civilian aspects of SSR and more recently defence reform through the launch of EUSEC Congo in 2005. The DRC is generally seen as an important test case for the EU in SSR, following the adoption in 2006 of the overarching EU policy framework, in terms of civil-military coordination, cross-pillar coordination, sequencing of short and long term instruments and EU coordination and cooperation with national and international actors. This is the first time the EU has engaged in defence reform, undertaking police and justice reform at the same time. It is unlikely that there will be another case on the same scale and level of political commitment for some years. In most geographical locations the main focus of EU support is likely to continue to be on civilian aspects of SSR. However, there are other countries and regions where the EU is starting to take a more holistic and coordinated approach to SSR, as in the case of Kosovo, Afghanistan and Guinea Bissau and, undoubtedly, there remain many cases where overall security sector reform is needed.

While the Stability Instrument provides a flexible and integrated response in a single consolidated financing instrument to promote peace and security, new long-term geographic and other thematic instruments also have a central role in promoting peace and security, including in the area of SSR. Indeed, the majority of the new instruments need to provide support in this sector if the EU is going be a key international player in SSR in the future, including the Instrument for Pre-Accession Assistance[16], the European Neighbourhood and Partnership Instrument[17], the Development

Cooperation and Economic Co-operation Instrument and the Instrument for the Promotion of Human Rights.[18] Mainstreaming within the Commission to ensure that SSR is being integrated into the various strategies and programmes these instruments cover is thus vital. In the Commission, mainstreaming is a particular preoccupation for directorates general within the External Relations family, both at headquarters' level and in the field. Both desk officers and delegations require the necessary knowledge and skills to plan and provide SSR support. The Inter-Quality Support Group in DG Development is responsible for ensuring that key policies are being mainstreamed.[19] They achieve this through Country and Regional Strategy Papers as the main tools for long-term planning of geographical instruments. Thematic instruments also have their own strategy papers. SSR needs and potential EC support are now identified in strategy papers covering the 2007-2013 period, so that long-term funding can be ensured. The relevance and importance of coordination and common approaches with other donors in addition to training and tools for implementation is underlined by the fact that many partner countries lack comprehensive SSR analyses and the consequent need for the EC to prioritise a limited number of areas, with most strategies focusing on one or two sub-sectors.

In order to enhance cross-pillar cooperation, the EC Communication underlined the need to establish better coordination between EC and ESDP activities, including joint needs assessments and improved complementarily in implementation. To enhance the professionalism of staff involved, ongoing work includes internal training of desks and delegations on how to conduct security sector analyses and how to prepare support programmes. Member states and EU institutions have also begun joint work on common training standards for personnel to be sent on international missions and on the establishment of pools of experts. This includes Commission support to a network of member states' training institutions and the European Training Group, which provides training for experts to be deployed in the field. Member states' experts are being deployed in twinning or other types of security sector reform programmes or ESDP missions. Steps have also been taken to establish crisis response teams in the framework of ESDP, and Commission assessment teams. A number of joint assessment missions have taken place in 2006 and 2007, which enable common analyses and better coordination and sequencing of support. Mechanisms are also being set up at field level to enhance coordination. The DRC and Kosovo are prime examples.

The EC Communication also recommended improvements of planning and implementation tools, including comprehensive SSR analyses and operational guidelines. The Commission is currently following up on existing guidelines for Integrated Border Management (IBM) for the Western Balkans with the development of IBM Guidelines for Central Asia, as well as general IBM guidelines. Here, joint work with other donors in the OECD-DAC is especially important. The DAC SSR Handbook, which was launched in the spring of 2007, will provide donors with tools for analysis and operational guidance. It will also constitute a framework for coordination at field level.

Conclusion – Assessing the Impact of Policy Change

SSR is clearly an area in which the EU has a significant role to play, through the range of security and development cooperation instruments at its disposal. The level of EU support is already relatively high in many parts of the world. Yet, the range of instruments and approaches used has made it more difficult for the EU to take a coordinated approach, so it is too early to assess fully the impact of the adoption of a comprehensive EU framework and efforts to provide the EC with a stronger policy base for security sector reform. In terms of behavioural change it will take time before new perceptions and policy approaches by the various EU actors lead to significant changes on the ground in the way the EU provides support. In addition, the EU is one player amongst several other international actors providing support. While the EU is already providing multi-sector SSR support to countries like Albania and South Africa through Community support and through a combination of ESDP and Community activities in the case of DRC, in the majority of cases the EU will continue to provide support to specific sectors, where it is seen to have a comparative advantage in relation to these other donors and international actors.

On the positive side the conceptual work carried out in the EU since 2005 is beginning to have an impact on the way assistance is provided. It does, however, need to be followed up with resources and mechanisms to ensure that concepts materialise in optimal operational support. This requires better assessment and analysis, prioritisation of SSR in the planning of support programmes and staff training. Cooperation with other actors will continue to be of central importance given the capacities and resources needed for the generally agreed holistic and multi-sector approach to be effective. For the Commission operational cooperation with member states and other bilateral and multilateral donors in the DAC has been and remains especially fruitful. It has provided a sound basis and a productive learning process resulting in the development of the DAC SSR Handbook. And it has provided for better coordination in the implementation of support. Importantly, local ownership and agreed definitions of security needs in partner countries are recognised as the most effective basis for cooperation. Here, much remains to be done to ensure that the perspectives and lessons learned from partner countries are fully understood and taken on board by the EU and other international actors. The aim has to be to further strengthen the provision of support to reform of security systems in partner countries.

Endnotes

1 Communication from the Commission to the Council and the European Parliament *A Concept for European Community Support for Security Sector Reform*, COM (2006) 253

2 *EU Concept for ESDP support to Security Sector Reform (SSR)* (Council doc. 12566/4/05)

3 Council Conclusions on a Policy Framework for Security Sector Reform 15-16 June 2006

4 The European Commission *Communication on Conflict Prevention*, COM (2001) 211

5 The European Commission *Communication on Governance and Development*, COM (2003) 615

6 Especially the *Security System Reform and Governance, Policy and Practice*, DAC Guidelines and Reference Series (Paris: OECD 2004)

7 Ibid.

8 'The European Consensus' on development was adopted by the Council on 22 November 2005.

9 The Commission *Communication on Governance and Development*

10 Ibid, p. 8

11 Commission *Communication on SSR*, p. 4-5

12 Commission Staff Working Document, Annex to the Communication from the Commission to the Council and the European Parliament, 'A Concept for European Community Support for Security Sector Reform', SEC (2006) 658.

13 Regulation (EC) No 1717/2006 of the European Parliament and of the Council, 15 November 2006.

14 Measures should place special emphasis on good governance and be carried out in accordance with international law.

15 *Security System Reform and Governance, Policy and Practice,* DAC Guidelines and Reference Series (Paris OECD 2004)

16 Regulation (EC) No 1085/2006 of 17 July 2006 establishing an Instrument for Pre-Accession Assistance (IPA)

17 Regulation (EC) No 1638/2006 of the European Parliament and of the Council of 24 October 2006 laying down general provisions establishing a European Neighbourhood and Partnership Instrument.

18 Regulation (EC) No 1889/2006 of the European Parliament and of the Council of 20 December 2006 on establishing a financing instrument for the promotion of democracy and human rights worldwide.

19 The group was set up following the adoption of the RELEX reform in 2000, in order to improve the quality and coherence of the European Commission's external aid programmes.

3. Security Sector Reform: a Challenging Concept at the Nexus between Security and Development

Patrick Doelle and Antoine Gouzée de Harven

Introduction

As the manager of the European Community's development policy, the European Commission is a fervent promoter of the concept of security sector reform (SSR). But like most of its counterparts, it faces the challenges stemming from the rather modest experience in this new policy sector at the nexus between development and security. This chapter is divided into two parts. Part one examines the Commission's promotion of the concept of SSR and its response to the challenges of SSR at international and European Union (EU) level. Part two focuses on the recently reformed European Community (EC) external assistance architecture and its implications for the integration of the SSR concept into overall EU policy.

The concept of SSR first needs to be put into perspective. While the umbilical link between development and security is today fully recognised by both development and security actors, this was not always the case. During the Cold War, the nature of international relations was not conducive to acknowledgment of what today seems an obvious link. First, ideological enmity between the two superpowers meant that nascent conflict between developing countries was fuelled by the two superpowers, which used them as battlefields to wage proxy wars against each other. Second, the naive donor view that development and economic growth would alone reduce the potential for conflict, violence and criminality served to prevent further reflection on the issue. In sum, development aid was about generating economic growth, but it was coupled with the unspoken aim of securing the loyalty of developing countries.

The demise of the Soviet Union and the advent of a sole superpower were accompanied by a new commitment to end conflicts around the world and maintain international peace and security. A new debate on the link between security and development began to emerge, as security and development actors realised that mutually supportive action was perhaps the key to their common objectives. Particularly, it was felt necessary to bridge the gaps between the traditionally sequenced and dissociated approaches of humanitarian assistance, peacekeeping and post-conflict recovery, which made forty percent of affected countries relapse into conflict. As development and security actors began to collaborate in the same theatres, a 'hybrid' sphere of intervention called 'post-conflict peace-building' emerged. The point was no longer merely to manage conflict, but to address its root causes, be they of a security, political, economic, environmental or social nature.[1] Both groups of stakeholders understood not only that their respective fields of operations were mutually-reinforcing, but also that they had a role to play in each other's field. Meanwhile, the many intra-state wars following the end of the Cold War led to a shift from the traditional focus on external security to a focus on internal security. Peace and security appeared to the development community not only to be a prerequisite to sustainable development, but an obvious core concern for the most impoverished.[2] This led to the emergence of the concept of 'human' security as opposed to state security. The establishment of a well functioning and accountable security sector thus naturally became an aim of development and security policy in the framework of peace-building.

The time was thus ripe for the formulation of the SSR concept, a term first formulated by the then UK Development Cooperation Minister, Clare Short in 1998.[3] The need for reform of a state's security system had already been pointed out on an ad-hoc basis, but this was the first time reference was made to the role of the security sector in promoting human development and helping to reduce poverty. The concept of security sector reform had emerged from the recognition that states emerging from conflict frequently lack democratic and professional security forces, and that these need to be created or transformed following the end of a conflict, since they are usually inappropriate, unbalanced in size, budget and capabilities and are frequently guilty of human rights violations and other crimes. They constitute a threat rather than inspiring confidence. Yet, if SSR was originally (and sometimes still misleadingly) exclusively linked to post-conflict settings, since they offer valuable 'windows of opportunity'[4], in time the concept appeared equally relevant elsewhere. Stable, transitional, fragile, collapsing and failed states all need an efficient and accountable security system for their development, and the scope of security sector reform has thus been widened to support inclusion of the fight against crime, terrorism, human trafficking and smuggling.

International and European Union SSR Challenges: the Role of the EC as a Development Actor

The EU had had a long history of cooperation in security issues before the concept of SSR was formulated, in particular in the acceding and neighbouring countries. Indeed, an important learning factor for the EU has been its own enlargement, requiring the adoption of the *acquis communautaire* by candidate countries. Important elements of this include the democratic control of security forces and security-related measures, such as border management – necessary in terms of customs controls in addition to traditional security terms. Likewise, partnership with countries now falling under the European Neighbourhood Policy (ENP) required the overall stability and security of the region, given its proximity to the Schengen area. Yet, cooperation did not properly speaking take place according to the precepts of today's concept of SSR. Departing from old-fashioned practices in the field of security, the concept today views the security sector as an interconnected whole, as a 'system' incorporating the supposition that improvement of one of its sub-sectors will only be sustainable if accompanied by improvement in the others. The concept calls for an integrated strategic approach encompassing the whole security system and based on a long-term vision and operationally sequenced action. The added-value of the concept is its plea for a balanced approach between the democratic and civilian control of the security forces on the one hand and their efficiency as security providers on the other.[5]

Firmly convinced of the benefits of this new approach to cooperation in the field of security, the EU has become one of the most active promoters of the concept. However, like other donors, the EU, and particularly the European Commission as its development cooperation manager, faced numerous difficulties in translating the implications of the security sector reform concept into practice. This section reviews the four main obstacles with which the European Commission has to cope as a leading development actor, and puts them into EU perspective.

The Challenge of Promoting SSR within Development Policy

The potential benefits of security sector reform for poverty reduction and human development are uncontested. As the UK Department for International Development put it in the early years of the concept, the underlying reasons for SSR are: (i) to increase the resources available for investment in poverty-reduction (e.g. by encouraging economic growth and thus attracting investors to a safe investment environment or reducing expenditure on security forces in developing countries); (ii) to better protect society, especially vulnerable groups (because research suggests that poor people are disproportionably affected by crime and violence[6] and security forces are often themselves the source of wrongdoings); (iii) to improve the contribution of the security sector to conflict prevention, management and resolution. Security sector reform can reduce tension through, inter alia, confidence building, controlling arms proliferation and preventing potential crises from degenerating into open armed conflict, etc; (iv) cutting across the first three is the need to ensure greater democratic participation in decision-making on the security apparatus and greater access to justice.[7] The security sector reform agenda thus contains both clear normative and practical commitments to development.

Despite the fact that these objectives are commonly accepted and that the potential for SSR to achieve them is undisputed, integrating security into development cooperation policies remains a challenge for three main reasons. First, there is the fear that development policy might be 'hijacked' to the benefit of national security objectives by foreign-policy makers through 'politicisation' or 'instrumentalisation' of development aid. The fear is not unfounded. Stability is still sometimes achieved at the expense of democracy, the rule of law and good governance. Unconditional support to authoritarian regimes and the fight against terrorism illustrates how easy it can be to turn a blind eye to human rights violations for the sake of 'security'. Second, there is a concern that the scarce resources dedicated to development cooperation might be unduly diverted to security purposes, rather than devoted to objectives directly targeting poverty alleviation – the so-called 'securitisation' of development aid. Here again, the concerns are not unwarranted. With global military spending at around $1,001 billion in 2005[8] and Official Development Assistance (ODA) at $106.8 billion[9], there is reason for some to believe that funds for security sector reform might be better sought elsewhere. Third, some development actors still believe that their mandate is strictly limited to poverty alleviation and human development *stricto sensu*, and that they do not have the expertise necessary to engage in highly political security-related activities.

Despite these concerns, the concept of SSR emerged from the recognition that sidestepping the discussion on the interdependency between security and development and focussing exclusively on 'traditional' fields of development cooperation was not only a mistake but clearly doomed to failure. There are two main reasons why the development community has come to believe – though this belief still needs to be deeply embedded – that integration of security issues into its own work is crucial. First, if development is contingent on security, the reverse is also true. Be it thanks to long-standing experience in developing countries, its peculiar understanding of the interests and challenges these countries face, its long-term approach or its democratic perspective, development policy displays a number of comparative strengths that make it indispensable to the achievement of security. Security actors are well aware of this and they have come to see that development actors can draw on invaluable know-how to position themselves as indisputable actors in the security field. The final aim of development actors may not be to achieve security as an end in itself. But, it is clear that their core objectives of poverty eradication and the achievement of the Millennium Development Goals may pass through action in the security area. Second, human security underpins the approach of development actors to security as part of development policy. It is clearly a broader objective than that of state security. Human security is about the basic needs of people in developing countries. These are not always the priority in the approach traditionally adopted by security actors, nor are they systematically the core of their mandate. Development actors, on the other hand, prioritise this crucial need of the individual and society as a whole; they might be the only actors to do so.

In an ideal world, full convergence of the objectives of security and development policy would imply that promotion of good governance, socioeconomic development, democracy and human rights would be guiding principles for security actors. Conversely, for development policy actors it would suggest mainstreaming conflict and security sensitivity into all areas of intervention. It would also trigger a strategic division of labour between development and security policy actors. Some security-related activities are indeed legitimate candidates for full or shared responsibility with development policy. Conflict prevention, peace building, the fight against traditional and organised crime, terrorism, the proliferation of weapons of mass destruction (WMD) and small arms and light weapons, as well as trafficking in human beings and drugs are all prime examples. The EU and European Commission regularly emphasise this interdependence between security and development, as is demonstrated by a series of policy documents – the 2003 EU Security Strategy[10]; the 2005 *Communication on Policy Coherence for Development – Accelerating Progress Towards Attaining the Millennium Development Goals*; the 2005 *Communication on a Strategy on the External Dimension of the area of Freedom, Security and Justice*; the 2005 Consensus on Development; the 2006 EU Africa Strategy; the 2006 *Communication on Europe in the World – Some Practical Proposals for Greater Coherence, Effectiveness and Visibility*; as well as the 2006 *Communication on Governance in the European Consensus on Development*. The European Commission is thus at the forefront in the advocacy of enhanced integration of security issues into development cooperation policies, constantly emphasising that SSR is a prerequisite for poverty alleviation and social development. Here again, examples abound – the 2001 *Communication on Conflict Prevention*, the 2003 *Communication on Governance and Development* and the 2006 Concept for European Community Support for Security Sector Reform.

Practical integration of SSR into the Commission's development programming is also evident. Its Country and Regional Strategy Papers and Action Plans testify to the fact that SSR requires long-term strategies, long-term and sustained commitment and departure from the outdated approaches to development reflected in previous programming documents.[11] The concept has thus found its way into EC development cooperation. Needless to say, however, we are still far from the ideal described above. The European Commission thus needs to build on its valuable achievements and continue its endeavours not only to mainstream the concept of SSR into its development policy, but also to enter into strategic partnership with its security counterparts.

Budgetary Responsibility: Official Development Assistance or Just 'External Assistance'?

Effective strategic partnership presupposes agreement on sources of funding for security sector expenditure. This raises the basic question as to whether development funds should be used for security-related expenditure, and if so, to what extent. This delicate and still unresolved issue is all the more important since the smallest financial gap might put any attempt at SSR at risk.

Development budgets are progressively assuming additional SSR-related expenditure without being concomitantly and proportionally increased. Although not a problem as such, this conflicts with the still largely unmet commitment of donors to dedicate 0.7% of GDP as Official Development Assistance (ODA) to the attainment of the Millennium Development Goals (MDGs).[12] Notwithstanding the uncontested contribution of security to development, the fear is that further dispersion of meagre development resources by taking on additional security-related tasks would make it even more difficult to achieve the MDGs. As a result, a frequent complaint concerns the risk of jeopardising the concept of ODA, by continuous expansion of its definition to cover extra security-related expenditure. The opponents of its extension thus argue that ODA should continue to be primarily targeted at the promotion of the economic development and welfare of developing countries.[13] Donors willing to invest in security as a precondition to development are paradoxically between the devil and the deep blue sea. On the one hand, they must oppose an extension of ODA to preserve their limited resources. Yet, on the other, they must support it if their security-related expenditure is to be considered a contribution to their 0.7% GDP commitment. To escape this ironical situation, development actors must ineluctably benefit from additional funding, be it with or without an extension of ODA criteria, providing they can invest in security while at the same time keeping their promise to dedicate at least 0.7% of GDP to measures directly aimed at poverty alleviation and the attainment of the MDGs. Only thus will it be possible to diminish, if not eliminate, the reluctance of development actors to engage in security activities not covered by their foreign and security policy counterparts.

Yet, this has not been so far been the chosen option. Military spending continues to rise worldwide, while development assistance is failing to rise at the same pace and is so far not even on target to reach 0.7% of most donors' GDP. At UN level, for example, SSR and the Demobilisation and Reintegration components of DDR processes are still funded through voluntary contributions, rather than mandatory assessed contributions. To date, the trend has merely been to extend the criteria defining ODA so as to include more security-related expenditure, but without a commensurate increase in resources for development. True, in March 2005, the members of the Development Assistance Committee (DAC) of the OECD extended and supposedly clarified the criteria of eligibility, so as to include expenditure associated with non-military aspects of security sector reform, yet development budgets remain the same.

The OECD initiative is also controversial in that it allegedly aimed at clarification with the purpose of identifying boundaries and promoting transparent and activity-based reporting on ODA expenditure. But the new criteria are actually rather confusing. As they are currently defined, they do not give a clear picture of which security expenditure is eligible and which is not. This prevents frank and constructive discussion on the extent of development budget responsibility for security expenditure and risks financial shortfalls. DAC Statistical Reporting Directives use fainthearted, if not ambiguous, wording. In its Annex 5 to the relevant Directives, the DAC stipulates that the following expenditure is ODA-eligible: 'Technical co-operation provided to governments to improve civilian oversight and democratic control of budgeting, management, accountability and auditing of security expenditure, including military budgets, as part of a public expenditure management programme'. It then adds: 'Assistance to civil society to enhance its competence and capacity to scrutinise the security system so that it is managed in accordance with democratic norms and principles of accountability, transparency and good governance'. Finally, it includes: 'Technical co-operation provided to parliament, government ministries, law enforcement agencies and the judiciary to assist review and reform of the security system to improve democratic governance and civilian control. Eligible assistance is limited to non-military competence/capacity building and strategic planning activities that promote political, institutional and financial accountability, civilian oversight, and transparency. In addition, support to defence ministries must be part of a national security system reform strategy and be approved by the partner country ministry with overall responsibility for coordination of external assistance'.[14] A literal interpretation of the text of this last paragraph implies that eligibility as ODA would require technical co-operation to be aimed at improving democratic governance and civilian control and this is clearly how many development actors understand it, above all NGOs.[15] Yet, the assertion that the issue has been satisfactorily clarified is questioned both by scholars and practitioners. Acrimonious debates on which expenditure is eligible have been rife.

What, though, of the improvement of the efficiency of security forces? Are activities aimed at increasing security forces' capacities to provide security eligible? The DAC has provided a partial response to these questions in a fact sheet published in October 2006, explaining that with regard to civil police work, 'expenditure on police training is ODA, unless the training relates to paramilitary functions such as counter-insurgency work. The supply of the donor's police services to control civil disobedience is not reportable'. Likewise, with regard to peacekeeping operations (whether UN-administered or UN-approved, or outside the UN), it points out that 'ODA does include the net bilateral costs to donors of carrying out the following activities [...] monitoring and training of administrators, including customs and police officers [...]'.[16] Capacity-building of the police, at least with regard to activities constituting 'training', is thus to be considered reportable. But this raises two issues. First, it seems rather odd that the criteria are not specified in the official directives themselves. Second, if police training is eligible, what of other types of capacity-building, notably the provision of equipment? And what is the status of the other security services? That many questions remain unanswered because of an inadequately drafted policy document may be a reflection of the quality of drafting skills, but it may also be the consequence of a lack of consensus and thus reluctance on the part of DAC Ministers to commit to unambiguous definitions.

Ambiguity leaves room for interpretation. Some favour a strict interpretation of the texts, claiming that ODA eligibility is restricted to training of the police and customs and border guards. The provision of equipment to any law enforcement agency or training of intelligence services would thus be excluded.[17] Others (principally security actors but also development actors working on security sector reform) support a wider interpretation of the OECD DAC document. They hold that the DAC Directives should be understood to allow the reporting of all SSR-related activities as ODA, including those aimed at enhancement of civilian control, democratic oversight and improvement of the efficiency of security forces, but excluding those benefiting military staff and Ministry of Defence officials. The adoption of a 'residual' approach in the wording of the texts seems to imply that all security-related activities are included, except those specifically excluded, i.e. the military. Tellingly, in its fact sheet, the DAC indicates under a point entitled 'exclusion of military aid' that 'supply of military equipment and services, and the forgiveness of debts incurred for military purposes, are not reportable as ODA'. Yet, the supply of equipment and services to other security forces might then be eligible – an equally logical assumption, which actually appears to be the 'official' one, for it is adopted by national and international development agencies. This interpretation was also supported by Ministers and Heads of Aid Agencies during the 2005 extension/clarification negotiations, when they decided to postpone their formal agreement on two 'remaining' items – training the military in non-military matters, such as human rights, and extending the coverage to peacekeeping. The decision to postpone agreement on these issues could be seen as an indication that agreement on the other issues referred to above was uncontroversial.

In sum, then, there is no clarity on the issue of ODA eligibility of SSR-related expenditure, so differing and equally convincing alternative interpretations co-exist. This is, of course, an impediment to constructive collaboration between development and security actors in the field of security sector reform. Yet, clarification of which security expenditure is ODA eligible affects the credibility of ODA itself, not least because the ambiguity precludes analysis of the 'financial gaps' with which SSR designers and implementers have to cope. The aim must be to enable the development community to argue that additional funding from other sources such as defence and foreign affairs budgets is required and that their own governments should provide it; or alternatively that they should be given more resources. Clarifying objectives and methods would facilitate the rebalancing of the tools and working methods of both security and development actors.

One indirect attempt at clarification – at least with regard to EC development aid – was undertaken by the European Parliament (EP), which introduced a formal complaint before the European Court of Justice in 2005 requesting the annulment of a Commission decision in 2004 to finance a project on border management in the Philippines. The Commission's decision was based on a 1992 EC Regulation on external assistance for Asian and Latin American countries (the ALA Regulation). The EP opposed the decision on the grounds that its stated objective, namely the fight against terrorism through assistance to the Philippines in implementing UN Security Council Resolution 1373[18], was neither covered by the relevant EC Treaty provisions on EC Development Cooperation (Articles 177-181 of the EC Treaty) nor the ALA Regulation, and that the Community was thus not legally competent to adopt the decision. In its defence, the European Commission argued that the fight against terrorism was only one among several objectives of the project. The main purpose was to strengthen the Philippines' border management system in general, and even if it was not explicitly mentioned in the relevant EC Treaty provisions and the ALA Regulation, support to governance in the area of security, including the fight against terrorism, contributed to the establishment of the necessary preconditions for sustainable development. It was thus implicitly covered by the provisions on rule of law and respect of human rights contained in Article 177 of the EC Treaty and the ALA Regulation. To underpin its argument, the European Commission retraced the evolution of development policy, arguing that the inclusion of governance and security issues was now a given. It explicitly referred to the broadening by the OECD of the ODA eligibility criteria with regard to SSR.

In its judgment of 23 October 2007[19], the Court did not follow this argument and annulled the Commission decision on the ground that the ALA regulation did not constitute an appropriate legal basis for actions in the area of anti-terrorism. However, very interestingly the Court also explicitly recognised the security-development nexus as well as a broad scope for

Articles 177-181 of the EC Treaty, and thus that measures in the fight against terrorism could be foreseen under EC external aid instruments, such as the new Instrument for Stability which is given as an example by the Court. Meanwhile, the European Commission, as a member of the OECD DAC, shares responsibility with other members to provide coherence, effectiveness and efficiency to the SSR concept. As mentioned above, the March 2005 discussions on two controversial proposals for ODA criteria adjustment – reform and training of security and military forces in non-military practices and 'peace support operations capacity' of developing countries' armed forces – ended in no agreement. In the first case, the issue stemmed from the need to ensure that security forces in developing countries benefit from training in human rights, international humanitarian law, gender equality, etc. and the question was whether funding should come from ODA or non-ODA sources. Some members argued that it could be funded from ODA resources, since such training would be conducted by civilians outside regular military training programmes. The military would thus not be directly funded. In the second case, the issue was that for some donors it was inappropriate to make support to OECD members' peacekeeping troops ODA eligible, while support for peacekeeping troops from developing countries was not. The arguments advanced by some European donors for a further expansion of ODA eligibility were valid in both cases.[20]

If the credibility of development assistance risks being undermined by the continuing ambiguity, some donors also question the increases in the proportion of their GDP devoted to the alleviation of poverty. A moratorium on the debate was agreed first until 2007 and then further extended until 2009. The Commission supported the extension, since it allows time to consider the reasoning in international context and ensure that arguments for further extension of ODA – to the detriment of development aid – are not integrated into its own discourse or that of its counterparts. The challenge is to convince other DAC committee members to adopt a clear position on security-related expenditure. A firm stance by all actors is clearly vital.

Despite these hurdles, some initiatives have meanwhile been taken. The Dutch government has created a Stability Fund with resources from its development (ODA eligible) and foreign policy budget (non-ODA eligible). The aim of the fund is provision of rapid and flexible support for peace, security and development in countries where violent conflicts threaten to erupt or have already erupted.[21] The fund is flexible enough to be used in developed, transitional and richer developing countries. And it can be used to support peace processes, military peacekeeping capacity, security sector reform, small arms and light weapons issues and crisis management. The Dutch government has specifically stated that the 'fund will not result in the contamination of development cooperation' and that 'if certain activities do not meet the OECD/DAC requirements for ODA, they will simply not be attributable to ODA'.[22] It is worth underlining that the Dutch Stability Fund, though a useful initiative for financing endeavours such as SSR, does not constitute genuine pooled funding, since it is financed by one single actor. The Dutch Ministry of Foreign Affairs incorporates development cooperation. Others, such as the Ministry of Defence or the Ministry of the Interior do not contribute financially. Likewise, analysis of the EC's new external assistance architecture demonstrates that the EC has adopted a legal framework enabling it to cope with the same challenge by softening elements of its financial instruments, notably the strict conditionality on funding exclusively ODA-eligible security expenditure in support for security sector reform abroad. It is thus able to assist its partners more comprehensively and therefore more effectively and durably. The UK Global and Africa Conflict Prevention Pools go further, since all participating ministries fund them.

Although laudable, these initiatives do not completely solve the financing issue, since the challenge of ensuring balanced integration of both ODA and non-ODA funds remains, precisely because of the equivocal distinctions discussed above. Indeed, 'mixed' funds such as in the Netherlands and the EC and genuine pooled funding mechanisms such as in the UK may still be undermined by interministerial competition for inevitably limited resources.

The Challenge of Internal Coordination: the 'Whole-of-Government' Approach

One of the biggest challenges to reforming a security system lies in the nature of cooperation between the various actors involved. Interaction between the different stakeholders within the partner country undergoing reform is one important component of the overall objective of better performance of the whole system. But cooperation and coordination between the relevant actors in the donor community and the partner country is the real issue. Expertise and commitment are required for the design and implementation of a SSR strategy to be effective. Human security, the final aim of SSR, is a core Global Public Good (GPG).[23] It can only be achieved through genuine aggregation of all stakeholders. As Biscop explains: 'the key word in a policy based on the notion of GPG is integration. Because the cores of GPG are inextricably linked, action must be undertaken simultaneously and in coordination between all relevant actors in all fields of external policy, putting to use the various instruments at their disposal, including trade, development, the environment and legal cooperation, diplomacy and security and defence.'[24] For an operation to engage these different actors effectively it must bridge institutional divides and reach out across different disciplines. Experience has shown that this is easier said than done. Political, security, human rights and development actors all have their own views on what must be accomplished in an insecure and unsafe country. Each is perhaps rightly convinced of the importance of its objectives. Yet, notwithstanding the fact that objectives often appear divergent, the key factor is that they are nonetheless closely related. Effective cooperation may be risky because it requires concessions and compromises on all sides, but it is clearly vital. Getting different ministries to act as a coherent whole is commonly termed a 'whole-of-government' (WGA) approach. Joined-up mechanisms aiming to bring together the different services of a donor or recipient country's government to ensure more coherence, effectiveness and efficiency has expanded apace in the international donor community.

The 1997 report 'Renewing the United Nations – a Programme for Reform', by the Secretary-General of the United Nations called for a more integrated and unified UN, both at headquarters and in the field. The

Secretary-General gave his Special Representatives increased authority and created a 'system of integrated missions'[25], emphasising that 'the reform process is designed to maintain and reinforce the distinctive nature of UN entities while seeking to facilitate their functioning in a more unified, cooperative and coherent framework as members of the United Nations family'.[26] Following the reiteration of this policy agenda in the main recommendations of the Report of the Panel on United Nations Peace Operations (the Brahimi Report, 2000), an important operational measure was the establishment of Integrated Mission Task Forces for peacekeeping and peacebuilding, comprising officials across UN departments. Another UN initiative is the creation of the Peacebuilding Commission, an intergovernmental body acting in an advisory role to the General Assembly and Security Council on early planning and implementation of peace-building activities. The aim is to use international resources to advise and propose integrated strategies for post-conflict peace-building and recovery, focusing attention on reconstruction, institution-building and sustainable development, and developing best practices on issues requiring extensive collaboration between political, military, humanitarian and development actors. Finally, the current 'One UN' initiative goes in the same direction. Based on the recommendations of the Secretary-General's High-level Panel on UN System-wide Coherence in the Areas of Development, Humanitarian Assistance, and the Environment[27], it stems from the recognition that the UN's work on development and the environment is often fragmented and weak, and that cooperation between organisations has been hindered by competition for funding, mission creep and outdated business practices. The High Level Panel recommended that the UN deliver a stronger practical commitment to cooperation in the implementation of one strategy in pursuit of a single set of goals. The Panel has made several recommendations potentially able to change radically how organisations operate at headquarters and in the field. The aim is to enable the UN to achieve more than the sum of its parts. At country level, this means the establishment of one UN with one leader, one programme, one budget and, where appropriate, one office. At headquarters, it means the creation of a UN Sustainable Development Board to oversee One UN Country Programmes. It also implies the appointment of a UN Development Coordinator with responsibility for the performance and accountability of UN development activities.

World Bank policy on fragile states takes the same kind of approach. In 2002, it established a task force on 'Low Income Countries Under Stress' (LICUS), on the principle that 'state-building is the central objective in fragile states, and that effective donor programs require integrated approaches across the political-security-development nexus'.[28] A multitude of similar activities are also taking place at regional level within sub-regional and continental organisations. Examples also exist at the national level, where the joined up government approach first emerged in the field of conflict prevention and post-conflict peace-building. The UK, for example, established in 2001 two Conflict Prevention Pools (CPP). The Africa Pool covers sub-Saharan Africa, and the Global Conflict Prevention Pool covers the rest of the world. These are standing inter-departmental bodies, combining the expertise of the Foreign and Commonwealth Office, the Ministry of Defence and the Department for International Development. The aim is to coordinate interventions and ensure that appropriate measures are taken at the different stages of failure a country might experience. The rationale is that the UK's contribution to conflict prevention 'could be even more effective if it was coordinated across departmental boundaries'.[29] Linking military intervention with peace settlement, DDR, SSR and long-term development is vital. Both pools are overseen by Cabinet committees and are managed at the working level by a joint steering team composed of officials from each department who decide on priorities, budgets and management.[30] Based on this model, the UK further established a Post-conflict Reconstruction Unit in September 2004 with an interdepartmental staff of approximately 28 drawn from five Government Departments and charged with providing 'HMG [Her Majesty's Government] and its partners with integrated assessment and planning support, underpinned by an operational capability, to deliver more effective stabilisation operations'.[31] Its capabilities are focused on governance, security and justice.

Likewise, in May 2004, the German Federal Government agreed an Action Plan on 'Civilian Crisis Prevention, Conflict Resolution, and Post-conflict Peace-building' which defines conflict-related foreign policy activities as cross-departmental tasks.[32] Its objective is to develop the Federal Government's capabilities and to make greater use of foreign, security and development policies in civilian crisis prevention. An inter-ministerial steering group, comprised of representatives from all federal ministries, under the supervision of the Foreign Office, was established in September 2004. The Netherlands has also developed a WGA on post-conflict reconstruction, encompassing the Ministries of Foreign Affairs (comprising Development Cooperation), Defence and Economic Affairs.

Outside the EU, the Government of Canada has adopted a 3-D (Defence, Development and Diplomacy) model, ensuring interdepartmental cooperation between National Defence, Foreign Affairs Canada, the Department of International Trade and the Canadian International Development Agency (CIDA). At the 2003 Diplomatic Forum in Toronto, Deputy Minister of Foreign Affairs Peter Harder described the model as a 'priority in the current transition [of government] that places greater emphasis on horizontal thinking'.[33] Whether the much-needed 3-D approach has stopped at the reflection stage is a moot point, however, since there is in practice no joined-up pool of resources, from which joined-up planning could be managed.[34] In addition, the 3-D picture also lacks joint planning, joint policy, joint implementation and joint views on end-states. Its detractors argue that such an inchoate strategy precludes the possibility of strategic thinking at the highest levels, a task which, ironically, should be the primary aim of such an exercise.

The US established an Office of Reconstruction and Stabilization within the State Department in August 2004 to oversee interagency coordination of civilian conflict prevention and post-conflict reconstruction capacities. The approximately 35 staff includes representatives from the Departments of State and Defence, the Agency for International Development (USAID), the CIA, and the military's Joint Staff.[35] As part of its 'transformational diplomacy' initiative launched in January 2006, the United States announced a restructuring of USAID with the objective of promoting 'integration between development, diplomacy, democracy, and security'.[36]

All these initiatives establishing WGA mechanisms and structures relate primarily to policy towards countries prone to, affected by or ridden with conflict, but they might also be deemed to cover countries falling under the broader and somewhat vague notion of fragile states or to transitional and stable countries. But, lack of visibility of the security sector reform issue area and the predominant trend to cure rather than to prevent has meant that SSR has so far failed to become part of the donor mindset. Yet, the stakes in WGAs are obvious, particularly in post-conflict settings or fragile states.[37] The overall objective is further coherence, effectiveness and efficiency to replace independent policies driven by different departmental mandates and implemented in parallel. Policy coherence can make policies mutually reinforce rather than undermine each other. It may be stating the obvious, but more coherence means more effectiveness as well as more efficiency. In addition, local ownership and more coherence usually mean more legitimacy and therefore greater responsiveness and commitment to partnership. WGAs enable donors to view the security sector as a whole. Since the different sub-sectors of a security system are interconnected, effective performance is contingent on all parts functioning together and donors being in a position to tackle all the various elements. Alternatives risk bringing about insecurity rather than security.[38] Action to strengthen police, for example, if unaccompanied by reform of corrupt and weak judiciaries, is unlikely to bring results. Likewise, if a strengthened police force is violent and if it violates human rights, there is a clear risk of increasing insecurity, riots and insurgency.

If the stakes are high, so are the challenges in developing and operating WGAs at strategic, planning and field levels. A first challenge lies in reaching agreement on objectives and priorities. They may be complementary, but the objectives of foreign policy, defence and development actors differ and their priorities do not always match. This often results in a lack of political incentive to engage in WGAs with other government colleagues. A second challenge is the constitutional, legal and regulatory framework. This can impede, if not prevent, smooth collaboration between stakeholders. Linked to this is the question of clarity of mandates and alleged 'overlapping' competences as well as that of their hierarchical status.[39] A third challenge stems from varying organisational cultures in ministries. Understanding and accommodating each other's idiosyncrasies takes time and the benefits of cooperation are only apparent in the longer term. Cooperation thus risks being considered as time-consuming and cumbersome. Last there is the issue of financial and human resources. These are inevitably the weakest links. Pooling funds and staff in fact constitutes a major challenge to administrative culture and questions the sense of policy ownership by ministerial officials.

If WGAs are usually linked to a donor's government, the challenges are the same in recipient countries. The local partners of each donor's ministries are usually different and may conflict with each other. If coherence is to deliver effective policy implementation, it is imperative for cooperation and coordination in security sector reform between security and development actors to take place both within and between donors and their partners.

To meet these challenges, an overarching policy with clear guidelines is key. Guidelines set the general aims, objectives, structures and processes for WGAs. Clear distribution of responsibilities or firm and formal recognition of overlapping responsibilities is essential. Clearly defined and commonly agreed objectives are required so as to federate the different stakeholders in the framework of an overall long-term strategy. Political leadership needs to come from above the actors involved, the prime minister's office being the normal focal point. Finally, effective implementation involves coordinating mechanisms and structures being viewed as important as basket funds and instruments such as information exchange, joint training, joint assessment[40], joint planning[41], joint deployment[42], joint reporting, joint monitoring and evaluation, etc. Of course, all these factors should ideally be institutionalised rather than ad-hoc. Formalisation makes them less subject to internal dissension between the various stakeholders.

The challenges are perhaps greater in the EU setting. The EU has embarked on WGA, though in this case a more appropriate term would be a 'whole-of-organisation' or 'whole-of-institutions' approach. To a certain extent, the EU's 'pillar' structure could be compared to the division of ministries in national governments, with the European Commission acting as the 'EU' development cooperation ministry, the Council as the foreign affairs and defence ministries and as justice and interior ministries. There are similarities with national ministries, notably with regard to the objectives of development, foreign, defence and internal policies, but the comparison stops there, however. The main difference is the level of integration of the EU institutional structures – its three pillars. Contrary to national foreign, development and defence ministries led by a single minister and interacting within a coherent whole, the first, second and third pillars are parallel, separate and unequal structures. The existence of different levels of integration between the pillars has several consequences. The first pillar is supranational, with a voting system based on qualified majority and exclusive right of initiative for the Commission. The second and third inter-governmental pillars decide by unanimity and shared right of initiative between the Commission and Member States. This imbalance between the pillars in terms of integration complicates coordination. The constraints of the decision-making system in the highly political inter-governmental pillars reduce the capacity of the Council to adapt to the Commission's policies and projects.[43] The current lack at EU level of an overarching coordinator equivalent to a 'prime minister' in national systems is also a key constraint resulting in the absence of a formal guarantee of the policy coherence nonetheless explicitly required by the treaties. A European Minister for Foreign Affairs would fill the vacuum. The post was proposed in the Constitutional Treaty and remains part of the alternative arrangements under negotiation in the second half of 2007.

For the EU, the 'whole-of-organisation approach' means cooperation and coordination between ad-hoc short-term security and diplomatic measures and long-term development measures. The European Commission has well-anchored delegations in more than 130 countries, cooperating with its partners on the basis of jointly elaborated strategic frameworks. The Council of the EU has very limited external representation structures. It intervenes on a short-term and ad-hoc basis outside the permanent bilateral cooperation frameworks maintained by the Commission. Ensuring effective coordination between these two complementary but divergent approaches may be vital to EU coherence, but it is less than perfect.[44] Nevertheless, the EU

Policy Framework for SSR adopted by the General Affairs Council meeting in Luxembourg on 12 June 2006 was a major breakthrough in the integration of the two approaches.[45] The framework comprising the November 2005 Concept for ESDP Support to Security Sector Reform[46] and the May 2006 Concept for European Community Support for Security Sector Reform[47], provides the EU with common conceptual guidance defining the principles for EU engagement in SSR and underlining the importance of a comprehensive and cross-pillar approach. The problem remains, however, that this policy framework with its two integral components, though highly symbolic and perhaps a precursor to enhanced inter-institutional coordination, remains silent on the issue of how to implement security sector reform in practice. It clearly does not deliver all the expected results and is merely a declaratory document, in practice risking the status of wishful thinking.

The origins of the approach are significant. Though the intention was initially to draft a single document, this proved impossible in practice and the result was two separate concepts simply linked together by an overarching Council declaration.[48] Neither the Common Framework nor the Concepts explicitly address the sensitive issue of the division of competence between the pillars. This is clearly a shortcoming, since the rapid growth of the CFSP/ESDP in recent years and the concurrent acknowledgment of the security/development nexus have dramatically underlined the grey areas between the Community's and the Council's competences in EU external relations.[49] These predominantly concern the second (CFSP) pillar and increasingly relate to third pillar police and judicial cooperation in criminal matters, where the external dimension is increasingly important. Provisions in the Treaties establishing the European Community and the European Union provide a basis for smooth cooperation between the two institutions, notably with regard to human rights and democracy. Yet, though the Treaty on European Union (TEU) and most policy documents[50] stress the need for the Union to 'ensure the consistency of its external activities as a whole in the context of its external relations, security, economic and development policies'[51], some areas are much more controversial. This is the case for election monitoring, dual-use goods, defence industrial aspects, conflict prevention, civilian crisis management, Small Arms and Light Weapons (SALW) and issues of external representation. Instead of leading to a formal recognition of overlap between their respective responsibilities and strengthening cooperation and coordination, the two institutions continue to wage turf wars, which occasionally end up in the European Court of Justice.[52]

An illustrative case is the action brought by the European Commission against the Council of the EU on 21 February 2005; the small arms and light weapons (SALW) case.[53] The Commission requested the annulment for lack of competence of a Council decision of December 2004 regarding an EU/CFSP contribution to ECOWAS in the framework of its Moratorium on SALW.[54] The Commission was already in the process of adopting a similar measure and had informed the Council. The proposed Council assistance took the form of a financial contribution and technical assistance to set up the Light Weapons Unit within the ECOWAS Technical Secretariat and to convert an ECOWAS moratorium into a Convention on SALW between its member states. The case illustrates the often conflictual relationship between the Commission and the Council. The potential impact of what could be a landmark case on the issue of competence is extensive. The Commission questioned the legality of the Council's decision on the basis that it encroached on Community competence, the aim and content of the impugned decision falling under the Community's competence in development cooperation under Articles 177 and 181a of the TEC. Art. 47 TEU states that 'nothing in this Treaty shall affect the Treaties establishing the European Communities or the subsequent Treaties and Acts modifying or supplementing them'. The Commission therefore argued that the Council decision impinged on the first pillar's area of competence, recalling that the European Court of Justice (ECJ) in case 176/03[55] established that the notion of encroachment is a direct consequence of the fact that the decisions could have been taken on the basis of Art. 177 TEC. Some would respond, as did the Council, that development is a shared competence between the Community and the Member States. But, the Court ruled in case 176/03, that Art. 47 TEU protects shared competence just as much as it protects exclusive competence of the Community. So Member States cannot pool their powers in the field of development aid and exercise them separately in the second pillar framework, as this would give the latter a competence it does not have, thereby infringing the Community's competence as set out in Art. 47 TEU. In mid-2007 it still remained to be seen which institutional view the Court will uphold.

The SALW case, though intellectually and legally pertinent, is entirely based on the pivotal assumption that the aim of the Council's decision was, as stated by the act, notably to counteract the reduction of the 'prospects for sustainable development' – thus a developmental objective – and that its content amounts to capacity building for a regional organisation, a type of intervention that 'primarily' takes place in the field of development cooperation (i.e. the first pillar). The decision has a second aim however, namely to diminish the 'threat to peace and security', a second pillar competence, since Art. 11 TEU stipulates that the preservation of peace and the strengthening of international security is one of the objectives of the CFSP. Thus, arguably the fight against the proliferation of SALW also falls within this competence. With regard to the content criteria, it could possibly be demonstrated that 'capacity-building' actions may also take place within the framework of CFSP. If the Council decision had simply not mentioned the objective of sustainable development, it might not have been challenged or at least the Commission's case would not have been so solid.

The outcome would not be significant were there not potential to disrupt the EU's role as a global security actor. Depending on the findings and final decision of the Court, the EU may either move a major step forward or a major step back. It is not so much which institution the Court will agree with that is important in this particular case, but rather the general approach it will take with regard to the 'grey area' between the first and second pillars. That the Court, apart from its decision in this particular case, formulates some guiding principles on inter-pillar cooperation is of paramount importance. After all, the consistency of overall EU external action is at stake. Ideally, such 'guidelines' would be based on the formal recognition that, though distinct but complementary, both the Commission's and the Council's respective competences within the first and second pillars find application within a 'grey zone' lying at the nexus between security and development and thus appear to overlap. This would amount to implicit acknowledgement of the right of both institutions to exercise their attributed competences in domains that are convergent, such as domains that are not primarily security or development-related. This should also imply the recognition that beyond the complementarity of their competences, there is also a complementarity of the means at the disposal of the Council and the Commission which makes the strength of the EU as a single organisation. There are of course limits to this apparent 'grey zone' and the Court could also usefully defin`e them. If they fail to do so, the judges of the ECJ would miss the opportunity sought by the Commission to transform this legal dispute into a positive landmark case for the benefit of EU external policy. A fainthearted decision would keep the door open for further disputes potentially leading both institutions to become risk-averse and hesitant to adopt measures falling in the perceived grey area. By cautiously sticking to their incontrovertibly exclusive competences, they would fail to make use of the EU's capabilities as a single entity, thereby inevitably entailing huge gaps in the EU contribution to tackling the intertwined challenges of insecurity and underdevelopment.[56] So the Commission made a plea before the Court for a judgment that would not only decide the case, but from which more general guidelines on inter-pillar relations could be established. This ought not to be necessary for the EU and EC security sector reform concepts, but it is noteworthy that the two (EU and EC) concepts for SSR implicitly acknowledge the need by listing respective current and potential areas of support to SSR that are largely convergent, even though they do not formally recognise each other's exclusive right to intervene in this sphere of competence.

The opinion of Advocate-General Mengozzi delivered on 19 September 2007 may stir up mixed feelings in this respect. Irrespective of the fact that the advocate-general proposes that the action be dismissed to the detriment of the Commission, the opinion does not appear entirely satisfactory in light of the above. On the one hand, he adopts a rather flexible position when he states in indent 166 that: 'delimiting the objectives of development cooperation in that way, without the matters which may be the subject of such cooperation falling a priori outside its scope, makes it possible to ensure the dynamic nature of that policy, while ensuring that the Commission observes the principle of the distribution and the assignment of the objectives laid down in Article 5 EC'. In indent 167, he then goes on to state that: 'this approach is consistent with the general scheme of the EC Treaty, which aims to attain limited objectives with the aid of extensive means, and not the reverse.' This leads him to the conclusion that measures connected with security may fall within the ambit of development aid provided that they serve exclusively or primarily to attain the objectives of social and economic development of Article 177. Using a word of caution, he further explains that: 'it would be erroneous and excessive to consider that any measure which fosters the economic and social development of a developing country falls within the competence of the Community pursuant to Title XX of the EC Treaty', and this despite the exactly similar wording of Article 177(1) EC which provides that: 'Community policy in the sphere of development cooperation… shall foster: the sustainable economic and social development of the developing countries…'. In doing so, he almost implicitly recognises that the Council and the

Commission can undertake within their respective competences of the second and first pillars similar activities with different objectives. On the other hand however, despite providing a long series of evidence between indents 181 and 189 that the Council itself recognises, in its 1997 programme for preventing and combating illegal trafficking in conventional arms and its 21 May 1999 resolution on SALW, the competence of the Community to intervene in the whole bunch of SALW-related actions, he dangerously adopts a restrictive position in indent 217 by categorising SALW-related activities according to their exclusive or primary security or development objective. Since the opinion of Advocate-General Mengozzi does not prejudge the ruling of the Court and that in any case, it feeds both positions, there is still room for hope that the Court will recognise the overlap of the sphere of action of the Council and Commission distinct competences.

To conclude, the reason for the Commission's appeal to the Court in the SALW case was the unwillingness of the Council to coordinate policymaking with the Commission and its concomitant refusal to admit that genuine and constructive inter-institutional collaboration is a responsibility shared by the Commission and the Council; a responsibility which requires not only declaratory commitment, but the existence of agreed coordinating mechanisms to ensure fulfilment. Adequate management through coordination arrangements is a challenge for WGAs in general. It is clearly a vital element of any successful whole-of-government approach. The EU has made substantial progress, but there still exist no genuine coordinating mechanisms. Instead, there are rather limited consultative structures or ad-hoc coordination attempts brought about by individual crisis situations. In both the Political and Security Committee (PSC) and the Committee for Civilian Aspects of Crisis Management (CIVCOM),[57] the Commission is represented by one of its officials. Does this thereby ensure balanced debate and joint decisions? Or is the *raison d'être* of the Commission's presence in CFSP/ESDP decision-making bodies no more than provision of information exchange between Council and Commission? If they fall short of enabling both Commission and Council to gain strategic oversight of all EU activities, it is perhaps fair to conclude that the emperor has no clothes.

At the planning level, there are positive achievements, however, even if SSR coordination still occurs largely on a case-by-case basis. In 2005 the Commission adopted its communication on reinforcing EU disaster and crisis response, even though some of the proposals it was making were still not fully formulated. The Commission argued that it 'would see great value in developing a common and authoritative analysis of the situation on the ground with Member States and the General Secretariat of the Council … [to]…. be used to make decisions as to the respective priorities for the Community, CFSP and bi-lateral assistance programmes'[58], adding that it would look for 'opportunities for joint assessments with colleagues in the General Secretariat of the Council' and proposing as a first step to 'improve exchange of information with the Council Joint Situation Centre and sharing of relevant commission capabilities'.

There are two separate Commission and Council fact-finding teams. In order to ensure high quality needs assessments at an early stage and to create flexibility in implementation capacity to deliver in time, the Commission established Assessment and Planning Teams (APTs). These brought together desk officers and sectoral specialists from across the Commission and its 130 Delegations. One role of the Teams was to contribute to CFSP fact finding missions organised by the Council Secretariat and conducted by the Council's own Civil Response Teams (CRTs), whose aim is to provide background for potential CFSP Joint Actions.[59] Underlining that the 'Secretariat and the Commission should seek to undertake joint assessment missions wherever possible', the Council foresaw that CRT missions could potentially contribute 'in agreement with the Commission, to possible action to be developed in the framework of Community instruments'.[60] The arrangements have been used to assess support to SSR in the Democratic Republic of Congo and in Guinea-Bissau, though these remain separate initiatives, again with only ad-hoc coordination. The Commission's proposal to link them through joint training programmes, needs assessment methodologies and personnel rosters have so far remained dead letters in the aftermath of the French and Dutch rejections of the Constitutional Treaty. As one outside observer has observed, following the insistence by some Member States on preserving the purely inter-governmental character of the second pillar and 'to avoid moves that might be seen as introducing further integration 'through the back-door' [...] it was decided not to fuse these instruments, but rather to maintain the distinct roles and mandates of CRTs and APTs within their respective institutional context'.[61]

Other interesting coordination structures are the Crisis Response Coordination Teams (CRCTs). These teams are ad-hoc task forces in Brussels. They were established in 2003 by the Council to provide coherent, comprehensive crisis management. A civilian official – at the highest level Javier Solana but otherwise a director-general – chairs them. They are composed of senior officials from the Commission and the Council Secretariat.[62] But they lack decision-making powers, so their role amounts to discussion of the development of crisis management and helping to plan ESDP missions decided by the PSC. In its communication on reinforcing EU disaster and crisis response, the Commission commits itself to present proposals for improving the functioning of the CRCTs by strengthening co-ordination with the Secretariat General of the Council.[63]

A further important innovation in terms of planning was the appointment of two EC liaison officers to the Civil-Military Planning Cell, so as 'to promote coherence between the planning assumptions of EC and CFSP measures, and to identify practical arrangements for the use of military assets in support of civilian Community programmes'. The Civilian-Military Planning Cell was established by the Council in 2005 to help plan integrated ESDP action. Though not a coordination mechanism as such, the secondment of two Commission officials to this structure was supposed to ensure that ESDP action would become more consistent with first pillar activities. Yet the Civilian-Military Cell has not so far succeeded in delivering its full added-value, notably owing to the need for civilian (Council and Commission) and military staff to familiarise themselves with each other's *modus operandi*.

While laudable, initiatives to ensure enhanced coordination between the first and second pillars so far lack real unity of command and thus merely amount to cross-representation. They use only political/administrative rather than operational staff, and thus fall short of ensuring a strategic vision for EU support to SSR and beyond. The proposal to create an EU Foreign Minister and an integrated European External Action Service addresses both this strategic deficit and the issue of coordination at field level by the creation of a single command chain in Brussels and in partner countries. Without these, it is unlikely that further significant improvements will be made. Coordination will thus continue to be ad-hoc and limited in scope. Unless the 2007 Intergovernmental conference on an alternative, less ambitious treaty retains the features of the Constitutional Treaty relevant to coordinated policymaking, the Commission will need to convince Member States and the Council Secretariat to create new coordination arrangements by other means, such as the creation of an SSR task force ensuring a permanent working relationship between the institutions.

The ultimate navel-gazing question on inter-institutional cooperation and coordination is which institution will be brought to adapt to the other. Former External Relations Commissioner Chris Patten believed that

> '[the] important point is that – however awkward they may be – the new structures, procedures and instruments of CFSP recognise the need to harness the strengths of the European Community in the service of European foreign policy. That is why the Treaty 'fully associates' the European Commission with CFSP. We participate fully in the decision-making process in the Council, with a shared right of initiative which we shall exercise. Our role cannot be reduced to one of 'painting by numbers' – simply filling in the blanks on a canvas drawn by others. Nor should it be. It would be absurd to divorce European foreign policy from the institutions which have been given responsibility for most of the instruments for its accomplishment: for external trade questions, including sanctions; for European external assistance; for many of the external aspects of Justice and Home Affairs.'[64]

Some believe that it is logical for the CFSP to adapt to the long-term engagements of the Commission and not vice-versa. Yet, by definition, sporadic action under the CFSP responds to concrete and usually unforeseen needs. The Commission thus also needs to demonstrate a higher degree of flexibility on its side if it is to guarantee adequate first pillar follow-up to CFSP decisions. So a wise alternative might thus be to agree that the Council and the Member States should be ready to bring political and strategic support to the Commission's action. When necessary, the Commission should also be bound to ensure smooth follow-up to Member States' responses to a crisis within the framework of the second pillar. Yet, the slow decision-making process within the first pillar is often inappropriate. This chapter later analyses the new EC external assistance architecture. It demonstrates that the Commission is well aware of this shortcoming and has thus introduced more operational flexibility, notably in the new Instrument for Stability,[65] which allows for short-term action of up to eighteen months without the cumbersome decision-making procedures entailing 'comitology'.[66]

The Challenge of Coordination with Other Donors

In addition to the issue of coordination within governments and organisations, as Hauck and Gaspers argue, 'the next step in coordination and joint action would be to use this *whole of government approach* for coordination and harmonisation with other donors and an alignment with systems and procedures at the recipient's side – a highly complex undertaking, but necessary to make the contributions to both individual countries and the continent as a whole coherent'.[67] For the EU, 'vertical' coordination with Member States – as opposed to 'horizontal' coordination with the other European institutions – is crucial if it is to be perceived as a single organisation. But interaction with Member States should not only be seen as 'donor' coordination. It might involve development actors and security or defence actors.

Though often criticised by beneficiaries and donors for its alleged lack of coordination and effectiveness in the field of external aid, the European Commission has been one of the driving forces behind the international reform process set in motion at the Monterrey conference,[68] which culminated in the famous 'Paris Declaration on Aid Effectiveness' adopted at the High Level Forum on 2 March 2005 by over one hundred countries and organisations.[69] This reform process aims at eventual achievement of the Millennium Development Goals (MDGs). It fits perfectly within the goals of aid effectiveness, in particular since its stated objective is enhanced coherence and sustainability.

The Paris Declaration paved the way for the so-called 'European Consensus on Development'[70] proposed by the European Commission[71] and jointly adopted on 20 December 2005 by the Council, EU Member States, the European Commission and the European Parliament. The European Consensus on Development is a demonstration of commitment to aid effectiveness, reflecting the EU intention to contribute decisively to the eradication of poverty by ensuring coordination of EU and Member State capabilities. The Consensus sets out principles, a common vision and a common implementation policy and fully endorses the five Partnership Commitments of the Paris Declaration (Ownership, Alignment, Harmonisation, Managing for results and Mutual accountability).

Significantly, during the negotiations on the adoption of the Paris Declaration, the EU imposed more rigorous standards on itself than other donors, fixing concrete targets known as the 'four additional commitments'. These were (i) to provide all capacity-building assistance through coordinated programmes with an increasing use of multi-donor arrangements; (ii) to channel 50% of government-to-government assistance through country systems, including by increasing the percentage of EU assistance provided through budget support or sector wide approach (SWAP) arrangements; (iii) to avoid the establishment of any new 'project implementation units'; and (iv) to reduce the number of un-coordinated missions by 50%.

To implement the ambitious commitments of the Paris Declaration and the European Consensus for Development, the Commission adopted on 2 March 2006 an 'Aid Effectiveness Package', consisting of three distinct but interlinked communications.[72] The 'Aid Effectiveness Package' was discussed on 10-11 April 2006 by the Council, which agreed to further measures to step up aid effectiveness.[73] The Council approved the Commission proposal of a joint programming framework aligned with partner countries' strategies. Here, the Commission, partner countries, interested EU Member States and all other interested donors were to undertake joint multi-annual programming based on a two-step approach entailing a common needs analysis and a common response strategy. The third communication of the Aid Effectiveness Package included a format for a detailed Common Framework for Country Strategy

Papers (CFCSP), intended as a basis for joint analysis as a preliminary to creating country strategies.

The European Community's New External Aid Architecture and SSR

We argued above that in spite of its broad acceptance by donors, the concept of SSR remains subject to a dialectic between security and development. How therefore to ensure that the concept delivers its full potential added-value? The EU's adoption of a new financial framework for 2007-2013 triggered negotiations on revision of the legal instruments for EC external aid, with new regulations entering into force in 2007. These provide a simplified but ambitious framework which ought, in principle, to allow the EC to better address the issues involved in designing and implementing support to SSR. This section analyses how the EC has met the challenges involved, though it is clearly too early to analyse how successful the new framework is.

The New Legal Framework for EC External Aid

Before the last multi-annual financial framework (2000-2006) for the EC budget was due to expire, the European Parliament, the European Commission and the Council of the EU entered difficult negotiations on the next financial framework for 2007-2013. This eventually led to the adoption of an inter-institutional agreement in May 2006.[74] The three institutions agreed that over the next seven year period the EU would concentrate its action on three priorities, two of which were directly relevant for security and SSR. The priorities were the completion of the EU's common area of freedom, security and justice and the establishment of the EU as a global player assuming its regional responsibilities, promoting sustainable development and contributing to both civilian and strategic security in the world. These two priorities cover EU action inside and outside its borders. They may not seem at first sight directly related, but they are linked by the fundamental principle that EU external policies are deemed to reflect internal policies and vice-versa.

Until 2006, external aid had been managed through a very broad and disparate range of geographical and thematic instruments adopted ad-hoc over time.[75] The plethora of instruments, their inconsistency and the complexity of different legal bases, objectives, programming and procedures made efficient and coordinated management of these instruments well nigh impossible. With a new financial framework for 2007-2013 imminent, the Commission proposed in September 2004 a rationalised and simplified set of instruments to replace the old, inappropriate external aid programmes from 2007 onwards.[76] The Commission's proposed new architecture comprised only six instruments: four new ones to complement the surviving Humanitarian Aid Instrument and the Macro Financial Assistance Instrument.[77] The Commission's initial proposal was subsequently altered as two years of negotiations between the Commission, the Council and the European Parliament led to an increase in the number of instruments (see below). A tripartite meeting at political level held on 26 June 2006 finally identified elements for a compromise and a political agreement was reached. While the structure of the initial Commission proposal was somewhat altered in that some of the proposed instruments were divided, notably at the insistence of the European Parliament[78], the final architecture nonetheless respects the overall objective of simplification and increased effectiveness.

In parallel with these negotiations, a new financial framework for 2007-2013 was negotiated. This considerably increased financial allocations to external aid overall. The new external aid instruments and the reference amounts allocated under the new financial framework 2007-2013 are: (i) the Instrument for Pre-Accession Assistance (IPA), providing €11,468 million assistance to candidate countries and potential candidate countries for accession to the EU[79]; (ii) the European Neighbourhood and Partnership Instrument (ENPI), with €11,181 million for greater political, economic, cultural and security cooperation between the EU and its neighbours[80]; (iii) the Development Cooperation Instrument (DCI), composed of geographic programmes for developing countries not covered by the IPA, the ENPI or the EDF[81], as well as of five thematic programmes supporting actions in all developing countries (including those covered by the ENPI and the EDF) and global action, with an allocation of €16,897 million[82]; (iv) the Industrialised Countries Instrument (ICI) for specific cooperation with countries excluded from ODA-eligibility, with an allocation of €172 million[83]; (v) the Instrument for Stability (IfS), which will contribute to stability in crises and build capacity in stable conditions to address specific global and trans-regional threats having a destabilising effect, with an allocation of €2,062 million[84]; (vi) the European Instrument for Democracy and Human Rights (EIDHR), which will support the development of democracy, the rule of law and human rights, in particular in countries where these issues are not considered priorities, with an allocation of €1,104 million;[85] and finally (vii) the Instrument for Nuclear Safety Cooperation, which will finance measures to support a higher level of nuclear safety, with a reference amount of €524 million.[86] In addition, the African, Caribbean and Pacific (ACP) countries will continue to be financed through the EDF on the basis of the 2000 Cotonou Agreement, revised in 2005.[87] The 10th EDF, comprising over €24 billion and managed by the Commission on the basis of a specific financial regulation adopted by the Council,[88] starts to run in 2008.

The need for simplification and rationalisation of the EC legal framework explains why there is no specific external aid instrument for security sector reform. But the geographical instruments (with the exception of the ICI), as well as the IfS and, to a lesser extent, the EIDHR, allow the EC to address SSR or parts of it. Before briefly analysing each of these instruments as to their potential contribution to SSR, it is worth recalling that despite the fact that the concept of SSR was developed and used in the area of development cooperation, in particular in post-conflict situations, other EU objectives and policies relevant to SSR intersect with EC development policy and thus play a role in determining the extent, standards and tools with which SSR may be addressed in third countries. On the other hand, EC Development policy[89]applies, of course, to all developing countries and not just those covered by the DCI and EDF.

(a) The Instrument for Pre-Accession Assistance (IPA)

SSR is a fundamental element in the context of EU Enlargement policy. Candidate countries are required to conform to the Copenhagen criteria set out at the 1993 European Council. These comprise stability of democratic institutions, rule of law and human rights and effective implementation of the *acquis communautaire*, including the whole EU *acquis* in the field of Justice and Home Affairs. Security sector reform is not explicitly mentioned in the IPA, but it is covered by the very broad scope of Article 2 IPA[90], which must be considered in light of the adoption of the IPA on the basis of Article 181a of the EC Treaty, the sole article of Title XXI ('Economic, financial and technical cooperation with third countries') inserted in the 2000 Treaty of Nice next to Title XX ('Development cooperation') whose Articles 177-181 were already added by the 1992 Treaty of Maastricht. This legal basis may seem surprising, as all countries covered by the IPA currently belong to the list of ODA recipient countries, and as it has been argued that Article 181a would only be applicable to non-developing countries.[91] However, the choice of this legal base follows the requirements of EU Enlargement policy, which could not afford to be subject to the frequently changing OECD-DAC criteria for ODA eligibility and its corresponding list of recipient countries.[92] Thus, even if the IPA has to be implemented consistently with the principles of EC Development policy – as explicitly follows from Article 181a (1), the assistance provided under the IPA is not linked to the ODA eligibility criteria and may thus cover – at least in principle – the full range of activities in the area of SSR.

(b) The European Neighbourhood and Partnership Instrument (ENPI)

The European Neighbourhood Policy (ENP) takes a new and ambitious approach towards most countries previously covered by the MEDA and TACIS programmes, which are now at the external borders of the enlarged EU.[93] While the ENPI, as indeed the IPA, does not explicitly mention SSR, its Article 2 defines the scope of EC assistance as covering a very broad range of issues, including *inter alia* all aspects of SSR.[94] It aims in particular to promote the implementation of the association agreements as well as the partnership and cooperation agreements concluded with various neighbourhood countries. As these agreements comprise policy areas going well beyond classical development issues, such as cooperation in Justice and Home Affairs, the ENP offers a more elaborate and comprehensive framework than the TACIS and MEDA programmes. This also explains why the ENPI was adopted on the basis of both Articles 179 and 181a of the EC Treaty. As for the IPA, EC assistance in SSR would thus not need to be subject to strict ODA eligibility.

(c) The Development Cooperation Instrument (DCI)

While the European Commission initially proposed an instrument including all third countries not geographically covered by the IPA or the ENPI, the final instrument covers only geographic programmes for those developing countries which are not ACP countries.[95] The Commission proposal to adopt this instrument on the basis of both Articles 179 and 181a of the EC Treaty was rejected. The DCI is thus based solely on Article 179, with a strong focus on the achievement of the Millennium Development Goals

(Article 2 (1)) and an explicit reference to the requirement that the geographical measures adopted under the DCI fulfil the criteria for ODA established by the OECD-DAC (Article 2 (4)). Even if SSR is implicitly covered by the DCI,[96] this means that comprehensive SSR may not figure among the priority areas and that not all actors and activities falling under the scope of the OECD definition of SSR may be addressed under the DCI.

The more restrictive approach taken by the DCI towards security issues has also to be seen in the context of the complaint of the European Parliament (EP) to the European Court of Justice against the 2004 Commission decision on the financing of the EC border management project in the Philippines referred to above. This approach was again demonstrated in the controversial discussions preceding the adoption of the Country Strategy Papers (CSP) for the DCI countries, where the DCI Committee representing the EU Member States opposed any reference to the fight against terrorism in the CSPs, and where the Development Committee of the EP disagreed with the CSP of certain countries, arguing that some of the actions identified by the Commission were not eligible as ODA, for example the planned EC project on money laundering in Pakistan. It remains to be seen how far the DCI will be used in practice for SSR activities, given the further restriction mentioned in its Article 2 (6) in relation to measures covered under the IfS, analysed in detail below under point e).[97]

(d) The European Development Fund (EDF)

The EDF may, at some future point, be integrated into the general EC budget, as the European Commission has frequently proposed and will doubtless propose again during the discussions beginning in 2009 on the revision of the EC 2007-2013 financial framework. Meanwhile, the 10th EDF, based on the Cotonou Agreement revised in 2005[98], finances all geographic programming for ACP countries from 2008 until 2013.[99] The provisions of the Cotonou Agreement are generally less explicit on SSR than those of the various new EC external aid instruments, but their broad formulation (referring to the general principles of human rights, democracy, rule of law, good governance, peace-building as well as conflict prevention and resolution)[100] should allow SSR to be addressed in a more comprehensive way than it was the case so far with most of the projects financed in ACP countries in the area of police and justice. Yet, because the EDF is a traditional development instrument, its funding is in principle linked to ODA eligibility, even if, unlike in the DCI, this requirement is not explicitly included and a few exceptions actually exist, most notably the African Peace Facility.[101] The importance of Article 11 ('Peace-building policies, conflict prevention and resolution') in the architecture of Title II on the political dimension of the Cotonou Agreement, illustrates that SSR in ACP countries still often seems to be understood as related to conflict and post-conflict situations, with the possible risk of ignoring its relevance for (relatively) stable countries.

(e) The Instrument for Stability (IfS)

Under the new legal framework for EC external assistance, the new Instrument for Stability complements the geographic instruments. Even before its adoption, it raised a good deal of questions and expectations with regard to security issues, including SSR. While the IfS undoubtedly reflects the growing importance of security in EC external aid and is the only instrument explicitly mentioning the security system, its importance for SSR should not be overestimated in comparison with the geographical instruments. Article 2 (1) IfS clearly states that IfS assistance is only complementary to the assistance provided under the other (notably geographic) external aid instruments, and that it can 'be provided only to the extent that an adequate and effective response cannot be provided under those instruments.' In other words, the IfS cannot be a substitute for action in those areas of security sector reform where the relevant geographical programmes could be used for funding. Furthermore, the relatively low level of funding of the IfS – compared to the geographic instruments – puts a clear financial limit on extensive use of this instrument.

What is more, the two objectives of the IfS and their related constraints make it unsuitable for anything other than ad-hoc and short-term support to national SSR in crisis situations or long-term but indirect support in stable conditions. This instrument follows a twofold objective; it distinguishes between a situation of crisis or emerging crisis on the one hand (Article 1 (2) a), and stable conditions on the other (Article 1 (2) b). In the first case, according to Article 3 (1), the aim of the IfS is to provide a rapid and flexible 'response to a situation of urgency, crisis or emerging crisis, a situation posing a threat to democracy, law and order, the protection of human rights and fundamental freedoms, or the security and safety of individuals, or a situation threatening to escalate into armed conflict or destabilise the third country or countries concerned.' Technical and financial assistance measures under Article 3 may cover a very broad range of activities, including in the field of SSR[102], and can be adopted very quickly thanks to more flexible procedures, but they constitute so-called 'Exceptional Assistance Measures' which according to Article 5 (2) IfS may not last longer than 18 months. While this already represents a clear improvement with regard to the former Rapid Reaction Mechanism (RRM) where measures were limited to a period of six months[103], it is only sufficient to launch some activities with the sole aim of preparing the ground for more comprehensive security sector reform. By definition this is a long-term process and would thus need to be financed through a geographic programme.

In stable conditions for cooperation, the IfS aims to 'help build capacity both to address specific global and trans-regional threats having a destabilising effect and to ensure preparedness to address pre- and post-crisis assistance.' Global threats include terrorism and organised crime, which were already identified by the 2003 European Security Strategy as key threats to international security. The assistance measures foreseen by Article 4 IfS may contribute to SSR in the beneficiary countries in this regard.[104] The measures adopted under Article 4 IfS are programmed as are any other long-term measures under EC external aid instruments, but their relatively low level of funding compared to the funds available under Article 3 IfS will limit assistance measures in the fight against terrorism and organised crime to very few projects of a global or trans-regional nature. Thus, their contribution to national SSR may be very limited.[105]

While the relatively low level of funding of the IfS underpins its complementary function with regard to the geographic instruments as enshrined in Article 2 (1), their relationship will require further clarification in practice, in particular with the DCI of which Article 2 (6) seems in apparent contradiction with Article 2 (1) IfS. Indeed, the wording of both provisions might give the impression that they mutually exclude any 'long-term' assistance in the area of security and stability (except with regard to trans-regional and global threats for the Stability Instrument) thereby passing responsibility for such funding to each other. While Article 2 (1) IfS clearly states that assistance can 'be provided only to the extent that an adequate and effective response cannot be provided under those instruments [including the DCI]', Article 2 (6) DCI creates confusion by stipulating that 'measures covered by Regulation (EC) No 1717/2006 [IfS] and in particular Article 4 thereof, and eligible for funding thereunder shall not, in principle, be funded under this Regulation'. This somewhat clumsy formulation may wrongly imply that the IfS will be the primary source of funding for all the types of measures it covers. Though this will be the case 'in practice' with regard to crisis management measures (Art. 3) and measures addressing trans-regional and global threats (Art.4), Art. 2 (6), DCI omits that 'theoretically' this should only be so to the extent that they cannot be adequately and effectively adopted under its own regulation. Because of the inconsistency and lack of precision of both articles owing to their negative wording, the DCI could be confusingly and mistakenly presented as subsidiary to the IfS with regard to security issues. Some would argue that this contradiction between the two regulations is not problematic. It could be a purely legalistic argument since, in practice, all the various types of measures are covered. Yet this does not take into account the fact that the confusion induced creates the risk of relying unduly, in geographic programming exercises, on the financially limited IfS for long-term funding of security activities such as support to SSR. During the recent geographic programming cycle, which accompanied the adoption of the new instruments, this confusion was already apparent and, as outlined below, it has not been without consequences with regard to programming for security sector reform under the DCI.

Finally, even if the IfS was adopted like the ENPI on the double legal basis of Articles 179 and 181a of the EC Treaty and is thus not constrained by ODA eligibility, its scope with regard to SSR activities is nevertheless not unlimited. Due to the fears of the Council of the EU that the IfS might infringe its own competencies under Title V of the EU Treaty, the IfS carefully avoids mentioning certain specific areas which the Council considered to be exclusive CFSP/ESDP competence during the negotiations on this instrument, notably disarmament, military reform and arms control.

(f) The European Instrument for Democracy and Human Rights (EIDHR)

In the initial Commission proposal for reform of the external aid package, democracy and human rights were to form a thematic programme covered by the Development Cooperation Instrument. But following pressure from the European Parliament the EIDHR was finally adopted as a separate instrument based on Articles 179 and 181a of the EC Treaty. Its focus is on the development and consolidation of democracy, rule of law and human rights, and thus closely linked to SSR.[106] As its programming is not conditioned, unlike other EC external aid instruments, by the approval of the partner country's government, EIDHR funds are mainly channelled through civil society organisations. The EIDHR is thus not meant to support SSR comprehensively, though its support may contribute to the accountability and civilian oversight aspects of SSR in a given country.

SSR within EC Programming and Aid Implementation

If the EC legal framework for external aid instruments has been profoundly simplified and rationalised, in principle providing a better basis for SSR support, the main characteristics of EC programming and aid implementation remain basically the same, albeit with a few adaptations to further improve aid effectiveness.

EC External Aid Programming

The principles of the Paris Declaration are reflected in the procedures of the programming phase of EC external aid foreseen by the new external aid instruments. In particular, all geographical programming documents have to be established in close partnership with the beneficiaries, covering not only their national, but also regional and local authorities as well as other relevant stakeholders. The purpose is to ensure that EC assistance complements the partners' strategies and respects the principle of local ownership.

Nevertheless, other EU objectives and policies intersect with EC Development policy and may thus influence how sensitive and highly political issues such as SSR are addressed in partner countries or regions during the programming phase. This applies of course to Enlargement and European Neighbourhood Policy, but also Justice and Home Affairs. As Justice and Home Affairs (JHA) policy has implications beyond EU borders, the Council adopted in December 2005 a 'Strategy for the External Dimension of the EU's area of freedom, security and justice'.[107] The need for coherence between EU internal and external policies implies that strategic considerations under EU JHA policy may influence significantly in third regions and countries where the EU and the EC are more likely to engage in SSR.

With the exception of the candidate and potential candidate countries covered by the IPA, where a somewhat different procedure is applicable[108], EC aid delivery through geographic instruments is first programmed on the basis of Country Strategy Papers (CSP) and Regional (or multi-country) Strategy Papers (RSP). For countries covered by the ENPI, these Strategy Papers have to reflect Partnership and Cooperation Agreements as well as ENP Action Plans. CSP and RSP are generally adopted for the whole period of validity of the relevant geographic instrument (currently 2007-2013), but with an obligatory mid-term review as well as an ad hoc review, if necessary.[109] Each CSP and RSP also contains a national or regional multi-annual indicative programme (NIP/RIP) setting out the priority areas and objectives for EC financing. The new NIP/RIP cover the first period until the mid-term review (2007-2010) and in general identify one or two focal, as well as a few additional non-focal, sectors of EC intervention, together with specific objectives, expected results, a timeframe and indicative financial allocations. As the CSP/RSP and NIP/RIP are in principle agreed with the relevant partner country or region, and following the Paris Declaration increasingly with other donors[110], the selection of SSR as a focal or non-focal sector, or its inclusion under a focal or non-focal sector focusing in more general terms on 'good governance' or 'rule of law', depends very much on the partners' priorities and the activities of other donors.

As observed above, the outcome of the first programming phase of the new EC external aid instruments indicates mixed results as to inclusion of security sector reform, despite the improvement over the previous programming phase. SSR-related activities figure prominently in national and regional programming documents for all countries covered by the IPA. The requirements of the Copenhagen criteria and the *acquis communautaire* in the area of JHA are clearly reasons, but the direct security threat for the EU posed by ongoing ethnic tensions and organised crime in the Balkans and Turkey are also an obvious incitation. For the countries covered by the ENPI, the picture is much less homogeneous, and this despite the fact that SSR-related activities were already carried out in many of these countries under the previous CSP/NIP and that the new European Neighbourhood Policy boosted JHA issues via their inclusion in the Partnership and Cooperation Agreements and ENP Action Plans. In the Eastern ENP (most of the ex-TACIS) countries, SSR issues continue to be covered, and continuity with the previous CSP/RSP seems ensured.[111] There is still a heavy focus on border management and the fight against trafficking and organised crime, but also clearly greater emphasis on justice reform and governance. The situation in the Southern ENP (ex-MEDA) countries is somewhat different. Even if all CSP/RSP include a general reference to governance, rule of law and human rights, as well as to cooperation in the field of JHA, many NIP only cover reform of the judicial and penitentiary systems.[112] So there is a risk that reforms in the area of SSR initiated under the previous CSP may not receive appropriate follow-up. It thus seems that the political sensitivity of SSR, coupled with the diverging priorities of the beneficiary countries, has meant that the potential of the ENP and its new instrument, the ENPI, has not yet been fully exploited in the area of security sector reform.

As to the countries and regions covered by the DCI, SSR is even more fragmented than in ENPI countries. In Asia, the CSP/NIP of certain countries cover SSR issues extensively[113], while in others it is addressed only partly[114] or not at all.[115] In the CSP/NIP for Latin-American countries, SSR figures even less, with very few of them foreseeing activities in this field.[116] In South Africa, the only ACP country where geographical programming falls under the DCI, governance and SSR constitute a non-focal sector and are broadly covered. Since the programming phase for the ACP countries covered by the EDF is not yet complete, the 10th EDF only starting in 2008, it is too early to make an accurate assessment of how SSR will be addressed under the new CSP/RSP. But the consultation process seems to indicate that there will be as equally scattered results as under the DCI.

The discrepancies in coverage of security issues, in particular SSR, in the CSP/RSP and NIP/RIP of the countries and regions receiving EC external aid can also be explained in part by the different approaches and priorities of those responsible for geographic programming. This demonstrates, as argued above, that security, external relations and development actors often fail to share the same vision and political agenda. The preponderant role of development actors in the European Commission, the European Parliament and EU Member States in programming for the DCI and the EDF probably explains overall reluctance to engage in SSR.[117] Reluctance is less prevalent in countries covered by the IPA and ENPI, where other actors have a greater say.

Geographical programming for a given country or region may be complemented by specific activities adopted under thematic programmes and instruments, where programming displays similar features to the geographical instruments. These are generally programmed via multi-annual Thematic Strategy Papers and related Multi-annual Indicative Programmes. In the case of the IfS however, only its longer-term component (Article 4) is subject to programming, as the crisis response component (Article 3) is by definition not programmable. Because of the new and innovative character of the IfS, the first strategy paper for longer term action only covers 2007-2011 and will likely be revised in 2009 following an assessment of the first results achieved. The related indicative programme only covers 2007-2008. As mentioned above, the low level of funding for action under Article 4 (1) IfS does not allow for substantial activities at global or trans-regional level to support national or regional programmes in the area of SSR.

The situation is somewhat different with regard to Exceptional Assistance Measures funded under Article 3 IfS, which benefit from a considerably higher allocation of funds.[118] However, to be sustainable in the case of SSR, these short-term measures need to be coherent, complementary and coordinated with long-term programming under the relevant CSP and RSP. As observed earlier, problems easily arise in cases where the CSP or RSP do not foresee assistance in SSR to follow up initiatives launched under the IfS. The geographic instruments do of course allow for revision of priorities and focal sectors in the CSP and RSP. The IfS also allows for so-called 'Interim Response Programmes', potentially bridging the gap between Exceptional Assistance Measures and long-term programmes. Nonetheless, the highly political nature of emergency measures adopted under the crisis response component of the IfS, the necessity to coordinate them with CFSP/ESDP missions and the potentially ensuing competition between the Commission and the Council, risk focussing attention on the complementarity between first and second pillar activities, and much less on the complementarity between short and long-term EC external aid measures. Experience with the Rapid Reaction Mechanism is a case in point.

As to programming of the EIDHR, the five objectives addressed in the Strategy Paper and the related multi-annual Indicative Programme, which both cover 2007-2010, do not address specific SSR issues. Again, this does not preclude some of the supported projects eventually having an impact on SSR.

EC External Aid Implementation

There are three types of aid delivery method for the implementation of EC external aid: the project approach, the sector approach and the 'macro' or general approach. While the project approach follows the classical EC contract and finance rules laid down in the EC Financial Regulation[119], the macro approach operates via general or sectoral budget support.[120] Finally, the sector approach allows for all types of implementation: sector budget support, EC contract and finance rules or participation in so-called 'pool', 'basket' or 'trust' funds managed by the leading donor in the sector. Problems of sustainability have been experienced in the public sector of partner countries where the traditional project approach has been adopted. These were due to frequent lack of ownership and coherence with partner policies, as well as high transaction costs. The new EC Development policy thus prioritises budget support and sector approaches, in line with commitments made in the context of the 2005 Paris Declaration on Aid effectiveness.

The relevance of these three aid delivery methods differs with regard to SSR. While general budget support is by definition not related to a specific sector and thus cannot address SSR as such[121], sectoral budget support or pool funding can result in donor harmonisation, alignment and, to some extent, whole-of-government approaches in the field of SSR. There is as yet no EC experience with sector budget support in this area.[122] And for various reasons the conditions for pool funding are often not met. So EC external aid in this field will continue to be implemented through traditional projects as well; in particular where technical assistance is needed to build capacity in partner countries. Furthermore, the project approach, though not the 'ideal' aid delivery method for SSR support, offers useful opportunities, notably to engage on entry points for subsequent reforms, for instance in order to help in the elaboration of an SSR strategy.

The new EC external aid instruments thus continue to allow the full range of measures for implementation as before, but they also include several improvements. Pool funding is now much easier than under the previous instruments. The European Commission is explicitly allowed to contribute to funds set up by partner countries or regions, by donors or by international organisations for joint financing and implementation of activities. At the same time, the European Commission may now also receive and manage funds on behalf of EU Member States, other donor countries or international organisations, thus allowing it to play the role of lead donor. These improvements should allow the EC to make its support to SSR part of coordinated donor approaches.

Finally, another challenge for implementation is the availability of expertise. Most development actors are not security experts. Hence, 'twinning', which was initially developed for the candidate countries to the EU, has now been integrated into all new EC external aid instruments and thus been extended to all partner countries and regions. Twinning occurs when an EU Member State administration seconds an expert to the corresponding administration of an EU partner country or region. Although the seconded expert comes from a Member State, the entire process is managed and funded by the EC. Twinning is thus a good illustration of coordination at EU level. In the former candidate countries, which joined the EU in 2004 and 2007, and in the countries covered by the CARDS and MEDA programmes, twinning has frequently been used to second EU Member State experts from law enforcement or judicial authorities to assist partner countries implement reforms in JHA – in most cases contributing to SSR.

The twinning procedure now needs to be adapted under the new EC external aid instruments, as its applicability has so far depended on a very specific context and strict rules.[123] The growing realisation of the need for experts for technical assistance assignments in third countries is reflected in various European Council Conclusions[124], but the operational implications have not yet been sufficiently integrated into the staff regulations and human resource policies of the EU Member States' administrations. Aid recipients tend to give more legitimacy, credibility and trust to security sector reform experts who are civil servants. Security sector reform involves highly sensitive security issues, so while this is not surprising, it underlines the need to find ways to facilitate their recruitment. Yet, with the exception of twinning, EC procedures for external aid are still rather ill suited to contracts with EU Member State administrations and recruitment of their civil servants.

In addition, many civilians assigned by Member States demonstrably lack adequate training or do not have relevant previous experience. The Commission therefore launched in 2001 an 'EC Project on Training for Civilian Aspects of Crisis Management'. The aim was to support Member States' efforts to establish trained personnel pools for rapid deployment in crisis management operations involving rule of law and civilian administration. A further aim was to create an agreed basis for common civilian training modules in the EU and thus establish common training standards.[125] This ongoing project promotes EU training co-operation, identifies joint approaches to civilian training, develops training modules and organises joint EU training itself. Furthermore, the Commission's Strategy Paper and Indicative Programme 2007-2008 for the longer term component of the IfS envisage an Expert Support Facility to overcome some of the present shortcomings. Here, Member State experts would be made available for short, medium and long-term missions.

However, despite the efforts of the Commission, the Council and Member States, in practice the number and availability of trained EU Member States' staff remains limited. The Commission will undoubtedly be constrained to continue relying on other implementing partners to provide technical support to SSR.

Conclusion

After decades of development cooperation, the results are unsatisfactory. Globally, poverty and inequality have not been significantly reduced. There is a quest for alternative approaches, but failure or only relative success of development cooperation in some regions and countries has many reasons. Two intertwined prerequisites for development have clearly been overlooked: good governance and security. The recent shift within development cooperation from a quantity to a quality or result-oriented approach has highlighted the need for a closer and stronger focus on security issues in developing countries. But, changing well-embedded habits is not easy, particularly when doubts persist about the necessity to do so.

We observed earlier that some development actors are still reluctant to engage in this non-traditional field of work, not only because of the politics and competition involved, but also owing to risk aversion. Despite a broad acknowledgment of the interdependency between security and development, some feel that the integrity and added-value of development assistance may be jeopardised by diversion from its primary purpose and collaboration with security actors. Nonetheless, continuing the traditional approach of focusing aid only on classical areas of development risks complacency – betraying the poor who rank insecurity as high as hunger in their core concerns. If insecurity and instability are root causes of poverty and underdevelopment, there is an incontrovertible need to address them. The European Commission has demonstrated its commitment to face the challenges entailed by the new approach epitomized by the concept of security sector reform. The recent programming exercise demonstrated, albeit with mixed and varied results depending on the regions involved, that overall, and compared to the previous programming cycle, the Commission's effort has borne fruit.

Challenges remain however. One is the question of funding and the as yet unresolved issue of the eligibility criteria for Official Development Assistance. As a member of the Development Assistance Community of the OECD, the European Commission has a potentially important role to play in finding a balanced and definitive compromise. At EU level, despite the stalled ratification process of the Constitutional Treaty, the Commission has endeavoured to ensure further coordination and complementarity between its long-term development activities in the first pillar and short-term CFSP/ESDP measures in the second pillar. Yet, as this chapter has argued, the responsibility for promoting the EU as a global and unique security actor lies with both the Commission and the Council. It might be better exercised if they accepted their own complementarity as equal institutions of a single organisation. A quibbling and legalistic approach to the issue of their respective competences runs the risk of leaving their much-needed cooperation and coordination characterised as bitter and unproductive. The inevitable result would be continued EU incapacity to deal with the security-development nexus, and this to the detriment of the victims of insecurity in developing countries and the interests of EU tax payers. The hope must be that the European Court of Justice will prove instrumental in facilitating the relationship between both institutions. It has a good opportunity to soften current tensions by speedy resolution of the 'Small Arms and Light Weapons' case.

Funding and coordination challenges remain at international and EU level, but the European Community's recent overhaul of its external assistance architecture has created more opportunities and increased the quality of support to SSR. Yet, full exploitation of the new external assistance architecture for support to SSR will depend on enhanced articulation between the different instruments. This will clearly be a progressive process and there is likely to be only a provisional and partial solution. The nexus between security and development clearly conditions the use of the SSR concept. Development actors have a prime responsibility for further progress. They are, after all, the biggest potential beneficiary of enhanced coordination; second, of course, to those communities development policy is intended to assist.

Endnotes

1 Report of the Secretary-General, *An Agenda for Peace, Preventive Diplomacy, Peacemaking and Peace-keeping*, A/47/277 – S/24111, 17 June 1992. First restricted to post-conflict transition, the concept later came to encompass conflict prevention.

2 See *Voices of the Poor*, Narayan and al., 2000, a series of studies commissioned by the World Bank: www.worldbank.org/poverty/voices/reports.htm

3 Clare Short (1998) was the first Minister for International Development in the Department for International Development (DFID) newly-created by the Labour government that came to power in Britain in 1997.

4 As Brzoska rightly points out: 'The link between the reform of the security forces and the

promotion of development is most obvious in post-conflict situations where a facilitating political framework for security sector reform is generally provided. Usually security sector reform has already been planned, or is even underway, and has been initiated and supported by national actors including, where applicable, peacekeeping forces'. See Brzoska, M., *Development Donors and the Concept of Security Sector Reform*, Occasional Paper No. 4, Geneva Centre for The Democratic Control of Armed Forces, Geneva, November 2003, p. 38. See also Schnabel, A., and Ehrhart, H.-G., *Security Sector Reform and Post-conflict Peacebuilding*, United Nations University Press, 2005.

5 As Brzoska summarises: 'the visionary concept of security sector reform adds value to these previous attempts in that it looks at all institutions involved in the provision of security in a comprehensive way and focuses all reform activities on the promotion of development goals, particularly the reduction of poverty. Security sector reform marks the effort to overcome a 'blind spot' in much development donor policy of the past, namely an engagement with those actors within developing countries charged with the provision of security' . See Brzoska, M., *Ibid.*, p. 46.

6 This is true both with respect to violence in 'peace time', for instance from common criminality (see Ball, N., Brzoska, M., Kingma, K. and Wulf, H., *Voice and Accountability in the Security Sector*, Bonn International Centre for Conversion, July 2001) as well as during war (see Collier, P., Lani, E., Hegre, H., Hoeffler, A., Reynal-Querol, M. and Sambanis, S., *Breaking the Conflict Trap: Civil War and Development Policy*, Oxford University Press and World Bank, New York, 2003).

7 See 'Policy Statement on Security Sector Reform', UK Department for International Development, London, 1999 and 'Security Sector Reform and the Management of Military Expenditure. High Risks for Donors, High Returns for Development', UK DfID, London, 2000.

8 Stockholm International Peace Research Institute Yearbook 2006.

9 Final ODA Data For 2005, Organization for Economic Cooperation and Development (OECD), http://www.oecd.org/dataoecd/52/18/37790990.pdf

10 'Policy Coherence for Development. Accelerating Progress Towards Attaining the Millennium Development Goals', Commission Communication COM (2005), 134 final, 12 April 2005. See for instance p. 10 where the Commission asserts that 'the EU will treat security and development as complementary agendas, with the common aim of creating a secure environment and of breaking the vicious cycle of poverty, war, environmental degradation and failing economic, social and political structures'.

11 This is even one of the recommendations made in the 2006 Concept for EC Support to Security Sector Reform.

12 The 0.7% target was proposed in 1969 by the Pearson Committee and accepted by member countries of the Development Assistance Committee (DAC) of the Organisation for Economic Cooperation and Development (OECD) in 1970 – the Western donor countries' 'club'. The Pearson Committee was set up by the World Bank in 1968 to review development assistance and make recommendations for aid, taking into account domestic and external factors, and assessing how aid could be used most effectively if it were increased.

13 'DAC Statistical Reporting Directives', OECD DAC, Development Co-operation Directorate, DCD/DAC(2007)34, 6 April 2007.

14 'DAC Statistical Reporting Directives: Addendum', OECD DAC, Development Co-operation Directorate, DCD/DAC(2000)10/ADD1/REV1, 7 April 2005.

15 See notably Robinson, C., *Whose Security? Integration and Integrity in EU Policies for Security and Development*, APRODEV, Brussels, June 2005, p. 22, who stresses with respect to the three paragraphs reproduced above that: 'With the first three, it could be argued that the security services should be democratically controlled in the first place, without the need for ODA support: why is management more acceptable as ODA than security force activity on the ground?' Interestingly, earlier in the text, he also states with regard to the DAC that: 'While advocating whole-of-government approaches to reform, it makes a distinction between [...] governance activities and those designed to strengthen the operational' capability of security forces, while acknowledging that partner governments in developing countries concerned with providing security effectively need to address both dimensions.'

16 'Is it ODA?' OECD DAC Factsheet, October 2006, http://www.oecd.org/dataoecd/21/21/34086975.pdf

17 See Conflict, Security and Official Development Assistance (ODA): Issues for NGO advocacy, British Overseas NGOs for Development (BOND), http://www.bond.org.uk/pubs/advocacy/gsdpaper.pdf

18 Adopted on 21 December 2001 in the immediate aftermath of the '9/11' attacks, this milestone Resolution requires full cooperation from all states in the fight against terrorism, including by preventing the movements of terrorists by effective border controls.

19 Case No. C-403/05, European Parliament against European Commission. http://eur-lex.europa.eu/LexUriServ/LexUriServ.do?uri=CELEX:62005J0403:FR:HTML; to be published in the European Court Reports.

20 'Should the criteria be expanded? Frequently Asked Questions on ODA criteria and security expenditures', Canada's Coalition to End Global Poverty (CCIC), May 2006, http://www.ccic.ca/e/docs/002_aid_2006-05_oda_security_criteria.pdf

21 Netherlands Ministry of Foreign Affairs, *Mutual Interests, Mutual Responsibilities: Dutch Development Cooperation en Route to 2015*, Policy Memorandum, October 2003.

22 *Ibid.*

23 'Global Public Goods can be grouped under four broad headings, which can be related to the UN Secretary-General's definition of 'larger freedom': (i) physical security and stability – 'freedom from fear'; (ii) political participation and an enforceable legal order that guarantees the human rights and equality of all; (iii) an open and inclusive economic order that provides for the wealth of everyone – 'freedom from want'; (iv) social well-being in all of its aspects – access to health services, to education, to a clean environment'. See Biscop, S., 'Security and Development: a positive agenda for a global EU-UN partnership' in Biscop, S., Francioni, F., Graham, K., Felicío, T., Laurenti, J. and Tardy, T., *The European Union and the United Nations. Partners in effective multilateralism*, European Union Institute for Security Studies, Chaillot Paper, n° 78, June 2005, p. 18.

24 Biscop, S., *Ibid.*, p.19-20.

25 The Secretary-General declared that system-wide integration in the field would be one of his key objectives particularly when it came to peacekeeping and peace-building activities, both in the field and at headquarters. See Secretary-General Annual Report, 1997, paras. 116 and 117.

26 A/51/950, 14 July 1997, para 149. The problem of inadequate coordination was revisited in a report by a later Secretary-General's High-level Panel (United Nations, 2004) and the Secretary-General's subsequent report, *In Larger Freedom* (United Nations, 2005), which argues for a coherent approach by all parties concerned with conflict management.

27 'Delivering as One', Secretary-General's High-level Panel on UN System-wide Coherence in the Areas of Development, Humanitarian Assistance, and the Environment, New-York, 9 November 2006.

28 LICUS Overview, http://web.worldbank.org

29 *The Global Conflict Prevention Pool: A Joint UK Government Approach to Reducing Conflict*, Foreign and Commonwealth Office, London, 2003, p. 6.

30 For more information, see Ball, N., *Evaluation of the Conflict Prevention Pools, The Security Sector Reform Strategy*, UK Department for International Development, Evaluation Report EV 647, March 2004.

31 http://www.postconflict.gov.uk/

32 http://www.auswaertiges-amt.de/www/en/aussenpolitik/friedenspolitik/ziv_km/aktionsplan_html.

33 Harder, P., Speech presented at the opening of the Diplomatic Forum, Toronto, Ontario, 4 December 2003.

34 Fitz-Gerald, A.-M., 'Addressing the Security-Development Nexus: Implications for Joined-up Government', IRPP, *Enjeux Publics*, vol. 5, n°5, July 2004, p. 14.

35 http://www.state.gov/s/crs; see also Krasner, S., D. and Pascual, C., 'Addressing State Failure,' Foreign Affairs, July/August 2005, pp. 153-163.

36 Condoleezza Rice, Remarks on Foreign Assistance, U.S. Department of State, 19 January 2006, http://www.state.gov/secretary/rm/2006/59408.htm; See also Graham, B. and Kessler, G. 'Rice Explains Aid Restructuring to USAID Employees', *Washington Post*, 20 January 2006. Innovations include the creation of a new Director of Foreign Assistance within the State Department, who will double-hat as the lead administrator of USAID. This shift aims to consolidate authority over the budgeting, planning, and implementation of all State and USAID foreign aid programs – which were previously scattered throughout both departments, sometimes to redundant or contradictory effect – within one office.

37 The three following paragraphs lean heavily on the OECD DAC reference document:

'Whole of Government Approaches to Fragile States', Governance, Peace and Security, 2006. See: http://www.oecd.org/dataoecd/15/24/37826256.pdf

38 Wulf, H., *Security Sector Reform in Developing Countries*, Eschborn, GTZ, 2000.

39 Some countries such as the UK have separate foreign affairs and development ministries. Others do not have separate development ministries but have development ministers such as Belgium, the Netherlands and Sweden for instance. Others again have neither separate development ministries nor development ministers.

40 Interesting examples of such mechanisms for joint assessment/analyses include the UK Drivers-of-Change and Strategic Conflict Assessments and the Netherlands Stability Assessment Frameworks.

41 Interesting examples of such mechanisms for joint coordination/planning include the UK Closer Working Action Plan as well as the Swedish Joint Preparation Process which is a more formal mechanism entailing obligations at the governmental level to coordinate for a specific purpose. Such mechanisms could also be linked to joint reporting to the Parliament.

42 Interesting examples of such mechanisms for joint deployment of staff include the integrated Security Sector Reform Pool set up by the Netherlands in 2005 and the UK Security Sector Development Advisory Team (SSDAT) both comprising military and civilian experts in police, justice, governance.

43 As Catriona Gourlay points out: 'Under the pressure of producing a swift result and a political signal in response to a crisis, coherence with ongoing or planned EC actions is often assumed rather than explored'. See Gourlay, C., 'Civil-Civil Co-ordination in EU crisis management in Gourlay', C., Helly, D., Ioannides, I., Khol, R., Nowak, A., and Serrano, P., *Civilian crisis management: the EU way*, Institute for Security Studies, Chaillot Paper No. 90, June 2006, p. 105.

44 For a review of the turf wars that prevent effective coordination see D. Spence, 'The Commission and the CFSP' in D. Spence (ed) *The European Commission*, John Harper, 2006.

45 Council Conclusions on a Policy framework for Security sector reform, 2736th, General Affairs Council meeting, Luxembourg, 12 June 2006.

46 EU Concept for ESDP support to Security Sector Reform (SSR), 12566/4/05, Brussels, 13 October 2005.

47 Communication from the Commission to the Council and the European Parliament, *A Concept for European Community Support for Security Sector Reform*, Brussels, 24.5.2006, COM(2006) 253 final.

48 If the security sector reform concept was incoherent, the common EU concept for support to Disarmament, Demobilisation and Reintegration adopted by the Commission and the Council of the EU respectively on 11 and on 14 December 2006, avoided this pitfall.

49 In the field of civilian crisis management, the Feira European Council in June 2000 set a target, within the European Security and Defence Policy (ESDP), of development of civilian capabilities in four priority areas: police, rule of law, civilian administration and civil protection. In the framework of the CFSP/ESDP, the Council has thus a wide range of competences with regard to SSR. In the field of military crisis management, in 2004 the range of 'Petersberg tasks', already including 'Humanitarian and rescue tasks, peacekeeping tasks and tasks of combat forces in crisis management, including peacemaking' as defined in the Amsterdam treaty', was upgraded to include joint disarmament operations, support for third countries in combating terrorism and security sector reform. See GAERC and Defence Ministers Council Conclusions, 17-18 May 2004.

50 One of the two main documents is the 2003 EU Security Strategy, which states: 'Over recent years we have created a number of different instruments, each of which has its own structure and rationale. The challenge now is to bring together the different instruments and capabilities: European assistance programmes and the European Development Fund, military and civilian capabilities from Member States and other instruments. All of these can have an impact on our security and on that of third countries. Security is the first condition for development. Diplomatic efforts, development, trade and environmental policies should follow the same agenda. In a crisis there is no substitute for unity of command. Better co-ordination between external action and Justice and Home Affairs policies is crucial in the fight both against terrorism and organised crime. Greater coherence is needed not only among EU instruments but also embracing the external activities of the individual member states.' (See EU Security Strategy, *Ibid.*, p. 14) This is also the idea at the heart of the European Consensus for

Development which stipulates in its introduction that: 'To this end, the 'European Consensus' sets out, for the first time in fifty years of cooperation, the framework of common principles under which the EU and its twenty-five Member States will implement their development policies in a spirit of complementarity'. (See European Consensus for Development, *Ibid.*, p. 5)

51 Art. 3 § 2 TEU: 'The Union shall in particular ensure the consistency of its external activities as a whole in the context of its external relations, security, economic and development policies. The Council and the Commission shall be responsible for ensuring such consistency and shall cooperate to this end. They shall ensure the implementation of these policies, each in accordance with its respective powers.'

52 Commission challenges to the Council have been mounted on a number of occasions for allegedly infringing Community competences in external relations. Common positions adopted in 1994 on Rwanda and the Ukraine were both criticised for the inclusion of Community matters in CFSP 'common positions'. Similar examples have been cited of the 'overly pervasive' use of CFSP instruments in electoral observation missions in Russia and South Africa as well as the Korean Peninsula Energy Development Organization initiative. Other issue areas, cutting across a number of countries, such as the export of dual-use goods have also been points of contention between the Community and the second pillar. Conversely, the Council challenged the Commission's competence to act when it supported conflict-prevention programmes in West Africa (through The Southern Africa Development Community and the Economic Community of West African States) as well as in Nepal; supported peace-building and mediation in Aceh, Liberia and Sudan; promoted peace-building efforts in Bolivia; and support for UN good offices in Colombia. See S. Duke, *Areas of Grey: Tensions in EU External Relations Competences,* European Institute of Public Administration, EIPASCOPE 1 – 2006, p. 2-3, http://www.eipa.eu/files/repository/eipascope/Scop06_1_3.pdf

53 'Action brought on 21 February 2005 by the European Commission against the Council of the European Union', Case C-91/05 in O.J., C 115/10, 14 May 2005. For further discussion see D. Spence, The Commission and the CFSP in D. Spence (ed) *The European Commission*, John Harper, 2006.

54 Council Decision 2004/833/CFSP of 2 December 2004 based on Article 3 of Joint Action 2002/589/CFSP.

55 In this case (C-176/03: Commission of the European Communities v Council of the EU), the Commission, supported by the European Parliament, had asked the ECJ to annul Council Framework Decision 2003/80/JHA of 27 January 2003 on the protection of the environment through criminal law. The judgment (13 September 2005, O.J., C 315/03, 10.12.2005, p. 2) clarifies the distribution of powers between the first and third pillars as regards provisions of criminal law even though, as a general rule, criminal law does not fall within the Community's competence.

56 With regard to any attempt to delineate first and second pillar competencies: 'the danger is that a clear division of roles might have the effect of limiting EU security action to short-term CFSP actions rather than fostering more needs-based short and long-term security sensitive assistance across the pillars'. See Gourlay, C., 'Civil-Civil Co-ordination in EU crisis management', *Ibid.*, pp. 105-106.

57 These are Council bodies responsible within their specific mandate for the planning and management of ESDP operations.

58 Communication from the Commission, *Reinforcing EU Disaster and Crisis Response in third countries*, COM(2005) 153, 20 April 2005, p. 9.

59 EU Doc. 10462/05, 23 June 2005, Multifunctional Civilian Crisis Management Resources in Integrated Format – Civilian Response Teams.

60 EU Doc. 9126/3/05 Rev 3, 21 June 2005, p.4. For more information see also: EU Docs.: 12825/05, 3 October 2005, Towards CRT Implementation, 15406/05 of 5 December 2005, CRT Generic Terms of Reference, 15740/05, 13 November 2005, CRT Training Concept.

61 Gourlay, C., 'Community Instruments for Civilian Crisis Management', in Gourlay, C., Helly, D., Ioannides, I., Khol, R., Nowak, A., and Serrano, P., *Civilian crisis management: the EU way*, Institute for Security Studies, Chaillot Paper No. 90, June 2006, p. 61.

62 Suggestions for Procedures for Coherent, Comprehensive EU Crisis Management, Doc. 11127/03, 3 July 2003.

63 *Ibid*, p. 10.

64 Speech by The Rt. Hon Chris Patten, Institut français des relations internationales (IFRI), Paris, 15 June 2000.

65 In this regard, Aline Dewaele and Catriona Gourlay deplore that the 'negotiations on this new financial instrument have not been carried out in the spirit of inter-institutional solidarity, but rather been reduced to legalistic arguments over the precise delineation of institutional competences'. See Dewaele, A. and Gourlay, C., *The Stability Instrument: defining the Commission's role in crisis response*, ISIS Europe, 27 June 2005, p. 6.

66 On comitology see R. Pedler: 'The Commission and comitology' in D. Spence, *The European Commission*, John Harper, 2006.

67 Hauck, V. and Gaspers, J., *Capacity Building for Peace and Security. A look at the African continent*, European Centre for Development Policy Management, Contribution to the International Task Force on Global Public Goods, Maastricht, February 2005, p. 29.

68 UN doc. No° A/CONF.198/11.

69 The Paris Declaration of March 2005 is available on the OECD website: www.oecd.org

70 Official Journal of the EU, C 46, 24.2.2006, p. 1.

71 Communication of 13 July 2005 of the European Commission to the Council, the European Parliament, the Economic and Social Committee and the Committee of Regions: Proposal for a Joint Declaration by the Council, the European Parliament and the Commission on the EU Development Policy, 'The European Consensus', COM(2005) 311 final.

72 'EU Aid: Delivering more, better and faster', COM (2006) 87 final; 'Financing for Development and Aid effectiveness – The challenge of scaling up EU aid 2006-2010', COM(2006) 85 final; and 'Increasing the Impact of EU Aid: a common framework for drafting strategy papers and joint multi-annual programming', COM(2006) 88 final.

73 The Council noted the progress made by the EU with regard to scaling up ODA and set new concrete targets of ODA increases, with the EU collectively providing 0.56% of its GNI by 2010, as an intermediate step to achieving the UN target of 0.7% by 2015. With its increase in aid volume, the EU currently contributes about 80% of the promised scaling up of ODA worldwide, providing collectively at least 50% of this increase to Africa. The Council conclusions are available on its website at:

http://www.consilium.europa.eu/ueDocs/cms_Data/docs/pressdata/en/gena/89219.pdf

74 Inter-institutional Agreement between the European Parliament, the Council and the Commission on budgetary discipline and sound financial management, Official Journal of the European Union, C 139/1 of 14 June 2006.

75 While the African, Caribbean and Pacific (ACP) countries had benefited since the 1960s from external aid under the European Development Fund (EDF), which is separate from the EC budget, the other regional instruments were adopted in the 1990s following the profound political and economic changes at the end of the cold war. These included the PHARE programme for the (then) candidate countries in Eastern Europe, the CARDS programme for the countries of the Western Balkans, the TACIS programme for the new countries emerging from the collapsed Soviet Union, the MEDA programme for the countries in Northern Africa and the Near East, and finally the ALA programme for the countries in Asia and Latin America. In addition to these regional instruments more than 20 other geographical and thematic programmes with often very specific objectives were adopted.

76 Communication of 29 September 2004 from the Commission to the Council and the European Parliament on the Instruments for External Assistance under the Future Financial Perspective 2007-2013, COM(2004) 626 final.

77 The package proposed by the European Commission comprised three geographical instruments (an Instrument for Pre-Accession Assistance, a European Neighbourhood Policy Instrument and a Development and Economic Cooperation Instrument), as well as an Instrument for Stability as a specific thematic instrument.

78 The European Parliament asked for a separate Democracy and Human Rights instrument, as well as a split between development and industrialised countries. Further, the Council decided to split the issue of nuclear safety from the Instrument for Stability and did not follow the Commission proposal to incorporate the EDF in the EC budget. The effect of this was that the ACP countries are not covered by the geographic programmes of the Development Cooperation Instrument.

79 Council Regulation (EC) No 1085/2006 of 17 July 2006, Official Journal of the EU, L 210/82 of 31 July 2006. Current candidate countries are Croatia, the Former Yugoslav Republic of Macedonia (FYROM) and Turkey, while the potential candidate countries are Albania, Bosnia and Herzegovina, Montenegro and Serbia (including Kosovo).

80 Regulation (EC) No 1638/2006 of the European Parliament and of the Council of 15 November 2006, Official Journal of the European Union, L 310/1 of 9 November 2006. The ENPI will cover the following countries: Algeria, Armenia, Azerbaijan, Belarus, Egypt, Georgia, Israel, Jordan, Lebanon, Libya, Moldova, Morocco, Palestinian Authority of the West Bank and Gaza Strip, Russia, Syria, Tunisia and Ukraine.

81 Regulation (EC) No 1905/2006 of the European Parliament and of the Council of 18 December 2006, Official Journal of the EU, L 378/41, 27 December 2006. Geographic programmes under the DCI will exist for the following regions: Latin America, Asia, Central Asia, Middle East and South Africa.

82 The five thematic programmes are: human and social development, environment, non-state actors in development, food security, migration and asylum.

83 Council Regulation (EC) No 1934/2006 of 21 December 2006, Official Journal of the EU, L 405/41 of 30 December 2006.

84 Regulation (EC) No 1717/2006 of the European Parliament and of the Council of 15 November 2006, Official Journal of the EU, L 327/1 of 24 November 2006.

85 Regulation (EC) No 1889/2006 of the European Parliament and of the Council of 20 December 2006, Official Journal of the EU, L 386/1 of 29 December 2006.

86 Council Regulation (Euratom) No 300/2007 of 19 February 2007, Official Journal of the EU, L 81/1 of 22 March 2007.

87 Council Decision of 21 June 2005 concerning the signing, on behalf of the European Community, of the Agreement amending the Partnership Agreement between the members of the African, Caribbean and Pacific Group of States (ACP), of the one part, and the European Community and its Member States, of the other part, signed in Cotonou on 23 June 2000, O.J., L 209, 11.8.2005. The full text of the revised version of the Cotonou Agreement can be found on the website of the European Commission: http://ec.europa.eu/development/body/cotonou/pdf/agr01_en.pdf#zoom=100

88 Council Regulation EC No 617/2007 of 14 May 2007 on the implementation of the 10th EDF, Official Journal of the EU, L 152/1 of 13 June 2007.

89 Legal basis and principles laid down in Articles 177-181 (Title XX) of the EC Treaty.

90 According to article 2 (1) IPA, assistance shall support the 'a) strengthening of democratic institutions, as well as the rule of law, including its enforcement; b) the promotion and protection of human rights and fundamental freedoms (...); c) public administration reform (...); h) regional and cross-border cooperation.' Article 2 (2) and (3) IPA refers to the assistance to be provided to the candidate and potential candidate countries to conform with the *acquis communautaire*.

91 See Zimmermann, comment on Article 181a EC Treaty in von der Groeben/Schwarze, 'Vertrag über die Europäische Union und Vertrag zur Gründung der Europäischen Gemeinschaft' (Nomos, 2003), part III, p. 1522.

92 Furthermore, Article 181a is the only provision in the EC Treaty which makes reference to association agreements and to agreements concluded with states which are candidates for accession to the EU.

93 The ENP covers all former MEDA and TACIS countries with the exception of the Central Asian countries, which are now covered by the DCI, and of Russia, which refused to be part of the ENP, but which is nevertheless covered by the ENPI as the EU and Russia are linked by a Partnership Agreement.

94 Article 2 (2) ENPI covers in particular the following areas of cooperation: 'd) promoting the rule of law and good governance, including strengthening the effectiveness of public administration and the impartiality and effectiveness of the judiciary, and supporting the fight against corruption and fraud; (...) k) promoting human rights and fundamental freedoms (...); l) supporting democratisation, inter alia, by enhancing the role of civil society organisations and promoting media pluralism (...); q) ensuring efficient and secure border management; r) supporting reform and strengthening capacity in the field of justice and home affairs, including issues such as (...) the fight against, and prevention of, trafficking in human beings as well as terrorism and organised crime, including its financing, money laundering and tax fraud; (...)'

95 See endnotes 77 and 78. The only exception is South Africa, which is the sole ACP country geographically covered by the DCI, as it was already previously covered by a specific EC regulation instead of the EDF.

96 Article 5 (2) covers in particular the following areas of cooperation: 'f) promoting and protecting fundamental freedoms and human rights, strengthening democracy, the rule of law, access to justice and good governance (...); g) supporting an active civil society (...); h) fostering cooperation and policy reform in the fields of security and justice, especially as regards (...) the fight against drugs and other trafficking including trafficking in human beings, corruption and money laundering; (...) w) reconstructing and rehabilitating, in the medium- and long-term, regions and countries affected by conflict (...), including support for (...) demobilisation and reintegration actions (...); y) in fragile or failing States, supporting the delivery of basic services and building of legitimate, effective and resilient public institutions (...).' The subsequent articles related to specific regions or countries identify more specific actions of which some are linked to SSR, as for instance 'the fight against drugs and other trafficking' in Asia (article 7 f) or 'border management' and 'fight against drugs and other trafficking' in Central Asia (article 8 c and d).

97 According to Article 2 (6) DCI, 'measures covered by Regulation (EC) No 1717/2006[NB: the IfS] and in particular Article 4 thereof, and eligible for funding there-under shall not, in principle, be funded under this Regulation, except where there is a need to ensure continuity of cooperation from crisis to stable conditions for development.'

98 It is to be noted that the revision has put more emphasis on political dialogue and on the role of national parliaments, two areas of great importance for the support to SSR.

99 The EDF also covers 20 Overseas Countries and Territories, but not South Africa which is covered by the DCI (see also endnote 95).

100 These principles are in particular referred to in Articles 9-11 of the Cotonou Agreement.

101 The Peace Facility for Africa was created on 11 December 2003 by the ACP-EC Council of ministers in accordance with Article 11 (4) of the Cotonou Agreement and with an allocation of €250 million funded by the 9th EDF. Its aim is, on the one hand, to strengthen the capacities of the African Union to engage in peace support and peace-keeping operations in Africa and, on the other, to support financially African led and staffed peace support operations. Though the operational component of the Facility excludes funding for arms, ammunition, salaries for soldiers, military training, etc. and as a result covers only expenses such as per diems, communication equipment, medical facilities, transport, logistics, etc., it is considered that only around 15% of the Peace Facility expenditure is reportable as ODA. Interestingly, in the ongoing discussions on the follow-up to the Facility under the 10th EDF, the possibility of extending it to SSR activities was contemplated both from the capacity-building perspective and from the operational viewpoint. Another good example of EDF funding of non-ODA eligible expenditures is the support provided to the army integration in the Democratic Republic of Congo through the so-called 'centres de brassage'.

102 Article 3 (2) covers *inter alia* the following areas: 'c) support for the development of democratic, pluralistic state institutions, including (...) effective civilian administration and related legal frameworks at national and local level, an independent judiciary, good governance and law and order, including non-military technical cooperation to strengthen overall civilian control and oversight over the security system and measures to strengthen the capacity of law enforcement and judicial authorities involved in the fight against the trafficking of people, drugs, firearms and explosive materials; (...) f) support for civilian measures related to the demobilisation and reintegration of former combatants into civil society (...), as well as measures to address the situation of child soldiers and female combatants; g) support for measures to mitigate the social effects of restructuring of the armed forces; (...) l) support for measures to promote and defend respect for human rights and fundamental freedoms, democracy and the rule of law, and the related international instruments (...).'

103 The RRM was the predecessor of the 'crisis component' of the IfS and expired at the end of 2006.

104 According to Article 4 (1), 'assistance shall cover: a) strengthening the capacity of law enforcement and judicial and civil authorities involved in the fight against terrorism and organised crime, including trafficking of drugs, people, firearms and explosive materials and in the effective control of illegal trade and transit. (...) With regard to assistance to authorities involved in the fight against terrorism, priority shall be given to supporting measures concerning the development and strengthening of counter-terrorism legislation, financial law,

implementation and practice, customs law, implementation and practice, immigration law, implementation and practice, and the development of international procedures for law enforcement.'

105 In the EC budget for 2007, €100M are available for Exceptional Assistance Measures under Article 3 IfS, while €44M have been allocated to longer term measures under Article 4 IfS, of which only €9M are devoted to the fight against terrorism and organised crime. According to the evolution of the budgetary amounts as foreseen by the EC financial framework 2007-2013, the budget allocation for crisis response will almost quadruple to reach €371M in 2013, while the budget allocation for longer term measures to counter global threats will only double to reach €80M in that year.

106 According to Article 2 (1) a) EIDHR, its scope notably extends to: 'ii) strengthening the rule of law, promoting the independence of the judiciary, encouraging and evaluating legal and institutional reforms, and promoting access to justice; [...] iv) supporting reforms to achieve effective and transparent democratic accountability and oversight, including that of the security and justice sectors [...]'.

107 Council conclusions of 1 and 5 December 2005. The Council conclusions and the Strategy are available on the website of the Council: www.consilium.europa.eu

108 Each year, the Commission adopts an enlargement strategy paper covering all IPA countries, together with annual country reports. The Multi-annual Indicative Financial Framework covering a period of three years and giving the indicative breakdown of the overall IPA envelope for the different countries has been adopted for 2008-2010, due to the delays in agreeing the EU Financial Perspectives 2007-2013 and the IPA.

109 The new CSP and RSP for ACP countries covered by the EDF will cover the period of validity of the 10th EDF (2008-2013).

110 Significantly, all the new EC external aid instruments explicitly stress for the first time the importance of close coordination between the Commission, the Council and the EU Member States. Under the new programming exercise for the period beginning in 2007 following the entry into force of the new EC external aid instruments, South Africa was chosen as a pilot country for a joint programming exercise between the European Commission and the EU Member States, with encouraging results which have led to an extension of this exercise to other third countries.

111 With the exception of Belarus where the political situation has meant that EC financing in this area is currently limited to the strengthening of civil society, all CSP and the RSP cover all or most of the SSR areas eligible for EC support, notably justice and law enforcement/police. This has been translated into the related NIP of Ukraine, Moldova, Georgia, Armenia and the RIP, with the exception of Azerbaijan where no concrete activities in this area are planned under the NIP 2007-2010. In the case of Russia, which is not formally part of the ENP but where a specific EU-Russia Partnership Agreement exists on the creation of four common spaces, the second common space relates to cooperation in JHA and the NIP 2007-2010 thus foresees several activities in this area.

112 This is the case of the NIP of Algeria, Morocco, Jordan, Syria and Lebanon. Only the NIP for Egypt covers SSR issues in a broad sense, while the NIP for Tunisia does not address any of them. The new RSP/RIP on the Euromed Partnership foresees a follow-up to the MEDA JHA programmes initiated under the MEDA regulation, which cover cooperation in the three areas of police, justice and migration.

113 This is notably the case for Afghanistan, Indonesia, Kazakhstan, Kyrgyzstan, Bangladesh and, to a lesser extent, Cambodia. The programming documents for Iraq cover SSR extensively, but the precarious situation in Iraq has meant that they are temporarily adopted on an annual basis.

114 In the CSP/NIP of Pakistan, Thailand, Philippines, Yemen, Laos and Sri Lanka, only certain very specific SSR-related areas are covered. These often correspond to the fight against certain forms of organised crime, to reform of the judiciary, to cooperation in the area of JHA or to the strengthening of civilian oversight mechanisms with regard to human rights abuses. Regional cooperation for the Central Asian countries covers border management and the fight against organised crime, while the RSP/RIP for ASEAN covers border management and the fight against trafficking of human beings.

115 This is notably the case of the CSP/NIP for China, India, Vietnam, Malaysia and Mongolia.

116 The CSP/NIP of the three Central American countries Honduras, Guatemala and El Salvador, which all face huge crime problems, put a heavy focus on SSR activities. The CSP for Colombia and Venezuela cover it to a lesser extent, while the CSP/RIP of all the other Latin-American countries do not plan any activities in this area. The RSP/RIP for the Andean Community only foresees activities in the fight against drugs.

117 At the European Commission, the ACP countries are dealt with by DG Development, the candidate and potential candidate countries by DG Enlargement and all other third countries by DG External Relations. At the European Parliament, the Development Committee has the prime responsibility for the ACP and DCI countries, while the Foreign Affairs Committee has the prime responsibility for the Enlargement and Neighbourhood Policies. At the level of the EU Member States, ACP and DCI countries fall in general, where they exist, under the responsibility of the Ministries for Development Cooperation, whose representatives participate in the committees created under the relevant external aid instruments.

118 In 2007, exceptional assistance measures related to SSR were adopted by the European Commission notably for Afghanistan, Chad, the Democratic Republic of Congo, Guinea Bissau, Lebanon and Somalia.

119 Financial Regulation applicable to the general budget of the European Communities, Council Regulation (EC, Euratom) No 1605/2002 of 25 June 2002 (OJ L 248, 16.9.2002), revised by Council Regulation No 1995/2006 of 13 December 2006 (OJ L 390, 30.12.2006). The details of the rules for external aid are laid down in the Practical Guide to contracting procedures for EC external actions, which is available at the following website: http://ec.europa.eu/comm/europeaid/tender/gestion/index_en.htm.

120 Budget support is the transfer of financial resources of an external financing agency to the National Treasury of a partner country, following the respect by the latter of agreed conditions for payment. The financial resources thus received are part of the global resources of the partner country, and consequently used in accordance with the public financial management system of the partner country. While general budget support represents a transfer to the National Treasury in support of a national development or reform policy and strategy, sector budget support represents a transfer to the national treasury in support of a sector programme policy and strategy.

121 General budget support may nevertheless have an effect on SSR through the strengthening of control of the national budgetary authority on state expenditure or through establishing SSR as one of the conditions for disbursement.

122 One difficulty stems from security not being a specific 'sector' but rather a 'system' involving a series of actors (and thus ministries) in the beneficiary country. This makes it difficult to channel sector budget support to one single ministry, as occurs in the traditional areas for sector budget support, such as health or education. However, this method is currently under consideration for SSR activities in certain ACP countries under the 10th EDF.

123 So far twinning programmes have been linked to the harmonisation or approximation with the *acquis communautaire* and mainly covered the secondment of an expert for 18-36 months, and thus did not allow covering broad reform activities without additional contracts.

124 For instance in the Conclusions of the European Council of 4 and 5 November 2004 which adopted the 'The Hague Programme on strengthening freedom, security and justice in the European Union'. All European Council Conclusions are available on the website of the Council: www.consilium.europa.eu

125 See http://www.eutraininggroup.net.

4. The Difficulties of a Donor: EU Financial Instruments, SSR and Effective International Assistance

Catriona Gourlay

Executive Summary

This chapter begins by tracing the conceptual history of security sector reform (SSR), noting that the EU now embraces a holistic approach to SSR, which encompasses the core security actors including law enforcement institutions, security management and oversight bodies, justice institutions, and non-statutory forces. As the scope of the SSR concept has increased, so too has the number and range of activities that comprise SSR assistance and the actors that implement it. Donor assistance was traditionally bilateral, but is increasingly channelled through international organisations (IOs). In most cases it is implemented directly by states or IOs, but they are increasingly using non-governmental organisations (NGOs) and private companies as implementing partners.

One consequence of the broad SSR remit is that SSR does not typically have a single institutional home within donor countries or international organisations, nor a consolidated means of budgetary support. Rather, international assistance for SSR is scattered across different institutions and departments, delivered in the context of various policy frameworks and subject to different funding mechanisms. These depend on the nature of the activity and the recipient (military or civilian), the time-scale of assistance (emergency or long-term) and the political context (post-conflict, transition or developmental).

The fragmentation of SSR assistance presents a number of challenges for donors. Evidence suggests that the effectiveness and sustainability of SSR interventions has been undermined by a lack of long term, predictable donor funding, and multiple financing channels, often leading to incoherent and poorly coordinated support. This has led to relative gaps in assistance, notably in the governance dimension of SSR, as well as a mismatch between short-term security and long-term development assistance. In this context, donor coordination, both within and between organisations, is particularly challenging whilst at the same time fundamental to the effectiveness of SSR interventions.

The donor coordination challenge has been addressed at a number of different levels. At the national level this has included, in a few cases, the development of whole-of-government approaches and common funding pools. International initiatives in relation to post-conflict SSR include the increased use of Multi-Donor Trust Funds as well as the establishment of the UN Peacebuilding Commission and Peacebuilding Fund. International organisations, notably the UN and the EU are also currently engaged in efforts to improve the internal coordination of their assistance. Nevertheless, the coordination challenge remains formidable and it is unclear whether effective international assistance ultimately requires the designation of lead agencies and hierarchical management and/or the development of common and comprehensive assessment frameworks and a development approach.

The main body of this chapter explores these generic challenges in relation to the EU, detailing the diverse funding instruments that can be used to support dimensions of SSR, while demonstrating that SSR assistance is not central to any of them. Funding sources for SSR can be divided into those that relate to crisis management and post-conflict situations, and those that are designed to support long-term activities in developing or transition contexts. In the case of short-term 'crisis management' assistance, SSR assistance has been delivered either through the dozen civilian inter-governmental missions of the EU, drawing on the Common Foreign and Security Policy line of the EU budget, or through short-term rapid funding mechanisms, notably the Rapid Reaction Mechanism, managed by the Commission.

The majority of the 70 countries that have received European Community (EC) funding for SSR assistance are politically stable developing countries or countries in transition. In these cases, SSR assistance has typically focused on long-term capacity building of the police and judicial sectors and support for strengthening democratic oversight. While some funding to support the democratic control of the security sector has been provided through the thematic budget line of the European Initiative for Democracy and Human Rights, the vast majority of support has been channelled through the geographical instruments of the EU budget as well as the European Development Fund (EDF). The EDF is separately funded by member states and is the main instrument of Community aid for development cooperation in the African Caribbean and Pacific (ACP) region. It has the additional advantage of being a more flexible source of development funding, able to support security activities on the basis of partnership agreements or requests.

In 2006 the principal financial mechanisms to deliver EC assistance (with the exception of the EDF) were rationalized in order to streamline funding during the current budgetary period of 2007-2013. This chapter details how past financial instruments have been merged into a handful of larger instruments and the potential impact of these changes on SSR funding. Of the new instruments, the Instrument for Stability is the only one that explicitly provides for SSR assistance and is designed to provide short-term assistance in politically unstable or post-conflict contexts. The three new geographic instruments also have the potential to support SSR activities, although to what extent this will be realized will depend on policy and programming priorities.

In the past two years, the profile of the SSR agenda has risen within the EU and a number of attempts have been made to promote a more coordinated approach to SSR assistance. In 2006 an SSR framework was agreed, conceptually linking the Commission and Council approaches. This was followed by the first attempt to join-up Council and Commission planning processes in relation to future SSR assistance in the Democratic Republic of Congo. Nevertheless, in crisis or post-crisis contexts where both inter-governmental and Community instruments are relevant, Commission and Council relations are still plagued by inter-institutional turf wars. These were exacerbated in 2005 and 2006 by the Commission taking the Council to court over the dividing line between security and development policy. The fall-out from this case included efforts by the Council and some member states to curtail the ability of the Commission to use the new financial instruments to fund security assistance. Thus, the effectiveness of EU SSR assistance demands on-going efforts to improve cross-pillar cooperation where both Council and Commission instruments are activated as well as efforts to improve the implementation of EC SSR assistance where the Commission is the only EU actor, as in the majority of development, transition and peacebuilding contexts.

Background: Implications of a Broader Approach to SSR

The European Commission's 2006 Concept for Support for Security Sector Reform (SSR) notes that SSR 'has been an integral part of EU integration, enlargement and external assistance for many years'.[1] Similarly, most of the civilian operations that the EU has launched since 2003 in the context of its inter-governmental crisis management capacities, have been designed to support the reform and strengthening of police and justice sectors. However, Commission-funded activities are not organised into SSR programmes as such and few project objectives make specific mention of SSR. Similarly, in only one of the twelve civilian operations managed by the Council – 'EUSEC DR Congo', which aims to provide advice and assistance contributing to the successful integration of the Congolese army – is SSR mentioned explicitly in the mission mandate.

There is no contradiction in the EU's claim to have been long engaged in SSR with only recent formal mention of it. Rather, the relative invisibility of SSR within the EU context can be explained by the expansion of the conceptual definition of SSR over the past five years. Originally, the concept was limited to the military and was primarily used in connection with downsizing in post-Cold War Warsaw Pact countries. Even when applied to post-conflict settings as in the Balkans, this was the common definition and approach. For example, in 2001, the EU-initiated Stability Pact working group on Security and Defence issues defined SSR as 'right-sizing, re-orientation, reform, and capacity-building of national defence forces'.[2] As development actors took a more active interest in the subject, the definition expanded to include police and the intelligence services, and then, largely driven by the development of guidelines within the OECD DAC framework in 2004, the definition expanded beyond the military and state. The Council and Commission Concepts for SSR, agreed in 2005 and 2006 respectively[3], use this broad definition which includes: the core security actors including law enforcement institutions, security management and oversight bodies, justice institutions, and non-statutory forces.[4]

The expanding definition of SSR is linked to the shift in emphasis from state security to human security, and the recognition that weak security sector governance often constitutes a threat to the population. The

Commission Concept for SSR, the EU Development Policy statement[5] and the EU Africa strategy[6] all propose greater support for SSR as a way of promoting human security and development. More specifically, the Commission Concept argues that support for SSR can help address the challenges of 'oversized and underpaid regular forces, irregular forces and security firms operating outside the law, lack of judicial independence, status and resources, lack of capacity, legal competence and sometimes political will by parliament to ensure accountability of security services, human rights abuses by police and defence forces, a culture of state impunity and the inability to protect the population against terrorist acts'.[7]

A key feature of the expanded definition of SSR is its emphasis on political and governance aspects in addition to the technical and capacity requirements of enhancing the delivery of justice and security. Advocates of this holistic approach point to the utility of combining capacity building and governance aspects in terms of efficacy and sustainability.[8] Yet the broadening of the SSR agenda has been criticized by some for 'making any serious SSR programme impossibly large and complex' and for 'turning SSR questions themselves into more general questions of governance'.[9] Similar concerns over the practicality of a comprehensive SSR concept, are, for example, evident in on-going efforts within the UN to agree a common definition or conceptual framework for SSR. There is a growing appreciation of the importance of SSR to post-conflict peacebuilding. This is reflected in statements of the Security Council, in the 2006 Inventory of UN peacebuilding capacity[10] and in the mandate of the newly established Peacebuilding Commission, which is due to address country-specific SSR strategies. Yet the UN's definition of and role in SSR remains contested in on-going interagency efforts to define SSR policy. Whereas some UN entities such as UNDP have explicitly embraced a holistic approach[11], others, notably DPKO[12], question the operational utility of an expanded conceptual framework for SSR. Rather they favour a narrower SSR concept, focused on post-conflict reform of the defence, police and corrections sectors.

Where, as in the EU, the 'holistic ethos'[13] that underpins the expanded SSR concept is accepted, SSR necessarily encompasses a number of technical and political objectives. For instance, the OECD DAC working group tasked with developing an implementation framework for SSR, has found that SSR activities are most effective when they address three parallel objectives: i) the improvement of basic security and justice delivery, ii) the establishment of an effective governance and oversight system and iii) the development and local leadership of a reform process.[14] It follows that a wide range of activities can support SSR objectives. These include activities typically undertaken by civilian development agencies or NGOs in the area of governance and democracy promotion. Examples of such activities include: technical cooperation provided to parliaments, government ministries, law enforcement agencies and the judiciary to assist, review and reform the security system; technical cooperation provided to governments to improve civilian oversight and democratic control of budgeting, management, accountability and auditing of security expenditure, including military budgets; and assistance to civil society to enhance its competence and capacity to scrutinize the security system. These are in addition to efforts typically undertaken by military actors to assist the development of capacity within the military sector and support military transformation, including demobilization. Examples of assistance that could be undertaken by the military in the context of European Security and Defence Policy (ESDP)[15] include, but are not limited to, activities to: define defence policies, organise defence structures, define military planning procedures, train armed forces, reorganise armed forces, and advise national and local authorities on military governance, procurement and defence policy.

As the scope of the SSR concept has increased, so too has the number and range of actors that can be said to be implementing SSR assistance. The principal actors in the provision of external assistance for SSR include member states as well as a host of intergovernmental organisations including the UN, EU, Organisation for Security and Cooperation in Europe (OSCE), North Atlantic Treaty Organisation (NATO), Council of Europe, African Union, Economic Community of West African States (ECOWAS) and Organisation of American States (OAS).[16] In addition, an increasing number of non-governmental organisations (NGOs) are active in this field both in terms of policy development and as implementing partners.

In most national and international organisations, including the EU, assistance is scattered across different institutions or departments, delivered in the context of various policy frameworks and subject to different funding mechanisms, depending on the nature of the activity and the recipient (military or civilian), the time-scale of assistance (emergency, short-term or long-term) and the geographical region or political context (post-conflict, transition or developmental). Consequently, international assistance for SSR, as currently defined by the OECD DAC and the EU, is typically fragmented both between and within organisations. The next section highlights some of the common challenges that this presents for the mobilization of adequate funding and the development of strategic and comprehensive approaches to SSR. Section two examines EU assistance to SSR in light of these challenges, with a view to highlighting how EU financial instruments and structures shape the EU's provision of SSR assistance.

Challenges for the Donor Community

The breadth and complexity of the issues addressed in SSR combined with the large number and diversity of actors engaged in SSR activities mean that donor coordination and coherence is a persistent challenge, both between and within organisations. This is often compounded by the cultural and doctrinal differences in approach between development and security actors, notably in their strategic and policy approach to the objective of local ownership, and the fact that the convergence of security and development agendas remains elusive in practice. While overlapping and sometimes contradictory agendas can be problematic in areas of high strategic interest and post-conflict settings, more commonly limitations in organisational mandates and financial regulations lead to gaps in engagement and organisational expertise. Indeed, lack of institutional capacity is often cited as a critical obstacle to more effective engagement in SSR by both security and development sectors.[17] It is beyond the scope of this chapter to review the full extent of the challenges that the donor community is currently addressing in connection with SSR.[18] Rather, this section looks specifically at the common challenges donors face in the mobilization and coordination of resources.

Resource Mobilisation

As indicated above, funding for SSR is disbursed across a broad range of organisations, departments and programmatic activities, making attempts to aggregate financial commitments to SSR difficult. Conversely, even within departments or institutions it is often impossible to disaggregate figures in line with SSR activities. This is, for example, the case within UN (DPKO) mission budgets, where budgets do not differentiate between civilian and military activities.[19] Furthermore, similar activities are often labelled differently, depending on which programme or institution they are supported by. Thus, as the OECD has discovered in its attempts to produce guidelines for SSR assistance, definitional issues militate against gaining an accurate understanding of financial commitments to SSR.[20] This is also true of the Commission where funding commitments are organised by region or theme and tracking commitments by sector or activity is notoriously difficult. This is illustrated by the internal mapping exercise undertaken by the Commission in preparation for the development of the Commission SSR Concept. Although the exercise sought to capture SSR related activities supported by the Commission in the period 2003-2005, the final report did not claim to be comprehensive[21] and delivered little quantitative data on Commission financial commitments to SSR activities over and above selected illustrative examples of projects funded.

Despite the difficulty of quantifying international SSR assistance, it is widely recognized that there are gaps in SSR funding, or at least dimensions of SSR that receive relatively less support. One such area relates to security governance, and the support of activities designed to promote the accountability of the security sector.[22] Security sector governance has not traditionally been a focus of bi-lateral assistance provided though defence and foreign affairs ministries, and only recently has it been recognized as a legitimate activity for development actors. This is reflected in the 2005 decision that an increased range of security related support is eligible to be reported as Official Development Assistance (ODA). ODA eligibility criteria are governed by the OECD DAC and define what constitutes appropriate uses of development assistance for the promotion of economic development and welfare of developing countries. Following discussions in the OECD DAC in 2004 and 2005, it was agreed that current criteria should include a wider range of security related activities.[23] These encompass all civilian aspects of SSR, as well as activities in relation to the civilian control of the military, including financial and administrative management of defence issues.[24]

It is possible that past restrictions on reporting security governance assistance as ODA may have constrained the use of donor development assistance for SSR. Certainly they had a normative impact, implying that SSR assistance was not a core development business. However, it is unclear whether restrictive ODA criteria were an obstacle to development donor funding of SSR. The fact remains that even where activities are ODA eligible, there is often poor commitment on the part of development donors to support activities specifically related to the security sector. Only between 1 and 2 percent of ODA is currently spent on activities related to security. This is exacerbated by pressure from many development NGOs who fear that increased support for SSR will lead to aid being tied to a narrow security agenda. Consequently, despite revised ODA eligibility criteria and SSR doctrinal and policy advances, the engagement of international donors in the support of security governance activities remains limited.

In general, donors still tend to concentrate on the efficiency of security actors as opposed to their governance and accountability, particularly in post-conflict contexts. This is not to say that development funding is used to support capacity of the defence and security sector. Even the revised ODA eligibility criteria still prohibit development funds from being used for direct support for military expenditures or the training of military personnel. Rather, such support is typically bilateral and managed by national defence or foreign policy departments. Similarly, the EU's potential role in supporting military planning, management and governance though training and advising, as identified in the 2005 ESDP Concept, would be funded by participating member states directly and through the CFSP budget line – subject to consensual inter-governmental decision-making (see below). Likewise, assistance for capacity building of the security sector is not usually implemented by development actors. Rather, it is normally undertaken either directly by military and police from donor states or, as is increasingly the case, by private service providers.[25]

The reform of the military has traditionally been seen as a prerogative of nations, addressed through bilateral assistance. This goes some way to explaining why the role of international organisations in defence reform has been constrained. The NATO Alliance is a notable exception, whereby defence reform has routinely formed part of the membership action plans developed for aspirant NATO members, as well as the action plans that pertain to its 20 partner countries.

The UN has relatively little experience or in-house capacity in defence reform.[26] While mandates for UN peacekeeping operations now often include provisions for disarmament and demobilization funded by member state assessed contributions to the UN peacekeeping budget, they rarely extend to support for broader issues of defence management, governance and reform.[27] The UN also lacks the standing capacity to offer advice and support for defence governance and the development of core operational military functions.[28] Similarly, while the EU has been deeply engaged in the provision of assistance for defence conversion and restructuring in transition states, especially in the context of EU enlargement, its ambitions in post-conflict countries have traditionally been more limited. The 'EU SEC DR Congo' mission is the only ESDP operation that specifically addresses defence reform – providing advice on the reform and integration of the Congolese army, although a follow-on integrated ESDP mission, designed specifically to support the defence and justice elements of a comprehensive SSR package for the DRC is currently being considered. Likewise, non-ODA eligible assistance on defence reform has only been provided by the EC in very few cases – notably also in support of army integration in the DRC.[29] Nor do other international organisations typically engage in defence reform. This is true of the OSCE, Council of Europe, AU, ECOWAS and World Bank and reflects the traditional reluctance by member states to cede authority to international organisations to engage directly in matters relating to the organisation and governance of state security.

The fact that member states have not found it suitable to channel funding for post-conflict defence reform beyond disarmament and demobilisation through international organisations, has resulted in a cleavage in the funding and provision of SSR assistance. Activities to improve defence reform and capacity are typically funded bilaterally and managed and implemented by security actors, whereas activities to promote security governance are typically (under)funded, from development budgets and by development actors, including international organisations and are typically implemented in politically stable countries and countries in transition. Not only does this cleavage exist between organisations, explaining the relative lack of competence in defence capacity building and reform in most international organisations, but within organisations – both at national and international level.

The impact of this fragmentation is exacerbated by the fact that security and development assistance follows different time-frames with distinct objectives and funding channels. For example, in the UN many short-term SSR activities have been funded from UN assessed contributions in the framework of peacekeeping operations, including disarmament and demobilisation activities[30] and initial quick impact projects in the justice sector.[31] However, longer-term activities necessary for effective reform led by UN agencies are reliant on the less forthcoming voluntary donor contributions. These programmes often collapse after the short-term emergency funding either from the Consolidated Appeals Process (CAP) or assessed contributions to peace operations is spent. There is no venue within the UN for medium to long-term security-relevant development assistance tailored to post-conflict countries. Indeed, the acknowledgment of this funding gap was one of the principal drivers for the establishment of the Peacebuilding Commission and Peacebuilding Fund.

There is evidence to suggest that the widespread mismatch between short and long-term funding reduces the efficiency of SSR interventions. For example, a 2006 lessons-learned study on SSR in UN peace operations found that the predominantly short-term approach serves as an impediment to effective implementation, since planning for 'quick wins' may set up weak political, legal and structural foundations for development initiatives in the security sector.[32] Similarly, it is widely recognized, including in the European Security Strategy and EC SSR Concept that an outstanding challenge for EU assistance is to link short term funding for SSR including through Common Foreign and Security Policy (CFSP) or emergency funding budgets, with long-term funding from geographic development budget lines.

Thus the effectiveness and sustainability of SSR interventions more broadly has been undermined by a lack of long-term, predictable donor funding, and multiple financing channels, often leading to incoherent and poorly coordinated support. This has led to relative gaps in assistance, notably in the governance dimension of SSR, as well as a mismatch between short-term security and long-term development assistance. In this context donor coordination, both within and between organisations, becomes particularly challenging whilst at the same time fundamental to the effectiveness of SSR interventions. The following section elaborates on the nature of this coordination challenge and identifies how donors are attempting to address it with respect to SSR.

Donor Coordination

There is broad consensus that donor coordination should deliver a number of efficiency benefits. Coordination should reduce duplication of effort and the likelihood of critical 'gaps' in donor information and assistance. Given that SSR is political, with political benefits and costs for the recipients of assistance, donor unity *vis-à-vis* partners is also critical to donor efficacy in negotiating assistance and reform. Similarly, it is widely acknowledged that the overall SSR assistance should be strategic, requiring the identification of priority objectives and coherent approaches to achieving them. As Neclâ Tschirgi writes: 'While peacebuilding is a multi-faceted process requiring holistic approaches, it needs to be guided by a hierarchy of priorities established in response to the specific needs and political dynamics in a given context. Establishing such a hierarchy requires an overall political strategy'.[33]

While the benefits of coordination are uncontroversial, how this should best be achieved, and the extent to which coordination requires hierarchical 'management' is less clear. The principal international forum within which donors have addressed these coordination challenges has been the OECD DAC. Discussions within its Network on Conflict Peace and Development Cooperation (CPCD) have aimed to foster a shared understanding and a more coordinated approach to SSR among different actors. This has resulted in key policy statements such as the 2005 OECD DAC Guidelines on Security System Reform and Governance as well as follow up efforts to devise a common implementation framework on SSR.[34]

One of the findings of the CPCD working group was that 'the coordination of technical and financial assistance benefits from the leadership of a bilateral or multilateral agency or donor that is recognized as credible by donors and aid recipients'. Such leadership is also particularly useful for the conduct of negotiations with partners, enabling donors to speak with one voice. However, the OECD DAC also argues that such leadership should not involve 'substantial control of the various elements present'. Rather, coordination is seen as benefiting from a diversity of approaches and should not inhibit rapid responses and innovation by individual donors.[35]

While leadership may benefit cooperation, it is not necessarily a pre-requisite for it. Rather the OECD DAC findings indicate that the use of common and comprehensive assessment frameworks and the sharing of the main facets of a development approach are fundamental for improved donor coordination. Thus, the OECD's efforts to agree an implementation framework on SSR are premised on the fact that donor coordination requires a common conceptual framework, guiding principles, a shared commitment to a developmental approach and to processes for developing common strategies.

The finding that effective coordination requires more than better information-sharing between the various actors engaged in SSR is not new. There are a number of case studies that demonstrate that poor coordination in SSR resulted from fundamentally different conceptions of how to approach post-conflict state-building and reform rather than an absence of formal mechanisms for coordination. For example, Bruce Jones, Elizabeth Cousens and Susan Woodward have all observed that the lack of coordination in Bosnia stemmed from differing policy goals by the major powers and international agencies.[36] This is despite the fact that the coordination mechanisms between the principal international agencies were relatively well established and clear. The political nature and cross-government interest in security issues makes coordination of SSR all the more difficult, as does the fact that many actors engaged in SSR do not necessarily share long term development approaches. If, as the OECD DAC argues, propitious conditions for donor cooperation include common analysis frameworks, a development approach, and, ideally a designated lead agency, it follows that the goal of efficient donor coordination will remain an elusive one where these conditions are not met. Since the majority of post-conflict capacity building and defence reform assistance is still provided bilaterally in accordance with national security policies, it remains the exception rather than the rule that such assistance follows a development approach, informed by common analytical frameworks, and led by a commonly identified international agency.

Hence, further efforts are required to generate internal cross-government or cross-agency and external cross-donor common approaches to providing SSR assistance. This challenge is necessarily addressed on a number of levels. Where governments or organisations have launched initiatives to do so, these have typically included: efforts to improve information exchange and policy practice, including through institutional innovations (including the UN Peacebuilding Commission) or restructuring, as well as complementary actions to mobilize resources, including through the pooling of funds or increasing the flexibility of funding rules.

'Whole-of-government' or 'joined-up' approaches to SSR have been pioneered by a few donor countries. In the UK, attempts to forge a common security and development agenda involved institutional change including the cross-departmental initiative by the Ministry of Defence (MoD), the Foreign and Commonwealth Office (FCO) and the Department for International Development (DFID) to create a Defence Advisory Team (DAT) – later renamed the Security Sector Development Advisory Team (SSDAT). This was linked to efforts to consolidate funds for activities from across government departments, which led to the establishment of the African Conflict Prevention Pool (ACPP) and the Global Conflict Prevention Pool (GCPP) in 2001. Similarly, other countries have created special funds for providing assistance for transitional or post-conflict contexts that are distinguished from long-term development assistance and short-term humanitarian aid. Examples include the 'Stability Fund' in the Netherlands, the Office of Transition Initiative in USAID and the Peacebuilding Fund and the Peacebuilding Programme in the Canadian Department of Foreign Affairs and Canadian CIDA respectively.

Whereas relatively few countries have engaged in extensive internal reforms to improve the coherence of their post-conflict assistance, an ever growing number have chosen to pool their assistance in Multi Donor Trust Funds (MDTFs) administered by the World Bank: for example in Afghanistan, West Bank and Gaza, Timor Leste, Bosnia, Cambodia, Kosovo, Iraq and Sudan. These funds are used to address immediate post-conflict reconstruction priorities as well as long-term institutional development.

Separate MDTFs have been established specifically for demining or disarmament and demobilisation activities including in Sierra Leone and the Greater Great Lakes. The argument for MDTFs is that a well-designed umbrella funding arrangement can promote aid coordination and effectiveness. However, they tend not to be used to finance police or prisons, and often political issues prevent the World Bank from disbursing funds for 12 to 18 months.[37] The World Bank also acknowledges that MDTFs are neither necessary nor sufficient for ensuring aid effectiveness. Separate donor funding can be equally effective if it is coordinated and programmed to support an agreed coherent programme with realistic budget. 'Conversely, a single umbrella MDTF will accomplish little for aid effectiveness if its design is faulty'.[38] The restrictions on what MDTFs can fund and the fact that political issues prevent MDTF funds from being disbursed in the short-term, mean that the increased use of MDTFs has not led to increased engagement in the early phases of post-conflict security sector reform. Nor can MDTFs alone promise to resolve the challenge of donor coordination, since this requires international agreement on a coherent programme.

The internal coordination challenge is perhaps felt less keenly in international organisations that specialise in specific dimensions of SSR. For example, NATO has approached SSR from a security perspective, while the Council of Europe has focused on democratic governance. This is not the case for the UN and EU, both of which engage in most if not all aspects of SSR, with potentially global reach. The breadth of their engagement places a premium on internal coherence and coordination. This has been recognised in principle, but both organisations are still exploring how internal procedures might be adapted in order to deliver a more comprehensive and joined-up approach in practice.

Within the UN, DPKO and UNDP have described their activities as addressing 'dimensions' of SSR and acknowledge that the UN's approach to SSR has been piecemeal.[39] This is currently being addressed on various levels and in different consultation forums and processes. For example, the UN's conceptual framework for SSR will be reviewed in the Security Council in 2007, DPKO and UNDP are reviewing their conduct of SSR within integrated peace operations[40], an inter-agency process to establish integrated standards on SSR has been launched, and the Secretary-General's Policy Committee is addressing issues of inter-agency coordination. These measures are intended to be complemented by the 2006 institutional innovation of the Peacebuilding Commission and the standing Peacebuilding Fund. The Peacebuilding Commission and Fund are intended to promote coordination amongst the international community and help deliver predictable financing in post-conflict recovery, including in the area of SSR. SSR is already being addressed in the two first country cases that the Peacebuilding Commission is focussing on, with UNDP's piloting in 2007-8 of the OECD DAC implementation framework guidelines in Burundi and Sierra Leone. Taken together, these initiatives constitute the UN's first thorough assessment of its past and potential role in SSR. Yet it is still unclear whether these deliberations will yield more resources and a more comprehensive approach to SSR within the UN family. Similarly, although the Peacebuilding Commission and Peacebuilding Fund clearly have the potential to bring all the relevant stakeholders together to formulate and mobilise resources for country-specific SSR strategies, it is too early to tell whether this potential will be realised.

The EU is the other international actor with potential to engage in the full spectrum of SSR activities. The following section briefly outlines how EU SSR assistance has been funded and managed to date, and to what extent new policies and financial instruments might address the key issues of resource mobilization and donor coordination.

EU SSR Assistance[41]

Similarly to other organisations, SSR does not have a single institutional home in the EU context, nor a consolidated means of budgetary support. Despite concerted attempts by the Commission and Council to agree a conceptual framework on SSR, there is no single SSR concept. Rather two concepts were agreed – one in 2005 that pertains to the support of SSR activities through the 'second pillar' intergovernmental context of European Security and Defence Policy (ESDP) and one in 2006 that relates to Community assistance for SSR delivered through the first pillar. Nevertheless, the two concepts were later formally linked by the European Council in December 2006. The Council decision states that taken together the two concepts constitute a policy framework for EU engagement in SSR and outlines common principles to guide SSR assistance.[42]

SSR-relevant assistance is also provided to partner countries through the third pillar of the EU's institutional architecture – the policy area encompassing justice, liberty and security (JLS). This policy area is principally managed by the Council of the European Union, although a number of issues outside the core areas of criminal justice and police are being 'communitarized' and will therefore be managed by the Commission in the framework of the first-pillar in the future. These include some of the external dimensions of JLS policies that are most relevant to EU SSR assistance. Current policy priorities in this area include the security threats of terrorism and organised crime and the challenge of managing migration flows. Practical examples of assistance to third countries in line with these policy objectives typically include broad measures to build security and justice sector capacity, as well as targeted activities to build capacity in border management and provide assistance in the fight against corruption, organised crime, terrorism and money laundering.[43] Thus, a key factor in how the EU chooses to support SSR relates to the institutional context of that support. Funding approved through the ESDP framework, is, for example, the sole source of assistance for military or intelligence reform and is particularly relevant for supporting the early stages of SSR in a crisis or post-crisis situation. This differs from the majority of civilian SSR activities that are delivered through medium to long-term Community funding instruments that have been developed to support a range of first pillar policy frameworks and objectives managed by the Commission. Consequently the nature of Community support to SSR depends very much on the geographical and policy context of a country.

Community funding instruments have been tailored to countries in conflict or in post-conflict situations, countries in the process of acceding to the EU and subject to the EU Enlargement policy, countries near to the EU and subject to the European Neighbourhood Policy, as well as developing countries. Regional distinctions are important for developing countries too, with different funding instruments and rules for supporting the African, Caribbean and Pacific (ACP) countries from the European Development Fund to those for funding developing countries from EU geographic development budget lines. In addition, governance aspects of SSR can also be funded through thematic budget lines, for example those supporting democratisation and the promotion of human rights. Thus, Community funding for SSR is disbursed across a number of geographically and thematically specific budget lines, each with different funding procedures and constraints. Financial instruments have been designed according to geographical region or country-specific political context. Within crisis or post-conflict contexts they are further differentiated depending on whether assistance is channelled though Community instruments or the intergovernmental actions of the Council.

This section outlines how some of the crisis management, development and democratisation financial instruments have supported SSR assistance in the past and briefly discusses the implications of the rationalisation of the financial instruments for the budget period 2007-2013 for future SSR support.

Short-Term EU Crisis Management Financing

Council Missions Supported by the CFSP Budget

According to Article 28 of the Treaty on European Union (TEU), administrative and non-military operational expenditure for Common Foreign and Security Policy (CFSP) can be charged to the budget of the European Union under a separate heading for CFSP[44], henceforth referred to as the 'CFSP budget'. It covers the operational costs of CFSP Joint Actions, including ESDP civilian operations with relevance to SSR. These tend to be short-to-medium term operations of one to three years. Since the ESDP became operational in 2003, twelve civilian and four military operations have been launched. The early EU civilian missions were designed to strengthen policing capacities through monitoring, mentoring and advising host-country police in the Balkans, but the geographical and substantive scope of ESDP activities has increased to include missions to strengthen the rule of law more broadly (Georgia and Iraq), monitor borders and demobilisation (Palestinian Territories and Aceh, Indonesia) and, in the case of the defence reform mission in Congo (EU SEC DR Congo), to assist with the transformation of the defence sector. These missions are managed in the Council with the Presidency responsible for the overall achievement of the objectives of ESDP actions. They are directed by the Political and Security Committee (PSC), which is in turn supported by the Committee for Civilian Aspects of Crisis Management (CIVCOM) and the Council Secretariat (DG E IX), which conducts strategic and operational planning as well as elements of mission support.

The most significant limitation of this funding instrument has been its meagre size. In 2005 the CFSP budget exceeded €60 million for the first time. This represents just over 1% of the budget for external relations allocated under the first pillar. However, the CFSP budget has been significantly increased since then, to €102.6 million in 2006 and €159.2 million in 2007. The CFSP budget allocation for the 2007-2013 period is €1980 million, indicating that the annual budgetary allocation is set to double. Nevertheless, funding increases have consistently fallen short of demand. This is true for the early missions whereby the launch of the EU Police Mission in Bosnia and Herzegovina (EUPM), for example, required that the Union 'scratch around for leftovers from different budgetary chapters, and even devise bureaucratic stratagems to put together a mere €14 million…'.[45] But it also remains true today; it is anticipated that the EU's Police Mission to Kosovo alone will absorb the majority of the budget in 2007.

Over and above the budgetary constraints, the process of funding CFSP Joint Actions from this budget is cumbersome. The decision-making framework for CFSP is inter-governmental (second pillar), with political control exercised by the Political and Security Committee (PSC) in the Council. The release of CFSP funds requires a legislative act – a 'Joint Action'. However, administrative responsibility for the execution of the CFSP budget rests with the Commission, in accordance with Art. 274 TEC. The Joint Action by the Council, therefore needs to be followed by subsequent administrative action by the Commission, conducted within the External Relations Directorate General (DG Relex), which is then subject to various procedures by the Court of Auditors[46], the European Court of Justice and the European Parliament. In practice, therefore, member states often explore the possibility of finding a legal basis for funding action under the Community budget before any decision is taken to use CFSP budget funds. Similarly, member states have often resorted to using first pillar allocation lines when access to the CFSP budget had proved too lengthy or difficult.[47] This helps explain why many actions that were originally funded from the CFSP budget have been transferred to the external relations subsection of the Community budget. This was the case with many human rights actions, now funded through the thematic budget line of the European Initiative for Democracy and Human Rights (EIDHR) or the Rapid Reaction Mechanism (RRM). It is also true for mine clearance.

In short, while the CFSP budget is the principal source of funding intergovernmental missions designed to build capacity in police or the rule of law as well as defence reform, the pressure on this limited budget line, exacerbated by the rapid increase in ESDP crisis management operations, means that this funding instrument is most likely to be used in a limited number of cases. It will be drawn upon for actions in which member states identify a clear added value in mobilising their domestic police and rule of law experts for capacity building and reform operations, usually in post-conflict situations, and will enable new areas of support, such as reform of the defence and intelligence sectors, that cannot easily be supported by Community instruments given development policy and ODA eligibility constraints.

Community Instruments to Promote Political Stability

The **Rapid Reaction Mechanism (RRM)** was a Community funding mechanism, established in 2001 to allow the Commission to rapidly disburse funds with the explicit purpose of promoting political stability. Its annual budget of approximately €30 million was used to finance non-combat, civilian activities aimed at countering or resolving emerging crisis and serious threats or outbreaks of conflict. Illustrative examples of SSR-relevant funding through this instrument since 2003 include: support for the transitional government of Afghanistan, including the National Security Council; funding to restore the legal system in Bunia and support the establishment of an Integrated Police Unit in Kinshasa, DRC[48]; support for a rule of law package of activities including support for prisons, the ministry of justice, ministry of conflict resolution and parliament in Georgia; and support for policing and border management in Central Asia, Moldova and Ukraine. RRM funding decisions were managed by four staff within the Conflict Prevention and Crisis Management Unit in Directorate A (CFSP) of the Commission's Directorate General on External Relations (DG Relex).

The advantage of the instrument, unlike other EC funding instruments subject to 'comitology' – the elaborate process whereby EC funding decisions are approved by specialist committees comprised of member state representatives – was that it was a flexible funding instrument that could deliver rapid funding in crisis situations to serve broadly political objectives. One disadvantage was that the RRM could only be used to fund actions for up to six months, after which follow-on funding was required from longer-term thematic or geographic funding instruments or other donors. This timeline was often too short in practice. Even where the EC Country Delegations and desk officers were committed to a project from its inception, the rigidity of EC programming procedures, involving lengthy decision-making procedures with comitology, meant that it often took over eight months for follow-on funding to be secured, leaving a funding gap. This is just one example of the gap between funding through short-term instruments and long-term funding. Similar gaps also exist in relation to other budget lines. One of the first formal recognitions of the disjointed nature of EC crisis response was the Commission Communication on Linking Relief, Rehabilitation and Development[49], which also emphasised the need to ensure more effective bridging between operations financed from different Community financing instruments in the context of a crisis. Consequently, one of the ambitions of the rationalisation of EU financial instruments for the 2007-2013 budgetary period was to improve the linkage between short-term crisis response instruments and longer-term follow-on funding.

The rationalisation of the external relations budget lines (in Heading 4 of the EU budget) has been part of an on-going process of simplification of EU aid management.[50] The past system was based on a series of aid instruments or budget lines[51], with their respective legal bases adopted through a co-decision process between the Parliament and the Council. Since January 2007, this has been abandoned in favour of a more flexible system based on a few large instruments. Four of the new financial instruments are geographic: the pre-Accession instrument (IPA)[52], the European Neighbourhood and Partnership Instrument (ENPI)[53], an Instrument for Development Cooperation (DCI)[54], and an instrument for cooperation with industrialised and other high-income countries and territories (ICI)[55]. The other five are thematic: the Instrument for Stability (IfS), the Humanitarian Aid instrument, the Civil Protection Financial Instrument[56], the Macro-financial assistance instrument and the instrument for the promotion of democracy and human rights (EIDHR)[57].

The new instruments were designed to better align policies with funding instruments. Their development was not therefore a legal consolidation or mainstreaming exercise and hence there is no neat correlation between past instruments and new ones. Nevertheless, in most cases there is continuity with funding programmes launched in the past. In some cases, such as in the case of macro-financial assistance or humanitarian assistance, there is little change, while in other cases, notably the Instrument for Stability (IfS), the instrument is new and aims to provide a single source of funding for a range of security-related activities that were previously conducted under various budgetary headings. However, some past instruments have been split. For example, aspects of the old Nuclear Safety instrument that pertain to issues of proliferation are now included in the Stability Instrument, while other aspects of nuclear safety assistance are now funded through a new Nuclear Safety instrument.

Table 4: *SSR-relevant European Community thematic financial instruments – past and present**

*New financial instrument (2007-2013)	Budget and principal changes	Past instrument (- 2006)	Budget and possible actions
Instrument for Stability (IfS)	€144.3 million in 2007, of which €100 million is for crisis response (€1.6 billion for crisis response from 2007-2013) Can fund crisis response actions for up to two years and long-term crisis response capacity building of other organisations. Also supports activities to address global and trans-regional threats, including terrorism and organised crime, and reduce risks relating to chemical, biological and radiological substances. Incorporates the RRM, rehabilitation and reconstruction regulation and aspects of the past Nuclear safety instrument.	The Rapid Reaction Mechanism (RRM) €30 million in 2006 Could fund actions for six months only	Provided short term support for: mediation, arbitration, reconciliation; rule of law and civilian administration; rehabilitation and reconstruction; civil society development; high level policy advice; disarmament, demobilisation and reintegration. Also funded technical assessment and fact-finding missions.
		Rehabilitation and Reconstruction Regulation	In principle, financed the first phase of relief, including efforts to develop institutional capacities for political stability. In practice, provided long-term top-up funding to a small number of countries whose conflicts were in the distant past.
		Nuclear safety Instrument	Provided support for efforts to improve nuclear safety particularly in central and eastern Europe and the former Soviet Union.
Instrument for the Promotion of Democracy and Human Rights (EIDHR)	€1104 million over 2007-2013 (average of €157 million a year) New EIDHR instrument puts greater emphasis on supporting non-state actors. Human rights also supported by long-term geographic instruments	European Initiative for Democracy and Human Rights (EIDHR) €122 million in 2006	Operates without host government consent Provided support for human rights monitoring and observer missions; support for elections; conciliation; support to international criminal tribunals; rehabilitation of victims of torture; promotion of the rule of law and independent media.

* The table above indicates roughly how the new thematic financial instruments that are most relevant for SSR - the Stability Instrument and the thematic human rights instrument - relate to past instruments for funding. It is not comprehensive and does not include other instruments that are important for the EU's humanitarian response to crises, notably the Humanitarian Aid Instrument (€700 million in 2007) and the Civil Protection Instrument (€5 million for external actions in 2007). Nor does it include the thematic instrument for macro-financial assistance.

The **Instrument for Stability** replaces and effectively extends the Rapid Reaction Mechanism. It is intended to deliver an immediate and integrated response to situations of crisis in third countries within a single legal instrument until normal cooperation under one of the other instruments for cooperation and assistance can resume. Previously a crisis response could trigger as many as seven separate EC financing instruments[58], each with its own decision-making procedures and budgetary constraints. Like the RRM, the Stability Instrument will enable the Commission to make rapid funding decisions (without comitology). It integrates the RRM budget line and improves upon it by allowing more time (two years) to secure follow-on funding from the geographic budget lines. It has therefore been designed to improve the linkages between the initial response and follow-up assistance delivered under the main long-term geographic instrument, and to strengthen the coherence between EC assistance and the EU's foreign policy response using inter-governmental CFSP instruments.

The 2007 budget for the Stability Instrument is €144.3 million of which €100 million is for crisis response, with a total of €2.5 billion projected over the next seven years, €1.6 billion of which is for crisis response.[59] The scope of activities that it can support was subject to intense negotiation between member states, the Council and the European Parliament in 2005 and 2006. These negotiations were made more difficult by the Commission taking the Council to the European Court of Justice over its support for ECOWAS in the area of small arms and light weapons. The Commission argued that if the Community has a legal basis for acting under its development policy mandate, the Council actions in the same area of policy are illegal under the EC Treaty. The Council's counter position made a legal case for restricting Community powers to areas that do not come under the objectives of CFSP. Hence issues of institutional competence dominated negotiations over the nature of security-related support that the EC could provide through the Stability Instrument. The final compromise details the activities that the Stability Instrument can be used to support in response to situations of crisis or emerging crisis, as well as other security related activities to promote cooperation in tackling organised crime, terrorism, non-proliferation and the protection of critical infrastructure. In relation to SSR, the instrument provides for 'support for the development of democratic, pluralistic state institutions [...] an independent judiciary, good governance and law and order, including non-military technical cooperation to strengthen overall civilian control and oversight over the security system and measures to strengthen the capacity of law enforcement and judicial authorities...'.[60] In addition, the instrument allows for support for demobilisation and reintegration of former combatants as well as measures to mitigate the social effects of restructuring the armed forces and strengthen the role of civil society and its participation in the political process. It also provides for measures aimed at strengthening the conflict prevention and post conflict recovery efforts of international regional and sub-regional organisations, which potentially include support to African regional organisations as well as the UN Peacebuilding Fund.

The Stability Instrument therefore improves upon past instruments for short-term EC financing in so far as it has led to important streamlining of decision-making in the crisis response phase. It also clarifies that short-term

Community instruments can be used to support the full range of civilian activities designed to promote capacity building and governance of the security system and provides for support to regional and international organisations in post conflict recovery. It does not extend to support for defence reform however, and therefore an integrated approach to SSR will necessarily continue to require concerted cross-pillar action, combining EU support for defence reform through ESDP, drawing on the CFSP budget, and EC support for so-called 'flanking' measures, potentially kick-started through the Stability Instrument and followed up with funding from long-term geographic instruments (see Figure 1 below for EC crisis-related funding instruments).

Figure 1. *EC funding instruments for crisis and post-crisis situations.*

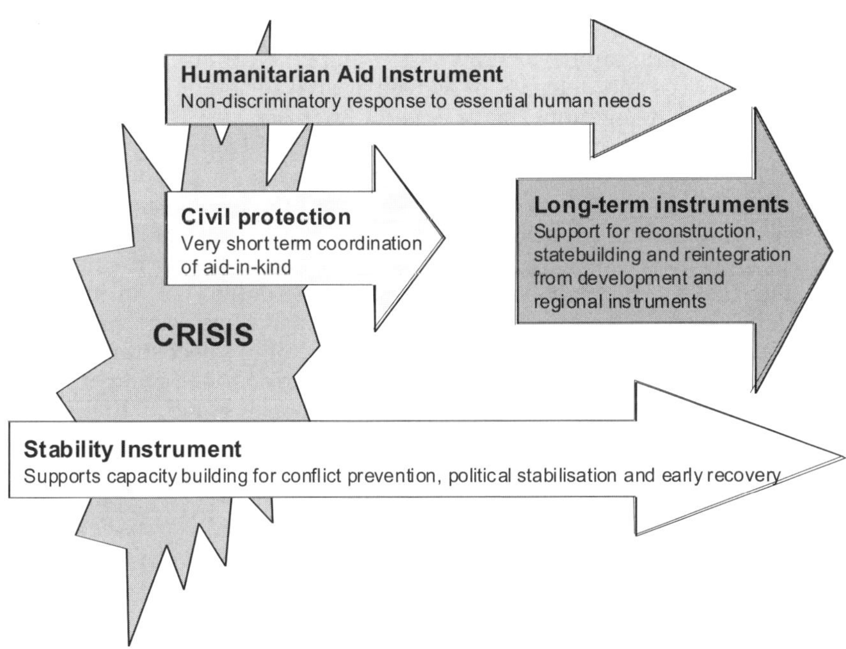

Thematic Instruments to Promote Democracy and Human Rights

The **European Initiative for Democracy and Human Rights (EIDHR)**[61] was established in 1999 to complement the EC's geographic instruments and CFSP actions by supporting actions implemented by NGOs and international organisations in particular.[62] Crucially, it can be used without host government consent and in some regions provides the only legal base for activities including the promotion of political and civil rights, election observation and conflict resolution initiatives. EIDHR tendering and project management is conducted by the EuropeAid Cooperation Office. In 2006, the amount available for the activities of the EIDHR was €122 million. While the EIDHR has been used to support the organisation of elections and electoral monitoring in transition and post-conflict countries (Afghanistan, Iraq, DRC and the Palestinian Authority, West Bank and Gaza, Ethiopia, Lebanon, Guinea Bissau and Burundi), since the mid 1990s funds have gradually shifted away from a priority focus on elections.[63] EIDHR-funded activities of particular relevance to SSR include: support for training in human rights standards for public administrators, army and police officers and judges; support for ombudsmen and truth commissions; the provision of legal aid to broaden access to the judicial system (Latin American and Nepal); and the mainstreaming of the rule of law into development policies. A conflict dimension has also been introduced with support for social and economic reintegration, including vocational training for ex-combatants and the creation of local mediation and power-sharing forums. The proportion of funding for 'conflict prevention' activities remains low, however, at 4% of funding from 2002-2004.

In 2001, the Commission found that this instrument did not promote coherent human rights and democratization actions across the EC.[64] Subsequent programming documents, developed with input from EC geographical services and delegations as well as civil society organisations and member states' delegations, have sought to place greater emphasis on focused strategic actions in a selected number of 32 focus countries. While the EIDHR programming documents are intended to promote coherent intra-pillar and cross-pillar action, there are a number of reasons why the programme falls short of these ambitions in practice. These are documented in a comprehensive assessment of the EIDHR programme for the European Parliament.[65] Of a number of relevant weaknesses identified in the study, the link between programming and political analysis has been shown to be wanting with the result that: 'It has proven difficult to select strategic initiatives that could potentially contribute to transformational change in third countries, and to avoid assistance to projects which could actually harm locally driven reform processes'.[66] Moreover, the unique characteristics of the instrument, namely its ability to be employed without government assent in non-democratic states, have been used extremely sparingly in practice and the instrument has therefore been of limited use in more sensitive political contexts. Finally, the instrument's cumbersome and lengthy funding procedures, including its reliance on calls for proposals, means that it is not suitable for rapid and flexible assistance in crisis situations.

Of particular relevance to the instrument's value for SSR is the conclusion that 'EIDHR input into mainstream institution building assistance has remained negligible' and that overall EC assistance for 'democracy building' through geographic and thematic instruments remains 'projectised' and disconnected from each other.[67] In short, much remains to be done to ensure a genuine integration of democracy and human rights within mainstream development aid. This has implications for potential future efforts to develop a comprehensive and coherent approach to SSR and highlights the persistent challenge of ensuring 'cross-instrument' co-ordination and synergies.

Although the Commission had initially proposed that the EIDHR be incorporated into the Stability Instrument, there was strong resistance to this proposal from the European Parliament and human rights groups principally on the grounds that this reduced parliamentary control over human rights funding decisions. Consequently, the new financial instruments include 'a financing instrument for the promotion of democracy and human rights worldwide'[68], which is similar to its predecessor EIDHR instrument. The annual budget of the instrument is in line with past EIDHR assistance and is set to increase from €130 million in 2007 to €320 million in 2013.

It is unclear whether the new EIDHR instrument will improve EU SSR support. On the one hand, its provisions more clearly provide for support to strengthen the rule of law, promote independence of the judiciary, encourage and evaluate institutional reforms and 'promote effective and transparent democratic accountability and oversight, including that of the security and justice sectors'[69]. On the other hand, support will depend on SSR being prioritised in the instrument strategy papers and action plans. It remains to be seen how far SSR activities will be prioritised, and to what extent EIDHR strategies are developed to complement or fill gaps in SSR assistance provided through other instruments.

Long-Term Development Funding

The European Development Fund

The European Development Fund (EDF) is the main instrument for Community aid for development cooperation in the 78 African, Caribbean and Pacific (ACP) countries and the 20 Overseas Countries and Territories (OCT). Articles 131 and 136 of the 1957 Treaty of Rome provided for its creation and, following a request by the European Parliament, a heading has been reserved for the Fund in the Community budget since 1993. The EDF does not come under the general Community budget.[70] It is funded by the member states, covered by its own financial rules and managed by a specific committee. The member states set the EDF budget in the Council via agreements that are subsequently ratified by the national parliament of each member state. Each EDF is typically concluded for a period of five years, following that of the partnership agreements.

The European Commission and other institutions established under the partnership play a key role in the day-to-day management of the Fund. The Commission Directorates-General for Development and External Relations, together with the European Commission country delegations set programming priorities and formulate Country Strategy Papers in cooperation with partner countries. In addition to the funds programmed under the regional and country strategies, there is an additional 'governance incentive tranche' that may be awarded to each country, pending the Commission's positive evaluation of governance in the country. The EDF also includes 'intra-ACP funds' which are available for facilities including, most notably the African Peace Facility used to support African Union peacekeeping. Policy and programming tasks are institutionally separated from the tasks of project management, which are conducted by the EuropeAid Cooperation Office – the implementing agency for projects funded from the EDF and geographic instruments funded from the Community budget.

The current 9th EDF budget funds the vast majority of activities in ACP countries. Likewise, the new 10th EDF covering the period 2008-2013 (€22.7 billion) will continue to provide a good basis for support to SSR with the strong legal underpinning of Article 11 of the Cotonou Agreement. The EDF has the additional advantage of not being constrained by ODA eligibility criteria in the same way as Community instruments[71], although non-ODA uses of the EDF are still so small that member states can report all their contributions to the EDF as ODA. In some cases EDF funds have been used to support military aspects of SSR, as for example in the DRC where funds were used to support Centres de Brassage for army integration, complementing the ESDP operation EU SEC Congo.

The Commission states that since 2003 SSR assistance has been provided through the EDF to at least 35 ACP states[72], whereby the majority of support has been provided in support of the rule of law, through justice and police reform and capacity building. The EDF has also been used to support civil oversight mechanisms, including parliaments, as in the case of Chad and Kenya for example. And many EDF recipient countries receive funding to improve public financial management. In post-conflict countries, EDF funds are also used to support DDR efforts, increasingly through Multi-Donor Trust Funds.

EDF funding is governed according to the partnership principle, whereby funding decisions are subject to joint donor and recipient decision-making procedures. In relation to security-relevant assistance, the specificities of the rules governing EDF funding decisions have the advantage that funding is not as constrained by ODA criteria. Conversely, despite the Cotonou agreement, there are no provisions that require EDF funds to support SSR, conflict prevention or good governance objectives more broadly. Hence, the use of EDF funds for SSR objectives required donor and host-government buy-in on a country-by-country basis in accordance with lengthy programming procedures. In practice, support for governance reform still represents a small proportion of EDF assistance, even in countries affected by conflict. This is due to the general preference by recipient states for 'concrete' assistance in traditional areas such as infrastructure to more politically sensitive governance-related assistance. But it can also be explained by inflexible and lengthy programming procedures, with insufficient attention to political analysis and impact assessments on the part of the Commission.[73] Hence funding for SSR from the EDF continues to be piecemeal and fall short of the comprehensive strategic approach advocated in the Commission Concept for SSR.

Another obvious limitation of this budget line is geographical, since it only applies to the ACP group of countries that are signatories to the Cotonou Agreement. SSR actions in other regions must be funded from other geographic instruments or individual country budgets (see below).

Geographic Instruments

Development and economic assistance co-operation in other regions is funded from other geographic instruments or individual country budgets within the EU external relations budget heading 4. Regional programmes total some €5 billion per annum. They include programmes targeted at Asia and Latin America (ALA)[74], Eastern Europe and Central Asia (excluding accession countries)[75], Mediterranean countries (MEDA)[76], South Africa[77], South Eastern Europe, the Balkans (CARDS)[78], the West Bank and the Gaza Strip[79]. All can be used for activities relating to post conflict reconstruction and institutional capacity building. These programmes are managed by DG Relex and DG Enlargement, in the case of the Western Balkans and Accession countries, with the EuropeAid Cooperation Office responsible for project management.

While it is difficult to establish what proportion of funding is directed to activities related to SSR due to the lack of appropriate classification codes, a review of country and regional strategy papers conducted by DG Development suggested that €2 billion out of a global programmable envelope of €10 billion (including EDF) was allocated to 'governance-related' activities.[80] For illustrative purposes, a brief description of the range of areas and countries funded by these instruments is provided below.[81]

In Asia, support has been provided from the Asia Latin America (ALA) budget line for a number of programmes to promote civilian oversight and strengthen civilian management and capacity of the justice and police sectors (Afghanistan, East Timor, Indonesia, Nepal, Philippines, Vietnam and Sri Lanka). The ALA has also been used to support justice reform, law enforcement and civilian management in Latin America (Colombia, El Salvador, Guatemala, Mexico, Nicaragua, Panama and Uruguay).

In the South and East Mediterranean and the Middle East, support has been provided through MEDA to modernise and reform the justice and police system (Morocco, Algeria, Tunisia, Yemen and the Palestinian Authorities) and strengthen civilian oversight and capacity building (Algeria, Morocco, the Palestinian Authorities, Egypt and Jordan).

In Eastern Europe and Central Asia, support has been delivered through the TACIS instrument for capacity building and reform of the justice, law enforcement and border control sectors as well as for measures to improve civilian oversight (Armenia, Azerbaijan, Belarus, Georgia, Kazakhstan, Moldova, Russia, Tajikistan, Ukraine and Uzbekistan). In Georgia, TACIS assistance was also designed to follow-up the ESDP rule of law mission to Georgia – EUJUST Themis.

In the Western Balkans, the majority of support has been delivered in the area of justice reform, police and internal security, through the CARDS programme. Beneficiary countries include Albania, Bosnia-Herzegovina, Croatia, Serbia-Montenegro, Kosovo and the Former Yugoslav Republic of Macedonia. This includes extensive programmes to strengthen the police and legal system (complementing the EU ESDP police and military operations) as well as efforts to efforts to improve financial management of SSR related expenditure and build capacity in custom, border control and regional cooperation.

The new geographic financial instruments that have been established to channel long-term development assistance from the EU budget in the 2007-2013 financial perspective are: the pre-Accession instrument (IPA – €10.2 billion), the European neighbourhood and partnership instrument (ENPI – €10.6 billion), and the Development Cooperation and Economic Cooperation Instrument (DCEC – €15.1 billion). In principle, all three geographic instruments can be used to support SSR actions just as geographic instruments have supported SSR activities in the past. While SSR is not mentioned as a cross-cutting issue to be mainstreamed in all programmes, the Development Instrument specifically mentions that 'particular attention shall be given to strengthening the rule of law, improving access to justice and supporting civil society, as well as promoting dialogue, participation and reconciliation, and institution-building'[82]. The Development Cooperation Instrument is also fairly flexible in so far as up to 10 percent of its funding need not be ODA eligible, providing significant scope for its use to fund activities with good governance and peacebuilding objectives, including SSR. However, some fear that drawing attention to these activities will be more difficult in the absence of parliamentary pressure and debate over individual budget lines and their legal basis.[83]

Conclusion: Outstanding Challenges for the EU[84]

Despite the rationalisation of EU financial instruments in the new financial perspective 2007-2013, EU SSR assistance remains scattered across a number of large regional and thematic instruments that have been largely tailored to support major regional and thematic policy objectives. These include crisis management, enlargement policy, European neighbourhood policy, development policy, human rights and democracy, and the external dimension of the EU's internal security and justice policies. In relation to conflict affected countries, the new short-term Instrument for Stability has the potential of delivering more rapid and flexible support of early phases of SSR. This still precludes most assistance for defence reform, however, and therefore a comprehensive approach will in many cases continue to require inter-pillar coordination with complementary ESDP interventions and close coordination with member states' bilateral activities. All of the financial instruments described above have the potential to support dimensions of SSR, but SSR assistance is not central to any of them. Thus the level and sustainability of the EU's SSR engagement will depend on its implementation of EU cross-cutting policy commitments to deliver a comprehensive and sustainable approach to SSR.

It follows that effective SSR support is not just about obtaining a supportive policy framework and suitable funding instruments, it is about the willingness and ability of EU staff to give sufficient priority to these activities within country and regional strategies and programmes. In this regard there are a number of recent developments which should facilitate the implementation of SSR activities. These include the agreement of a clear conceptual framework for SSR in the Commission and Council concepts for EU support to SSR, which should also help identify comparative institutional advantages and raise awareness about SSR norms amongst officials. Furthermore, the new Common Framework for drafting country strategy papers and joint multi-annual programming[85] provides for a more strategic approach to SSR. Importantly, the framework states that greater attention should be given to analysing measures taken to ensure security and stability, including SSR, within the context of country analysis.

Translating these developments into better programming practice will require further steps, however. A number of these were outlined in the Concept for Commission support to SSR assistance and include the development of: tools for comprehensive SSR analysis, guidelines to assist the integration of SSR support into country and regional strategy papers and programming dialogue, and operational guidelines for implementing SSR assistance. It will also require efforts to improve the capacity and expertise of the EU, including though SSR training for Council and Commission officials, and the development of mechanisms whereby both the Commission and Council can draw on external SSR experts.

Over and above efforts to improve the implementation of Commission assistance, there is a recognised need for increased efforts to foster intra- and cross-pillar complementarity. This might include joint needs assessments or fact-finding missions to assess possible ESDP and Commission contributions to SSR activities in countries and regions affected by conflict. Similarly, efforts could be made to join up approaches at different stages of the planning and evaluation cycle. There is also room for innovation regarding joint evaluation/lessons-learned work by Council and Commission, which should be aimed at promoting best practice with regard to the coordination of the overall EU effort. This could take the form of after-action reviews following each SSR-relevant ESDP operation as well as regular reviews of the implementation of the ESDP SSR concept and Commission Concept for SSR.

There is reason to be optimistic that the EU is taking the internal coordination challenge seriously. Although there are few formal links requiring concerted EC and ESDP planning, on-going planning for a comprehensive approach to SSR in the Democratic Republic of Congo (DRC) has been exemplary. The planning of both a potential future integrated ESDP mission to DRC and future EC assistance for SSR has been informed by a comprehensive review of the DRC, drafted jointly by the Council Secretariat and the Commission Services as well as by a follow-up joint Commission/Council evaluation mission. On-going joint planning efforts are based on commonly agreed principles and address the potential roles of the EU – identifying ESDP and EC activities – over the short, medium and long term. They also envision the development of a new coordination mechanism to improve information exchange between all EU actors in the field and in Brussels.

Similarly, the EU has an ambitious agenda with regard to the issue of donor coordination in the DRC case. On 15 September 2006 the General Affairs and Cooperation Council concluded that 'in view of the need for a comprehensive approach combining the different initiatives underway, the EU would be ready to assume a coordinating role in international efforts in the security sector, in close coordination with the United Nations, to support the Congolese authorities in the field'. The on-going planning process thus also addresses the development of new mechanisms (mixed committees in the defence, police and justice sector) to ensure coordination between the DRC authorities and the international community.

Finally, the EU has an opportunity to work internationally to support efforts in the area of SSR funding. The EU and its member states have played a major role in the OECD DAC discussions that have led to a broadening of the scope of ODA definitions to include these issues. The EU will continue these efforts, working to ensure that ongoing discussions within the OECD DAC develop operational guidelines based on best practice and current understanding of the linkages between poor security and poverty.

The EU also has an important role to play in improving financial support for SSR in the UN context. This includes support to the UN's Peacebuilding Commission, including through the provision of assistance to implement its recommendations and by contributing to the Peacebuilding Fund. Importantly, the EU and its member states should also support the position that assessed contributions need to be made available to UN agencies, such as UNDP, involved in the longer term aspects of SSR, so as to improve the sustainability of UN SSR efforts conducted within the framework of peace operations.

Endnotes

1 European Commission (2006) 'A Concept for European Community Support for Security Sector Reform', Brussels, 24 May 2006, COM (2006)253 final.

2 Special Co-ordinator of the Stability Pact for South Eastern Europe, Working Table III, Security and Defence issues, 'Security Sector Reform', paper for the Regional Conference, Bucharest, 25-26 October 2001.

3 Council of the European Union, 'EU Concept for ESDP Support to Security Sector Reform (SSR)', Brussels, 13 October 2005, 12566/4/05 REV 4, and the Commission Concept referred to in note 1.

4 *Security System Reform and Governance, Policy and Practice*, DAC Guidelines and Reference Series (Paris: OECD 2004).

5 Council of the European Union (2006), 'The European Consensus on Development'. Official Journal No C 46 of 24 February 2006.

6 Council of the European Union (2005), 'The EU and Africa: Towards a Strategic Partnership' 15702/1/05 Rev1.

7 European Commission (2006), 'A Concept for European Community Support for SSR' *ibid.* p. 5.

8 See, for example, Williams, R. (2002), 'Development Agencies and Security-Sector Restructuring'. *Conflict, Security & Development* 2 (1) 145-9.

9 David Chuter (2006), 'Understanding Security Sector Reform', *Journal of Security Sector Management*, Volume 4, Number 2, April.

10 This Inventory of UN Capacity in Peacebuilding included security sector governance, law enforcement and defence reform as part of the 'security system reform' sector, as distinct from the justice, rule of law, human rights and governance sectors.

11 UNDP's Bureau for Crisis Prevention and Recovery has developed a comprehensive approach to 'justice and security sector reform'. See (2003) 'Security Sector Reform and Transitional Justice. A Crisis Post-Conflict Programmatic Approach', UNDP.

12 Interviews with DPKO officials, 18-21 December 2006.

13 Chanaa, J. (2002) 'Security Sector Reform: Issues, Challenges and Prospects', *Adelphi Papers* No. 344. Oxford: Oxford University Press.

14 OECD DAC Network on Conflict Peace and Development Cooperation (CPDC) 'Key Messages and Preliminary Findings from the Implementation Framework on Security System Reform' (IF-SSR), July 2006.

15 As stipulated in the ESDP Concept for SSR, *ibid.*

16 For an overview of the involvement of international organisations in SSR see 'Intergovernmental Approaches to Security Sector Reform', Background Paper prepared by DCAF in *Developing a Security Sector Reform (SSR) Concept for the United Nations*, Proceedings of the Expert Workshop held in Bratislava, Slovakia on 7 July 2006.

17 See for example, Wulf, H. (2004), Security *Sector Reform in Developing and Transitional Countries*. Berlin: Berghof Research Center for Constructive Conflict Management.

18 This is done well, for example, in Neclâ Tschirgi, (2004) 'Post-Conflict Peacebuilding Revisited: Achievements, Limitations, Challenges' International Peace Academy.

19 See Shepard Forman and Stewart Patrick, *Good Intentions: Pledges of Aid for Post-Conflict Recovery* (Boulder, CO: Lynne Rienner Publishers, 2000).

20 OECD, 'Security System Reform and Governance: Policy and Good Practice', High Level Meeting, 15-16 April 2004.

21 Annex 2 'Areas of European Community Support to SSR' to the Communication from the Commission to the Council and the European Parliament 'A concept for European Community Support for Security Sector Reform' COM (2006) 253 final. The mapping exercise did not include assistance provided in connection with the accession process or the EU's internal security and did not claim to include relevant information on all partner countries.

22 This is supported by the findings of a study on post-conflict SSR assistance in Afghanistan, Bosnia and Herzegovina, Haiti, Kosovo, Sierra Leone and Kosovo by David Law. See David M. Law (2006), *The Post-Conflict Security Sector*, DCAF Policy Papers No. 14, Geneva Centre for the Democratic Control of Armed Forces (DCAF), p16.

23 OECD note of 3 March 2005, 'Conflict Prevention and Peacebuilding: What Counts as ODA?'

24 These include: technical cooperation provided to parliament, government ministries, law enforcement agencies and the judiciary to assist, review and reform the security system and thus improve democratic governance and civilian control; technical cooperation provided to governments to improve civilian oversight and democratic control of budgeting, management, accountability and auditing of security expenditure, including military budgets, as part of a public expenditure management programme; assistance to civil society to enhance its competence and capacity to scrutinise the security system so that it is managed in accordance with democratic norms and principles of accountability, transparency and good governance.

25 For a discussion of the private sector as implementers of reform see Peter Wilson, 'Private Security Actors, Donors and SSR,' Alan Bryden and Marina Caparini eds., *Private Actors and Security Governance*, (Lit: Zurich, 2006), pp. 247-263.

26 This is one of the findings of the 2005 UN Peacebuilding Inventory.

27 Advice and training for the reform of national defence capabilities was provided in a few cases, notably in the DRC, Liberia and Timor Leste.

28 Anthony Craig, (2005) 'The Role of the UN in Defence Reform', DPKO.

29 European Commission, (2005), 'Background Paper on EC support to Security Sector Reform'.

30 See E. Barth Eide, A. T. Kaspersen, R. Kent and K. von Hippel (2005), *Report on Integrated Missions: Practical Perspectives and Recommendations*, Independent Study of the Expanded UN ECHA Core Group, NUPI. (2005) p. 26

31 Scot Carlson (2006) *Legal and Judicial Rule of Law Work in Multi-Dimensional Peacekeeping Operations: Lessons – Learned Study*, Peacekeeping Best Practices Unit (New York: United Nations)

32 Edward Rees (2006), *Security Sector Reform and Peace Operations: 'Improvisation and Confusion' from the Field*, March – External Study, New York: Department of Peacekeeping Operations.

33 *Post Conflict Peacebuilding, ibid*. p. 10.

34 Security System Reform and Governance, A DAC Reference Document, OECD, 2005 and OSCE DAC IF-SSR, *ibid* – note 14.

35 OSCE DAC IF-SSR, *ibid* – note 14.

36 See, for example: Jones, Bruce (2001) *The Challenges of Strategic Coordination: Containing Opposition and Sustaining Implementation of Peace Agreements in Civil Wars*, International Peace Academy, New York; Cousens, Elizabeth M. (2001) 'Building Peace in Bosnia,' in Elizabeth M. Cousens and Chetan Kumar with Karin Wermester, ed., *Peacebuilding as Politics: Cultivating Peace in Fragile Societies (Boulder*, Colo.: Lynee Rienner) pp. 113-152, and Woodward, Susan (2002), 'Economic Priorities for Successful Peace Implementation,' in Stephen John Stedman, Donald Rothchild and Elizabeth M. Cousens, eds., *Ending Civil Wars: The Implementation of Peace Agreements* (Boulder, Colo.: Lynne Rienner), pp.183-214.

37 Susan L. Woodward, 'Peace Operations: the Civilian Dimension. Accounting for UNDP and the UN Specialised Agencies', A discussion paper prepared for the Center on International Cooperation, New York University, for the Government of Denmark's Meeting on Strengthening the UN's Capacity on Civilian Crisis Management, Copenhagen 8-9 June 2004. p. 13.

38 Salvatore Schiavo-Campo (2003), 'Financing and Aid Management Arrangements in Post-Conflict Situations', Working Paper No. 6, World Bank Conflict Prevention and Reconstruction Unit, p. 2.

39 These views were expressed by representatives of DPKO and UNDP in conferences on SSR, co-organised by DCAF, in Brussels in June 2006 and in Geneva in October 2006.

40 In a project supported by the Government of Canada and implemented by DCAF.

41 This section draws on earlier publications by the author, including Gourlay, C. 'Community instruments for civilian crisis management' pp. 49-67 and 'Civil-Civil Co-ordination in EU crisis management' pp. 103-119 in *Civilian Crisis Management: the EU way*, Chaillot Paper, No. 90, European Union Institute for Security Studies, Paris, June 2006.

42 These principles broadly correspond to those outlined in the 2005 OECD DAC guidelines.

43 See chapter 6 in this book by Jörg Monar for a description of the EU's activities undertaken in the context of the justice and home affairs policy area.

44 For military ESDP operations, participating member states cover the costs on the basis of 'costs lie where they fall'. For civilian ESDP operations, only the agreed 'common' operating costs are borne by the CFSP budget.

45 Missiroli, *ibid* p. 8.

46 The European Court of Auditors reports annually on the management of the EU's external expenditure from the EU budget. It also periodically conducts special reports on the management of the CFSP budget. The last of these, Special Report No. 13/2001, recommended further measures to improve the transparency of the financing of CFSP actions, address delays in the launching of actions and improve reporting and evaluations of CFSP actions to the Commission and European Parliament.

47 See S. Duke 'The Rhetoric-Resources Gap in EU Crisis Management' EIPASCOPE no. 3, 2002, pp. 2-8 and C. Gourlay, 'Fixing EU crisis management financing', *European Security Review*, issue 8, October 2001, available at www.isis-europe.org.

48 At the time of writing, further funding for police reform was being considered in connection with an integrated approach to SSR reform in the DRC. See 'Draft Commission Decision regarding a RRM action of support to the reform of the security system, in particular the reform of the Congolese National Police', Ref: C (2006) 6959/1 of 15/12/2006.

49 European Commission, 'Linking Relief, Rehabilitation and Development – An Assessment' COM (2001) 153 final.

50 These proposals were advanced in the two Commission Communications on the Financial Perspectives that were published in February and July 2004: 'Building our common Future, Policy Challenges and Budgetary Means of the Enlarged Union 2007-2013, COM(2004) 101, February 2004 and COM(2004)0626 'Communication from the Commission to the Council and the European Parliament on the Instruments for External Assistance under the Future Financial Perspective 2007-2013' July 2004.

51 There are currently 91 budget lines in the RELEX family policy areas and EU external assistance is carried out through over 30 legal instruments.

52 Regulation (EC) No 1085/2006 OJ L 210, 31.7.2006, p. 82.

53 Regulation (EC) No 1638/2006, OJ L 310, 9.11.2006, p. 1.

54 Regulation (EC) No 1889/2006 OJ L 386, 29.12.2006, p. 1.

55 ibid.

56 Council Decision establishing a Civil Protection Financial Instrument, 5215/07, Brussels, 26 February 2007.

57 Regulation (EC) No 1889/2006 OJ L 386, 29.12.2006.

58 In Iraq, for instance, the response has included the Rapid Reaction Mechanism, the Human Rights Regulation, the Mine Action Regulation, and Humanitarian aid. Other options include the regulations on 'Aid to uprooted people' and 'Rehabilitation'.

59 The Stability instrument is by far the smallest of the EC external relations instruments. Budgetary allocations in billion euro for the other principal financial instruments over 2007-2013 are as follows: Humanitarian Aid 5.6, Development Cooperation 15.1, European Neighbourhood Policy 10.6, and Pre-Accession instrument 10.2. All figures are based on a working document of the Commission services 'Multiannual Financial Framework, Indicative breakdown of expenditure within individual headings' April 2006.

60 Regulation of the European Parliament and of the Council establishing an Instrument for Stability, PE-CONS 3634/06, 20 October 2006.

61 The legal basis for the EIDHR is Council Regulations (EC) 975/1999 and 976/1999.

62 From 2001-2004, 80% of funds went to NGOs, the rest to international and regional organisations.

63 From 50% to 15% in 2002.

64 Commission Communication on the EU's role in promoting Human Rights and Democratisation in Third Countries COM (2001) 252 final, May 2001.

65 'No Lasting Peace and Prosperity without democracy and Human Rights: Harnessing debates on the EU's future financial instruments' by Richard Youngs et al. External Study for the Directorate general for External Policies of the Union, Directorate B, European Parliament,

EP/ExPol/B/2004/09/10. This study provides a comprehensive overview of the EIDHR programme and provides a number of concrete recommendations for how the EU could adopt a more strategic approach to democracy and human rights through institutional reform, and improve the quality of its human rights assistance through procedural reform, including the reform of the Financial Regulation and funding procedures.

66 *Ibid* p 14.

67 *Ibid.* 15.

68 Regulation (EC) No 1889/2006 of the European Parliament and of the Council of 20 December 2006.

69 Regulation 1889/20006 Article 2, subsections ii and iv.

70 However, since 2004 the Commission has sought to integrate the EDF into the EU budget, where it would be dispersed according to EU budgetary rules and programming priorities, rather than objectives and rules agreed between all signatories to the Cotonou Agreement. The Commission contends that the budgetisation of the EDF would increase efficiency and public accountability by allowing the European Parliament to scrutinise EDF funds as it does the EU budget. However, the proposal was ultimately rejected for the 10th EDF since a number of member states resisted the move fearing increases in their net contributions. Moreover, the European Parliament opted not to incorporate the EDF into the Financial Perspective 2007-2013, fearing that this would lead to a decrease in the funds available to poor ACP countries.

71 This is illustrated by the fact that the 9th EDF was used to fund the African Peace Facility of which only 10-15% is classified as ODA – the rest has been spent on a contribution to costs of African military peacekeeping forces. The 10th EDF will also be used to support the Facility.

72 The 'Commission Services background paper on EC support to Security Sector Reform' states that at least the following countries have received SSR assistance: Angola, Benin, Burkina Faso, Burundi, Cameroon, Comoros, Dominican Republic, Democratic Republic of Congo, Eritrea, Fiji, Guinea Bissau, Equatorial Guinea, Guinea Conakry, Haiti, Ivory Coast, Jamaica, Kenya, Liberia, Madagascar, Malawi, Mauritius, Mozambique, Niger, Nigeria, Republic of Congo, Rwanda, Seychelles, Sierra Leone, Solomon Islands, South Africa, Sudan, Somalia, Chad, Togo, Vanuatu and Uganda.

73 For more detailed critiques of conflict (in)sensitivity in EU country-programming, see 'Improving the impact of Country Strategy Papers and programming on peace and stability. Lessons learned, best practice and recommendations from the Horn of Africa', Saferworld, April 2006, and Saferworld's 'submission on the Country Strategy Paper for Kenya: Prioritising safety, security and conflict prevention', July 2006.

74 Based on Council Regulation EC NO. 443/92 (ALA)

75 Based on Council Regulation EC No 99/2000 (TACIS)

76 Based on Council Regulation EC No 2698/2000 (MEDA)

77 Based on Council Regulation EC No. 1726/2000

78 Based on Council Regulation EC No. 2666/2000 (CARDS)

79 Based on Council Regulation EC No. 1734/94 (amended by Council Regulation 2840/98)

80 See 'No Lasting Peace and Prosperity without Democracy and Human Rights' *ibid.* p 12.

81 For a more comprehensive overview of EC assistance for SSR activities, see 'Commission Services Background Paper on EC Support to SSR, 2006 and the Commission paper 'Support to Peacebuilding: examples of EU action', Memo/05/313, 12 September 2005, available at:

http://europa.eu.int/rapid/pressReleasesAction.do?reference=MEMO/05/313&format=HTML&aged=0&language=EN&guiLanguage=en

82 Regulation (EC) No 1889/2006, p. 19.

83 See CONCORD paper 'Principles on Promoting Cross-cutting issues and Thematic Approach in EU Development Cooperation'. April 2005.

84 This section draws on an unpublished briefing paper by Sarah Bayne and Catriona Gourlay, prepared for the Finnish Ministry of Foreign Affairs, 'Approaches Toward Ensuring Effective Support for Peace Support/Keeping Missions in Africa', May 2006.

85 Communication from the Commission to the Council and the European Parliament, 'Increasing the impact of EU Aid: A common framework for drafting country strategy papers and joint multiannual programming', COM (2006) 0088 Final. 2 March 2006, Brussels.

5. Security Sector Reform: CFSP, ESDP and the International Impact of the EU's Second Pillar

Willem van Eekelen

Security sector reform (SSR) became a special theme when the ending of the Cold War led to the emergence of new pluralistic democracies on the periphery of the European Union. The transition from a communist and Soviet dominated system implied far-reaching changes in civil-military relations leading to transparent and democratic control of the security sector. A common element in the various definitions of SSR was the inclusion of all uniformed services having part of the state monopoly of the use of force. The reform process contained a technical dimension, covering modern force planning, and a more conceptual one, stressing fundamental concepts of democratic governance. Sometimes, the two were linked under the caption of 'transformation', but in practice that new concept remained primarily military in nature. Gradually, the declining priority of collective defence of national independence and territorial integrity impacted on all European countries and led to the downsizing of forces and their restructuring for new missions. Simultaneously, examples of asymmetric warfare coupled with new technological developments enabling a 'revolution of military affairs' through network-centric warfare led to a reorganisation of NATO and the creation of Allied Command Transformation in Norfolk, Virginia. Consequently, SSR had implications for both new and old democracies.

With the new emphasis on peace support operations – the catch-all phrase for the whole spectrum of missions ranging from humanitarian assistance to peace enforcement – 'defence' became more selective and therefore more political. At first, peacekeeping remained what it had been before: military presence with the agreement of the parties in the conflict under the umbrella of a seemingly durable cease-fire. That was the time when peacekeeping was often deemed not to be a soldier's job, though only soldiers could do it. That has changed fundamentally; first in Bosnia, then Kosovo and currently in Afghanistan, a transition to robust peacekeeping and then to undiluted combat duties has taken place. The military profession has become more dangerous, and repeated absences from home have become the norm.

Governments had to apply the basic democratic principles of 'reveal, explain and justify' to their decisions to send forces abroad to fight terrorism, to bring stability to failed states or to intervene in countries torn by ethnic or religious strife. At first, the main focus was on the creation of democratic structures and the rule of law in the countries emerging from the Soviet Union and the Warsaw Pact. Somewhat paradoxically, however, SSR did not formally become a criterion for EU accession, although it could be assumed to be implicit in the Copenhagen Criteria of 1993, which stressed pluralistic democracy and the rule of law. The issue did not arise prominently as the accession of the Central and Eastern European countries to the EU was only effected after they had already been admitted to NATO. The Partnership for Peace Framework Document of 1994, in paragraph 6, committed the subscribing states to 'exchange information on the steps they have taken or which are being taken to promote transparency in defence planning and budgeting and to ensure the democratic control of armed forces'. So it was understood that security sector governance had not been an obstacle to NATO membership and – *a fortiori* – would not play a role in the EU negotiations. Another reason was that these negotiations were being conducted by the European Commission, which lacked specific military expertise (and was not given competence in these matters by the member states either). Their substance centred on the traditional *acquis* of European integration. Paradoxically, however, NATO had also done little in the field of SSR. At first, there had been reluctance on the part of the US and others to embark on this sensitive field, since it might detract from the need to build up credible military capabilities. Subsequently, the term SSR was resisted by France which did not see a political role for the Alliance in this area and preferred to see it dealt with by the EU. Nevertheless, the Partnership for Peace in its various activities and the subsequent Membership Action Plans covered much of what could be considered SSR, though they did not formally use the term.

Despite this general observation, the prospect of EU membership implied a series of very specific obligations with a bearing on the security sector. Fulfilling the requirements under the 'EU policy of freedom, security and justice', particularly in the areas of border controls, migration, asylum and visa policy, police cooperation and judicial cooperation in criminal and civil matters, was not only a matter of transposing the related EU *acquis* into national legislation in the process of accession negotiations under Chapter 24 (Justice and Home Affairs), but also required the candidate countries to demonstrate their capacity to implement successfully these measures in line with generally accepted EU standards and best practice.

Before the European Union was created by the Maastricht Treaty, the predecessor of the Common Foreign and Security Policy (CFSP) – European Political Cooperation – had already played an important role in the Helsinki process of the Conference (later the Organisation) for Security and Cooperation in Europe. In fact, the emphasis on the so-called 'third basket' of human rights was the result of a coordinated effort by the EPC member states. The Helsinki Final Act of 1975 had made the discussion of how a state treated its own nationals a legitimate subject of international intercourse. It could no longer be refused on the grounds of interference in internal affairs. A further important step was taken in December 1994 with the adoption of the 'Code of Conduct on politico-military aspects of security'. Its 42 paragraphs covered many subjects which still remain topical, such as the commitment not to support terrorist acts and the obligation to prosecute and extradite terrorists. An extensive section VII considered democratic political control of military, paramilitary and internal security forces as well as of intelligence services and the police to be an indispensable element of stability and security. Thus the Code provided an early definition of what was going to be called the security sector. It also stated in article 21 that the participating states would at all times provide and maintain effective guidance for control of these forces by constitutionally established authorities vested with democratic legitimacy. Subsequent articles dealt with legislative approval of defence expenditures, measures to guard against accidental or unauthorised use of military means, ensuring that the recruitment or call-up of personnel is consistent with obligations in respect of human rights and fundamental freedoms, the commitment to reflect in laws or other relevant documents the rights and duties of armed forces personnel, instruction of such personnel in humanitarian law and making them aware of their individual accountability under international law. Section VIII contained provisions that defence policy and doctrine should be consistent with international law, as well as the command and training of the armed forces. If recourse to force could not be avoided in internal security missions, it was deemed to be commensurate with the needs of enforcement and obliged to avoid injury to civilians or their property.

Reviewing the application of the Code of Conduct ten years later, Victor-Yves Ghebali criticised its lack of a global vision and general principles.[1] In particular, he referred to the absence of formal references to the judiciary branch, the lack of operative provisions on internal security, intelligence and police forces and the omission of the category of border guards. Similarly, there was no specification of the rights and duties of armed forces personnel, while the references to international humanitarian law obligations and the provisions on the domestic use of force were considered too weak. This led Ghebali in a subsequent publication to call for a comprehensive set of agreed norms, standards and procedures reflecting the inter-linkage between all of the institutional components of the security sector.[2]

Regrettably, member states did not attempt to remedy these shortcomings in an otherwise excellent document, which could be properly called the legacy of the Final Act. One area of which better use could be made was the questionnaire for reporting on national practices, which could be used for some careful 'naming and shaming' in objective reporting on the 'State of the OSCE'. The EU member states (in the context of CFSP) could take the lead and agree unilaterally on more substantial reporting. However, the Panel of Eminent Persons set up to make recommendations for the future tasks of the OSCE did not make any recommendations on SSR in its 2005 report. As a result, the OSCE, after its promising start with the Code of Conduct, did not manage to follow it up with a modern concept of SSR.

Linking Security and Development

A paradigm shift occurred with the growing acceptance of the link between security and development by the developed nations in the Organisation for Economic Cooperation and Development (OECD).

Through the angle of development, SSR obtained a prominent place and even became a 'mainstreamed' element of foreign policy, particularly in managing post-conflict situations. The OECD 'Development Assistance Committee Guidelines: Helping Prevent Violent Conflict' of 2001 recognised that security was increasingly viewed as an all-encompassing condition in which people and communities live in freedom, peace and safety, participate fully in the governance of their countries, enjoy the protection of fundamental rights, have access to resources and the basic necessities of life, and inhabit an environment which is not detrimental to their health and wellbeing. This understanding of security was seen as consistent with the other new concept, the notion of 'human security' – promoted by UNDP and development actors. It was given practical importance by the debate on which form of security-related assistance could be counted under the heading of Official Development Aid (ODA).

The Guidelines were followed up in 2005 by a 'Reference Document Security Sector Reform and Governance' containing a Policy Statement and an extensive analysis of the problem in general and its regional aspects in particular. The DAC agreed on ten recommendations for action in order to promote peace and security as fundamental pillars of development and poverty reduction. These stressed a 'whole of government' approach to SSR and the role OECD governments should play in addressing security related issues, such as: international corruption; money laundering; organised crime; perpetuation of militia-linked private security forces, including support from multinational enterprises; human trafficking; the proliferation of weapons of mass destruction; terrorism prevention; and illicit trade in small arms and light weapons.[3]

As might be expected from such a long list of issues, the DAC approach to the security sector went beyond the uniformed services and the civil authorities responsible for their oversight. It encompassed judicial and penal institutions and civil society, including human rights organisations and even the press. While such a wide scope could have compromised its effectiveness, the DAC managed to draft specific recommendations. As suggested by its title, the ultimate objective of the Reference Document was better governance. By broadening the focus of security policy from state stability and regime security to the wellbeing of populations and respect for human rights, the path was opened to mainstreaming security as a public policy and governance issue. The military were seen as only one of the instruments of security policy and greater attention was given to traditional legal, social and economic instruments.

The resulting principles were sufficiently concrete to apply to the uniformed services: under point 4 it was recommended that the security system should be managed according to the same principles of accountability and transparency that apply across the public sector, in particular through greater civil oversight of the security processes. Point 5 stated three core requirements of a well-functioning security system:

- Development of a nationally-owned concept of security;
- Strengthened governance of the security institutions responsible for formulating, executing, managing and monitoring security policy;
- Building institutional mechanisms for implementation and capacity

throughout the security system, including building civil control and supervision bodies in order to avoid an increase in the power and influence gap between military and civil bodies.

By its very nature, the Document was donor-oriented. This gave rise to the criticism that it was too limited, since it did not draw in the receiving countries which were supposed to fulfil its objectives. Yet, it was considerably more than a declaratory statement of desirable aims. It also contained examples of good practice among member countries. In the context of the present chapter, two of these merit specific mention. Much of the work carried out by the UK is undertaken through its Global Conflict Prevention Pool and the Africa Conflict Prevention Pool, enabling timely planning and rapid action. The pools contain components for both peacekeeping and aid programming. In the field of more effective and flexible funding, the Netherlands Stability Fund was mentioned. This aimed at an integrated approach to peace, security and development and allowed development money to be used for some specific aspects of a military operation. This was made possible by the OECD agreement to add six new themes to the list of activities which might be financed under Official Development Assistance: democratic control and management of security expenditure; strengthening the role of NGOs in the security field; support for legislation against recruiting child-soldiers; improving democratic governance in the security sector; non-military activities in peace-building, conflict prevention and conflict resolution; and finally, control, prevention and reduction of small arms/light weapons.

The development community did not welcome all the changes. For example, the creation of the African Peace Facility was criticised for spending more on short term peacekeeping than on preventive action and long-term capacity building.[4] But, the debate is set to continue, hopefully leading to the conclusion that all three core requirements of a well-functioning security system are necessary in the relations between security and development.

Towards an EU Concept of SSR

In 2003 High Representative Javier Solana took a major initiative in formulating a European Security Strategy as a conceptual underpinning of the increasing number of policy statements and other activities in the context of the Common Foreign and Security Policy.[5] The main points were the comprehensive listing of the main current challenges and threats, the emphasis on 'effective multilateralism' with the UN Charter as its fundamental framework, and the recognition that crises cannot be solved by military means alone. The Strategy concluded that 'security is the first condition for development' and contained a brief reference to SSR:

> As we increase capabilities in different areas, we should think in terms of a wider spectrum of missions. This might include joint disarmament operations, support for third countries in combating terrorism and security sector reform. The last of these would be part of broader institution building.

On 19 July 2005, after discussing a paper on the 'Initial elements for an EU Security Sector Reform Concept', the Political and Security Committee of the

EU tasked the Council General Secretariat, in close cooperation with the Commission, to draft an EU Concept for ESDP support to SSR. A draft appeared in October as a joint effort of four different support elements[6], which made clear at the outset that the Commission would develop, albeit again in close cooperation with the Council Secretariat, a separate EC concept for SSR covering first pillar activities. At a later stage consideration would be given to bringing the two strands together, but – not atypical for their mutual relations – this never happened. The ESDP document was adopted by the Council in November 2005, complementing existing concepts for missions in the field of Rule of Law and in Civilian Administration in crisis management.[7] It began with an expression of support for SSR in partner countries as one of the core areas for EU action identified in the European Security Strategy, contributing to:

> an accountable, effective and efficient security system, operating under civilian control consistent with democratic norms and principles of good governance, transparency and the rule of law, and acting according to international standards and respecting human rights, which can be a force for peace and stability, fostering democracy and promoting local and regional stability.

EU support would be based on respect for local ownership and coherence with other areas of EU external action. It would be defined in the political dialogue and in close consultation with the partner government, and adapted to the specific country situation. In the absence of a partner government in a crisis situation or in the immediate aftermath of a conflict, the early stages of EU support were to pave the way for long-term country-owned SSR reforms based on participatory and democratic processes. The paper distanced itself somewhat from the OECD/DAC guidelines by stating that an EU Concept for ESDP support to SSR should take due account of their key elements 'although they (the guidelines) do not reflect the specificities of the EU, nor those security aspects that fall under the ESDP'. Another reservation was made in relation to Disarmament, Demobilisation and Reintegration (DDR), which could constitute a significant pillar of SSR and was regarded as central to conflict resolution and internal stability. In such cases, SSR would call on DDR-type activities, but the point was made that SSR went well beyond DDR and should be considered as the primary concept. Therefore, DDR should be addressed separately, but consistently with this SSR concept, noting that the Commission was particularly active in the field of reintegration. A concept for DDR was put on the EU agenda during the second semester of 2006.

The EU definition of the security sector took the OECD/DAC Guidelines as a basis and included four main categories:

- *The core security actors*: armed forces, police, gendarmerie, paramilitary forces, presidential guards, intelligence and security services (both military and civilian), coast guards, border guards, customs authorities, reserve or local security units (civil defence forces, national guards, militias).
- *Security management and oversight bodies*: the Executive, national

security advisory bodies, legislature and legislative select committee; ministries of defence, internal affairs and foreign affairs; customary and traditional authorities, financial management bodies (finance ministry, budget office, financial audit and planning units) and civil society organisations (civilian review boards and public complaint commissions).
- *Justice and law enforcement institutions*: judiciary, justice ministry, prisons, criminal investigation and prosecution services, human rights commissions and ombudsmen; customary and traditional justice systems.
- *Non-statutory security forces, with whom donors rarely engage*: liberation armies, guerrilla armies, private bodyguard units, private security companies, political party militias.

Again, as with the DAC guidelines, the question arises as to the practical significance to be attached to such an extensive list, particularly in terms of the 'holistic' approach advocated in the Concept. Most of the institutions mentioned have a function in relatively mature states and can play a role only when stability has been restored to a considerable extent. More pertinent is the view that SSR can be a useful instrument to prevent conflict in fragile states, a core task in countries emerging from conflict and a central element of the broader institution-building and reform efforts in countries in a more stable environment. But the scope of its activities would of necessity be limited.

The Concept states first that in an immediate post-conflict situation the military are likely to be deeply involved in politics and in the whole security sector. Security would likely be ensured by an external military or police presence. Equally political authority might be exercised by an external actor for a limited period of time. This observation leads to the comment that it is questionable whether the word 'reform' is applicable to such a situation, which requires disarmament, demobilisation and subsequent reintegration of ex-combatants, before a return to a situation nearing normal conditions. The point is reinforced by the admission later in the document that ESDP action in support of SSR can be implemented only where a basic degree of security and order (possibly ensured by an international military or police presence) exists in the state concerned. It is true that these measures may be part of an exit strategy for a more complex crisis management operation, but, again, the word 'reform' seems hardly appropriate, and an exit strategy without follow-up of the initial entry seems doubtful.

The Concept continues, secondly, that in a transition and stabilisation phase, local political authorities would likely be in place, at least until elections have taken place or other permanent arrangements effected. ESDP actions would then be undertaken in a more stable environment and in the spirit of prevention of a return to violence. Support for SSR could become a mission of its own and local ownership could be expected to a larger degree than in an immediate post-conflict situation.

Thirdly, in an environment that is assessed as stable and where no return to significant conflict is to be expected, support for SSR could assist the ongoing development of democratic institutions, but should be tied in closely with other governance reforms conducted by the state concerned.

The Concept lists an extensive range of measures in support of reforming the defence sector and the police and of strengthening justice and the rule of law. The legal basis for an EU action should either be a resolution of the UN Security Council or an invitation by a host partner state or International/Regional/Sub-regional organisation. Such action might be initiated by an EU member state or the Commission and would, as a general rule, take the form of a Joint Action under article 14 of the Treaty on European Union, and be set up under the control of the Political and Security Committee. A general concept describing the management of a specific EU action should be developed defining its desired end state and benchmarks and include an evaluation mechanism based on these objectives.

The Concept certainly has its merits, but like many EU documents it suffers from its undue length and statements of the obvious. Its main weakness seems to be the lack of linkage between the various sectors and measures. As outlined later in this chapter, the EU finds it difficult to identify a chain of measures and events that lead to the desired outcome of reform.

The Views of the European Commission

The European Commission sent a Communication to the Council and the European Parliament containing 'A Concept for European Community Support for Security Sector Reform' on 24 May 2006.[8] It was accompanied by a Commission Staff Working Document containing annexes on EC policy frameworks relevant to support in the area of SSR, areas of European Community support to SSR, the European Commission programming cycle, and examples of international standards relevant for support in the area of SSR.[9]

Although the Commission also took the OECD/DAC definition as its basis, its detailed description of SSR was somewhat different from the ESDP document described above. In the first place the Commission preferred the term 'security system'. This underlined that reform went beyond the notion of effectiveness of individual services and should be seen as part of governance reform policy and public sector strategy. Secondly, it defined the security system as all state institutions and other entities with a role in ensuring the security of the state and its institutions. In the category 'security management and oversight bodies' it changed the ESDP order and put parliament first, reverting to the OECD list by adding 'media, academia and NGOs' as elements of civil society. It deleted the civilian review boards and public complaint commissions, presumably because these would belong to the ombudsman and other functions listed under the Justice institutions. Under non-statutory forces no reference was made to political party militias, but the list was not exhaustive.

The Commission summed up the challenges faced by EU partner countries, which hampered common efforts to achieve sustainable development. It was an impressive list: oversized and underpaid regular forces, irregular forces and security firms operating outside the law, lack of judicial independence, status and resources, lack of capacity, legal competence and sometimes political will by parliaments to ensure accountability of security services, human rights abuses by police and defence forces, a culture of state impunity and inability to protect the population against terrorist acts. In helping to meet these challenges the European Community (EC) was engaged in over 70 countries through both geographical and thematic programmes. Crucial for successful reform was 'taking into account the close interlinkages between security, development and governance, including democratic principles, rule of law, human rights and institutional capacity building'. To do so the EC had a vast array of instruments, which formed part of its regular external assistance and the EU political dialogue. The Commission emphasised that the Community needed to focus more clearly on the governance aspects of SSR, including the strengthening of parliamentary oversight, judicial independence and media freedom, and take a more holistic approach by engaging in coordinated support for the different sectors of the SSR process. It advocated more short to medium-term engagement to kick-start and complement long-term instruments.

Among the policy recommendations of the Commission the following deserve specific mention:

- Strengthening policy and programming dialogue by including international standards on SSR;
- Integrating SSR in Country and Regional Strategy papers, Action Plans and programming tools;
- Considering joint missions with the Council Secretariat and/or Member States to further coordinated assessment and planning;
- Expanding the expertise and pool of experts for field missions and programmes;
- Developing SSR specific training for the mainstreaming of security system reform.

The Commission Staff Working Document drew attention to the fact that the Rapid Reaction Mechanism (RRM) set up in 2001 to enhance European ability to intervene quickly and effectively in crisis or potential crisis situations would be replaced in 2007 by the Stability Instrument. Its short-term funding would enable the EC to act rapidly and more flexibly with support for the early stages of the reform process.

The Commission Communication was introduced in the advisory CivCom and the Pol-Mil groups and subsequently in the Political and Security Committee, but it was hardly discussed, since it was only a Commission Communication. Nevertheless, the EU Council of Development Ministers on 12 June 2006 welcomed the Communication, which together with the CFSP concept would constitute a policy framework for an EU role in SSR. The Council stressed the importance of a cross-pillar approach to this long term process. A specific point concerned the norms for accountability and transparency, which should be the same as for the entire public sector. During the Finnish Presidency in the second semester of 2006 an EU approach to disarmament, demobilisation and reintegration (DDR) was elaborated, together with the Commission. No attempt was made to integrate the two SSR documents. This did not contribute to an image of effective coordination. Yet, in the field there was less competition, as the joint Council Secretariat – Commission assessment teams to Kinshasa and Afghanistan demonstrated in the autumn of 2006. The envisaged

Commission contribution of 10 million euros to the civilian work of the Provincial Reconstruction Teams in Afghanistan would be a major step, also for the improvement of EU-NATO cooperation.

EU Missions in the Field

Looking at the missions performed first by the Western European Union and later the European Union, non-military missions constituted a majority. The first time European nations took responsibility outside their own continent was the mine-clearing operation coordinated by the WEU in 1987-8 during the Iran-Iraq war. It was not directed against anyone, bar the mines which were threatening international passage in the Gulf and the Red Sea as well as the supply of oil. For a while, WEU had an advantage over NATO, which was limited by the debate about whether it could go 'out-of-area'. That issue was settled in 1995 when the German constitutional court in Karlsruhe agreed that the concept of out-of-area missions did not infringe the German Constitution. Until then Germany could not contribute military units. It did, however, circumvent the problem by contributing police, border-guards and customs officers to a number of operations. In fact, the WEU task of 'elaborating and implementing decisions having defence implications', in practice was more often police-oriented than military.

In the Kuwait crisis of 1990 the WEU played a military role. It took a major part in enforcing the UN naval embargo against Iraq, as it later did from 1992 with a flotilla in the Adriatic blockading the coasts of former Yugoslavia, first in parallel with NATO and later in a joint operation. The following embargo on shipping on the Danube was enforced by police and customs officers. In 1994 the WEU provided the police contingent to the EU administrator of the Bosnian district of Mostar. When in 1997 Albania was ravaged by the upheaval following the collapse of the 'pyramid' scheme, the WEU sent a Military Assistance Police Mission (MAPE) to help stabilise the situation. Between 1999 and 2001, at the request of the EU, the WEU Demining Assistance Mission (WEUDAM) supported the Croatian Mine Action Centre in clearing anti-personnel mines.

On 13 November 1999 the WEU Ministerial Council, meeting in Marseilles, transferred its crisis management functions to the European Union, but for a while NATO remained in the lead on the Balkans after it had initiated air operations against the Milosevic regime. The Essential Harvest arms collection operation from Albanian fighters in Macedonia, and the subsequent operation Amber Fox for protecting election monitors there, were conducted by NATO. In March 2002 the European Council in Barcelona announced its willingness to take over NATO's operations in Macedonia. At the same time the first-ever EU operation was launched, as the EU took over the tasks of UN International Police Task Force in Bosnia. The Macedonia Operation Concordia, consisting of 350 lightly armed personnel, was launched on 31 March 2003, first for six months but later extended until 15 December 2003, when it was succeeded by a 200-strong police mission under the name of Proxima, aiming to help develop domestic police forces.

The first substantial EU military operation took place in the Democratic Republic of Congo, when violence escalated around Bunia, capital of the Ituri province. The UN was not able to mount a peacekeeping operation quickly enough and the EU started operation Artemis, involving 1800 personnel with France as the lead nation on 12 June 2003. It lasted until 1 September when full responsibility was handed back to the UN with its Mission in the Congo (MONUC). In December the EU decided to continue its activities in the form of a police mission, EUPOL Kinshasa, and later added an advisory mission, EUSEC, to assist the government in determining the size of the Congolese armed forces and improving their chain of payment. EUSEC managed to reduce the size of the army from an alleged 350,000 to 150,000 at first and later to 90,000, thus combating gigantic fraud in the payment of salaries by eliminating a host of 'ghost soldiers'. No wonder it took the eight officials of the mission five months of its one year mandate to overcome opposition from corrupt officers. During the two rounds of the presidential elections of 2006, EUPOL made a significant contribution to maintaining law and order and extended its mandate until 30 November. Operation Artemis was an important precursor of the EU's battle-group concept, envisaging permanent availability of two EU battle-groups each with some 1500 personnel with fighting capability to be ready within a week.

The largest EU military operation so far has been Althea, with 7000 personnel in Bosnia. NATO decided at the Istanbul Summit of June 2004 to terminate SFOR and transfer it to the EU under the so-called Berlin Plus arrangements, which provide for an EU-led operation using NATO assets and a role for Deputy SACEUR – always a European general – in the military chain of command. European defence ministers decided to maintain its troop level during 2006. The assessment of the first year of EUFOR Althea was positive. Major General David Leakey, its first commander, had instructions 'to be new and distinct and make a difference'. Through combining the military and civil operations the EU achieved a collective and politically significant impact in Bosnia, especially by promotion of the EU 'brand' in the public's perception. Yet, Leakey wrote that ministers need to be clear on what they expect the military to undertake, the military needs to be flexible and the requirements for adaptation of their conventional military skills and capabilities to new and unorthodox tasks: 'a military force cannot stand apart and aloof from the main challenges to the rule of law facing the society to which it is deployed. Otherwise it risks irrelevance and erosion of its credibility'.[10]

In addition to the military and police missions, the EU embarked on a number of civilian missions to strengthen good governance and the rule of law. On 16 July EUJUST THEMIS was launched for Georgia, consisting of 10 civilian legal experts from different member countries attached to various departments connected with justice and home affairs ministries in order to address urgent challenges in the criminal justice system and to assist in developing a coordinated approach to the reform process. Somewhat similar was the EUJUST LEX Rule of Law Mission to Iraq, agreed on 21 February 2005 and operational by 1 July, to train some 770 judges, investigating magistrates, senior police and penitentiary officers at a cost of €10 million over a period of one year.

An unexpected task arose in the wake of the tsunami that wrought havoc in the Aceh province of Indonesia. The longstanding battle between the government and the Free Aceh Movement (GAM) ended with a memorandum of understanding signed on 15 August 2005, the anniversary of Indonesia's declaration of independence. The EU responded quickly with a Joint Action decided on 9 September to deploy the Aceh Monitoring Mission (AMM) together with Norway, Switzerland and countries from ASEAN. AMM become operational on 15 September, the date agreed for the beginning of the decommissioning of GAM armaments and the relocation of 'non-organic' Indonesian and police forces. The first phase of both programmes was completed on 27 September, so that the agreed 'allocations' to former GAM combatants could start on 12 October. The operation was an outstanding success through its speedy action in seizing a window of opportunity for monitoring a fragile agreement and doing so effectively on the ground.

In 2005 the EU also became active in Palestine, but more carefully. As of 4 January police experts headed by a British chief superintendent were deployed in the area, but not as an EU unit. On 20 April an exchange of letters between Ahmed Qurei, the Palestinian Prime Minister, and EU Special Representative Marc Otte, established the EU Coordinating Office for Palestinian Police Support housing four officers in the interior ministry in Ramallah and a satellite office in Gaza City. They produced a three-year development programme consisting of transformational and operational plans and providing a 'blueprint for building a modern, democratic and accountable police service and as a framework for donor assistance'.

Politically more spectacular was the involvement of the EU in the opening of the border between Egypt and Gaza at Rafah after the Israeli withdrawal from the strip. Israel had wanted to keep control of the external border, but accepted a European intermediary role after the intervention of US Secretary of State Condoleezza Rice. The agreement, which took effect on 25 November 2005, allowed Israeli access by means of television monitors, though the actual monitoring of the security forces of the Palestinian Authority on the border was undertaken by a 60-strong EU police force.

In the 'frozen conflict' of Transnistria several Chairmen-in Office of the OSCE had tried their hand at a solution, but to no avail. A new opportunity arose after the Orange revolution in Ukraine, when its authorities sought to strengthen border controls to stop smuggling. At the joint request of the presidents of Moldova and Ukraine the EU agreed to the Border Assistance Mission (BAM) providing 50 border guards plus 19 staff from 1 December 2005 for a period of two years to monitor the entire border between them, including the Ukrainian border with Transnistria. The guards had the right to make unannounced visits, open containers and visit offices where border formalities were being conducted. The agreement was concluded outside the OSCE and the negotiating mechanism, which includes Moldova, Russia and Ukraine with the EU and US as observers. Equally, it did not affect the presence of the 1200 peacekeepers in a zone of 10 kilometres on both sides of the Moldovan-Transnistrian border, one-third of whom are Russians.

If these EU missions could be put into categories, the following might apply:[11]

- Supporting EU objectives: ARTEMIS in the Congo, EUJUST LEX in Iraq and the Rafah Border Assistance Mission (BAM) between Gaza and Egypt.
- Supporting the transatlantic relationship: CONCORDIA and ALTHEA, the two Balkan operations with a military-civilian flavour.

- Supporting regional organisations: AMIS II in Sudan for the African Union, the Aceh Monitoring Mission for ASEAN and the Moldova/Ukraine BAM for OSCE objectives.
- Supporting good governance with EUJUST, THEMIS in Georgia and EUSEC in the Congo.

Another characteristic of several of the missions was their rapid response with very little preparation. This was particularly the case with ARTEMIS (which depended heavily on France as the lead nation and so far is the only truly autonomous European military mission) and the much smaller Aceh Monitoring Mission. In itself, this was a compliment to the ability and flexibility of the Brussels mechanisms. Whether it would have been achievable for a larger mission is a moot point.

Major General Messervy-Whiting, the first Chief of Staff of the EU Military Staff, concluded that for the European Union the name of the game had become conflict prevention, peace implementation, stabilisation and strengthening the ability of fragile democracies to adopt best practices, all on a case by case and solid legal basis, worldwide. 'The EU is in the business of steady, piece by piece construction, sometimes moving slowly but on occasion quite rapidly – but still striving for evolution rather than revolution'.[12]

With ARTEMIS as an example, the EU developed the battle-group concept: some 1500 men available within 5-10 days and consisting of forces of up to four member states. Some groups would be made up of units of a single nation. Thereby, multi-nationality was diminished, but fighting capability increased. Almost all EU member states were prepared to contribute to a system of rotation, which by the beginning of 2007 would result in two battle-groups being permanently available for rapid deployment.[13] These units of limited size reduced the power differential between the larger and the smaller members. For an EU or UN operation a battalion-sized contribution was already quite substantial, but for an autonomous EU operation an entry force of two battle-groups would be rather small and certainly unsuitable for actual war combat. Only the NATO Response Force envisaged some brigade-sized national units. Nevertheless, most countries struggled with the expeditionary character of their contributions. Only a few, like France and the UK, had historical experience with this task, but most were used to stationary defence forces in their own country, or close to home.

How to Assess Urgency and Success

A survey of success and failure of military operations for humanitarian purposes in the 1990s, somewhat paradoxically, has shown that, despite the fact that they were all at the bottom of the hierarchy of power application, success was greatest in the easier missions (delivery of aid) and the hardest (defeating the perpetrators). The intermediate missions (protecting aid operations and saving the victims) had a high degree of failure.[14] In various ways the EU operations discussed above all contributed to restoring stability in an environment of fragile or failed states and to preventing post-conflict situations from relapsing into violence. But, in order to judge adequately the efficiency of their integrated approach and to formulate criteria for ultimate success, the development of assessment frameworks for the urgency and utility of envisaged operations was necessary. Likewise criteria were needed for designing integrated approaches to security, governance and development and, more specifically, for enhancing democratic governance.

The first framework – the rationale for commencing an operation – basically boils down to the following questions: how serious is the crisis in political and humanitarian terms; is there public support in the country about to intervene; what are the chances of success of a military-civilian operation; and which countries are prepared to participate in its conduct or financing. A more detailed check-list could include the availability of a clear mandate and rules of engagement, the associated risk of large scale casualties, the probable duration of the commitment, the availability of successors in a process of rotation, and the credibility of an exit strategy.[15] One of the lessons learned in recent peace support operations is the increased problem of national limitations put on the use of the forces they have contributed. Constraint management has become a major headache for multinational force commanders, severely limiting the flexibility of their operations. The willingness of countries to contribute to an operation, both in terms of personnel and money, has been much greater in humanitarian relief operations than for concrete efforts in crisis management. And if there was preparedness to join the mission, again it was easier to obtain non-combat support than fighting soldiers. Both NATO and the EU have a financing problem, particularly since the same countries – those with expeditionary capabilities – are always called upon. The EU has the Athena instrument for financing common costs, but in NATO every nation pays its own way. 'Costs lie where they fall' is a euphemism for 'going Dutch'.

The second framework, a Stability Assessment Framework, is a tool for analysing stability in a particular country and for developing strategic planning that assists in developing institutional capacities. The Netherlands Institute for International Relations in Clingendael has developed twelve indicators usable in a concrete situation.[16] The first four relate to governance:

1. The legitimacy of the State, representing the people as a whole.
2. Is public service delivery progressively deteriorating or improving?
3. Is a basic rule of law established, arbitrarily applied or suspended, and are human rights violations easing?
4. Leadership – are elites factionalised or do they have national perspectives; are leaders capable of winning loyalties across ethnic, tribal or religious lines?

Then two security indicators:

5. Does the security apparatus operate as a 'state within the state', or as a professional military, answerable to legitimate civilian control?
6. The regional setting. Are destabilising regional cross-border interventions increasing or decreasing?

And six socio-economic development indicators:

7. Are demographic pressures mounting or easing?
8. The presence of refugees and internally displaced persons.

9. The existence of group-based hostilities and a legacy of vengeance-seeking.
10. Emigration and human flight.
11. Are economic opportunities organised along group lines?
12. The state of the economy.

The Clingendael framework groups these indicators into a rating sheet, which makes it possible to draw an aggregated trend line, which in turn might prove helpful in identifying potential trigger events and hazard zones. It then takes a further step by mapping and analyzing the institutional capacity of the military, the police and corrections system, judiciary, civil service, and parliament. Dividing the analysis into categories of effectiveness and legitimacy, important questions are suggested as sample guidance. Those related to the effectiveness of the military include:

- Does the military have the necessary expertise to fulfil its functions effectively?
- Do they guarantee internal stability and order?
- Do monitoring and evaluation of performance occur?
- If performance is poor, are the problems addressed?
- Is the role of the military based on a wide ranging assessment of the country's internal and external security environment?

Guidance questions to assess legitimacy are:

- Does the military accept both the democratic political process and the need for accountability to civil authorities?
- To what extent is the military considered to operate autonomously, operating independently of factions in society?
- Does the military respect human rights?
- Are formal policies and plans guiding the defence sector?
- Does the military seek undue influence over policy development?

The aim of these frameworks is to arrive at a reference document per country as a basis for judging progress and effectiveness. As such these documents could be an important instrument for underpinning public policy, particularly when the assessments are shared in a multinational context like the CFSP.

Concluding Remarks

Security sector reform has become a mainstreamed element of development policy and thereby of foreign policy. As with most mainstreamed policies, it has become broad, maybe even too broad. Through its broadness it allows people to say that it is merely what they have already been doing for a long time, but under a new name. That is why this chapter has included a description of policy assessment frameworks, for the momentum of reform can be maintained only if it is seen to be effective and to lead to more stability and better development. Concepts, frameworks and strategies are fine, but in the end only results matter. Common assessments need to be applied to concrete policies, including elements of conditionality to the use of the spectrum of instruments available to the EU. The great advantage of these joint assessments will be their objectivity and their availability as the basis for a policy dialogue with the countries concerned. This will also be pertinent to the ESDP, for the objectives of civil-military operations will need to be made more specific than the general aims of stability and good governance. They have to be translated into daily working practices, both in Brussels and in the field.

Governments will have to do better in defining the desired outcome of an operation and the efforts needed to achieve it. Lessons for future EU action can be learned from the crises in Iraq and Afghanistan. Long term success needs to be predicated on quick impact statements, because local populations are likely to be disheartened if conditions do not improve rapidly. And the best way to obtain 'local ownership' is to transfer financial means and authority as quickly as possible to local authorities.[17]

Major problems of coordination are encountered on the spot, not only among the official institutions, internal and external, but also with the dozens and sometimes hundreds of non-governmental agencies. Post conflict reconstruction is broader than SSR, and in places like the Congo there is no chance for either unless large scale demobilisation has been achieved. Part of the problem is the impossibility of a clear demarcation of responsibilities. In the UN the Department of Peace Keeping Operations (DPKO) does not deal with SSR, because it is not hard core peacekeeping. UNDP has its Bureau for Crisis Prevention and Reconstruction (BCPR), but that also deals with natural catastrophes such as the tsunami disaster. Yet, the UNDP's unit for the rule of law and transitional justice is very relevant, because the initial successes of police reform are often hampered by an inadequate judiciary and a lack of prisons. If the aim is a 'whole of government approach', the whole chain of events needs to be taken into consideration.

The military, after their initial task of restoring order, can do a great deal in winning public confidence by restoring infrastructure or building schools. Some resent this as 'mission creep', but the effort is worth many patrols. The major contribution by the Dutch contingent in Iraq in relaunching a damaged cement factory, thus creating jobs for many unemployed and building material at the same time, is a case in point.

Within the EU the bizarre situation continues of a High Representative with responsibilities but no money, and a Commissioner for External Relations with access to the EU budget but competence limited to civilian crisis management, both with bureaucracies keen to guard autonomy and thus seemingly reticent to envisage enhanced collaboration. As a result the ESDP approach is more military and the Commission's more development oriented. A Minister for Foreign Affairs, envisaged by the stalled Constitutional Treaty, could have remedied this artificial separation between military and civilian crisis management, itself largely due to the refusal of France and the UK to recognise the competence of the European Commission and the European Parliament in CFSP matters.

Following the UN example, High Representative Solana has increasingly made use of Special Representatives, thus avoiding micro-management from Brussels. However, their work has mainly been directed to political mediation during and after the conflict phase. The advisory and training activities of SSR have often been left to NGOs, some of which had little inclination to be coordinated by anybody. Yet, the impact of SSR on society depends on myriads of personal contacts, individual persuasion and awareness of cultural specificity.

A crucial question remains: where should the emphasis of EU action be – on the conflict phase or on post-conflict stabilisation? ARTEMIS was a short term military operation, restoring order before the UN was ready to take over, thus saving the credibility of the following MONUC operation. ALTHEA in Bosnia is the continuation of a long term presence in order to maintain stability. So far, ESDP deployments have been largely demand driven, but in future they would be arguably more effective if inserted into a strategic framework. The development angle will, of its nature, focus on peace building and human rights. Development funds are likely to be spent on countries which have mastered their conflict. ESDP is more concerned with immediate operational efforts to restore a minimum of law and order. Both admit that in many cases a relapse into violence has occurred. A peace agreement in the Congo has led to new chaos because of inadequate arrangements for its implementation. In Bolivia the army and police did not cooperate in avoiding civil war. The causes of conflict do not disappear easily, so the problem remains of which action is most appropriate given the nature of each situation: crisis, post-conflict, or more advanced stability. The EU has the enormous advantage over other international organisations of possessing a wide spectrum of instruments, which, if properly coordinated, could make the difference in a crisis. The willingness to envisage joint action between the ministries of foreign affairs, development assistance and defence is a major step forward.

Endnotes

1 Victor-Yves Ghebali and Alexander Lambert, *The OSCE Code of Conduct on Politico-Military Aspects of Security. Anatomy and Implementation*, The Graduate Institute of International Studies, Geneva, Vol. 5. Martinus Nijhoff Publishers, Leiden/Boston, 2005.

2 Ghebali presented a draft of 'Preliminary elements for an integrated OSCE concept for security sector reform and governance' in a Food for Thought Paper for a DCAF seminar in July 2006. See also his DCAF Policy Paper No. 10 of November 2005, 'The OSCE between Crisis and Reform: Towards a New Lease of Life'.

3 Another follow-up was the decision of the OECD/DAC High-Level Meeting of Development Ministers and Heads of Agencies (HLM) of 3 March 2005 which agreed that the principles drafted by the Fragile States Group on 'good international engagement in fragile states', by both development and security stakeholders, should be piloted in 9 fragile states until the end of 2006 and be considered for adoption by the HLM in 2007.

4 Damien Helly, 'Assessing the Impact of the European Union as an International Actor', in *Securing Europe? Implementing the European Security Strategy*, Ed. Anne Deighton with Victor Mauer. Zürcher Beiträge zur Sicherheitspolitik, Nr 77, 2006, p. 86.

5 Adopted by the European Council in Brussels on 12 December 2003 under the title *A Secure Europe in a Better World*. It might be argued that the document was more of a pre-strategic concept, because it did not give precise guidance for force planning. Nevertheless, it was a remarkable attempt to formulate current threats in a way compatible with US and NATO strategy, while insisting on European views for tackling them. See also my *From Words to Deeds. The Continuing Debate on European Security*. CEPS Brussels, 2006, pp. 181-198.

6 Doc 12566/4/05 REV 4, COSDP 613, PESC 784, produced by the EUMS/CIVMIL CELL/DG E VIII/DG E IX.

7 *Comprehensive EU Concept for Missions in the Field of Rule of Law in Crisis Management*

(Council doc. 9792/03 of 26 May 2003) and *EU Concept for Crisis Management Missions in the Field of Civilian Administration* (Council doc. 15311/03 of 25 November 2003).

8 COM (2006) 253 final. SEC (2006) 658.

9 SEC(2006) 658 of 25.5.2006.

10 'ESDP and Civil/Military Cooperation: Bosnia and Herzegovina, 2005', in *Securing Europe?* Op. cit. in note 4, p.67.

11 *Ibid.*, p.38 in the contribution of Major General Graham Messervy-Whiting, 'ESDP Deployments and the European Security Strategy'.

12 *Ibid.* p. 40.

13 The EU started in 1999 with the Helsinki Headline Goals, aiming at 50-60,000 men available within 60 days and sustainable for a year, and a police component of 5,000 men. NATO followed suit with the NATO Response Force, smaller (first 20,000, now 25,000 personnel) available within two weeks as a three service fighting force with the capability of an 'insertion force'. There was an element of competition in this leap-frogging, but both NRF and Battlegroups aimed at rapidly available combat capabilities. So far, neither has been deployed, except for the earthquake assistance in Pakistan in a NRF mode.

14 Taylor B. Seybolt, *Humanitarian Military Intervention. The conditions of success and failure.* SIPRI, 2007, p. 272.

15 For the Netherlands decisional framework see W. van Eekelen *Debating European Security 1948 – 1998*, CEPS Brussels 1998, p. 293.

16 *The Stability Assessment framework: Designing Integrated Responses for Security, Governance and Development*. Prepared by the Clingendael Institute for the Netherlands Ministry of Foreign affairs, 2005. A similar study was prepared earlier (2003) on *Enhancing Democratic Governance of the Security Sector: An Institutional Assessment Framework*. These frameworks for external actors are a useful complement to the guidance for internal parliamentary action and questions contained in the DCAF/IPU *Handbook for Parliamentarians No.5 (2003) Parliamentary oversight of the security sector. Principles, mechanisms and practices.*

17 See for a fuller treatment Willem van Eekelen, *From Words to Deeds, the continuing debate on European Security*. CEPS/DCAF Brussels/Geneva, 2006, which made use of Rupert Smith, *The utility of force, the art of war in the modern world*. Allen lane, London, 2005, and Marc Houben, *International Crisis Management: the approach of European states*, Routledge, Abingdon, 2005.

6. Justice and Home Affairs: Security Sector Reform Measures as Instruments of EU Internal Security Objectives

Jörg Monar

Introduction

The term 'justice and home affairs' (JHA), which has firmly entered EU jargon, requires some initial clarification with regard to security sector reform (SSR) as the subject of this book. The term is used in the EU context to denote a range of policy-making areas falling within the remit of the ministries of interior and justice, based on Title IV of the Treaty establishing the European Community (TEC) and Title VI of the Treaty on European Union (TEU): asylum, immigration, border controls, judicial cooperation in civil matters, forming part of the so-called first (EC) pillar, and judicial cooperation in criminal matters and police cooperation, forming part of the third (EU) pillar. Since the entry into force of the Treaty of Amsterdam in 1999 these areas have been brought together under the fundamental treaty objective laid down in Article 2 TEU of establishing and maintaining the EU as an 'area of freedom, security and justice' (AFSJ). The term JHA is actually no longer used in the Treaties, but the EU Council grouping the ministers of justice and of the interior still meets under the label of the 'JHA Council' and the term continues to be used in many official documents.

The six JHA areas indicated above may look like a bit of a motley collection of areas and issues. At first sight there is, for instance, no obvious link between judicial cooperation in civil matters and border controls, or asylum policy and judicial cooperation in criminal matters. Yet apart from all these areas being within the remit of the ministries of justice and interior they have another element in common which is that all of them are a response to the opening-up of borders between the member states, be it through the abolition of controls on persons at internal borders in the Schengen context or in the broader economic context of the completion of the Internal Market. The 'vanishing' internal borders have reduced the effectiveness of purely national management instruments on issues such as asylum and the fight against serious crime and have thereby forced the member states to compensate for this by enhanced cross-border cooperation and common measures. The original rationale of the AFSJ is therefore in every respect an 'internal' one, and the treaty provisions indeed make no reference at all to any specific 'external' objective of the AFSJ, let alone a contribution to SSR in third countries.

Yet there has been a growing 'externalisation' of JHA objectives since the end of the 1990s as the EU has tried to complement or better achieve certain of the 'internal' AFSJ objectives through 'external' action. A major driving force of this ongoing externalisation have been the internal security interests of the EU which – enhanced by the post-9/11 terrorist threat and the 'securitisation' of illegal immigration challenges – have come to dominate the entire AFSJ project. By developing new or enhanced forms of cooperation with third-countries and by encouraging and supporting JHA capacity building abroad, the Union has *de facto* developed a growing role in SSR as far as the JHA domain is concerned.

In this chapter we will first look at the EU's internal security concept in the context of the AFSJ and its 'external dimension', which is important for understanding both the potential and the limits of JHA-related EU action in the SSR domain. We will then analyse the main objectives and instruments of external action with SSR relevance in the context of the AFSJ, starting with the specific context of the EU enlargement of the AFSJ and continuing with the main issues and regional priorities of JHA-related SSR as they can thus far be ascertained in the 'neighbourhood' and 'global' dimensions of EU external action in the JHA domain. This will lead to some general conclusions about the performance, potential and problems of the EU as a protagonist of SSR in the JHA domain.

The Security Concept of the AFSJ: The Primacy of Internal Objectives

Of all the EU policy-making domains, the AFSJ has the peculiarity that its label comprises no less than three fundamental public goods: 'freedom', 'security' and 'justice'. Of these three 'security' probably has the most concrete meaning and corresponds best to the 'normal' understanding of the term from a public policy perspective. The Treaties are helpful in this respect as they clearly spell out that providing internal security to EU citizens is a central objective of the AFSJ project: Article 29 TEU establishes it as the Union's objective for the remaining 'third pillar' JHA fields to provide citizens with 'a high level of safety' within the AFSJ, and Article 61(e) TEC provides for measures in these fields to be 'aimed at a high level of security'. That this objective of enhanced security for citizens is primarily understood in a law enforcement sense is not only made clear by the law enforcement aspects, which are explicitly linked in the Treaties to the two articles but also by the main programme documents of the AFSJ. Thus, the Tampere European Council Conclusions of October 1999 already stated that 'the high level of safety in the area of freedom, security and justice presupposes an efficient and comprehensive approach in the fight against all forms of crime', that 'people have the right to expect the Union to address the threat to their freedom and legal rights posed by serious crime', and that the 'the joint mobilisation of police and judicial resources' is necessary as a consequence.[1]

While the fight against serious crime – in particular organised crime and terrorism – is central to this internal security concept, over the last few years it has been gradually widened by the member states to include the fight against illegal immigration, and this as a priority area. Referring to the 'new urgency' of the security of the EU and its member states, the current 2004 to 2010 multi-annual programme for the development of the AFSJ, the Hague Programme, actually lists illegal migration as the first of a number of cross-border problems which require a joint response, even before terrorism and organised crime.[2] This 'securitisation' of illegal immigration has been much analysed and criticised.[3] Yet it must be seen as part of the response of member state governments to the political radicalisation and racism high illegal immigration levels can generate, the growing involvement of organised crime in the lucrative trade of bringing people over the external borders, and the exploitation and crime potential of immigrants without work or residence permits.

With its current focus on the fight against crime and illegal immigration, the internal security concept of the AFSJ does not differ much from that of national systems. However, there is one important difference in that in the security domain the EU is regarded only as a provider of 'added value' with respect to action taken at the national level, its role being considered only supplementary to the internal security function of the member states which remains primary. The Vienna Action Plan of December 1998 – the first of the multi-annual programme documents for the AFSJ – explicitly stated that the aim was not to create a 'European security area' with uniform detection and investigation procedures and that the responsibilities of member states to maintain law and order and safeguard internal security should in no way be affected by the AFSJ[4], as this is also provided for by Article 33 TEU. Although no specific reference is made in Titles IV TEC and VI TEU to subsidiarity, this principle lies very much at the core of the AFSJ *security* concept in the sense that the EU should only address internal security issues which – because of their cross-border nature – can potentially be handled more effectively through common action at EU level. In practice this has meant that forms of crime with no cross-border dimension – such as youth crime or burglaries – have so far remained almost totally outside the scope of EU action, which has focused primarily on serious cross-border crime, such as transnational organised crime and terrorism and the fight against illegal immigration. The EU therefore has no comprehensive internal security mandate in the JHA domain: it can only act if there is a clear cross-border dimension and if its action is expected to provide an 'added' level of security which national action alone cannot achieve.

The internal security concept of the AFSJ has implications for the potential and the limits of EU action aimed at SSR in third-countries. The primary objective being to provide European citizens with an enhanced level of security within the EU, contributions to SSR abroad on the basis of competences and instruments relating to JHA policies in the context of the AFSJ are necessarily strongly determined by the EU's current internal security objectives, the fight against serious cross-border crime and illegal immigration. In that sense SSR measures – from an EU JHA policies perspective – are essentially instruments of AFSJ objectives and not aimed at the transformation of third-countries for foreign or development policy objectives. This may appear as a major restriction on the SSR potential of the EU JHA policy-making domain. Yet if one looks at the growing external dimension of the AFSJ it becomes clear that the SSR potential is actually quite significant.

The External Dimension of the AFSJ and its SSR Potential

Although focused on internal security problems, the AFSJ security concept also has an external dimension. Already in the second half of the 1990s the member states recognised that internal JHA measures would need to be complemented by external policies in order to be fully effective. This recognition led, *inter alia*, to the introduction in the Treaty of Amsterdam of treaty-making powers regarding external aspects of the AFSJ, both in the 'first' and 'third pillar' fields.[5] Yet, in spite of increasing JHA-related external action (to which we return below) it took the Union until 2005 to develop an overall approach in this respect. On the basis of the enhanced external action provided for by the 2004 Hague Programme, a mandate from the European Council of June 2005 and a Commission Communication of October 2005[6], the Council adopted in December 2005 a Strategy for the External Dimension of JHA: Global Freedom, Security and Justice.[7] This document starts with the programmatic statement that in order to respond to the 'security threats of terrorism, organised crime, corruption and drugs and to the challenge of managing migration flows' the EU can only be effective if it works with third-countries, which means 'to make JHA a central priority in its external relations and ensure a co-ordinated and coherent approach'.[8] As regards the objectives and the form of such 'work' with third-countries, the Strategy could have been limited to traditional forms of international cooperation in the JHA domain with primarily operational objectives such as information exchange and judicial assistance. Yet the Strategy goes distinctly beyond those, and it is there that the SSR potential of the JHA domain comes to the forefront.

While traditional cooperation in the JHA domain tries to work with an international partner on the basis of its current structures and capabilities, the EU's external JHA dimension Strategy makes frequent reference to actually transforming structures and capabilities of third-country partners. Within the wider context of the structural causes of international migration challenges the EU has to tackle, the document states that 'addressing weak governance and state failure in third countries are key to breaking the vicious cycle of conflict, poverty and instability'. In this context EU police and judicial expertise is described as 'essential to the rebuilding and transformation of weak law enforcement institutions and court systems'.[9] Here we have a clear system transformation objective which ties in perfectly well with the declared EU 'efforts to reduce insecurity and eradicate poverty through strengthening good governance and the rule of law in third countries' as part of the EU 'Policy Framework on Security Sector Reform', which was endorsed by the Council half a year after the Strategy in June 2006.[10] The same rationale of trying in the JHA domain to transform third-country partners rather than just cooperating with them appears in the reference to the 'benefits' to be expected for the AFSJ from the engagement 'to tackle problems at source through actions to build capacity in third countries and supporting a more secure global, rules-based environment'.[11] It is also stated – without too much modesty – that already 'EU funding and expertise provide important support for institutional and capacity building in third countries across a range of JHA areas, from law enforcement to border control'.[12] The Strategy also indicates specific areas where further steps are needed to develop capacity in third-countries, such as the fight against drug-trafficking and production.[13]

The external dimension of the AFSJ therefore has a clear SSR dimension and potential: it consists of the aim of encouraging and contributing to institutional and capacity building of third countries in fields of relevance to AFSJ objectives in the fight against crime and illegal immigration. Although no explicit reference is made to SSR in the external JHA Strategy, it is evident that support for enhanced capacities of third-countries on a broad range of law enforcement issues is of considerable relevance to what the European Commission in its May 2006 Communication on Community support for SSR has defined as the essence of SSR, the 'reform of both the bodies which provide security to citizens and the state institutions responsible for management and oversight of those bodies'.[14]

Because of its focus on internal JHA objectives, engaging in the logic of SSR measures abroad is not the most natural area of AFSJ policy-making. The primary preoccupation of ministers of the interior and justice and their officials, who largely determine policy outputs in the AFSJ context, is naturally with internal issues of security and justice. This accounts for a heavy influence of the internal JHA agenda on external JHA action, which also means that any SSR-related measures tend to be strongly 'inspired' by AFSJ internal security objectives. An important testing ground for, and experience with, such measures has been the enlargement of the AFSJ, which for this reason merits particular attention in this analysis.

The Enlargement of the AFSJ: A 'Model' for SSR in the JHA domain?

The December 2005 external JHA dimension Strategy contains a forceful statement about the importance of enlargement in the context of this Strategy:

> The prospect of enlargement is an effective way to align with EU standards in justice and home affairs in candidate countries and those with a European perspective, both through the adoption and implementation of the acquis and through improvements in operational contacts and co-operation.[15]

It is probably not an exaggeration to say that – although never put under the SSR label – the enlargement of the AFSJ has been the most extensive and successful SSR policy of the EU in the JHA domain so far. By making the adoption and implementation of the full JHA *acquis*, including that of the Schengen system incorporated in 1999, part of the accession conditions[16], the EU has actually forced the ten new members which joined in 2004 and Bulgaria and Romania in 2007 as the latest new members to engage in wide-ranging reforms of their internal security systems. The process of joining the AFSJ – which is not yet fully complete as the new member states are not yet integrated into the operational parts of the Schengen border control system[17] – meant not only bringing national legislation into line with the steadily growing legally binding JHA *acquis*[18] but also adapting policies, priorities, structures and standards so that this *acquis* could be implemented effectively and ensure full participation in the operational aspects of the AFSJ internal security system. A few examples can bring out the extent of the reforms the new member states had to go through in the internal security sectors.

As regards border controls the new member states not only had to shift their main border control capacity to the EU's new external borders – which for Poland, for instance, meant a transfer from Western to Eastern borders – but also to demilitarize border guard forces, to transform them into a special professional border police force under the control of ministries of interior or of justice with specific legally defined responsibilities, to train border guards in line with the border control and mobile surveillance techniques provided for by the Schengen rules and standards, to build up IT capabilities for participation in the SIS and to provide for an effective cooperation and division of responsibilities with other law enforcement authorities.[19]

In the field of police cooperation national structures had to be reorganised to create central units with responsibility for specific forms of serious crime prioritised by the EU (especially organised crime) Police training and inter-agency cooperation had to be improved, national strategies for the fight against challenges like trafficking in drugs and human beings had to be developed and cross-border cooperation capabilities had to be enhanced through legislative, organisational, IT and training means.[20] Preparations for taking over the *acquis* also involved a considerable adaptation of national policing techniques and cultures aimed at both enhanced effectiveness and rule of law standards, which were supported by a range of EU training and expertise transfer measures.[21]

As regards transformation of the criminal justice systems in preparation for accession, the EU not only requested the adoption of the legal *acquis* on judicial cooperation in criminal matters (including relevant Council of Europe Conventions), but also introduced benchmarks for changes in the judiciary. These included constitutional amendments removing any ambiguity regarding the independence and accountability of the judicial system and measures ensuring a more transparent and efficient judicial process, notably by enhancing capacity and accountability of senior magistrates and the conduct of and report on professional, non-partisan investigations into any allegations of high-level corruption.[22]

While not all parts of the JHA requirements have been fully met, there is no denying that the EU has, overall, been rather successful in bringing about substantial changes in the internal security systems of the former candidate countries and the now twelve new member states. The JHA-relevant chapters of the Commission's annual monitoring reports of the candidate countries provide ample evidence for this. This SSR in all but name has been achieved not only by the threat of non-compliance with the *acquis*, potentially delaying or even endangering accession and tight monitoring both by the Commission and the Council, but also by the use of a wide variety of pre-accession aid instruments for JHA-specific supporting measures. On the basis of the Commission's monitoring reports and joint evaluations with each candidate country, these measures were regrouped in annually updated national action plans. Besides financial instruments for infrastructure development (e.g. for external border control equipment) the supporting measures focused on the identification of deficits, the transfer of expertise and the provision of training, most of it being funded through the PHARE programme. A substantial part of the expertise transfer was achieved through the 'twinning' arrangements under which experts from ministries in the old member states were seconded to partner ministries in the candidate countries. These 'twinning' projects also extended to more sensitive security sector aspects such as the fight against public sector corruption.[23] For training in the fields of judicial cooperation in criminal matters and police cooperation, funding was also provided by other programmes focusing on specific JHA challenges such as GROTIUS-II (criminal justice), OISIN-II (law enforcement cooperation), STOP-II (trafficking in human beings), HIPPOKRATES (crime prevention) and FALCONE (organised crime) whose objectives were continued by the 2003 to 2006 AGIS programme.[24]

With the pre-accession strategy in the JHA domain for the 2004 and 2007 enlargement being considered as overall successful, the EU is pursuing a largely similar strategy *vis-à-vis* the currently remaining candidate countries: Croatia, Macedonia and Turkey. The support measures are now funded under the new 2007 to 2013 Instrument for Pre-Accession Assistance (IPA).

Can the JHA reforms which were encouraged – in most cases actually imposed – be regarded as a 'model' for JHA related SSR measures of the Union? In some respects probably yes: in the context of the enlargement process the EU has developed a whole system of SSR- relevant measures in the JHA domain comprising the setting of targets to be achieved (the *acquis* and the capacity to implement it, including the use of benchmarks), the identification of deficits which need to be addressed (in the monitoring reports and joint evaluations leading to national action plans) and the development of a whole range of instruments to support the changes considered necessary (infrastructure support, transfer of expertise, training etc.). Much of this could also be used for SSR in a non-accession context, and at the very least one can say that the AFSJ enlargement has provided the EU with a huge laboratory to test the greater or lesser effectiveness of the instruments applied.

Yet in other respects the AFSJ enlargement related reforms cannot be regarded as an easily transferable 'model' for SSR: the incentive structure of the enlargement context is clearly a uniquely forceful one. *Vis-à-vis* third countries with no accession perspective or interest the EU finds itself obviously in a much weaker position when it comes to encouraging JHA-related SSR. The massive 'export' of AFSJ objectives, standards and procedures which has taken place in the context of enlargement appears quite unthinkable in the case of countries not on an accession path. The conditionality of certain financial and economic measures upon compliance with EU objectives, which the EU often uses *vis-à-vis* other third countries will never be able to match the accession prospect as an incentive. In addition, it will in many cases simply not make sense to push third countries to reform their security sector, which may be necessary for accession purposes but do not significantly add to effectiveness of their respective systems or their cooperation capabilities with the EU. There would be little point, for instance, in aligning national law enforcement data collection and analysis standards and procedures to the requirements of the SIS without any prospect for ever acceding to it. A further consideration is that for third countries not on the accession path the EU is much less likely to provide similar levels of financial support for JHA system transformation. Investing in internal security capabilities of a current or future new member state will inevitably rank higher in the order of priorities than JHA-related SSR in other countries.[25] The same applies to member states' willingness to make personnel available for capacity building as this was done on a relatively large scale in pre-accession 'twinning' arrangements.

While JHA-related SSR measures in the accession context may not be an easily transferable model as whole, quite a few elements of these measures – as will be shown in the following – can be found in other forms of action in the 'external dimension' of the AFSJ.

JHA-Related SSR Regarding 'Neighbouring' Countries: a 'Glacis' for the AFSJ

The above mentioned December 2005 Strategy for the External Dimension of JHA can be regarded as a milestone in the conceptualisation of SSR measures as part of the external side of the AFSJ. Yet before the adoption of the strategy the EU had already engaged in measures which can be regarded as pursuing SSR objectives in a number of JHA fields. Most of the EU effort in this respect has been focused on the EU's 'neighbourhood', a term which has grown from the immediate bordering countries to include even more remote partners such as Azerbaijan, Israel and Lebanon.

For obvious reasons the Western Balkans, as a major region of origin and transit of organised crime and illegal immigration, have ranked high on the EU's external JHA agenda. As part of the EU's 'Stabilisation and Association Process' (SAP) for the Western Balkans the 'Community Assistance for Reconstruction, Development and Stabilisation' (CARDS) Programme for countries in the region has included since its start in 2000 distinctive capacity building elements in the JHA domain with obvious SSR implications. The CARDS 'Regional Strategy Paper' for 2002 to 2006 provided, for instance, for institution-building support, expertise transfer via twinning-type arrangements and training measures with a view to creating more effective border security systems and enhanced capabilities of police and judicial authorities in fighting crime.[26] CARDS reflects rather nicely the influence of the EU's internal security objectives on this type of neighbourhood external action. In line with the EU's concerns about the securitization of illegal immigration, for instance, the Regional Strategy has explicitly included the objective of enhanced capabilities in the combat against illegal immigration under the heading of the 'fighting of national and international crime' and has put a major emphasis on that as regards JHA reforms in the beneficiary countries. Enhancing interconnectivity of regional police forces with Europol is one of the objectives, and in many fields legislative alignment with the EU JHA *acquis* is also part of the Strategy.[27] An example for a CARDS project is the 'Modernising the Police Service' project with Albania which was implemented in 2003 to 2004 via the Police Assistance Mission of the European Community to Albania (PAMECA) and was focused on improving standards and practices at the senior levels of the Albanian police force as well as the creation of better training facilities.[28] The proliferation, often on a fairly ad-hoc basis, of different bilateral and multilateral measures have led to criticisms of compartmentalisation, lack of strategic direction and coordination as well as duplication problems of JHA-related action in the Western Balkans.[29] In response to these criticisms the Council adopted in May 2006 a new 'Action Oriented Paper' (AOP) with more emphasis on strategic objectives and effective coordination in law enforcement and judiciary capacity building, this also in view of counter-terrorism and anti-corruption objectives.[30] Both in terms of objectives and of instruments, CARDS assistance has shown considerable similarities to the EU pre-accession approach in its EU sponsored JHA-related SSR measures, despite the fact that the 'European perspective' and the accession prospects of at least some of the Western Balkan countries continue to be much less certain. The AFSJ system export aimed at and eventually largely achieved in the context of enlargement has clearly served as model for JHA-related SSR in the Western Balkans.

To some extent the same is true with regard to the Euro-Mediterranean Partnership and the MEDA Programme as its main funding instrument. The MEDA Programme also has a substantial JHA section under the general objective of 'enhancing the rule of law, human rights and good governance'. In line with the AFSJ international objectives, reforms in the Mediterranean partner countries targeted at capacity building in the fight against illegal immigration and cross-border crime – with a focus on drug-trafficking and terrorism – have been identified as MEDA priorities in the JHA domain. Measures of SSR relevance in this context include advice on legislative measures, the training of police and customs officers in crime prevention and crime-fighting techniques, both general and technical training of judges, prosecutors, lawyers and court officials to enhance the efficiency and rule of law standards of the judiciaries, and the promotion of expertise through the exchange of officials and training activities targeted at 'modern and effective systems of border controls'.[31] In the context of the MEDA Regional Indicative Programme 2005-2006 the objectives have been partly redefined and refined, with a slightly stronger focus on the fight against money-laundering and judicial reform. As regards SSR-related measures greater emphasis has been placed on special 'centres' for training and the exchange and transfer of expertise, the definition of 'good practices' and the drawing-up of 'charters' or 'guides' of such practices, 'twinnings' between ministries and courts and the involvement of EU agencies such as Europol, Eurojust and the European Police College.[32] As with CARDS, MEDA has been primarily implemented through bilateral cooperation with individual Mediterranean partners, which means that the particular 'mix' of objectives and measures varies from one country to the other.

The MEDA Programme is now part of the instruments of the European Neighbourhood Policy (ENP). Introduced in 2003 with the aim of developing a prosperous and friendly neighbourhood zone for the EU (a 'ring of friends')[33], the ENP has included right from the start a strong JHA dimension aimed, in particular, at enhancing the effectiveness of the border control, police and criminal justice systems.[34] The ENP has absorbed and further developed a number of already existing special JHA cooperation and assistance mechanisms regarding neighbouring countries. One example is JHA cooperation with the Ukraine which has since 2002 been based on a special EU Action Plan and comprises a range of measures in support of governance capabilities regarding the fight against serious crime and illegal immigration.[35] All the current national Action Plans in the context of the ENP comprise a JHA dimension, but there are considerable variations in the priorities and extent of JHA-related SSR measures provided for. Generally it can be said that the reforms encouraged and supported by the EU reflect again very much internal JHA priorities. In the case of Morocco, for instance, which is a major country of transit and origin for illegal immigration into the EU, heavy emphasis has been placed on the build-up of enhanced capabilities as regards migration management, border management and trafficking in human beings[36], and the December 2006 progress report has also focused on measures in this domain which have included a first 'twinning' arrangement.[37] The Moldova Action Plan also has a strong focus on migration management although a major emphasis is also placed on capacity building in the fight against organised crime, which is an area of particular concern to the EU because of the weak state structures in the country. As part of the implementation Moldova has already introduced central investigative units for the fight against organised crime and an inter-agency centre to combat trafficking in human beings, which correspond to EU demands in the domain of institutional capacity building.[38]

EU objectives regarding SSR in the JHA domain are inevitably more modest as regards ENP countries which pose less immediate challenges to AFSJ objectives – or over which it simply has less political leverage. An example is Israel which not only constitutes much less of a problem from the migration and organised crime perspective but would also certainly resent any declared EU objectives as regards the transformation of its own internal security systems. As a result the Action Plan and its implementation focus on a logic of enhanced cooperation rather than any reforms of the Israeli security sector, with exchanges of best practices in fighting terrorism financing and human trafficking constituting the only elements with some – admittedly rather limited – SSR potential.[39]

There can be no doubt about the SSR relevance of many of the JHA measures adopted under the different EU neighbourhood instruments. These measures have focused primarily on enhancing law enforcement, judiciary and migration management capacities, and they have obviously been very closely related to the EU's internal security objectives and priorities in the context of the AFSJ. Although this has naturally not been put this way in the relevant programme documents, JHA-related SSR measures have *de facto* served primarily the capacity of neighbouring countries to reduce challenges to the EU in terms of serious cross-border crime and illegal immigration, helping the Union thereby to construct a sort of protective JHA *'glacis'* around the AFSJ. This is also nicely reflected in the Vienna Declaration on Security Partnership, which was adopted at a ministerial conference with the neighbourhood countries on the subject of internal security relations in Vienna on 5 May 2006. The Declaration identified migration and asylum as fields of 'particular challenges' requiring the longest list of measures, although this field is clearly less of a concern to most neighbouring countries than to the EU.[40] All this does not mean, however, that the EU- sponsored reforms of the security systems are not also of genuine benefit to the countries in question, which all have problems of serious crime and also some of migration of their own for which the enhanced capabilities are in many cases urgently needed.

Implementing the JHA External Dimension Strategy: The Global Dimension of SSR-related Measures

The various JHA measures regarding the EU's wider neighbourhood are now all part of the December 2005 Strategy for the External Dimension of JHA. Yet the Strategy comprises a claim to a global reach[41], and some JHA-related SSR measures can actually be identified well beyond the neighbourhood dimension.

EU investments in enhancing migration management capacities in countries of origin and transit have increased considerably since 2005, mainly because of the increased migratory pressures from and via Northern Africa. Apart from providing expertise and training to Northern African countries as part of the ENP (the example of Morocco has been given above), a range of special assistance measures regarding migration management involving the sending of experts and exchanges of best practices and training needs were started during 2006.[42]

As regards the fight against serious forms of international crime, the fight against terrorism, organised crime and drug-trafficking are priority areas for the implementation of the External Dimension Strategy.

In the field of counter-terrorism much of the EU's external activities of SSR relevance have focused on the objectives defined in UN Security Council Resolution 1373(2001) with its emphasis on suppressing the financing of terrorist acts and international counter-terrorism capacity building. The EU has made extensive use of political dialogue to encourage third countries to adapt their legislation in line with UNSCR 1373 and has started to systematically introduce enhanced anti-terrorism clauses in agreements with third countries which also provide for exchange of experience, technical assistance and training.[43] Assistance measures on financial legislation include projects on money laundering as well as study of existing legislation in Andean Pact countries to implement recommendations of the Financial Action Task Force (FATF) on money-laundering and terrorist financing. Assistance regarding customs legislation comprises border control and management programmes in the Western Balkans, Eastern Europe and Turkey. Extradition assistance provides training for international judicial cooperation. EU police and law enforcement capacity building specifically supports counter-terrorism capabilities, and more general law enforcement in Algeria, Central and Eastern Europe, the Western Balkans, and Palestinian Authority (PA) areas. EU judicial capacity building includes projects for stronger court systems and public prosecution in the Western Balkans and Eastern Europe, judicial modernization in Morocco and Tunisia and – an example for the rather specific nature of certain measures – technical assistance to the Indonesian Attorney-General on forensic accounting.[44]

International EU measures in the fight against organised crime largely overlap with those in the fight against terrorism as regards international capacity building and legislative alignment in the fight against money-laundering and terrorist financing (see above). Organised crime involvement in illegal immigration and trafficking in human beings is a cross-cutting theme in the capacity building measures on migration management, both inside and outside the neighbourhood dimension. A high priority is given to helping third-countries upgrade their law enforcement capabilities in the fight against drug-trafficking. This involves advice on legislation, expert missions, sharing of best practices and training programmes.[45] Cooperation with Latin American countries is well developed in this respect, a recent example being a 2004 to 2006 project with the countries of the Andean Community on enhancing capabilities in the fight against synthetic drugs which involved the posting of EU experts in the region.[46] Encouraging reforms in Asian countries of origin and transit has also been of growing importance, often in conjunction with other law enforcement objectives. An example of such a cross-cutting programme is the 2003 to 2009 Border Management Programme in Central Asia (BOMCA) which is funded under the technical assistance programme TACIS and focused on Kazakhstan, Kyrgyzstan, Tajikistan, Turkmenistan and Uzbekistan. JHA-related measures with SSR relevance include high-level advice and guidance in upgrading legislation and providing expertise on airport security or the use of dogs to detect drugs.[47]

Many of the EU's 'global' JHA measures are again very much driven by internal AFSJ security objectives. A prominent example is that of the 'Action Oriented Paper' (AOP) on Afghanistan which was adopted under the JHA External Dimension Strategy on 22 May 2006.[48] After a considerable reduction during the time of the Taliban, over 90 percent of the heroin consumed in the EU is again coming from Afghanistan[49] – a nice example of military intervention reducing one security threat (terrorism) while increasing another (drugs). The AOP provides for additional support from the EU for criminal justice reform with a strong emphasis on legislative reform, legal training and mentoring and capacity building support for national and border guard police forces. Some of these measures are also to be extended to neighbouring countries, involving, for instance, the provision of training for Pakistani law enforcement and customs officers.[50]

Overall there is clearly a growing global dimension in external EU action in the JHA domain which has SSR implications. The primary objective is – as in the neighbourhood context – capacity building of third-countries in the fight against serious forms of cross-border crime and illegal immigration, the primary internal security concerns of the AFSJ. Yet this global dimension is less developed than the neighbourhood dimension, more fragmentary in its geographical coverage and also more limited in the available funding instruments.

Conclusion

SSR in third countries is currently not a primary objective of JHA as an EU policy-making domain. Both from the political perspective of the JHA Council and the treaty objectives and competences of the EU in this field the internal security objectives of the AFSJ are paramount. Yet there is obviously a lot of SSR potential in the JHA domain, and the growing externalisation of internal security objectives in the fight against cross-border crime and illegal immigration since the end of the 1990s has gradually made the EU realise some of this potential. The most successful example in this respect has clearly been EU enlargement, where the EU has been able to bring about comprehensive reforms in the accession candidates' internal security systems through a combination of accession conditionality and extensive pre-accession supporting instruments. Quite a few of the pre-accession JHA reform objectives and instruments have found their way into the various neighbourhood programmes, but the EU's political leverage here depends much on whether or not countries have a credible accession perspective. The global dimension, newly emphasized by the 2005 External JHA Dimension Strategy, tends to be more issue-oriented – anti-terrorism and drugs capacity building being among the priorities – and fragmentary in its geographical coverage.

There has been a huge proliferation of the number and different types of measures of SSR relevance in the external JHA dimension. In some geographical areas of dense activity – such as the Western Balkans – problems of coordination, duplication and the effective use of resources have appeared. These problems have been recognised and more recently – especially in the AOPs on the Western Balkans and Afghanistan – have also been addressed. Yet effective targeting and coordination will remain a challenge for a complex actor such as the EU which also has to struggle with different priorities and often separate action by its member states. Of crucial importance therefore is a close and effective monitoring of the implementation and effectiveness of measures. In the context of the accession process the monitoring and reporting procedures have been developed to high standards. It is less certain that this is also the case for the neighbourhood instruments – and much less certain with regard to the global dimension, if one takes the rather vague and superficial first two implementation reports of the Commission on the JHA External Dimension Strategy as indicators.[51]

It cannot be denied that the focus of SSR-related external EU action on law enforcement, judiciary and illegal migration management capabilities in third countries reflects very closely EU internal security objectives. Yet this does not mean that the EU is simply pursuing a ruthless externalisation of its internal security objectives. Apart from the fact that these enhanced capabilities are in many cases urgently needed for these countries' own internal security problems the EU's external JHA action has its own more general normative dimension. The enhancing of rule of law standards, with an emphasis on human rights protection and principles such as the independence of the judiciary, and the promotion of good governance are in fact cross-cutting themes of JHA training activities and expertise transfer on legislation and law enforcement reform abroad. Yet what may be referred to as the primacy of EU internal security objectives has meant a prioritisation of the above indicated JHA aspects, with little or at least less emphasis placed on other aspects such as, for instance, petty or juvenile crime within those countries which normally contribute greatly to citizens' feeling of insecurity. But this should not be regarded as a point for criticism: the EU cannot possibly be expected to act on all of the ills of the world, and ultimately its primary interest must be to deliver added value for its own citizens. There can be no doubt that carefully targeted, well coordinated and effectively monitored SSR-related measures in the JHA domain can deliver such added value.

Endnotes

1 European Council (1999) *Presidency Conclusions, Tampere European Council.* Bulletin EU 10-1999, paragraphs 6 and 40.

2 Council of the EU (2005) *The Hague Programme: Strengthening Freedom, Security and Justice in the European Union,* OJ C 53 of 3 March 2005, paragraph 2.

3 See, inter alia, Christina Boswell, *European Migration in Flux: Changing Patterns of Inclusion and Exclusion,* London: Blackwell Publishing, 2003 and Alessandra Buonfino, 'Between unity and plurality: the politicization and securitization of the discourse of immigration in Europe', *New Political Science,* 26(1), 2004: 23-49.

4 Council of the EU (1999) *Council and Commission Action Plan of 3 December 1998 on how best to implement the provisions of the Treaty of Amsterdam on the creation of an area of freedom, security and justice,* OJ C 19 of 23 January 1999.

5 Jörg Monar, "The EU as an International Actor in the Domain of Justice and Home Affairs", *European Foreign Affairs Review,* 9(4), 2004: 395-415.

6 COM(2005)491 of 12.10.2005.

7 Council document no. 15446/05 of 6.12.2005.

8 *Ibid.*, paragraph 1.

9 *Ibid.*, paragraph 6.

10 Council Conclusions on a Policy Framework for Security Sector Reform (adopted on 12.6.2006), Council document no. 9946/06, paragraph 2.

11 Council document no. 15446/05 of 6.12.2005, paragraph 8.

12 *Ibid.*, paragraph 12.

13 *Ibid.*, paragraph 3.

14 COM(2006)253 of 24.5.2006, p. 3.

15 Council document no. 15446/05 of 6.12.2005, paragraph 10.

16 It should be recalled that Article 8 of Protocol 2 annexed to the TEU by the Treaty of Amsterdam on the incorporation of the Schengen *acquis* introduced the obligation for new members states to accept 'in full' the Schengen *acquis* in spite of the opt-outs granted to the UK and Ireland.

17 After some delays both on the EU side (because of delays with the introduction of the second generation Schengen Information System, SIS) and the side of the new member states (because of capability deficits) this is now foreseen for 2008.

18 Which by October 2006 had expanded to a list of 43 pages of individual legal texts (European Commission, DG Justice, Freedom and Security, JAI-Acquis Update October 2006).

19 For more details see Arto Niemenkari, 'EU/Schengen requirements for national border security systems', Geneva Centre for the Democratic Control of Armed Forces (DCAF) Working Paper Series, 8, 2002, and the declassified parts of the 'Common Manual' in OJ C 313 of 16.12.2002.

20 See Richard Crowe, *The Schengen 'Acquis' in police cooperation: implementation in an enlarged Europe,* ERA-Forum: scripta iuris europaei, no. 3, 2004, 415-433, and – as examples for required action taken or not taken – pp. 35-37 of the Commission's 2006 Monitoring Report on Bulgaria (SEC(2006)595 of 16.05.2006) and pp. 34-36 of the 2006 Monitoring Report on Romania (SEC(2005)596 of 16.05.2006),

21 For some examples see Frank Gregory, *'Good Cops': Issues related to EU Enlargement and the 'Police' Requirements of the JHA acquis,* ESRC 'One Europe or Several?' Programme Working Papers, 24/01, 2001.

22 See, for instance, the benchmarks which continue to apply to Bulgaria and Romania even after accession and whose non-observance could entail the suspension of membership rights in the Commission's Monitoring Report on the state of preparedness of Bulgaria und Romania for EU membership of September 2006 (COM(2006)549 of 26.9.2006), p. 10.

23 An example is the 2003 Estonian-German Twinning Covenant on Reducing corruption in Estonia under the 2003 Phare National Programme for Estonia, no. EE03-IB-JH-02 http://www.korruptsioon.ee/orb.aw/class=file/action=preview/id=9437/Korruptsiooni_v2hendamine_Eestis_2004-2005.pdf

24 For examples see the Commission's third annual AGIS implementation report, COM(2006)1535 of 21.11.2006.

25 Under the PHARE JHA 'horizontal programme' alone the EU spent in 1997-2004 over 600 million euro (Commission DG FSJ information). This does not take into account other institution and capacity building measures of JHA relevance and expenditure under other relevant programmes.

26 European Commission External Relations Directorate General, 'CARDS Assistance Programme to the Western Balkans. Regional Strategy Paper 2002-2006', pp. 33-34 and 40-42.

27 *Ibid.*, pp. 40-41.

28 CARDS Project Description no. 7 (http://ec.europa.eu/enlargement/pdf/financial_assistance/cards/cases/007_en.pdf).

29 See, for instance, the critical 'Friends of the Presidency Report' of October 2004, Council document no. 13385/04 of 13.10.2004.

30 Council document no. 9272/06 of 12.5.2006.

31 European Commission, 'EURO-MED Partnership. Regional Strategy Paper 2002-2006', 2002, pp. 33-35.

32 European Commission, 'MEDA. Regional Indicative Programme 2005-2006', 2004, pp. 21-25.

33 COM(2003)104 of 11.3.2003, p. 4.

34 See the European Commission's 'European Neighbourhood Strategy Paper', COM(2004)373 of 12.5.2004, pp. 16-17 and 23.

35 See the 'EU Action Plan on Justice and Home Affairs in the Ukraine' (OJ C 77 of 29.3.2003) which was adopted by the Council in December 2001.

36 European Commission, 'EU/MOROCCO Action Plan', June 2005, pp. 21-22.

37 European Commission, 'Rapport de suivi PEV MAROC', SEC(2006)1511/2 of 4.12.2006, p. 11.

38 European Commission, 'ENP Progress Report Moldova', SEC(2006)1506/2 of 4.12.2006, p. 11.

39 European Commission, 'ENP Progress Report Israel', SEC(2006)1507/2 of 29.11.2006, pp. 8-9.

40 Council document no. 8501/06 of 8.5.2006, pp. 6-7.

41 The Strategy's sub-title actually reads 'Global Freedom, Security and Justice' (Council document no. 15446/05 of 6.12.2005, p. 1).

42 In particular with regard to Mali, Mauritania and Senegal. See COM(2006)735 of 30.11.2006.

43 See Council document no. 14458/2/04 of 11.5.2005 on 'EU Counter-Terrorism Clauses' (declassified parts).

44 Latest available version of the 'EU Action Plan on Combating Terrorism' (Council document no. 11882/1/06 of 7.9.2006), latest implementation report by the EU Anti-Terrorism Coordinator (Council document no. 15266/1/06 of 24.11.2006) and supplementary interview information.

45 See the 'EU Action Plan on Drugs 2005-2008', OJ C 168 of 8.7.2005, pp. 13-15.

46 European Commission, *Revised Regional Indicative Programme 2004-2006: The Andean Community*, 2004, pp. 9-10.

47 For a description see European Commission, *Boosting Border Management Control & Drug Control in Central Asia*, http://ec.europa.eu/europeaid/projects/tacis/publications/case_studies/pf_centralasia_border_en.pdf

48 Council document no. 9370/1/06 of 22.5.2006.

49 *Ibid.*, p. 3, and Interpol fact-sheet on Heroin http://www.interpol.int/Public/Drugs/heroin/default.asp

50 Council document no. 9370/1/06 of 22.5.2006, p. 8 and 13.

51 Council documents no. 15001/06 and 15363/06, both of 20.11.2006.

7. Parliamentary Control over European Security Policy

Elmar Brok

Introduction: An Emerging Security and Defence Policy with No Real Democratic Control

Security structures are intrinsic to the concept of a united Europe even though it has only been in the course of the last decades that the European Union has become an actor in security and defence policy. In fact, a common defence policy for Europe has been advocated continually since the outset of European integration. One could even argue that the creation of a common defence structure is essential in the transition from an economic to a political community embracing common values. The fact is, of course, that in order to support their collective ambitions in European Security and Defence Policy, the EU member states have made significant and rapid progress in creating an EU-level policy framework. Since the end of the Cold War Europe has benefited from a unique window of opportunity to pursue its own concepts of security and defence. Some argue that the EU's added value as a comprehensive humanitarian, economic and military security provider and its use of soft power has enabled the Union to establish itself as a plausible normative alternative to the US's reliance on military dominance.

International relations is a world in flux. The changing global security environment would undoubtedly bring about further diversification in forms of military conflict. It is thus natural for European Security and Defence Policy to be in similar flux. As ESDP matures, the European Union would doubtlessly be called upon to assume new responsibilities and to make a greater contribution to regional crisis management. These new responsibilities cannot be met by military means alone, but by using the broadest spectrum of non-military instruments available to prevent conflicts and to counter violence and terrorism. This implies, in particular, the reinforcement of cross-frontier mechanisms of co-operative security, including media communication, judiciary co-operation and co-operation of police forces, as well as assistance to countries outside the EU in the development of democratic structures and civil society institutions.

But, if the European Union is ideally placed to grasp the opportunity of developing into both an independent player and a key contributor to the existing security and defence framework, the consequent increase in EU civilian crisis management or civil-military crisis management operations ought to engender an enhancement of democratic accountability within the EU's decision-making framework. Parliamentary scrutiny of ESDP both by the national parliaments of the EU member states and the European Parliament is ill suited to fulfil this function within the present institutional structures. The reason is quite simple. The shift of decision-making powers to the European level has created an accountability gap as national parliaments increasingly lose the ability to exercise democratic scrutiny and control over security and defence policy made in what is now an intergovernmental and even supranational context. Meanwhile, the European Parliament is legally and politically unable to absorb the national parliaments' lack of democratic credentials.

The European Defence Context

The challenge to the EU of playing a role in defence matters is one feature resulting from the underlying consensus of EU member states on the need to work more co-operatively to overcome structural obstacles and to achieve enhanced and more efficient capabilities in order to accomplish their security ambitions. But, defence transformation is about more than a political reorientation to meet new threats in a changing security environment. It is also about reaching all levels of the defence establishment to create appropriate defence instruments to support security policy priorities. Perhaps the most significant motive for Europeans to work collectively on defence matters is the need to restructure European defence, including the defence industrial base and national defence expenditure. The introduction of new security concepts and the need to co-operate in order to tackle the new security challenges are forcing defence planners to re-orient towards communications in 'network-enabled warfare' and concepts such as 'effects-based warfare'.[1] There is a distinct trend away from the Cold War emphasis and from large military platforms. Yet, the generation of defence capabilities remains locked in Cold War procurement practices, but with much reduced defence budgets. Specifically privileged relationships developed between defence establishments and national defence industries believed essential during the Cold War to ensure security of supply are now seen as a structural obstacle to transformation of national defence postures. Worse, in some cases arms exports have been used to support inefficient industries with the unsavoury result that European exports exacerbate conflicts in the developing world.[2]

Most commentators believe that the current levels of defence spending are likely to remain broadly stable for the foreseeable future. An increase in spending would anyway not necessarily provide for more military capability, unless accompanied by reform of inefficient procurement processes, ministerial bureaucracies and relevant industrial sectors. The current argument is that if defence spending is not to increase, one obvious way of bridging the capability-expectation gap is through increased armaments co-operation. Joint procurement of the necessary equipment offers an increase in cost effectiveness through economies of scale and reduced duplication. Importantly, however, politicians and publics must be aware, and be seen to be aware, that this also requires common structures for democratic scrutiny.

The EU's Common Foreign, Security and Defence Policy since the 1990s

The first steps towards a European Security and Defence Policy (ESDP) were taken as far back as 1952, but were ultimately rejected by the French National Assembly in August 1954. Although agreement was reached in the following year to create the Western European Union (WEU), this did comparatively little to impart a cutting edge to the European Community's security and defence profile, neither then nor in the years leading to the partial dissolution of the WEU on 13 November 2000.

A milestone came with the European Single Act of 1986, when the ambitious objective of European Political Cooperation was postulated, triggering fresh discussion on security issues. However, it was not until the Maastricht Treaty of 1992 that European Union responsibility in the area of foreign and security policy was endorsed. The WEU was identified at that time as the core vehicle for its development. The Maastricht Treaty first introduced the Common Foreign and Security Policy – not as an integral part of Community law but, instead, as a stand-alone intergovernmental pillar. As a result, it admitted intergovernmental cooperation at member state level only, granting a shared but no sole right of initiative to the European Commission, as it would have done had the Community method been adopted. This institutional basis meant that the adoption of principles and general guidelines relating to the Common Foreign and Security Policy were subject to unanimous vote in the Council of Ministers. The Commission, of course, had no vote, and since CFSP business was outside the European Community pillar, the European Parliament's role was correspondingly less than democratically optimal.

The new policy endorsed in Maastricht implied the need for a definition of European Defence Policy, but it was the subsequent Treaty of Amsterdam of 1997 which substantially enhanced the Common Foreign and Security Policy by introducing the post of a High Representative and creating potential for reinforcement of the European pillar of NATO by ramping up the Union's European Security and Defence Policy and incorporating some of the competence of the WEU into the EU's common structures. The Treaty of Amsterdam also integrated the Petersberg tasks, declared by the WEU in 1992, into the Treaty on European Union, building the basis of the ESDP in the realm of humanitarian and rescue tasks, peace-keeping and tasks of combat forces in crisis management, including peacemaking.

Coping with the fallout of the collapse of Yugoslavia after the end of the Cold War had shown all too clearly the futility of underpinning EU political goals without military means. So, the Franco-British declaration at St. Malo in December 1998 injected a new urgency by stressing the desirability of European Union military autonomy at international level and proposing functions and mechanisms for European Union crisis management. As a result, responsibility for implementing the Petersberg Tasks was transferred from the WEU to the European Union. At the European Council in Cologne in June 1999, under the auspices of the German presidency, it was finally agreed that the necessary institutional and military preconditions for military response should be in place by the end of 2000. In the autumn of 1999 the Helsinki Council agreed on the creation of politico-military structures that were subsequently institutionalised in the Treaty of Nice: the Political and Security Committee, the European Union Military Committee and the European Union Military Staff. The 'Headline Goals' defined that the European Union should be in a position to deploy a force of up to 60,000 troops worldwide, within sixty days, capable of operating out-of-area for a minimum of twelve months by 2003. Input to the European Union-NATO interface and the potential for non-European Union states to participate in EU-led missions were also discussed. Additionally, the European Council held under the auspices of the Portuguese presidency in Feira in June 2000 reached an agreement on a concrete Headline Goal for civilian capabilities.[3] As of 2003, up to 5,000 police officers were to be available for international missions, with up to 1,000 deployable within thirty days. As to the mooted contribution of third-parties to EU military missions, it was agreed that non-EU member states could take part without involving NATO, provided they were invited by the EU to take part in the operation. The Nice Summit saw no substantive developments in the area of security and defence other than the articulation of rules concerning crisis intervention of non-European Union members of NATO and those with official candidate status. In sum, in less than a year, two medium-term objectives had been endorsed to enable efficient civilian and military crisis management. In addition, a complementary Rapid Reaction Mechanism provided the European Commission with a new first-pillar tool to circumvent the time-consuming process of consultation and agreement for funding operations and to facilitate prompt allocation of financial resources for civilian crisis intervention.

The Gothenburg European Council in June 2001 then endorsed the *Commission Communication on Conflict Prevention* and the *EU Programme for the Prevention of Violent Conflicts*, signalling the intention to make conflict prevention a central objective of European security policy. The Gothenburg European Council further developed the EU's civilian elements of crisis management by establishing four priority areas: policing, rule of law, civil administration and civil protection. Consequently, it formulated 'Headline Goals' for the establishment of a Rapid Reaction Force (RRF) with a force up to 60,000 troops as part of its crisis management tools. The initiatives set out in the programme represented ambitious goals for future Presidencies and revealed a new determination to combine the concepts of European foreign policy with conflict prevention and crisis management. But this was no simple task. The Capabilities Improvement Conference of November 2001 came to the sobering conclusion that the contributions of member states to attainment of the Headline Goals was falling short in a number of areas, especially in intelligence-gathering, logistics, communications and transport. A study released by the International Institute for Strategic Studies warned that these shortfalls could delay the capacity building required for the completion of the Petersberg Tasks by ten or fifteen years. The Laeken Council of December 2001 saw political agreement on the deployment of a European Rapid Reaction Force, which is now operational, but member states nonetheless took note of the shortcomings.

The EU as an International Security Actor

In January 2003, the EU's first EU civilian crisis management operation, the EUPM Police Mission in Bosnia-Herzegovina, marked the beginning of an increasing number of ESDP operations conducted in the context of CFSP. The EU's commitment did not limit itself to civilian missions. It soon extended to military operations, such as the EUFOR mission Concordia in the Former Yugoslav Republic of Macedonia, which was established on 31 March 2003. By 2007 there had been a total of seven completed missions, with eight ongoing. Of these fifteen operations only four have been purely military, with the remainder either civilian or a combination of civilian and military components, such as the supporting action to the African Union Mission in Sudan (AMIS III), and the advisory and assistance mission for security reform in the Democratic Republic of Congo (EUSEC). In addition, by early summer 2007, the EU was preparing for an EU crisis management operation in Kosovo in the field of rule of law and a take-over of selected tasks from the United Nations Interim Administration Mission in Kosovo (UNMIK). As discussions on the future status of Kosovo continued the scope of the mission was set to lead to further extension of the terms of reference.

The trend towards more operations with both civilian and military components is likely to continue. This is not only due to the changing security environment but also to two fundamental incentives arising from changes in the EU's concept of security, manifested first in the 2003 European Security Strategy. The ESS envisaged Union action increasingly outside its immediate vicinity, and this manifest ambition of a global role for the EU was grounded in the EU's position as a comprehensive humanitarian, economic and military security provider able to respond to needs in conflict zones all over the world. In addition, there was (and remains) increasing demand at home and abroad for it to do so.

It thus becomes clear why the 'Europeanisation' of security and defence policy creates a democratic accountability gap that needs to be addressed. As decisions to engage in military or civil-military operations are increasingly taken at the European level, the parliaments of member states are left with insufficient mechanisms and power to control their governments' decisions. Within the existing legal framework the European Parliament's scrutiny of ESDP is also limited – policy-making structures formally belong in the second pillar and are therefore intergovernmental by nature. Only conflict prevention and civilian crisis management, which increasingly overlap with ESDP tasks, fall under the first pillar and consequently under the EP's scrutiny. The salient issue is that democratic accountability of decision-making processes is an indispensable element in Europe's democratic framework, and that legitimacy thus ought to be enforced through increasing the participation of citizens' representatives.

Democratic Control and the European Parliament

The European Parliament has recognised the need for an EU level security and defence policy and supports the efforts of EU member states to develop it further. It also recognises that a balance between the principles of security, confidentiality, practicality and flexibility of procedures is essential. Neither can be compromised. Nonetheless, the European Parliament is insisting on enhancing transparency and control over decision making and budgetary issues within the framework of the General Budget of the European Union as well as in its access to information. In 2004 the European Parliament created a sub-Committee on Security and Defence (SEDE) within the overall responsibility of the Foreign affairs Committee (AFET) to account for its growing responsibility in this field. Although the European Parliament is not a decision-maker in CFSP and, by extension, ESDP, it does have a role in shaping it. It exerts substantial influence on matters relating to the CFSP budget and Commission programmes. In practice, it assumes budgetary responsibility for foreign aid disbursements four times higher than those currently allocated by the US Senate.

According to the provisions of the Treaty on European Union's Article 28, administrative and operational matters pertaining to the Common Foreign and Security Policy are financed from the European Community budget. To that extent, Parliament and Council appear as equal partners, although shared budgetary responsibility – developed over years of discussion and negotiation – does not include military or defence policy issues or matters otherwise decided unanimously by the Council. In addition to these budgetary rights, the European Parliament has wide-ranging powers to monitor and consult. The Council has to take the Parliament's opinion into account in formulating and modifying the CFSP. Both the Commission and the Council are obliged to provide regular reports to the Parliament on the latest developments in CFSP, and the EU High Representative Javier Solana and Commissioner Benita Ferrero-Waldner address the Parliament at least four times annually. The Chair of the Council is at the disposal of the European Parliament for comments at the beginning and end of his term of office as well as immediately after Council meetings. Additionally, the President of the Council briefs the Parliament's Committee on Foreign Affairs, Human Rights and Security and Defence Policy following each meeting of the Council of Ministers. Member state defence ministers also present reports to the Parliament's Committee twice a year. In addition, the Parliament can assume a proactive role in the policy process by submitting specific queries and recommendations to the Council of Ministers. Every member of the European Parliament is entitled to submit questions relating to foreign and security policy issues. Questions can also be addressed to the European Commission, as it is equally under a statutory obligation to inform the European Parliament. The influence of the Parliament has been further bolstered by inter-institutional agreements. One agreement, in effect since 6 May 1999, formally strengthened the Parliament's position in foreign policy. It obliged the Council to present the Parliament with an annual account of major Common Foreign and Security Policy developments, together with details of the financial resources assigned to them.

In sum, the Parliament has acquired substantial rights over time to monitor and discuss Common Foreign and Security Policy issues. It is on an equal footing with the Council with regard to the financing of common foreign and security measures. Yet, in practice, the Parliament's strong position in the budgetary field has frequently resulted in watered-down Council initiatives, though by using its budgetary powers as leverage, the European

Parliament has succeeded in acquiring advance information on aspects of policy options in the Common Foreign and Security Policy. During the negotiations for the 2007-2013 financial perspectives the Parliament placed funds foreseen for the CFSP budget into reserve, thereby threatening drastically to cut the budget. Settlement of the issue was agreed under the Finnish Presidency, so as the EU prepares for a potential crisis management operation in Kosovo, where it takes over selected tasks of the United Nations Interim Administration Mission in Kosovo (UNMIK), the European Parliament has for the first time received prior, as opposed to late, information about the status of the preparations for the mission and the future role the EU is intending to play in the process of political stabilisation.

Room for Improvement: Parliamentary Scrutiny of the ESDP

In contrast to national parliaments' involvement in the democratic control of security and defence policies, the European Parliament is not actively involved in decision-making structures for the European Union's security and defence policy. Yet, despite this built-in deficit of democratic accountability, the European Parliament maintains a strong position through its access to ESDP-related information. The Parliament enjoys a formal right to regular information on 'the development of the Union's foreign and security policy' and a consequent corollary right to issue opinions or reports. Nonetheless, the European Parliament has repeatedly criticised the Council's *a posteriori* approach, which too often consists merely in informing the Parliament by submitting a descriptive list of Common Foreign and Security Policy activities carried out in the previous year instead of involving the EP in forthcoming policy debates and choices. At present, too often, the Council is only able to report to Parliament whether – and, if so, how – its contribution has been taken into account. This is provided for in Article 21 of the Treaty on European Union and in the Interinstitutional Agreement of 6 May 1999. Only a change in this practice would guarantee that the European Parliament's views have a substantial impact on future policy options.

The European Parliament has frequently underlined its readiness to hold a debate with the Council and its High Representative, Javier Solana, at the beginning of each year in order to discuss the basic orientation for the CFSP in the forthcoming year. It also encourages both the Council and member states to further strengthen parliamentary scrutiny of ESDP, by ensuring that the European Parliament plays a major role, using the structured dialogue mechanism provided for in a new Interinstitutional Agreement, signed on 17 May 2006.[4] Furthermore, the recognised deficit of parliamentary scrutiny could be redressed and transparency increased by strengthening cooperation between the European Parliament and national parliaments. In its latest report on CFSP, adopted by the AFET Committee on 27 March 2007, the European Parliament proposed measures to strengthen parliamentary scrutiny, especially with regard to the intelligence and security services. Measures include, for example, granting Parliament the right to appoint and dismiss the Counter-Terrorism Coordinator and the Directors of the Joint Situation Centre, as well as of the EU Satellite Centre and the European Union's Judicial Cooperation Unit EUROJUST. The EP is also demanding that these officials submit an annual report on their activities and budget in order to ensure that recommendations and remarks from Parliament are duly taken into account. As the Interinstitutional Agreement of 20 November 2002 sets out, the role of the existing EP Special Committee, in which its members can access sensitive information of the Council in the field of security and defence policy, should be enhanced in order for it to scrutinise the new intelligence organs of the European Union as well as the EU Military Staff.

The Financing of CFSP/ESDP

Only when it comes to decision-making powers over the CFSP/ESDP budget, can the European Parliament be regarded as on an equal footing with the Council. Here the EP already exerts important *ex ante* control. The Parliament has continuously underlined its difficulties in assessing the financial coherence and effectiveness of financing ESDP operations, owing to the increasing complexity of funding options and the lack of sufficient information. At the same time, the European Parliament does acknowledge that more funds must be allocated to the CFSP/ESDP budget in order to make the EU a credible and capable actor at international level. The total amount of €1.74 billion allocated to the CFSP for the period 2007-2013 may be insufficient to match EU ambitions, but the agreed funding for the CFSP in 2007, amounting to €159.2 million, is an important step in the right direction.

The difficulty for parliamentary scrutiny of the EU's CFSP and ESDP operations arises in part from the complications introduced by the broad range of budget lines concerned. Civilian missions have been financed directly under the CFSP budget, whilst all military missions remain outside the scope of the democratic scrutiny of both national parliaments and the European Parliament. So far, the military operations have been funded under the NATO principle of 'costs lie where they fall', meaning that they are directly covered by the contributing member state. Any agreed common costs are managed under a mechanism known as ATHENA and agreed on 3 February 2004. Another problem is that multiple tasks and demands in crisis management operations usually require an integrated combination of instruments and rapid response mechanisms, so a clear-cut distinction as to whether such missions are civilian or military and consequently which sources of financing apply is not always possible. Thus, the European Parliament has only limited information concerning political objectives under the budget and can therefore only assess general 'trends' in spending on CFSP. The Parliament lacks in-depth information on how funds are allocated in terms of policy objectives. It is thus not in a position to adequately assess the effectiveness of such spending. This has led the Parliament to recommend placing all mechanisms, including the ATHENA mechanism, within the General Budget of the European Union.

On 1 January 2007, a new Interinstitutional Agreement on budgetary discipline and sound financial management came into force. This increases the Parliament's participation in the CFSP decision-making process and allows for greater democratic scrutiny of the external action of the Union.[5] But, it does not change the existing rules on ESDP operations. It does not explicitly provide for the joint costs of military operations within the framework of the ESDP to be financed from the Community budget, and thus does not, as the Parliament would have wished, discontinue the existing practice of having recourse to member states' subsidiary budgets or start-up funds. In its report on the annual report from the Council to the EP on the main aspects and basic choices of CFSP, including the financial implications for the general budget of the European Communities[6] the European Parliament criticised the fact that the current arrangements perpetuate the financial burden of those member states which make the biggest contribution, thus jeopardising future participation in ESDP operations and creating a situation which could easily be avoided by financing such operations from the EU budget. It also calls upon the Council to ensure the Parliament's right to be consulted annually *ex ante* on aspects of and options for CFSP, an ever more important requirement in the absence of the Constitutional Treaty, because key proposals to improve inter-pillar coordination are now on hold. Features such as the mutual assistance clause, structural co-operation, the European External Action Service and the single legal personality, all provided for in the Constitutional Treaty, are thus urgently needed if further progress in ESDP is to be assured.[7] The European Parliament has again urged the Heads of State and Government to finalise the Constitutional Treaty by the end of 2008, not only as a prerequisite for further enlargement but also in order to enable the Union to work more effectively, more transparently and more democratically in the fields of both external action and CFSP/ESDP.

Further Enhancement of ESDP through the Constitution

The Constitution would have introduced significant new elements into European Security and Defence Policy. The Treaty binds the EU to the principles of the United Nations Charter, and especially to preserving world peace and international security. With the Constitution, civilian measures would have priority over military means for solving conflicts. Nevertheless, the Treaty also envisages that the EU may, in certain circumstances, resort to the use of military means to defend European values with armed force. There needs, however, to be a unanimous decision from the Council for such operations. The Constitution also obliges member states to improve their civilian and military capabilities. First and foremost, this means a more efficient interlocking of national capabilities administered by the European Defence Agency. With Europe-wide co-ordination and co-operation it would be possible to reduce parallel structures and consequently costs. Finally, the Constitution would confer legal personality on the Union. This would allow the EU to participate more actively and exert more influence in multilateral affairs through representation in certain international/multilateral organisations, in particular the United Nations, the International Criminal Court (ICC), the Organization for Security and Cooperation in Europe (OSCE) and the Council of Europe. Above all, a seat in the UN's Security Council would be the most genuine expression of a true and effective common foreign policy and would enable the Union to support effectively the reform of the United Nations.

A desirable objective would be a move away from strict adherence to the principle of unanimity and provision of more qualified majority voting across the full spectrum of the EU's Common Foreign and Security Policy. This said, exceptional situations would have to be catered for. Indeed, the existing Treaty provision provides for constructive abstention with regard to the Common Foreign and Security Policy and the principle has been extended by the Constitutional Treaty to co-operation in military issues (Article III-208). Whether the 'mini-treaty' signed at the June 2007 summit will reinforce the point remains to be seen. The requisite scope for action can be achieved via a 'coalition of the willing', a pragmatic approach proposed in the draft constitution. A decisive point in this respect was that a 'coalition of the willing' should on no account be a 'closed shop'; any coalition would hopefully remain open to subsequent participation by other countries which meet the requisite criteria.

The European Union now comprises twenty-seven member states. If those states are to act in a concerted manner, sooner or later the Union has to provide for action by qualified majority voting. Where a common position is discussed and agreed, there is less temptation to proceed to unilateral action by an individual member state. This would appear to be the only way towards expression of a common political will which, after all, is the ultimate objective. The achievement of democratic control of the security sector thus remains as much an internal imperative for the EU as it constitutes a desirable norm for external policy-making and the funding of EU action abroad.

Endnotes

1 Much of this is associated with debates surrounding the so-called Revolution in Military Affairs. See Freedman, L., 'The Revolution in Strategic Affairs', *Adelphi Paper* 318, The International Institute for Strategic Studies, Oxford University Press, 1998.

2 Miller, D., *Export or Die: Britain's defence trade with Iran and Iraq*, London, Cassell, 1996.

3 Council of the European Union, ESDP Presidency Report, annex 1 'Headline Goal 2010,' Brussels 15 June 2004. The 2010 Headline Goal was first introduced in a French 'Non Paper' entitled 'Towards a 2010 Headline Goal.' This was further elaborated by an Italian Presidency Paper and again by a UK 'Non-Paper' focussing on implementation entitled 'The Road to 2010.' 'Draft Joint Action on the establishment of a European Defence Agency (EDA)', No. 10450/04, Brussels, 11 June 2004.

4 Interinstitutional Agreement on budgetary discipline and sound financial management of 17 May 2006, COM (2006) 327 final, OJ C 139 of 14.6.2006.

5 Interinstitutional Agreement on budgetary discipline and sound financial management of 17 May 2006, COM (2006) 327 final, OJ C 139 of 14.6.2006.

6 Report on the annual report from the Council to the EP on the main aspects and basic choices of CFSP, including the financial implications for the general budget of the European Communities (point H, paragraph 40 of the Interinstitutional Agreement of 6 May 1999) - 2005 (A6-0130/2007) by Elmar Brok, adopted during AFET meeting on 27 March 2007.

7 *ibid.*

8. Beyond the External–Internal Security Divide: Implications for EU Policies of Protection

Magnus Ekengren

Introduction

The necessities of transnational protection and crisis management in a globalised world are compelling the EU to take on a new, proactive security responsibility.[1] In the last few years the European Union (EU) has given assistance to those affected by the Asian tsunami, supported American authorities during the Katrina disaster, coordinated water-carrying aircraft to fight forest fires in Southern Europe and rescue teams in Turkey and Morocco after earthquakes. The Union has sent military peace keeping missions to Bosnia and the Democratic Republic of Congo, taken measures to prevent the further spread of avian influenza and to respond to the challenges of international terrorism, and coordinated EU member states in bringing home thousands of refugees after the war in Lebanon in the summer of 2006. The list of activities is growing with extraordinary pace and provides a striking evidence of the fact that the new security agenda is truly global.[2]

The Union's policies and instruments of protection have had a hard time keeping up with the demands stemming from this development.[3] Unfortunately, the many tragic events since the beginning of the 1990s have forced the EU onto the defensive. The development of the EU's security policies has so far been a reaction triggered by conspicuous events.

- Experience from the Balkan wars resulted in the formation of a European Security and Defence Policy (ESDP) for *external* crises, backed up with a military and civil crisis management capability and new organs.
- '9/11' led to the intensification of EU *internal* security efforts. Currently almost every area of cooperation in all Union pillars has a security plan, a security committee and a network for rapid communication and reaction.
- The events in Madrid on 11 March 2004 led the EU to adopt the 'Solidarity Declaration' on mutual support for the prevention of terrorism and aid in the event of a terrorist attack on EU territory.
- The Asian tsunami disaster at the end of 2004 resulted in closer EU con-

sular cooperation and the establishment of civilian teams for international rescue missions.

- The bomb attacks in London in the summer of 2005 have led to closer EU cooperation on intelligence and discussions of a Programme for the protection of critical infrastructure in Europe.[5]

Thus, the Union has tended to fall into the same traps as the nation states; i.e. basing its defence on the last crisis (or war) and making a strong distinction between internal and external security. This has been the root of many problems. In fact, most of the external actions listed above were forced to be carried out by EU instruments that were initially created for 'internal' crisis management. The consequence is that the new globalised tasks often have to be handled by *ad hoc* arrangements. For instance, due to the lack of a capacity for external civilian crisis, it was the *enlargement* department (and budget line) of the EU Commission that suddenly had to take the lead for Union support to affected candidate states during the floods in Central Europe in 2002. For similar reason Union responsibility for the safety of EU citizens abroad was 'invented' and developed only during the acute phases of the tsunami disaster.[6]

The 2003 European Security Strategy declares that 'internal and external aspects are indissolubly linked'.[7] However, the implications of this merger for EU protection are not (yet) reflected in the analysis and making of Union policies, institutions and operational planning. It is widely acknowledged that there is great potential in a more efficient combination of the EU's external and internal crisis management capacities.[8] Indeed, the future development of the ESDP and the Solidarity Clause in the draft Constitutional Treaty[9] constitute a crucial test for the Union's ability to retake the initiative internationally when it comes to shaping transboundary security in an innovative and strategic manner. This has never been as important as it is today when we see the shortcomings of civilian crisis management as well as more traditional uses of warfare and arms in Iraq and in the Russian suppression of terrorism.

The aim of this chapter is to examine some central policy and operational implications of the closer interface for EU protection policies. To this end it presents a conceptual framework for the analysis of EU security that transcends today's artificial boundary and can inform the debate about policy and institutional reform. The chapter begins with a theoretical background to why the internal-external distinction has had such a strong influence on our thinking. The subsequent section sketches a global approach to European and EU security in terms of concentric circles in contrast to a sharp division between home and abroad. In the light of this perspective implications are discussed first with regard to the ESDP, second in relation to EU civil protection, third within the framework of the Solidarity Clause and finally with a special focus on national military capacities needed for the implementation of the Clause. The goal is to pin-point key challenges that must be met for a more efficient EU role in the protection of its core values and citizens.

From the Internal-External Divide to Circles of Security

EU between National and International Security

The Union has always essentially been a transboundary security project. For the first forty years of the Union's existence, it promoted inter-state security through a system of networks that crossed state borders. External security relations among states were turned into 'domestic' European politics. Now – in an era of transboundary threats – the task is to create a common defence and security through similar networks beyond the internal-external divide.

An unhelpful theoretical development in recent years is the use of concepts and frameworks borrowed from the study of *national* security to study supranational security. Consequently, an unhelpful distinction has been made between internal 'desecuritization' of relations between EU member states[10] and an external Common Foreign and Security Policy (CFSP), which has been analysed in the context of international security dynamics.[11] This division originates in the tradition of territorial security and border defence. In practice the division is cemented by the EU's 'pillar' construction where the second pillar (the CFSP) has been set in contrast – formally as well as analytically – to the 'internal' security domains of the first (civil protection, health etc.) and, more recently, the third pillar (police, border control).[12] However, the question is to what extent a line between external and internal security can be drawn for a political entity that is not first and foremost territorially defined and one of whose aims was to erode borders for the purpose of inter-state security. The questions of what is inside and what is outside the Union[13] and external and internal EU security[14] should thus arouse significant analytical interest.

By combining domestic and international perspectives on EU security this section sketches the contours of a European security field stretching from inside the EU to beyond its borders. The field for Union security action can thus be defined as a sequence of concentric circles of different concerns and dynamics, rather than on the basis of a strict distinction between internal and external security. In this way, the approach builds upon and extends earlier conceptual attempts such as those associated with an 'enlarged European security space'[15], the 'internal' European security area[16] or as 'sub-regional institutional security frameworks'.[17] It also relates to studies of Europe's increasingly decentralised decision making and metaphors such as 'Olympic Rings'.[18]

Theories on the dissolution of boundaries between internal and external *national* security have demarcated a new transboundary 'field of security' in Europe.[19] The role of the EU is often here described as a 'platform' for negotiations between the security agencies of the member countries, such as the police and military forces. The roles of national actors are changing; both the police and military forces[20] are now increasingly oriented towards the common task of 'internal' European security. This has led to the fact that security analysis and planning are preoccupied with crisis situations and the prevention of conflicts and international crimes rather than traditional wars.[21] EU measures are gradually leading to a Europeanisation of the national obligation to protect citizens. The challenge to current theory, therefore, is to make sense of the EU as more than just a platform: it now possesses both internal and external safety and security instruments of its own. Consequently, the EU increasingly reflects the characteristics of a *domestic* system that could be understood by using theories of system and societal vulnerability, i.e. major disturbances on society (system effects).[22]

What is the *international* security threat to the EU? The confusion evoked by this kind of question is due to the fact that the EU traditionally has not been conceived of as an international security entity; it has, for example, no collective defence in the traditional sense.[23] Nor has it been analysed as an actor pursuing an active security policy because 'security policy' has been adjudged to remain within the competence of the EU member states (or to be taken care of in other organisations such as the North Atlantic Treaty Organisation). The EU has traditionally most often been viewed as an outcome or reflection of the considerations of other players organising for other concerns. Its success was that it created security by not discussing security. The consequence is that the EU until recently has lacked its own international security identity, which makes it difficult to capture in theoretical language the explicit and active EU security role that is taking shape today. The way in which the ESDP has evolved since 1999 has been interpreted as 'the end of territorial defence' for the EU[24], but the definition of the EU's security identity cannot be made with negations alone. Before we can understand how the 'internal' and 'external' dimensions overlap, the reference object of EU security must be further defined. What values, systems, 'functions' or perhaps territory do both 'internal' and 'external' policies aim to protect?

Internal and External Security: Common Objects of Protection

Over the years, new security referent objects have evolved incrementally within the Union as a result of its growing field of competences. Owing to the gradual expansion of the tasks of EU institutions, those institutions have also been forced to take on a growing responsibility for safeguarding and protecting the EU functions and 'systems', new policy competences have been created. The question of *whom, what* and *from what* EU security is protecting can be explained in the light of what the Union has considered to be a crisis throughout its history, and considering how the list of what should be safeguarded for the common good has grown. Since the 1950s the EU has provided *national* security.[25] In the 1970s and 1980s, economic welfare and stability came to be perceived as a critically important object for EU members to secure jointly. A crisis for the functioning of the common market and the institutional and legal measures taken to uphold the 'four freedoms' of intra-European exchange became an EU crisis.[26] By focusing on safeguarding the vital flow of resources for the welfare and identity of EU member states, the Union in effect took steps towards transnational *societal* security.[27] In the 1990s, the outbreak of war and violence in the Balkans also forced EU leaders to define this crisis as a crisis for the Union. The value of peace and stability in the neighbourhood – the 'near abroad' – was added to the EU's core goals. The aim of protecting peace and the safety of civilians was no longer limited to EU member states. Consequently, the reference object for the Union's endeavours became the same within and outside its borders: to secure states or ethnically based groupings from fighting each other. Thus a threat or event that undermines peace and stability in wider Europe also presents a potential crisis for the EU today. In this way the concept of human security[28] could also be added as a label for characterizing the aim of European security. This development was further underlined in subsequent years when natural disasters increasingly became defined as EU crises. The Commission and its Directorate-General (DG) for Humanitarian Aid (ECHO) gave a high priority to helping Turkey when the country was hit by two earthquakes in 1999.[29] If early practices set a precedent for future EU crisis management, EU security might increasingly refer to all humans in grave international crises.[30]

The 1990s saw a new development in internal EU safety. The BSE ('mad cow disease') crisis in 1996 was a serious threat to the common market and at the same time to the safety of European consumers. The EU had to reconcile the protection of both aspects of the growing multidimensional character of its referent object of security.[31] The events of 11 September 2001 started a chain of policy responses that have more clearly stated 'EU citizens' as an object of security. The Solidarity Clause constituted the next step by declaring that the EU aims should be to 'protect democratic institutions and the civilian population' not only from terrorist attack but also in the event of natural or man-made disasters (Article I-43).[32] Therefore, the referent object of security is not just a matter of infrastructure or flow, but also concerns the ability to govern society and to articulate political goals – the *functional* security areas.[33]

The historical overview shows how the Union has come to play a security role in four 'core' areas transcending the external-internal divide. In this way the Union is protecting certain fundamental values such as peace and stability (both within the EU and the near abroad), the European economy and the safety of people and society wherever under threat. These values are the main referent objects of security that members of the community seem to agree about in terms of joint protection. In other words, the Union has developed its policies for the protection of these fundamental EU values.[34] The EU's role in

Figure 2. *The four core areas for EU security*

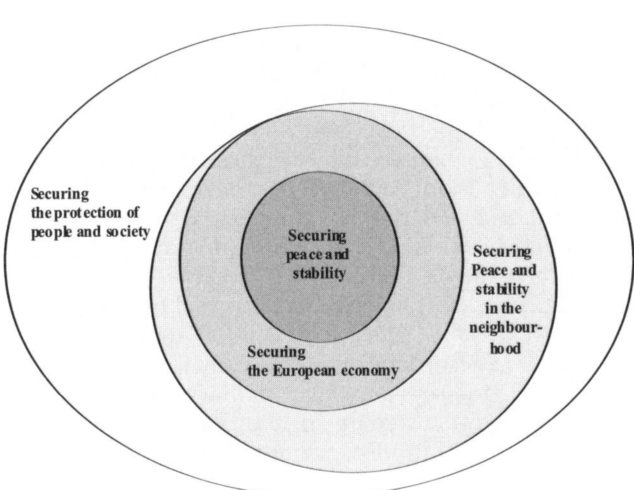

the four core areas could be said to embrace all the security concepts referred to above: national, societal, human and functional.

Figure 2 illustrates how the Union security role has evolved over the years in the form of the protection of four 'core areas'.[35] The figure could in fact be seen as depicting the chronological evolution beginning in time with the inner circle as well as the geographical extension of the Union's security commitment, ranging from member states in the inner circle to anybody in need of protection in the outer area.

EU Actions in Circles of European Security

The circle approach can now be translated into descriptions of specific security complexes. For instance, the Union has mainly responded to its neighbours not as a traditional security actor but by extending its internal system of governance through enlargement and through the integration of external actors into joint policy-making processes[36] – that is, through the EU's traditional fostering of security community. The consequence is a blurred boundary between 'outsiders' and 'insiders' in many EU security initiatives such as security sector reform.[37] In the light of earlier CFSP history[38], the capabilities developed for the ESDP will probably be used primarily in the areas bordering the EU. These areas are defined not only by the incidence of transboundary threats and risks, but also by expanding economic and security networks – the EU's traditional method of crisis and conflict prevention. The networks include first pillar systems to minimise societal vulnerabilities and prepare for emergencies. The main task of the new military and civilian capabilities of the ESDP is formally to manage crisis and conflict outside the borders of the EU.[39] This is intended to make the EU better-equipped as an 'international' security actor in the same boundary land for which it is attempting to build a 'domestic' European infrastructure through *inter alia* the Solidarity Clause on terrorism. Forthcoming enlargements and the 'European neighbourhood policy'[40] only underline the need for a circle approach in an EU security space that is steadily moving east and south.

Further away from the Union heartland, the security identity of the EU is gradually changing character. The Union is a hybrid of an international organisation and a would-be polity whose object is both the protection of EU and universal values wherever they are threatened in the world and the safety of EU citizens in a more narrow sense.[41] Threats closer to the core EU security crises might best be defined by threats to free trade and EU citizens, the EU Charter of Fundamental Rights, and so on – and, further out, to international law and the values embodied by the United Nations.[42] According to the proposed EU constitution, ESDP missions should be carried out for the purpose of peacekeeping, conflict prevention and the strengthening of international security in accordance with the principles of the UN Charter.[43] The EU's first independently launched military operation – Operation ARTEMIS in the Democratic Republic of the Congo, in 2003 – was carried out at the request of the UN (under a Chapter VII resolution).[44] If the early practices involving UN requests and mandates have set a precedent for future ESDP operations, EU security might increasingly encompass all people who are involved in a grave international crisis, as predicted by our circle approach. The evolving security role of the EU might then perhaps best be characterised as that of a regional body for the implementation of UN decisions. In that case, the 'outer' EU security circle would equal international security, and there would – by definition – exist no external security dimension in relation to which internal security could be distinguished.

Thus, the internal-external divide has in practice to a large extent lost its importance as analytical as well as political guideline for EU security action. The initial plan for the deployment of EU battle groups was 'within a geographical radius of 6000 kilometres from Brussels'. The obvious analytical implication of this kind of definition of European security is the concentric circle approach presented above. But what are the policy and operational implications?

Implications for ESDP

EU Level

ESDP has given rise to fundamental discussions about how to develop a more global EU concept that would seek to combine external and internal approaches more closely. This is thought to be essential if ESDP is to be successful and proactive.[45]

The EU's security answer to the 11 September 2001 attacks was non-military in nature. The focus was put on the crisis management capacities that exist in all three EU pillars. In practice, this made the EU responsible for the paradox of 'internal' and 'external' non-territorial security. In general, the events of 9/11 started a process which has led the EU to rethink its previous demarcation lines between trade, aid, diplomacy and the new crisis management capacities created under the ESDP. Discussions on whether or not to include the capacities of the EU's third pillar, Justice and Home Affairs – for example, in the areas of personnel and threat identification – signalled a development towards a broad transboundary security approach to the ESDP. For internal as well as external security reasons, many observers argued that there was an urgent need for better coordination between non-military ESDP activities, work under the Justice and Home Affairs pillar and the European Commission. It was also suggested that security thinking should be 'mainstreamed' into other areas of EU cooperation as well.[46] However, most of the issues still remain to be solved as of writing (2007).

The Union's strength as a crisis manager lies, above all, in the possibility of gathering together the full range of instruments that it has acquired over the years. Just as it will be difficult to separate internal security policy aspects from the external ones, it will probably be difficult to separate non-political aid instruments from protection activities with a security-political dimension. However, these sort of problems must be resolved quickly. The EU's potential as a crisis manager will crystallise through the development of new and innovative networks over and above the pillars of the EU. Therefore, to be really successful as a crisis manager, the EU must find ways to bridge the pillar structure, which currently militates against effective coordination of the various resources that the Union has at its disposal. Already, international crisis management instruments have developed within the EU's first pillar in the form of coordination by CIVCOM and the Commission's Rapid Reaction Mechanism

(RRM).[47] The cross-pillar coordination that has already begun will help to break down the divisions between external and internal policies of protection. The challenge of different principles for decision making in each pillar will, however, remain. Some analysts, for instance, predict that CFSP crisis management in the long run will remain intergovernmental due to weak incentives for member states to delegate to supranational organs.[48] Others, in contrast, argue the institutionalisation of EU protection policies in some sectors is leading to more supranational solutions.[49] In this perspective it is in the long term possible to envisage an all-embracing 'fourth pillar' for EU protection that will standardise decision making structures between pillars.[50]

National Level

To a greater degree than EU level coordination, perhaps, effective capability depends on member states being prepared to break up or redefine corresponding barriers on the home front: barriers between internal vulnerability and external defence, between defence and police forces, military and civilian intelligence agencies, between defence, justice and foreign ministries, and between defence policy, emergency planning and rescue agencies.[51] All of these barriers originate from a strong distinction between internal and external security. Many observers conclude that the future structure of EU institutions and their relationships with member states is the key dimension for efficient ESDP instruments.[52]

Ability is not just about having material resources to hand; it is also – as in the 1950s – about being ready to think in new ways and with new priorities. Current ESDP capability will never be greater than the contributions by member states. For example, to what extent EU security policy is intertwined with national security is largely a national question. Nowhere is this more clearly illustrated than in the current EUFOR operation in Bosnia-Herzegovina, which replaced NATO's SFOR in December 2004. One reason that the EU Police Mission (EUPM) in Bosnia (starting 2003) received such a strong response to its request for national experts in organised crime was the great interest in the issue amongst justice ministries and police forces in member states. It was understood at an early stage that drug smuggling and crime syndicates, which threaten the EU's major cities, are best countered by being on the spot in the Balkans.[53] The question was how much security the member states achieve at home for money invested in the Balkans through the EU.

Member states have differing views about certain issues in joint operations, which are of central importance to breaking up the internal-external divide. For example, there are ongoing discussions about the extent to which there should be strict demarcation between military and police tasks in EUFOR operations. Member states have emphasised that in Bosnia, the EU will be seen as an actor only with a well-coordinated contribution. Certain countries have made moves seeking to place the EU Commission under the authority of ESDP in the form of the EU Special Representative. Others have maintained that the objective of the Union has always been to turn European security policy into a matter of EU domestic policy; therefore, they have resisted any attempts to subordinate what they see as the engine for the whole process – the EU Commission – under the infrastructure for Union foreign policy in the second pillar.

The realisation of an ESDP beyond the internal-external divide requires not only long-term vision, but also unified concepts that can give direction and impetus to the national work at hand. The current establishment of multinational EU battle groups is one indication of the capabilities that will be required for future global security. As indicated by this chapter, however, there is still much thinking to be done about the political and strategic use of such resources; for what purposes should these groups be used?

Implications for the Solidarity Clause

As mentioned previously, the Solidarity Clause was adopted in March 2004 after the Madrid bombings in the form of a political declaration.[54] The Clause builds on the fundamental character of the Union and contains a range of forward-looking elements, which can help in the removal of boundaries between EU internal and external security and between crisis management and defence. The Clause was initially developed in the European Convention's Defence Working Group in 2002-2003.[55] The Clause states that: 'The Union shall mobilise all the instruments at its disposal, including the military resources made available by the Member States, to:

- Prevent the terrorist threat in the territory of the Member States;
- Protect democratic institutions and the civilian population from any terrorist attack;
- Assist a Member State in its territory, at the request of its political authorities, in the event of a terrorist attack;
- Assist a Member State in its territory, at the request of its political authorities, in the event of a natural or man-made disaster.'

The Clause brings to the fore several central issues addressed by the theoretical section of this chapter: Whose security? What will the EU secure? What constitutes a crisis for the EU? What is the EU providing security against? Does EU security apply to democracy and institutions in member states and/or at the EU level? To the member states' or the EU's population? Were the bomb attacks in Madrid an EU crisis? If so, what made them an EU crisis? Why was the Clause not invoked in the case of the London underground bombings in the summer of 2005?[56] This adds up to a number of 'when', 'where' and 'how' questions.

Where? The Clause applies to efforts within the Union's territory, not beyond. Territorial integrity was the goal of nation states. Will the integrity of societal functions be the goal of EU defence? The Solidarity Clause can take the EU a step closer to a new sort of transnational societal defence of the civilian population and democratic institutions. This 'total' EU defence could be seen as distinct from collective territorial defence as well as traditional EU conflict prevention. The EU as defence union rather than defence alliance? A successful defence union would probably be of great importance in consolidating a European identity.

How? The Clause emphasises the need for capabilities embracing all sectors – including military resources. The thinking is that, in the long term, member states should move in the same direction in their defence policy in order to meet the new terrorist threat. The assumption is that, today, member states are converging in terms of values and have reached a sufficient degree of integration in terms of cooperative networks. Another condition for the Clause to be successful is that preventive measures and national infrastructures are coordinated to the point that member states can act jointly at times of crisis. This readiness to act can, to a limited extent, be legislated through the EU, but must be based on a long-term common viewpoint and, perhaps, on the development of new forms of cooperation within the EU. Practical requirements for the Clause include a new transnational, cross-sector EU infrastructure of 'working networks' between member states in the protection field. This should include national public administrations as well as the civilian community, private business and voluntary organisations, the military, police forces, the judiciary and intelligence agencies. Discussions are currently taking place about how such cooperation can best be achieved. Thinking in this area has included the idea of 'EU preparedness guidelines' as a basis for an all-encompassing European societal defence.[57] Other far-reaching questions are how EU candidate countries and neighbouring countries can best be involved in this process, and what links there should be between the EU, the USA and Russia in these matters.

More than perhaps any other EU instrument, the Clause has the potential to be an instrument that contributes to the dissolution of the boundary between internal civil protection for emergencies and external crisis management for security.[58] It could be interpreted as bridging the two main views that have coexisted so far on the *finalité* of EU defence: collective defence through military alliance, on the one hand, and security through networks on the other. An EU defence *within* expanding European security circles is more easily reconciled with European integration's traditional role of creating a long-term zone of peace (security community), in contrast to the defence of territory for its own sake. The latter is more closely associated with traditional military instruments of power, which could be detrimental to relations with certain third countries and to the image of the EU as a security model. The EU could thus become a defence power while simultaneously avoiding a new and potentially destabilising balance-of-power relationship with neighbouring regions. The EU candidate states could be involved at an early stage of the accession process, and neighbouring and other states would be allowed to participate as far as possible. The Clause could be a step that, with time, might be a model also for other parts of the world. Perhaps Europe could be linked together with similar regional systems into a global defence network to combat today's network-based global terrorism.

The Clause legally codifies the external-internal interface by formally recognising the new object of EU security discussed in the theoretical parts: the functions of democratic institutions are to be safeguarded and populations are to be protected. Compared to the case of the traditional nation state, functional specification is given a relatively stronger position than territorial delimitation as a basis of EU security and defence. This weakens the rationale for a dividing line between internal and external EU security, in practice as well as analytically.

Implications for EU Civil Protection

EU civil protection cooperation demonstrates the Union's expanding concern for protecting 'people', 'property' and 'democratic institutions'. Civil protection cooperation first began in the mid-1980s largely as the result of a Commission push for more coordination to manage natural disasters internal to the Union. The then-commissioner for environment argued strongly that his directorate-general should do more in the wake of forest fires and heat waves in Southern Europe. Several Council resolutions adopted since 1985 approved the move toward joint training and an exploration of resource sharing. A legal basis for the actual deployment of such resources, however, would not come until 2001. The 11 September attacks led to the creation of a Community 'mechanism' for the compilation and use of member state resources, not only for natural disasters but also terrorist attacks.[59] Moreover, with the rise of the EU's external role in the European Security and Defence Policy (ESDP), member states ensured that the mechanism could be used to coordinate events both inside and outside the EU.[60] However, the elaboration of a capacity able to transcend this boundary has in practice shown to be more cumbersome than expected. This section tries to explain why.

The Community civil protection mechanism concerns the response phase of a disaster, and involves the pooling of civil protection resources amongst the 27 EU member states plus three non-EU states.[61] Member states are obliged to 'identify in advance intervention teams which might be available for such intervention' (Council of the European Union 2001, Article 2). Moreover, the 'member state in which the emergency has occurred shall notify those member states which may be affected by the emergency' along with the European Commission (Council of the European Union 2001). Member states have committed themselves to make available civil protection intervention teams of up to 2000 persons at short notice by 2003.[62] Community civil protection activities are managed by the directorate-general for environment, in the unit for civil protection. Monitoring and coordination of disasters takes place through the Monitoring and Information Centre (MIC), which operates a 24/7 communication and rapid alert network between member states called the Common Emergency Communication and Information System (CECIS).[63]

The adoption of the Community mechanism not only strengthened the EU's competences in civil protection: it also made pooled civil protection resources potentially available for use abroad. The EU, operating through pillar I, thus took an explicitly external role in civil protection alongside its traditional internal role. In turn, a question soon arose as to whether the Community mechanism might also be deployed as part of pillar II's ESDP. The Feira European Council in June 2000 agreed that the civilian crisis management component of ESDP should include civil protection. After several years of negotiation, the Commission and the Council agreed on a joint declaration in 2003 setting out how the Community mechanism might be employed for an ESDP mission.[64]

The mechanism has been employed several times since its establishment. After the 11 September 2001 events more than 1,000 rescue workers from the member states were co-ordinated through the mechanism for missions across the Atlantic.[65] The MIC has launched requests for assistance in connection with the oil accident caused by the *Prestige* tanker off the Spanish coast in the autumn of 2002.[66] This resulted in ships, aircraft, equipment and experts from different participating countries being put at the disposal of the Spanish, Portuguese and French authorities. The mechanism was also used for a request for high capacity pumps during the floods in France in

December 2003 and again in February 2004, when Morocco was hit by an earthquake. In 2006 the mechanism was used for the first time in a war situation when it helped member states evacuate their citizens from Lebanon and coordinated European experts for the education of locals to clean up the oil spill caused by Israeli bombing. Several capacities have been tested in these first EU interventions. The value added by the mechanism over the system of bilateral requests for assistance is its provision for more consolidated and theoretically quicker and more precise response. The mechanism performed well as a clearing house for assistance. A number of technical problems have, however, been highlighted. These had mainly to do with communication problems between the various national teams.[67] Many of the problems, however, seem to originate in a mindset still strongly shaped by a distinction between internal and external security. Although the formal mandate to use civil protection tools outside Union territory now exists, implications for operational planning seem to have been largely ignored.

The Internal–External Challenge

Floods – 2002

On 14 August 2002, Czech president Vaclav Havel phoned Commission president Romano Prodi – at that time on vacation in his home town of Bologna – to explain the acute flooding situation in Central Europe.[68] Prodi travelled immediately to Prague and promised that the Union would assist the Czech Republic. Contacting most of the high-level civil servants in the Commission (largely from the directorate-general for environment and directorate-general for enlargement), Prodi urged them back from vacation to lead the work of coordinating the assistance of the EU member states and putting together an EU aid package for the affected areas. One of the first to be contacted was the Head of Unit for the Czech Republic team at directorate-general for enlargement at the European Commission.[69] Later that same day, Czech Republic authorities made a formal request to the MIC of the directorate-general for environment to activate the Community mechanism. The request prioritised portable dryers, floating pumps, and electric submersible pumps. The request was notified from the MIC to the competent national authorities.

Some EU states used other mechanisms for assistance in addition to the MIC. Others went ahead with bilateral contacts even while the MIC was trying to coordinate activities. This led to confusion at the European level, 'rather than better coordination'.[70] Member states were free to send whatever resources they had available, rather than the ones targeted by the requesting country.[71] That too led to problems, including the provision of assistance that could not be used by the Czech Republic. Czech foreign minister Stanislav Gross announced on 14 August that, while grateful for the aid, some of it was unnecessary. He emphasised that assistance with reconstruction was, by that point, a higher priority.[72] By 21 August, the Czech Republic had received assistance in the form of dryers, pumps, blankets, stoves, disinfectants, hygienic materials, generators, emergency grants, personnel and other humanitarian items from twenty countries. Throughout the disaster, Commission president Romano Prodi kept a close watch over developments and reiterated the wider Europe's 'solidarity with the victims of the flooding'.[73] After several days, a Commission delegation that included commissioners Margot Wallström, Gunther Veurheugen, and Michel Barnier visited Prague and Germany to assess the damage. This was the largest visit by a Commission delegation at this level for a civil protection incident, displaying a concern, in the words of one Commission official, for an EU response to disasters '*wherever* they happen' (italics added).[74]

Tsunami – 2004

Within hours of the Asian tsunami of December 2004, the Commission's directorate-general for environment began collecting information and critical intelligence for dissemination through the MIC. As for any use of the civil protection mechanism, however, no action could proceed without a formal request from the country in need. For external deployment of the mechanism, a further approval needed to be granted from the current holder of the EU's rotating presidency.[75] The Sri Lankan government made a formal request to the MIC while the Dutch presidency signed off on the use of the mechanism.[76] The MIC notified all EU states (and the five other participants in the Community mechanism) of the appeal from Sri Lanka through the MIC's rapid alert network.[77] The receiving countries were later broadened to include Indonesia and the Maldives, in addition to Sri Lanka and Thailand.[78]

After several days the Union was forced to take on a new responsibility that had never been included in its crisis preparation. This was the need to support and evacuate EU citizens affected by the tsunami. The Dutch presidency focused considerable attention on this task.[79] The MIC took part in the inter-consular telephone conferences organised by the presidency, which aimed at coordinating the evacuation efforts in Thailand. The result of these conferences was a new request by the MIC to member states, stipulating the need for medical assistance and search and rescue teams for European citizens.[80] In the aftermath of the crisis, the Union admitted its shortcomings and lack of imagination. The Union had had a preparedness for assisting its own citizens in its territory and for aiding third country nationals hit by catastrophes. However, there had been no operational planning for helping EU citizens abroad.

In the aftermath of the tsunami, the Commission attempted to remedy these shortcomings. It launched a consultation process with the member states on the development of the existing civil protection tools into a broader instrument addressing prevention of, preparedness for and response to disasters.[81] The Commission proposed that member states in some form should declare their 'firm commitment' to cooperate with each other in delivering civil protection assistance and the reinforcement of EU coordination capacities, such as an 'operational planning capacity' of the MIC of the Commission and a common function on site with the formal authority to coordinate the assistance. The idea was to make the MIC more able to mobilise military means, hire equipment that cannot be obtained by member states, and promote a system of specialised national modules for European use. These standby modules should, according to the Commission, be deployed 'quasi-automatically' on the request of 'appropriate European authority'.[82]

In their response, many member state authorities emphasised the need to respect national sovereignty and the principles of subsidiarity, and warned against any reform that did not strengthen the added value of the EU capacity. According to many member states, the role of the EU was first and foremost to provide coordination support to national interventions. For this reason, many were in favour of the proposals to improve the MIC. There was also a broad consensus on the need to strengthen the Union's capacity in the area of prevention, preparedness and information to the public. In contrast, most member states hesitated to adopt the idea of creating a standby capacity for mutual European assistance, not least because they thought the composition of national and European teams needed to be as flexible as possible in a situation where future disasters were 'unknown'. According to member states, different compositions were needed for different interventions and teams should be composed of personnel working with emergencies on a daily basis. The idea of a flexible modular system could, according to some member states, be further discussed.[83] The so-called Barnier report of Spring 2006 suggested the establishment of a standing European civil protection force – 'Europe aid' – supported by an EU Council for civil protection and permanent sites around the globe for the quick provision of assistance.[84] Yet, according to interviews with national officials, this proposal has not been favourably received by national ministries.

As for the ESDP, the basic challenge of transcending the internal-external divide is an expression of the tensions between the need for common action, national sovereignty concerns and practical sector specific needs.[85]

Implications for National Armed Forces

The ability of the EU member states to provide for capacities such as military assistance to internal protection will be decisive for the EU's possibilities to transcend the internal-external security boundary. In order to illustrate an important case of national policy adaptation, this section investigates the positions of the three Nordic EU countries – Finland, Sweden, Denmark – with regard to the use of military assistance in domestic counterterrorism activities. The emerging new internal role of the Nordic armed forces is a significant example of the national reforms needed for the implementation of the EU's Solidarity Clause. The national and Union levels are closely linked because national military assistance for internal EU use is of great importance for the effective implementation of the Solidarity Clause, which calls upon the member states to make available 'military resources'. Again, the closer internal-external interface makes the development of the EU's security policies increasingly dependent on the contributions of the member states. In order to put the national resources requested at the disposal of the EU, governments must fundamentally rethink the traditional division of roles between the police and the military.

Traditionally, the EU member states have adopted many different solutions for providing and regulating these functions.[86] In all of the Nordic countries there has historically been a strict division between the military's defence of the state border and national security and the maintenance of order by the police. In the aftermath of September 2001, however, the Nordic governments have begun to re-examine their legal frameworks with regard to the use of military assistance to combat terrorist attacks on their territory.

Finland's 1980 act on the provision of assistance by the defence forces to the police allows military assistance to be given only in cases where the resources of the police are inadequate. After September 2001, a commission established to consider the act proposed amendments in areas related to the combating of terrorism. Under the proposal, the police can ask the Ministry of the Interior to request assistance from the Ministry of Defence. The two ministers together decide whether this type of assistance ought to be provided. The naval and air force units of the defence forces can be put at the disposal of the police if the nature of the terrorist threat calls for these resources.[87] The 2004 amendment to the 1980 act also specifies the conditions for military assistance. The police may receive assistance from the armed forces in order to prevent or avert certain criminal acts as specified in the Finnish Criminal Code. In emergency situations when there is a 'serious' and 'direct' threat to 'particularly important' functions of society, the police force's request for assistance can be made directly to the top military command.[88] In the Finnish Government's strategy for national preparedness, the basic functions of society are defined as 'state leadership, external capacity to act, the nation's military defence, internal security, functioning of the economy and society, securing the livelihood of the population and its capacity to act, and their ability to tolerate a crisis'.[89]

Military assistance by the Swedish Armed Forces to the police has not been permitted since 1931, when the military opened fire on a strike demonstration in Ådalen and several participants were killed. In 2003 the Swedish Ministry of Justice published the report of a government commission on the implications of the attacks of 11 September 2001, suggesting legal reforms to enable military assistance.[90] The report proposed that, on the request of the police or the coastguard, the armed forces could intervene against non-state actors with the degree of force necessary to avert immediate danger to the safety of the state or human life or to prevent extensive destruction of property. The commission suggested that the government could deploy the armed forces to combat an armed attack against the Swedish state even if the attack did not emanate from a foreign state. This opened a new field in which the armed forces could be used: military assistance would be allowed in cases of large-scale terrorist attacks threatening the security of the state. Less serious terrorist attacks that could be classified as armed attacks against the security of the state would continue to be a matter for the police. Currently, Swedish armed forces may respond to surprise attacks against the Swedish state by a foreign state without awaiting a decision by the government. The report suggested that this condition should also apply in the event of threats from terrorists.[91] The proposed bill did not, however, obtain political support. Instead, a new commission proposed the framing of a new act to regulate the conditions for military assistance to the police in the event of a major terrorist act on (Sweden's) democracy beyond the current capacity of the police.[92] The new legislation was adopted by parliament in June 2006. In the framework of the EU Solidarity Clause on terrorism, the Swedish Government predicts that military support for civilian crisis management, including the police, will most likely concern the provision of nuclear, biological and chemical expertise, logistics and command resources.[93]

One of the tasks of the Danish Armed Forces, according to the 2001 defence forces act, is assistance to the civilian authorities, including both assistance in rescue operations and assistance to the police.[94] The guiding principle is that military units providing assistance are subordinated to the command of the requesting authority and should obey the latter's rules of engagement. There are no particular statutory limitations concerning the character of the assistance.

According to the act, among the assets that could be provided by the armed forces are helicopters and boarding expertise. The Danish police do not possess their own helicopters, and it is primarily the Royal Danish Navy that could provide boarding expertise to the police. Danish law does not exclude assistance for combating organised crime. Decisions on this kind of assistance are taken jointly by the ministries of Justice and Defence.[95]

Towards a New Type of Transnational Security Community?

This chapter elaborates the concept of European security in concentric circles as a way to understand the new landscape for EU protection policies. By putting the ESDP, the Solidarity Clause, EU civil protection and national armed forces in this landscape it is able to reveal key questions and a need for reform in a way not possible for approaches constrained by the internal-external security divide.

Viewed over the last five decades, the transformation of European security into increasingly wider circles is nothing new. In the 1950s the European Community helped the West European states to think ahead in terms of common security through transnational cooperation. With the EU's transcending of national internal-external boundaries, Western Europe emerged as a security community: defined by Karl Deutsch as a group of people integrated to the point where there is a 'real assurance that the members of that community will not fight each other physically, but will settle their disputes in some other ways'.[96] For the European security community, there was no sharp division between 'internal' and 'external' security. The community faded away the further you moved from its centre.

The current challenge is to try again to make the most of European innovative thinking on security. A key to success is to think and act beyond the internal-external divide. In the 1950s the European Union was able to transcend the division between external and domestic security for its member states by generating cooperation and community through transnational networking. Fifty years later, it has begun to dissolve the boundary between external and internal EU security by expanding its internal safety, police and defence cooperation to neighbouring areas and linking it to the EU's contribution to international security. This chapter examines some of the clearest and most visible signs of this development. It also shows that much remains to be done. However, the trans-governmental security and safety cooperation that has evolved since September 2001, and that has been codified by the Solidarity Clause on terrorism, might provide the EU with an opportunity to take the lead again in the creation of post-national security systems and communities.

As in the case of the security community, the new EU security role does not imply the transformation of Europe into a state. It is also unlikely to be based on a military defence alliance. Instead, the Solidarity Clause and the ESDP point to a Union fostering a new type of regional security identity. The question is whether the EU will manage to deepen the European security community into a secure European community – a homeland defence *à la* Europe.

A secure community could tentatively be defined as 'a group of people that is integrated to the point where there is real assurance that the members of that community will assist each other to protect their democratic institutions and civilian populations – the basic functions of their societies and governments'.[97] In this kind of community there would also be no clear distinction between internal and external security. It is in the light of this emerging new European – and perhaps transatlantic – secure community that the implications for the EU's protection policies should be assessed.

Endnotes

1 The author would like to thank Arjen Boin, Philipp Fluri, Sue Lai Suying, Mark Rhinard and David Spence for most valuable comments on earlier versions of the chapter. I am also indebted to the members of the programme 'Creating EU Crisis Management for a Secure European Community' conducted by the Leiden University Crisis Research Center (CRC) in the Netherlands and the Programme for European Security Research at Swedish National Defence College. More information at www.eucm.leidenuniv.nl.

2 Duke, S., *The Elusive Quest for European Security* (Macmillan: Basingstoke, 2000); Van Ham, P. and Medvedev, S., *Mapping European Security after Kosovo* (Manchester University Press: Manchester, 2002).

3 Boin, A., Ekengren, M., Rhinard, M. (eds) (2006) 'Special Issue: Protecting the Union: The Emergence of a New Policy Space', *Journal of European Integration*, Vol. 28, No 5, December.

4 European Council, 'Declaration on combating terrorism', Brussels, 25 Mar. 2004, URL <http://ue.eu.int/ueDocs/cmsUpload/79635.pdf>.

5 European Commission (2005) 'Commission Green Paper on a European Programme for Critical Infrastructure Protection', COM (2005) 576 final, Brussels, 17.11.2005.

6 Ekengren, M., Matzén, N., Svantesson, M. (2006) *The new security role of the European Union: transnational crisis management and the protection of Union citizens*, EUCM report 2, ACTA 35 B 2006, Stockholm: National Defence College. In this regard, however, the EU displayed a similar pattern as some member states.

7 Council of the European Union, 'A Secure Europe in a Better World: European Security Strategy', Brussels, 12 Dec. 2003, URL <http://ue.eu.int/cms3_fo/showPage.ASP?id=266>, p. 2.

8 Duke, S. and Ojanen, H. (2006) 'Bridging Internal and External Security: Lessons from the European Security and Defence Policy', *Journal of European Integration*, Vol. 28, No 5, December, pp. 477-494.

9 European Union (2004) 'Treaty establishing a Constitution for Europe.' Official Journal of the European Union, C 310, 16 December 2004, p. 32. Adopted as a political declaration in the aftermath of the Madrid train bombings in 2004. See more on the Clause in section five.

10 Buzan, B., Wæver, O. and de Wilde, J., *Security: A New Framework for Analysis* (Lynne Rienner: London, 1998).

11 Ginsberg, R. H., *The European Union in World Politics: Baptism of Fire* (Rowman & Littlefield: Lanham, Md., 2001); and Smith, M. E., *Europe's Foreign and Security Policy: the Institutionalization of Cooperation* (Cambridge University Press: Cambridge, 2004).

12 Winn, N. and Lord, C., *EU Foreign Policy Beyond the Nation State: Joint Actions and Institutional Analysis of the Common Foreign and Security Policy* (Palgrave: Basingstoke, 2001); and Hill, C., 'The capability-expectations gap, or conceptualising Europe's international role', eds S. Bulmer and A. Scott, *Economic and Political Integration in Europe: Internal Dynamics and Global Context* (Blackwell: Oxford, 1994).

13 Walker, R. B. J., *Inside/Outside: International Relations as Political Theory* (Cambridge University Press: Cambridge, 1993).

14 Wæver, O. et al., *Identity, Migration and the New Security Order in Europe* (Pinter: London, 1993); and Sjursen, H., 'Security and defence', eds W. Carlsnaes, H. Sjursen and B. White, *Contemporary European Foreign Policy* (Sage: London, 2004), p. 62.

15 Lenzi, G., 'Defining the European security policy', ed. J. Zielonka, *Paradoxes of European Foreign Policy* (Kluwer: The Hague, 1998), pp. 111-14.

16 Wæver, O., 'The EU as a security actor: reflections from a pessimistic constructivist on post-sovereign security orders', eds Kelstrup and Williams, *International Relations and the Politics of European Integration: Power, Security and Community* (Routledge: London, 2000), pp. 250-94.

17 Jørgensen K. E. (ed.), *European Approaches to Crisis Management* (Kluwer Law: The Hague, 1997), p. 211.

18 Browning, C. (2005) 'Westphalian, Imperial, Neomedieval: The Geopolitics of Europe and the Role of the North', in C. Browning (ed.) *Remaking Europe in the Margins* (London: Ashgate).

19 Bigo, D., 'When two become one: internal and external securitisations in Europe', eds Kelstrup and Williams, *International Relations and the Politics of European Integration: Power, Security and Community* (Routledge: London, 2000), pp. 171-204; and Bigo, D., 'The Möbius ribbon of internal and external security(ies)', eds Albert, Jacobson and Lapid, *Identities, Borders, Orders: Rethinking International Relations Theory* (University of Minnesota Press: Minneapolis, Minn., 2001), pp. 91-116.

20 Bigo, 'When two become one' (note 19), p. 183.

21 Bigo, D., *Polices en Réseaux: l'Expérience européenne* [Police in networks: the European experience] (Presses de la Fondation nationale des sciences politique: Paris, 1996); and Mitsilegas, V., Monar, J. and Rees, W., *The European Union and Internal Security: Guardian of the People?* (Palgrave: Basingstoke, 2003).

22 Jervis, R., *System Effects: Complexity in Political and Social Life* (Princeton University Press: Princeton, NJ, 1997).

23 Sjöstedt, G., *The External Role of the European Community* (Saxon House: Farnborough, 1977); and Whitman, R. G., *From Civilian Power to Superpower? The International Identity of the European Union* (Macmillan: Basingstoke, 1998).

24 Gärtner, H., 'European security: the end of territorial defense', *Brown Journal of World Affairs*, vol. 9, issue 2 (winter/spring 2003).

25 Technically speaking, the European Union has only existed since 1992. I take the history of the EEC (which began in the late 1950s) into account as well.

26 Boin, A., Ekengren, M., Rhinard, M. (2006) 'Functional Security and Crisis Management Capacity in the European Union. Report', No B 36 ACTA-series, National Defence College, Stockholm, chapter 2.

27 Buzan, B., Wæver, O. and de Wilde, J., *Security: A New Framework for Analysis* (Lynne Rienner: London, 1998); Møller, B. (2001) 'Global, National, Societal and Human Security, A General Discussion with a Case Study from the Middle East', Paper presented at the 4th Pan-European Conference at the University of Kent at Canterbury, UK, 8-10 September 2001.

28 Paris, R. (2001) 'Human Security: Paradigm Shift or Hot Air?', *International Security*, 26,2. pp. 87-102.

29 Ekengren, M., and Ramberg, B. (2003) 'EU Practices and European Structure of Crisis Management: A Bourdieuian Perspective on EU Foreign Policy – The cases of Earthquakes in Turkey and Recon-struction of Kosovo, 1999' Paper presented at ECPR Conference, September 2003 Canterbury, UK.

30 It is perhaps significant that 'A Human Security Doctrine for Europe' recently was proposed as a doctrine for Europe's security capabilities. (Kaldor, M., *A Human Security Doctrine for Europe, The Barcelona Report of the Study Group on European Security*. Presented 10 November 2004, led by Professor Mary Kaldor in 2003 at the request of EU Secretary-General Javier Solana. Online. Available HTTP: <http://www.lse.ac.uk/Depts/global/> (accessed 6 October 2005)

31 Grönvall, J. (2000) *Managing Crisis in the European Union: The Commission and 'Mad Cow' Disease*, Stockholm: CRISMART/Swedish National Defence College, p. 89; and Grönvall (2001) 'Mad Cow Disease: The Role of Experts and European Crisis Management,' in Rosenthal, U., Boin, A. and Comfort, L. (eds), *Managing Crises: Threats, Dilemmas, Opportunities*. Springfield: Charles C Thomas.

32 European Union (2004) 'Treaty establishing a Constitution for Europe', Official Journal of the European Union, C 310, 16 December 2004, p. 32.

33 Sundelius, B. (2005) 'Disruptions – Functional Security for the EU', in Elbe, S. Luterbacher, U. Missiroli, A., Sundelius, B. and Zupi, M. (2005) *Disasters, Diseases, Disruptions: a new D-drive for the EU*, Chaillot Paper, no. 83, September.

34 Boin, A., Ekengren, M., Rhinard, M. (2006) 'Functional Security and Crisis Management Capacity in the European Union. Report', No B 36 ACTA-series, National Defence College, Stockholm, p. 20. This characterisation of an EU crisis builds on a classical crisis definition according to which a crisis should be understood as a 'serious threat to (...) fundamental values and norms of a social system (...)' (Rosenthal, U., Charles, M.T. and 't Hart, P. (eds.) (1989) *Coping with crisis: The management of disasters, riots and terrorism*. Springfield, Charles C Thomas.

35 The figure was first presented in Ekengren, M., Matzén, N., & Svantesson M. (2006) *The New Security Role of the European Union* (Stockholm: Swedish National Defence College, Acta B35), p. 120.

36 Filtenborg, M. S., Gänzle, S. and Johansson, E., 'An alternative theoretical approach to EU foreign policy: network governance and the case of the Northern Dimension initiative', *Cooperation and Conflict*, vol. 37, no. 4 (2002), pp. 387-407.

37 Hänggi, H. and Tanner, F. (2005) 'Promoting security sector governance in the EU's neighbourhood', Chaillot Paper, No 80, July, Paris: Institute for Security Studies.

38 On the basis of the growing collection of case studies of the EU's external actions it is safe to conclude that the CFSP has been politically strongest within ('collective at any cost') and on the EU's frontiers. See Piening, C., *Global Europe: The European Union in World Affairs* (Lynne Rienner: London, 1997). This development has been underlined as a consequence of the extended cooperation with candidate states in the 1990s. See Friis, L. and Murphy, A., 'The European Union and Central and Eastern Europe: governance and boundaries', *Journal of Common Market Studies*, vol. 37, no. 2 (1999), pp. 211-32.

39 See the Treaty of Amsterdam, 2 Oct. 1997, URL <http://www.europarl.eu.int/topics/treaty/pdf/amst en.pdf>; European Council, 'Presidency conclusions', Helsinki, 10-11 Dec. 1999, URL <http://europa.eu.int/council/off/conclu/dec99/dec99_en.htm>; European Council, 'Conclusions of the Presidency', Santa Maria da Feira, 19-20 June 2000, URL <http://www.europarl.eu.int/summits/fei1_en.htm>; and European Council, Gothenburg, 15-16 June 2001, URL <http://europa.eu.int/comm/gothenburg_council/index_en.htm>.

40 Commission of the European Communities, 'Communication from the Commission: paving the way for a new neighbourhood instrument', Brussels, 1 July 2003, COM (2003) 393 final, URL <http://europa.eu.int/comm/world/enp/document_en.htm>.

41 Whitman, R. G., 'The fall, and rise, of civilian power Europe?', Paper presented at the Conference on the European Union in International Affairs, National Europe Centre, Australian National University, 3-4 July 2002; and Manners, I., 'Normative power Europe: a contradiction in terms?', *Journal of Common Market Studies*, vol. 40, no. 2 (2002).

42 Haaland Matlary, J., 'Human rights', eds Carlsnaes, Sjursen and White (note 14), pp. 141-54. On the EU Charter of Fundamental Rights see URL <http://www.europarl.eu.int/charter/>.

43 United Nations, 'Charter of the United Nations', URL <http://www.un.org/aboutun/charter/>.

44 Ulriksen, S., Gourlay, C. and Mace, C., 'Operation Artemis: the shape of things to come?', *International Peacekeeping*, vol. 11, no. 3 (autumn 2004), pp. 508-25.

45 Duke, S. and Ojanen, H. (2006) 'Bridging Internal and External Security: Lessons from the European Security and Defence Policy', *Journal of European Integration*, Vol. 28, No 5, December, pp. 477-494; Protecting Europe – Policies for enhancing security in the EU, International Conference organised by The Security & Defence Agenda, 30 May 2006, Brussels. 'Session four: Is Europe getting the politics of security right?'

46 See Dwan, R., 'Capabilities in the civilian field', Speech at the Conference on the European Union Security Strategy: Coherence and Capabilities, Working Group 2, Capabilities, Swedish Institute of International Affairs, Stockholm, 20 Oct. 2003, URL <http://www.sipri.org/contents/conflict/nonmilitary.htm>,

47 Boin, A., Ekengren, M., Rhinard, M. (2006) 'Chapter 18: The Commission and Crisis Management', in D. Spence (ed.) *The European Commission*, London: John Harper Publishing, pp. 481-501.

48 See Wessels, W., (2003) 'Why the EU's Common Foreign and Security Policy will remain Intergovernmental: a rationalist institutional choice analysis of European crisis management policy, *Journal of European Public Policy* 10: 4, pp. 576-595.

49 Boin, A., Ekengren, M., Rhinard, M. (eds) (2006) 'Protecting the European Union – Policies, sectors and institutional solutions', Report, Swedish National Defence College, October.

50 Ekengren, M. (2002) 'EU som civil krishanterare – nätverksbyggare eller aktör?', i S. Myrdal (red) *EU som civil krishanterare, Säkerhetspolitiska rådet*, Utrikespolitiska Institutet, Stockholm.

51 Sundelius, B., 'The seeds of a functional security paradigm for the European Union', Paper presented at the Second Pan-European Conference on EU Politics of the ECPR Standing Group on European Union Politics., Bologna, 2004.

52 Smith, M. E., *Europe's Foreign and Security Policy: the Institutionalization of Cooperation* (Cambridge University Press: Cambridge, 2004).

53 See Dwan, R., 'Capabilities in the civilian field', Speech at the Conference on the European Union Security Strategy: Coherence and Capabilities, Working Group 2, Capabilities, Swedish Institute of International Affairs, Stockholm, 20 Oct. 2003, URL

54 de Wijk, R., 'Civil defence and solidarity clause: EU homeland defence', Paper prepared for the Directorate-General for Research of the European Parliament, Brussels, 5 Jan. 2004.

55 Ekengren, M. and Larsson, S., 'Säkerhet och försvar i framtidens EU: an analys av försvarsfrågorna i det europeiska konventet' [Security and defence in the future EU: an analysis of the defence questions in the European convention], Report no. 2003:10 (Swedish Institute of European Policy Studies (SIEPS): Stockholm, 2003), URL <http://www.sieps.se/_eng/forskning.htm>. See also the SIEPS Internet site at URL <http://www.sieps.se/>.

56 Boin, A., Ekengren, M., Rhinard, M. (2006) 'Chapter 18: The Commission and Crisis Management', in D. Spence (ed.) *The European Commission*, London: John Harper Publishing, pp. 481-501.

57 Ekengren, M. (2006) 'New Security Challenges and the Need for New Forms of EU Co-operation – the Solidarity Clause and the Open Method of Coordination', *European Security*, Vol. 15, No. 1, pp. 89-111.

58 de Wijk, R., 'Civil defence and solidarity clause: EU homeland defence', Paper prepared for the Directorate-General for Research of the European Parliament, Brussels, 5 Jan. 2004.

59 Ekengren, M., Matzén, N.,, Rhinard, M., Svantesson, M. (2006) 'Solidarity or Sovereignty? EU Cooperation in Civil Protection', *Journal of European Integration*, Vol. 28, No 5, December, pp. 457-476.

60 Duke, S. and Ojanen, H. (2006) 'Bridging Internal and External Security: Lessons from the European Security and Defence Policy', *Journal of European Integration*, Vol. 28, No 5, December, pp. 477-494.

61 The non-EU states participating in the mechanism include Iceland, Liechtenstein, and Norway.

62 These commitments were made at the European Council meeting in Göteborg in June 2001.

63 CECIS is linked with a number of other networks operating in different sectors, including those dealing with radiological, health, and biological-chemical disasters. See European Commission (2004) 'Communication from the Commission on Reinforcing the Civil Protection Capacity of the European Union', Brussels, 25 March 2004, COM(2004)200 final. 2004a, pp. 11-12.

64 Joint Declaration (2003) 'Joint Declaration by the Council and the Commission on the use of the Community Mechanism in Crisis Management referred to in Title V of the Treaty on the European Union of 29 September 2003', Internal Document.

65 de Wijk, R., 'Civil defence and solidarity clause: EU homeland defence', Paper prepared for the Directorate-General for Research of the European Parliament, Brussels, 5 Jan. 2004.

66 Personal interview with an official from the Commission's civil protection unit, directorate-general for environment, 13 February 2003.

67 Woodbridge, J. (2002) 'Civil Protection Against Terror Attacks: testing EU cooperation', *European Security Review*, (ISIS), 2002(15), pp. 7-8.

68 Personal interview with an official from the Commission's directorate-general for enlargement, 13 February 2003.

69 Personal interview with an official from the Commission's directorate-general for enlargement, 13 February 2003.

70 Woodbridge, J. (2002) 'Civil Protection Against Terror Attacks: testing EU cooperation', *European Security Review*, (ISIS), 2002(15), pp. 7-8.

71 Personal interview with a member of the Commission's civil protection unit, directorate-general for environment, 11 February 2003.

72 Radio Free Europe/Radio Liberty, 15 August 2002 transcript of broadcast found on Relief Web (available at: http://www.reliefweb.int/w/rwb.nsf, accessed February, 2003).

73 European Commission (2002) 'Commission expresses solidarity with victims of floods – ANNEX.' Press release, IP/02/1220. Brussels, 15 August 2002.

74 Personal interview with a member of the Commission's civil protection unit, directorate-general for environment, 11 February 2003.

75 For further assessment of the general procedures of the MIC within the directorate-general for environment, see Ekengren, M., Matzén, N., Rhinard, M., Svantesson, M. (2006) 'Solidarity or Sovereignty? EU Cooperation in Civil Protection', *Journal of European Integration*, Vol. 28, No 5, December, pp. 460-462.

76 European Commission (2005) 'EU Civil protection assistance in South East Asia', Memorandum, MEMO/05/6, Brussels, 11 January 2005.

77 European Commission (2005) 'Commission's civil protection mechanism takes effective measures to coordinate technical assistance in South Asia', Press Release IP/05/4, Brussels, 5 January 2005.

78 European Commission (2004) 'The European Commission coordinates EU civil protection support to catastrophe areas in South Asia', Press Release IP/04/1544, Brussels, 31 December 2004.

79 European Commission (2004) 'European Commission mobilises the Civil Protection Mechanism for victims of the earthquake and tsunami in South Asia', Press release IP/04/1543, Brussels, 27 December 2004.

80 European Commission (2005) 'EU Civil protection assistance in South East Asia', Memorandum, MEMO/05/6, Brussels, 11 January 2005.

81 European Commission, 'Consultation on the future instrument addressing prevention of, preparedness for and response to disasters: Issue Paper', 31 January 2005, Brussels. Commission, Directorate General Environment, Directorate A. ENV. A.5. -Civil Protection. http://www.europa.eu.int/comm/environment/civil/consult_new_instrument.htm. Accessed on 20-02-2006.

82 European Commission, 'Consultation on the future instrument addressing prevention of, preparedness for and response to disasters: Issue Paper', 31 January 2005, Brussels. Commission, Directorate General Environment, Directorate A. ENV. A.5. -Civil Protection.

http://www.europa.eu.int/comm/environment/civil/consult_new_instrument.htm. Accessed on 20-02-2006, p. 11.

83 European Commission, 'Consultation on the future instrument addressing prevention of, preparedness for and response to disasters: Questionnaire', Brussels. Commission, Directorate General Environment, Directorate A. ENV. A.5. – Civil Protection, 2005.

84 Barnier Report (2006) 'For a European Civil Protection Force: Europe Aid', Independent report commissioned by the Austrian Presidency (Spring 2006) and Commission President José Manuel Barroso. Delivered May 2006.

85 Ekengren, M., Matzén, N.,, Rhinard, M., Svantesson, M. (2006) 'Solidarity or Sovereignty? EU Cooperation in Civil Protection', *Journal of European Integration*, Vol. 28, No 5, December, pp. 472-473.

86 The French Gendarmerie Nationale is made up of paramilitary forces and is organised under the Ministry of the Interior. Austria, Belgium, Greece (to a certain extent), Italy and Luxembourg have similar forces. All these forces are specialised in terms of training, equipment (often comprising heavy weaponry, armed vehicles, etc.) and lines of command for tasks that straddle the border between internal order and security and external security. E.g., the Italian Arma dei Carabinieri is responsible for certain military operations as well as for 'internal' civilian tasks, such as maintaining order. In some countries the forces are under the control of the defence ministry, in others, of the interior ministry. In some states (e.g., Italy) the authority, chain of command and rules of engagement change depending on the particular task. See Benyon, J. et al., *Police Forces in the European Union* (University of Leicester, Centre for the Study of Public Order: Leicester, 1994); and Stålvant, C.-E., 'Questioning the roles of the military and police in coping with functional security: some assertions about national variations and their impacts', Paper presented at the Second Pan-European Conference on EU Politics of the ECPR Standing Group on European Union Politics, Bologna, Italy, 24-26 June 2004.

87 Finnish Prime Minister's Office, Finnish Security and Defence Policy 2004, Government Report no. 6/2004 (Prime Minister's Office: Helsinki, 2004), URL <http://www.vnk.fi/vn/liston/vnk.lsp?r=88862&k=en>, pp. 127-28.

88 Republic of Finland, 'Hallituksen esitys Eduskunnalle laiksi puolustusvoimien virka-avusta poliisille annetun' [Government proposition to parliament concerning amendment of the act on the provision of assistance by the defence forces to the police], Government proposition to parliament no. 187/2004, 8 Oct. 2004, URL <http://www.finlex.fi/linkit/hepdf/20040187/>.

89 Finnish Ministry of Defence, Government resolution on securing the functions vital to society and strategy for securing the functions vital to society, Helsinki, 27 Nov. 2003. http://www.defmin.fi/index.phtml/page_id/369/topmenu_id/7/menu_id/369/this_topmenu/368/lang/3/, p. 5.

90 Swedish 11 September Commission, Vår beredskap efter den 11 September [Our preparedness after 11 September], Statens Offentliga Utredningar no. 2003:32 (Swedish Ministry of Justice: Stockholm, 2003), URL <http://www.regeringen.se/sb/d/108/a/424>.

91 Swedish 11 September Commission (note 90), pp. 24-25.

92 Swedish Support Inquiry, Polisens behov av stöd i samband med terrorismbekämpning [The police's need for support in connection with combating terrorism], Statens Offentliga Utredningar no. 2005:70, (Swedish Ministry of Justice: Stockholm, 31 Aug. 2005), URL <http://www.regeringen.se/sb/d/108/a/48806/>.

93 Bjurner, A., 'The development of the European Security and Defence Policy', Statement in the Committee on Foreign Affairs, Swedish Parliament, 20 Apr. 2004, p. 10.

94 Kingdom of Denmark, 'Lov om forsvarets formål, opgaver og organisation m.v.' [Act on the defence force's aims, tasks and organisation, etc.], Act no. 122, 27 Feb. 2001.

http://www.retsinfo.dk/_GETDOCI_/ACCN/A20010012230-REGL.

95 Mäkelä, J. (Lt Com.), 'Combating terrorism in Nordic countries: a comparative study of the military's role', C level thesis, Swedish National Defence College, Stockholm, May 2003. http://bibliotek.fhs.mil.se/publikationer/uppsatser/2003/chp0103/

96 Deutsch, K. W. et al., *Political Community and the North Atlantic Area: International Organization in the Light of Historical Experience* (Princeton University Press: Princeton, 1957).

97 Ekengren, M. (2007) 'From a European Security Community to a Secure European Community – Tracing the New the Security Identity of the EU', in: H.B. Brauch et al. (eds.) *Globalization and Security Challenges* (New York: Springer Verlag).

II: EUROPEAN UNION SECURITY SECTOR REFORM IN PRACTICE

9. EU Conditionality and Security Sector Reform in the Western Balkans

Alex G W Dowling

Introduction

The European Union has played a key role in the emergence of the Western Balkans from authoritarianism and war, becoming the principal sponsor of the new republics of the former Yugoslavia (FY) and presenting the prospect of EU membership in return for the implementation of specific reforms. This bargain is the essence of conditionality, the strategic means through which the EU conducts security sector reform (SSR) in the sub-region. This chapter seeks to evaluate how successfully the EU has conducted SSR through the use of membership conditionality in the six countries of the sub-region, as a means to improving standards of security sector governance (SSG).[1]

The needs for SSR in the Western Balkans are immense, based on the dual challenges of post-authoritarian and post-conflict transition. The security sector was involved in the gravest excesses of the wars and had been built for the purpose of territorial conflict, thus providing a burdensome post-conflict legacy.

Oversized military forces must be downsized to levels commensurate with peacetime needs, with disarmament, demobilisation and reintegration (DDR) providing a considerable socio-economic challenge. The creation of all-professional armies designed to fulfil new tasks such as peacekeeping also require significant resources not readily available in post-war, post-authoritarian economies. Effective and democratic policing is also essential to improving the relationship between state and citizen. Police, security and paramilitary forces were defenders of state security in the communist era, and were subsequently deployed in the wars of the 1990s by one ethnic group against another. In all the countries of the region, the low level of effectiveness and independence of the judiciary, coupled with high levels of official corruption and organised crime, are fundamental problems that threaten national, regional and international security. The symbiosis of organised crime and the security sector indeed arguably remains one of the greatest impediments to regional stability.

Beyond provision for an effective and efficient security sector, the necessary conditions for effective oversight of its activities have yet to be established. Empowering parliaments with the capacity, will and knowledge is one important element of oversight. Another is the empowerment of civil society and independent media, capable of scrutinising the activities of the security sector and informing the public that it is in principle committed to serve. Effective oversight presupposes transparency and accountability and the removal of the cloak of secrecy surrounding the activities of the security sector in the recent authoritarian past of the six countries. However, embedding reform not only in institutions but also in the mentalities of their agents is ultimately a generational challenge, requiring at once far reaching endorsement of new norms and the elimination of prevailing mindsets. It involves, for example, embedding such concepts as human security and a core commitment to protection of the security of the state's citizens, as opposed to its elite.

EU SSR Monitoring Mechanisms

Unlike in the countries of Central and Eastern Europe (CEE), SSR-relevant conditionality has featured significantly in the regular reporting on the Western Balkans countries' progress towards fulfilling European standards. Although not articulated as such until the recent development of an EU SSR policy framework, issues related to SSG have been some of the key criteria applied to countries of the sub-region. The logical rationale was that building a security sector that functions in accordance with the highest SSG standards would be one of the most compelling means of stabilising the region.

The primary means through which the EU identifies priorities and progress in SSR is through the European Commission's annual evaluations of developments in each country, based on the 1993 Copenhagen Criteria. The Criteria have provided the blueprint for reforms, specifying the standards expected of those countries that wish to join the EU. They stipulate the need for any aspiring member to ensure: (1) the stability of institutions guaranteeing democracy, rule of law, human rights and respect for and protection of minorities (political criteria); (2) a functioning market economy as well as the capacity to cope with competitive pressures within the Union (economic criteria); and (3) the ability to take on the obligations of membership – meaning effective implementation of the *acquis communautaire* (administrative criteria).[2] As Heiner Hänggi has outlined, those criteria relevant to SSG derive from both democratic conditions (under part 1 of the Copenhagen Criteria) and *acquis* conditions (under part 3).[3] Whilst similar conditions were also demanded of the countries of Central and Eastern Europe, culminating in the 2004 enlargement round, they have been partially reinterpreted in their application to the countries of the Western Balkans. The imperatives of security and stability that belatedly compelled the international community to intervene in the sub-region in the 1990s have fundamentally influenced EU involvement. This is evident not only in the presence of both military and civilian ESDP missions but in the type of conditionality that has been applied to the region.

Although reform in the area of defence has traditionally been the preserve of NATO, the EU has acknowledged its importance in the Western Balkans. Early reporting by the European Commission made reference to the ongoing process of military reforms, though acknowledging NATO's lead in the area. On the other hand, civilian democratic control of armed forces and security agencies was considered by the EU to be an important element in long-term stability and remains a key issue in evaluating compliance with democratic criteria. Ensuring the integration of military and security forces into effective democratic structures is a core priority.

The most pressing SSG concern in the Western Balkans is improving provision for the rule of law. As well as being part of the EU's *acquis* conditionality in the area of Justice, Liberty and Security (JLS – formerly Justice and Home Affairs), the rule of law is assessed more broadly under the democratic Copenhagen Criteria. Resolving problems of corruption and criminality have been principal criteria for EU membership. Police and judicial standards are carefully scrutinised by the Commission. In the JLS field, the EU has outlined criteria for the functioning of border police through the implementation of the Integrated Border Management (IBM) concept. IBM was conceived as a comprehensive approach to border problems across administrative and national dividing lines under the management of dedicated professional skills and including the demilitarisation of borders and passing authority from the military to the Ministry of Interior.[4] The issue of border management in the sub-region, itself an area bordering the EU, is of particular importance in light of its role as a corridor for the trafficking of contraband and people to Western Europe. The Western Balkan countries still have considerable deficiencies in border management, as monitoring reports consistently testify.

The broader democratic architecture in which the security sector operates also has a significant impact on SSG standards. The EU's regular reporting monitors transparency, accountability, the role of the media and civil society participation. Although not monitored in the context of SSG, improving the functioning of these democratic attributes is an important component of SSG in its broader sense, both in the provision of external oversight and in ensuring civil society's investment in its security sector.

The effective use of the conditionality tool in promoting SSR in the Western Balkans is dependent on the prospect of eventual membership of the EU. The 1999 Stabilisation and Association Process (SAP) was thus tailored to the sub-region's dual needs of post-conflict stabilisation and eventual integration into the EU. It tentatively held out the prospect of membership, with an interim contractual framework provided by the signing of Stabilisation and Association Agreements (SAA), whilst promoting regional cooperation. The Thessaloniki summit of June 2003 declared that the sub-region's future lay in membership of the European Union, through the same process as that applied to CEE states.[5] Community Assistance for Reconstruction, Development and Stabilisation (CARDS) was the financial mechanism through which the European Commission supported SAP. CARDS committed €4.6 billion to the region between 2000 and 2006 with objectives that included: reconstruction, democratic stabilisation, and institutional and legislative development. These were intended 'to underpin democracy and the rule of law, human rights, civil society and the media'.[6] As of January 2007, the CARDS programme has been replaced by the

Instrument for Pre-accession Assistance (IPA), which seeks to bridge the gap between external and internal assistance as countries prepare for eventual EU membership.[7]

This comprehensive approach to the integration of the Western Balkans has indeed resulted in a considerable transformation. There is no longer a prospect of conflict in the region in the foreseeable future. The issue of Kosovo, currently a UN protectorate, remains the last hurdle to finalising statehood in the region. Meanwhile, SSR remains an ongoing process likely to demand a long-term, intensive engagement if Euro-Atlantic standards of SSG are to be met.

Of the six states that constitute the Western Balkans sub-region, each has experienced a distinct combination of factors that account for current-standards SSG. Since SSR is primarily a political, rather than a technical endeavour, it remains hostage to the political environment in each country. Each is at a varying stage in relations with the EU. Currently, no official benchmarking exists by which to review progress in SSR. The clearest means to judge the success of EU conditionality in this area is thus by an overview of current SSG standards in the sub-region.[8]

This chapter splits the sub-region into potential candidate countries (Albania, Bosnia and Herzegovina, Serbia, and Montenegro) and candidate countries (Croatia and the Former Yugoslav Republic of Macedonia, hereafter Macedonia). Since Kosovo remains under international supervision with the issue of its statehood unresolved at the time of writing, it is not dealt with as a case where conditionality is applied.

The State of SSG in the Western Balkans

The Potential Candidates

Albania[9]

As the only country of the Western Balkans that was not a product of the disintegration of Yugoslavia, Albania has experienced a divergent and marginally less tumultuous recent past. The ethnic divisions that contributed to war between the other countries of the region have not been a significant source of political instability. Nonetheless, a wide range of factors continue to undermine Albania's transition to democracy. Not least is the authoritarian legacy left by President Enver Hoxha's forty-year rule. Albania was isolated and backward and its political culture was consequently void of experience of democratic practice when the transition to democracy began in 1991. Political polarisation, clientelism, corruption, crime and economic underdevelopment all continue to blight the country's progress. Bitter feuds between the Democratic Party (PDSH) and Socialist Party (PSSH) and within them have combined with the pursuit of personal interests by leading politicians to prevent the level of consensus necessary to pursue a strong reform agenda.[10]

In 1997, widespread internal disorder followed the collapse of pyramid investment schemes in which many Albanians lost their life savings. The episode encapsulated the perilous combination of political infighting, corruption and poverty that threatened the stability of the country, leading to the downfall of the government.[11] During the disorder, it is thought that more than half a million small arms were dispersed within society as military and police depots were targeted by looters.[12] In response to the crisis, a multinational force mandated by the UN Security Council intervened militarily in Operation Alba. The international community thus played a fundamental role in imposing a degree of political stability and consensus. It subsequently provided the incentives required to keep the reform process from stagnation. Strong public and political commitment to democratic transformation and Euro-Atlantic integration is one of the few areas of broad cross-party agreement. The goal of NATO membership has been pursued virtually since transition began, with Albania joining the then North Atlantic Cooperation Council in 1992. In keeping with this membership ambition, reform of the Albanian Armed Forces (AAF) has been underway for more than a decade, in an attempt to downsize, professionalise and modernise forces in line with NATO demands, whilst struggling to attain a defence budget at 2% of GDP. There is no doubt that the prospect of NATO membership has been the key driver of reforms, with the 2004 Military Strategy labelled the 'Strategy for NATO-integration'.[13] Amongst the political elite, the ambition remains that Albania will be included in a 2008 enlargement round, thus maintaining substantial pressure to meet rigorous reform targets. NATO's permanent mission in Tirana monitors the fulfilment of agreements and provides political and technical advice on achieving the aims of the reform strategies.

Albania's relationship with the EU intensified in June 2006 with the signing of a Stabilisation and Association Agreement. Although defence reform has remained outside the scope of EU monitoring, it is clearly an important issue in terms of the country's broader path to stability and democracy. European Commission Stabilisation and Association reports demonstrated this over the years through references to reform of the armed forces, whilst acknowledging that NATO led the way in this field.[14] The focus on democratic standards and the rule of law, as elsewhere in the region, reaches the heart of arguably Albania's greatest challenges. Amongst the key concerns identified by the European Union are: corruption; judicial effectiveness and independence; organised crime; media freedom and civil society participation. The EU linked the 2005 election, deemed to be the freest in the country since 1991 (although it 'only partially' complied with international standards, according to the OSCE), to Albania's progress in integration.[15] Both front-runners, incumbent Prime Minister Fatos Nano and Sali Berisha, could not afford to risk responsibility for a breakdown in relations with the EU and the result was thus not contested. As in 1997, the direct involvement of the international community played a key role in avoiding the political crises that had occurred in previous elections.

The victory of Berisha's Democratic Party was in part based on an anti-corruption campaign. Progress on the issue is closely observed by the EU. Endemic corruption, nepotism and abuse of power lie at the heart of Albania's malfunctioning institutions. Civil service appointments are politicised within the climate of feuding between the main parties and officials show more allegiance to patronage networks than to the law. Particularly troublesome has been the functioning of the judiciary, which retains little independence from political interference or public trust. As outlined in the European Commission's most recent progress report, judicial proceedings remain lengthy, poorly organised and non-transparent. A new Law on the Judiciary in 2006 in fact failed to address important outstanding problems, such as the constitutional protection of judges.[16] An effective judiciary is crucial to the criminal prosecution of corruption, yet the institution itself is marred by corruption whilst judges and lawyers are not trained to satisfactory standards.[17]

Reform of the Albanian State Police has seen progress, with a comprehensive draft Law on State Police awaiting approval at the time of writing. The law foresees increased decentralisation in so far as the police will retain a greater degree of operational independence from the Ministry of Interior, as recommended by the European Commission. There remains a need to improve coordination between different police agencies, whilst there has been a habit of creating new agencies that lack the capacity to carry out their designated functions. Although Albania is a signatory to a number of international conventions on policing, there is not the implied capacity to fulfil certain obligations or a broad knowledge amongst officials and police of the conventions. In agreements with international organisations, lip service is often paid to these conventions with the likely ambition simply to content the international community that obligations are met. Amnesty International has noted that Albania's commitment to the UN Convention against Torture has not stopped police ill-treatment nor remedied the inhuman and degrading conditions of detention in police stations.[18] Although the Border Police force is now part of the State Police and thus under the jurisdiction of the Ministry of Interior, Albania's blue border continues to be patrolled by the Coast Guard, under the jurisdiction of the Ministry of Defence, with a police officer on board patrol boats to exercise 'civilian control'. This is not considered compatible with EU IBM standards, which require borders to be guarded by civilian police.

The role of international donors and institutions in shaping Albania's reform agenda is fundamental. PAMECA, the EU's Police Assistance Mission, has been one of the sources of expertise used for technical and strategic guidance. A risk has been that such guidance encourages the post-authoritarian tendency of resorting to hierarchical instructions instead of seeking initiative and developing local ownership. Although local civil society is developing, its influence is based largely on the government's desire to be seen to act in ways agreeable to the international community, whilst independent think tanks and NGOs survive largely on the basis of international support. In the field of security, expertise is limited and decision-makers have no record of utilising or nurturing civil society organisations for policy guidance purposes.

Oversight and accountability of security institutions also remains limited. Although the legislative framework is fairly developed, practice is far less so. The State Police Internal Control Service is not transparent in its investigations and dismissals of officers. Oversight through the Parliamentary Commission for National Security is in practice negligible. The Parliamentary Commission, charged with oversight of police, border and intelligence structures, lacks the expertise, capacity and most importantly the political will to exercise genuine oversight. Parliamentary commissions are controlled by the political majority which in turn act solely on the basis of the government's consent. The role of the media in oversight of security institutions is also unsatisfactory, with the European Commission concerned that it remains subject to political and economic interests and demonstrates an inadequate legal framework and low professional and ethical standards.[19]

Although Albania has made great efforts to reform laws and structures related to the security sector, implementation is thus in its infancy. Breaking down networks of criminality and corruption and, more broadly, developing a democratic culture capable of delivering SSG commensurate with Western standards remain Albania's core challenges.

Bosnia-Herzegovina[20]

The Dayton Peace Agreement (DPA) that brought an end to war in Bosnia-Herzegovina (BiH) in 1995 established a quasi-State that reflected the country's ruinous ethnic divisions. The institutional structure in the Constitution, provided for by Annex IV of the General Framework Agreement for Peace in Bosnia and Herzegovina, defied the formation of a functional state. Instead it created a number of federal layers to appease the patchwork of ethnicities within it. As the principal battleground in the wars of Yugoslavia's dissolution, Bosnia-Herzegovina was a post-conflict society on a level beyond that of its neighbours. For these reasons, SSR began from a distinctly lower level than in other countries of the region. Additionally, the intrusive level of international management, directed primarily through the Office of the High Representative of the UN Secretary-General (OHR), who also functions as the EU Special Representative, limits the potential for functional democratic institutions able to assume responsibility for running the state, ironically the OHR's own *raison d'être*.

The decentralisation of authority to the Entity and cantonal levels has allowed illegal networks and practices developed in the war to endure, whilst draining the state's limited resources. The main political parties continue to derive their legitimacy from existing divisions.[21] Strong resistance to strengthening the central state is ingrained at the local level, primarily in Republika Srpska (RS). The resulting standoff between these vested interests and the international community – which sees the development of stronger State-level institutions as crucial to improving the State's functioning – accounts in large part for slow progress in reforms. Nowhere has this been more evident than in the reform of security structures.

Dayton heavily circumscribed the powers of the central State, leaving all powers relating to the provision of security in the hands of the Entities.[22] Not only did this ensure the lack of coordination and direction required to ensure nationwide security provision, but also allowed the intelligence services of the entities to be deployed against each other. These unsatisfactory circumstances belatedly led the international community, particularly the EU, to demand the creation of efficient State-wide security services as a condition of further Euro-Atlantic integration. Initially, the international community had been most concerned with defence reform, since the maintenance of national armies was perpetuating a state of mistrust not unlike that during the war.[23] Sarajevo's interest in joining NATO's PfP led in 2001 to NATO stating that a State-level Ministry of Defence and army was a prerequisite. Resistance from RS officials to succumb to international pressure and relinquish defence powers to the State level was overcome after the Orao Affair, in which an RS state-owned aviation firm, Orao, was found to be exporting arms to Iraq, contravening a UN embargo.[24] This strengthened international resolve to push through reforms, undermined RS attempts to defend its 'sovereignty' and led the OHR to establish a Defence Reform Commission to guide the process, combining international experts and local political figures.[25] The Laws on Defence of 2003 and 2005 created State-level defence institutions, setting a precedent for other sectors. Competencies placed at the Entity level by the DPA could be transferred on the basis of the existing Constitution. As of 1 January 2006, Entity Ministries of Defence and commands were succeeded by a new State-level Ministry. Separately, downsizing and professionalisation are ongoing, as stipulated in the October 2005 Law on Service in the Armed Forces.

The role of the EU in BiH accelerated after 2000, as the aim of preparing the country for EU membership, through the SAP, became the primary mission of OHR. The UNHR merged with the position of EU Special Representative in 2002. Additionally, the EU Police Mission (EUPM) succeeded the UN International Police Task Force (IPTF) in the same year, whilst EUFOR took over the NATO-led SFOR in 2004. The use of conditionality, providing economic assistance (through the CARDS programme) and the lure of eventual membership in exchange for reforms, became key to progress in security sector reform, as in all areas of reform.[26] Yet, the use of the OHR's formidable executive powers to push through unpopular changes in the face of resistance was and remains a significant additional instrument. Indeed, the importance of conditionality in BiH is somewhat debatable. In practice, often reforms have been conceived and carried out by the international community, circumventing obstructionist forces when necessary.

Following the handover by EU Commissioner Chris Patten to BiH Foreign Minister Prlic of a Road Map for BiH in March 2000, the European Commission conducted a Feasibility Study in 2003 to assess the country's readiness to open negotiations on an SAA. The study contained close analysis of democratic and JHA conditions. On the issue of policing, it highlighted the inefficiency and ineffectiveness of a system in which forces were organised on an array of tiers, with 10 FBiH cantonal police forces, one Brcko force, FBiH and RS police forces, the State Border Service, the State Information and Protection Agency (SIPA), the judicial police and financial police. This cost the country €180 million per year and required 17,000 staff but produced fundamental coordination and effectiveness problems. The study concluded that BiH must 'now consider further restructuring and rationalising police services in order to enhance efficiency and improve crime fighting capabilities.'[27] Police reform was thus one of the sixteen priority areas for BiH in the report's conclusion.

The lack of consistent and coordinated police practice throughout the State allowed impunity for criminals, as arrest warrants issued in one jurisdiction were not enforced in another. Bosnian police forces have at times even relied on Interpol for the exchange of information rather than direct contacts. Even today the Federation Ministry of Interior often has to rely on the goodwill of cantonal ministries to tackle crimes, even when they lie within the Federation's remit, while cantonal ministries remain resistant to Federation interference. These problems are further compounded by legislative inconsistencies between cantons and the Entity level. The establishment of the State Intelligence and Protection Agency (SIPA) in 2004 was the first attempt to provide State-level coordination of the many separate police forces, but it is still only running at around one third of its capacity.[28] In October 2005, agreement was reached between BiH political leaders on the principles of police reform, as specified by the European Commission, foreseeing the establishment of a Police Restructuring Directorate (PRD) to develop maps of the future police boundaries and a timeline that would result in legislation being submitted to parliament by December 2006. The whole process is to be overseen by the EUPM, itself the subject of criticism.[29] The main sticking point has been the principle that functional police areas be determined by technical criteria and not ethnic boundaries. This would mean establishing policing regions crossing the boundaries between the two Entities.[30] RS leaders are currently obstructing the implementation of the 2005 agreement, still insistent that policing remain an Entity competence.[31]

As was the case with defence reform, overcoming RS intransigence towards police reform will likely require OHR to exercise its extensive Bonn Powers. The same was true in the case of intelligence reform, another prerequisite for opening negotiations on an SAA.[32] Having been left in the hands of political parties by the DPA, intelligence services were used for political and criminal ends. This included protection of the various figures indicted by the International Criminal Tribunal for former Yugoslavia (ICTY) in The Hague. While military intelligence was dealt with through defence reform measures, establishing a State-level agency in the 2005 Law on Defence, the reform of civilian agencies required a separate framework. The approach to intelligence reform largely mirrored the process and timeframe of defence reform, though with far less public attention. OHR established an Intelligence Reform Commission to draft and amend legislation in May 2003, which consequently tabled a draft law foreseeing the establishment of a State-level Intelligence and Security Agency (OSA) through the merger of Entity agencies. As with the draft defence laws, the High Representative bypassed the Council of Ministers, given its intransigence, submitting the draft law directly to the Parliamentary Assembly for approval, which it gave in April 2004. Judging the effectiveness of the OSA in operational terms is difficult, since it failed to deliver a public annual report on its activities, thus contravening the law by which it was established.[33] Structurally, however, the reform process is complete; the country now has a single, civilian, state-level and multi-ethnic intelligence agency, within the necessary legal and regulatory frameworks and with executive, parliamentary, judicial and internal oversight mechanisms. Since July 2006, the agency has been under full domestic ownership, albeit with international monitoring.

The legal and structural reform of BiH security mechanisms has seen the shift of competencies from Entity to State level in the case of the defence, intelligence and border sectors[34], yet notably not the BiH police. Legal provision does not guarantee operational effectiveness, but it is the basis for meeting conditions for opening SAA negotiations and is thus central to OHA's work. Extensive problems also remain in the provision of free and effective media, another key EU condition. The press remains territorially and ethnically divided, efforts are made to exert political influence, there is a lack of professional conduct, and expertise on security issues is limited. Transparency is also limited by the opaque bureaucratic structures of government.[35] The EU demands the creation of a legal framework and necessary institutions to restructure public broadcasting.[36]

Reforming the splintered policing structures, creating a national broadcaster and delivering key suspects to the ICTY now remain the final obstacles to BiH signing an SAA. Whilst political leaders in the Federation have largely met conditions for the sake of Euro-Atlantic integration, it remains to be seen whether RS obstruction can continue to be sidestepped in order to meet them. Fundamentally, the methods used to meet EU SSR conditions in BiH defy the principles of democratic governance and local ownership. International oversight has failed to achieve local engagement and the objective of a separation of powers remains unattainable in a state where the High Representative has ultimate executive, legislative and judicial authority. As Marina Caparini has argued, the choice would appear to be between effective SSR and democratic SSR.[37]

Serbia[38]

Serbia has experienced pervasive political instability since the fall of President Slobodan Milosevic in October 2000. During his reign, he created a semi-authoritarian system, reinforced by a clientelist network that penetrated all the important institutions of the state, not least the security sector. Whilst in the other countries of the region a linear, if occasionally precarious, path towards democratic development and stability may be broadly observed, the same is not easily discernible in Serbia. The ebb and flow of progress towards European standards reflects the view of some stakeholders that the compliance costs of reform are not worth the sacrifices involved. In addition, the case for reform has never been convincingly sold to the public. The democratic consensus, supported by the two rival reformist parties, the Democratic Party of Serbia (DSS) and Democratic Party (DS), has been susceptible to the influence of populism in the governing coalitions.

A further source of instability has been the issue of Serbia's uncertain statehood. The country's legal foundation has taken numerous guises. The 1992 Federal Republic of Yugoslavia became the State Union of Serbia and Montenegro (SCG) in February 2003. The State Union was partly an external construct, imposed by the Council of the EU in the name of short term European security and stability, against the view of the European Commission that longer term interests were at stake.[39] It proved an ill-judged policy, creating a weak and ineffectual centre, lacking popular support and merely delaying the inevitable; the Union's Constitutional Charter contained provisions for a referendum on independence after three years, which promptly led to Montenegro opting to break from the Union in May 2006[40], leaving Serbia as an independent state.

Attempts to pursue SSR have been no less troubled. In the immediate post-Milosevic era, then Yugoslav President Vojislav Kostunica was deeply reluctant to undertake substantial reform of the Yugoslav Army or of wider defence structures, seeing reform as a potential cause of instability, whilst also opposing cooperation with the ICTY. Ironically, Kostunica's adversaries also had few objections, since they believed his link with Milosevic-era institutions damaged his credibility. Additionally, Serbia has suffered from a tenuous legal framework resulting from the fluctuating legal status of the country and this has hampered security sector reform. Valuable time was lost during the SCG period owing to the stalemate between the republics. Since the Army was one of the few areas under State Union jurisdiction, effective reform was impossible without the coordination of all levels of power. A brief period of intensive defence reform activity was led by the then Minister of Defence Boris Tadic in 2003. The subordination of the General Staff to civilian control under the Ministry of Defence was established for the first time and appears to have been genuinely implemented, although the subordination of military intelligence remains questionable[41] and the military leadership was purged of some of the reform obstructionists.[42] Although the momentum slipped, the belated release of a White Paper on Defence in April 2005 offered a credible technical reform path.[43]

Following the end of the State Union, the government had planned to transfer the Ministry of Defence to Serbia and follow this with parliamentary discussion of a Strategic Defence Review, laying out Serbia's medium-term defence reform strategy, a process delayed by post-election political wrangling. Evidently, Serbia is in a state of flux, with a new constitution recently approved, finally replacing that of the Milosevic era, and elections in January 2007 followed by months of negotiations over the formation of a new government. The new Constitution contains little on defence issues, leaving much to be defined in future laws, dependent on the political climate, which will be further disrupted by local elections provisionally planned for the end of 2007. Such an uncertain environment makes a stable reform process impossible to design and implement, with the Milosevic era Law on Defence still in effect. Despite the armed forces being under civilian and formally democratic control, problems regarding the division of powers between the President and Prime Minister persist and the relationship between President Tadic and Prime Minister Kostunica's governing coalition has been strained. Whilst the position of President has entailed a prominent role for Tadic in the military since the Milosevic era, the Defence and Finance Ministries remain under the jurisdiction of the government. No national security strategy exists, with separate draft documents prepared by the Cabinet and President, again highlighting turf battles within the Executive branch. Parliamentary oversight was limited within the State Union set-up[44], with strong executive and party influence on Committee action, whilst the new Serbian parliamentary Committee for Defence and Security is unlikely to differ much in character from its predecessor. Although democratic civilian oversight is ensured in the new Constitution, the European Commission remains dissatisfied, particularly with the parliamentary dimension, which is seen as 'a key priority of the European partnership'.[45]

A principal deficiency in defence reform therefore remains the lack of a legal framework, explained by the various changes in the status of the state and the sense of perpetual transition that has accompanied it. Yet, the reform measures implemented so far have been sufficient to win Serbia an invitation to join NATO's PfP in November 2006, possibly as a means of placating the country in preparation for the possible independence of the southern, Albanian-dominated, province of Kosovo. In light of ICTY conditionality exercised by NATO for so long, it could be said that such politically-influenced decisions undermine the conditionality tool.

Within the field of justice, liberty and security (previously JHA), police reform began after the fall of Milosevic. The stated objective was implementing the 'Four Ds': de-politicisation, de-centralisation, de-militarisation and de-criminalisation. Yet, these aims have never been systematically developed in government policy. Reforms have been driven by crises and necessities. An early attempt to articulate a reform strategy saw the creation of a Ministry of Interior 'Vision Document', finally released in 2003 and subsequently over-shadowed by the assassination of Prime Minister Zoran Djindjic, thereby losing its momentum. The Serbian Government announced in March 2003 that it was disbanding the elite Red Berets, the Special Operations Unit (JSO), owing to its mooted connection with the assassination.[46] Serbia lacks a police strategy. The process of defining priorities in reform is thus based on the 2001 OSCE Study on Policing.[47] However, significant advances on police reform were not possible without a new Law on Police, a deficiency regularly highlighted by the European Commission[48], finally remedied by its adoption in November 2005. A structural innovation in the document was the separation of the police service from the Ministry of Interior, with the Director of the police no longer an Assistant Minister. It remains to be seen whether the Ministry resists the urge to exercise its still considerable power.

Police oversight became a central issue after Djindjic's assassination, but the Inspectorate General, an internal control department, has been painfully slow to develop and it has faced a lack of cooperation from within the police itself.[49] *Post facto* external oversight through the parliament's Committee for Defence and Security also remains insufficient. It clearly lacks expertise, capacity and interest in exercising effective oversight and there is no alternative independent external oversight body. In fighting organised crime, a widespread problem in the country, the launch of Operation Sabre following Djindjic's death had a significant impact. The creation of the Organised Crime Directorate (UBPOK) under the General Police Directorate is considered a positive step, though the development of a national criminal intelligence system is much needed. The establishment of a war crimes unit, prosecutor's office and court chamber were also symbolically important, despite a lack of significant results to date. The de-militarisation of Serbia's borders, another EU demand, has been slow and remains incomplete, with the Law on State Borders long delayed. The slow implementation of the Law on Police has also meant that border police reforms have dragged.[50] Education and training are evidently vital elements in improving police practices but relevant strategic planning and legislation have been absent.

The link between the security services and criminality expanded greatly in the 1990s, during the period of international sanctions, whilst the removal of senior security officials was not carried out early after the transition to democracy in 2000, thus allowing criminality to remain ingrained. As the European Commission's Regular Report of 2004 noted, only half-hearted attempts (such as the abolition of the JSO) have been made to purge the security sector of the old guard.[51] Reform of intelligence agencies has been a key component of Euro-Atlantic conditionality for Belgrade. Legal changes, notably the 2002 Law on Security Services, met only minimum requirements. There is no dedicated coordinating body for the five security services, spread over three different ministries and currently the responsibility of the government. Attempts to establish a national security council were thwarted by political arguments over who would chair such a body. Parliamentary oversight of intelligence remains more theoretical than applied, with the relevant committee lacking specialisation, understaffed and limited in its scope of enquiry, partly because its hearings are public. There is also a lack of will to exercise effective oversight. There remains insufficient separation between police and security forces, since security officials are mandated to use all police measures, whilst democratic civilian control is not much understood as a concept below the top ranks.

The state of the judiciary also makes the fight against corruption and organised crime less effective. Although independent by law, it is restricted by political interference, low professional standards, financial restrictions, carelessness and corruption.[52] The reform strategy, another priority identified by the European Commission, appears inadequate effectively to tackle this array of deficiencies.[53]

Reforming security and rule of law structures impacts upon Serbia's commitment to cooperation with the ICTY. Dismantling the structures used to shelter fugitives is a significant element in fulfilling the international community's demand for high-profile indictees, particularly Ratko Mladic – believed to be resident in Serbia – to be sent to The Hague. Serbia has paid a high price for non-compliance. NATO PfP membership was denied until November 2006 and the EU suspended SAA negotiations in May 2006 on account of the failure to apprehend Mladic. The ICTY's Chief War Crimes Prosecutor, Carla Del Ponte, claimed that the government failed to arrest Mladic in January 2006, instead hoping that he would voluntarily surrender.[54] The instability of Serbia's political landscape and the influence of populist and nationalist parties makes the issue highly politically sensitive, requiring more political capital than governing coalitions have so far possessed. In addition, the impending resolution of the question of Kosovo's future further threatens political stability and support for the goals of Euro-Atlantic integration. Laying the Kosovo issue to rest, in turn resolving Serbia's long-term statehood, may help the country to break the cycle of political short-termism for which the international community has been partly to blame. Serbia needs the opportunity to catch up with its neighbours if regional stability is to be assured.

Montenegro

Montenegro's decision by referendum to end the State Union with Serbia in May 2006 represented one of the final phases in the dissolution of Yugoslavia. With the EU stipulating a 55% threshold for the vote to be legitimate, the victory margin was tight with 55.5% in favour of independence, reflecting deep divisions in society. The State Union of 2003-2006 was clearly a failed project, largely enforced by the EU and characterised by disagreement and failure to reform. The lack of domestic reform coupled with Serbia's failure to comply with ICTY demands appear to have been decisive factors in the population's decision.[55]

The undisputed outcome of the referendum augurs well in light of the substantial minority of unionist Serbs that remain in the new state. Nonetheless, Montenegro is a small and fragile state with a population of just 650,000. Though it has exercised substantial self-government for more than a decade, the current ruling elite has a reputation for corruption and links with organised crime.[56] Adopting policies to placate Serb unionist voters will be an important test of the new Montenegrin government, as will the management of national minorities representing around a quarter of the population. These minorities remain under-represented in public institutions. The current political scene has been built around the issue of independence and is split along ethnic lines.

One of the main arguments employed in the referendum by then Prime Minister Milo Djukanovic was that Montenegro had a better chance of Euro-Atlantic integration outside the State Union. The suspension of SAA talks with Serbia and Montenegro in May 2006 would, for example, no longer apply to Montenegro alone. Nonetheless, as the SCG Constitution deemed Serbia the successor state, Montenegro has to build from scratch not only those institutions, including the Ministries of Foreign Affairs and Defence, previously under the SCG, but also its international relationships. Untangling the SCG has involved a time-consuming process of political bargaining. Whilst Serbia holds leverage due, among other factors, to the large Serb population in Montenegro, Podgorica could offer access to the Adriatic Sea and the SCG navy.[57]

The opening of negotiations on an SAA with the EU in September 2006 combined with NATO's decision to grant PfP status in November 2006, were significant steps in line with the government's stated ambition to seek membership of both organisations. The EU clearly remained opposed to the idea of Montenegro's independence from Serbia throughout the referendum period, a fact manifested in its qualified majority requirement (the 55% threshold). The EU's use of conditionality is entering a new phase following Montenegro's independence. No longer can failure to progress in reform be blamed on the dysfunctional State Union or the obstructionism of Serbia, with Montenegro's politicians now fully accountable. Creating capacity to carry out reforms was a challenge for the Republic during the SCG period and represents a key short-term priority for the EU. Montenegro may be in advance of Serbia in terms of the political consensus on integration – as demonstrated by the higher degree of legislative reform activity from 2003-6 – but it has lacked the human and material resources at the disposal of Belgrade.[58]

In the field of SSR, strategy policy documents will need to be developed to map out policy on key threats and objectives for the Armed Forces. This was previously a State Union-level competence. Montenegro inherited significant military capacity from SCG, yet it is largely outdated and clearly unsuitable for the country's needs. Disposing of it in a cost-effective manner is a key issue.[59] The reform and downsizing process, which aims at a force level of 2,500, will be difficult to finance in light of the country's limited resources, though PfP membership will open access to international advice. The European Commission's November 2006 draft European partnership placed parliamentary control over defence and security sectors as a key early priority for the newly created state, thus providing an indication of how the issue is now valued in Brussels.[60] Oversight is currently a token concept, not only in the parliamentary field but also in internal, external, ombudsman, media and civil society forms.[61]

In the rule of law area, corruption and organised crime are priority issues for the state to address. Capacity building is needed in police, judicial and anti-corruption areas, along with the finalisation and implementation of respective strategy documents. Organised criminal networks with political connections took root, as they did in Serbia, under Milosevic's regime and the period of economic sanctions. Whereas the democratic shift in 2000 and then the launch of Operation Sabre after Djindjic's assassination dealt a significant blow to crime in Serbia, comparable networks in Montenegro were less hard-hit.[62] The seventeen year rule of Djukanovic also allowed the consolidation of networks of favour, with Djukanovic himself implicated in a smuggling ring.[63] The country's reputation as a regional trafficking hub is of serious concern to the leadership and efforts to tackle it, such as the creation of the Anti-corruption Initiative Agency, have been made. Again, implementation will be the proof of a true commitment to tackling corruption.

EU conditionality in these areas is set to take on a new form, no longer weighed down by the issue of the State Union. Montenegro may prove able to accelerate the integration process if political consensus can be maintained and capacity developed with the help of international guidance.

The Candidate Countries

Croatia

Croatian citizens and officials alike tend to view their country's trajectory as distinct from its eastern and southern neighbours. Croatia is certainly the region's clearest example of the virtuous circle linking reform and Euro-Atlantic integration. The creation of the EU's SAP in 2000 for the Western Balkans introduced the differentiation needed to allow each country to move at its own reform pace, no longer reducing progress to the level of the slowest. Despite Croatia's participation in the war, the early resolution of the country's status, a resilient economy, erosion of the Serbian security threat, and strong political consensus on EU aspirations all allowed the country to strive towards integration following the death of President Franjo Tudjman in 1999.[64] Acknowledging Croatia's rapid progress, NATO invited Croatia to participate in PfP in May 2000 and then in the Membership Action Plan (MAP) in May 2002, designed to prepare countries for Alliance membership. Similar progress was initially seen in relations with the EU; an SAA was signed in October 2001 following the European Commission's favourable Feasibility Study. This was followed by the decision to open membership negotiations in June 2004.

Although Croatia has been less hampered by the nexus of authoritarianism and conflict than its neighbours, the legacy is nonetheless evident and must be overcome in order to achieve European standards of democracy and governance. Nowhere is this more true than in the security sector, arguably the area where least reform progress has been made. By gaining independence in the context of a civil war, Croatia's security sector was built specifically for the purpose of fighting the so-called Homeland War. This process, of course, did not prioritise governance and professionalism. The aim was rather to place the maximum number of men under arms to fend off Serb aggressors in what was, and still is, perceived as a purely defensive war.[65] Following the end of hostilities, President Tudjman maintained a centralised system of power and transformed the military into a praetorian guard, manipulating its image of heroism and tying it intimately with his Croatian Democratic Union (HDZ) party.[66] This ensured that the army retained a position of political favour, reinforced by public support and thus establishing a formidable resistance to reform. The military commanded significant state resources and experienced no external oversight, beyond that exercised by Tudjman himself.

Following the death of Tudjman, the failure of the HDZ in the elections of January 2000 reflected public dissatisfaction with the corrupt and internationally isolated Presidential system that took root after the war. The subsequent Social Democrat-led coalition introduced constitutional amendments in November 2000 and March 2001 that dismantled the Presidential system and shifted greater power to the legislature.[67] Defence reform was set in motion with the Laws on Defence and Security Services in 2002, which introduced provisions for civilian control and defined the roles of president, government and parliament. National Security and Defence Strategies were also adopted to increase compatibility with NATO and a resolution was passed by the parliament in December 2002, declaring Croatia's commitment to EU accession. Indeed, the rationale for defence reform was almost entirely externally driven. The shift from territorial defence, the emphasis both in Tito's Yugoslavia and Tudjman's Croatia, to a defence posture compatible with NATO interests demanded considerable downsizing, professionalisation and investment in human capital, delicate issues in light of the Croatian Armed Forces' (CAF) special position in society. The completion of the Strategic Defence Review (SDR) in 2005 and subsequent adoption of the Long Term Development Plan (LTDP) in 2006 signalled a stronger willingness on the part of the government to see the defence reform process through, after much political wrangling in the Ivica Racan government of 2000-2003 that saw little achieved beyond paper declarations.[68] In the area of civil-military relations, there are still considerable problems with the MoD structure, allowing for overlapping responsibilities of the administrators and the General Staff. Mechanisms for oversight remain somewhat chaotic. Efforts to resolve the Tudjman-era concentration of power in the President's hands led to changes that will rely on personal relations to function effectively. Parliamentary oversight remains a largely formal exercise and suffers from a lack of will on the part of Committee members to genuinely scrutinise the CAF.[69]

Defence standards in Croatia remain not only short of Euro-Atlantic standards but are not even the most advanced in the region. It is surprising that the European Commission has failed to identify this shortcoming in its reporting process, contenting itself to note that the army is under civilian, executive and parliamentary control.[70] This seems inconsistent with the rigorous monitoring of civil-military relations in Turkey or parliamentary oversight in what was then Serbia and Montenegro.[71] More rigorous conditionality was applied in the ICTY's demands for the capture of General Ante Gotovina. Efforts to submit Gotovina to The Hague to face charges in relation to the campaign against Krajina Serbs in August 1995 were highly politically sensitive, owing to the favourable popular perception of the military. The issue became the cause of a breakdown in relations between Croatia and the EU in 2005. Accession negotiations had been scheduled to begin in March but were delayed until October.[72] When Gotovina was eventually captured in the Canary Islands in December 2005, with Croatian cooperation, there was widespread public opposition to his arrest.[73]

Much like the CAF, the intelligence services developed in wartime Croatia were wholly unsuitable for peacetime and Euro-Atlantic SSG standards. With the loss of an external threat, the security services turned on internal dissidents to Tudjman's single-party rule, whilst Parliament was reluctant to establish a committee charged with intelligence oversight until the democratic change in 2000.[74] In light of scandals involving abuses by the services, the new government committed itself to reform them. The body of legislation that developed – most notably the March 2002 Law on Security Services – was rather more comprehensive than the practical application. Oversight mechanisms such as the Parliamentary Internal Affairs and National Security Committee have failed in practice to provide independent scrutiny of the security services. In July 2006, the Law on Intelligence and Security Services was adopted following amendments in response to criticism from civil society organisations. The law provides for civilian oversight, despite initial attempts by the government to curtail it. The law's adoption fulfils a commitment included in the Government's Action Plan for the apprehension of Ante Gotovina.[75] Widely reported abuses of the human rights of a number of journalists by the Counter-Intelligence Agency led to the dismissal of the Agency Head in December 2004. However, although the Parliamentary Committee concluded in March 2005 that there was reason to believe that human rights violations had occurred, no follow-up measures were taken.[76] The European Commission subsequently concluded that civilian oversight mechanisms of the agencies had to be monitored.

The EU has been deeply engaged in rule of law reforms in Croatia. The reform of the police services has been closely observed. The wartime service lost its popular legitimacy in the late 1990s, owing to the high incidence of police corruption and the consequent popular support for reform.[77] The current reform programme is guided by the Croatian Police Action Plan 2004-07, aiming to transform the force into a 'service', including the implementation of community policing.[78] But, the pace of police reform remains slow and subject to political interference, despite the fact that specific areas are in need of improvement, such as protection of minority rights[79] and data protection[80].

The issue of corruption is regarded as an important indicator of Croatia's readiness for EU membership and was perceived by the public actually to have worsened in 2006.[81] An anti-corruption programme was launched in March 2006, and the Office for Combating Corruption and Organised Crime (USKOK) strengthened, though considerable capacity building is still needed, according to the European Commission.[82] One of the institutions perceived to be most corrupt by the public is the judiciary, another reform priority for EU accession. In line with European standards, the government increased the judicial budget by 16% in 2003 and has continued to do so in subsequent years. However, it still faces a huge backlog of cases and must rationalise procedures.[83]

Although Croatia stands apart from its neighbours in the degree to which it has enacted reforms, there remains work to be done in order to achieve the necessary standards of SSG. The defence sector, where the army's special position in society has increased its resistance to change and oversight, arguably remains the greatest reform challenge. The European Commission's regular reporting has failed to monitor progress sufficiently in this area beyond ICTY compliance. Significant work also remains to be done in judicial reform and tackling corruption, both under close scrutiny from the EU.

Macedonia

Although not dragged into the wider wars of Yugoslav secession, the Former Yugoslav Republic of Macedonia has nonetheless experienced familiar ethnic tensions and violence. Inter-communal tensions between ethnic Macedonians and minority ethnic Albanians lingered under the surface as Yugoslavia disintegrated and Macedonia's independence in 1991 saw the restriction of minority rights previously guaranteed under the Yugoslav federation. Albanians were drastically under-represented in state institutions, whilst almost all aspects of society were characterised by ethnic separation. The first President of the Republic, Kiro Gligorov, aimed to alleviate divisions through a power-sharing system, the reinstatement of minority protection measures and increased decentralisation of government. However, the 1998 elections led to a coalition of nationalist parties that institutionalised separation rather than dismantling it.[84] By February 2001 tensions, stoked by events in Kosovo, surfaced as the National Liberation Army (NLA), comprising Kosovo-Albanian and local insurgents, clashed with the Macedonian security forces in the northwest of the country, in protest against discrimination against the Albanian population.[85] Fearing a repeat of its failures in Bosnia, the international community responded swiftly and effectively, brokering the August 2001 Ohrid Peace Agreement. The settlement envisaged a political restructuring process that would provide greater rights and representation to the ethnic Albanian minority in official institutions, as well as a decentralisation of powers to municipal level. One of the key provisions was to secure proportional ethnic equity for Albanians in the police force, which at the time stood at a just 5 percent.[86]

As elsewhere in the region, international intervention proved decisive in securing peace. The Ohrid agreement foresaw the immediate deployment of the NATO operation Essential Harvest to oversee the collection of weapons of NLA fighters. This was followed by the Amber Fox mission to protect international monitors of the peace implementation. Subsequently, in March 2003, the EU inherited the peacekeeping mantle in the shape of Operation Concordia, part of its emerging ESDP identity. The increasingly secure environment then allowed for the replacement of the peacekeeping force in December 2003 with two successive EU Police Missions, EUPOL PROXIMA and the EU Police Advisory Team (EUPAT).

As the progressively lower profile of the international presence demonstrates, the threat of conflict has receded as Ohrid has been implemented. Nonetheless, a tumultuous period in late 2004 underlined that the country remained fragile. A referendum on the issue of territorial redistribution, stipulated in the Ohrid Agreement, was forced by a collection of ethnic Macedonian nationalist parties in November 2004, essentially becoming a vote on Ohrid itself. Two weeks before the vote was due, reports of an armed ethnic Albanian militia group based in the village of Kondovo added to the impression that the referendum was reigniting ethnic strife.[87] A timely intervention by the newly re-elected US administration a day before the vote helped to ensure its failure, by recognising the constitutional name of the 'Republic of Macedonia', and thus keeping the peace process on track.[88] Although spoilers linger on the political landscape, there is a consensus amongst the main political parties on achieving stability through the Ohrid framework and the aim of eventual Euro-Atlantic integration. The EU's decision to grant Macedonia candidate status in November 2005 was no doubt partly a reward for the implementation of Ohrid, rather than recognition of European standards met, for no firm prospect or deadline for membership was offered.

The Ohrid Agreement was never intended as a complete blueprint for the Macedonian state, but rather a means of removing the causes of conflict. Crucial legal reforms have been undertaken and practical implementation is ongoing but the opening of accession talks remains a distant prospect. EU and NATO conditionality are vital to the process. As a key component of the Ohrid settlement, police reform is a high-profile endeavour. With considerable support from the EU as well as the OSCE, progress has been made. Increased Albanian representation, civilian control of border police, community policing schemes and the development of a Professional Standards Unit (PSU) are examples of the significant achievements.[89] The belated adoption of the Law on Police by the National Assembly in November 2006 was another milestone, though it was not supported by the Albanian opposition coalition, which thus complicated and delayed its implementation.[90] Problems remain, however, in a number of areas of implementation: the Ministry of Interior is resistant to facilitating oversight and decentralisation; transparency and meritocracy are deficient; and inter-agency cooperation does not meet international standards.[91]

Perhaps the greatest deficiency in the police reform process is the lack of comparable progress in judicial reform, which was not demanded in the Ohrid Agreement. As the European Commission's 2006 report acknowledged, 'reform is at an early stage and improving the independence and the efficiency of the judiciary remains a major challenge.'[92] The 2004 Strategy on the Reform of the Judicial System laid out a legislative reform timetable and the constitutional and legal framework for an independent and efficient judiciary is now in place.[93] Yet, practical implementation, the real test of the reform process, has been neglected. Macedonians see their judiciary as inefficient and corrupt, with their politicians wielding excessive influence. There remains a backlog of hundreds of thousands of cases and legal procedures often last for years. Many question whether the political will exists to match the judicial reform rhetoric.[94] Corruption is also high in political and bureaucratic circles, whilst measures to combat it are often reduced to political weapons with which to attack opponents.[95]

Unlike police and judicial reforms, defence reform has a longer history, since Macedonia joined NATO's PfP in 1995. The Strategic Defence Review (SDR) of 2003-4 foresaw most priority targets for reform of the Army of the Republic of Macedonia (ARM) being met by 2007, though achieving proportional ethnic equity of 25 percent Albanians is not expected until 2013. This ethnic redistribution is made more difficult given the context of ongoing downsizing and professionalisation and the resulting high redistribution of positions to achieve a trim and representative personnel strength of 8,460 by 2007.[96] Undertaking such personnel changes without a tradition of meritocracy is another area of concern, as are budget constraints. Parliamentary oversight is also not yet adequately exercised, with the National Assembly often acting as a rubber stamp to decisions by the executive branch. Although competence exists in the Defence and Security Committee, personal and party loyalties determine the strength of willingness to hold the government to account. Intelligence oversight by parliament has been non-existent, in part because the relevant Committee's chair, Ljubo Boshkovski, was charged with war crimes offences, leading to its paralysis.[97]

A major challenge of SSR in Macedonia will be to ensure that Albanian communities develop greater trust in their security institutions, through ethnic representation and community input. Strong support for EU and NATO membership within the Albanian population is explained by their belief that integration will help to secure their rights within governance structures. Yet, ethnic Slav Macedonians see integration as a means to reinforce their sovereignty in a historically insecure neighbourhood. To conclude, most political obstacles appear to be surmountable for SSR in Macedonia as long as a strong momentum towards EU and NATO integration is sustained. The ideal of EU membership is the motor driving the key issues of judicial and police reform but clearly it relies on the careful handling of the Kosovo settlement, if the process is not to destabilise its southern neighbour.

Conclusion

Significant challenges remain to be surmounted if the countries of the Western Balkans are to attain Euro-Atlantic standards in security sector governance. That SSR remains a work in progress is natural, in light of the sub-region's recent emergence from war and authoritarianism. Whilst some commentators have questioned the slow progress to date made in reforms, building functioning and effective democratic institutions – a prerequisite to successful SSG – is clearly a generational challenge. Fostering a culture wherein democratic norms are 'internalised' is the final phase of the process of norms transfer, a process that is as yet incomplete.[98]

In the absence of the internalisation of the highest democratic standards of SSG, the role of international actors has been the primary driver of reform in the security sector. The prospect of membership of the EU and NATO has been the most effective means of inducing change in SSG. NATO has been involved in SSR, specifically in defence reform, through the use of conditionality but it is the EU that is leading the reform process in the Western Balkans. Democratic and *acquis* conditionalities within the Copenhagen Criteria demand reform of all aspects of the security sector, from rule of law institutions to mechanisms for effective democratic oversight. Where conformity costs have been seen as too high, less effort has been made to adapt. Perhaps the most obvious example here is in the case of ICTY cooperation. The demand that Ratko Mladic and Radovan Karadzic be delivered to The Hague has been seen as too politically costly for leaders in Serbia and BiH. Maintaining a delicate balance between what could be termed 'supply' (membership prospects) and 'demand' (reform criteria) is imperative for EU conditionality to function effectively. It means ensuring that a clear European perspective is evident to the countries of the sub-region.

In gauging the EU's success in implementing SSR in the Western Balkans, various shortcomings remain evident. Provision for the rule of law remains inadequate; official corruption and organised crime continue to occur frequently and often with the collusion of the security sector, thus undermining both security and economic progress. Ingrained networks of patronage continue to operate within the public administration, preventing the emergence of meritocratic practice. The capacity of the police and the judiciary to tackle such problems requires radical improvement. Public institutions remain centralised, thus obstructing the development of more efficient practices and leaving excessive control in the hands of the executive. This in turn impacts upon transparency and accountability mechanisms. A feature of SSG throughout the sub-region is the subservience of parliament to the executive in defence and security matters. There is neither sufficient capacity nor willingness to hold government genuinely to account. The same holds true in the areas of media and civil society, where a lack of expertise or interest in security and defence issues prevents more effective public oversight of the security sector. In defence reform progress is more evident, in large part due to the longer engagement of NATO in the region. But, even here significant problems remain in civil-military relations and democratic oversight in most of the countries examined here.

The substantial shortcomings in SSR testify to both the difficulty of the challenge and the limits of conditionality. Whilst Euro-Atlantic integration is the strongest incentive for reform, it is not always sufficient to overcome obstructionism in the short term. It is evident throughout the region that much more progress has been made in legislative provision for SSR than implementation. In the absence of a strong domestic consensus to reform in a given area, legislating may simply placate international demands without confronting the challenges of implementation. There is a danger that excessive stock is put by the international community in legal and regulatory reform, rather than implementation, reducing conditionality to a 'box-ticking' exercise. Nevertheless, the EU's regular reporting tool is the most effective means through which this problem may be overcome. Continuing to monitor implementation efforts on an annual basis is thus vital.

There is a lack of explicit, rigorous benchmarking in SSG, resulting from the vagueness of the Copenhagen Criteria. The result is a degree of arbitrary and inconsistent monitoring by the European Commission. For example, in the case of civilian democratic oversight of armed forces, Croatia still has much work to do but it has not been highlighted as readily in the monitoring process as in other countries. Indeed, those aspects of SSG that fall solely under the democratic criteria have arguably been the most inconsistent. In the field of armed forces reform, much has been left to NATO. Although a division of labour is sensible, there is no obvious reason to exclude more comprehensive commentary on the subject. NATO may be the technical implementer, but the emerging ESDP identity makes defence reform directly relevant to EU needs. Indeed, the EU's emerging ambitions in SSR may well come to improve the lack of coherence and rigour in the sub-region. The EU's emerging ambitions in SSR may well improve problems associated with the lack of coherence and rigour in the sub-region. The poorly-defined democratic Copenhagen Criteria are insufficient on their own to offer a comprehensive approach to SSR. Whilst the acquis criteria are much more closely defined, they too do not include an explicit SSR component.

Another issue of concern is the inherent contradiction between the mantra of local ownership and the use of rigorous conditionality. By imposing a reform agenda on an unwilling recipient, the democratic process through which consensus is achieved and sustained is bypassed. As Timothy Edmunds has argued, the use of 'pre-conditionality' by the international community has been highly effective in this regard. Instead of using conditionality as a weapon, punishing laggards by withholding benefits, it instead rewards successful reformers with a greater prospect of membership, allowing countries to identify their own reform path and thus retain legitimacy in the eyes of target populations.[99] Nonetheless, conditionality has been undermined by the lack of sovereignty in some states of the sub-region. Most notably in BiH, but also to some degree in Macedonia and the former State Union of Serbia and Montenegro, outside interference in state sovereignty has complicated the conditionality process by imposing demands on the state. In BiH, it is contentious even to talk in terms of conditionality, since the High Representative has imposed the will of the international community where local consensus was not forthcoming. Where the security and stabilisation imperative has – at times understandably – trumped longer term efforts to encourage institutional reform, conditionality has been compromised.

It has been argued that the unique challenge faced by the EU in the Western Balkans, of combining stabilisation and integration, requires a different approach from that of conditionality. According to this argument, integration is a condition of stabilisation, rather than the other way around, and thus requires a fast track to membership.[100] However, in the midst of the EU's current identity crisis and questions over 'absorption capacity', prospects for rapid membership look bleak. The pre-conditionality tool has represented one of the most effective means through which to foster the process of 'Europeanisation', and changing the rules of the game would certainly undermine its utility. For conditionality to continue to be a potent force for reform, it is imperative that the European perspective of the Western Balkans remains clear, with the EU firmly engaged in the region.

Endnotes

1 For a comprehensive definition of security sector governance, see Hänggi, Heiner, 'Making Sense of Security Sector Governance', in Hänggi, H. and T. H. Winkler (eds.), *Challenges of Security Sector Governance* (Lit Verlag: Munster, 2004)

2 Copenhagen European Council, 21-22 June 1993, Presidency Conclusions, Relations with the Countries of Central and Eastern Europe.

3 Hänggi, Heiner, *The Role of Security Sector Governance in the EU's Democratic and Acquis Conditionality* (Forthcoming, DCAF)

4 Hobbing, Peter, 'Integrated Border Management at the EU Level', Centre for European Policy Studies, CEPS Working Document No.227 (August 2005), p.3

5 'EU-Western Balkans Summit – Declaration' Press release, 10229/03 (Presse 163) Thessaloniki (21 June 2003). Available at: http://ec.europa.eu/enlargement/enlargement_process/accession_process/how_does_a_country_join_the_eu/sap/thessaloniki_summit_en.htm

6 Information on the CARDS programme may be found on the DG Enlargement website at: http://ec.europa.eu/enlargement/financial_assistance/cards/index_en.htm

7 For more information on the IPA, see: http://ec.europa.eu/enlargement/financial_assistance/index_en.htm

8 There is no universally recognised set of criteria for good practice in security sector governance but Part I of this volume details the evolution of the concept.

9 Information on SSR in Albania was in part derived from: Sulstarova, Enis, *Survey on the Armed Forces in Albania*; Hroni Sotiraq and Enis Sulstarova, *Republic of Albania: Survey on Intelligence*

Services; Hroni, Sotiraq, Republic of Albania: *Survey on the Albanian State Police* (all Forthcoming, LaVAK: Vienna 2007); 'Internal Political Struggles', *Southeast European and Black Sea Studies*, Vol.6, No.1 (March 2006), pp.25-41

10 *Ibid.*

11 'Albanian Scam Victims Riot, Turn on Government', CNN World News, 25 January 1997. Available at: http://www.cnn.com/WORLD/9701/25/albania/index.html

12 Turning the Page: Small Arms and Light Weapons in Albania', Center for Peace and Disarmament Education / Saferworld, December 2005, pp.5-7

13 Pietz, Tobias, 'Defence Reform and Conversion in Albania, Macedonia and Croatia', BICC Brief 34, July 2006, p.10

14 See for example, European Commission, *Commission Staff Working Paper: Albania Stabilisation and Association Report 2003*, {COM(2003) 139 final}, 26 March 2003, p.4. Available at: http://ec.europa.eu/enlargement/pdf/albania/com03_339_en.pdf

15 Albania vote met 'some standards', BBC News, 4 July 2005. Available at:

http://news.bbc.co.uk/2/hi/europe/4645643.stm

16 European Commission, *Commission Staff Working Document: Albania: 2006 Progress Report*, {COM (2006) 649 final}, 8 November 2006, p.7. Available at: http://ec.europa.eu/enlargement/pdf/key_documents/2006/Nov/al_sec_1383_en.pdf

17 Feilcke-Tiemann, *Albania: Gradual Consolidation*, p. 29. For a general overview of the state of Albania's justice system, see: 'Analysis of the Criminal Justice System of Albania: Report by the fair trial development project', OSCE Presence in Albania, September 2006. Available at: http://www.osce.org/documents/pia/2006/11/21952_en.pdf

18 'Albania: Obligations under the UN Convention against Torture – a gap between law and practice', Amnesty International, 1 February 2005. Available at: http://web.amnesty.org/library/Index/ENGEUR110012005?open&of=ENG-ALB

19 European Commission, *Albania 2006 Progress Report*, p.12

20 Information on SSR in Bosnia and Herzegovina is derived in part from: Hadzovic, Denis, *Defence reform in Bosnia and Herzegovina*; Hadzovic, Denis, *The Intelligence Sector in Bosnia and Herzegovina*; Ahic, Jasmin, *Bosnia's Security Sector Reform: Reconstruction of BH police*; Ahic, Jasmin, *Bosnia's Security Sector Reform: State Border Service BH as an efficient Border Management Agency* (all Forthcoming, LaVAK: Vienna 2007)

21 'Bosnians Left Divided After Poll', BBC News, 2 October 2006. Available at: http://news.bbc.co.uk/2/hi/europe/5398928.stm

22 The full text of the constitution may be found at: http://www.ohr.int/dpa/default.asp?content_id=372

23 Vetschera, Heinz and Matthieu Damien, 'Security Sector Reform in Bosnia and Herzegovina: The Role of the International Community', *International Peacekeeping*, Vol.13, No.1 (March 2006), p.30

24 'Bosnia Warned Over Arms to Iraq', BBC News, 27 October 2002. Available at:

http://news.bbc.co.uk/2/hi/europe/2366523.stm

25 For an overview of the DRC's work, see: Locher III, James R. and Michael Donley, 'Reforming Bosnia and Herzegovina's defence institutions'. *NATO Review*, No. 4, 2004, Winter 2004

26 Chandler, David, 'From Dayton to Europe', *International Peacekeeping*, Vol.12, No.3 (Autumn 2005), p. 342

27 European Commission, *Report from the Commission to the Council on the preparedness of Bosnia and Herzegovina to negotiate a Stabilisation and Association Agreement with the European Union*, COM(2003) 692 final, 18 November 2003 pp.25-6. Available at: http://eur-lex.europa.eu/LexUriServ/site/en/com/2003/com2003_0692en01.pdf

28 Briefing by Brigadier General Coppola, Head of EUPM, March 2006, Sarajevo

29 For an indictment of EUPM's performance, see: 'Bosnia's Stalled Police Reform: No Progress, No EU', International Crisis Group, *Europe Report* N°164, 6 September 2005, pp.12-14

29 *Ibid.*

31 European Commission, *Commission Staff Working Document: Bosnia and Herzegovina: 2006 Progress Report*, {COM (2006) 649 final}, 8 November 2006, p.48. Available at: http://ec.europa.eu/enlargement/pdf/key_documents/2006/Nov/bih_sec_1384_en.pdf

32 European Commission, *Report from the Commission to the Council on the preparedness of Bosnia and Herzegovina to negotiate a Stabilisation and Association Agreement*, p.42

33 A confidential report was presented to Parliament in February 2006. See: 'Police and Intelligence Reforms in Bosnia and Herzegovina: Urgent Action Needed', Centre for European Integration Strategies, 7 April 2006, p.4 (published with the support of DCAF)

34 The State Border Service (SBS) was established in 2000, under UN stewardship, with much less political acrimony than in other sectors. It is proving operationally effective where it has sufficient capacity but resource shortfalls must be overcome.

35 For an overview of the Media and SSR in BiH, see: Fittipaldi, Mariangela, 'Security Sector Reform and Media in BiH: The Way Ahead to Security Sector Good Governance', Centre for Security Studies, February 2006 (published with the support of DCAF). Available at: http://www.css.ba/docs/Media&SSReformENG.pdf

36 According to the 2006 Progress Report, 'Adopting all necessary legislation at State and Entity level and ensuring its implementation is a key priority of the European Partnership.', European Commission, *Bosnia and Herzegovina: 2006 Progress Report*, p.14

37 Caparini, Marina, 'Security Sector Reform and Post-Conflict Stabilisation: The Case of the Western Balkans', in Bryden, Alan and Heiner Hänggi, *Reform and Reconstruction of the Security Sector* (DCAF: Geneva, 2004), p.13

38 Information on SSR in Serbia and Montenegro was provided in part by the following sources: Bakic, Branka and Novak Gajic, *Police Reform in the Republic of Serbia*; Djurdjevic-Lukic, Svetlana, *Defence Reform in Serbia and Montenegro: Hampering Exceptionalism*; Jankovic, Sasa, *Intelligence/Security Systems of Serbia and Montenegro* (all Forthcoming, LaVAK: Vienna 2007)

39 Emerson, Michael et al, 'The Reluctant Debutante: The EU as Promoter of Democracy in its Neighbourhood', in Emerson, Michael (ed.), *Democratisation in the European Neighbourhood*, Brussels: CEPS, 2005, pp.184-5

40 'Montenegro's Referendum', International Crisis Group, Europe Briefing 42 (30 May 2006), p.2.

41 Glisic, Jasmina, 'Sluggish Security Sector Reform in Serbia and Montenegro', Centre for Civil Military Relations, Belgrade (19 May 2006). Available at: http://www.ccmr-bg.org/analize/rec/word61.htm

42 Optimism regarding this period of reform activity is seen in the EC's 2004 Report. European Commission, *Commission Staff Working Paper: Serbia and Montenegro: Stabilisation and Association Report 2004*, {COM(2004) 206 final}, undated, 2004 , pp.7-8 Available at: http://ec.europa.eu/enlargement/archives/pdf/serbia_and_montenegro/cr_s-m_en.pdf

43 Boonstra, Jos and David Greenwood, 'Serbia and Montenegro' in: Greenwood, David (ed.), 'The Western Balkan Candidates for NATO Membership and Partnership', *Harmonie Papers* No, 18, Centre for European Security Studies (CESS), Groningen, 2005, pp.88-9

44 This was observed by the European Commission, though in the context of broader observations on the functioning of the State Union parliament. European Commission, *Commission Staff Working Document: Serbia and Montenegro: 2005 Progress Report*, {COM (2005) 561 final}, 9 November 2005, p.10. Available at:

http://ec.europa.eu/enlargement/archives/pdf/key_documents/2005/package/sec_1428_final_progress_report_cs_en.pdf

45 European Commission, *Commission Staff Working Document: Serbia 2006 Progress Report*, {COM (2006) 649 final}, 8 November 2006, p.9. Available at: http://ec.europa.eu/enlargement/pdf/key_documents/2006/Nov/sr_sec_1389_en.pdf

46 'Serbia's 'Elite' Enemy Within', BBC News (26 March 2003). Available at: http://news.bbc.co.uk/2/hi/europe/2888943.stm

47 The OSCE has been strongly involved in assisting police reform in Serbia and Montenegro. An outline of their law enforcement programme can be found at: http://www.osce.org/serbia/13164.html

48 European Commission, *Serbia and Montenegro 2005 Progress Report*, p.50

49 European Commission, *Serbia 2006 Progress Report*, p.37

50 *Ibid.*, p.35

51 European Commission, *Serbia and Montenegro: Stabilisation and Association Report 2004*, p.45

52 Brussis, Martin, 'Serbia and Montenegro: Democratic Consensus Susceptible to Populist Actors', *Southeast European and Black Sea Studies,* Vol.6, No.1 (March 2006), p.108

53 European Commission, *Serbia 2006 Progress Report*, p.37

54 'European Union Suspends Talks with Serbia', Radio Free Europe/Radio Liberty (RFE/RL) (3 May 2006). Available at: http://www.rferl.org/featuresarticle/2006/05/8013AFCD-6A1B-4338-AEAC-E94B328BBF0B.html

55 Watkins, Amadeo, 'New Montenegro and Regional Stability', Conflict Studies Research Centre (CSRC), Balkans Series, 06/26 (June 2006), p.1

56 Batt, Judy, 'Endgame in the Balkans – from fragmentation to integration', *EUISS Newsletter*, No 17 (January 2006)

57 'What Next for Montenegro?', BBC News (22 May 2006). Available at: http://news.bbc.co.uk/2/hi/europe/5005344.stm

58 European Commission, *Serbia and Montenegro 2005 Progress Report*, p.8

59 Watkins, *New Montenegro*, p.6

60 European Commission, *Proposal for a Council Decision on the principles, priorities and conditions contained in the European Partnership with Montenegro* {SEC (2006) 1388}, 8 November 2006, p.6. Available at: http:/ec.europa.eu/enlargement/pdf/key_documents/2006/Nov/mn_com_654_partnership_en.df

61 Gajic, Novak, *Police Reform in the Republic of Montenegro* (Forthcoming paper commissioned by DCAF), pp.24-5

62 *Ibid.*, p.17

63 Kahn, Jeremy, 'Old ways die hard in Montenegro', CNN Money.com (25 August 2006). Available at: http://money.cnn.com/magazines/fortune/fortune_archive/2006/09/04/8384863/index.htm

64 Vlahutin, Romana, 'The Croatian Exception', in: Batt, Judy (ed.), 'The Western Balkans: Moving On', *Chaillot Papers*, No.70, EU Institute of Security Studies, Paris, October 2004, p.35

65 The process of constructing a territorial defence force is described in: Silber, Laura and Alan Little, *Yugoslavia: Death of a Nation* (Penguin Books: London, 1997), pp.107-13

66 Volten, Peter, 'Croatia' in: Greenwood, David (ed.), 'The Western Balkan Candidates for NATO Membership and Partnership', *Harmonie Papers* No, 18, Centre for European Security Studies (CESS), Groningen, 2005, pp.44

67 Kusic, Sinisa, 'Croatia: Advancing Political and Economic Transformation', *Southeast European and Black Sea Studies*, Vol.6, No.1 (March 2006), p.67

68 Pietz, *Defence Reform and Conversion in Albania, Macedonia and Croatia*, pp.36-7

69 Volten, Peter, 'Croatia', pp.47-9

70 European Commission, *Commission Staff Working Document: Croatia 2005 Progress Report*, {COM (2005) 561 final}, 9 November 2005, p.13. Available at: http://ec.europa.eu/enlargement/archives/pdf/key_documents/2005/package/sec_1424_final_progress_report_hr_en.pdf

71 See note 34 above

72 Rather than the capture of Gotovina, it appears that the reason for beginning the negotiations was in fact political. Austria lifted its objections to opening accession talks with Turkey in exchange for clearing the path for Croatia, its ally, to do so as well in a dramatic deal in Luxembourg on 3 October 2005. It remains unclear whether Carla del Ponte's unexpected announcement on the same day that Croatia was cooperating with the ICTY was politically influenced or simply fortuitous. See: 'EU and Turkey Agree Terms', *The Guardian* (3 October 2005). Available at: http://www.guardian.co.uk/turkey/story/0,12700,1583966,00.html

73 'Massive Rally for Croatia Suspect', BBC News (11 December 2005). Available at: http://news.bbc.co.uk/2/hi/europe/4518946.stm

74 Zunec, O., 'Democratic oversight and control over intelligence and security agencies', in: Fluri, Philipp and Jan Trapans (eds.), *Defence and Security Sector Governance and Reform in South-East Europe: Insights and Perspectives, A Self-Assessment Study*, vol. 1, Albania, Bulgaria, Croatia (Geneva Centre for the Democratic Control of Armed Forces (DCAF): Geneva and Belgrade, 2003), pp.71-4

75 OSCE Mission to Croatia, *News in brief*, 25 July 2006. Available at: http://www.osce.org/documents/mc/2006/07/20036_en.pdf

76 European Commission, *Croatia 2005 Progress Report*, p.14.

77 Caparini, *Security Sector Reform and Post-Conflict Stabilisation*, p.15

78 European Commission, *Commission Staff Working Document: Croatia 2006 Progress Report*, {COM (2006) 649 final}, 8 November 2006, p.6. Available at: http://ec.europa.eu/enlargement/pdf/key_documents/2006/Nov/hr_sec_1385_en.pdf

79 *Ibid.*, p.12

80 *Ibid.*, p.53

81 Freedom House, *Croatia Country Report 2006*. Available at: http://www.freedomhouse.org/template.cfm?page=47&nit=397&year=2006

82 European Commission, *Croatia 2006 Progress Report*, p.8

83 Sinisa, *Croatia: Advancing Political and Economic Transformation*, p.69

84 Williemsen, Heinz, 'Former Yugoslav Republic of Macedonia: Persisting Structural Constraints to Democratic Consolidation', *Southeast European and Black Sea Studies*, Vol.6, No.1 (March 2006), p.85

85 This armed movement was not supported by mainstream Albanian politicians however, who condemned its actions. Steele, Jonathan, 'Nowhere near the brink', *The Guardian* (19 March 2001). Available at: http://www.guardian.co.uk/comment/story/0,,458971,00.html

86 'Agreement on Macedonia Police', CNN World News (5 August 2001). Available at: http:/edition.cnn.com/2001/WORLD/europe/08/05/macedonia.talks/index.html

87 'Macedonia: Not out of the Woods Yet', International Crisis Group, *Europe Briefing* No 37 (25 February 2005), p.4

88 'Macedonia's Referendum: A Narrow Squeak', *The Economist* (11 November 2004). Available at: file:///Users/admin/Documents/DCAF%20Related/Conditionality%20Article/Latest%20journalism%20on%20W%20Balkans/Economist_com%20%20Macedonia's%20referendum%20Nov%202004.htm

89 'Macedonia: Wobbling toward Europe', International Crisis Group, *Europe Briefing* No 41 (12 January 2006), p.7

90 'Macedonia's Parliament adopts new Law on Police', *Southeastern European Times* (3 November 2006). Available at: http://www.setimes.com/cocoon/setimes/xhtml/en_GB/features/setimes/features/2006/11/03/feature-02

91 *Wobbling toward Europe*, International Crisis Group, p.8

92 European Commission, *Commission Staff Working Document: The former Yugoslav Republic of Macedonia 2006 Progress Report*, {COM (2006) 649 final}, 8 November 2006, p.44 Available at: http://ec.europa.eu/enlargement/pdf/key_documents/2006/Nov/fyrom_sec_1387_en.pdf

93 *Ibid.*, p.10

94 Nikolovska, Kristina, 'EU Gives Cautious Welcome to Macedonia's Judicial Reforms', Institute for War and Peace Reporting (IWPR), *Balkan Insight* (9 November 2006). Available at: http://www.iwpr.net/?p=brn&s=f&o=325431&apc_state=henpbrn

95 Williemsen, *Persisting Structural Constraints to Democratic Consolidation*, p.87

96 Pietz, *Defence Reform and Conversion in Albania, Macedonia and Croatia*, p.24

97 Boonstra, Jos, 'Macedonia' in: Greenwood, David (ed.), 'The Western Balkan Candidates for NATO Membership and Partnership', *Harmonie Papers* No, 18, Centre for European Security Studies (CESS), Groningen, 2005, pp.63-4

98 Cole, Eden and Philipp H. Fluri, 'Security Sector Reform Norms Transfer in South East Europe', in Hänggi, Heiner and Theodor H. Winkler, *Challenges of Security Sector Governance* (LIT: Münster, 2003)

99 Edmunds, Timothy, 'Political Conditionality and Security Sector Reform in Post-Communist Europe', *Conflict, Security and Development*, Vol. 3, No. 1 (April 2003), pp. 139-44

100 See : Batt (ed.), *The Western Balkans*, p.19. This was also argued by the International Commission on the Balkans.

10. EU Support for Security Sector Reform in the Former Soviet Union: A Piecemeal Success

Duncan Hiscock

Introduction

This chapter looks at the evolution of EU policy and assistance towards the states of the former Soviet Union in the sphere of security sector reform (SSR). It starts by outlining the overall context in which the security relationship between the EU and the post-Soviet region is developing. It then goes on to look in more detail at different sub-regions, considering the quality of security sector governance in each area and the transformations that have taken place since these countries gained independence.

The central argument of this chapter is that although the EU has sponsored many security-related initiatives and reforms in the former Soviet Union, little has been done to promote SSR as the 'holistic, multi-sectoral approach' advocated by the European Commission's Concept for ESDP Support to Security Sector Reform.[1] This is understandable, but should be a cause for concern: the quality of security sector governance is poor in much of the region, being neither very democratic nor very effective. Unreformed security sectors are a major obstacle to democratisation in many post-Soviet countries; in some they are a threat to security in themselves.

The EU's authority in the former Soviet Union is growing, but it is not yet always perceived as a major security actor. Only by using its limited resources and influence more efficiently can it have a noticeable effect on the quality of security sector governance in the region. This chapter suggests some possible steps in this direction, whilst accepting that in most post-Soviet states truly comprehensive SSR remains unlikely.

The Former Soviet Union: Security Partner, Security Threat

With the Soviet military threat gone and widespread optimism about the inevitability of democratisation in the post-socialist world, it is easy to understand why the region was afforded relatively little attention in the early 1990s. However, EU enlargements in 2004 (including the post-Soviet states of Estonia, Latvia and Lithuania) and 2007 have literally brought the former Soviet Union closer to home. Yet it is not simply a matter of physical proximity. The EU's security agenda continues to evolve, and the CIS region figures prominently in many of the key security challenges: energy supply and security; Islamist terrorism; illegal migration; and the trafficking of human beings and drugs.

The EU emphasises that these are shared problems, which can only be addressed through cooperation. This is undoubtedly the case, and is also diplomatic good sense. Yet, in practice this approach blurs one problem, and ignores another. The first problem is that shared problems do not necessarily translate into shared solutions. Though the EU and post-Soviet states can agree that they face similar threats, often they do not share the same opinion of how best to respond. Too often, post-Soviet security actors still prefer heavy-handed, over-centralised state interventions, which are questionable both in their effectiveness and democratic credentials. This is because these security actors are still heavily influenced by their Soviet legacy: the security context has changed faster than perceptions of what constitutes security and how best to provide it. The second, related, issue is that this pervading Soviet influence on post-Soviet security sectors constitutes an obstacle to democratic development. Some security actors are as much of a threat to as a provider of security. Unfortunately, this problem was overlooked throughout the 1990s, and only now, with the new emphasis on SSR, is it beginning to be addressed.

The Legacy of the Soviet Security Sector

The level of security sector governance in the USSR was, unsurprisingly, extremely low. Since the state had few mechanisms by which personal or social grievances could be addressed legitimately (or adequately), the only alternative was repression. The main domestic security organs – the KGB, the Ministry of Internal Affairs, the General Prosecutor's Office, and the judicial system – were thus designed to protect the interests of the state and the regime rather than its citizens' rights. These closed, secretive institutions were not subject to any form of civilian control (except by the Communist Party). The legal system was riddled with contradictions and the justice sector was largely subservient to the will of the executive, meaning that although to some extent a 'rule through the law' existed, there was no rule of law.

Given this unpromising legacy, the challenge for those pursuing 'democratisation' or 'transition' should be clear. Full democratisation is impossible without strengthening democratic governance of the security sector. Key security ministries that are not under full democratic control risk either becoming over-powerful actors in their own right or being controlled by specific groups for their own political or economic interests. This is exactly what has been allowed to happen in the majority of post-Soviet states.

Unfortunately, in the 1990s both local and international reformers supporting 'democratisation' ignored this problem, concentrating mostly on economics and democratic elections. It is easy to be critical of this approach with the benefit of hindsight, and it would be unfair to criticise the EU for not taking this into account when 'security sector reform' was undeveloped as an academic or policy discipline. Nonetheless, it is now time for the EU to approach the issue in a more comprehensive and strategic fashion. The danger of not doing so is not only the continuation of an unsatisfactory status quo. Unreformed, undemocratic security sectors may act as an obstacle to reforms in other sectors and undermine the EU's ability to achieve its policy goals with respect to these countries; they may even become threats to security in themselves, whether as accomplices to rejuvenated authoritarianism or as actors in reignited 'frozen' conflicts. The following sections analyse the state of the security sector in various post-Soviet states and consider the role of the EU so far in supporting SSR.

Different Sub-Regions, Different Problems, Different Approaches

Although the successor states of the Soviet Union share the same heritage, they have developed along different vectors in the 15 years since independence. This is due to different levels of infrastructure, different security challenges, and different geopolitical outlooks. It thus makes little sense to look at them all through the same lens. Indeed, the EU itself does not do so, making a distinction between the Western CIS and South Caucasus states (except Belarus) on the one hand, which are dealt with under the European Neighbourhood Policy (ENP), and the Central Asian states on the other hand, where the EU's primary tool is the Development Cooperation Instrument (DCI). In keeping with its size and strategic importance, there are distinct bilateral relations between the EU and Russia. Meanwhile, Belarus receives little technical assistance, as it is the subject of EU sanctions in response to Aleksandr Lukashenka's authoritarian style of government.

This paper follows the same subdivision, looking first at the countries included in the ENP, and then at Central Asia.[2] Russia will not be considered, since the EU lacks any real levers to support security sector reforms in the country and has little ability even to influence Russian attitudes about security sector governance. These sections aim to discuss the following key issues with regard to each region and/or country:

a) *Security sector governance:* What is the level of security sector governance, and how does this relate to the overall level of democratic governance in the country?
b) *Security sector reform:* How has the security sector developed over the last 15 years? Is it possible to attribute such changes to a coherent reform strategy?
c) *The role of the EU:* What influence has the EU had on promoting reform so far? What are the EU's stated plans for supporting reform in the next five years?

The intention is not to catalogue the entire range of security sector related activities supported by the EU across the region, so much as to highlight the overall direction of this support and its strengths and weaknesses.

Security Sector Reform in the ENP Zone

The five post-Soviet countries currently covered by the ENP do not form a coherent region either geographically or in terms of the challenges they face. The main thing they have in common is that they are recognised as

'European' countries (though less so with the South Caucasus countries). Hypothetically, they could thus one day become EU member states, though the EU has made clear that it cannot make any promises of membership for the time being. The ENP, which also covers the EU's Mediterranean neighbours, is thus an attempt to develop a coherent approach to all the countries on the EU's periphery that are not currently membership candidates. Nonetheless, the EU develops an individual ENP Action Plan with each country, which rightly allows for considerable variation in the exact form of cooperation.

Ukraine

Ukraine might be considered a 'test rod' for SSR in the former Soviet Union, since it has always been one of the most westward-looking post-Soviet states. Under President Viktor Yushchenko (since 2005) this Western orientation has increased, and Ukraine has repeatedly stated its long-term goal of EU membership. Similarly, integration with NATO has gradually intensified, even if Viktor Yanukovych, Prime Minister since summer 2006, has advocated a more cautious approach to membership. This means that significant levers of influence are available to the EU to promote and support SSR.

In the Annexes to the European Commission's Concept for European Community Support for Security Sector Reform, Ukraine is held up as a 'good example ... where the EC has given substantial support to the SSR process in ... a context [where] ... the country is undergoing a process of transition towards good governance, rule of law, respect of democratic principles and human rights.'[3] It is certainly the case that Ukraine has made significant progress in recent years towards the respect of democratic principles and human rights, and also that the EC has given substantial support to various parts of the security sector – but is it really possible to claim that there is a coherent SSR process taking place in the country? And even if so, how much influence has the EU had? And has support from the EU been implemented within a recognisable SSR framework?

Although the EU's efforts to support reforms in the security sector are admirable, it is probably misleading to classify it as 'support for SSR', because neither the donor nor the recipient has really conceived of it in these terms. This is an important point, which to a greater or lesser extent applies to all EU support in the security sector across the former Soviet Union. This should give pause for thought, since over the long run, assistance that deals with the issues at the heart of SSR – security sector governance, democratic control, the rule of law, professionalisation of security actors, civilianisation of security institutions, etc – is likely to be of more benefit both to the recipient country and to the EU than piecemeal measures that have limited effect on the overall functioning of the security sector.

On one level, it is clear that Ukraine has made considerable progress in reforming its security sector. The Armed Forces are in the middle of a major transformation, including large troop reductions, professionalisation, improved democratic civilian control and greater operational separation of the Ministry of Defence from the General Staff. The Security Service of Ukraine has been stripped of many of the functions it inherited from the KGB, and the intelligence services as a whole are slowly being reformed according to Western models. The State Border Guard Service is being demilitarised and procedures and infrastructure strengthened. Across the sector, legislation and regulations have been elaborated to bring Ukraine into line with international best practice.

Yet despite these positive signals, it would be hard to argue that these reforms are part of a holistic or systematic approach to SSR. While it is possible to point to progressive reforms in some parts of the security sector, such as the Armed Forces, in other agencies, such as the Ministry of Internal Affairs or the General Prosecutor's Office, reform has been a much slower process. Corruption remains rife in the judicial system and there is little public trust in the courts or belief in the rule of law. The result is that reforms in different agencies have been moving at different speeds, and quite possibly different vectors. Little effort has been made to develop and implement a centralised, coordinated vision for reform. In fact, it is unclear how such a concept could be developed without prior agreement on what Ukraine perceives as its main security threats and how it intends to address them. A National Security Concept has long been under preparation, but yet to be officially agreed, and it is doubtful how much guidance it will provide even when it is published. Lastly, in most cases little has been done to tackle the way in which the ministries are managed: reforms have mostly focused on training and renewal of infrastructure, while issues such as financial, resource, personnel and strategic management have been left largely untouched.

It is equally hard to argue that the EU has been the leading actor promoting reform in the security sector – so far, at least, NATO has played that role. Inevitably, this has focused primarily on the Armed Forces, explaining why reforms in this field are more advanced than elsewhere in the sector, though NATO has recently expanded its focus, including SSR issues into its Joint Working Group on Defence Reform and becoming more engaged in intelligence reform.[4]

In fact, much of the EU's assistance has been focused on a limited number of agencies and issues (Border Guards and Customs; migration, drug trafficking and organised crime[5]), reflecting both the EU's security concerns far more accurately than a Ukrainian SSR agenda and reflecting also the fact that EU assistance has focussed primarily on the European Commission's first pillar competence. This is not to say that these issues are not also of great concern to Ukraine; it does suggest, however, that despite the EU's stated commitments to SSR, holistic approaches and local ownership, in practice it has tended to support initiatives which most suit its own security priorities. Again, this is a pattern that is repeated in the EU's dealings across the region. However, one of the EU's most recent programmes, the assistance mission on the Ukrainian-Moldovan border (EUBAM, see below) suggests that the EU is gradually adopting the principles of SSR, even if the mission was primarily designed with other motives in mind.

Moldova and EUBAM

Until recently, Moldova was perceived as a largely unreformed, conflict-ridden corner of Europe which held little interest for the EU – a separate delegation did not even open in Chisinau until October 2005. Three main factors have pushed Moldova up the political agenda. Firstly, with Romania joining the EU on 1 January 2007, Moldova – and the unresolved conflict in Transnistria – is now on the EU's border. Secondly, for the past couple of years President Vladimir Voronin has pursued a more avowedly pro-European position, opening the country up to greater European influence. Thirdly, the EU has decided to take a more active role in resolving the 'frozen' conflicts on the European continent, both because it recognises the security challenges they present and because it wishes to demonstrate that it can be a serious foreign policy actor. In this regard, the Transnistria conflict appears the most immediate and the easiest to resolve.

It is unsurprising, therefore, that support for finding a viable settlement to the Transnistria conflict figures heavily in the EU-Moldova Action Plan agreed in February 2005, alongside commitments to strengthen the rule of law, improve the management of migration, and combat organised crime and drug trafficking. Observers are pessimistic about the implementation of much of the Action Plan, however, suggesting that Moldova has been more ready to make statements about its EU aspirations than to implement decisions that might make integration a reality.[6]

On the topic of Transnistria, however, the EU has certainly been active. In November 2005 the EU launched the European Union Border Assistance Mission to Moldova and Ukraine (EUBAM), an ambitious initiative aimed at helping these two states modernise border management on the internationally recognised Moldovan-Ukrainian border – most of which is in practice Ukraine's border with Transnistria. This is intended to support the conflict resolution process by reducing smuggling and organised crime and improving border control standards on this politically sensitive border. EUBAM has no powers to monitor or police the border itself; instead its role is to provide advice and training to Ukrainian and Moldovan border and customs officials (including while they are actually carrying out their duties) and assist with the upgrade of infrastructure.

A year after EUBAM started, it has been hailed as a major success by local and EU officials alike.[7] It was deployed quickly and effectively and became operational in a very short space of time. It was soon uncovering evidence of smuggling and highlighting inefficiencies in the current control regime. It also catalysed the implementation by Ukraine in March 2006 of a customs regime that allowed Transnistrian goods only if they were accompanied by Moldovan tax documentation, which has had a major political impact on conflict dynamics – even if, as a recent Crisis Group report argues, its impact on preventing smuggling has so far been more limited.[8]

From an SSR perspective, however, what is most interesting is that many of the issues that EUBAM is addressing – or uncovering – fall within a wider concept of SSR, even if the mission has never been referred to as such. As the EUBAM's annual report illustrates, the focus has been not only on upgrading officials' practical skills, but also to changing the working culture. The report highlights EUBAM's efforts in areas such as human resource management, organisational culture, and the rule of law.[9] EUBAM has put great emphasis on inter-agency cooperation at both the operational and senior levels, another central focus of SSR where post-Soviet countries have a great deal to learn. It is clear that this hands-on approach could act as an entry point for broader SSR activities in future, since it is catalysing a greater understanding, both within the country itself and among EU officials, of the problems caused by a lack of SSR in post-Soviet countries. One analyst sums this up succinctly: 'You cannot change the [Moldovan] border guards without changing the entire security sector. What ails the border guards is deeply entrenched in their mentality'.[10]

The question is whether EUBAM will be sufficient to build on this momentum, and whether the EU is prepared to grasp the nettle. EUBAM's mandate is currently due to expire at the end of 2007, and there are fears that the new Ukrainian government headed by Viktor Yanukovych since August 2006 might resist attempts to extend or expand EUBAM's mission. Even if EUBAM does gain a multi-year extension, however, its potential to influence greater reforms across the security sector may be lost.

There is a strong argument to be made that SSR could act as part of a long-term resolution to the Transnistrian conflict (and other post-Soviet conflicts, particularly in Georgia). Simply put, Chisinau will never be able to persuade Transnistria to willingly reintegrate into Moldova unless it can convince Transnistrians that Moldova offers them a better standard and quality of living. Economic opportunities are crucial, as the Crisis Group report argues.[11] However, the security sector should not be overlooked either. Security sector institutions are particularly sensitive in conflict resolution, because of the role they may have played in the initial conflict and because they may continue to be perceived as instruments of discrimination or repression. Over time, efforts to reform the Moldovan security sector by improving democratic governance, professionalism and efficiency could have a major impact in creating more promising conditions for an eventual settlement.

To do so, however, would require greater commitment from the Moldovan government itself, and for the EU to play a more active role in both promoting and supporting such reforms. A survey of SSR in Moldova concludes that 'progress towards SSR in Moldova may be identified as minimal' and that it has been reduced to 'periodic downsizing of the armed forces and the redistribution of tasks among the institutions responsible for national security'.[12] The EU (and NATO) should encourage the Moldovan government to implement comprehensive SSR, both by making SSR more central to the technical assistance it provides and by stressing the links between successful SSR and conflict resolution. The EU may be reluctant to do so, however, cautious of being seen to interfere in the most sensitive areas of state policy, and also aware that it still may not have enough capacity to provide SSR-related assistance if it is requested.

The South Caucasus: Armenia, Azerbaijan and Georgia

On the very periphery of Europe, Armenia, Azerbaijan and Georgia were initially left out of the European Neighbourhood Policy, but this decision was reversed in 2004, largely as a consequence of the 'Rose Revolution' in Georgia in November 2003 that brought Mikheil Saakashvili to power. The South Caucasus's importance to the EU stems from its strategic location between the Caspian Sea and Central Asia, Russia, the Middle East, and the Black Sea and Turkey and its potential as a transit corridor and supplier of oil and gas from the Caspian and beyond. Though to many EU member states the South Caucasus appears even more remote, unstable and ungovernable than Ukraine or Moldova, there is still a general acknowledgement that developments in the region could have a major impact on peace and stability on the European continent, and this has led the EU to engage more fully with the region, including the three unresolved conflicts in Abkhazia, Nagorno Karabakh and South Ossetia.

In Armenia and Azerbaijan, the development of the security sector has been strongly influenced by the unresolved conflict in Nagorno Karabakh. A study of security sector reform in Armenia from 2005 by this author noted that since the violent conflict had escalated before the two countries had even gained independence, the development of their security sectors was strongly influenced by the war.[13] In Armenia's case, this meant that building up the security sector was prioritised within the Armenian state, and given the urgency of this process and the lack of other models, this was done largely along Soviet lines. The perceived 'victory' in Karabakh has allowed the security agencies, in particular the Ministry of Defence, to maintain their privileged position within the state, and has made them very resistant to any reforms they fear might weaken Armenia's military preparedness. There may be more space for reform in the policing and judicial sectors, but even here, progress is slow.[14]

In Azerbaijan's case, the effective loss of Karabakh led the country to the brink of collapse, and it took the return of Heydar Aliyev, who had run the Azerbaijan Soviet Republic during the USSR, to conclude a ceasefire and rebuild the country. He was quite successful in this mission, though the system over which he presided was regularly criticised by opponents as undemocratic and corrupt. Despite declarative statements in support of democratic control, little has been done to reform security sector institutions that are still largely run according to Soviet-style procedures and approaches, even after Heydar Aliyev's son, Ilham, came to power in October 2003. Recent years have seen large year-on-year increases in defence spending, financed out of Azerbaijan's growing energy wealth. This cannot be thought of as SSR, however, since the emphasis is not on democratic governance but on boosting Azerbaijan's military capabilities; the main aim is to strengthen Azerbaijan's hand *vis-à-vis* Karabakh, with the spectre of a new war if peace negotiations over Karabakh were to fail completely.[15]

If nothing approaching SSR can be identified in either Armenia or Azerbaijan, then Georgia represents the other extreme – no other country in the CIS has exhibited such zeal for reform over the last couple of years. Among the many ambitious goals it has set itself, it has already began a complete overhaul of the police force (including the establishment, virtually overnight, of a new 'Patrol Police'); it is restructuring, retraining and re-equipping its armed forces (with a view to achieving NATO membership, says the Government; in order to re-ignite the conflicts in South Ossetia and Abkhazia, claim politicians in these areas and in Moscow[16]); and it also aims to reform the justice sector along Western lines, based in part on the recommendations presented to Georgia by EU advisers under the EUJUST Themis mission – another significant example of EU support for security sector reform in recent years.

EUJUST Themis was a one-year mission between June 2004 and July 2005 which placed nine legal experts across the Georgian justice sector (the Ministry of Justice, the Ministry of Internal Affairs, the Prosecutor's Office, the Ombudsman's Office, the Council of Justice, the Appeal Court and the Supreme Court) with the aim of advising and coordinating the development of a criminal justice reform strategy. Themis was the first such rule-of-law mission to be deployed by the EU under the ESDP, and it inevitably suffered from a number of teething problems. These related partly to the over-ambitious nature of the mission within the set time-frame, and the difficulties of pursuing reform in the sometimes chaotic world of Georgian politics, but also to a number of internal challenges relating to funding mechanisms and instruments and the relationship between the Commission and the Council.[17] This experience has provided plenty of lessons learned for the EU in terms of deploying rule-of-law and crisis management missions globally; it should also be used as an opportunity to assess the challenges and opportunities for similar EU support missions for SSR in the former Soviet Union.

The European Neighbourhood Policy

The ENP has received mixed reviews since being unveiled in 2004, and is expected to undergo some kind of revision during the German Presidency in the first half of 2007. This provides the perfect opportunity for the EU to integrate its new SSR concepts, which were only finalised in 2005, into the revised ENP. This would be in keeping with the sensible recommendation made within the Commission's 'Concept for European Community Support for Security Sector Reform' on 'integrating SSR in Country (CSP) and Regional (RSP) Strategy Papers, Action Plans, and programming tools'.[18] However, recently released documents suggest that this integration is slow to be realised.

The original ENP Strategy Paper, released in May 2004 [19], makes no direct mention of SSR, though it does refer to many of its central elements: the need to promote good governance and the primacy of the rule of law on the one hand, and a range of security threats (under the rubric of 'justice, security and home affairs') on the other. However, no direct link is made between the two. Furthermore, the chief priority that is identified – migration and border management – is questionable from an SSR perspective. Although there is no question that these issues are important to the EU's partner countries and do present them with certain security challenges, the primary security challenges caused by migration and weak border management are to the EU itself, rather than to its ENP partners. This gives the strong impression that despite the emphasis on 'local ownership', the EU has been successful in imposing its own priorities on ENP partner states when developing its priorities. Meanwhile, the wider question of the democratic governance of the security sector has been largely ignored, with virtually no emphasis on reform of internal security agencies (e.g. policing and intelligence ministries) and less on the judiciary than is perhaps needed. After all, over the long term even a strong border and migration management regime along the EU's perimeter is unlikely to really provide the EU with security if these states – and particularly their security sectors – remain mismanaged and corrupt.

In December 2006, the Commission issued a communication on strengthening the ENP.[20] From an SSR perspective, this document is disappointing. The word 'security' is barely mentioned, even though much is written about border management and migration. There is an acknowledgement at the beginning that the ENP has so far failed to have much of a role in conflict resolution, but provides few pointers on how to address this problem (apart from increased political dialogue). SSR is not mentioned at all, and of the concrete list of instruments suggested in the Council's Concept for ESDP Support to SSR (support in reforming the defence sector; support in reforming the police sector; support in strengthening justice/rule of law elements; support in strengthening the border and customs sector; support in reforming the financial and budgetary aspects of the security sector[21]), most are not considered.

The continuing lack of consideration for SSR in the ENP's main strategy documents is largely reinforced by the ENP Action Plans for the three South Caucasus countries released in November 2006.[22] None of them contain any reference to SSR, although like the ENP from which they are derived, they do contain considerable measures on border management and migration and a few more general commitments regarding the rule of law. A positive exception to this trend is the fact that the implementation of the above-mentioned criminal justice reform strategy for the criminal justice system has been made Priority 1 in the new Action Plan for Georgia.[23]

If this lack of emphasis on SSR is disappointing, it can hardly be said to be unexpected. The EU is still only beginning to get to grips with SSR, and mainstreaming SSR across EU and member state institutions (another sensible recommendation of the Concept for EC Support for SSR) will take considerable time. Attempts to address SSR more directly in ENP countries may also come up against significant resistance, both internal and external. Within the EU, certain member states and officials may be reluctant to roll out SSR initiatives that they fear are over-ambitious, too sensitive and have the potential to anger Russia. In ENP countries themselves, the principle of local ownership may be seen to preclude the possibility of undertaking SSR activities where local elites may be suspicious. Yet a distinction should be made between local ownership in terms of how projects are planned and managed, and the EU simply avoiding engaging in areas that it fears may be sensitive. On the contrary, the EU needs to have the conviction that democratic security sector governance is essential to the health of the states that are on the EU's doorstep, and that since they have made strong public commitments to democracy and upholding safety and stability, the EU's experience in SSR is not only useful, but essential. In short, the specific content of SSR in any given country must indeed be locally owned, but the EU should not flinch from putting the topics of security sector governance and SSR firmly on the bilateral agenda.

Central Asia

Until 11 September 2001, Central Asia barely figured on the EU's radar. Despite a civil war in Tajikistan and outbreaks of violence in the Ferghana Valley, the region generally seemed too distant to worry about. After the invasion of Afghanistan, however, the EU and NATO 'discovered' the region's strategic importance. Although there are currently no major conflicts in the area, the security threats to the region are grave. There are extremely high levels of poverty, most of the states in the region have weak institutions and cannot provide more than the most basic of services, and corruption is rampant. This creates a fertile soil for social unrest, as the shooting of protesters by Uzbek government troops in Andijon in 2005 highlighted. It is expected that any major outbreak of violence could result in a major refugee crisis that Central Asian states are ill-equipped to cope with.[24] Poverty, poor education and distrusted state institutions also have the potential to fuel the spread of radical Islamist movements, though it can be difficult to judge the real size of such threats due to limited transparency and the tendency of governments in the region to exaggerate the Islamist threat in order to booster their own credentials in the 'War on Terror'. Lastly, since the fall of the Taliban, Afghanistan has once again become the world's number one exporter of opium/heroin, with around 30% of drug trafficking passing through Central Asia's vast and poorly protected borders. All of these factors suggest that the potential for a major security crisis is high.

Central Asian leaders have largely responded to these threats by using their internal security agencies as instruments of repression in order to keep a lid on these forces. To a greater or lesser extent, all Central Asian states have built on the Soviet legacy of using the security sector to maintain their regimes, making minor adaptations to the functioning of the sector in order to suit their own needs but essentially leaving it unchanged. Anna Matveeva notes that 'this preoccupation with the security of the regime leads to an emphasis on internal security and the suppression of political opponents. Increasingly, the state presents itself to its citizens in a police uniform, rather than as a provider of goods and services'.[25] The level of authoritarianism differs from country to country, with Turkmenistan and Uzbekistan the most oppressive – in recent years both have been virtually closed to Western access, Uzbekistan abandoning its flirtation with the West after criticism of its actions in Andijon.

The EU's approach to Central Asia has focused on regional cooperation. It has argued that the challenges faced by Central Asian states – terrorism, drug trafficking, illegal migration, environmental degradation, etc – can only be dealt with effectively at a multilateral level, and the majority of its assistance has been provided in the form of regional programmes. It is telling that unlike the countries now covered by the ENP, the EU has never developed specific country strategies for each country in Central Asia, preferring to deal with them through a regional strategy paper. This is currently the Strategy Paper for 2002-2006, with assistance provided under TACIS.[26] This will soon be phased out, to be replaced by the Development Cooperation Instrument (the Central Asian counterpart of the ENP), although commentators expect that it will take a long time for this instrument to become operational.[27]

The EU's obsession with regional cooperation has been widely criticised as being ineffective.[28] Though it may make perfect theoretical sense to handle essentially regional problems at the regional level, this approach will bring few results if the states in question have neither the resources nor the will to develop a serious response to these problems at the national level. Effectively, by focusing on all countries at once, no country feels under enough pressure to respond adequately. Furthermore, as Matveeva argues, Central Asian leaders have tended to respond to regional security threats in exactly the opposite way, by constructing further obstacles to cross-border communication in the hope that they will not get infected by the same ailments as their neighbours.[29]

Nonetheless, the EU's flagship programme in Central Asia has had some limited success. The Border Management in Central Asia (BOMCA) programme established in 2003, and the Central Asia Drug Action Programme (CADAP) from 2001 that was merged into it, have had some success in promoting border management reforms, though their impact falls far short of EUBAM in Moldova and Ukraine. Many reasons have been suggested for the frustrating progress of BOMCA/CADAP, including the over-ambitious goals it had set itself, the insufficient level of on-the-job training, and the sheer size of the challenge in a region of vast, undemarcated borders and badly paid, poorly trained state officials.[30] A further problem is that despite providing the financing for the programme, the EU has not taken full responsibility for the project; it is implemented by UNDP and has so far received limited political guidance from the EU. This reduces the EU's understanding of the challenges the programme faces or how to respond to them, and means that the EU is not building up its own experience of providing security-related assistance in the region.

Despite its failings, however, BOMCA/CADAP – like EUBAM – has significant potential as an entry point into wider questions of SSR in the region. Matveeva argues that 'BOMCA/CADAP can be used as a vehicle and a pilot case for advancement of EU thinking on common security policy, including security sector reform', but that 'neither the Commission nor the member states presented BOMCA/CADAP as an exercise in SSR, although there are good grounds to regard it as such'.[31]

Again, though, no mention of SSR has yet found its way into the EU's official policies towards the region. The draft Regional Strategy Paper for Central Asia for the period 2007-2013[32] puts a very strong emphasis on security, making it clear that managing the security threats listed above is a high priority for the EU in the region. The other emphasis is on poverty reduction, and the idea is that the Development Cooperation Instrument should be used primarily as a tool to help Central Asian states implement the Millennium Development Goals. Yet few direct links have been made between security and development, despite the massive growth in international understanding of this topic over the past few years. It is unrealistic and possibly unwise to expect the EU to launch a full SSR strategy for Central Asia, which would be coldly received by local regimes who fear it would undermine their power bases, but the total omission of SSR suggests that the EU is not making the best use of the instruments that it has at hand.

The Crowded Neighbourhood: Other Actors Promoting SSR

Lastly, it is worth briefly considering the wider context in which the EU is operating. As this paper has noted, the EU is far from the only international actor in the region: NATO, the OSCE, and the UN are all active and there is significant potential for coordination – or overlap. Furthermore, various states (most obviously the US) provide significant support on a bilateral basis. If this were not enough, Western actors must always be conscious of Russia, which is suspicious of their motives for promoting SSR in the region and has tried to build its own security dialogue through bilateral relations and the CIS. It is beyond the scope of this paper to analyse each actor's role in promoting SSR across the former Soviet Union. However, it may be useful to make some general observations about the compatibility (or otherwise) of these roles, and the challenges of coordinating between them.

As noted, the most active international security actor in the region is NATO. NATO has a security relationship with all post-Soviet states through the Partnership for Peace (PfP), which was established in 1994 as a way of boosting cooperation with its new partners across Eastern Europe, and particularly the successor states of the former Soviet Union. As time has passed, countries that wish to further develop their relationship with NATO have requested greater support and cooperation, and NATO has responded by establishing a range of mechanisms short of full membership: the Individual Partnership Action Plans (IPAP), Intensified Dialogue, and the Membership Action Plan (MAP). In recognition of their size and importance, NATO has also maintained a bilateral relationship with Russia (the NATO-Russia Council) and Ukraine (the NATO-Ukraine Commission). In all of these mechanisms, NATO agrees action plans jointly with the state in question. The amount to which SSR is emphasised within these plans thus depends on the overall attitude of the particular state, though it is made clear that major reform will be required before any membership application is approved, and therefore countries that are most interested in NATO integration (most notably Georgia and Ukraine, though also to some extent Armenia, Azerbaijan and Moldova) are encouraged to place SSR on the agenda.

The difficulties in the relationship between NATO and the EU are well acknowledged.[33] Despite similar, though not identical memberships, they have different roles, different capabilities and many member states have very different perspectives on how each organisation should be used and how tasks should be divided between them. This has often led to competition and mutual suspicion of each other's methods and motives. This is a particular concern for EU support to SSR, since both NATO and the EU are seeking to promote reform, partly through the possibility of further enlargement. The problem is not at the level of objectives, since they generally share the same vision for strengthening democratic security sector governance in the region, but in the priorities and mechanisms that are used to achieve these goals, and the compatibility and coordination between them. A natural division of responsibilities exists, which allows NATO to focus more on military reform while the EU and other actors deal with other aspects of SSR. Coordination at the local level is often good, especially given that the host states often find it hard to coordinate their own position, let alone ensuring that there is a match between foreign and local priorities. Unless they are properly coordinated at a high level, however, they are unlikely to fit together into a comprehensive strategy for reform, and the current relationship between the two organisations in Brussels leaves a lot to be desired.

Unlike the EU and NATO, all post-Soviet states are members of the OSCE and the UN. This has some advantages, in that all states are automatically part of any dialogue on SSR, but it is also a disadvantage in that agreeing a combined vision for SSR between 56 or 192 states is extremely hard. The UN is involved in conflict resolution in parts of the FSU, particularly with regard to the Georgian-Abkhaz conflict, but it has not linked this to SSR. Likewise, it is not surprising that the OSCE does not have an overt SSR agenda. Nonetheless, building on its experiences in the Balkans, it has engaged heavily in certain aspects of SSR, most notably police reform in Georgia and Kyrgyzstan (with smaller projects elsewhere). In Georgia, the EU has been keen to coordinate support for police reform and to channel much of its donor support through the OSCE. The OSCE faces a major challenge at the present time, however, due to increasing hostility towards the organisation from Russia and many other post-Soviet states, which claim that it focuses unduly on 'democratisation' in their sub-region at the expense of other tasks. The weakening of the OSCE is thus starting to create a vacuum of influence in much of the post-Soviet region that Russia, the US, the EU and NATO are all keen to fill.

The success or failure of SSR in the region will be strongly influenced by the outcome of this battle for influence. The likelihood is that the EU will be able to promote SSR only if it cooperates more closely with other Western actors – particularly NATO – at a multilateral level, and if its member states coordinate more effectively to ensure that bilateral aid is in line with the EU's wider objectives and positions are agreed in other multilateral and international forums (such as the OSCE and the UN). The danger is that until the EU-NATO relationship improves and their symbiotic relationship is better understood, the attempts of both the EU and NATO to promote SSR in the former Soviet Union will be undermined by their lack of coordination.

Conclusion

This chapter has argued that although the EU has provided considerable support to post-Soviet security sectors, this support has rarely been systematic or comprehensive. Though some recent initiatives suggest that the principles of SSR are gradually being taken on board, the concept still has little visibility in the former Soviet Union. Given that SSR remains a relatively new idea at the theoretical, policy-making and practical levels, it would be unfair to criticise the EU for not having approached security-related assistance from this framework in the past. It will take time and commitment to mainstream SSR internally across Commission delegations and directorates and to integrate the contributions of the EU's three pillars into a comprehensive and operational set of SSR policies. It will also take time and resources to build up the necessary networks and staff to respond promptly to future requests for SSR assistance. Furthermore, the EU must negotiate with legitimate governments that generally display a high-level of caution when 'security' matters are discussed; in practice, EU delegations may often feel unable to promote comprehensive SSR if the states in question do not wish them to do so.

It would be naïve to imagine that the EU can suddenly play a major role in improving security sector governance across the post-Soviet world in the near future. The EU does not yet have the complete toolkit of physical or policy resources necessary to undertake such reforms in the region. Weakened by its own internal problems and limited by an increasingly assertive Russia, the EU also lacks suitable levers of influence to persuade local elites to roll out unsettling long-term reforms that may undermine their existing power bases. Nevertheless, the EU can still do much to promote SSR in the former Soviet Union. Despite teething problems, operations such as EUBAM and EUJUST Themis suggest that when it puts its mind to it, the EU can play a significant role in supporting reforms that have a more comprehensive element. The challenge will be to integrate this experience more deeply into the EU's future cooperation with post-Soviet countries.

Internally, more can be done to ensure that the principles of SSR are more overtly referred to in regional policy documents such as the European Neighbourhood Policy (ENP) and the Development Cooperation Instrument (DCI) and the national action plans that stem from them. For internal mainstreaming, an initial focus might be on boosting links with the three EU Special Representatives (EUSR) for Moldova, the South Caucasus and Central Asia, who are central actors in the development of the EU's future strategies towards these regions. If the EUSRs can be convinced of the potential benefits of SSR to local governance, conflict and security dynamics, they are likely to play a key role in developing the SSR agenda in the post-Soviet world. This, in turn, will imply enhanced relations between the EUSRs and the Commission delegations and services. Another option would be to draft policy papers or frameworks that review how the EU's SSR concepts could best be utilised in post-Soviet sub-regions (e.g. Moldova and Ukraine; the South Caucasus; and Central Asia) in order to bridge the gap between the overarching theoretical concepts and the specifics of policy-making and technical assistance on the ground in specific countries or regions. If this path is followed, care must be taken to ensure that such proposals remain integrated with regional and country strategy papers.

In states that show limited desire to learn from European standards of democratic security sector governance, the EU should nonetheless link security-related assistance in specific areas (such as border control or customs modernisation) to project activities that seek to encourage more comprehensive dialogue on SSR. In other words, where possible such assistance should serve as an 'entry point' rather than as stand-alone assistance; EUBAM and BOMCA/CADAP have considerable potential in this regard. Meanwhile, in countries that are more overtly open to the EU's influence, such as Georgia, Moldova or Ukraine, the EU should not be afraid to make SSR a more central part of bilateral cooperation. To do this, more attention will also have to be paid to coordination and cooperation with NATO and the OSCE to ensure that these actors are acting in concert rather than duplicating or contradicting each other. There are also significant opportunities in Moldova and Georgia (and to a lesser extent in Azerbaijan and Armenia) to promote SSR as a long-term component of conflict resolution. Countries with improved security sector governance and a genuine commitment to the rule of law should help to reassure separatist regions that the states that they fought to break away from have changed and are truly able to respect and protect their human rights. Stronger rule of law is also essential for the economic regeneration of these areas.

The EU stands at a crossroads with regard to SSR. The EU is still not always perceived as a serious security actor in the region (indeed, Russia's relaxed attitude to the EU in comparison to NATO stems in part from the fact that it is not seen as a threat to Russian influence in security affairs). This is both a strength and a weakness. It is a strength because the EU is not seen as being so threatening, and if it is careful it can handle more sensitive issues without provoking a knee-jerk rejection. However, it is a weakness because it is partly based on truth – the EU is still in the early stages of developing its ESDP and CFSP, and security-related assistance has so far been patchy in both design and implementation, not least because some of its constituent elements have been outside the CFSP/ESDP framework, falling into the European Commission's first pillar ambit.

Yet, seen as a whole, the EU's SSR strategy provides the nucleus of a vision for the way forward. Implementing it successfully will be an extremely tough challenge, but the potential benefits are huge: if post-Soviet states were to make genuine steps towards European standards of security sector governance and the rule of law, this would be likely to have a much greater and longer-lasting impact on the security of both the EU and the states themselves than any number of projects focusing only on border controls and migration.

Endnotes

1 Council of the European Union, *EU Concept for ESDP Support to Security Sector Reform (SSR)*, Brussels, 13 October 2005, 12566/4/05 REV 4. Paragraph 15 (page 8). http://register.consilium.europa.eu/pdf/en/05/st12/st12566-re04.en05.pdf

2 The three Baltic States – Estonia, Latvia, and Lithuania – are not considered since their separateness from the rest of the Soviet Union was soon recognised by the EU and they became EU member states in 2004.

3 Annexes to the Commission Communication, *A Concept for European Community Support for Security Sector Reform*, Brussels, 24 May 2006, COM(2006)253F. Annex II, pg. 7. http://ec.europa.eu/comm/secretariat_general/regdoc/rep/2/2006/FR/2-2006-658-FR-1-0.Pdf

4 The Joint Working Group on Defence Reform was established in 1998 under the NATO-Ukraine Commission. More information can be found at: http://www.nato.int/issues/nato-ukraine/jwgdr.html. Intelligence reform is outlined as a priority in the NATO-Ukraine Action Plan (http://www.nato.int/docu/basictxt/b021122a.htm) and a number of working-level meetings and seminars have been organised in this regard over the past 2-3 years.

5 EU/Ukraine Action Plan, agreed February 2005. http://ec.europa.eu/world/enp/pdf/action_plans/ukraine_enp_ap_final_en.pdf

6 International Crisis Group, *Moldova's Uncertain Future*, Europe Report No. 175, 17 August 2006, pp.14-15. http://www.crisisgroup.org/library/documents/europe/moldova/175_moldova_s_uncertain_future.pdf

7 *Ibid.*, pp. 5-8.

8 *Ibid.*, pp. 6-7.

9 European Union Border Assistance Mission to Moldova and Ukraine, *Annual Report 2005/2006*. http://www.eubam.org/files/100-199/191/Report_ENG.pdf

10 Iurie Pintea, UNDP, quoted in International Crisis Group, *Moldova's Uncertain Future*, p.7

11 International Crisis Group, *Moldova's Uncertain Future*, pp. 15-18.

12 Bonn International Centre for Conversion, *Security Sector Transition in Moldova*, p.1, part of an *Inventory of Security Sector Reform Efforts in Partner Countries of German Development Assistance*, http://www.bicc.de/ssr_gtz/index.php

13 Duncan Hiscock and Gagik Avagyan, *Security Sector Reform in Armenia*, London: Saferworld, 2005. http://www.saferworld.org.uk/images/pubdocs/Armenia_English.pdf

14 *Ibid.*, p.7

15 The threat of renewed conflict is regularly raised by Azerbaijani politicians. For example, in January 2006, the Defence Minister, Safar Aliyev, said that if Armenia did not 'liberate' the territories it occupies in Nagorno Karabakh, this 'could lead to a resumption of military activ-

ities'. Quoted by RFE/RL, http://www.rferl.org/featuresarticle/2006/01/6acc8b50-7aec-4774-898d-ef30d3ebd46a.html

16 See for example Russian President Vladimir Putin's comments on Russian television in October 2006 that in Abkhazia 'people are very worried about the militarisation of Georgia', quoted by the BBC, http://news.bbc.co.uk/1/hi/world/europe/6083644.stm

17 Damien Helly, 'EUJUST Themis in Georgia: An ambitious bet on rule of law' in Institute for Security Studies (ed. Agnieszka Nowak), *Civilian Crisis Management: The EU Way*, Chaillot Paper No 90, Paris: June 2006. http://www.iss-eu.org/chaillot/chai90.pdf

18 European Commission (2006), *A Concept for European Community Support for Security Sector Reform*, Brussels, 24 May 2006, COM(2006)253F, p. 10 http://eur-lex.europa.eu/LexUriServ/site/en/com/2006/com2006_0253en01.pdf

19 European Commission (2004), *European Neighbourhood Policy Strategy Paper*, Brussels, 12 May 2005, COM (2004) 373 final. http://ec.europa.eu/world/enp/pdf/strategy/strategy_paper_en.pdf

20 European Commission (2006), *On Strengthening the European Neighbourhood Policy*, Brussels, 4 December 2006, COM (2006) 726 final. http://ec.europa.eu/world/enp/pdf/com06_726_en.pdf

21 Council of the European Union, *EU Concept for ESDP Support to Security Sector Reform (SSR)*, pp. 13-16.

22 *EU/Armenia Action Plan*, Brussels/Yerevan, November 2006; *EU/Azerbaijan Action Plan*, Brussels/Baku, November 2006; *European Union-Georgia Action Plan*, Brussels/Tbilisi, November 2006. Available at http://ec.europa.eu/world/enp/documents_en.htm

23 *European Union-Georgia Action Plan*, Brussels/Tbilisi, November 2006, p.7

24 International Crisis Group, *Central Asia: What Role for the European Union?*, Asia Report No. 113, 10 April 2006, p. 1. http://www.crisisgroup.org/library/documents/asia/central_asia/113_central_asia_what_role_for_the_eu.pdf

25 Anna Matveeva, *EU Stakes in Central Asia*, Chaillot Paper No 91, Institute for Security Studies, Paris: July 2006, p. 18. http://www.iss-eu.org/chaillot/chai91.pdf

26 TACIS stands for Technical Assistance to the Commonwealth of Independent States, and has been the EU's main mechanism for providing assistance to CIS states over the last decade. With the introduction of the ENP and the DCI, it is now being phased out – partly as a recognition that it makes little sense to treat all CIS states with the same approach.

27 International Crisis Group, *Central Asia: What Role for the European Union?*, p.11-12.

28 *Ibid.*, p. 23.

29 Matveeva, *EU Stakes in Central Asia*, pp. 49-50.

30 International Crisis Group, *Central Asia: What Role for the European Union?*, p.13-14; Matveeva, EU Stakes in Central Asia, pp. 88-90.

31 *Ibid*, p. 97.

32 European Community, *Regional Strategy Paper for Central Asia for the Period 2007-2013*, draft of 15 June 2006.

33 NATO Secretary General Jaap de Hoop Scheffer discussed these in detail at a keynote speech in Berlin on 29 January 2007 entitled 'NATO and the EU: Time for a New Chapter'.

11. Security System Reform in the Democratic Republic of the Congo: The Role Played by the European Union

Rory Keane[1]

Introduction

This chapter outlines the major security system reform (SSR) challenges facing the Democratic Republic of the Congo (DRC), and provides an overview and critique of how EU security and development policies have endeavoured to assist the SSR process. The chapter does not specifically outline each EU member state's bilateral contribution to such reforms, but focuses rather on the joint contribution of the European Commission (the EU's first pillar) and the European Security and Defence Policy (ESDP – the EU's second pillar).[2]

The chapter is divided into three sections. First, a brief historical overview provides the political context and reasons why the DRC faces such tremendous challenges in the security sector. Section two focuses on these SSR challenges and reviews the responses in the areas of DDR (Demilitarisation, Demobilisation and Reintegration) and reform of the defence, police and judicial structures of the DRC. In addressing these three principal areas, the role played by the international community and notably the European Union is highlighted. SSR is much broader than DDR/defence, police and justice reform, but the analysis in this chapter is limited to these three fields, as they constitute the 'priority of the SSR priorities' in the DRC. Finally, the ongoing EU response to SSR in the DRC is analysed through the lens of the EU comprehensive approach to SSR for the DRC, as set out by the EU's Political and Security Committee on 1 December 2006.

The Sun City Agreement and the Input of the International Community

The politics and security of the Democratic Republic of the Congo (DRC) are the key to war and peace in Central Africa. Yet, its recent history has been characterised by conflict and war in which seven countries were entangled from 1996 to 2002, resulting in a modest estimate of some two million victims. As a result of the 2002 Inter-Congolese Dialogue in Sun City a transitional government was established, known as the '1+4 system' (one president and four vice-presidents representing the main warring factions).[3] As with other post-conflict peace deals such as the 1995 Dayton Peace Accord in Bosnia or the 1998 Good Friday Agreement in Northern Ireland, the focus was on power-sharing between former belligerent factions. This transitional system came to an end on 29 October 2006 with the democratic election of a new DRC president for the first time since 1960. The question in the post-election period is whether the newly elected DRC authorities can deliver peace, security and, ultimately, prosperity. There is of course no clear answer to this question. Clearly, peace and prosperity will largely depend on whether the SSR agenda in the DRC is actually implemented.

The rebirth of the DRC began on 17 December 2002, when the so-called All Inclusive Agreement was signed, creating the transitional authorities of the DRC. The transition was to last four years and was finally brought to a close on 29 October 2006 with the confirmation in power of President Joseph Kabila. The All Inclusive Agreement had established an interim president (Joseph Kabila, son of Laurent Kabila), who governed with four vice-presidents, representing the various fighting groups that signed the peace agreement. The main challenges facing the transitional authorities were the adoption of a new Constitution, the holding of democratic elections and the maintenance of peace and security in the country, especially in the East. The Constitution was finally adopted on 18 December 2005, with strong support from the international community. Democratic elections (parliamentary elections and the first round of Presidential elections) were held on 31 July 2006 and the second round of Presidential elections was successfully concluded on 29 October 2006. Maintaining peace in the East implied managing an inter-ethnic low-level war in Ituri, the Kivus and Northern Katanga, which was complicated by significant arms transfers throughout the 1990s, mainly from Rwanda and Uganda. The conflict in the East was a legacy of the Rwandan genocide. In Northern Ituri certain Ugandan backed rebels, including NALU (National Army for the Liberation of Uganda) and Hutu Rwandan rebels (the FDLR – Front Démocratique de libération du Rwanda) were the main concern. The issue of the Banyamulenge (Congolese ethnic Tutsi group) dissidents was an additional problem. In South Kivu the FDLR were also active along with the Mai-Mai tribe, who were also active in North Katanga.

The East resembled a failed state. The 'territory existed' but the 'state did not'.[4] After Sun City the objective of the UN and the international community was therefore to 'put the state back into the equation', a difficult task given the plundering during decades of the Mobutu regime. While documents such as the EU's 2005 Africa Strategy proclaim that development should go hand in hand with security, it became clear after the Sun City Agreement that security would be a vital prerequisite of sustainable development in the DRC. Reform of the army, police and justice sector thus became pressing priorities. While numerous plans were developed in order to make progress in these sectors, clearly domestic political will was the precondition of progress. Yet, there was no specific plan for SSR in the Sun City Agreement – the agreement focused on ending the fighting rather than building the peace. This lack of clear political will – on all sides – made the case for army reform especially difficult. The Mobutu regime had created an army with parallel command structures and ethnic allegiances. The objective was now to create an integrated army including the DRC's former fighters and militia groups. It is not surprising that Laurent Kabila's Alliance of Democratic Forces for the Liberation of Congo (AFDL) managed to take power in 1997 without much resistance. He was supported by Rwanda, Uganda, Angola, Burundi and Eritrea. Yet success did not induce Laurent Kabila to move army reform forward after taking power. He relied heavily, for example, on his elite Presidential Guard (GSSP) for protection. Additionally 'his attempt at army reform was disastrous, in no small part because he entrusted it to a Rwandan general, James Kaberebe, who established the new Armed Forces of the Congo with Rwandan strategic interests in mind.'[5] One symptom of the lack of army reform was the ability of Congolese rebel forces in August 1998, backed by Kabila's former allies, Rwanda and Uganda, to gain control of a large portion of the country until Angolan, Namibian and Zimbabwean troops came to Kabila's aid.

In 1999 the Lusaka Accord was signed by all six of the countries involved and by rebel groups.[6] But peace remained elusive. In January 2001 Laurent Kabila was assassinated by his own bodyguard, while war still raged. It is little wonder that Joseph Kabila, his son, distrusted the army after becoming DRC President as part of the Sun City transitional deal. His father's death had clearly taught him to be on his guard. He thus focused rather on boosting his Presidential Guard and increasing training – effected largely under the aegis of his neighbouring ally Angola. Significantly, his Presidential Guard was not required to partake in the national army reform process advocated and supported by the international community. Another symptom of the complexities that existed between Kabila and his vice-presidents was the allocation of military command posts and structures. This became a central negotiating issue, with, eventually, the positions of chief of staff and chief of the air force given to Joseph Kabila's party, while the RCD party of Vice-President Ruberwa received the ground forces and the MLC party of Vice-President Bemba the naval command. Ruberwa also became the chair of the SSR joint government–international community steering committee, though this body did not in fact meet before January 2005 and since then has acted more as a donor coordination body.

After the all-inclusive peace agreement came into effect, international support for the transition process accelerated considerably. The United Nations peacekeeping Mission (MONUC) was substantially increased. It had been on the ground since the Lusaka Accords in 1999 and was to become the biggest UN peacekeeping operation in the world, with over 16,000 troops. The European Commission also re-engaged with the country in 2002, subsequently financing 80% of the election process (€165 million). In total it allocated €800 million to the DRC between 2002 and 2007. In diplomatic terms the EU also began to play a more prominent role, most notably through the EU Commissioner for Development and Humanitarian Aid, Louis Michel, the EU High Representative for the CFSP, Javier Solana, and the EU Special Representative for the Great Lakes, Aldo Ajello. A French-led EU mission (operation Artemis) to Bunia in 2004 helped to secure the territory, while two ESDP missions were launched in 2005 supporting the police (EUPOL) and army (EUSEC) respectively, while a short-term EU military mission (EUFOR) was posted to Kinshasa in 2006 in order to help secure the election process. Bilateral donors – including South Africa, Angola, France, Belgium, the UK and the Netherlands – also accelerated their cooperation, while the World Bank financed large scale reforms, outlined in its Poverty Reduction Strategy Paper (PRSP). Meanwhile a political mechanism developed in Sun City – *'Le Comité International d'Accompagnement de la Transition'* (CIAT) – enabled key international donors to steer the domestic political process in the DRC.

SSR in the DRC

International Assistance to DDR and Defence Reform

Demilitarisation, Demobilisation and Reintegration (DDR) are key aspects of SSR. In recent years the DDR paradigm has developed and become more streamlined through the UN Integrated DDR Standards (IDDRS), the Stockholm Initiative on DDR (SIDDR) and the World Bank led Multi Country Demobilisation and Reintegration Programme (MDRP) in Central Africa, which includes a large programme in the DRC. Strongly influenced by the above, the EU is now in the process of developing its DDR approach. A joint Commission-Council DDR paper outlines the parameters and makes clear the EU ambition to play an ever more influential role in DDR in the future.[7] As one NGO puts it, and other chapters of this book describe, 'In post-conflict contexts, the EU is often one of the biggest players in supporting peace processes, through both the 1st and 2nd pillars ... This is not only due to the funding provided to DDR programmes through multilateral trust funds, but also its capabilities in the political, trade and development assistance fields, which enable it to address relevant issues related to security, governance, livelihood, justice and reconciliation.'[8]

The World Bank's MDRP is the largest initiative of its kind, supporting DDR in seven central African countries. The MDRP is financed through two separate but complementary sources: World Bank/IDA funds amounting to an estimated $200 million and a multi-donor trust fund of an estimated $300 million, of which $200 million is currently committed. As to the EU, the European Commission – through the European Development Fund (EDF) – alone committed €20 million to the MDRP process in the DRC. As local ownership is a key principle of the MDRP, the programme is run by National Commissions for DDR in each country. In the DRC, political challenges – specifically the lack of progress on key army reforms – prevented the national commission – *Commission Nationale de Désarmement, Démobilisation et Réinsertion* (CONADER) – from launching the DDR programme until June 2005. By October 2006 over 140,000 ex-combatants had gone through the process, with 46,000 of those choosing to join the new reintegrated DRC army (FARDC) through the *Brassage* process – a mixing and integration of various former warring factions – while the remainder returned to civilian life. Of these approximately 90,000 returning to civilian life, only a little over 60,000 had benefited from reintegration projects by January 2007.

The demobilisation phase of the DDR process in the DRC will probably end formally in 2008, as it is unlikely that a further extension of the current MDRP process would lead to additional voluntary demobilisation. By then the programme will most probably have reached saturation point. Yet, a relatively large number of ex-combatants in the Kivus and Katanga have refused to join the DDR process and will likely be dealt with using alternative procedures by the new DRC authorities, with support from the UN mission MONUC. There are three potential options that the new DRC authorities may consider for ex-combatants who do not in the meantime sign up to the MDRP process. They may repatriate a number of the Combatants on Foreign Soils (COFS); it may prove feasible, through political pressure and confidence building measures, to bring some combatants into the FARDC through a special targeted *Brassage* process, and a small number may be willing to demobilize and enter a community reintegration process.[9] This latter option might prove sensible for some Mai-Mai combatants.

Apart from the complex issues in Ituri, the Kivus and Katanga caused by the fact that certain groups were not ready to demilitarise for a myriad of political, military and economic reasons, large scale DDR has taken place with some degree of success nationwide. The objective of the MDRP henceforth must be to consolidate the gains made. As is evident from other large-scale DDR processes in the past, demobilised combatants will not remain demobilised if the reintegration phase in not properly handled. Reintegration training is thus essential, and the international donor community must adequately ensure that ongoing and planned relief and development programmes benefit both demobilised combatants, for example through rapid employment schemes, as well as the community at large.

As to progress on defence reform, a number of challenges still remain. Only fourteen of a targeted eighteen military brigades have so far been formed, for example, and these are poorly trained, lack basic equipment and in some cases even basic accommodation and vital services, such as health care. Consolidation is thus key to military reform in 2007. The brigades need further training and donors need to provide funding to support them. Here, the problem is likely to be that OECD ODA compatibility issues make it difficult for donors directly to support military reform in the DRC. Intense discussion between donors on whether to support a redefinition of ODA, so as to facilitate army reform in fragile states such as the DRC is underway (see also Catriona Gourlay, chapter 4). On the positive side, however, it must be stressed that despite the many challenges in the military reform sector, the sector has benefited from a 'chain of payments' project, implemented by the ESDP's executing agent EUSEC in 2006. The chain of payments project regulated the payment of salaries, ensuring that soldiers based in the integrated brigades received their full salary on time and regularly. The project also assists in stamping out financial corruption at senior level within the military.

Police Reform and EU Assistance

As with the army, the DRC police is also in need of structural reform, training and equipment. Mobutu used the police as an instrument to safeguard his own power base. When Laurent Kabila came to power in 1997 he made a feeble attempt to merge the Civil Guard and the National Gendarmerie with the aim of creating a unified national police structure. However, the subsequent civil war produced a politicised and marginalised police force. In addition, many police in the country received no training, still receive a minimal salary and work under very poor conditions. The police also continue to be denounced as perpetrators of petty corruption and human rights abuses.

On the positive side, since 1999 MONUC has provided a series of police training programmes such as trainers' training, refresher courses, judiciary policing and general intelligence. Other specialised MONUC training modules include judicial identity, interrogation techniques, public security, traffic police, static guards and escorts, command structures, airport security and police intervention. Some 40,597 Congolese police officers have been trained, of which 1,208 received trainers' training by MONUC. Other DRC partners also participated in the training of the Congolese police – mainly South Africa (2,719), Angola (3,042), France (3,800) and the European Union (1,008). MONUC is also indirectly involved at the operational level of the *Police Nationale Congolaise.*

The situation in the capital, Kinshasa, is slightly better than in the rest of the country, as the creation of integrated police units in Kinshasa was enshrined in the Sun City Agreement and key donors, including Angola, France and the EU have supported their training and development. Both Angola and France have also trained Rapid Intervention Police in Kinshasa, while the EU has trained an integrated police unit focusing on security provision for state institutions and high-level protocol security. Yet, outside these training activities in Kinshasa, nationwide police training in the DRC has been very basic. It has almost wholly occurred in the context of securing the election process. In the run-up to elections in 2006 donors created a UNDP-managed $48 million fund to equip and train the police to secure the process. From January 2005, the UN (MONUC) provided basic training for approximately 50,000 territorial police officers, so as to secure the election process. Since election security was the priority and owing to financial and time constraints, basic policing skills were placed on the back burner. A systematic training needs profile was never undertaken. The lack of a systematic approach to police reform in the DRC was also hampered by the fact that the number of existing police officers in the country was uncertain. While a consultancy company undertook a police census in 2005, estimating that there were between 70,000-80,000 police officers in the country, the methodology of the research has been strongly questioned. A further major hindrance was the view that national police integration was considered in 2004 to be too costly and too complicated. Finally, police reform in the DRC has been based on local level assessments of needs, thus rendering it difficult to assess the level and standard of reform across the board. Standards vary from region to region.

The EU's support to the Congolese National Police consists of staff training, equipment and operationalisation of the new Integrated Police Unit (IPU) with three specific strands; the rehabilitation/functioning of a training centre and the provision of equipment to the IPU, training of the IPU itself (1,008 personnel) and the mentoring of IPU operations. The European Commission provided finance for the resumption of training activities within the IPU, donating €9 million. From 1 May 2005, the 1,008 IPU police officers were advised, monitored and mentored by the EU's ESDP Police Mission (EUPOL). EUPOL was extended in November 2005, when additional focus was put on crowd control in the run up to and during the elections, coordination of other intervention units and further training of the IPU.

A more coherent, long-term and coordinated approach to police reform in the DRC was clearly necessary. In February 2006 the DRC Ministry of Interior invited the European Commission and MONUC, in cooperation with the *Police Nationale Congolaise* (PNC), to establish a *Groupe de Réflexion* in order to map out police reform priorities for the DRC. The group included the PNC, the EU (EUPOL and the Commission), the UN, South Africa, Angola, France and the UK. The group's final report was endorsed by the DRC Minister of Interior. If requested by the DRC authorities, this process will lead to the creation of an implementation body (*Comité de Suivi*), financially and technically supported by the EC and other actors, but chaired by the DRC authorities and including all the major donors. The EC will support key police reform priorities at a cost of €10 million in the 2007-2008 period. Reform priorities now include support for human resource management and a national police census, while the ESDP Mission (EUPOL) continues its important role as mentor and adviser, also with a stronger focus on key police reforms within the context of SSR.

Justice Reform

A comprehensive audit conducted in the justice sector was carried out by a number of key donors (European Commission, Belgium, France, the UK, the UN – MONUC, UNHCHR and UNDP) active in the sector in 2003[10]. The audit shows the extent to which the sector is institutionally weak, procedurally incoherent and severely lacking in equipment, infrastructure and training. The DRC judicial system has roots in the colonial past. Many of its structures and procedures mirror the French or Belgian legal systems with a judicial system divided between military justice and civilian justice institutions. The civilian system is based on a Supreme Court, an appeals court, *tribunaux de Grande Instance, tribunaux de commerce* and *tribunaux de Paix*. On the military justice side a high military court, military courts, military tribunals at garrison level and military police tribunals are the main institutional blocks.

Economic failure and poor governance has meant that the judicial system has operated well below minimum standards for decades. The main problem identified by the audit was the almost absolute lack of independence of the justice system from government. In addition to the strong political influence exerted over the judicial branch, (especially during the Mobutu era), court houses are in neglect, there are not enough judges to service the needs of the entire country and judicial training is minimal or non-existent. In addition there are serious budgetary constraints. In 2004 a mere 0.6% of the state budget was allocated by the transitional government to justice, and the figure is even lower today. Donors (most notably the European Commission) have invested heavily in reforming the judicial system since 2002, but support needs to continue in the medium to long term.

In terms of the penal justice system, priorities include a return to the moratorium on the death penalty, ensuring that a procedural hierarchy exists, answerable and accountable to ministers and parliament, protection and support for juvenile delinquents and reform of the system of presidential pardons. An important issue, of course, is transitional justice. Human suffering in the DRC included political crime, human rights violations and victimisation. The Inter-Congolese Dialogue between the warring factions – which led to the Sun City Agreement – created two specific mechanisms as the basis of transitional justice: an Amnesty Law and a Trust and Reconciliation Commission. Both have been criticised. The application and definition of the Amnesty Law has been less than required, while the Trust and Reconciliation Commission failed to take on many of the 'best practice' recommendations made by the international community.

Prison administration also requires support, both in terms of infrastructure and best practice. It is still difficult to ascertain how many people are in prison. The official audit on the judicial sector showed that 9,000 were imprisoned in 2004, yet some NGOs held that the figure was as high as 55,000. Irrespective of the numbers imprisoned the actual conditions in prisons continue to be unacceptable and show little respect for the human rights of prisoners – medical care and nutrition are often minimal and in 2004 only 0.14% of the state budget was attributed to prison management. A further complicating factor is the lack of formal training for prison guards. Military justice is another vexed issue. It is estimated that up to 80% of human rights abuses are carried out by the military or police. In the short term the key justice reform priorities include: ensuring that magistrates and judicial personnel are installed in key institutional locations nationwide, clarifying and supporting the role of the judicial police of the prosecutor,[11] creating and implementing a plan to develop and enhance key infrastructure and procurement of vital equipment.

Work in all these areas has begun. In November 2004 the DRC transitional government agreed with donors a structured reform programme. The Minister for Justice created the justice joint committee in October 2005 as the basis for donor coordination and strategic planning. The committee is co-chaired by the Minister for Justice and the resident Head of the Commission Delegation. The committee's work led to the drafting of a number of key organic laws, including on the *Conseil Supérieur de la Magistrature* (the High Council of Justice) and a law on the Statute of Magistrates. The new DRC Constitution – adopted by referendum in December 2005 – foresees the creation of a High Council of Justice, which will effectively become the managing body of the judiciary, responsible for the organisation and functioning of both civilian and military courts.

The EU's Future SSR Strategy in the DRC

As outlined by Buxton in chapter 2, the EU approach to SSR is based on the OECD DAC definition of SSR, in particular the 2006 OECD DAC Implementation Framework.[12] The EU Concept for ESDP Support to Security Sector Reform (adopted in November 2005) together with the Concept for European Community Support for Security Sector Reform (adopted in May 2006) formed an important backdrop for the development of the first ever joint ESDP–European Commission paper on SSR in the DRC, which was completed in December 2006. The development of the strategy followed a request by EU Foreign Ministers in the context of the

General Affairs Council on 15 September 2006, when EU Foreign Ministers concluded that the EU should play a coordinating role for SSR in the DRC, together with the UN, subject to agreement by the DRC authorities. The EU paper for SSR in the DRC emphasizes three key principles:

1. Development of a DRC nationally-owned SSR concept designed to strengthen good governance, democratic norms, the rule of law and respect for human rights in line with internationally agreed norms.
2. Strengthening governance of the security institutions with a focus on the core requirements of a well functioning security system, including the development of well-defined policies and sound governance of security institutions – features directly in line with the objectives in the DRC Governance Contract (see endnote 10).
3. Enhance service delivery in the security sector, ensuring that Congolese security actors (military, police, judicial) become a source of security, rather then insecurity for citizens and thus with a focus on the fight against impunity for crimes committed by members of these services.

As noted in the paper, subject to a request by the DRC authorities, the EU will continue to play a support role to the DRC authorities based on the following features:

- Political dialogue as established by article 8 of the Cotonou Agreement between the EU (led by Presidency and Commission) and new DRC authorities will focus on the SSR agenda in the DRC.[13]
- The credibility of ESDP missions represents a major asset in addressing both cooperation with the new government and coordination within the international community.
- Substantial additional funds for SSR will be allocated under the 9th EDF, which is coming to an end, and SSR will be included as a sector for Commission activity under the 10th EDF, notably in the justice and police sectors.
- Several EU member states are already engaged in effective bilateral support programmes in the field of SSR.

Conclusion

A number of key principles guide the constructive and progressive relationship between DRC authorities and the EU. There is clear potential for successful realisation of the priorities in the SSR agenda for the DCR. The successful completion of the democratic election process in the DRC enables the principle of local ownership to become a key priority to efficient donor intervention. The DRC-led mixed committees in the justice, police and defence sectors can contribute to the creation of a sense of local ownership in partnership with the international community. But, effective coordination between EU member states, the Commission Delegation in Kinshasa and ESDP missions clearly remains vital for the various EU actors to ensure a common voice in dealing with the DRC authorities.

The justice (2004) and police (2006) audits conducted by the relevant DRC authorities and donors were clearly necessary. They constitute highly valuable forerunners to a programmatic approach to SSR. But, it is important for SSR to be viewed through a broad governance lens, including institutional and parliamentary oversight. The DRC Governance Contract[14] includes SSR priorities as a key feature in the overall governance agenda. With the European Commission's inclusion of SSR within its governance agenda for the10th EDF (2008-2013), perspectives for reform of the security sector in the DRC look decidedly brighter than hitherto.

Endnotes

1 The opinions in this chapter are expressed solely in the name of the author and do not necessarily represent European Commission policy.

2 The European Security and Defence Policy or ESDP is a major element of the Common Foreign and Security Policy pillar of the European Union (EU). The European Security and Defence Policy is managed by the Council of the European Union, which is an intergovernmental body in which the EU member states are represented. For an overview of ESDP see: Jean-Yves Haine, 'ESDP: An Overview', The Institute for Security Studies, Paris. http://www.iss-eu.org/esdp/01-jyh.pdf

3 For a detailed overview of the transition period in the DRC, see Hoebeke, Hans, 'The Politics of Transition in the DRC', *Africa Policy and Research Notes*, IRRI-KIIB, October 2006.

4 Pourtier, R. (1997), 'Du Zaïre au Congo': un territoire en quête d'Etat', *Afrique Contemporaire*, No. 183, 3ème trimestre.

5 International Crisis Group, 'Security Sector Reform in the Congo', 13 February 2006, page 3.

6 The main components of the Lusaka Accord consisted of a cease-fire, the creation of a Joint Military Commission, deployment of UN peacekeepers, disarmament of militias, and national reconciliation.

7 See the EU concept for Support to Disarmament, Demobilisation and Reintegration endorsed by the European Commission and Council of the EU in December 2006, reprinted as an annex to this book.

8 'DDR: Supporting Security and Development: The EU's added value', *International Alert Report*, September 2006, p. 5.

9 The *Brassage* process was a process whereby different militia and army elements were brought together for a 45 day period in one place (*les centres de Brassage*) and integrated together into a working army brigade.

10 Audit Organisationnel du Secteur de la Justice en RDC – Rapport d'état des lieux synthèse, May 2004.

11 The judicial police of the prosecutor only has 300 inspectors and the question is open as to what extent the independence of that corps will improve if its integration within the PNC takes place, as is currently considered.

12 For an overview of SSR approaches, see 'Intergovernmental Approaches to Security Sector Reform' Background paper for the workshop on 'Developing a SSR Concept for the United Nations', DCAF, 7 July 2006, Bratislava.

13 The Cotonou Agreement, signed between the EU and the group of African, Caribbean and Pacific states (ACP countries) in 2000, aims to fight poverty while contributing to sustainable development and to the integration of ACP countries into the world economy. Article 8 states that the 'Parties shall regularly engage in a comprehensive, balanced and deep political dialogue leading to commitments on both sides'.

14 Following the successful election process in the DRC, the DRC authorities have developed a Contract on Governance, which includes key government priorities for the DRC in key sectors, such as SSR, public finance management, public administration reform, transparency and human recourse management.

12. The EU and its Southern Neighbours: Promoting Security Sector Reform in the Mediterranean Region and the Middle East

Derek Lutterbeck and Fred Tanner

Introduction

This chapter takes stock of the EU's SSR-related activities in the countries of its southern neighbourhood, i.e. the Mediterranean region and the Middle East. Needless to say, this is a region which is characterised by important deficits in terms of security governance, as well as democratic governance more generally. Thus, according to the ratings of Freedom House, the Middle East and North Africa is the region of the world which contains the highest percentage (61%) of countries which are rated as 'not free' in terms of political and civil liberties.[1] Among the Arab countries of the Euro-Mediterranean Partnership (EMP), no country is considered 'free', and only Jordan and Morocco qualify as 'partly free'.[2] Similarly, the Arab Human Development Report of 2004 has pointed to the 'freedom deficit' in the Arab world, i.e. to the lack of freedom of expression, of association and of making political choices.[3]

This general lack of democracy and accountability is also reflected in deficiencies in the governance of these countries' security sectors. In practically all countries of the region, there is only limited, if any, civilian participation in and oversight over security policy-making, which largely remains the preserve of executive powers and military establishments. In countries such as Algeria or Turkey, the military has traditionally also played an important political role, virtually yielding a veto power over the political process.[4] Moreover, the misuse of the armed forces for internal purposes, and in particular to suppress political opposition, has been rather widespread. Military spending, too, is not only very high in the countries of the region, but also unaccountable, as the militaries, in addition to formal defence budgets, typically have various informal sources of income over which there is no independent control.[5]

Despite these important deficits in terms of democratic security sector governance, as this chapter will argue, the EU has thus far been rather reluctant to become involved in SSR activities in the Mediterranean region and the Middle East. With the exception of Turkey, where the EU has made the country's EU membership contingent on significant reforms of its security sector – in particular with regard to the National Security Council – the EU has so far largely failed to address the issue of SSR in its relationship with its southern neighbours, despite the fact that the EU would have several instruments at its disposal to do so. And while over recent years the EU has shown growing interest in closer security cooperation with the countries of the Mediterranean and Middle Eastern region – in particular in fields such as crisis management, immigration-control and counter-terrorism – these collaborative efforts have been largely devoid of a reform or governance dimension, focusing instead mainly on strengthening the efficiency of security institutions. Nevertheless, recent EU documents and, to some extent, policies with regard to the Palestinian Territories and Lebanon suggest that SSR could become an increasingly important field of activity for the EU in the Mediterranean and the Middle Eastern region.

The EU and Security Sector Reform in Turkey

The country in the region where the EU has had the most decisive impact in terms of SSR has been Turkey. While the EU has not been involved in actual reform projects in Turkey, it has used the carrot of EU accession in order to push for rather far-reaching reforms of the country's security sector. This has not been an easy or self-evident task, as the Turkish military establishment has traditionally played an important political role and practically had a *droit de regard* over national politics. In fact, as recently as 1997, the Turkish military removed politicians from power and overthrew a democratically elected government. Moreover, even though Turkey has been a member of NATO since 1952, there has always been great reluctance among NATO countries to raise the issue of democratic governance of the Turkish armed forces.

Turkey's aspiration to join the EU – it formally submitted its application to the European Community in 1987 – and the pre-accession process have been key factors behind reforms of the country's security sector over recent years. In order to meet the political conditionalities contained in the Copenhagen criteria, Turkey undertook to implement a number of significant reforms of its security sector, including both its armed and internal security forces. While the security sector is not mentioned explicitly in the Copenhagen criteria, which contain references to democratic governance and respect for the rule of law and human rights, the EU has identified a number of specific reform objectives which have been of direct relevance for the country's security sector. These have included in particular the removal of the 'guardianship' role of the military in Turkish politics and limiting the powers of the National Security Council (NSC), whose 'recommendations' were practically binding on the government. Other reforms which the EU has been pushing for, and which have concerned the country's security sector, include improving respect for human rights, eliminating the use of torture by Turkish security forces, preventing arbitrary detention, and the abolition of the death penalty. The main instrument of the policy of conditionality to encourage security sector reforms in Turkey has been the yearly progress reports through which the EU has been evaluating the progress Turkey has been making in the light of European standards.

While at the Luxembourg Summit of 1997 Turkey was excluded from the enlargement process, ostensibly because of its human rights record, a number of developments that took place within the EU since then – such as the change of government in Germany, and the more benign attitude of Greece towards Turkey in the aftermath of the earthquake in 1999 – eventually paved the way for Turkey's formal recognition as an EU candidate country at the Helsinki Summit in 1999. However, even though Turkey was formally granted the status of candidate country in Helsinki, the European Commission continued to point out that Turkey still failed to meet the political requirements of the Copenhagen criteria. As mentioned in earlier progress reports, the main obstacles were seen in the political power of the military, lack of minority rights, and insufficient respect for human rights more generally.[6]

For the EU, a core concern has always been the important political role and lack of civilian control of the armed forces in Turkey. However, until rather recently, the EU shied away from demanding comprehensive reforms from Turkey in the area of civil-military relations, and limited itself largely to one specific institution, the aforementioned NSC. Thus, subsequent to the Helsinki summit, the specific requirements for Turkey to join the EU were outlined in the Accession Partnership Document of 2000, which sets out a number of short and medium term reform objectives. Among the 17 short terms 'priority areas' that are listed in the Accession Partnerships Document there is no explicit reference to the reform of the security sector.[7] Possibly as a matter of convenience, the EU largely reduced the complex issue of security sector reform or civil-military relations to the question of the NSC. Here, the EU called upon Turkey to 'align the constitutional role of the National Security Council as an advisory body to the Government in accordance with the practice of EU Member States'. The document also demanded that Turkey take all necessary measures to fight against torture practices, bring detention conditions into line with international standards, strengthen respect for human rights by Turkish authorities, and improve the accountability of the police.[8] At the 2003 review of the Accession Partnership with Turkey, the EU Council explicitly referred to the civilian control of the armed forces by recommending to 'adapt the functioning of the National Security Council in order to align civilian control of the military with practice in EU Member States'.[9]

Since 2005, however, the EU has been adopting a significantly broader approach to security sector reform and civil-military relations in Turkey. The 2005 progress report of the European Commission for the first time contains an entire section on 'civil-military relations' in Turkey, whereas previous reports focused almost exclusively on the NSC. Reforms of the NSC remain a key concern, but the EU is now also calling for reforms with regard to a number of other aspects of civil-military relations, such as enhancing the expertise of parliamentarians in security matters, ensuring civilian participation in the drafting of Turkey's National Security Policy Document, or strengthening civilian control over the (paramilitary) Gendarmerie.[10]

In Turkey, its official recognition as a 'EU candidate' did spark a gradual but nevertheless far-reaching reform process which has involved in particular the political role of the NSC as well as parts of the country's internal security services. It is noteworthy in this regard that these reforms only began in earnest once Turkey was formally recognised as a 'candidate country'. Earlier calls for reform by the EU had not been heeded by the government in power, as they were considered by many domestic actors within Turkey as too costly to enact solely to please the EU.[11]

Major reforms of the NSC were initiated as part of the legislative package on democratic reform which was launched in 2003 in order to bring Turkey into line with EU requirements. The main elements of these have been to strip the NSC of its executive powers and to transform it into a mere 'advisory' body, and to increase the number of civilian members, which are now in the majority.[12] In August 2004, the first civilian Secretary General of the NSC was appointed. In addition, there has been an effort to increase the NSC's transparency: in late 2004 the NSC for the first time organised a press briefing at its headquarters, which was attended by some 200 Turkish and foreign journalists.[13]

Reforms have also aimed at reducing the power of the military with regard to other state institutions. For example, the formerly military-dominated Higher Education Board has been brought under civilian control. Moreover, the military's formerly easy access to financial resources has been limited by new legislation on transparency of defence expenditures. In this regard, the 2004 Regular Report on Turkey noted that budgetary transparency has been enhanced by the permission granted to the civilian Court of Auditors 'to audit military and defence expenditures'.[14] Progress has also been made in curbing the formerly far-reaching powers of the military courts. Under legislation introduced in 2006, no civilian shall be tried by military courts during peacetime, except under very specific circumstances.[15]

Regarding the country's internal security apparatus, important reforms over recent years have been enacted mainly through amendments of the country's Penal Code, the Anti-Terror Act, and the Law on Political Parties. This has involved, *inter alia*, the abolition of the death penalty, an increase in penalties for torture-related crimes, and the strengthening of a number of basic freedoms, such as freedom of expression, freedom of association, and gender equality. Similarly, at the procedural level, retrial rights have been established for individuals in cases that have been in conflict with rulings of the European Court of Human Rights. In addition, the infamous State Security Courts have been abolished. In order to ensure effective implementation of this new legislation, human rights boards have been set up in major towns and cities which are responsible for adjudicating human rights complaints.[16] An important focus of EU accession-driven police reforms has been to enhance the country's police forces (National Police and Gendarmerie) in the fight against organised crime and drug trafficking through capacity-building and training programmes.[17]

It is evident that EU conditionalities alone have not been sufficient to push Turkey ahead with reforms that re-distribute the political control of military power within Turkish society. Rather, the reform process needed to be sustained from within the security system. Such support mainly came from General Hilmi Ozkök, former Chief of Staff of the Turkish Armed Forces and member of the NSC. By putting himself behind these reforms,

General Ozkök clashed with the euro-sceptics within the Turkish armed forces as well as with the land army, army intelligence units, and the corps of the gendarmes 'that oppose such reforms, which they find excessively constraining'.[18] One main obstacle to sustained reform has been that the Turkish army continues to use international or national crises such as Cyprus or the fight against Kurdish insurgents in southeast Turkey to reassert its standing in domestic politics. The army's main argument against reform has been that national security and unity need to take precedence over democratisation and reform of civil-military relations. Moreover, General Özkök's successor, General Yasar Buyukanit, who took office in mid-2006, is known to be a euro-sceptic, and many analysts expect a slowing down, if not a partial reversal, of the reform process during his term of office.

Despite Turkey's progress in the field of security sector governance over recent years, the EU remains generally sceptical about, and vigilant over, the implementation of these reform packages, and the extent to which changes in legislation actually have an impact on political and social life in Turkey. For example, in its 2004 Progress Report, the European Commission, while welcoming the reforms of the NSC and observing that 'civil-military relations are evolving towards European standards', also voiced concern about the various 'informal mechanisms' though which the NSC continues to influence political life in Turkey.[19] In 2005, the Commission expressed its relative satisfaction with the 'good progress' which had been made by Turkey in reforming civil-military relations, but by 2006 the tone became considerably more critical as the reform process seems to have lost momentum.[20] Areas in which Turkey is expected to make further progress in bringing civil-military relations in line with European standards, include in particular the still significant political influence of the armed forces, as senior military officers continue to publicly express their opinion on a broad range of policy issues, and the still limited role of the parliament in overseeing defence expenditures as well as in security policy making more generally. For example, the National Security Policy Document adopted by the government in 2005 has not been discussed by parliament. Moreover, while the commission has noted improvements made over recent years in bringing defence expenditures under parliamentary control, it has also pointed out that parliamentary reviews are only very general in nature and do not cover military projects and programmes. Moreover, extra-budgetary funds are excluded from parliamentary scrutiny and there is no internal audit of military property.[21]

The European Parliament, which has traditionally been much more vocal in criticizing the lack of democratic governance and respect for human rights in Turkey, also continues to be sceptical about the reforms of the country's security sector enacted by the Turkish leadership over recent years. In its March 2004 report, it too welcomes the efforts of the Turkish government to bring defence expenditure under parliamentary control, but at the same time points to the 'influential (formal and informal) army network comprising *inter alia* think tanks, businesses and funds, which could prove to be a an obstacle to reform of the state'. Similarly, it notes that that 'torture practices and mistreatment still continue' and that 'little progress' has been made in this regard. In general, the European Parliament considers that there remains a 'wide gulf between the principles of the European rule of law and judicial principles in Turkey'.[22] In 2006, the European Parliament also deplored the 'slowing down of the reform process' in Turkey and the 'persistent shortcomings' in a number of areas, including civil-military relations. A particular reason for concern for the European Parliament has been the anti-terror law adopted in June 2006, which provides for a broad definition of terrorism, potentially limiting the accountability of security forces and intelligence agencies in the fight against terrorist activities.[23]

Overall, significant reforms of the Turkish security sector have thus been enacted over recent years, even though considerable shortcomings continue to persist, and EU institutions have been voicing concerns about the slowing down of the reform process of late. The Turkish case also illustrates the important role played by the EU and the prospect of EU membership in this regard. EU conditionality seems to have been one if not the most important driving force behind the transformation of Turkey's security sector towards European standards, even if internal forces have also played an important part. The EU's policies towards Turkey are also indicative of a certain learning curve on the part of the EU and of its adoption of an increasingly explicit and broad concept of security sector reform and civil-military relations. After long focusing almost exclusively on the reform of one institution – the National Security Council – the EU has been adopting an increasingly comprehensive approach to the transformation of civil-military relations in Turkey which in particular also encompasses the role of parliament in security policy making. One challenge for the EU that remains, however, will be to better coordinate and eventually combine its efforts with regard to defence reform on the one hand, and those concerning internal security reform on the other, as a common EU approach to these areas still seems to be lacking.

The EU and Security Sector Reform in the Southern Mediterranean

In contrast to Turkey, where the EU has placed the transformation of the country's security sector – in particular reforms of the NSC – high on the bilateral agenda, the EU has thus far largely neglected this issue in its relationship with (other) southern Mediterranean countries. The main reasons have not only been the EU's more limited leverage over these countries, which in contrast to Turkey do not have the prospect of joining the EU in the foreseeable future, but also a lack of political will on the part of the EU to raise the issue of democratic governance – of the security sector as well as more generally – with the countries of the southern Mediterranean. Nowadays, the EU pursues its security policy towards the southern Mediterranean through a number of instruments, including the Euro-Mediterranean Partnership (EMP) or Barcelona Process, the European Neighbourhood Policy (ENP), and the ESDP, on which a dialogue has been established since the Naples Euro-Mediterranean Conference in December 2003.

The Barcelona Process and the European Neighbourhood Policy

The Euro-Mediterranean Partnership is a framework for developing a 'zone of peace and stability'. It includes a politico-security dialogue, economic relations that should lead to a free trade zone, and social-cultural relations. This multilateral framework is underpinned by a network of association agreements that regulate the bilateral relations between the EU and individual partner states. However, there has been little progress in the domain of security cooperation in the Euro-Mediterranean framework. Efforts to establish a comprehensive framework on security issues in the region have been blocked ever since 1999, when the Euro-Mediterranean Charter for Peace and Security proposed by the EU was rejected by some Arab states. After 10 years of existence, the lack of visible results in the political and security chapter of the EMP has given rise to considerable criticism, both by government officials and policy analysts.

The association agreements do not explicitly deal with the issue of security sector governance or reform. While they all contain a clause committing the partner countries to respect democratic principles and human rights (Article 2), a provision which in principle would allow the EU to address the issue of democratic governance of the security sector in its relationship with southern Mediterranean countries, in practice, the EU has thus far never invoked this clause *vis-à-vis* its partner countries. In fact, as has been pointed out by many analysts and critics of the Barcelona process, democracy and human rights issues have practically remained taboo within the EMP framework, as the EU seems to have been driven by other policy objectives such as maintaining good relations with the regimes in power and ensuring access to strategic resources from the region, such as oil and natural gas.

The new European Neighbourhood Policy launched in 2004 aims to further political, economic and social reforms in the countries neighbouring the EU by offering partner states access to the EU's four freedoms (free movement of goods, persons, services, and capital). It is conceived as an instrument to promote prosperity, security and stability in the EU's post-enlargement neighbourhood. The main instruments for implementing the Neighbourhood Policy are the action plans, which are elaborated jointly with the partner countries, and which set out short- and medium-term reform objectives.[24] In contrast to the association agreements, the action plans put more emphasis on institutional reforms and the promotion of 'good governance' in the partner countries. However, most of the action plans adopted thus far for EMP countries do not contain specific references to SSR or democratic governance of the security sector. Provisions which are most directly relevant for SSR are those relating to judicial reform and human rights training for security forces. Notable exceptions, however, are the action plan adopted for the Palestinian Territories and the recently proposed action plan for Lebanon. The action plan for the Palestinian Authority makes reference to 'reforms of PA security services', although it does not further specify what these reforms should entail. The proposed action plan for Lebanon is the first one which contains an explicit provision on 'security sector reform', and sets forth the objective 'to ensure consistency of the management and operation of the security system with respect for human rights and democratic norms'.[25]

Thus in general, within the EMP/ENP framework, neither the EU nor southern Mediterranean states have so far formally embraced the concept of SSR or democratic governance of the security sector, even though the recent ENP action plans for the Palestinian Authority and Lebanon suggest that this could change in the future. There have, however, been a number of specific policy areas where the EU has been involved in activities which are, or could be, relevant for SSR in the countries of the southern Mediterranean. These include in particular its democracy and human rights promotion programmes, judicial and police reform projects, and the ESDP, in the framework of which the EU recently launched a police reform mission in the Palestinian Territories. The (few) EU-sponsored activities in these areas are, however, linked to security sector reform mostly by approximation and not by design.

Democracy and Human Rights Promotion Programmes

The EU's policy on human rights and democratisation in the Mediterranean has been 'presented by the EU as a strategic, not merely ethical imperative'.[26] However, as already mentioned previously, human rights and democratisation have been low on the EMP agenda, 'despite the fact that the EU does have a range of tools at its disposal to exercise pressure for the respect for human rights and democracy in the Mediterranean'.[27] Critics of the EU's policies in this respect typically point out that, despite the rhetorical commitments to furthering democratic governance in the region, the EU is ultimately not committed to this objective, its main concern being to ensure 'stable' regimes and continued access to natural resources in the countries of the region.

The EU's main funding instruments for its democracy and human rights activities in the region are the European Initiative for Democracy and Human Rights (EIDHR) and the MEDA programme. However, funding for democracy-building under both of these programmes has generally remained very limited. Under the EIDHR, the Middle East has been the region in the world which has received the lowest amount of EIDHR funding. During the years 2001-2004, the Middle East received 12% of the roughly €100 million in EIDHR funds per year. Moreover, the main focus of these projects has been on relatively apolitical areas such as the promotion of women's rights, campaigns against torture, or support for human rights NGOs. Thus far, no SSR-relevant projects seem to have been carried out in the EIDHR framework.[28]

The same can also be said of the MEDA programme, under which only limited funds have been allocated to governance-related projects. Of the roughly €1 billion a year MEDA fund, during the period 2001-2003 only €232 million were devoted to institutional reform projects, and most of the available funds were devoted to 'soft' projects, such as support for NGOs in the fields of development assistance and environmental protection. And of those projects which have been governance-related, the large majority have concentrated on technical or regulatory aspects, in particular the harmonisation with the EU's single market rules.[29]

Justice and Home Affairs (JHA) Cooperation and Judicial and Police Reforms

More relevant from an SSR perspective have been the EU's activities in the field of JHA in the Mediterranean region. Noteworthy in this context is that over recent years, the EU has generally been devoting more attention to internal security or JHA cooperation with EMP partner countries, reflecting not only deepening integration among EU countries in this area but also growing concerns with internal security challenges such as illegal immigration, drug trafficking and organised crime in the Mediterranean region. From early 2001 onward, JHA has generally become a priority area within the EMP, with regular meetings of senior officials of interior ministries in parallel to meetings on political and security matters.[30] In the aftermath of 9/11, these efforts also increasingly focused on terrorism in addition to illegal migration, drug trafficking and organised crime. A framework document on a regional cooperation programme on JHA issues was adopted at the Valencia conference of 2002. The development of this programme has resulted in regional and bilateral cooperation in the area of justice, freedom and security.[31]

At the EU level, several relatively large projects on judicial reform have subsequently been launched in Algeria (€15 million), Morocco (€28 million) and Tunisia (€30 million). Moreover, in Algeria, a police reform project (which was initiated in 2000) has been carried out in the framework of the EU's Neighbourhood Policy. The main objective of this project has been to professionalize Algerian police forces, and to enhance respect for human rights and the rule of law. In addition, an important goal of the EU has been to improve the capacity of the Algerian police to manage migratory flows. A total of €10 million has thus far been allocated for this project.[32]

The official view within the EU is that closer security cooperation with Arab EMP partner countries is consistent and indeed supportive of its objective of promoting democracy and 'good governance' in the region.[33] It is however often pointed out that the EU's enhanced focus on counter-terrorism has actually been detrimental in terms of improving accountability of, and respect for human rights by, security forces of Arab EMP countries. Morocco, for example, has been criticised by human rights organisations for its anti-terror legislation and policies adopted in the aftermath of the Casablanca bombings in 2003. According to Human Rights Watch, for instance, Morocco's campaign against Islamist militants, which has also involved fast-track convictions, has been undermining the considerable progress made by Morocco in this field over recent years.[34]

Moreover, there is evidence that the EU as well as individual EU countries have devoted resources mainly to enhancing the efficiency of (internal) security forces of Southern Mediterranean countries in preventing undocumented migration across the Mediterranean and less to actual reforms. In October 2002, for example, the EU allocated €40 million to Morocco for the construction of a coast-control system along the country's northern shores aimed at preventing migration and drug trafficking across the Straits of Gibraltar.[35] Another example is the increasingly close cooperation between EU countries, and in particular Italy, and Libya. In 2003 alone, the Italian government spent more than €5.5 million on cooperation with Libya on immigration control. Moreover, in order to supply Libya with military equipment to beef up its border controls, Italy has also been pushing to lift the arms embargo imposed on Libya since 1986, which the EU agreed to end in 2004. Subsequently, in 2005 Italy promised to provide Libya with further equipment worth €15 million to beef up its borders.[36] Most recently, Italy and Libya also reached an agreement on the carrying out of joint sea patrols along the Libyan coast.[37]

Overall, EU and EU countries' policies in this area have thus been driven mainly by operational considerations and short-term security concerns with illegal migration, drug trafficking and terrorism as opposed to institutional reform objectives, such as enhancing respect for human rights, accountability and civilian oversight over security forces of Southern Mediterranean countries.

ESDP Mission in the Palestinian Territories – and Lebanon?

The most directly SSR-related activity of the EU in the region thus far has been its assistance to the Palestinian Authority (PA), and in particular the recently launched ESDP police mission in the Palestinian Territories. EU assistance to the Palestinians not only has a long history – dating back to the early 1970s – but over the years, the EU has also emerged as the main donor supporting the Palestinian Authority. Between 1994 and 2004, EU support for the Palestinians amounted to a total of more than €2 billion, and it was mainly thanks to the EU that the PA has been able to avoid collapse.[38] This assistance has focused on both long-term institution-building as well as on humanitarian assistance, this latter aspect becoming increasingly important after the outbreak of the second Intifada in 2000.

It was mainly the growing awareness of the problem of corruption within the PA, as well as mounting allegations that EU aid was being diverted to finance terrorist activities, that led the EU to focus more strongly on 'institutional reforms' of the PA, such as independence of the judicial system and financial transparency. Some of these efforts have directly touched upon the Palestinian security sector. Thus, in 2002-2003, judicial reform programmes amounting to a total of €7 million were launched aimed at modernising the Palestinian judicial system. These programmes comprise both material assistance and the training of judges and prosecutors. Moreover, the EU has been organising human rights training for Palestinian security services.[39]

More recently the EU, aware of the growing need for effective policing after the Israeli pullout from the Gaza strip, also initiated a police reform project in the Occupied Territories within the framework of the ESDP. In June 2004, the European Council declared its 'readiness to support the Palestinian Authority in taking responsibility for law and order, and in particular in improving its civil police and law enforcement capacity'.[40] Subsequently, the EU set up an EU Coordination Office for Palestinian Police Support (EU COPPS), consisting of four EU police experts based in East Jerusalem and Ramallah. Its official objectives include both immediate operational elements, in particular the delivery of technical equipment, as well as longer-term transformation of the Palestinian police forces, such as the reform of management structures and the development of proper accountability mechanisms.[41] In January 2006, these efforts were further stepped up when the EU launched the European Union Police Mission for the Palestinian Territories (EUPOL-COPPS), under which a total of 33 unarmed police officers are to be deployed with the aim of supporting the PA in establishing sustainable and effective policing arrangements under Palestinian ownership in line with international standards.[42]

However, when Hamas won the elections and took over power in March 2006, the EU decided to suspend aid payments to the Hamas-led PA – while continuing to channel support to the Palestinian people through the Temporary International Mechanism – pointing to Hamas' unwillingness to renounce terrorist violence and recognise Israel. This has also meant that the EU's assistance to the Palestinian security sector has practically come to a standstill. As of early 2007, less than half of the planned 33 officers had been deployed within the framework of EUPOL-COPPS, and due to political constraints the mission has practically remained in a stand-by mode.

Whether or not one agrees with the EU's decision to cut off assistance to the Hamas-led government, it is indicative of the rather political nature of the EU's SSR assistance in the region. It suggests that the EU's policies in this area are driven more by political considerations than by concerns about the security situation in the Occupied Territories, where the need for effective and well-governed security services seems to be as great as ever.[43] This politicised approach in turn seems to be an important reason why among the Palestinian population trust in EU assistance – while stronger than in assistance from the US – is currently very low. In a recent opinion poll carried out in the Occupied Territories, fewer than one-third of the respondents expressed trust in assistance coming from the EU.[44]

Another country in the region where there currently might be an opening for SSR projects is Lebanon. At least according to some commentators, the Syrian military departure from Lebanon following the public outrage caused by the assassination of the former Lebanese Prime Rafik Hariri, and the election of a new parliament in 2005, opened a unique opportunity for reforming Lebanon's security services.[45] Deficiencies in Lebanon's security sector have been highlighted in particular by the UN Fact-Finding Mission which has been inquiring into Hariri's assassination. Its report pointed to a general lack of effective oversight of the Lebanese security sector, and put the main responsibility for the absence of law and order in the country on both Lebanese security services and the Syrian Military Intelligence.[46] Among Lebanese political forces, the need for reforming the country's security sector has been emphasised, for example, by General Aoun's Free Patriotic Movement, which won 21 seats in the 2005 parliamentary elections. General Aoun's reform programme calls, for example, for the de-politicisation of the Lebanese armed forces and for subjecting them to stricter control by the country's civil authorities.[47]

A request for external support in reforming Lebanon's security forces was reportedly made by Prime Minister Fouad Siniora in 2006, after the cessation of hostilities between Hizbollah and Israel, and the launching of the enlarged UNIFIL mission, for which EU countries agreed to provide the backbone. At a meeting of EU defence ministries in October 2006, the EU High Representative Javier Solana declared that the EU would respond positively to the request from the Lebanese Prime Minister for assistance in reforming the country's security sector. An EU mission would be dispatched shortly to Lebanon, he declared, to assess 'the parameters of help for armed forces and security sector reform'.[48] In Lebanon, as in the case of Palestine, the question, however, remains to what extent the EU will be committed to establishing a well-governed security sector in Lebanon and to initiating real reform processes of the country's security services regardless of political obstacles, or whether its policies will be driven mainly by political considerations and the objective to support the Siniora government.

EU-NATO Relations in SSR Assistance

As the EU intends to strengthen its involvement in SSR-related activities in the Mediterranean and Middle Eastern region, cooperation with other organisations which might become active in this field, such as NATO, will also become increasingly important. As evidenced by NATO's Istanbul Cooperation Initiative (ICI), which was launched at the Istanbul Summit in 2004, NATO too aims to enhance its outreach efforts in the region. The initiative's initial focus is on the Gulf States, but it is open to all interested countries of the 'broader Middle East'. Moreover, while the ICI's main focus is on cooperation in fields such as counter-terrorism and WMD proliferation, defence reform and civil military relations are also part of the 'ICI menu', although it remains to be seen to what extent NATO will be willing to become involved in this politically sensitive area. The recently concluded agreement between NATO and Kuwait suggests that also for NATO practical cooperation and intelligence-sharing, in particular in the field of counter-terrorism, will be more important than political reform processes.[49]

The EU's and NATO's past experience with defence and security sector reform in the countries of Central and Eastern Europe, have shown that the two organisations can find effective solutions and a workable division of labour in providing external assistance to SSR, even though their respective tasks have differed somewhat depending on the countries concerned. The predominant division of labour has, of course, been that the EU has concentrated on the reform of police and other internal security institutions while NATO has focused on defence reform, but in some cases the EU has also increasingly ventured into the defence area.[50] In the case of the Western Balkans, as well as in Turkey, for example, the EU has made membership contingent on reforms of these countries' armed forces and the strengthening of democratic oversight over the military, and thus to some extent also taken ownership of defence reform in these countries. Moreover, in the Democratic Republic of Congo the EU has also carried out actual reform projects of the country' security services including its armed forces (EUSEC DRC). While thus in the Central and Eastern European context, the EU and NATO have acquired rather rich experience in providing assistance to both internal and external security services, the more important question will be whether the two organisations will have sufficient political will to address these sensitive issues and support real political reform processes in the Mediterranean and Middle Eastern region.

Conclusion

As the adoption of key EU documents in 2005 and 2006 suggests, the EU is in the process of developing an increasingly explicit and comprehensive strategy on SSR in a number of policy fields, such as development cooperation, enlargement, conflict prevention, and democracy and human rights promotion.[51] There seems to be a growing recognition within the EU that SSR is an 'important part of conflict prevention, peace building and democratisation and contributes to sustainable development.' Moreover, the EU holds the view that SSR 'goes beyond the notion of effectiveness of individual services and instead focuses on the overall functioning of the security systems as part of a governance reform policy and strategy of the public sector.'[52]

The analysis above, however, suggests that the EU's involvement in, or promotion of, SSR-relevant projects in the Mediterranean and Middle Eastern region has thus far remained rather limited, in contrast to its activities in Central and Eastern European countries.[53] The main exception to this rule has been Turkey, where in the context of the accession process the EU has been pushing for significant reforms of the country's security sector over recent years. While the EU has been involved in certain governance-related projects in the region, for the most part these have not focused on the security sector but have rather been confined to more technical issues such as regulatory harmonisation. Moreover, in so far as the EU's activities have centred on the security services of southern Mediterranean countries, the aim has been mainly to enhance their efficiency, in particular in fighting irregular immigration from and through these countries, and less on strengthening their governance or oversight.

The EU's reluctance is, of course, to a large extent a consequence of the fact that SSR, at least when it involves the strengthening of democratic control of security services, implies a redistribution of political power away from executive powers and military establishments towards civilian institutions – a transformation which few if any of the countries of the region are currently willing to contemplate. In addition, the EU has shown a general lack of political will to raise the issue of democratic governance with the countries of the Mediterranean and Middle Eastern region, the main reasons arguably being the EU's overriding objective of securing the cooperation of the regimes in power in areas which are of key concern to the EU, such as preventing illegal migration, countering terrorism and securing access to natural resources, and the fear of EU countries that political reforms in southern Mediterranean countries could bring Islamist movements to power. A further reason for the EU's low key approach to democracy in the region seems to be the considerable concern among European policy-makers at being perceived as seeking to impose democracy from the outside.

In addition, given that, with the exception of Turkey, the countries of the southern Mediterranean do not have the prospect of joining the EU, it anyhow holds only limited leverage over these countries in pushing for reforms. In this vein, critics often also point out that the EU's new Neighbourhood Policy, as well, despite the original promise that it would offer 'everything but institutions', does not provide sufficient incentives to elicit significant reforms from the partner countries either, in particular given the EU's reluctance to liberalise its agricultural markets and current trends towards increasingly restrictive immigration policies *vis-à-vis* southern Mediterranean countries.[54]

Nevertheless, the cases of the Palestinian Territories and, possibly, Lebanon suggest that the EU might in the future become increasingly involved in SSR in the countries of the Mediterranean and Middle Eastern region. These cases, however, also highlight that this is most likely to occur, or might only occur, when there is a genuine willingness or a perceived need on the part of the 'recipient' country to reform and strengthen good governance of its security sector. Moreover, the EU's current policies *vis-à-vis* the Occupied Territories in particular also highlight the need to adopt a less politicised approach to SSR assistance in the region. If external support for security sector reform is to be effective, it will need to be trusted by the recipient population. Such trust, however, can only be built if assistance is perceived as being aimed first and foremost at improving the security situation of the country concerned, and not as being driven by a hidden or overt political agenda.

Endnotes

1 Freedom House, 'Freedom in the World 2006. Selected Data from the Freedom House's Annual Global Survey of Political Rights and Civil Liberties', available at: http://www.freedomhouse.org/uploads/pdf/Charts2006.pdf (accessed December 2006).

2 See Freedom House, *Freedom in the World Comparative Rankings: 1973-2006*, available at: http://www.freedomhouse.org/template.cfm?page=15&year=2006.

3 UNDP, Regional Bureau for Arab States, *Arab Human Development Report 2004. Towards Freedom in the Arab World* (New York: United Nations Publications, 2005).

4 Kees Koonings and Dirk Kruijt, eds., *Political Armies: The Military and Nation Building in the Age of Democracy* (Zed Books, New York, 2002).

5 Robert Springborg, *Military Elites and the Polity in Arab States*, Development Associates, Occasional Paper no 2., Arlington, Virginia, 1998, p. 6

6 Regular Report from the Commission on Turkey's Progress towards Accession, COM(2000) final, 8 November 2000.

7 Council Decision of 8 March 2001 on the principles, priorities, immediate objectives and conditions contained in the Accession Partnership with the Republic of Turkey, Official Journal of the European Communities, 24 March 2001.

8 *Ibid.*

9 Council Decision of 19 May 2003 on the principles, priorities, intermediate objectives and conditions contained in the Accession Partnership with Turkey, Official Journal of the European Union, 12 June 2003.

10 European Commission, Turkey 2005 Progress Report, (COM 2005 561 final), Brussels, 9 November 2005, pp. 12-15.

11 Nathalie Tocci, 'The European Neighbourhood Policy: Responding to the EU's Post-Enlargement Challenges', *Document IAI*, 2004, p. 7.

12 Umit Cizre, *The Catalysts, Directions and Focus on Turkey's Agenda for Security Sector Reform in the 21st Century*, DCAF Working Paper no. 148 (Geneva: Geneva Centre for the Democratic Control of Armed Forces, 2004), p. 16.

13 Commission of the European Communities, Turkey 2005 Progress Report, COM (2005) 561 final, 9 November 2005, p. 13.

14 Commission of the European Communities, Recommendation of the European Commission on Turkey's progress towards accession, Communication from the Commission to the Council and the European Parliament, COM(2004) 656 final, 6 October 2004, p. 11.

15 Commission of the European Communities, Turkey 2006 Progress Report, COM(2006) 649 final, 8. November 2006, p. 7.

16 Tocci, *op. cit.*

17 Cizre, *op. cit.*, p. 19.

18 David L. Phillips, 'Turkey's Dream of Accession', *Foreign Affairs*, vol. 83, no. 5 (Sept/Oct 2004), pp. 92-93.

19 Commission of the European Communities, Regular Report on Turkey's progress towards accession, COM(2004) 656 final, 6 October 2004, p. 23.

20 Commission of the European Communities, Turkey 2005 Progress Report, COM (2005) 561 final, 9 November 2005, p. 13-14.

21 Commission of the European Communities, Turkey 2006 Progress Report, COM (2006) 649, 8 November 2006, p. 8.

22 European Parliament, Report on the 2003 Regular Report of the Commission on Turkey's Progress Towards Accession, 19 March 2004, pp. 8, 9 and 13.

23 European Parliament, Report on Turkey's Progress Towards Accession, 2006/2118(INI), 13.9.2006

24 As of September 2006, ENP Action Plans have been adopted for Israel, Jordan, Lebanon, Morocco, the PA and Tunisia, see: http://ec.europa.eu/world/enp/documents_en.htm.

25 Commission of the European Communities, Proposal for a Council Decision, COM(2006) 365 Final, Brussels, 5.7.2006.

26 Richard Youngs, 'European Approaches to Security in the Mediterranean', *Middle East Journal*, vol. 57, no. 3, Summer 2003, p. 416.

27 Rosa Balfour, 'Rethinking the Euro-Mediterranean Political and Security Dialogue', *ISS Occasional Papers* no 52, Institute for Security Studies, May 2004, p. 20.

28 Richard Youngs (Ed.), *Survey of European Democracy Promotion Projects* (Madrid: Fride, 2005), p. 62.

29 Richard Youngs (Ed.) *ibid.*, p. 73.

30 Richard Gillespie, 'Reshaping the Agenda? The Internal Politics of the Barcelona Process in the Aftermath of September 11', *Mediterranean Politics*, vol. 8, 2003, p. 27.

31 See *Regional and Bilateral MEDA Co-operation in the Area of Justice, Freedom and Security*, Euromed Report no. 86, 1 March 2005, at

http://europa.eu.int/comm/external_relations/euromed/publication/2005/report_86.pdf

32 Euro-Med Partnership, National Indicative Programmes for Algeria, Morocco and Tunisia, 2005-2006.

33 See the conclusions of the Euro-Mediterranean Conferences in Naples, Dublin and The Hague.

34 Human Rights Watch, *Morocco: Human Rights at a Crossroads*, October 2004.

35 *El Pais*, 6 October 2002.

36 Human Rights Watch, *Stemming the Flow: Abuses Against Migrants, Asylum Seekers and Refugees*, September 2006, p. 101-102.

37 *Corriere della sera*, 23.11.2006.

38 European Commission, 'The EU's relations with West Bank and Gaza Strip', at http://europa.eu.int/comm/external_relations/gaza/intro/index.htm#4.%20EU%20financial%20assistance%20to%20the%20Palestinians.

39 *Ibid.*

40 Presidency Conclusions of the Brussels European Council, 17 and 18 June 2004 (10679/2/04 REV 2), p. 25.

41 EU Council Secretariat Fact sheet, 'EU Assistance to the Palestinian Civil Police', 25 February 2005.

42 EU Council Secretariat Fact sheet, 'European Police Mission for the Palestinian Territories (EUPOL-COPPS), 9 February 2006.

43 See, e.g., *Palestinian Security Sector Governance: Challenges and Prospects*, Palestinian Academic Society for the Study of International Affairs, Jerusalem; and Geneva Centre for the Democratic Control of Armed Forces, August 2006.

44 Roland Friedrich et al., *Government Change and Security Sector Governance: Palestinian Public Perceptions*, Summary Report, Geneva, 3 August 2006.

45 Rami G. Khouri, Security Sector Reform: Lebanon's Rare Opportunity', 3 July 2005, available at: http://www.agenceglobal.com/article.asp?id=570

46 Report of the Fact-finding Mission to Lebanon inquiring into the causes, circumstances and consequences of the assassination of former Prime Minister Rafik Hariri, 25 February-24 March 2005.

47 'General Aoun's Lebanon Reform Program', available at: http://www.lebanonwire.com/0605/05061601LW.asp

48 *Europe News*, 3.10.2006.

49 *Jane's Defense Weekly*, 20 December 2006.

50 Heiner Hännggi and Fred Tanner, *Promoting Security Sector Governance in the EU's Neighborhood*, Chaillot Paper No. 80, July 2005

51 Council of the European Union, *EU Concept for ESDP support to Security Sector Reform (SSR)*, Brussels, 12566/05, Rev 4., 13 October 2005; Commission of the European Communities, *A concept for European Community Support for Security Sector Reform*, COM(2006) 253 final, Brussels, 24.5.2006.

52 Commission of the European Communities, *A concept for European Community Support for Security Sector Reform*, COM(2006) 253 final, Brussels, 24.5.2006, p. 5.

53 See Heiner Hännggi and Fred Tanner, *op.cit.*.

54 Richard Youngs, *Europe's Flawed Approach to Arab Democracy*, Centre for European Reform Essays, October 2006.

13. Civilian Crisis Management in Asia: The Aceh Monitoring Mission

Suying Lai

Introduction

Two years after the first civilian crisis management operation was launched by the European Union in Bosnia, the EU embarked upon its first operation in Asia through the Aceh Monitoring Mission (AMM).* This EU-led mission, tasked to oversee the implementation of commitments undertaken by the government of Indonesia (GoI) and the former separatist group, Free Aceh Movement (GAM), has been widely praised for its contribution to the immediate post-conflict peace-building process. Beyond the AMM, the EU is contributing to peace-building and development in Aceh through its assistance to longer-term reforms and post-tsunami reconstruction, both of which are ongoing. This chapter examines the EU's contribution to short and long-term peace-building, highlighting those which constitute the building blocks of security sector reform (SSR), such as monitoring the disarmament, demobilisation and reintegration of former combatants, and support to police and judicial reform. To situate the relevance of the various measures undertaken by the EU, a first section provides an overview of the conflict and efforts to achieve a political solution.

The Conflict

When in 1949 the Netherlands recognised Indonesia's independence, Aceh – a former independent sultanate – became an autonomous province in Indonesia. It was subsequently incorporated into the province of North Sumatra in 1950.[1] Many Acehnese resisted this increased control over their territory by the central government, which only increased during the New Order period (1966-1998) characterised by centralism and uniformity with the aim of creating a single Indonesian identity.[2] As a response to the increased political control and perceived exploitation of Aceh's natural resources by the central authorities, the Free Aceh Movement (*Gerakan Aceh Merdeka* – GAM) launched a rebellion calling for Aceh's secession in 1976.

* The author would like to extend special thanks to Mr. Pieter Feith, Head of the Aceh Monitoring Mission, and his spokesperson Mr. Juri Laas for kindly having reviewed the chapter.

This was immediately viewed as a direct threat to the territorial integrity of the state by the GoI, to be diffused by military means. Since Indonesia's independence, the military had viewed itself as the guarantor of state unity. The militant groups which formed the predecessors of the Indonesian military had played a decisive role in the state's independence struggle and subsequent legitimisation, and after these groups organised themselves as the Indonesian armed forces, the military continued to exert great influence in politics, existing in parallel, and only partially subservient, to the civilian government.[3] Although the military was at times successful in temporarily suppressing the GAM rebellion, the GoI consistently failed to address the grievances of the Acehnese underlying the secessionist claim. The conflict thus remained unresolved.

From a Military to a Political Solution

In 1997, the Asian financial crisis exposed the structural weaknesses of the Indonesian economy. The crisis, and the ensuing political and economic unrest, led to the downfall of Indonesian President Suharto, setting in motion dynamics which prompted the government to seek a more conciliatory, political approach to the conflict in Aceh. In May 2000, a cease-fire, or 'Humanitarian Pause', was reached between the GoI and GAM. The cease-fire was facilitated by the Geneva-based Henry Dunant Centre for Humanitarian Dialogue, whose efforts were financially supported by the European Commission, UNDP and USAID.[4] However, the cease-fire was actively undermined by the military and soon collapsed.

In December 2002, the Centre for Humanitarian Dialogue brokered a second truce, the Cessation of Hostilities Agreement (COHA). This was an important departure from the 'Humanitarian Pause'. It saw greater international backing, with $8 million pledged to the Centre for the monitoring mission, which formed part of the agreement, and financial support for post-conflict reconstruction pledged by Japan, the United States, the EU and the World Bank.[5] The EU, through its Rapid Reaction Mechanism[6], donated €2.3 million to monitoring the COHA. It also funded other projects in Indonesia benefiting Aceh, such as assistance to Acehnese internally displaced persons.[7] Although the COHA began with a significant reduction in violence, it broke down within six months as progress towards a political settlement faltered and both sides accused each other of violations. In May 2003 the GoI declared martial law in Aceh.

Ironically, the subsequent year of intensified fighting saw crucial developments towards a final political settlement take shape. The GAM had suffered heavy losses and its leadership had come under increasing criticism. It thus began to reconsider its position. On the other side, the new President, Susilo Bambang Yudhoyono, and his Vice President, Jusuf Kalla, elected in October 2004, were both in favour of a negotiated, political solution.[8] They had both been involved in the previous peace talks. The December 2004 tsunami inevitably served to fast track the negotiations which had already resumed, not least because the large international humanitarian presence, including foreign military personnel, impeded the continuation of fighting and renewed international attention to the conflict.[9] One month after the tsunami struck, a first round of formal negotiations between the GoI and

GAM was opened in Helsinki under the auspices of a new, more authoritative mediator, former Finnish President Martti Ahtisaari[10], Chairman of the Board of the Crisis Management Initiative.[11] Ahtisaari was an experienced former senior diplomat with high-level institutional and personal access, especially to the EU, which enabled him to secure a brokered agreement with the necessary international backing to succeed.

In contrast to the previous two agreements where cease-fires were meant to lead to a political settlement, Ahtisaari demanded that the two sides first reach political consensus before signing an agreement. This approach placed great pressure on the parties to modify their positions, and with success. GAM made the strategic concession of accepting 'self-government' instead of full independence, and the GoI eventually permitted the establishment of local political parties in Aceh, previously a key stumbling block.[12] The resulting Memorandum of Understanding (MoU) was signed on 15 August 2005. It included provisions on the governing of Aceh, human rights, amnesty and reintegration of former combatants, and security arrangements. It also established an Aceh Monitoring Mission (AMM), tasked to monitor the implementation of the MoU, and provisions for dispute settlement. Although the EU was not directly involved in the peace talks, it supported the efforts of the Crisis Management Initiative financially. Moreover, behind the scenes it played an indispensable role. It became clear early on that the EU was the prime candidate for the monitoring mission. While the peace talks were taking place, the EU successfully garnered the political will and institutional resources to launch a monitoring mission at short notice. The mission was to be present on the ground when the MoU was signed. Indeed, on 15 August 2005, an 80-person strong Initial Monitoring Presence (IMP) was dispatched to Aceh. It stayed there for one month until the arrival of the AMM, the EU's first civilian crisis management operation in Asia.

The Aceh Monitoring Mission

The Aceh Monitoring Mission was led by the European Union and consisted of monitors from the EU, five ASEAN contributing countries, Norway and Switzerland.[13] Under the leadership of the Head of Mission (HoM), Pieter Feith, Deputy Director General for Politico-Military Affairs in the Council of the European Union, the AMM was tasked to:

a) monitor the demobilisation of GAM and decommissioning of its armaments,
b) monitor the relocation of non-organic military forces and non-organic police troops,
c) monitor the reintegration of active GAM members,
d) monitor the human rights situation and provide assistance in this field,
e) monitor the process of legislation change,
f) rule on disputed amnesty cases,
g) investigate and rule on complaints and alleged violations of the MoU,
h) establish and maintain liaison and good cooperation with the parties.[14]

To bolster its authority and effectiveness, the AMM enjoyed unrestricted freedom of movement, and neither the GoI nor GAM had a veto over the actions or control of AMM operations. In case of disagreement over the implementation of the MoU, the HoM had the authority to issue binding rulings on the parties. Since the AMM had no negotiating role, should the HoM be unable to resolve the dispute, this power would devolve to former mediator Martti Ahtisaari. Through both its composition and mandate, therefore, the AMM served to remedy the flaws of the previous peace agreements, namely the lack of authoritative neutral monitors and a mechanism for dispute resolution.[15]

Disarmament and Demobilisation

One of the AMM's principle tasks was to monitor the disarmament, demobilisation and reintegration (DDR) of GAM combatants and the relocation of non-organic[16] Indonesian military and police forces from Aceh. Although from the outset of negotiations it was apparent that agreement on DDR and its monitoring would be relatively easy, the importance of successful execution was crucial. A transparent and impartially monitored DDR process was not only to serve as a key early confidence-building measure, and thereby increase the prospects for peace, but DDR was also to result in improved security for the Acehnese. Although the security situation had already improved before the signing of the MoU, it remained frail with 'improved' being understood as GAM exercising restraint by refraining from attacking the Indonesian military, a measure matched by the ceasing of military operations on the government side.

To ensure the successful disarmament and demobilisation of GAM, it was of particular importance that the former separatist group saw AMM as monitoring its disarmament in parallel to monitoring and ensuring the relocation of Indonesian armed forces and police. Parallel steps by the former foes, in 'tit-for-tat' fashion, would provide incentives for each to fulfil its commitments. Strengthening GAM's faith in the peace process was of particular importance, as the Movement had 'agreed to disarm and reintegrate its members into village society before the political structures mandated by the agreement [were] put in place'.[17]

The disarmament and demobilisation of GAM and the redeployment of troops took place between September and December 2005. The operation went smoothly and according to schedule. In the MoU it was determined that GAM would demobilise 3,000 combatants and hand over 840 weapons to the AMM to be destroyed. The GoI, on the other hand, undertook to relocate as many non-organic soldiers and police as necessary, so that by the end of the relocation process it would have 14,700 soldiers and 9,100 police left, with the remaining personnel consisting only of Aceh-based military units and local police. The process was subsequently verified by the AMM. During each of the four rounds of weapons disarmament around a quarter of the total number of weapons (plus ammunition and explosives) to be turned in were eliminated by the AMM. Before each weapon was destroyed, AMM staff determined whether the weapon turned in would qualify, in order to counter the common problem of past DDR programmes in which ex-combatants turned in old and unserviceable weapons, with dozens of weapons being disqualified. The disarmament process was public and witnessed by the GoI and Indonesian military. Following each disarmament ceremony, the GoI relocated its troops and police. By the end, the military had relocated 25,890 soldiers and 5,791 police officers, a fact which served as a stark reminder of the differences in capability between the two parties.

As in any effective peace process, DDR must deal not only with the 'officially recognised' conflict parties, namely the military and GAM, but also with shadier elements such as militias, civilian defence groups and military auxiliary units, which may all pose a threat to the peace. Any violence they commit can be easily perceived or used as a justification by the other side to break its commitments. Such groups may also form a public security challenge during periods of post-conflict insecurity and lawlessness. In the Aceh case, such groups had reportedly been responsible for human rights violations.[18] The question of illegal armed groups was therefore addressed in the MoU, which allocated responsibility to the GoI for decommissioning all illegal arms, ammunition and explosives held by them.

Up to February 2006 there had been no significant incidents involving illegal armed groups, but during the 30th meeting of the Commission on Security Arrangements (COSA) the AMM indicated that such groups were attempting to sabotage the peace process. COSA had been created by the HoM to facilitate consultation between the GoI and GAM under the chairmanship of the AMM, and to diffuse conflicts before they could escalate.[19] Regular COSA meetings were held at both provincial (senior representatives) and local (district) levels. This way the AMM was able to steer and gauge progress on the various steps in the implementation of the MoU and help facilitate problem solving. Holding meetings at district level helped to disseminate information on the peace process, giving local leaders on both sides ownership and responsibility, and ensuring that local problems were solved at local level rather than being allowed to escalate and grow out of proportion. Further, by conducting regular district level COSA meetings, the number of items on the agenda at the provincial meetings could be maintained at a manageable level. Decisions in the COSA meetings at all levels were taken by consensus, which proved an excellent confidence building measure between the parties and the AMM.

After conducting an investigation, the HoM Pieter Feith expressed strong concerns about the activities of illegal armed groups, which he believed had been involved in attacking the GAM-linked Aceh Referendum Information Center (better known as SIRA) and in the abduction of a treasurer of a local cooperative.[20] At the meeting the HoM requested the GoI to investigate these incidents and report back to the AMM, and ensure disciplinary measures for those involved. When the GoI's investigation absolved the government of responsibility, the AMM accepted the outcome, although it did ask the government to confirm in writing 'its full implementation of the disbandment of any illegal armed groups or parties'.[21] Apart from handling these incidents, the AMM noted no further activity by illegal armed groups or parties. In the summer of 2006, it dismissed speculation that a host of shootings by unidentified gunmen days before the Indonesian parliament passed a new law on Aceh's governance were related to the former conflict. The Jakarta-based human rights group, Aceh Working Group, believed otherwise though. It maintained that the violence and high level of armed robberies during those months were part of a systematic campaign to disrupt peace in Aceh.[22] It also expressed concerns over the rising trade in illicit small arms and light weapons, which it claimed were falling into the hands of pro-government militias.

Amnesty

Under the MoU, the GoI committed itself to granting amnesty to all persons who had participated in GAM activities, including political prisoners and detainees. The amnesty process was to begin within 15 days of the signing of the MoU, thus before the DDR and relocation processes began and under the presence of the Initial Monitoring Presence. Already on Indonesia's Independence Day, on 17 August 2005, the GoI released 298 GAM prisoners as part of the annual amnesty. Although this was unrelated to the MoU, it was perceived as a clear sign of goodwill. The amnesty of undisputed prisoners and detainees, which totalled more than 1,400 individuals in the initial release, proceeded without incident and formed an important first step in building trust.[23] Upon leaving prison, former prisoners and detainees were provided with an initial reintegration package consisting of financial support, clothes and other goods, which would be followed by longer-term assistance.[24]

In addition to the undisputed cases, there were more than 100 disputed cases in which the government claimed that the individuals held had committed purely criminal offences, while GAM maintained that they were in fact political. COSA provided the GoI and GAM with an institutionalised forum to discuss these disputed cases, with the HoM acting as a facilitator with the authority to rule on cases to prevent deadlock. On the one hand, the HoM urged the government to examine the disputed cases and GAM to be cooperative, while on the other he maintained that he would use his authority to rule if necessary.[25] The aim was for the GoI to take into consideration, and for the two parties to reach consensus on, as many cases as possible without the AMM's involvement, not least in order to maximise ownership of the process and legitimacy of its outcome. In April 2006, a Swedish judge experienced in handling amnesties joined the AMM to assist with the resolution of the remaining cases, and in the following months agreement by consensus was reached on all of them.[26] Not all incarcerated GAM were amnestied, however; 34 individuals convicted of crimes including bombings, the possession of firearms and robbery remained in prison, despite the wishes of GAM's leadership.[27]

Reintegration of Former Combatants and Post-Tsunami Reconstruction

As the above-sections describe, disarmament and demobilisation took place rapidly after the signing of the MoU, reaching completion halfway through the AMM's first mandate in March 2006.[28] This meant that both domestic and international efforts could be focused on the reintegration of former combatants and on other issues crucial to ensuring sustainable peace and development. The MoU had contained provisions on the reintegration of GAM members, stating that the GoI and the Acehnese authorities would provide economic facilitation to former combatants, pardon political prisoners and affected citizens through the allocation of suitable farm land and financial assistance. In accordance with the MoU, the AMM monitored the reintegration process, while the GoI allocated funds for the rehabilitation of private and public property destroyed or damaged during the conflict.

Days after the signing of the MoU, the European Commission (EC) proposed granting €4 million of financial assistance to the 3,000 GAM combatants to be demobilised and to the 2,000 prisoners to be amnestied.[29] To ensure rapid disbursement of funds, the European Commission's Rapid Reaction Mechanism was foreseen, though the EC in fact only provided financial assistance to former prisoners, as the GoI decided to provide for the immediate needs of ex-combatants in order 'to show [its] commitment to the peace process and get political credit out of that'.[30] Starting in October 2005, the government made payments of one million rupiah (around $100) to 3,000 ex-combatants for a period of six months, to be followed by the provision of long-term assistance. For comparison, no financial assistance to demobilised combatants had been envisaged in the 2002 Cessation of Hostilities Agreement, which illustrates the more comprehensive nature of the MoU and the acceptance by the two sides of a far more permanent solution.[31]

Agreement between the GoI and GAM on the method of distribution of funds was reached in November 2005 with the help of the AMM, though this was not without prior disagreement. The GoI had been keen for ex-GAM members to register with the authorities, as it was concerned with the proper allocation of funds, not least because it feared that some of the money would be withheld by the GAM leadership and misused for political recruitment as it sought to transform itself into a political party.[32] This proposal, however, was not acceptable to GAM. Although GAM officially cited security concerns as its reason for opposing the registration process, it later become clear that the underlying reason was that a much larger number of GAM members required financial support. The figure 3,000 was only an approximation of the number of active GAM fighters and did not include those who had provided logistical support, 'civilian' GAM, and the families of deceased GAM fighters who were all expected to be provided for. Moreover, through control of the disbursement process, the leadership wished to maintain its chain of command, which would facilitate the Movement's transformation into a political player. During the negotiation process, in line with the AMM's ambition to maintain good cooperation with both parties, it 'encouraged the GAM leadership to authorise members to register on an individual basis with Indonesian authorities, while acknowledging that they [were] not obliged' to do so.[33] In the end, a compromise was reached and it was decided that the funds would be paid to GAM regional commanders based on a calculation of the number of fighters to be demobilised in each respective area; the commanders would be responsible for correctly allocating the funds.

The short-term reintegration funds were clearly not distributed according to ideal-type DDR best practice, in which individual assistance would have been accurately tracked via a DDR programme management system. Neither was it corruption free.[34] However, that the former foes were able to reach agreement on the disbursement of funds, and on terms favourable to the weaker party GAM, was an accomplishment in itself, serving to strengthen mutual trust and allowing the GoI to live up to its initial MoU obligations.

These were at least as important as the formal technical distribution of funds, especially since this initial financial assistance, nicknamed 'smoking money' by some ex-GAM, had little impact on the GAM members who received it.[35] For former GAM combatants to be able to contribute productively to society, longer term reintegration assistance was necessary, and Aceh as a whole had to develop economically and politically. From the outset, the EU recognized this interdependence between peace and development. In the case of Aceh it was understood as post-tsunami reconstruction, and the EU fulfilled and continues to fulfil a key contribution in this regard.[36]

The Link to Development

The EU has been the largest donor to the post-tsunami reconstruction effort. Together the EC and EU member states have channelled more than $460 million to the World Bank-managed Multi-Donor Tsunami Reconstruction Trust Fund for the rehabilitation and reconstruction of Aceh and Nias, and the EC sits as one of the Trust Fund's three co-chairs, together with the World Bank and the Indonesian Agency for Reconstruction and Rehabilitation (BRR).[37] This money, spent between 2005-2007, had been earmarked for the (re)construction of public infrastructure and services, restarting of economic activities, and securing the livelihood of tsunami-affected people.[38] Additionally, it was used to develop the administrative skills and capacity of the BRR and local government. Clearly, funds benefiting the development of Aceh in general could have a positive impact on GAM reintegration, and the EC has emphasised the coordination of its funding initiatives (the EU does not implement its own programmes) with the AMM.[39] Of particular relevance to the linking of humanitarian assistance with conflict resolution was the use of the Rapid Reaction Mechanism (RRM), which was useful for fast support to small political initiatives independent of the general relief effort.[40] The RRM not only financed the initial €7 million EC contribution to the Trust Fund, but also a number of short term programmes to strengthen the capacity of local authorities to design and implement post-tsunami assistance. It also financed a small project to consult Acehnese civil society on the government's reconstruction plans.[41] Last but not least, as described above, the RRM was used to fund the peace negotiations leading to the MoU and to support the reintegration of amnestied prisoners. The use of the RRM for these ends has been described as 'one of the most positive and relevant medium-term measures [taken] by the EU'.[42]

Another venue, Europe House, created by the EC in October 2005, also served as a forum to connect post-tsunami reconstruction with GAM reintegration and wider development. Serving to facilitate donor coordination and enhance policy dialogue with the local communities and authorities, it maintained close coordination with the AMM, especially in the spheres of Community reintegration programmes for former combatants and amnestied prisoners, and communication and information tools on the MoU and the peace process.[43] Nevertheless, international aid groups charged with post-tsunami reconstruction were criticised for their silence and lack of contribution to the peace process.[44] This allegation is supported by the fact that no reintegration-relevant projects were funded by the Multi-Donor Tsunami Reconstruction Trust Fund, through which the EU's post-tsunami humanitarian assistance for Indonesia was channelled. Moreover, to prevent discontent from non-tsunami affected persons who were also in need of assistance, post-tsunami support to the coastal population should have been provided in parallel to support to the equally poor population inland.[45]

In February 2006, the Aceh Peace-Reintegration Agency (BRA) was established by the Governor of Aceh. Its mandate was to implement the reintegration process in accordance with the MoU, as well as the coordination of government and donor post-conflict programming.[46] It benefited from input and support from the EU and other international actors. The creation of this Agency constituted a first step towards embedding the reintegration process into longer term programmes benefiting all affected citizens, and therefore making the reintegration and wider peace process 'self-sustainable', as consistently advocated by the EU.[47] Upon creation it was in no shortage of funds, having received $20 million from the Indonesian national planning agency before the end of the fiscal year in mid April. However, the BRA's capacity to distribute this money and exercise oversight were weak. Overwhelmed by 50,000 proposals for assistance from Acehnese citizens, the Agency 'all but [froze] the release of cash while [it] figured out' how to allocate the money.[48] Finally, with technical assistance provided by the World Bank, in August 2006 the BRA was able to launch the first phase of a community-level economic assistance programme for victims of the conflict. Notwithstanding this development, the AMM's HoM in his monitoring capacity commented that the reintegration process had not moved 'vigorously forward', a view shared by many within GAM who had publicly complained about the slow pace of long-term reintegration assistance.[49] GAM and civil society actors had also criticised the lack of transparency, the overly bureaucratic approach of BRA and corruption; all structural problems endemic to Indonesia which the EU could do little to alleviate in the short term.[50] In sum, at the end of 2006 the reintegration process still had a long way to go before being able to provide for all those who needed it.

Addressing the Root Causes of the Conflict

According to Rïzal Sukma, an academic, the underlying causes of the 29-year conflict between GAM and the GoI can be summarised as economic exploitation, excessive centralism and uniformity at the cost of Acehnese identity, military repression, and impunity for human rights abuses.[51] The MoU had sought to address these root causes to ensure sustainable peace and to enable Aceh to establish a democracy based on human rights and the rule of law. Economic exploitation and excessive centralism were to be eliminated through a new law on Aceh's governance, on which discussions began in the autumn of 2005 and which was drafted in 2006. Military repression, and human rights abuses and impunity thereof, would be resolved with the relocation of non-organic forces and human rights monitoring by the AMM, and sustained through human rights training for the police and the establishment of an independent and impartial court system. The creation of a Commission for Truth and Reconciliation would address the human rights abuses committed in the past and serve as a mechanism for transitional justice. The EU is providing both short and long-term support to rectify the latter two root causes.

The EU's short term measures were epitomised by the AMM. In addition to monitoring the relocation of Indonesian non-organic forces and GAM's DDR, hence preventing the recurrence of military repression and violence, the Mission encompassed a clear human rights component to ensure its upholding. This was the first time that the EU included human rights monitors in the context of a crisis management operation, forming a tangible expression of the emerging efforts by the EU to mainstream human rights into both civilian and military crisis management operations.[52] In this regard, EU Ministers at the November 2006 Civilian Capabilities Improvement Conference underlined the importance of raising awareness of human rights for civilian ESDP personnel for future missions.[53]

As stipulated in the MoU, the AMM would monitor the human rights situation following the end of conflict and provide assistance while monitoring the process of legislative change. Through the AMM's 11 district offices, human rights monitors investigated incidents, including the excessive use of power, extortion and intimidation.[54] In addition, in an attempt to embed human rights norms for the long-term, the AMM engaged in 'daily dialogue with civilian and military authorities at [the] local level to raise awareness of international standards of human rights protection and best police practice'.[55] This was complemented by the Mission's efforts to strengthen national institutions in the field of human rights and Acehnese civil society.[56] Although it is premature to evaluate the capacity development efforts by the AMM and the EU in general at this stage, a report on cooperation between EU civilian crisis management and civil society has already described the Mission's information exchange and outreach activities with NGOs as 'exceptional' in comparison to previous ESDP missions.[57] For example, during the deployment of the Initial Monitoring Presence, a meeting with NGOs was convened to explain the purpose of the upcoming monitoring mission, discuss how civil society groups planned to support the peace process, and how the AMM could best communicate with them.[58] Significantly, after the meeting efforts were made to establish sustained, substantive interaction with civil society through the appointment of an AMM staff member responsible for civil society liaison. This contact was maintained, and more than one year later, the HoM himself held a discussion with civil society on ensuring the self-sustainability of the peace process after the Mission's departure.[59]

Beyond the AMM, the EU, in line with its commitments to promote democracy, human rights and respect for the rule of law, is seeking to contribute to long-term human rights development in Aceh. This is exemplified through its assistance to police and judicial reform and its continuous presence on the ground through the European Commission's Permanent Delegation. Following the issuance of the comprehensive €15.9 million EC 'peace support package' in December 2005, the Commission is currently providing technical and capacity development assistance to support the Acehnese local police and civil judicial system.[60] Additionally, it is improving access to justice and assisting public administration and local government reform. It also assisted with the organisation of the 2006 local elections.[61] By seeking to facilitate the creation of a police force and judicial system which is effective, responsive and protective – as opposed to undermining – human rights, the EU is contributing directly to aspects of security sector reform at the local level. If reforms prove successful, Aceh could prove a model for similar situations elsewhere in the country, especially since the region is widely looked upon as a test case for implementing autonomy for Indonesia's regions in the future. Moreover, successful assistance to police reform in Aceh may also demonstrate to other actors of the security sector that their modes of operation are subject to outside involvement, even if only in the form of benign reform assistance. In contrast, at present the Indonesian military views the issue of training standards as its own domain, even though it is widely accepted that these standards are inadequate.[62]

Law on Governing Aceh

One of the key elements contained in the MoU was the stipulation that the legislature of Aceh would draft a new governing law for the territory. The peace agreement thereby empowered the Acehnese to rectify previous encroachments on their identity and autonomy by the central authorities – the root causes of the conflict. Given that the process of legislative change was a domestic affair, the AMM was not involved in the drafting of the law. However, it did actively conduct consultations with both parties, channelling between them information on their respective positions on the contents of the draft law, but never publicly commenting on individual articles. In addition, the AMM mediated between the parties on occasion and informally provided advice. Following the adoption of the Law on Governing Aceh (LoGA) in July, consultations with the two parties continued to help them find solutions to outstanding disagreements.[63] Given the centrality of human rights to the Mission, the AMM also specifically monitored legislative developments concerning human rights and their implementation.[64] Before the Mission was launched, the idea of providing assistance to set up the Human Rights Court and Commission for Truth and Reconciliation (CTR), both mandated by the MoU, had been floated within the EU.[65] But while the EU has repeatedly stated its support for the establishment of a Human Rights Court, by mid 2007 assistance to the CTR was still not on the cards, for the CTR was to be established by the Indonesian Commission of Truth and Reconciliation, a body authorised in 2004 but whose members had yet to be selected.[66] Ironically, pressure to create the CTR could jump-start the creation of the Commission tasked to establish it.

Given the significance the new governing law would assume, the drafting process was an arduous one, involving not only GAM and government parties but also broad consultation by members of the vibrant Acehnese civil society. After the draft law was drawn up, it was submitted to the GoI, which subsequently handed it to parliament for final approval. Finally, after a four month delay caused by fierce parliamentary deliberation, the law was adopted on 11 July 2006. The delay in the adoption of the LoGA caused a postponement of the local and district elections, originally scheduled for April but ultimately delayed until 11 December 2006. This had significant consequences for the AMM, whose mission had to be prolonged three times for it to be present while the elections took place. To observe the fairness of the elections and enhance public confidence in the electoral process, the EU deployed a 73 person-strong Election Observation Mission, tasked to observe the voting, counting of ballots and compilation of results, and to provide an evaluation of the election process.[67] This €2.4 million mission was financed through the European Initiative for Democracy and Human Rights, from which Indonesia had previously benefited.

Sharia Law

One of the most controversial developments following the August 2005 peace accords has been the expanding role of Islamic Law (Sharia) in Aceh. Aceh holds a unique position in that it is the only region in Indonesia where Sharia can be applied in full, a right originally granted by the central government in 1999 as a concession to the Acehnese in order to undercut support for GAM's secessionist claim and win back the support of the population. Although the fundamental compatibility of Sharia with international human rights norms is a contentious issue, unlikely to be resolved soon, the concrete implementation of Sharia in Aceh, which has resulted in corporal punishment and sporadic limitations on the freedom of women, constitutes a clear violation of European, if not, universal human rights standards. These developments have been cautiously noted by the EU. An internal Council document entitled 'Sharia Law in Aceh and EU Funding' addressed the issue, and questions have been raised concerning the Acehnese authorities' intention to expand the application of Sharia to non-Muslims, positing that this could endanger not only economic cooperation between the EU and Indonesia, but also the broader goals of human rights and democracy promotion.[68]

The most vocal EU actors on this issue have been members of the European Parliament. MEP Ana Gomes, a former Portuguese Ambassador to Indonesia, wrote in the *International Herald Tribune* following a raid on the World Food Programme's compound in Banda Aceh by the Sharia police, that the adoption of the LoGA, which had increased powers for local religious leaders, had served to create a theocracy out of Aceh, lacking accountability and making a 'mockery out of Indonesia's positive developments toward greater democracy and the rule of law'.[69] She also criticised the lack of efforts by the international community, including the EU, to raise the issue of women's interests and human rights.[70] Focusing on the economic implications of the implementation of Sharia, German MEP Hartmut Nassauer, who headed a delegation of MEPs to Indonesia, made clear that 'religiously based laws could harm Indonesia's reputation and scare off investors' and that attempts to regulate the behaviour of women were unacceptable to the EU.[71]

Beyond the general undesirability of the expansion of the brand of Sharia which has taken root in Aceh, Sharia also poses potentially long-term implications for security sector and legal reform. In the LoGA it was stipulated that 'responsibility for investigating Sharia violations [would rest] with the police and civilian investigators', which suggested that the vice and virtue police (*wilayatul hisbah* – WH), responsible for monitoring compliance with Sharia, would become recognised as civil servants.[72] This could undermine efforts by the EU and other international donors to assist police reform, since it is widely recognised, including by the local population, that members of the WH are poorly recruited and trained. On the other hand, improving the selection process could result in the employment of more religious officers. Given the current form Sharia has taken, this could undermine human rights. Accountability of the WH, especially if its powers were extended as it currently advocates, also poses the problem that the belief in religious infallibility could promote religious oversight independent of the democratic civilian oversight structure. Moreover, criticism of those mandated to enforce the observance of religious laws could easily be construed as 'anti-Islamic' and therefore be ignored; some have already become afraid to express such opinions for fear of wrong interpretation.[73] Given the destabilising potential of these developments, the International Crisis Group has expressed the concern that international donors could discontinue funding efforts at police reform if the WH were to assume an increased role.[74]

The Aceh Monitoring Mission in Retrospect

There is no doubt that the August 2005 peace agreement succeeded because both the GoI and GAM committed themselves to a political solution to stop the years of bloodshed. Capitalising on the political will from both sides to seek peace, the AMM, and hence the EU, played a crucial role in building confidence between the parties by monitoring the implementation of commitments undertaken and facilitating the resolution of disagreements, especially in COSA. The AMM therefore helped to solidify the momentum towards peace which existed following the MoU, enabling the two parties to move forward on critical issues such as the distribution of reintegration funds, resolution of disputed amnesty cases, and debate on the LoGA, all of which could have handicapped the peace-building process. That the AMM was formed by EU and ASEAN member states and henceforth enjoyed the backing of the international community ensured that its presence carried the necessary weight to execute its tasks with authority and deter rogue elements from sabotage. Moreover, the partnership with ASEAN allowed the EU to profit from that organisation's knowledge of the region and culture in order to enhance the legitimacy and regional ownership of the Mission.[75]

Upon the completion of the AMM in December 2006, the peace process had become firmly entrenched. Not only had GAM become part of the democratic process, but the GoI, which had been able to improve significantly its international reputation as a result of the success achieved in Aceh, also had incentives not to renege on its commitments. With this 'negative peace' in place, longer-term efforts towards the establishment of a 'positive peace' began, including police and judicial reform, which were already being funded by the EC and other international donors. The successful demobilisation and disarmament of GAM and the relocation of Indonesian troops provided the foundations for the above-mentioned reforms, which could eventually lead to system-wide security sector reform. Indeed, the EU has already stated that it would support reforms in Indonesia eradicating corruption, creating democratic control of the armed forces, as well as improving internal stability.[76] The process of DDR is not over, however, and continuing efforts to assist the reintegration of former combatants are crucial to dissuade ex-GAM members from criminal activity posing a public security threat. Before his departure, the HoM made it clear that the commitment of the EU to Aceh and the peace process extended to the long-term.[77] In this regard, the acknowledgement by the EU that security is a precondition for development bodes well for the integration of future EU activities in Aceh in the security and development domains, not least because Community development funds can be utilised to support all civilian aspects of security sector reform, as well as activities in relation to the democratic and civilian control of the military aspects of security sector reform.[78]

Of particular relevance to the AMM is the issue of local ownership, one of the key principles on which European Union ESDP support to security sector reform is based.[79] Inherent in the fact that the AMM had a monitoring as opposed to a more robust mandate, the former conflict parties were the principals in charge of the success of their peace process. To support the two parties during the tenure of the mission, the AMM continually sought to facilitate direct consultations and dialogue between the GoI and the GAM, institutionalised through regular COSA meetings. The HoM had underlined that these consultations be retained after the departure of the AMM and broadened to include other segments of Acehnese society.[80] A constant emphasis has also been placed on the self-sustainability of the peace process during the tenure of the AMM.

The Acehnese have greatly appreciated the AMM's presence and considered it 'extremely important and contributing to lasting peace'.[81] A survey conducted by the International Foundation for Election Systems in cooperation with USAID during the fall of 2006 elicited that 97% of the respondents claimed to be satisfied with AMM. This was a view shared by the international community. The AMM's success also attests to the fact that the EU is increasingly capable of speedy provision and successful integration of a broad range of instruments and expertise for its crisis management operations.[82] Such capabilities are expected to become increasingly in demand, as DDR and human rights monitoring will increasingly replace traditional peacekeeping in crisis management operations.[83]

Beyond the achievements of the AMM, the Aceh peace process has been hailed across the board as a clear success, expressed most prominently by the nominations of Indonesian President Susilo Bambang Yudhoyono and Martti Ahtisaari for the 2006 Nobel Peace Prize. The successful Aceh peace process has helped Indonesia to rehabilitate its international standing, previously tarnished by the political and economic turmoil ignited by the Asian financial crisis and which culminated in its 'defeat' in East Timor. The EU has already declared that it will support an enhanced role for Indonesia in ASEAN and in the region, and three months following the signing of the MoU, the United States resumed its Foreign Military Financing programme there. Such overt assistance could not have been possible had the military undermined the peace process as it has done in the past.[84]

Conclusion

Much has been achieved in a short period of time for the Acehnese and for Indonesia following the peace agreement. However, much remains to be done, whether concerning democracy development, human rights protection, or concerning the democratic, civilian control of the security sector. Concerning the latter issue, it is worth noting that the GoI allocated around $50 million to finance the partial relocation of the military from Aceh, a sum similar to what the military would have received from the war economy should the conflict have continued. In a country where the military obtains more than two thirds of its budget from off-budget sources, this offset paid to the military underscores the challenges facing Indonesia in terms of security sector reform. Through the AMM, the European Union with ASEAN have made a decisive contribution to peace in Aceh. This peace is now being built upon through longer-term reforms, which the EU is supporting in conjunction with its post-tsunami reconstruction efforts. These reforms, if not undermined by the future role of Sharia in Acehnese society, could in turn constitute part of the stepping stones of comprehensive security sector reform in Indonesia.

Endnotes

1 Caroline Bivar (2006) 'Emerging from the Shadows: The EU's Role in Conflict Resolution in Indonesia', European Policy Centre Issue Paper No. 44, p. 17.

2 Rizal Sukma (2004) 'Security Operations in Aceh: Goals, Consequences, and Lessons', East-West Center Washington, *Policy Studies* 3, p. 4.

3 John Bradford (2005) 'The Indonesian Military as a Professional Organisation: Criteria and Ramifications for Reform', *Working Paper* No. 73, Institute of Defence and Strategic Studies, January 2005, p. 6; Kingsburg quoted on p. 8.

4 Braud and Grevi *op. cit.*, p. 19.

5 Sukma *op. cit.*, p. 20.

6 The Rapid Reaction Mechanism (RRM) allows the Community to respond quickly to the needs of countries faced with political instability or disaster.

7 European Commission, *Indonesia National Indicative Programme 2005-2006*, p. 43.

8 Edward Aspinall (2005) 'The Helsinki Agreement: A More Promising Basis for Peace in Aceh?', East-West Center Washington, *Policy Studies* No. 20, pp. vi, 14.

9 Aspinall *op. cit.*, p. 20.

10 Ahtisaari had been approached to mediate by a Finnish businessman who had previously worked in Indonesia and befriended Jusuf Kalla's assistant when Kalla was still deputy coordinating minister for people's welfare under President Megawati (Aspinall *op. cit.*, p. 18).

11 The Crisis Management Initiative is an independent, non-profit organisation that works to promote sustainable security. It was founded by Martti Ahtisaari in 2000.

12 Aspinall *op. cit.*, pp. viii, 42.

13 The ASEAN contributing countries were Brunei, Malaysia, Philippines, Singapore and Thailand.

14 Memorandum of Understanding, 5.1, 5.2.

15 Bivar *op. cit.*, p. 21.

16 Non-organic forces were soldiers from battalions and police forces temporarily stationed in Aceh.

17 Aspinall *op. cit.*, p. 57.

18 Amnesty International (2005) 'Indonesia: A briefing for EU and ASEAN countries concerning the deployment of the Aceh Monitoring Mission to Nanggroe Aceh Darussalam Province', 9 September 2005.

19 'Strengthening Peace after Disaster: the Aceh Monitoring Mission' (2006) *ESDP Newsletter*, Issue 2, June 2006, p. 18.

20 AMM Press Statement (2006) 'On the Outcome of the Meeting of the Commission on Security Arrangements', Banda Aceh, 25 February 2006.

21 AMM Press Statement (2006) 'On the Outcome of the Meeting of the Commission on Security Arrangements', Banda Aceh, 12 March 2006.

22 'Indonesian Rights Group Warns of 'Systematic' Bid to Disrupt Peace in Aceh' *op. cit.*

23 International Crisis Group (2005) *op. cit.*, p. 2.

24 International Crisis Group (2005) *op. cit.*, p. 3.

25 Reuters (2005) 'Indonesia Asked to Examine Aceh Amnesty Cases', 4 October 2005.

26 AMM Press Statement (2006) 'On the Outcome of the Meeting of the Commission on Security Arrangements', Banda Aceh, 29 April 2006. 'Amnesty, Reintegration and Human Rights' (2006) Aceh Monitoring Mission Website. http://www.aceh-mm.org/english/headquarter_menu/amnesty.htm

27 Nina Afrida 'Freedom Tastes Good for Pardoned GAM Prisoners' (2006) *The Jakarta Post*.

28 The Council Joint Action 2005/643/CFSP establishing the AMM was to expire on 15 March 2006. It was extended three times to 15 December 2006.

29 Braud and Grevi *op. cit.*, p. 30.

30 Braud and Grevi *op. cit.*, p. 30.

31 Aspinall *op. cit.*, p. 45.

32 This paragraph draws heavily on information from the International Crisis Group (2005) *op. cit.*, pp. 4-5.

33 International Crisis Group (2005) *op. cit.*, p. 5.

34 On the distribution of reintegration assistance see Mark Knight and Alpaslan Özerdem *op. cit.*, p. 512.

35 Bank Dunia and World Bank (2006) *GAM Reintegration Needs Assessment: Enhancing Peace through Community-level Development Programming*, March 2006, p. 31.

36 Feith *op. cit.*, pp. 3-4.

37 Multi-Donor Fund Website. www.multidonorfund.org

38 'Post-Tsunami Reconstruction: Commission Finances First Long-term Activities in Aceh, Indonesia' (2005) European Commission External Relations Website: *The EU's Relations with Indonesia*. IP/05/1025, Brussels, 29 July 2005.

39 Braud and Grevi *op. cit.*, p. 30.

40 Marlies Glasius (2006) 'The EU Response to the Tsunami and the Need for a Human Security Approach', *European Foreign Affairs Review*, Vol. 11, No. 3, p. 377.

41 European Commission (2005) *Progress Report on the European Commission's Response to the Indian Ocean Tsunami of 26 December 2004 and Reinforcing EU Disaster and Crisis Response in Third Countries*, 18 November 2005, p. 6.

42 Glasius *op. cit.*, p. 359.

43 European Commission (2005) *Progress Report on the European Commission's Response to the Indian Ocean Tsunami of 26 December 2004 and Reinforcing EU Disaster and Crisis Response in Third Countries*, 18 November 2005, p. 10.

Council of the European Union (2006) 'Presidency Report on ESDP', Brussels, 12 June 2006, 10418/06.

44 Daniel Burdock (2006) 'Prospects for Peace: New Agreement to End Conflict in Aceh Creates Surprising Trust and Optimism', *Inside Indonesia*, April-June 2006.

http://www.insideindonesia.org/edit86/p28-29_burdock.html

45 Glasius *op. cit.*, p. 365.

46 World Bank/DSF (2006) 'Aceh Conflict Monitoring Update', 1–31 March 2006, p. 5. 'Strengthening Peace after Disaster: the Aceh Monitoring Mission', *op. cit.*, p. 18.

47 Feith op. cit., p. 4. 'Strengthening Peace after Disaster: the Aceh Monitoring Mission', *op. cit.*, p. 19.

48 Joe Cochrane (2006) 'Analysis: Re-integration Is Key to Peace in Indonesia's Aceh', *Deutsche Presse-Agentur*, 14 August 2006.

49 Cochrane (2006) *op cit*.

50 Renner (2006a) *op cit*.

51 Sukma *op. cit.*, pp. 3-5.

52 Council of the European Union (2005) 'Aceh Monitoring Mission – Human Rights Aspects', Brussels, 11678/1/05, pp. 1-2.

53 Council of the European Union (2006) 'Civilian Capabilities Improvement Conference 2006: Ministerial Declaration', Press Release, Brussels, 13 November 2006, p. 3.

54 Braud and Grevi *op. cit.*, p. 32.

55 Braud and Grevi *op. cit.*, pp. 31-32.

56 'Amnesty, Reintegration and Human Rights' (2006) Aceh Monitoring Mission Website.

57 Catriona Gourlay (2006) Partners Apart: Enhancing Cooperation between Civil Society and EU Civilian Crisis Management in the Framework of ESDP. CMI, ELPO, KATU, p. 24.

58 Gourlay *op. cit.*, p. 24.

59 'AMM Stresses the Importance of Dialogue', AMM Press Release, 3 November 2006, Aceh Monitoring Mission Website, p. 1.

60 The EU is not the only actor supporting security sector reform in Aceh. Norway, for example, which also participated in the AMM, is cooperating with the Indonesian Ministry of Justice and Human Rights to assist the Indonesian police in providing human rights courses for its police and municipal police officers, civilian state investigators, and Sharia police members in Aceh.

61 EU Council Secretariat Factsheet, 22 May 2006, p. 4.

62 Bradford *op. cit.*, p. 8.

63 'Ex-rebels in Indonesia's Aceh to Lodge Complaint over Autonomy Law' (2006) *Agence France Presse*, 3 August 2006.

64 'Amnesty, Reintegration and Human Rights' (2006) Aceh Monitoring Mission Website.

65 Council of the European Union (2005) *op. cit.*, p. 4.

66 International Crisis Group (2006a) 'Aceh's Local Elections: The Role of the Free Aceh Movement (GAM)', *Crisis Group Asia Briefing* No. 57, 29 November 2006, p. 13 footnote 71.

67 'EU Deploys an Election Observation Mission to the Indonesian Province of Aceh' (2006) Brussels, 16 November 2006, IP/06/1570.

68 Council of the European Union (2006) 'Sharia Law in Aceh and EU Funding', Brussels, 9 October 2006, 13750/06. Council of the European Union (2006) 'Introduction of Sharia Law in the Indonesian Province of Aceh', Brussels, 11 September 2006, p. 2.

69 Ana Gomes (2006) 'Aceh's Harsh Islamic Law Is an Ominous Sign; Islam in Indonesia II', *International Herald Tribune*, 14 September 2006.

70 Gomes *op. cit.*

71 Patung (2006) 'Sharia Warnings', www.indonesiamatters.com, 25 November 2006.

72 This paragraph draws heavily on International Crisis Group (2006b) *op. cit.*, pp. 1, 9, 14.

73 Shawn Donnan and Taufan Hidayat (2006) 'Aceh Enforces Sharia Law with the Lash of a Cane', *Financial Times*, 6 October 2006.

74 International Crisis Group (2006b) *op. cit.*, p. 14.

75 Feith *op. cit.*, p. 4.

76 'The EU in Aceh: Between Conflict Resolution and Peace-building', *Policy Dialogue*, European Policy Centre, 13 March 2006.

77 AMM Press Release (2006) 'Pieter Feith Discussed Reintegration with Former GAM commanders', 29 November 2006, p. 1.

78 European Commission (2006) 'A Concept for European Community Support for Security Sector Reform', Brussels, 24 May 2006, COM(2006)253F, pp. 6-7.

79 Council of the European Union, 'EU Concept for ESDP Support to Security Sector Reform (SSR)', Brussels, 13 October 2005, 12566/4/05 REV 4, p. 11.

80 'AMM Stresses the Importance of Dialogue', *op. cit.*, p. 1.

81 Pauliina Arola (2006) 'Civilian Crisis Management and the Role of Civil Society: Learning from the Past/Assessment of the Aceh Monitoring Mission by an NGO', speech presented in Conference on Enhancing Cooperation between Civil Society and EU Civilian Crisis Management, Helsinki, Crisis Management Initiative, 27 September 2006.

82 Feith *op. cit.*, p. 4.

83 Feith *op. cit.*, p. 4.

84 'The EU in Aceh: Between Conflict Resolution and Peace-building' *op. cit.* Marcus Mietzner (2006) 'The Politics of Military Reform in Post-Suharto Indonesia: Elite Conflict, Nationalism, and Institutional Resistance', Policy Paper 23, East-West Center Washington, p. 52.

III: SECURITY SECTOR REFORM IN INTERNATIONAL PERSPECTIVE

14. EU – NATO Cooperation in Post-Conflict Reconstruction

Karl-Heinz Rambke and Sebastian Keil

Introduction

After the end of the Cold War, the international community faced various new security challenges worldwide. The huge number of armed conflicts, causing more than eight million deaths from 1990 to 2004[1], was a main structuring element of the international system. When international organisations, nation-states and non-governmental organisations (NGOs) began to develop more effective measures for conflict management, they soon realized that peacebuilding and post-conflict reconstruction of war-torn states were complex and difficult tasks. In fact, around 50 percent of the conflicts of the past 20 years have relapsed within five years of the signing of a peace agreement.[2] Although the UN Agenda for Peace, issued in 1992, first described peacebuilding[3], the international community has used various terms to deal with the issue. Peacebuilding and post-conflict reconstruction are so closely linked, that this chapter uses the term 'post-conflict reconstruction' and bases itself on the G-8 declaration on 'future actions in stabilization and reconstruction'.[4]

Since the end of the Cold War the EU and NATO have been engaged in several war-torn countries. Afghanistan is the most current example, but their engagement in the Balkans was and remains vital. Yet, neither the EU nor NATO were well prepared for post-conflict reconstruction at the outset of their missions; the EU had to develop its role as a security actor and NATO had to revise its political role and its military strategy. Step by step, both organisations adapted their political and military approaches, integrating lessons learnt into their new policy choices. Today, both struggle with the same issue; how to establish a stronger link between political, military and civilian measures. This chapter analyses the cooperation mechanisms and various initiatives of both organisations. Its aim is to identify possible synergies potentially leading to enhanced performance.

All peace operations and reconstruction efforts are constrained by internal and external risks and threats. We address these challenges first. We then describe and analyse EU and NATO methods for post-conflict reconstruction and their policies for creating peace and stability. Basing our argument on the consultation and cooperation arrangements between the two organisations since January 2001, we examine their collaboration both at political level and in the field. The chapter does not attempt to cover all EU and NATO missions in detail, for this is ably undertaken in other chapters in the book. Our analysis focuses on three important operations: Bosnia and Herzegovina (BiH), Kosovo and Afghanistan.

Various politicians have criticised cooperation between the EU and NATO. The Polish Defence Minister Radek Sikorski characterised it as 'underutilized' and 'underdeveloped'[5] and NATO Secretary General Jaap de Hoop Scheffer postulated that 'we need to break the deadlock in the NATO-EU relationship.'[6] Should the two organisations renew their partnership and attempt to create a fruitful division of labour? We argue that some lessons have been learnt, and we offer recommendations and draw several conclusions as to how the EU and NATO might improve their capabilities and cooperation in post-conflict reconstruction.

What Does Post-Conflict Reconstruction Mean?

The process of post-conflict reconstruction is multifaceted. It covers diplomatic, political, military and economic factors, and encompasses two essential tasks. On the one hand, security and stability have to be achieved after the termination of hostilities, and on the other, the international and national actors have to be engaged in the parallel long-term process of consolidating peace by reconciling people, achieving justice and reforming and/or rebuilding institutions and the economy. Therefore, post-conflict reconstruction should be seen as a dynamic process in which security and consolidation are balanced and causes of conflicts are eliminated. The objective of ensuring security should not hinder development, and a comprehensive approach addressing all aspects at the same time is necessary.

The most important condition is the establishment of security, or at least a safe environment in order to start the societal rebuilding process. Necessary steps are the Demobilisation, Disarmament and Reintegration (DDR) of former combatants. As part of the reconstruction process, security sector reform (SSR) needs to be pursued with the objective of contributing to a secure environment conducive for development.[7] Often, a new structure for the military, border guards and police has to be created. In addition, the repatriation of refugees and the return of internally displaced persons must be facilitated. Another significant step is the establishment of self-sustaining governance under the rule of law. In order to achieve justice, warlords, war criminals and human rights violators need to be prosecuted. In addition, complete justice and law enforcement reform needs to be initiated. All these steps go hand in hand with the rebuilding of national institutions and economic recovery programmes. The challenge is to combine all necessary measures in a way that stabilises the country in the short- and long-term and at the same time is perceived as right and fair by the population and elites.[8] In short, post-conflict reconstruction is aimed at 'preventing the outbreak, the recurrence or continuation of armed conflict.'[9]

As other chapters in this book testify, bearing in mind the complexity of this process, a holistic approach is needed and an overall strategy must be developed by the mandated international actors as a first step. The strategy should describe the end-state, i.e. the desired final status to be achieved in the final stage of the post-conflict reconstruction process. Then, an implementation plan should be developed in conjunction with national actors. The plan would describe the tasks of all political, civilian, economic, humanitarian and military actors, all international organisations and, if possible, the NGOs working in the field. Ideally, the reconstruction process should be led from within the country, and local ownership should be enabled as early as possible. But, often the international conditions do not allow for such optimal solutions. There are frequently different political agendas and a lack of common political will. Moreover, no blue print exists for a successful post-conflict reconstruction policy and as each war-torn country is different, there is a need for a specific, tailor-made approach for each international operation.

Risks and Threats in Post-Conflict Environments

Post-conflict reconstruction confronts the international community with a range of security risks and threats, which domestic authorities and their security forces need to tackle. Apart from societal obstacles there are interlinked challenges: the prevalence of small arms and light weapons; the fight against belligerents, insurgents and terrorist groups; the influence of external and internal spoilers; corruption and bribery; organised crime; drug cartels and human trafficking.[10]

In every post-conflict society, an overabundance of small arms and light weapons (SALW) in private and governmental hands poses a serious threat for the stabilization process.[11] As a recent survey points out, between 60 and 90 percent of deaths in violent conflicts are caused by SALW.[12] One example illustrates the key issues. After the collapse of the Taliban regime in 2001, the new Afghan government and international actors failed to disarm paramilitary groups. Security experts have identified 500 illegal armed groups[13] and SALW are used by warlords and drug dealers to create or maintain local power bases. In addition, SALW have been employed in terrorist attacks against the International Security Assistance Force (ISAF) and civilians. What is more, Afghan drug cartels play a major role in international drug production with 89 percent of opium currently from Afghanistan,[14] and corruption, organised crime and warlords have seriously hampered economic recovery. The massive poverty in many regions has thus not been overcome.[15] In sum, security in Afghanistan has not been achieved and there is a high risk that the country will return to violence and conflict. BiH and Kosovo also face organized crime syndicates, which greatly undermine the local economy and thus security. There, the 40 to 50 percent unemployment rate clearly demonstrates that economic recovery has not been accomplished, and corruption and bribery are rife. According to Transparency International, BiH is highly corrupt and confidence in the national government is low.[16] One probable result is that foreign financial assistance is gradually siphoned off, thus slowing down economic investments as well. The acid rhetoric of some ethnic groups' political leaders, as witnessed in BiH, Serbia and Kosovo, do not support reconciliation. There is ethnic animosity, tensions and civil unrest. External spoilers from neighbouring countries or even from other regions have a strong, often negative, impact on future development. BiH and Kosovo still face dramatic structural deficits – for example 90 percent of the minorities in Kosovo remain unemployed.[17]

Add to this the absence of protection and preservation of minority rights and the challenge of integrating the continuous return of refugees and it is evident that the basic prerequisites for a stable and multi-ethnic society are simply not present. The occurrence of new violence and riots in Kosovo in March 2004 was clearly a direct result.

All these risks and threats require evaluation by a range of experts with political, economic, judicial, humanitarian, police and military credentials, coming from different countries and international organisations. In short: there is a need for a comprehensive risk analysis to identify the most critical areas of concern and provide policy-makers with a sound basis to begin planning their post-conflict reconstruction strategy.

EU Concepts and Post-Conflict Reconstruction

As van Eekelen argues in Chapter Five, the experience gained from the 1999 Kosovo crisis pushed the EU member states to develop a European Security and Defence Policy (ESDP) under the umbrella of the Common Foreign and Security Policy. Since then the EU has undertaken various steps along the path and direction of an original form of post-conflict reconstruction policy.

Since the first ESDP operation, the European Police Mission (EUPM) in BiH in January 2003[18], the EU has been fully engaged in post-conflict reconstruction and the Political and Security Committee (PSC) has become the main political body preparing decisions in the field of ESDP, with its supporting EU Military Staff (EUMS) and Military Committee planning military operations on the strategic level.[19] But, the European Commission is a critical partner of ESDP. Before its demise (or rather integration into other financial instruments) in 2007, the Rapid Reaction Mechanism (RRM) created in 2001 had become an effective tool. It allowed the European Commission to react fast to crisis or emergency situations[20], while civil-military co-ordination (CMCO) endeavoured to facilitate interlinkage between all the EU's component parts. Yet the institutional struggle for influence in Brussels between the Commission and the EU Council with its various sub-bodies has been compounded by the diversity of different programmes – initiated by both institutions – and the cumbersome method of financing arrangements for ESDP operations. A cohesive policy has not been attained.[21]

It was above all the Balkan region that became the main area of the European Commission's engagement and of ESDP operations. The creation of the Stability Pact for South East Europe at the EU summit in Cologne in June 1999 was the first important initiative to rebuild the Balkan region.[22] The Pact, to be succeeded by the Regional Cooperation Council in 2008, is divided into three working tables. Democratic, economic and security issues are discussed on a biannual basis with representatives of around 80 countries and organisations. In particular, the working table on economic reconstruction, development and regional cooperation, placed under the responsibility of the European Commission, plays a vital role in post-conflict reconstruction.[23] By creating the Stabilisation and Association Process for the Western Balkan countries, the EU has developed an efficient tool to strengthen cooperation between the three EU pillars and present a strong incentive for these countries to fulfil their political requirements. Since autumn 2005 the Commission has been negotiating with BiH to integrate the country into this process as a further step on the way to EU membership.[24]

As part of its stabilisation concept, in February 2000 the EU initiated a European Agency for Reconstruction (EAR). This became its main reconstruction arm, assisting the process of fast recovery in Kosovo.[25] Its main tasks have centred on management of the implementation of specific EU programmes funded by the Commission that are designed to support good governance, institution building and the rule of law as well the development of a market economy through investment in critical infrastructure and environmental protection. They also focus on social development and the strengthening of civil society. Today, the EAR is the main economic tool in preparing the Balkan countries for future EU membership. Since 2000, €5billion have been channelled to the Western Balkans[26] with the EAR supporting local ownership in the reconstruction process and working within the framework of the Community Assistance for Reconstruction, Development and Stabilisation (CARDS) programme.[27]

The European Security Strategy, adopted in December 2003, underlines the EU's comprehensive approach to security.[28] The 'Battlegroup concept' was recently designed to provide the forces required to mount a rapid response to a crisis and has been operational since 2007. The EU is now able to deploy and engage two concurrent single battalion-size task forces simultaneously; thus the EU now possesses a military capability able to respond to small crises.[29] On 20 July 2006 the EU Gendarmerie Force (EGF) was declared operational. The EGF will be engaged in crisis areas with up to 800 police officers in the spectrum of civil security actions, either on its own or in parallel with military forces.[30] The changing international situation and the challenges of post-conflict reconstruction led in 2005 to the creation of a Civil-Military Cell, established within the EUMS. This was an important milestone, as the EU thereby enhances its ability to coordinate and combine its capabilities and financial resources. This should address the rather artificial distinction between civil and military missions.[31] Finally, the EU Presidency and the European Commission have developed an EU concept for SSR, already intensely implicated in a range of SSR related activities. The clear understanding that a single EU concept was needed meant the EU's Council of Ministers welcomed the Commission's later 'Concept for European Community Support for SSR'[32] on 12 June 2006 and acknowledged that the EU should hereafter 'take a comprehensive and cross-pillar approach to SSR.'[33]

In sum, the EU has created, and is still creating a variety of civilian as well as military concepts, tools and capabilities. Yet there remain many difficulties within the EU and its institutions in terms of organising, financing, coordinating and carrying out missions. The EU bureaucracy and the national interests of the EU member states often hamper consistent action. In addition, the parallel engagement of the EU High Representative for CFSP, the EU Special Representative in the country, ESDP missions, the European Commission and the EU member states are not conducive to coherent policy-making. The EU should doubtless reinforce its capacities, improve its performance and the efficiency of its measures in the field, as other chapters in this volume underline and as the EU's external relations Commissioner has argued.[34] Without a comprehensive strategy for post-conflict reconstruction the coherence of all available EU instruments is clearly jeopardised.

NATO's Concept for Post-Conflict Reconstruction

After the fall of the Berlin Wall, NATO adapted its policy, strategy, military capabilities, integrated structure and the employment of its means. Its engagement in the Western Balkans has been crucial to the development of its concept of peace support operations and its role in post-conflict reconstruction. In its Strategic Concept, adopted in April 1999, NATO declared that it supports all efforts to rebuild and reconstruct the economies and democracies of war-torn regions and to be active in the peaceful resolution of conflicts.[35] Its missions and tasks in BiH, Macedonia, Kosovo and Afghanistan present valuable and insightful hints as to how NATO understands its role in stabilisation operations. From NATO's point of view, peace support operations are multi-functional. They include a range of different missions, from peace enforcement, peacekeeping and peacebuilding to humanitarian operations. In other words, peacebuilding 'covers actions which support political, economic, social and military measures and structures aiming to strengthen and solidify political settlements in order to redress the causes of conflict; this includes mechanisms to identify and support structures which can play a role in consolidating peace, advance a sense of confidence and well-being and supporting economic reconstruction.'[36]

NATO's experience over the last ten years has shown that it can cover the full spectrum of military missions, from conflict prevention (Macedonia), peacemaking and peacekeeping (IFOR/SFOR in BiH) to conflict resolution (Kosovo air campaign). For NATO it has been a constant process of learning, adaptation and political compromise.[37] NATO's primary role in peace support operations is to separate and keep apart warring factions, disarm militias and belligerents, control and destroy heavy weaponry and carry out demining operations, thus securing peace and bringing stability to a war-torn country in accordance with the relevant mandate. In addition, the employed military forces give direct and indirect assistance to all parties involved. They patrol cities and routes, guard military and civilian sites, escort civilian agencies, offer engineering support, rebuild infrastructure, inform the local population, support the political authorities in the pursuit of indicted war-criminals, support the election process and train domestic armed forces and advise policemen. In addition, NATO is involved in stabilisation activities (NATO HQ in Sarajevo, Skopje and Tirana) providing training and advice in SSR. Through the concept of civil-military cooperation (CIMIC), formal relations between the military commander and civilian national and local authorities are established in the field. Further, the population, international organisations and non-governmental organisations within NATO's area of responsibility are encouraged to participate as well. CIMIC is conducted in support of the mission and allows cooperation and co-ordination with civilian actors, the accomplishment of civilian tasks and/or access to civilian resources.[38] It should be noted that NATO's engagement is generally limited to military and defence organisations.

Since 12 June 1999 the Kosovo Force (KFOR) mission has aimed at creating a secure environment for a political solution and the reconstruction process. The KFOR operation implemented a process of demilitarisation, demobilisation and reintegration (DDR) of former combatants. As part of the overall objective of building self-governing structures and confidence within society, the process of DDR is crucial and always necessary. Armed groups have to be demilitarised and demobilised, under the auspices of military and police forces, and they must be reintegrated into civil society and the legal framework.[39]

Another major political decision, NATO's military concept for defence against terrorism, can be seen as a direct answer to 9/11. Since 2002 NATO's military operations have encompassed tasks such as Anti-Terrorism, Consequence Management, Counter-Terrorism and the active combat of terrorist activities in the field, in particular in Afghanistan.[40] Since August 2003 NATO has provided security in Afghanistan; ISAF conducts in parallel a peace support and post-conflict reconstruction mission. The aim of ISAF is to help stabilise the country and create long-term conditions for self-sustaining peace. During this operation a new concept was developed, known as the Provincial Reconstruction Team (PRT). These PRTs have numerous objectives and they facilitate the reconstruction through patrolling, monitoring, influence and mediation, and extending the authority of the central government. They are an effective method of providing assistance to rebuild provinces, and more importantly to establish security, build confidence and provide coordination and assistance in the actual reconstruction phase.[41] Several countries have chosen their own approach for PRTs, and only recently has co-ordination by HQ ISAF been established. In particular, the US PRT concept focuses mainly on counter-insurgency rather than on rebuilding.[42]

Lastly, NATO has also developed policies for combating organised crime and trafficking in human beings. It is NATO's aim to promote democratic control and implement all necessary requirements of an effective security sector through cooperation, common programmes and tailored training. In addition, NATO initiates long-term security enhancement through the Partnership for Peace (PfP) cooperation programme with Serbia, Montenegro and BiH.[43]

To conclude, NATO plays an essential military role in securing peace and security in former war-torn countries and it has demonstrated successfully that it is constantly implementing lessons learnt. However, NATO has not defined its role in post-conflict reconstruction[44], and it should clearly develop a strategy, which includes the political and civilian aspects of this important task.

EU – NATO Cooperation

The next section first provides a brief description of the formal decisions agreed by the two organisations and then an assessment of whether different national agendas have an impact on cooperation. A third section analyses their strategic partnership in the field and outlines how the EU and NATO are handling cooperation mechanisms. This should allow an answer to the key question of whether greater efficiency can be achieved through improved coordination of policies and capabilities or through a division of labour.

Formal Agreements between the EU and NATO

The EU and NATO share the same interests in managing international crises. Their common comprehensive framework in shaping a mutual strategic partnership determines that 'NATO and EU officials meet on a regular basis at different levels: at foreign ministers' level twice a year; at ambassadors' level – EU PSC and North Atlantic Council (NAC) – a minimum of three times per semester; at the level of the Military Committee twice every semester; at the committee level on a regular basis; at staff level on a routine basis.'[45] On 16 December 2002, the two organisations signed the 'NATO-EU Declaration on ESDP'. Both declared their willingness for effective mutual consultation, equality, due respect for autonomous decision-making and finally for a coherent, transparent and mutually reinforcing development of their military capabilities.[46] The shadow of the Iraq crisis severely hampered the implementation of this declaration and only step by step could a better basis for cooperation be achieved. In 2004, the logic of cooperation became even stronger with both organisations' respective enlargements. As of 1 January 2007, 21 of 27 EU member states are NATO allies; in addition 4 EU states are PfP members. However, the only cooperation on post-conflict reconstruction involving the top political bodies, PSC and NAC, has been the operation in BiH. By the end of 2005, both organisations also agreed to establish two liaison cells, one in SHAPE and the other in EUMS.[47] Finally, the EU High Representative for CFSP and the NATO Secretary General meet regularly to improve the cooperation framework.

The important 'Berlin Plus' agreement signed on 17 March 2003[48] is a practical framework allowing the EU access to NATO's planning capabilities, command facilities, collective assets and military capabilities. The agreement is a 'technical manual not … a political tool'[49] and has been used for two EU-led operations. On the highest political level, both organisations have declared their willingness to interact and cooperate in several Summit and Council communiqués. The joint meetings on all levels, especially those of PSC and NAC, show that long-lasting cooperation is possible. However, not all member states are willing fully to support the strategic partnership. The formal meetings, including the transatlantic dinner, where EU and NATO foreign ministers meet and discuss cooperation issues, have thus been unproductive and there is a lack of close cooperation in post-conflict reconstruction.[50]

National Agendas Hampering EU-NATO Cooperation?

If, despite the initiation of an institutional framework, the partnership remains far too limited in scope[51], the essential reason is that domestic agendas and national interests are influencing governments' policies and attitudes towards both the EU and NATO. Some examples of such different national policies illustrate the point. US policy is dominated by a global mindset, often strongly influenced by military considerations. Since the US sees NATO as the primary military decision-making body in Europe, it supports ESDP as long as it does not compete with NATO. In addition, the US government wishes to set policy on when and how to act, seeing itself as clearly leading the Alliance, including its relationship with the EU.[52] In contrast, France favours strengthening the EU and ESDP. France endeavours to limit NATO's role in the long-term. Consequently France does not support ambitions to develop civilian assets for NATO and pushes for autonomous EU decision-making without taking NATO's agenda into account.[53] A third country, Turkey, as a NATO member, has a strong impact on ESDP. Its national approach can easily lead to blocking NATO support for EU missions.[54] Since December 2004 Turkey has been obstructing all developments beyond the ongoing operations under the framework of Berlin Plus, because of its unwillingness to cooperate with Cyprus. Further, Malta and Cyprus are not included in high-level talks, since they do not possess bilateral security agreements with NATO.[55]

The Berlin Plus agreement only applies, in any case, to military cooperation and to a limited set of operations. Berlin Plus was never intended to facilitate the political decision-making process or give priority to NATO or the EU in case of the engagement of one or both organisations. The agreement only applies when a political decision has been taken and the result is an EU-led operation using NATO assets.[56] EU-NATO cooperation in times of crisis is decided on a case-by-case basis and requires unanimous consent in the EU Council and the NAC. In principle, NATO can also decide to recall its assets during an ongoing EU-led operation under Berlin Plus, though this is very unlikely. The Berlin Plus agreement is a political compromise that facilitated the first ESDP military operations. It is a reflection of the past and some of the needs of the present; but it does not present a vision for the future. New strategic tasks and interests demand new political, civilian and military approaches and new capabilities. Military crisis management always has to be combined with political and civilian measures for recovery and reconstruction. A further constraint is the simultaneous employment of assigned military forces by the EU and NATO, because they have to be taken from a single set of national forces. The future employment of the NATO Response Force and the EU Battle groups may also cause political conflicts between the organisations and their member states. As a variety of member states see themselves in the driver's seat, every decision in each organisation is not only highly political, but clearly difficult to obtain. If the member states are not willing to overcome current difficulties, the different national approaches are likely to constrain future common post-conflict reconstruction efforts.

Institutional Cooperation in Operations

Although national agendas have hampered EU-NATO cooperation on the political level, considerable progress has been achieved in the field, in particular in BiH, which is regarded as a great success, and in Kosovo and Afghanistan which are analysed in detail below.

Bosnia and Herzegovina

After the Dayton agreement ended the war, the IFOR/SFOR missions stabilised the country, and during the last 11 years significant progress has been achieved and fundamental reconstruction efforts are visible on the ground. A special EU-NATO cooperative effort in the SSR process occurred when the reestablishment of police structures was supported by EUPM through the assistance of SFOR's Multinational Specialised Units. EUPM also created strong relations with SFOR and coordination between the two can be characterised to be very good.[57] The second operation under Berlin Plus, EUFOR, succeeded NATO's SFOR mission starting on 2 December 2004.[58] Overall, the handover from SFOR to EUFOR can be considered the most successful example of cooperation. Despite some political quarrels at the beginning, the organisations have worked together pragmatically, and EUFOR and NATO share the same building in Camp Butmir. While EUFOR is now providing day-to-day security in the country, the small NATO Headquarters primarily assists BiH and its government in defence reform and in preparation for PfP membership. Additionally, both EUFOR and NATO are engaged in the pursuit of war crimes fugitives.[59]

The EU Special Representative (EUSR)[60] has played and still plays a vital role in promoting EU policy and representing the international community. He coordinates all EU efforts, giving political guidance to EUFOR and EUPM, thus linking civilian and military actions. To coordinate and guide all activities in BiH, he chairs regular meetings with EUFOR, EUPM, the EU Monitoring Mission, the EU Presidency and if feasible with the European Commission delegation.[61] In addition, he coordinates his activities and initiatives with other international organisations such as the OSCE and NATO, and on a personal basis he meets regularly with NATO political and military representatives. However, a specific role of the EUSR in the handover process from SFOR to EUFOR was not visible.[62]

As its efforts concentrated on the smooth handover process, the EU failed to create strong cooperation between EUPM and the EUFOR Althea operation in the beginning, in particular in the fight against organized crime. This changed in 2005 and EUFOR was able positively to shape the situation of the country.[63] In addition, EUFOR established multinational Liaison and Observation Teams (LOT) as a means of ensuring closer cooperation with the population and local administration.[64] In the field, cooperation between EUFOR and the Commission's delegation on a number of high-value CARDS projects has been sound.[65] Despite the EU having parallel structures under the umbrella of ESDP and the programmes of the Commission, these instruments are sensible tools to support reconstruction. They are paving the way for BiH's progress towards integration in the EU. Since 1991 the EU has committed more than €2.5 billion to BiH.[66] However, political reconciliation in the country has not yet been achieved; the three ethnic entities do not share a common vision for the future. Peace has thus not yet been secured. Parliamentary and presidential elections have recently shown that BiH is still deeply divided along ethnic lines.[67] A continuous EUFOR presence will thus be necessary, according to Bosnian government officials.[68]

The EU and NATO have demonstrated in BiH that their cooperation can be very fruitful. Implementing the lessons learnt in Macedonia, the political and in particular the military bodies of the two organisations worked together closely before and after the handover from SFOR to EUFOR. Unfortunately, the EU and NATO have not been innovative enough to elaborate together a strategic assessment of the future development of BiH, to consolidate all SSR issues within the EU and to ensure that the international community speaks with one voice with common objectives. Even the EU still has work to do in order to persuade all member states that they should provide national assistance in line with the agreed EU policy.

Kosovo

Under UNSC Resolution 1244, responsibilities are divided between the UN (police, justice reform and civil administration), the OSCE (democratisation and institution building) and the EU (reconstruction and economic development).[69] Co-operational approaches within the established mandates were not on their agendas. KFOR was not part of UNMIK and its objective was 'to maintain a safe and secure environment and to foster understanding and tolerance in a multi-ethnic society.'[70] Each KFOR Commander worked closely with the UN Special Representative of the Secretary-General, thus supporting the political objectives of UNMIK. As intelligence gathering remained a military task, KFOR elaborated its own threat analysis, thus preventing the development of a comprehensive risk analysis on the political level. The military contribution to reconstruction was coordinated through CIMIC teams and initiatives of several national contingents. In this context, KFOR Headquarters could not streamline the national policy of the assigned contingents, which resulted in often conflicting methods of engagement and sometimes contradictory agendas.[71]

The EU's contribution started in 1999, when it took the lead in the reconstruction efforts. Within UNMIK, the EU was responsible for pillar IV, economic development, and it has devoted over €1.6 billion to Kosovo for that task.[72] Reconstruction operations were conducted under the auspices of the European Agency for Reconstruction (EAR). For EAR it was obvious from the very beginning that it would not be able to assist in reconstructing the region without the support of KFOR. However, this did not cause EAR to consult regularly with KFOR before planning their projects.

It appears almost certain that the EU will take over part of UNMIK's role in Kosovo once the status talks are terminated and the UN Security Council has agreed upon a new mandate. On 10 April 2006 an EU Planning Team (EUPT) was initiated to prepare the EU for that task. In the beginning EUPT only focussed on a smooth transfer of authority from selected tasks of UNMIK,[73] thus a linkage with KFOR was not created. Subsequently cooperation in the field has strongly improved, and the KFOR Headquarters fully supports the planning process of the EU. On the highest political level however, Turkey is currently blocking closer cooperation between NATO and the EU.

The eruption of violence in March 2004, the current difficult economic situation and the dwindling confidence in international actors need to be analysed thoroughly. The open status question clearly led to growing discontent, and as long as the final status is not decided, economic recovery and successful reconstruction is unlikely to be possible. Despite some remarkable progress on the ground, the international community has not been able to govern Kosovo as a promising quasi-protectorate in an effective manner and to solve the root causes of the conflict. As Wim van Meurs rightly argues: 'With no real stake in these territories, international representatives insist on quick results to complex problems; they dabble in social engineering but are not held accountable when their policies go wrong.'[74] In order to start a more effective reconstruction process, a long-term perspective for Kosovo has to be created as soon as possible. A coherent and unified strategy of the international actors – the UN, OSCE, EU and NATO is – vital.[75]

The stabilisation and reconstruction mission combines an equal place for military forces, for international police and for civilian experts in political, economic, judicial and social affairs. Cooperation between the EU and NATO in Kosovo has been far too limited. Owing to the acceptance and use of the 'stovepipe principle'[76], both organisations have developed their contribution to Kosovo's security and development more or less in isolation and on an ad-hoc basis. Not surprisingly, they have concentrated their efforts on their key mandates: NATO has achieved its military mission by securing peace and by ensuring a safe environment for reconstruction, and has thus remained a purely military instrument. The EU has been the key driver in economic recovery and rebuilding of infrastructure, thus remaining a fundamental donor and the international economic mechanism for the development of the country. Yet, both organisations failed to create the necessary synergies among themselves and the international agencies involved. As long as the political leaders of some EU member states and NATO nations negate the necessity of enhanced cooperation, structural deficits will continue and no coherent reconstruction policy is likely to be developed and implemented.

Afghanistan

Since August 2003 NATO has led the UN-mandated ISAF operation in 'assisting the Afghan authorities in providing security and stability, paving the way for reconstruction and effective governance.'[77] NATO has gradually expanded its mission throughout the country and since October 2006 its operation has indeed covered the whole territory. ISAF troop levels have increased to 35,000 with the assignment of former US Coalition Forces from Operation Enduring Freedom (OEF).[78] It works closely with the Afghan government on all levels, ISAF forces fulfilling a variety of tasks, from fighting the Taliban insurgents and terrorists to training the Afghan National Army, humanitarian assistance, reconstruction and development projects in cooperation with international agencies and NGOs.[79] The ISAF concept for stabilisation includes the use of CIMIC to integrate local authorities in the reconstruction process. Projects, such as the rebuilding of schools, the reestablishment of water and power supplies and support in health, education and technical issues, have been carried out successfully by ISAF. In particular, the Provincial Reconstruction Teams (PRTs) serve as one of the focal points for international reconstruction assistance, and they work closely with UNAMA[80] field representatives.

The EU is engaged in the reconstruction of Afghanistan through its support of the Bonn (political) process and the Afghanistan Compact for a stable and democratic Afghanistan. The Joint Declaration of 16 November 2005 outlines increased cooperation, based on Afghan ownership, across a range of areas. These include support to political and economic governance; SSR and judicial reform; counter-narcotics; development; human rights, civil society and refugee return; education and culture.[81] The European Commission and the EU member states pledged more than €3 billion in aid for the period 2002–2006.[82] And on 29 January 2007 the EU Commissioner Ferrero-Waldner presented her plans for 2007-2010, a package worth €600 million.[83]

The EU and NATO have not signed a specific document clarifying their roles and cooperation, albeit a monthly meeting is held among senior international officials to increase cohesion of effort. In addition, the EUSR in Afghanistan[84] regularly visited NATO political authorities in Kabul and Brussels in order to enhance cooperation. According to Afghan officials, both organisations are making 'an effective contribution to the training of the armed forces and the police, as well as to the renewal of central and administrative structures in Afghanistan.'[85] However, a co-operative framework between ISAF and the EU is not visible, although EU member states and European NATO nations are highly involved in reconstruction.[86] Here again, significantly, the EU does not speak with one voice.

The Bonn process, the parallel military operations of Operation Enduring Freedom (OEF) and ISAF as well as ISAF's concentration in Kabul in the beginning of the operation did not allow a comprehensive approach for post-conflict reconstruction. Moreover, the willingness of various countries, including the key players within the EU, to take over responsibility for specific functions in rebuilding Afghanistan, without detailed coordination with NATO or the EU, demonstrates engagement without an overall strategy. The reasons for the lack of institutional cooperation between the EU and NATO are multi-faceted. The different PRT approaches, the parallel initiatives of EU member states, the activities of the European Commission, the limited responsibilities of EUSR and the different national policies *vis-à-vis* ISAF, clearly prove that nation-states decide, picking their part of the reconstruction efforts. But, they do not use the EU and NATO to create synergies.

In the run-up of the NATO summit in Riga in November 2006 it became evident that international engagement has only been partly successful on the ground. Various reasons need highlighting. First, NATO's mission is 'the most under-resourced international stabilisation operation'[87] since it has been engaged in peace operations. Second, less international aid per capita has been delivered in comparison to many other countries.[88] Third, the PRT approach goes in the direction of regional stabilisation, but a long-term approach for the entire country is still underdeveloped. Fourth, despite threats such as Taliban insurgents, terrorist attacks, warlords, organized crime, SALW, mines, drug production and trade being identified, their eradication is not yet part of a common and comprehensive security and reconstruction concept. Fifth, problems arising from the unsecured border between Afghanistan and Pakistan, refugee camps in Pakistan, and failing Pakistani political control in some border regions have not so far been tackled. Finally, different national policies are not helpful in profiling a coherent assistance program towards Afghan society. Reconciliation and confidence building are dwindling, the state institutions are far from functioning adequately, and the influence of religious fanatics is currently again increasing.[89] These signs should alarm the EU and NATO. Both organisations should, ideally, adjust their Afghanistan policies together with the Afghan government as quickly as possible and further increase considerably their political, military and civilian engagement.[90]

Lessons Learned and Best Reconstruction Practices

For several years the EU and NATO have been highly involved in post-conflict reconstruction. The handover in Macedonia and the transition from SFOR to EUFOR has provided proof of their ability to cooperate successfully. The EU-led Operation Althea is often quoted as a good example of lessons learnt as the EU structures worked adequately and NATO's support functioned very well. Overall, military cooperation under the Berlin Plus agreement is working smoothly and the establishment of two liaison cells in EUMS and SHAPE is offering an even stronger link for future military cooperation. Nevertheless, political agendas in some capitals and the interaction between the EU institutions in Brussels are currently hampering effective cooperation. As we have seen, neither organisation has yet elaborated a comprehensive concept defining and describing how to stabilise and reconstruct a war-torn country.

As far as the EU is concerned, the establishment of a Civil-Military Cell within EUMS is a first positive approach to tackling post-conflict reconstruction as a holistic concept. Within the EU a single command structure on both the political/strategic and operational/field levels is needed, and cooperation between the three pillars must be significantly improved. The EU bureaucracy should no longer slow down the implementation of decisions. Reform of EU structures and procedures in Brussels is a prerequisite for the development of a coherent EU policy capable of rapid action and effective civil-military cooperation. The nominated EUSR in a country should have the political responsibility for all aspects of an EU mission, including political, military and economic issues. He or she should possess the authority to give clear directives to the military force commander and to all EU representatives. Both the political and the military leader should work together closely, having integrated military and civilian experts in their staffs to ensure a better understanding of political, economic, civilian and military thinking.[91] We recommend taking all these aspects into account when developing an EU post-conflict reconstruction concept.

NATO remains predominantly a military instrument and its engagement is mainly focused on military issues. It therefore has to change its policy and capabilities if it intends to become a key player in post-conflict reconstruction. Both CIMIC and the PRT approaches provide suitable measures for the long-term process of post-conflict reconstruction. However, stabilisation and reconstruction operations need much more than the military solutions NATO can provide. It is vital that NATO nations agree upon a comprehensive reconstruction strategy. This could lead to the build-up of specific stabilisation forces in addition to CIMIC forces, the establishment of guidelines for cooperation with other international organisations and civilian partners within a post-conflict reconstruction operation and the development of its own civilian assets. However, early creation of a stronger strategic partnership with the EU would be welcomed, as this would avoid duplication with available EU instruments.

With the EU taking the lead in civilian matters, such as police and judicial reform and economic recovery, and NATO responsible for military affairs, both seem to have established silently a natural division of labour. Yet this has only happened accidentally and varies from case to case, so it would be useful if this kind of task-sharing could become a deliberate policy, integrated into a comprehensive strategy. Parallel military engagement of both organisations as in BiH should be avoided or specifically aimed towards clearly identified objectives.

As current cooperation on the political level is considerably impeded by some governments, a 'common steering committee' between the EU and NATO as a preparatory forum might prove a sensible innovation. This forum could begin as an informal setting for some representatives, purely designed to develop options and recommendations for closer collaboration. These findings could then be discussed in joint PSC-NAC meetings. In addition, discussions might be envisaged related to cooperation on those cases where both organisations are currently involved. A project-oriented approach might achieve positive results. One case might be the need for stronger collaboration in Afghanistan. If the EU is to be drawn, at some point, to take over the responsibilities of UNMIK, close cooperation with NATO might prove more than a simple spin-off. The potential for the failure of post-conflict reconstruction in Afghanistan is substantial. In Kosovo it is still high. Increased cooperation between the EU and NATO in the field would be highly desirable. Creating 'operational steering groups' on a permanent basis might lead the way to more substantial cooperation in due course.[92] These groups would have the potential to enhance common understanding and facilitate cooperation. Further, all EU member states and NATO nations supporting reconstruction efforts on a bilateral basis might coordinate their additional assistance through these operational steering groups; the aim being to develop a common and coherent approach of the EU, NATO and their member states in the field.

Against this potential it is worth noting that some EU and NATO member states have recently created new national structures, which carry the potential to enhance cross-fertilisation. In particular, the United Kingdom and Germany have developed plans and institutions that allow for a better and more efficient use of national assets in post-conflict reconstruction. The UK concept is creative from an institutional and operational point of view. The establishment of a Post Conflict Reconstruction Unit within the national system enables the UK and its partners through an 'integrated assessment and planning support, underpinned by operational capability, to deliver more effective stabilisation operations.'[93] In particular, it focuses on governance, security and justice and is seen as an instrument to assist the UK government in post-conflict stabilisation through its 28 representatives from five government departments. The unit is already linked with the UK PRT in Helmand Province, Afghanistan, and is also represented in the UK embassy in Kabul. Germany focuses more on a civilian conflict resolution approach, though it does not neglect the role of the armed forces. The German concept includes NGOs, private local actors, social programmes and country-specific discussions – all necessary to cover the basic needs of a post-war society. The aim is to establish mechanisms for an overall concept via interministerial cooperation. The German PRT concept, based on a new interministerial approach, brings together the military, diplomats, police, humanitarian assistance and economic development experts in a single structure.[94]

These two national initiatives demonstrate the ability to link civil and military tasks and to overcome the traditional 'stovepipe' approach. The EU and NATO might profit from an evaluation of all structures, plans, lessons learnt and in particular the OECD initiative, which favours the establishment of a close link between security, development, good governance and democracy in post-conflict reconstruction. Most importantly, both organisations should cooperate under a common and coherent post-conflict reconstruction concept to prevent ineffectiveness and thus the recurrence of violence and conflict.

Conclusion

The EU and NATO have achieved encouraging results in their areas of responsibility. Their cooperation in BiH and the resultant stabilisation of the country is the most prominent example. The handover from SFOR to EUFOR using the Berlin Plus framework functioned effectively. In Kosovo and Afghanistan, EU-NATO cooperation has been very limited, in particular on the political level. No specific, tailor-made concept has been developed, and the traditional stovepipe approach prevails in both organisations. In the context of post-conflict reconstruction, a common understanding has not been elaborated and at present a strategic partnership exists only on paper.[95]

Overall, in contributing to reconstruction and sustainable peace, both organisations have achieved many goals in their respective operations and engagements, but this rather general comment should not hide the fact that neither organisation has established and initiated its own post-conflict reconstruction concept. Importantly, without a clear political strategy, the reconstruction of a war-torn country is unlikely to be successful. And such a strategy should include a series of criteria: end-state, risks and threats, securing peace, DDR, SSR, justice, rule of law, police, financial regulations, as well as ways and means to achieve these objectives. National caveats should be limited and made clear from the very beginning, so that political and military leaders are able to take them into account when planning their mission and acting on the ground. The implementation of this strategy should result in a safe environment, good governance, an effective security sector and successful economic recovery. By achieving these conditions, both organisations would finally be able successfully to terminate their missions.

The EU and NATO need to understand that neither organisation is able to rebuild a war-torn country alone. Both need to recognise their own strengths and limitations in post-conflict reconstruction. So far, the EU has not been successful in developing a coherent approach for ESDP operations and post-conflict reconstruction. Yet, it does possess all essential economic and civilian tools for effective implementation of the necessary measures in post-conflict reconstruction. NATO's military capabilities are highly suitable for stabilising a war-torn country, thus creating a safe environment for rehabilitation, reconciliation and recovery. But NATO does not possess the necessary tools to act as a key enabler for reconstruction. Both organisations need strong partners.[96] Both actors could profit from each other, because they share the same values and are directed towards the promotion of democracy, human rights, rule of law and market economics, including free trade. Both could use the capabilities and resources of the other organisation, provided both follow a common strategy for post-conflict reconstruction.

As the political struggle between the EU and NATO seems unlikely to diminish in the near future, we recommend the establishment of new mechanisms – the initiation of a common steering committee at the political/strategic level and operational steering groups at the operational/field level. Both organisations, bringing their strengths to the forefront and willingness to secure peace, need to cooperate in a more effective way both politically and operationally in the field, thus achieving a higher degree of complementarity and cooperation.

If the EU and NATO are not able to solve their political differences and rivalry during the coming years, duplication of tools and efforts will be unavoidable. Without strong partners, NATO is doomed to fail in Afghanistan, and the failure would have severe consequences not only for the country, but also its neighbouring states and for the Alliance as a whole. The danger of an even greater transatlantic rift cannot be underestimated. It should certainly be avoided by all EU member states and NATO nations. As the NATO Summit Declaration in Riga has shown, EU-NATO cooperation has not been given a high priority. We therefore recommend the establishment of an EU-NATO High-Level Policy Group as soon as possible. The Policy Group should consist of high-ranking politicians, practitioners with field experience (Heads of Missions, etc.) and academic experts. The group should make an independent evaluation of the EU and NATO and their future security policy challenges. It should assess the current and future political role of both organisations, their strengths and weaknesses, the possibilities of a truly strategic partnership and elaborate recommendations for a division of labour and the development of a common and comprehensive post-conflict reconstruction strategy. The report should be presented to the PSC and NAC in a joint meeting.

To conclude, an independent Policy Group along the lines advocated in this chapter would have the potential to develop essential proposals that could substantively improve overall cooperation between the EU and NATO. Further, it could lead to the development of a common post-conflict reconstruction strategy and a more effective, tailor-made contribution of all EU member states and NATO nations in future stabilisation and reconstruction operations.

Endnotes

1 See Dan Smith, *Towards a Strategic Framework for Peacebuilding: Getting Their Act Together: Overview of the Joint Utstein Study of Peacebuilding.* (Oslo: Royal Norwegian Ministry of Foreign Affairs, 2004)

2 Alan Bryden, Timothy Donais, Heiner Hänggi, *Shaping a Security Governance Agenda in Post-Conflict Peacebuilding,* (Geneva DCAF, November 2005), 1

3 Boutros Boutros-Ghali, *An Agenda for Peace: Preventive Diplomacy, Peacemaking and Peacekeeping,* A/47/277-S/24111. (New York: United Nations, 1992). Peacebuilding: 'Actions taken to identify and support structures which will tend to strengthen and solidify peace in order to avoid a relapse into conflict.'

4 http://en.g8russia.ru/docs/19-print.html *G-8 Declaration on Cooperation and Future Action in Stabilization and Reconstruction,* G-8 Summit, 15-17 July 2006 (accessed 24.10.2006).

5 Radek Sikorski, 17. Forum Bundeswehr und Gesellschaft, Berlin, 23.10. 2006 (Welt am Sonntag, 29.10.2006 Ausgabe 44/06, p. WS1)

6 Jaap de Hoop Scheffer, Global NATO: Overdue or Overstretch? (Brussels 6 November 2006) http://www.nato.int/docu/speech/2006/s061106a.htm (accessed 08.11.06)

7 A commonly agreed definition of SSR does not exist, although the OECD Development Assistance Committee has developed a very useful concept. See: Heiner Hänggi, Fred Tanner, *Promoting security sector governance in the EU's neighbourhood*, Chaillot Paper n. 80, (Paris July 2005), 16f; Jayantha Dhanapala, Keynote Address, (Brussels 28 June 2006): 'In a narrow sense, SSR can reflect a state-centric understanding of security, focusing on those public sector mechanisms responsible for the provision of external and internal security, as well as on the relevant civilian bodies responsible for their oversight, management and control. But SSR as part of post-conflict peacebuilding requires a far broader perspective.' As each conflict is different, 'there is no generic SSR model.' http://www.jayanthadhanapala.com/wsPeaceSecurity.html (accessed: 17.11.06)

8 OECD, *Policy Brief: Security System Reform and Governance: Policy and Good Practice*, (May 2004), www.oecd.org/dataoecd/20/47/31642508.pdf (accessed 24.10.2006)

9 S/PRST/2001/5 of 20 February 2001. in: Smith, *Towards a Strategic Framework for Peacebuilding*, 20.

10 International Crisis Group, *Countering Afghanistan's Insurgency: no quick fixes.* Asia Report N.123 (2 November 2006), 2 www.crisisgroup.org/home/index.cfm?id=4485&1=1 (accessed 06.11.2006)

11 Albrecht Schnabel; Hans-Georg Ehrhart, *Security Sector Reform and Post-Conflict Peacebuilding* (New York: United Nations University Press, 2006), 1.

12 Small Arms Survey, *Weapons at War* (Oxford: Oxford University Press, 2005), 3.

13 Christopher Alexander, 'NATO and the EU in Afghanistan: Post-Conflict Achievements and Challenges'. In: NATO Defence College, *NATO-EU Cooperation in Post-Conflict Reconstruction*, NDC Occasional Paper 15 (Rome: CSC. GRAFICA s.r.l., 2006), 67.

14 United Nations Office on Drugs and Crime, *2006 World Drug Report* (Vienna: United Nations, 2006), 1.

15 International Crisis Group, Report N. 123 (02.11.06), 8 www.crisisgroup.org/home/index.cfm?l=1&id=4485

16 For more information see: Transparency International, *Corruption Perception Index 2005* (2006). http://www.transparency.org/policy_research/surveys_indices/cpi/2005 (accessed: 29.08.06)

17 Marie-Janine Calic; *Der Westen beschönigt die Lage auf dem westlichen Balkan*, In: Internationale Politik, IP 61 (2006), S.86-95

18 EUPM supports local police forces in BiH in the fight against corruption and organised crime. 500 police officers from 30 countries help to establish sustainable policing arrangements under the control of BiH. The mission has been extended until the end of 2007. In: Hans-Georg Ehrhardt / Burkhard Schmitt, *Staatszerfall, Gewaltkonflikte und 'Nation-Building' als politische Herausforderung für die EU*. In: Hans-Georg Ehrhardt / Burkhard Schmitt (Hrsg.), *Die Sicherheitspolitik der EU im Werden*, 45ff; 51; 57. The EU launched its first military peacekeeping operation CONCORDIA in Macedonia (March-December 2003).

19 PSC is monitoring and controlling missions and giving strategic guidance to the responsible political authorities and/or military commanders on the ground. See Graf von Kielmannsegg, Sebastian, *Die Verteidi-gungspolitik der Europäischen Union* (Stuttgart: 2005), 276ff.

20 Reinhardt Rummel, 'Soft-Power EU. Interventionspolitik mit Zivilen Mitteln'. In: Hans-Georg Ehrhardt / Burkhard Schmitt (Hrsg.), *Die Sicherheitspolitik der EU im Werden* (Baden-Baden: 2004), 259ff.

21 Annika S. Hansen, *Against all Odds – The Evolution of Planning for ESDP Operations*, 36

22 Stability Pact for South Eastern Europe, *Achievements and Chronology. What is the Stability Pact?* (2006) http://www.stabilitypact.org (accessed: 31.08.06)

23 Gunther Hauser, *Regionale Sicherheit für Mitteleuropa. Militärische und polizeiliche Kooperationen* (Wien: 2005), 62.

24 Marie-Janine Calic; *Der Westen beschönigt die Lage auf dem westlichen Balkan*, In: IP 61 (2006), S.86f

25 EAR: an independent EU agency, accountable to the European Council and the European Parliament, overseen by a Governing Board composed of representatives from 25 EU Member States and the Commission.

26 see: European Agency for Reconstruction. http://www.ear.eu.int (accessed: 05.09.06)

27 CARDS is an EU programme supporting the participation of the countries of the Western Balkans in the EU's Stabilisation and Association Process, see Richard Zink, 'The EU and Reconstruction in the Western Balkans'. In: NATO Defence College. *NATO-EU Cooperation in Post-Conflict Reconstruction*, 45; see the EU Commission's description http://ec.europa.eu/enlargement/financial_assistance/cards/index_en.htm

28 European Union, *A Secure Europe In A Better World*. European Security Strategy (2003), 2; 6-9.

29 Jan Joel Andersson, *Armed and Ready? The EU Battlegroup Concept and the Nordic Battlegroup*, http://www.pana.ie/idn/010406.html (accessed 17.11.2006)

30 http://www.eurogenfor.org 800 persons in 30 days could be deployed.

31 It comprises both military and civilian planners including two representatives from the Commission. In: Council of the European Union, *Bulletin of the EU Military Staff. IMPETUS. The Way Ahead* (2006), 8.

32 Commission of the European Communities, *Communication from the Commission to the Council and the European Parliament*, (Brussels, 24 May 2006) COM (2006) 253 final

33 Council of the European Union, *Council Conclusions on a Policy framework for SSR* (12.06.06) www.ue2006.at/en/News/Council_Conclusions/1206SecuritySectorReform.pdf (accessed 17.11.06)

34 Benita Ferrero-Waldner, *Europa als globaler Akteur. Aktuelle Schwerpunkte Europäischer Aussen- und Nachbarschaftspolitik*. In: *Sicherheit+Stabilität*, No.1 (Berlin: Berliner Wissenschafts-Verlag, 2005), 7-22; 8, 13.

35 The Alliance is committed to a broad approach to security, which recognises the importance of political, economic, social and environmental factors in addition to the indispensable defence dimension. In: NATO, NAC-S(99)65 – 24 April 1999, (1999).

36 Military Technology, *Crisis management – A Fundamental Security Task. The NATO Experience and Euro-Atlantic Partnership* (No. 9/2006), 57-65.

37 Mihai Carp, 'NATO Policy and Perspectives on Reconstruction Operations and NATO-EU Cooperation'. in: NATO Defence College, *NATO-EU Cooperation in Post-Conflict Reconstruction*, 37ff.

38 Hänggi, Tanner, *Promoting security sector governance*, 23; NATO, MC 411/1. Reinhardt Rummel, *Soft-Power EU. Interventionspolitik mit Zivilen Mitteln*, 259f.

39 GTZ, NODEFIC, PPC, SNDC, *Disarmament, Demobilisation and Reintegration. A Practical Field and Classroom Guide* (Frankfurt 2004), 21.

40 The NATO Summit in 2002 endorsed the Partnership Action Plan against Terrorism. In: NATO, International Military Staff. *NATO's Military Concept for Defence Against Terrorism*, (Updated 14.04.05), 3. http://www.nato.int/ims/docu/terrorism.htm (accessed: 06.09.06)

41 NATO, ISAF (2006) http://www.jfcbs.nato.int/ISAF (accessed: 19.09.06); NATO, ISAF. *Primary Role* (2006) http://www.afnorth.nato.int/ISAF/mission/mission_role.htm (accessed: 08.06.06)

42 US PRTs contain 50-100 U.S. military personnel, civil affairs officers from the Defence Department, rep. from USAID, the state department and other agencies. In: Kenneth Katzman, *Afghanistan: Post-War Governance, Security and U.S. Policy*. RL30588 (Washington: CRS Report for Congress, updated 23.08.06) 24.

43 Other NATO tools are: the Planning and Review Process (PARP), the Membership Action Plan (MAP), the Individual Partner Action Plans (I-PAPs) and the Partnership Action Plan for Defence Institution Building.

44 See *Comprehensive Political Guidance*, endorsed by NATO Heads of State and Government on 29 November 2006, (Riga 29 Nov. 2006), http://www.nato.int/docu/basictxt/b061129e.htm (accessed 30.11.06)

45 The former NATO SecGen Lord Robertson and the Swedish EU Presidency exchanged letters to define the scope of cooperation and the modalities of consultation between the two organisations. NATO, Issues. NATO-EU: A Strategic Partnership (2006) http://www.nato.int/issues/nato-eu/index.html (accessed: 11.09.06)

46 see: *Ibid*. Declaration was based on decisions at the NATO Summit 1999 and the EU Council in Nice 2000; Riga Summit Declaration, 29 Nov.2006, http://www.nato.int/docu/pr/2006/p06-150e.htm (accessed: 30.11.06)

47 National Defense University, Institute for National Strategic Studies. *NATO and the European Union: Improving Practical Cooperation.* A Transatlantic Workshop organized by the Institute for National Strategic Studies in Partnership with the Ministry of Defence of Finland (Washington D.C, March 20-21, 2006), 2.

48 Paul Cornish, *EU and NATO: Co-operation or Competition?* European Parliament (Brussels October 2006), Policy Department External Policies, Briefing Paper, EP-ExPol-B-2006-14

49 Quoted from a participant on a conference in 2003. In: International Crisis Group, *EU Crisis Response Capability Revisited.* Crisis Group Europe Report No.160 (17 January 2005), 29.

50 Volker Heise und Peter Schmidt, *NATO und EU: Auf dem Weg zu einer strategischen Partnerschaft?* (Berlin: 2006), 10ff. http://www.kas.de/upload/dokumente/trans_portal/nato-eu.pdf (accessed: 12.10.06)

51 Rühle, Michael, *Different Speeds, Same Direction. NATO and the new transatlantic security agenda. In: Internationale Politik, Transatlantic Edition* (Berlin: Summer 2006), 81.

52 R. Nicholas Burns, *The US vision of NATO's future*, 17. Forum Bundeswehr und Gesellschaft, Berlin, 23.10. 2006 (Welt am Sonntag, 29.10.2006 Ausgabe 44/06, p. WS1) and Stuart M. Seldowitz, *EU and NATO Relationship.* see: http://www.defence-conference.de/pressebericht.asp (accessed: 09.10.06)

53 Annika S. Hansen, *Against all Odds – The Evolution of Planning for ESDP Operations*, p.43. During the planning process for the DARFUR engagement France blocked a NAC decision, as it wished to secure a leading role for the EU and therefore the EU had to decide first (24 May 2005).

54 Turkey is often not willing to work together with Greece and Cyprus in any decision making bodies.

55 These developments have led to informal NAC-PSC meetings after formal meetings in 2005 in order to talk about future operations, e.g. in Darfur. These meetings include Malta and Cyprus, too.

56 Paul Cornish, *EU and NATO*, 10

57 Annika S. Hansen, *Against all Odds – The Evolution of Planning for ESDP Operations*, 44

58 CONCORDIA is not covered in detail. EUFOR derives its mandate from UNSC Resolution S/RES/1575 (2004). For EUFOR the 22 EU member states and 11 non-EU countries provide 7,000 soldiers.

59 Julie Kim, *Bosnia and the European Union Military Force (EUFOR): Post-NATO* Peacekeeping, CRS Report for Congress. (CRS: The Library of Congress, Updated January 5, 2006), 3. (accessed: 04.10.06): http://www.usembassy.it/pdf/other/RS21774.pdf#search =%22NATO%2BBosnia%2BEUFOR%22

60 The EUSR is double-hatted since April 2002, when he took over the responsibilities of the former UNSR. The EUSR reports back through the PSC and the High Representative of CFSP and he briefs the Commission representatives in theatre.

61 Annika S. Hansen, *Against all Odds – The Evolution of Planning for ESDP Operations*, 36f; see the extended mandate of EUSR www.eusrbih.org/legal-docs/1/?cid=512,1,1 (accessed 28.05.07)

62 For more information about the EUSR see: http://www.eusrbih.org (accessed: 10.10.06)

63 David Leakey, Interview in: *ESDP newsletter*, Issue 1, December 2005, p.23

64 Rolf Schlüter, 'EUFOR – Der deutsche Beitrag im elften Jahr nach Dayton', in: *Europäische Sicherheit* 6/06,79

65 David Leakey, 'ESDP and Civil/Military Cooperation : Bosnia and Herzegovina, 2005', 69 in: Anne Deighton, Victor Mauer (Ed.), *Securing Europe?*, Zürcher Beiträge zur Sicherheitspolitik (Zürich 2006)

66 International Crisis Group, Europe Report N. 160 (17 January 2005), 50 http://www.crisisgroup.org

67 Gulfnews.com, *Bosnians split on country's future*, (AP: 10/02/2006)

http://archive.gulfnews.com/world/Bosnia-Herzegovina/10071929.html (accessed: 03.10.06)

68 Kim, *Bosnia and EUFOR: Post-NATO Peacekeeping*, 6.

69 NATO Review, *Istanbul Summit Special* (Brussels, NATO Public Diplomacy Division, 2004), 25.

70 NATO, Allied Command Operations. *SACEUR visit to Kosovo* (03 August 2006) http://www.nato.int/shape/news/2006/08/060803a.htm (accessed: 15.09.06)

71 Jean Callaghan, Mathias Schönborn (Ed.), *Warriors in Peacekeeping. A Comparative Study based on experiences in Bosnia* (Münster 2004), 419f and Andreas Heinemann-Grüder, Igor Grebenschikov, 'Security Governance by Internationals: The Case of Kosovo', 45 in: *International Peacekeeping* 13 (2006) H.1; This fact not only raised tensions among national contingents (force protection, mission picking due to national caveats, humanitarian initiatives), but it caused tensions between the military and the non-military actors and between some military contingents and the local population as well.

72 for more details see: http://www.euinkosovo.org/uk/about/about.php (accessed: 09.10.06)

73 Official Journal of the European Union, Council Joint Action 2006/304/CFSP (10 April 2006), Art.2,3; Annika S. Hansen, *Against all Odds – The Evolution of Planning for ESDP Operations*, 50

74 Wim van Meurs, *Europäische Politik für den Balkan und Kosovo neu gedacht. Überlegungen zum Report der Internationalen Balkankommission* in: Südosteuropa-Mitteilungen, 45/3 (2005), 11.

75 Cees Coops and Peter Faber, *Kosovo – Strategic Options for the Future?* Research Paper No.19 (Rome: NATO Defense College, May 2005), 7.

76 The 'stovepipe principle' means that each organisation or each department within an organisation works on its own without taking into account the responsibilities, tasks and performance of others.

77 NATO, *NATO in Afghanistan* (2006) http://www.nato.int/issues/afghanistan/index.html (accessed: 19.09.06)

78 see http://www2.hq.nato.int/ISAF/structure/structure_structure.htm (accessed 21.11.06)

79 General Ray Henault, Chairman of NATO MC. In: NATO, IMS, *NATO's Top Officer Comments on Expansion of ISAF operations* (2006) http://www.nato.int/ims/news/2006/n061005e.htm (accessed: 11.10.06)

80 United Nations Assistance Mission in Afghanistan, http://www.unama-afg.org

81 European Commission, *The EU's relations with Afghanistan* (2006) http://ec.europa.eu/comm/external_relations/afghanistan/intro/index.htm#intro (accessed: 22.09.06)

82 See http://europa.eu.int/rapid/pressReleasesAction.do?reference=MEMO/05/309&format=HTML&aged. Brussels, 08.09.05 *Afghanistan: How EU support is making a real difference* (accessed: 08.11.06)

83 http://www.delafg.ec.europa.eu/en/whatsnew/index.htm#7 (accessed: 28.05.07)

84 Klaus-Peter Klaiber, *The EU in Afghanistan, Impression on my term as Special Representative*, National Europe Centre Paper 44 (Canberra 2002); Klaiber was followed by Francesco Vendrell

85 Haquani, Zulmaï, 'NATO, The European Union, and Civil Reconstruction in Afghanistan'. In: NATO Defence College, *NATO-EU Cooperation in Post-Conflict Reconstruction*, 58.

86 Germany: Training of the national police; Italy: Judicial reform; UK: Combat drug production and trade; Japan: DDR; US: ANA and Canada: Demining.

87 Roland Paris, *NATO: Go Big or Get Out* (25 October 2006), in: *The Globe and Mail*, http://aix1.uottawa.ca/~rparis/Globe_25Oct2006.html

88 Roland Paris, *idem*; Der Spiegel, *Sterben für Kabul* (19.11.06), 34

89 International Crisis Group, *Countering Afghanistan's Insurgency: No Quick Fixes*, Asia Report N.123 http://www.crisisgroup.org ; NATO / Konrad Adenauer Stiftung, Conference Report 'The Challenge of Stabilization and Reconstruction: How to improve International Cooperation', Brussels 16/17 October 2006

90 Bert Koenders, President of the NATO Parliamentary Assembly, Speech to the NATO Summit, (Riga 29 November 2006)

91 ISIS Europe, *Future of ESDP: Lessons from Bosnia*, Number 29, (June 2006) http://www.isis-europe.org

92 Klaus Reinhardt, *KFOR. Streitkräfte für den Frieden* (Diessen: Balzek & Neumann, 2002), 549ff.

93 Post Conflict Reconstruction Unit, *PCRU & Stabilisation; Achievements* (London: Post Conflict Reconstruction Unit, 2006) http://www.postconflict.gov.uk (accessed: 18.09.2006)

94 Auswärtiges Amt, *Zivile Krisenprävention, Konfliktlösung und Friedenskonsolidierung* (Berlin: AA 2006) http://www.auswaertiges-amt.de/diplo/de/Aussenpolitik/Frieden Sicherheit/Krisenpraevention/Uebersicht.html (accessed: 09.10.06)

95 Riga Summit Declaration, 29 Nov. 2006, http://www.nato.int/docu/pr/2006/p06-150e.htm (accessed: 30.11.06)

96 Julian Lindley-French, *Big world, big future, big NATO*, (NATO Review 2005 Issue 4), http://www.nato/int/docu/review/2005/issue4/english/opinion.html

15. Supporting Security and Justice – the OECD approach to Security System Reform

Mark Downes and Graham Thompson[1]

Introduction

The challenge of tackling insecurity and conflict as a barrier to political, economic and social development remains high on the agenda of the international community. If states are to create the conditions in which they can escape from a downward spiral wherein insecurity, criminalisation and under-development are mutually reinforcing, socio-economic and security dimensions must be tackled simultaneously. The issues we face today – transnational crime, corruption, terrorism, etc. – are not new but have drawn more attention to the nexus of security and development issues. Donors have learned hard but valuable lessons from their efforts to help build peace and prevent slippage back into conflict in the aftermath of war. The experience of the Democratic Republic of the Congo, Kosovo and East Timor, to name but a few, have highlighted the important role that security system reform can play in creating viable and sustainable states and supporting the establishment of the rule of law.

In addition, a number of recent high profile reports have emerged which question the effectiveness of the current international aid architecture to pro-actively prevent, or effectively deal with, the outbreak of violence. The 2005 report from the UN Secretary General's High Level Panel on Threats, Challenges and Change, *A More Secure World: Our Shared Responsibility*, calls for a rethink in how to deal with conflict and underlines the interconnected nature of contemporary threats to security. This was further emphasised in the subsequent report from the UN Secretary-General, *In Larger Freedom: Towards Development, Security and Human Rights for All*, which reiterates the call for an effective international response to the new security paradigm.

This chapter aims to chart the development of OECD Development Assistance Committee (DAC) thinking on SSR, termed security *system* reform by OECD DAC, which underlines the positive role that SSR can play in stabilising fragile, conflict-prone or conflict-affected states. The DAC's 2005 *Guidelines on Security System Reform and Governance* underline that an accountable and efficient security system, operating under civilian control within a democratic context not only reduces the risk of violent conflict but is the necessary component for the creation of an enabling environment for development to occur.[2] Building on this work the OECD DAC has developed an operational manual, *The OECD DAC Handbook on SSR: Supporting Security and Justice* – that provides practical guidance to donors on supporting partner country SSR processes. This handbook was developed through a process known as the Implementation Process for Security System Reform (IF-SSR) which brought together lessons learned from the engagement of the international community in security and justice reform over the last decade. The lessons learned through this process will be critiqued in light of current donor practice. Finally, this chapter will put forward issues for consideration as part of the next generation of SSR engagement.

Role of the OECD DAC – Harmonising SSR Policy and Practice

The Organisation for Economic Cooperation and Development's Development Assistance Committee brings together the major bilateral donors with their multilateral counterparts from the UN, World Bank, IMF and EC to tackle issues of aid effectiveness, harmonisation and alignment. Established in 1961, the DAC has, over the last decade, been at the cutting edge of conflict, peace and security policy. In particular, its work on SSR has become the international point of reference and challenged donors to consider the nature of their support to security and justice reform.

The cost of neglect and the consequences of conflict, in terms of infrastructure, social capital and investment, is all too evident. According to the 2005 *Human Development Report*, 'violent conflict is one of the surest and fastest routes to the bottom of the HDI [human development index] table – and one of the strongest indicators for a protracted stay there'. The cost has been estimated to be somewhere between $4bn and $54bn.[3] With Official Development Assistance globally estimated to be approximately $100bn in 2006, it is clear that one conflict has the capacity to wipe out or undermine the potential benefits of the investment made in development assistance in any given year. With increasing awareness of the need to prevent the outbreak and slippage back into conflict, bilateral and multilateral actors work through the OECD DAC Network on Conflict, Peace and Development Cooperation (CPDC)[4] to improve their collective efforts to help conflict-prone and conflict-affected countries establish structures and mechanisms to manage change and political conflict through democratic and peaceful means.

The DAC has worked collectively to develop a joint policy on support to SSR. This policy, as outlined in the 2005 *DAC Guidelines on Security System Reform and Governance* (hereafter referred to as the DAC Guidelines on SSR), has helped donors think through the importance of support for the development and reform of security and justice structures. The enhanced focus on security in terms of service delivery and accountability provided a much needed governance approach to the traditional donor engagement in this field. The impact of this work can be seen in the inclusion of the DAC principles on SSR in both the Commission and Council Concepts of SSR.[5] Similar initiatives by other DAC members led to the development of specific national policies or strategies on supporting security system reform.

As with all development policies, without the knock-on effect on field level behaviour, policies are of limited value. For that reason the DAC has also focused on harmonizing donor practice through the development of practical guidance on supporting security system reform. The *OECD DAC Handbook on Security System Reform: Supporting Security and Justice* (hereafter referred to as the 'OECD DAC Handbook on SSR') has been developed through a two year process that brought together the development community with their security and diplomatic colleagues and also, most importantly, the views, perspectives and experiences of practitioners from partner countries. The result is a manual that incorporates knowledge on the political, governance and technical nature of SSR, and which is based on experience gathered on conflict prevention and peacebuilding over the last decade throughout the developing world. Almost as important as the handbook, is the process that helped develop it. The OECD DAC provides a forum for sharing lessons learned for tackling complex issues that require a collective response. As such the OECD DAC is viewed as a neutral broker in bringing together development, diplomatic and security actors.

Security for Whom?

The traditional concept of security is being redefined to include not only state stability and the security of states but also the safety, well-being and freedom from fear of their people. The recognition that development and security are inextricably linked is enabling security in partner countries to be viewed as a public policy and governance issue inviting greater public scrutiny of security policy. The manner in which the security system operates is central to the concerns of the poor and vulnerable. Ineffective policing, weak justice and penal systems, and corrupt militaries mean that the poor suffer disproportionately from crime and fear. Security and justice should be seen as a public good which it is the right of all citizens to enjoy and the responsibility of the state to guarantee. This understanding informs the need to see security and justice as a service delivery issue, which, like health and education, is of critical importance for supporting sustainable development and poverty reduction. A democratically run, accountable and efficient security system helps reduce the risk of conflict, thus creating an enabling environment for development to occur.

The recent debate within the donor community on the security–development nexus has not only placed the need for security square on the development agenda, but has also done much to shine a spotlight on the need for a coordinated and coherent approach to development from across donor governments. There is now a clear recognition that security of the state and security of the people are not the same, but they are mutually dependent. For this reason it is essential to recognise that the state itself can be the cause of insecurity, conflict and violence. Indeed in many environments, the absence of the state or the predatory nature of formal security and justice institutions can mean that in a range of contexts it is non-state actors who provide the natural recourse for people when it comes to both security and justice.

Such a recognition has a direct impact on the scope, focus, objectives and means of support for security and justice reform. Despite the key findings of the 2002 World Bank 'Voices of the Poor' report, which found that safety and security were top priorities of the poor, these issues are rarely considered in national development strategies. Understanding the security and justice needs of people is central to taking a developmental and governance approach to SSR. It moves away from the pure focus on developing the operational capacity of security forces, to enhancing service delivery and accountability. This does not exclude support for enhanced operational capacity but it does require that such support is conditional on there being progress in the development of adequate oversight and accountability.

It is important to recognise and understand who provides security and justice in countries. While donor support tends to focus on state structures, it is important to recognise the role that non-state actors play in the provision of security and justice services. It is estimated that in sub-Saharan Africa 70 to 80 percent of justice services are provided through non-state means.[6] While recognising the irreducible role of the state, this reality challenges how donors provide support to SSR processes and underlines the need to ensure more inclusive processes when defining SSR needs. That said, donors must recognise the risks associated with working with non-state actors who may also be the purveyors of insecurity and providers of injustice, and who, equally, may be unaccountable.

The Principles of Security System Reform

The security and justice system as defined by the OECD DAC includes all those institutions, groups, organisations and individuals – both state and non-state – that have a stake in, or can influence, security and justice provision. The DAC Guidelines on SSR state that the security system includes[7]:

- **Core security actors**: armed forces; police service; gendarmeries; paramilitary forces; presidential guards; intelligence and security services (both military and civilian); coast guards; border guards; customs authorities; and reserve or local security units (civil defence forces, national guards, militias).
- **Management and oversight bodies**: the executive; national security advisory bodies; legislative and legislative select committees; ministries of defence, internal affairs, foreign affairs; customary and traditional authorities; financial management bodies (finance ministries, budget officers, financial audit and planning units); and civil society organisations (civilian review boards and public complaints commissions).
- **Justice and the rule of law**: judiciary and justice ministries; prisons; criminal investigation and prosecution services; human rights commissions and ombudsmen; and customary and traditional justice systems.
- **Non-statutory security forces**: liberation armies; guerrilla armies; private security companies; political party militias.

Viewing the actors engaged in security and justice provision and/or oversight as a 'system' enables national authorities and international actors to consider how reform of one sector can affect another. Experience shows that international support to SSR is most effective when donor programmes take a strategic approach and help build linkages between reforms across the security system. For example, supporting the development of the police service in isolation of the broader criminal justice system often has limited impact.

It is also essential to be clear on the objective of support to security system reform. As outlined earlier, the change of focus from a state centric approach to security that entailed the provision of capacity to the 'core security actors' towards a more comprehensive understanding of security, places a focus on security and justice service delivery, governance and accountability. The main objectives of SSR, as defined by the OECD DAC, are to enhance security and justice service delivery (see Figure 3), which underlines the need to work with state, non-state and oversight actors. The need to take a comprehensive or holistic approach to understanding security requires understanding who provides security or justice and the array of actors that can influence the (in)security.

The focus on service delivery also forces donors to consider the impact of their support. The previous focus on the provision of 'training and equipment', meant that the evaluation of success of SSR programmes depended on the ability to train X number of police officers in Y number of months. However, when viewed in terms of service delivery, what is measured is the impact of training on experience and perceptions of (in)security or access to justice amongst beneficiaries, i.e. citizens. The overall objective, therefore, of international support to security system reform processes is to increase the ability of partner countries to meet the range of security and justice challenges they and their people face, 'in a manner consistent with democratic norms, and sound principles of governance and the rule of law'[8], as defined in the *DAC Guidelines on SSR*. SSR helps create a secure environment conducive to other political, economic and social developments, through the reduction of armed violence and crime.

The focus for international actors should be to support partner countries in achieving four overarching objectives:

i) Establishment of effective governance, oversight and accountability in the security system.
ii) Improved delivery of security and justice services that are responsive to people's needs.
iii) Development of local leadership and ownership of the reform process.
iv) Sustainability of justice and security service delivery.

Basic working principles for donor support to SSR processes, as agreed in the policy statement in the *DAC Guidelines on SSR*[9], underline that SSR should be:

- People-centred, locally owned and based on democratic norms and human rights principles and the rule of law, seeking to provide freedom from fear and measurable reductions in armed violence and crime.
- Seen as a framework to structure thinking about how to address diverse security challenges facing states and their populations through

more integrated development and security policies and through greater civilian involvement and oversight.
- Founded on activities with multi-sectoral strategies, based upon a broad assessment of the range of security and justice needs of the people and the state.
- Developed adherence to basic governance principles such as transparency and accountability.
- Implemented through clear processes and policies that aim to enhance the institutional and human capacity need for security policy to function effectively and for justice to be delivered equitably.

Figure 3: *SSR to enhance security and justice delivery*

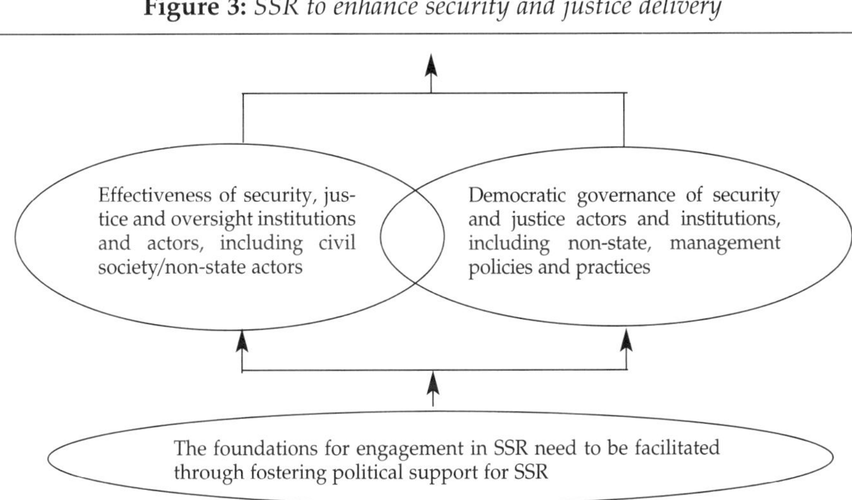

Source: OECD DAC Handbook on Security System Reform: supporting security and justice (2007)

Current Gaps in SSR Practice

While SSR is still a relatively new concept, there has been significant work undertaken and lessons learned in a number of security and justice sectors over the past decade. On the other hand, a number of challenges still remain. These challenges are outlined below:

Lack of a Coherent Strategy for SSR

The main challenge facing donors is the lack of a coherent strategy to support SSR, a strategy that encompasses the different resources available from across government. Donors continue to take an *ad hoc* approach to SSR, viewing the different sectors in isolation and not as an interconnected system. Donors, for example, continue to fund individual training programmes for the police without looking at how that training fits into the overall education system or how training on crime scene management needs to be understood in the context of how the police and prosecutors need to cooperate. Donors, collectively, need to view the system as a whole, to have a shared understanding of SSR and work collectively to provide coherent and coordinated support to partner countries.

Lack of Sufficient Capacity

The second main challenge facing donor governments is the lack of capacity available to support SSR. Bilateral and multilateral actors depend on serving police, military, prison and judicial officers to implement their programmes. While serving officers have technical expertise in their sectors, more guidance is needed to enable these officers to have a better understanding of: (i) the political nature of security reforms and (ii) the need to ensure reform linkages across the system. In addition, many have never been involved in a reform process and may require specific guidance on entry-points, programme design and SSR programme management. There is also the additional problem that there is a limited pool of serving officers, restricting the ability of donor governments to deploy such officers on SSR missions, when they are needed to ensure security and justice services at home.

A recognition that SSR is not only about increasing operational capacity but also about enhanced service delivery, governance and accountability, highlights that other skills are also required. Such skills include an understanding of institutional reform, change management, financial management, strategic planning, human resources and training. While there is a need to develop the strategic level skills to manage SSR support programmes, there is also the challenge for donor governments to ensure that the necessary skills (from either government or outside sources) are available and deployed at the right time.

Need to Enhance Oversight and Cross-Government Training

Programme officers in the field and in HQ could benefit from a stronger understanding of the technical as well as the political issues related to SSR. With the implementation of SSR programmes increasingly being subcontracted to private companies, programme officers need to have an in-depth understanding of SSR processes and sector-specific reform needs – to enhance the oversight of subcontractors and the development of an overall SSR strategy.

In tandem with a need to develop a comprehensive cross government strategy on SSR, there is a need to ensure that this is backed up with sufficient training and whole of government mechanisms to ensure a coherent approach to policy, planning and deployment. The DAC is developing training modules to support the dissemination of the *OECD DAC Handbook on SSR* and encouraging members to review their capacity and coherence across government.

Change of Approach Required to Make SSR Implementation More Effective

As the international community moves from an implementation approach that is designed around *ad hoc* projects focusing on specific aspect of sectoral forms, for example police training, towards a more strategic understanding of the linkages across the security system, there needs to be a requisite change in practice. Similarly, there needs to be a change in how the international community evaluates their actions in support of SSR, away from a focus on outputs (number of police, military or parliamentary personnel trained) and more towards looking at the impact of programmes and whether they have improved day-to-day security and access to justice for people.

The OECD Approach to SSR

Building on its 2005 policy guidance, the OECD has over the past two years focused on translating the policy guidance into an operational manual for donor government personnel. The process to develop the *OECD DAC Handbook on SSR* has brought together the development community with their security and diplomatic colleagues to harmonise their approaches and understanding of security system reform. The handbook largely follows the external assistance programme cycle and contains valuable tools to help encourage a dialogue on security and justice issues and to support an SSR process through the assessment, design and implementation phases. More importantly, it provides a platform to ensure a more coherent approach across donor governments and the international community by providing a framework that incorporates both the development and non-development aspects of SSR.

The OECD promotes a developmental or governance approach to SSR which aims to develop a security and justice system that is attuned to the needs of the public, tackles the causes of insecurity in a manner consistent with democratic norms and principles of good governance, including transparency and the rule of law. SSR is a long term process; in many cases it will require a culture change within security institutions, as the state's understanding of security evolves from one with an emphasis on regime security to one which espouses principles of human security. SSR is an inherently political process, dealing as it does with issues of power and control. It requires, however, significant technical input that encompasses a wide variety of expertise that include security and justice capacity, issues of management, and experience in the development of procedures for accountability and oversight.

In supporting SSR processes, donor governments need to draw on expertise from a number of government ministries if they are to provide the required assistance for a partner country's SSR process. As such, it is crucial that there is a shared understanding from the donor governments of the overriding principles that underline their SSR support. Respecting the competences and constraints of each party is essential to any co-operative arrangement across government. The best safeguard against possible abuse of the mandate of the agencies concerned is maximum transparency about objectives, allocations and operations.

Lessons Learned from the Process of Developing the OECD DAC Handbook on SSR

The process of developing the *OECD Handbook* included not only bringing together expertise from across government but also field-level experience from both national authorities and the international community. The international community has learned hard but valuable lessons over the last decade; these lessons challenge the international community to review how it provides assistance, have a more realistic view of time scales and an increased focus on ownership and sustainability.

Following the programme cycle the main lessons that have emerged from the IF-SSR process include:

Recognition of the Linkages between Security and Justice

The terms security and justice are often used throughout the handbook. This reflects the growing recognition that a people-centred approach to SSR requires that access to justice be placed at the forefront of this agenda. Security and justice are not the same and neither is subordinate to the other. However, in promoting an environment in which individuals and communities feel safe and secure, within which the rule of law is respected and sustainable development can flourish, it is important to recognise the linkages and the complementary nature of the relationship between security and justice. The handbook advocates an approach whereby desired outcome and context determine the priority, nature and scope of the programme. It argues that addressing the challenges faced by all citizens to achieve personal safety, security of property and access to justice should be the key determining factors in evaluating the success or otherwise of the donor programme of support. Generating public interest, understanding and engagement in SSR is therefore critical.

Preparing the (Political) Terrain for SSR (Building Dialogue, Understanding and Political Will)

The process leading up to reforms in the security system and ensuring political buy-in and local ownership can be as important as actually implementing the reforms. Incorporating an inception phase into programmes allows better understanding of the core problems and needs. An inception phase can be likened to a pre-assessment phase that would allow programmes to focus on building credibility and relationships through confidence-building measures with national interlocutors. The time spent developing local constituencies for SSR is a prerequisite for engagement on a technical level. The process of SSR is crucial, so time spent preparing the political terrain is time well spent. The inception phase will also allow the international community to gain an in-depth understanding of politics, security and the local situation, which will facilitate the identification of the major issues and reform needs. It will also allow an opportunity to assess possible strategies for supporting change initiatives; identify potential change agents; and seek out and understand any constituencies that may not favour reforms and their reasons, through, for example, undertaking a Drivers of Change and Power Analysis[10], and a Conflict Analysis.

Much of the engagement of the international community in this phase should be on identifying opportunities on which to build a broader SSR programme, for example, mapping experiences/programmes in-country, setting and managing expectations. This phase should also enable the development standards (baseline data) for monitoring and evaluation through, for example, experience and perceptions surveys within communities. The focus should be on building local ownership (identifying, supporting and building upon local initiatives; building local capacity to lead any reform programme into the future).

Developing an inception phase does not mean that donors cannot undertake programming. Indeed, quick impact programmes can help develop a donor's legitimacy, build local partners and help develop ownership. Examples of 'quick win/do no harm' activities include:

- South-South Dialogue;
- Roundtables on security and justice service delivery, parliamentary oversight, community policing, etc.;
- Training programmes and education: it is important to balance training on capacity with issues of accountability and governance, as there is a risk that security actors will latch on to capacity training and justify a narrow focus on certain specific issues;
- Exchanges.

The inception phase in many ways creates the space for a broader dialogue on issues of security and justice. It is important to be aware that the inception phase does not necessarily mean that a full scale SSR process will emerge. It may become evident that there is no added value from the engagement of the international community on the issue at a given time. In any donor government, different actors, with different interests may be engaged in aspects of SSR; it is therefore critical that during an inception phase development agencies ensure a coherent approach is taken within their government on how they will support the SSR initiatives of a partner government. Partners do not recognise distinctions between development, diplomatic and security actors: they perceive all activities emanating from a coherent donor government.

Engagement in post-conflict situations requires the need to differentiate between the stabilisation and development phase. It is important to recognise that each of the above phases have different objectives and require a different approach. The stabilisation phase can and should be used to prepare the ground for SSR, and the international community is not currently utilising sufficiently the potential role of DDR, peace support operations and peace agreements in preparing the terrain for SSR. Ensuring that these tools and approaches are designed and delivered in a coherent and coordinated manner, with each informing and supporting the other, is important in delivering effective support for the overarching peace-building objective. Financial sustainability of security structures developed in a post-conflict environment is also a key issue to be considered.

There are a number of contextual factors that make SSR more or less likely to occur. If the level of economic development, nature of the political system, and specific security situation are used as points of departure, a number of potential SSR contexts, or rather 'context clusters', emerge as typical – each reflecting a different rationale for reform:

- The developmental context in relatively stable developing countries (key criterion: socio-economic development);
- The post-authoritarian – primarily post-communist – context in transition countries (key criterion: political system);
- The post-conflict context in countries engaged in rebuilding the state after conflict (key criterion: security situation).[11]

Relatively good opportunities for externally-assisted SSR activities tend to exist in developing countries which have embarked on a process of democratisation after elections or other forms of peaceful change, in post-authoritarian transition states which aim at joining a regional organisation making democracy a requirement for membership (e.g. potential EU and NATO members), and in those post-conflict states in which international peace support operations offer a basis for reconstruction and local actors show a certain capacity and readiness for reform. In many other cases, however, prospects for externally-assisted SSR are rather difficult. In particular, this applies to countries in armed conflict, to fragile and 'post-conflict' states at early stages of conflict transformation, as well as to authoritarian regimes and so-called illiberal democracies where the will to reform is lacking. This does not necessarily mean that SSR should not be promoted in these countries, but that this task will be even more challenging with higher political risks attached than is the case in more conducive environments. The focus in these countries is less of a technical nature and more focused on providing support to non-state actors to enhance their scrutiny of security affairs and preparing the political terrain and understanding of SSR.

Conducting SSR Assessments

An SSR assessment should be undertaken in partnership with partner country actors in government and civil society. It should cover:

- Political analysis, the security context, capacity and governance, and the needs of the poor, marginalised groups and all citizens. Contextual analysis conducted in the inception phase and institutional assessment will help to identify constraints and opportunities in SSR.
- Ensuring a balance between building capacity (technical competence) and integrity (quality of governance) within security institutions is critical.

An SSR assessment can occur in tandem with, and be facilitated by, the inception phase. Unless an assessment is carried out in partnership with national authorities or is driven by local processes, the impact of the process will be limited, and in the long term it is highly unlikely that programmes will prove effective or sustainable. Assessment should also identify how donors' engagement can add value. How the reform process can be monitored and evaluated should be kept in mind throughout this phase. For instance, baseline data collection and other assessment activities need to ensure that basic standards are recorded that will facilitate future evaluations. Building local capacity and using local expertise is important when developing baseline data, though this may be more complex when conducting the political analysis component of the assessment.

Most work on conflict prevention and peace building requires a long-term commitment, and SSR is no exception. SSR requires improvements in the governance of security activities and, as such, is a particularly long-term task. It is also a politically sensitive endeavour. The international community needs to be realistic about what can be achieved in the short, medium and long term, and carefully match resources and policies to realistic programmes and strategies. There is a need to consider carefully a range of questions through analysis and assessment of the context. These include issues such as the risks of not engaging in SSR and, if engaging, what kinds of expectations and needs exist.

Designing SSR Strategies and Programmes

Central to a successful SSR process is the inclusion of capacity development for national planning, developing strategies and managing implementation. Programmes developed by the international community should not do the thinking and strategising for national counterparts. One-off or compartmentalised approaches should be avoided and a system-wide perspective is critical, though challenging.

Local Ownership needs to be the point of departure for the development approach to SSR. This will have a subsequent knock-on effect regarding the design of donor programmes to support a partner country's SSR process.[12] Such programmes should value process over product, for the unit of change for a reform process is the enhanced engagement of the state with the public on security issues, and not necessarily the policy document that results.

There are different approaches to designing an SSR programme or overarching strategy. A comprehensive/holistic understanding should inform a focused approach. Some options derived from practitioners and examples of current experience include taking or developing:

- An *issues-based/problem-solving approach* that involves focusing on one security issue as an entry-point to the wider security system. This approach may enable linkages to develop more naturally. Focusing on 'problem solving' can make the outputs of the reform process more visible and increase buy-in. Such an approach also results in the development of programmes that are designed to address key needs, as was the case in developing the Multi-Ethnic Policing Element in south Serbia in 2001 as part of the need to ensure basic security in a multi-ethnic and conflict prone environment.
- An *institutional approach* can be taken where there are existing pro-reform initiatives at an institutional level which can be supported, as was the case with prison reform in Nigeria in the late 1990s. There is also a need to support and strengthen linkages between security and justice institutions with this approach. For example, in South Africa

government policy is developed through clusters of ministries/departments whose work is interconnected. These clusters need to agree on key joint policies, objectives and priorities and then present them jointly, ensuring that ministries do not work in silos. They should also meet regularly to assess performance. One ministry can be a member of a number of clusters.
- *Government-initiated reviews* that facilitate a National Assessment process, as was the case in Jamaica in 2002.
- *Two-phased approaches* to post-conflict situations where the situation can range from executive authority (Bosnia/Timor Leste) to support to a post-conflict government (Sierra Leone/Sudan). In these instances, there is a need to differentiate between stabilisation and development. A two-phased approach involves securing the peace/stabilization, followed by ensuring stability through undertaking development oriented programming. Each phase requires different skills and focus.
- *Thematic-based engagement* which involves focusing on thematic issues such as juveniles, public order or elections, as is currently the case in DRC where the focus is on election security, or the role of sector-wide approaches (SWAps) in supporting planning and policy development as is the case in Uganda.
- An approach that creates the demand for reform by *working through civil society*. This approach was taken successfully in both in Ghana and Guatemala.
- *Poverty Reduction Strategies* (PRS) – or *National Development Strategies* that include the issues of SSR. This approach is under-utilised but helps put the issues on the national political agenda. Both Sierra Leone and Uganda (though their Poverty Eradication Action Plans) have utilised this approach to place security issues high on the government agenda.

Programmes need to be designed to be attuned to the political realities of both donor and partner country. This requires:

- Realism (achievable objectives, timescales, funding levels, political);
- Flexibility (knowledge management, encouraging innovation, rewarding lessons identified and acted upon); and
- Sustainability (building capacity, on-going affordability, local ownership, institutional absorption reflected in management processes, etc.).

The design phase should identify the right mix of skills required for implementation. Programmes also need to balance technical expertise with the necessary development skills, political awareness, change management, mentoring, communication skills, and project management skills. Time frames have to be carefully considered and realistic. Long-term time frames are needed. As already noted, donors and partners must work with an understanding of what is realistic when it comes to what reforms can be achieved. This realism has to be reconciled with the short-term donor financing mechanisms. There are risks inherent in the tension between what reforms are needed and what can be achieved in a short time frame and these need to be identified and managed.

Given the different skills required to support SSR, donors need to increase their national capacity, and provide joint training for government departments and technical staff (e.g. military, police, prison officers) on the developmental approach to SSR.

Implementing and Managing SSR

The process of developing an SSR strategy will vary from country to country and in different contexts. The chances of success will be significantly increased if it is a government-led process that is conducted in a participatory manner, supported by the international community as appropriate and local civil society organisations, women's groups and women leaders.

As national ownership and leadership are essential for effective SSR, it is important that structures, institutions and procedures are supported or developed from the outset that can manage and coordinate the change process. The implementation of SSR will require collaborative arrangements at the international, national and local levels. What should be avoided is an SSR process made up of, and implemented as, stand-alone projects with little or no co-ordination and consideration of larger national frameworks.

By utilising the inception phase, development agencies should be able to identify the most useful entry-point. When considering entry-points, agencies should look to balance short-term needs with an engagement that will help broaden out the reform process.

Some generic entry-points that have previously been used and which are highlighted in the *OECD DAC Handbook include*:

- *Capacity building*: the provision of training and equipment is the most obvious entry point and can help build confidence with national authorities. It also allows the transfer of norms and values from practitioner to practitioner, which can be a powerful tool in trying to change mindsets and institutional culture at a senior level. Such an entry point should be balanced with an agreement to tackle governance issues.
- *Development of a national SSR strategy*: this approach focuses on developing the analysis and strategy capacity at a national level and is useful for ensuring a sustainable reform process.
- *Good practice on managing public expenditure and public sector reform*: greater transparency and accountability in security spending and enhancing democratic accountability of the security services can lead to calls at a political level for more sweeping reforms. Including security institutions in public sector reforms places an emphasis on management procedure and practices, a central pillar of an SSR process.
- *Democratisation*: security issues should be included in any democratisation programme that aims to enhance civil society, the public, or national or local parliaments' understanding of their rights, responsibilities and obligations.
- *Legislative reforms*: in many cases, the legislative framework within which security institutions/actors operate is outdated. A legislative framework based on democratic principles or practices can have positive knock-on effects for how security institutions operate.
- *Addressing issues of crime*: places the focus on meeting the needs of the

public and can help make the change from a state-centric to a public-centred approach to security.
- *Building an attractive investment climate*: focusing on issues of insecurity and crime will also facilitate links to broader economic policies and rule of law reforms.

Some common challenges in SSR implementation are also addressed and the handbook provides practical advice on how these challenges can be overcome:

- *Develop an SSR Strategy*: a framework is required to guide the reform process, set benchmarks and highlight where development agency engagement is required and adds value.
- *Develop a communications strategy*: failures in communication have undermined many SSR programmes. Communication needs to happen at many levels, including between international actors, between international actors and national partner country governments, between government departments in the partner country, and between partner country governments and the public.
- *Focus on capacity-building*: international actors often get frustrated with the slow progress of programmes and begin to implement themselves, leaving local actors behind. While this may speed up the process, and sometimes lead to short-term outputs, it undermines long-term impact by alienating local stakeholders.
- *Don't weaken local institutions by poaching staff*: Experienced local staff are often in high demand in fragile states. International organisations are often tempted to poach local staff from partner governments and NGOs, but this can weaken the capacity of important local institutions.
- *Implement whole-of-government approaches*: coordinating the interventions of different departments in donor governments is sometimes as challenging as inter-donor coordination. The involvement of a myriad of actors, often with different agendas and objectives (e.g. counter terrorism vs. poverty reduction), can lead to different actors working at cross purposes.
- *Regulate private SSR contractors*: many donor-funded SSR programmes are now being implemented by private sector companies and NGOs. This trend towards contracting out has potentially significant implications for accountability and quality control.
- *Lack of continuity* of staff or having the right staff (at the right time) is a challenge: understanding the different personnel needs between crisis management (stabilisation) and stability (more development-oriented) missions is critical to ensuring the right expertise and technical skills are available for an SSR programme. Integrated teams that bring together technical expertise with the necessary political, management and communications skills are critical.
- *Oversight is often overlooked*: development agencies tend to focus on short-term, high visibility projects such as training; there is reluctance to engage in what can be difficult and challenging programmes that include accountability and management reform. With a balance between

enhanced capacity and governance, the impact of SSR programmes will be limited.

Donor Coordination and Harmonisation: Roles and Responsibilities

As with all development activities, donor coordination is a key but challenging endeavour. The political nature and cross-government interest in security issues, however, makes coordination of SSR all the more difficult.

When considering coordination mechanisms at field level, it is important to ensure that those coordinating the process will be there for the medium to long term, as that is the required timeline for SSR. In addition, there needs to be a clear discussion on the division of roles and responsibilities within the international community: contradictory roles will hamper implementation and undermine the legitimacy of engagement. For example, those who are evaluating the progress of the reform process cannot also be advisors to the government on reforms, as this would be tantamount to evaluating one's own engagement. So, a clear distinction between those who would coordinate and evaluate the engagement of the international community/the reform process and those who would work on programme/project implementation is essential if effective donor coordination is to be achieved.

Next Steps for the SSR Agenda

Identifying the Focus and Raising the Profile

SSR is still a relatively young agenda but significant steps have been taken in recent years to refocus its purpose around the objective of supporting human security. Central to this is the understanding of security as a public good and framing the SSR debate as a service delivery issue. It will be important that this service delivery approach informs how development agencies and the broader international community move forward with the SSR agenda. This understanding places citizens rather than institutions as the key beneficiaries of SSR support programmes. In turn, this demands that in the design of programmes the issue of who delivers security and justice services and the perceptions of beneficiaries are fully considered. Most importantly, it also requires that the success or otherwise of programmes is measured by their impact upon the levels of security and justice enjoyed by these beneficiaries. Given the growing consensus around the relevance of security and access to justice for individuals and communities in establishing an enabling environment to support sustainable development and poverty reduction, consideration should be given to establishing an overarching goal and benchmarks that will focus minds and provide incentives for both investing resources and measuring progress in this area – perhaps through a Millennium Development Goals equivalent of Security and Justice Development Goals.

Supporting the UN and other Multilateral Organisations to Develop their Corporate Strategy on SSR

The OECD work on SSR in many ways represents the latest thinking as regards SSR policy and practice. The OECD does not have field representation itself, but works through its members to gather practical experience, identify lessons and disseminate emerging good practice through encouraging the use of its materials at field level. The OECD work on SSR guidance has also actively sought to reach beyond the experience of its members alone. In this regard the process of developing the SSR handbook has benefited greatly from substantive input from practitioners from partner countries themselves who have to address the many challenges involved in taking forward SSR on a daily basis in a range of environments with or without assistance from the donor community. This range of inputs into the OECD guidance and the nature of the materials developed in seeking to bridge the gap between policy and practice and influence behaviour in the field should also be of benefit to others, particularly multilateral organisations, as they develop their SSR policies and guidance. As the UN, AU, and the OSCE (the EU has already developed its concept on SSR) for example begin to develop their corporate strategies on SSR, the OECD work should provide a platform from which to build. While it will be important not to 're-create the wheel', there is obviously a need to have a discussion within these organisations as to their mandate, focus and capacity to support SSR. The OECD DAC work will be a valuable input into that discussion and the need to ensure harmonisation of the basic principle and practices for supporting SSR, underlines the need for a continued dialogue between these organisations at a strategic but also field level.

Improving SSR Practice

The challenge for the SSR community is now to address the practical issues around improving its support for the delivery of security and justice. There are a number of high level policies in place and principles agreed. However, translating these principles into practical programmes that have real impact upon improving the lives of many people around the world who suffer insecurity, the fear of crime, violence and/or injustice on an on-going basis remains a work in progress. The devil, as they say, is in the detail and the focus for the SSR agenda needs to be around addressing the practical obstacles and hurdles in the field: gathering experience, identifying and sharing lessons and disseminating good practice in a manner that effectively influences policies in headquarters and behaviour on the ground. This requires dedicating resources to bring together policy makers and practitioners on a regular basis to share experience in forums which promote honest reflection and mutual learning. Participation in such forums should include practitioners, policy makers and civil society representatives from partner countries.

The OECD is well placed to support this approach amongst development actors, through the Security and Development task team of the DAC Network on Conflict, Peace and Development Cooperation (CPDC). Indeed the *OECD DAC Handbook on SSR* represents a significant step forward in addressing the gap between policy and practice, identifying key issues and providing guidance based on the evidence of experience. The process itself of developing the handbook has helped build a network of practitioners and policy makers from OECD and partner countries.[13] Further work on outreach and dissemination of the main messages from the handbook needs to continue to be developed and engaged as this work is disseminated. A community of users of the OECD DAC work should be developed which can provide regular feedback and enable future editions to be developed based on a broader evidence base. Issues such as the role of non-state actors in the delivery of security and justice need to be better understood and the OECD has made progress in this area with a guidance paper on the 'multi-layered'[14] approach to security and justice service delivery in fragile states. The next step will be for DAC members to identify opportunities to utilise this approach in the field. But there are other challenges as well where greater comparative experience from the field should be captured and shared. These include issues such as the politics of SSR and understanding decision making processes; addressing spoilers; building greater integration of approaches in a post-conflict environment, e.g. links between DDR and SSR; sequencing of programmes – particularly in post-conflict environments; and taking a justice sensitive approach to institutional reform within the security sector, to name but a few.

To complement the *OECD DAC Handbook on SSR*, the DAC Network on Conflict, Peace and Development Cooperation (CPDC) is in the process of developing an SSR training package and train-the-trainer course to help policymakers and practitioners. The modules aim to support staff in developing, delivering and evaluating development agency engagement in security system reform and conducting strategic planning for improved policies, practices and partnerships. For those participants not directly involved in SSR activities, this training will help their understanding of the security–development nexus, the role of SSR and the potential links across the development agenda.

Outreach

The recognition that SSR is at the nexus of the security and development agenda underlines the need for development, diplomatic and security actors to move towards a shared understanding of the subject, including the development of a common language and, most importantly, shared programme objectives. The range of skills and experience required to effectively support SSR highlights the need for collaboration and coordination within and between governments and multilaterals. Progress in this area is on-going and the OECD DAC is well placed to continue to play a leading role in representing the development community and promoting this dialogue. Again, the process of supporting the IF-SSR process has facilitated broad based and inclusive discussions. Indeed a range of UN agencies plus the EC have actively contributed towards the framework, but there is a need for this to continue and intensify if one of the main objectives of the IF-SSR process, promoting greater international community coordination in the field, is to be realised. The CPDC SSR task team is planning to support the implementation of the main operational commitments from the IF-SSR process in appropriate countries and this should help identify key issues and barriers to such coordination and ways to navigate through them.

However, in addition to outreach, there is also the need for those engaged on SSR within the development community to work closely with those who have been working on similar issues from a rule of law perspective. As SSR develops a greater focus on human security and the needs of individuals and communities, the potential overlap between these two schools of thought and practice has grown. Rather than allow supply side boundary issues to colour the debate it will be important that dialogue around a demand-led, needs-based approach is adopted which identifies how work in one area complements and strengthens the other. The OECD has sought to promote this synergy through the process of developing the *OECD DAC Handbook on SSR* and this is underlined through its reference to the equal importance, and complementary nature, of security and justice. The principle that desired outcome and context define the programme of support should be reiterated. This, in turn, should encourage a fusing of different development tools and approaches to allow an effective issues based approach to improving the delivery of security and justice to be realised.

Other critical audiences for greater outreach include implementation partners and, most importantly, the partner countries themselves. As stated earlier, development agencies and donor governments are increasingly contracting the private sector through consultancy companies, NGOs and, in some cases, private security/military companies as well as individual consultants. Building a dialogue with these implementing partners is therefore clearly an important step in influencing behaviour in the field and bridging the gap between policy and practice. Identifying how policy and principles should translate into programmatic approaches and behaviour by those engaged to implement programmes is vital if these principles are to have any meaning in reality. Again the IF-SSR process has sought to engage with implementing partners, but more needs to be done to build on these initial discussions and to build a common understanding. The *OECD DAC Handbook on SSR* provides a very useful vehicle to take this dialogue forward and encourage the private sector and NGOs to become part of the community of users of the Implementation Framework and to therefore inform its development over future editions.

Finally and most importantly, there is a clear role for the OECD in reaching out to partner countries and engaging with them around the principles and practice of SSR. The potential role that regional organisations can play in developing agreed common standards around the delivery of security and justice and the management and governance of security institutions could be critical in seeing a step change in the profile and implementation of this important agenda in the regions where it matters most. The OECD SSR policy guidelines and handbook represent the only internationally agreed set of principles and guidance on SSR. As such, there is potential for them to play a useful role in facilitating discussions with regional organisations around their relevance for addressing the challenges faced by their own member countries, or how they might need to be revised and/or tailored to reflect them more effectively.

In summary, the process of developing the *OECD DAC Handbook on SSR* has created a community of policy makers, practitioners and advocates. The challenge now is to build from here and expand the network. This outreach should seek to promote constructive dialogue with diplomatic and security communities; greater involvement of the rule of law community; understanding of principles and good practice with implementing partners; and, most importantly, the active engagement of partner countries themselves. In so doing the OECD can, utilising the *OECD DAC Handbook on SSR*, provide a focal point around which the international community shares it experiences and learns through doing. In short, the time for general principles and fuzzy policy statements is over; the challenge ahead is about addressing the very real challenges of implementation and improving the delivery of security and justice for the many people in the world today that currently enjoy access to neither.

Endnotes

1 The opinions in this chapter are expressed solely in the name of the authors and do not necessarily represent OECD policy or the policy of any of its member states. This article is based largely on the outcomes of the Implementation Framework for Security System Reform (IF-SSR) process, a multi-donor initiative to develop a standardized SSR field manual. This process was jointly led by the authors. The operational guidance accruing from the IF-SSR process has been published as the *OECD DAC Handbook on Security System Reform: supporting security and justice* and was endorsed by OECD DAC Ministers at the High Level Meeting in April 2007. See further www.oecd.org/dac/conflict/if-ssr.

2 See further *OECD Guidance on Security System Reform and Good Governance* (2004).

3 Collier and Hoffler (2004) *The Challenge of Reducing the Global Incidence of Civil War*, The Copenhagen Consensus Papers.

4 For further information on the OECD DAC Network on Conflict, Peace and Development Cooperation, see www.oecd.org/dac/conflict

5 See further European Commission (2006) *Concept for European Community Support for Security Sector Reform*, Brussels, 24 May 2006, COM (2006)253 final.

6 See further Chirayath, Sage and Woolcock (2005) 'Customary Law and Policy Reform: Engaging with the Plurality of Justice Systems', prepared as a background paper for the *World Development Report 2006: Equity and Development*; as quoted in OECD DAC (2007) *Security and Justice Service Delivery in Fragile States*, Paris.

7 DAC (2004) p. 20.

8 OECD (2005) p. 12.

9 *Ibid.* p. 14.

10 See further Department for International Development (2004) 'Public Information Note: Drivers of Change', DFID, UK; or OECD DAC (2005) 'Lessons Learned on the Use of Power and Drivers of Change Analyses in Development Co-operation – Final Report', OECD DAC Network on Governance (GOVNET) – both documents can be accessed at http://www.gsdrc.org/go/topic-guides/drivers-of-change.

11 These three contexts are drawn from A. Bryden and H. Hänggi (2005) 'Reforming and Reconstructing the Security Sector' in A. Bryden and H. Hänggi (eds.) *Security Governance in Post-Conflict Peacebuilding*, Münster: LIT.

12 See further Nathan, Laurie (2006), *Local Ownership in Security Sector Reform: a guide for donors* published by DFID accessible on http://www.crisisstates.com/download/others/SSR%20Reform.pdf

13 Through regional meetings held in Ghana (2005) and Bolivia (2006) and its links the Africa Security Sector Network (ASSN). For CPDC, see www.oecd.org/dac/conflict.

14 OECD DAC (2007) *Enhancing Security and Justice Service Delivery.*

Conclusion

David Spence and Philipp Fluri

Several chapters in this book argue that the EU is at a turning point as a global security actor in general and as a provider of assistance to security sector reform in particular. Times have changed since a visit to the Brussels institutions would not encompass discussions with uniformed officials. Today, no review of the EU's institutional structure would be complete without discussion of the many military and civil-military committees making up the administrative support structure of CFSP and ESDP. As this book went to press in December 2007, it followed the first formal meetings of EU defence ministers to decide policy in a sector which saw its first hesitant steps a mere ten years ago.

To illustrate how the EU's involvement in security policy has evolved, it is interesting to note that in just one meeting in May 2007 defence ministers adopted a joint action on deployment of the EU police mission in Afghanistan (EUPOL Afghanistan), sending 159 police officers to conduct training for the Afghan police force and to provide advice for improving the command chain and procedures. They validated a proposal for a concept of operations as part of security sector reform in the Democratic Republic of Congo and in parallel to its justice interface (EUPOL-DRC), including advisory activity for training, security structures, the payment chain and the development of cooperation between the police and the judicial sector, mainly in the context of criminal investigations. All these were new activities in addition to the police reform mission already underway (EUPOL), which had undertaken training of a unit of 1,000 police in Kinshasa since April 2005. Initially expected to last one year, the police mission could merge, in June 2008, with another EU programme set up in DRC since 2005, the mission for SSR assistance and reform advice (EUSEC DRC), a concept also reviewed during the Council. Defence ministers also suggested actions to enhance partnership with the African Union (AU) on crisis management and resolution capacities. The Council presented an action plan based on four areas to strengthen African capacities (conflict prevention, training of African troops, support of operations, and post-conflict reconstruction), on the basis of the principle of African ownership. They also adopted a joint action extending the planning mission for a possible crisis management operation in Kosovo, extending an existing joint action of 2006 on setting up an EU planning team (EUPT Kosovo), in respect of the EU crisis management operation in Kosovo in the field of rule of law and, possibly, in other areas once the question of the status of Kosovo has been settled. Their meeting also took stock of the reconfiguration of the European force (EUFOR) in the context of Operation Althea in Bosnia-Herzegovina and on cooperation with the United Nations, especially in the DRC. And it confirmed support to the African Union mission in Sudan (AMIS), both in terms of financing and in terms of member state contributions in military and civilian experts. Part of the Defence Ministers' work on the same day was a meeting of the European Defence Agency Steering Board, during which ministers approved a strategy for developing a European Defence Technological and Industrial Base. They also took stock of the development of EU military capabilities with a view to achieving the Headline Goal 2010, which provides for the setting in place of a European rapid reaction force by 2010, able to respond to crisis situations (crisis management including the use of force, peace and stabilisation missions, security missions, etc.). Their working lunch was devoted to the Balkans (Kosovo and the Althea mission in Bosnia-Herzegovina) and to Sudan (EU support of AMIS) and was attended by NATO Secretary General Jaap de Hoop Scheffer. Defence ministers also joined foreign ministers to approve essential points concerning Afghanistan, Kosovo and the Democratic Republic of Congo. All this in one meeting.

There is no doubt, therefore, of the EU's credentials as a security actor, but as the authors in this study argue, much work remains to consolidate the EU's character as an SSR actor regionally and internationally. The EU's SSR concepts acknowledge that the development of joint actions with other international organisations is necessary and that empowerment of regional organisations and actors is required if sustainable reform is to be achieved. Yet, how the EU is to manage this cooperation efficiently with international organisations and donors in the SSR field clearly needs further research and pragmatic policy-making. SSR does not have a single institutional home in the EU context, nor a consolidated means of budgetary support. Despite concerted attempts by the Commission and Council to agree a conceptual framework on SSR, there is no single SSR concept. Rather two concepts were agreed (both included as annexes to this book) – support of SSR activities through the second CFSP intergovernmental pillar as part of the European Security and Defence Policy (ESDP) and one that relates to European Community (first pillar) assistance for SSR. The two were formally linked by the European Council in December 2006, but the issue for the next few years is how effective practical implementation turns out to be, as SSR is mainstreamed throughout EC spending without the benefit of a strong political-administrative base providing strategic impulse and oversight.

Ultimately, the future of EU SSR very much depends on how not only the EU institutions but EU member states engage (or not) in SSR. If more member state governments seek to employ a 'whole of government' approach like that advocated by the OECD-DAC and employed by The Netherlands and the UK, there might also be greater political will to integrate development and security structures at the EU level. And if this were successful, SSR could well become a framework to steer other policy developments. On the other hand, if a 'whole of government' approach does not take hold at the EU level, EU SSR could end up being a catch-all term for a variety of policies from border management to police reform, all admittedly part of SSR, but not to be equated with an overall, comprehensive concept of SSR as such, not least because they were not devised to serve the end of comprehensive security 'system' reform in the first place. The risk is low levels of synergy and coherence. A concerted effort is clearly needed to obtain political backing for prioritising SSR at senior national and EU levels and to achieve a clear coordinating role for the EU in SSR.

In addition, development of the EU approach to SSR is very much contingent on external circumstances. If a future conflict sees the EU able to coordinate its civil-military response well and if open conflicts can be shown to lead in time, through EU action, to stabilisation and post-conflict reconstruction, this would serve to enhance the legitimacy of the EU approach to SSR. If the EU fails in this endeavour, the risk lies in the potential undermining both of the EU's legitimate aspirations in the SSR sector and the practical implementation of its strategies. Much, therefore, is riding on the Commission's and the Council's ability to mainstream SSR effectively in practice.

Annex 1

A SECURE EUROPE IN A BETTER WORLD

EUROPEAN SECURITY STRATEGY

Brussels, 12 December 2003

Introduction

Europe has never been so prosperous, so secure nor so free. The violence of the first half of the 20th Century has given way to a period of peace and stability unprecedented in European history.

The creation of the European Union has been central to this development. It has transformed the relations between our states, and the lives of our citizens. European countries are committed to dealing peacefully with disputes and to co-operating through common institutions. Over this period, the progressive spread of the rule of law and democracy has seen authoritarian regimes change into secure, stable and dynamic democracies. Successive enlargements are making a reality of the vision of a united and peaceful continent.

No single country is able to tackle today's complex problems on its own

The United States has played a critical role in European integration and European security, in particular through NATO. The end of the Cold War has left the United States in a dominant position as a military actor. However, no single country is able to tackle today's complex problems on its own.

Europe still faces security threats and challenges. The outbreak of conflict in the Balkans was a reminder that war has not disappeared from our continent. Over the last decade, no region of the world has been untouched by armed conflict. Most of these conflicts have been within rather than between states, and most of the victims have been civilians.

As a union of 25 states with over 450 million people producing a quarter of the world's Gross National Product (GNP), and with a wide range of instruments at its disposal, the European Union is inevitably a global player. In the last decade European forces have been deployed abroad to places as distant as Afghanistan, East Timor and the DRC. The increasing convergence of European interests and the strengthening of mutual solidarity of the EU makes us a more credible and effective actor. Europe should be ready to share in the responsibility for global security and in building a better world.

As a union of 25 states with over 450 million people producing a quarter of the world's Gross National Product (GNP), the European Union is inevitably a global player... it should be ready to share in the responsibility for global security and in building a better world.

I. THE SECURITY ENVIRONMENT: GLOBAL CHALLENGES AND KEY THREATS

Global Challenges

The post Cold War environment is one of increasingly open borders in which the internal and external aspects of security are indissolubly linked. Flows of trade and investment, the development of technology and the spread of democracy have brought freedom and prosperity to many people.

Others have perceived globalisation as a cause of frustration and injustice. These developments have also increased the scope for non-state groups to play a part in international affairs. And they have increased European dependence – and so vulnerability – on an interconnected infrastructure in transport, energy, information and other fields.

Since 1990, almost 4 million people have died in wars, 90% of them civilians. Over 18 million people world-wide have left their homes as a result of conflict.

In much of the developing world, poverty and disease cause untold suffering and give rise to pressing security concerns. Almost 3 billion people, half the world's population, live on less than 2 Euros a day. 45 million die every year of hunger and malnutrition. AIDS is now one of the most devastating pandemics in human history and contributes to the breakdown of societies. New diseases can spread rapidly and become global threats. Sub-Saharan Africa is poorer now than it was 10 years ago. In many cases, economic failure is linked to political problems and violent conflict.

45 million people die every year of hunger and malnutrition... Aids contributes to the breakdown of societies... Security is a precondition of development

Security is a precondition of development. Conflict not only destroys infrastructure, including social infrastructure; it also encourages criminality, deters investment and makes normal economic
activity impossible. A number of countries and regions are caught in a cycle of conflict, insecurity and poverty.

Competition for natural resources - notably water - which will be aggravated by global warming over the next decades, is likely to create further turbulence and migratory movements in various regions.

Energy dependence is a special concern for Europe. Europe is the world's largest importer of oil and gas. Imports account for about 50% of energy consumption today. This will rise to 70% in 2030. Most energy imports come from the Gulf, Russia and North Africa.

Key Threats

Large-scale aggression against any Member State is now improbable. Instead, Europe faces new threats which are more diverse, less visible and less predictable.

Terrorism: Terrorism puts lives at risk; it imposes large costs; it seeks to undermine the openness and tolerance of our societies, and it poses a growing strategic threat to the whole of Europe. Increasingly, terrorist movements are well-resourced, connected by electronic networks, and are willing to use unlimited violence to cause massive casualties.

The most recent wave of terrorism is global in its scope and is linked to violent religious extremism. It arises out of complex causes. These include the pressures of modernisation, cultural, social and political crises, and the alienation of young people living in foreign societies. This phenomenon is also a part of our own society.

Europe is both a target and a base for such terrorism: European countries are targets and have been attacked. Logistical bases for Al Qaeda cells have been uncovered in the UK, Italy, Germany, Spain and Belgium. Concerted European action is indispensable. Proliferation of Weapons of Mass Destruction is potentially the greatest threat to our security. The international treaty regimes and export control arrangements have slowed the spread of WMD and delivery systems. We are now, however, entering a new and dangerous period that raises the possibility of a WMD arms race, especially

The last use of WMD was by the Aum terrorist sect in the Tokyo underground in 1995, using sarin gas. 12 people were killed and several thousand injured. Two years earlier, Aum had sprayed anthrax spores on a Tokyo street.

in the Middle East. Advances in the biological sciences may increase the potency of biological weapons in the coming years; attacks with chemical and radiological materials are also a serious possibility. The spread of missile technology adds a further element of instability and could put Europe at increasing risk.

The most frightening scenario is one in which terrorist groups acquire weapons of mass destruction. In this event, a small group would be able to inflict damage on a scale previously possible only for States and armies.

Regional Conflicts: Problems such as those in Kashmir, the Great Lakes Region and the Korean Peninsula impact on European interests directly and indirectly, as do conflicts nearer to home, above all in the Middle East. Violent or frozen conflicts, which also persist on our borders, threaten regional stability. They destroy human lives and social and physical infrastructures; they threaten minorities, fundamental freedoms and human rights. Conflict can lead to extremism, terrorism and state failure; it provides opportunities for organised crime. Regional insecurity can fuel the demand for WMD. The most practical way to tackle the often elusive new threats will sometimes be to deal with the older problems of regional conflict.

State Failure: Bad governance – corruption, abuse of power, weak institutions and lack of accountability - and civil conflict corrode States from within. In some cases, this has brought about the collapse of State institutions. Somalia, Liberia and Afghanistan under the Taliban are the best known recent examples. Collapse of the State can be associated with obvious threats, such as organised crime or terrorism. State failure is an alarming phenomenon, that undermines global governance, and adds to regional instability.

Organised Crime: Europe is a prime target for organised crime. This internal threat to our security has an important external dimension: cross-border trafficking in drugs, women, illegal migrants and weapons accounts for a large part of the activities of criminal gangs. It can have links with terrorism.

Such criminal activities are often associated with weak or failing states. Revenues from drugs have fuelled the weakening of state structures in several drug-producing countries. Revenues from trade in gemstones, timber and small arms, fuel conflict in other parts of the world. All these activities undermine both the rule of law and social order itself. In extreme cases, organised crime can come to dominate the state. 90% of the heroin in Europe comes from poppies grown in Afghanistan – where the drugs trade pays for private armies. Most of it is distributed through Balkan criminal networks which are also responsible for some 200,000 of the 700,000 women victims of the sex trade world wide. A new dimension to organised crime which will merit further attention is the growth in maritime piracy.

Taking these different elements together – terrorism committed to maximum violence, the availability of weapons of mass destruction, organised crime, the weakening of the state system and the privatisation of force – we could be confronted with a very radical threat indeed.

II. STRATEGIC OBJECTIVES

We live in a world that holds brighter prospects but also greater threats than we have known. The future will depend partly on our actions. We need both to think globally and to act locally. To defend its security and to promote its values, the EU has three strategic objectives:

Addressing the Threats

The European Union has been active in tackling the key threats.

- It has responded after 11 September with measures that included the adoption of a European Arrest Warrant, steps to attack terrorist financing and an agreement on mutual legal assistance with the U.S.A. The EU continues to develop cooperation in this area and to improve its defences.

- It has pursued policies against proliferation over many years. The Union has just agreed a further programme of action which foresees steps to strengthen the International Atomic Energy Agency, measures to tighten export controls and to deal with illegal shipments and illicit procurement. The EU is committed to achieving universal adherence to multilateral treaty regimes, as well as to strengthening the treaties and their verification provisions.

- The European Union and Member States have intervened to help deal with regional conflicts and to put failed states back on their feet, including in the Balkans, Afghanistan, and in the DRC. Restoring good government to the Balkans, fostering democracy and enabling the authorities there to tackle organised crime is one of the most effective ways of dealing with organised crime within the EU.

In an era of globalisation, distant threats may be as much a concern as those that are near at hand. Nuclear activities in North Korea, nuclear risks in South Asia, and proliferation in the Middle East are all of concern to Europe.

In an era of globalisation, distant threats may be as much a concern as those that are near at hand... The first line of defence will be often be abroad. The new threats are dynamic... Conflict prevention and threat prevention cannot start too early.

Terrorists and criminals are now able to operate world-wide: their activities in central or southeast Asia may be a threat to European countries or their citizens. Meanwhile, global communication increases awareness in Europe of regional conflicts or humanitarian tragedies anywhere in the world.

Our traditional concept of self- defence – up to and including the Cold War – was based on the threat of invasion. With the new threats, the first line of defence will often be abroad. The new threats are dynamic. The risks of proliferation grow over time; left alone, terrorist networks will become ever more dangerous. State failure and organised crime spread if they are neglected – as we have seen in West Africa. This implies that we should be ready to act before a crisis occurs. Conflict prevention and threat prevention cannot start too early.

In contrast to the massive visible threat in the Cold War, none of the new threats is purely military; nor can any be tackled by purely military means. Each requires a mixture of instruments. Proliferation may be contained through export controls and attacked through political, economic and other pressures while the underlying political causes are also tackled. Dealing with terrorism may require a mixture of intelligence, police, judicial, military and other means. In failed states, military instruments may be needed to restore order, humanitarian means to tackle the immediate crisis. Regional conflicts need political solutions but military assets and effective policing may be needed in the post conflict phase. Economic instruments serve reconstruction, and civilian crisis management helps restore civil government. The European Union is particularly well equipped to respond to such multi-faceted situations.

Building Security in our Neighbourhood

Even in an era of globalisation, geography is still important. It is in the European interest that countries on our borders are well-governed. Neighbours who are engaged in violent conflict, weak states where organised crime flourishes, dysfunctional societies or exploding population growth on its borders all pose problems for Europe.

Enlargement should not create new dividing lines in Europe. Resolution of the Arab/Israeli conflict is a strategic priority for Europe

The integration of acceding states increases our security but also brings the EU closer to troubled areas. Our task is to promote a ring of well governed countries to the East of the European Union and on the borders of the Mediterranean with whom we can enjoy close and cooperative relations.

The importance of this is best illustrated in the Balkans. Through our concerted efforts with the US, Russia, NATO and other international partners, the stability of the region is no longer threatened by the outbreak of major conflict. The credibility of our foreign policy depends on the consolidation of our achievements there. The European perspective offers both a strategic objective and an incentive for reform.

It is not in our interest that enlargement should create new dividing lines in Europe. We need to extend the benefits of economic and political cooperation to our neighbours in the East while tackling political problems there. We should now take a stronger and more active interest in the problems of the Southern Caucasus, which will in due course also be a neighbouring region.

Resolution of the Arab/Israeli conflict is a strategic priority for Europe. Without this, there will be little chance of dealing with other problems in the Middle East. The European Union must remain engaged and ready to commit resources to the problem until it is solved. The two state solution – which Europe has long supported – is now widely accepted. Implementing it will require a united and cooperative effort by the European Union, the United States, the United Nations and Russia, and the countries of the region, but above all by the Israelis and the Palestinians themselves.

The Mediterranean area generally continues to undergo serious problems of economic stagnation, social unrest and unresolved conflicts. The European Union's interests require a continued engagement with Mediterranean partners, through more effective economic, security and cultural cooperation in the framework of the Barcelona Process. A broader engagement with the Arab World should also be considered.

AN INTERNATIONAL ORDER BASED ON EFFECTIVE MULTILATERALISM

In a world of global threats, global markets and global media, our security and prosperity increasingly depend on an effective multilateral system. The development of a stronger international society, well functioning international institutions and a rule-based international order is our objective.

We are committed to upholding and developing International Law. The fundamental framework for international relations is the United Nations Charter. The United Nations Security Council has the primary responsibility for the maintenance of international peace and security. Strengthening the United Nations, equipping it to fulfil its responsibilities and to act effectively, is a European priority.

Our security and prosperity increasingly depend on an effective multilateral system. We are committed to upholding and developing International Law.
The fundamental framework for international relations is the United Nations Charter.

We want international organisations, regimes and treaties to be effective in confronting threats to international peace and security, and must therefore be ready to act when their rules are broken.

Key institutions in the international system, such as the World Trade Organisation (WTO) and the International Financial Institutions, have extended their membership. China has joined the WTO and Russia is negotiating its entry. It should be an objective for us to widen the membership of such bodies while maintaining their high standards.

One of the core elements of the international system is the transatlantic relationship. This is not only in our bilateral interest but strengthens the international community as a whole. NATO is an important expression of this relationship.

Regional organisations also strengthen global governance. For the European Union, the strength and effectiveness of the OSCE and the Council of Europe has a particular significance. Other regional organisations such as ASEAN, MERCOSUR and the African Union make an important contribution to a more orderly world.

It is a condition of a rule-based international order that law evolves in response to developments such as proliferation, terrorism and global warming. We have an interest in further developing existing institutions such as the World Trade Organisation and in supporting new ones such as the International Criminal Court. Our own experience in Europe demonstrates that security can be increased through confidence building and arms control regimes. Such instruments can also make an important contribution to security and stability in our neighbourhood and beyond.

The quality of international society depends on the quality of the governments that are its foundation. The best protection for our security is a world of well-governed democratic states. Spreading good governance, supporting social and political reform, dealing with corruption and abuse of power, establishing the rule of law and protecting human rights are the best means of strengthening the international order.

Trade and development policies can be powerful tools for promoting reform. As the world's largest provider of official assistance and its largest trading entity, the European Union and its Member States are well placed to pursue these goals.

Contributing to better governance through assistance programmes, conditionality and targeted trade measures remains an important feature in our policy that we should further reinforce. A world seen as offering justice and opportunity for everyone will be more secure for the European Union and its citizens.

A number of countries have placed themselves outside the bounds of international society. Some have sought isolation; others persistently violate international norms. It is desirable that such countries should rejoin the international community, and the EU should be ready to provide assistance. Those who are unwilling to do so should understand that there is a price to be paid, including in their relationship with the European Union.

III. POLICY IMPLICATIONS FOR EUROPE

The European Union has made progress towards a coherent foreign policy and effective crisis management. We have instruments in place that can be used effectively, as we have demonstrated in the Balkans and beyond. But if we are to make a contribution that matches our potential, we need to be more active, more coherent and more capable. And we need to work with others.

More active in pursuing our strategic objectives. This applies to the full spectrum of instruments for crisis management and conflict prevention at our disposal, including political, diplomatic, military and civilian, trade and development activities. Active policies are needed to counter the new dynamic threats. We need to develop a strategic culture that fosters early, rapid, and when necessary, robust intervention.

We need to develop a strategic culture that fosters early, rapid and when necessary, robust intervention.

As a Union of 25 members, spending more than 160 billion Euros on defence, we should be able to sustain several operations simultaneously. We could add particular value by developing operations involving both military and civilian capabilities.

The EU should support the United Nations as it responds to threats to international peace and security. The EU is committed to reinforcing its cooperation with the UN to assist countries emerging from conflicts, and to enhancing its support for the UN in short-term crisis management situations.

We need to be able to act before countries around us deteriorate, when signs of proliferation are detected, and before humanitarian emergencies arise. Preventive engagement can avoid more serious problems in the future. A European Union which takes greater responsibility and which is more active will be one which carries greater political weight.

More Capable. A more capable Europe is within our grasp, though it will take time to realise our full potential. Actions underway – notably the establishment of a defence agency – take us in the right direction.

To transform our militaries into more flexible, mobile forces, and to enable them to address the new threats, more resources for defence and more effective use of resources are necessary.

Systematic use of pooled and shared assets would reduce duplications, overheads and, in the medium-term, increase capabilities.

In almost every major intervention, military efficiency has been followed by civilian chaos. We need greater capacity to bring all necessary civilian resources to bear in crisis and post crisis situations.

Stronger diplomatic capability: we need a system that combines the resources of Member States with those of EU institutions. Dealing with problems that are more distant and more foreign requires better understanding and communication.

Common threat assessments are the best basis for common actions. This requires improved sharing of intelligence among Member States and with partners.

As we increase capabilities in the different areas, we should think in terms of a wider spectrum of missions. This might include joint disarmament operations, support for third countries in combating terrorism and security sector reform. The last of these would be part of broader institution building.

The EU-NATO permanent arrangements, in particular Berlin Plus, enhance the operational capability of the EU and provide the framework for the strategic partnership between the two organisations in crisis management. This reflects our common determination to tackle the challenges of the new century.

More Coherent. The point of the Common Foreign and Security Policy and European Security and Defence Policy is that we are stronger when we act together. Over recent years we have created a number of different instruments, each of which has its own structure and rationale.

The challenge now is to bring together the different instruments and capabilities: European assistance programmes and the European Development Fund, military and civilian capabilities from Member States and other instruments. All of these can have an impact on our security and on that of third countries. Security is the first condition for development.

Diplomatic efforts, development, trade and environmental policies, should follow the same agenda. In a crisis there is no substitute for unity of command.

Better co-ordination between external action and Justice and Home Affairs policies is crucial in the fight both against terrorism and organised crime.

Greater coherence is needed not only among EU instruments but also embracing the external activities of the individual member states.

Coherent policies are also needed regionally, especially in dealing with conflict. Problems are rarely solved on a single country basis, or without regional support, as in different ways experience in both the Balkans and West Africa shows.

Working with partners There are few if any problems we can deal with on our own. The threats described above are common threats, shared with all our closest partners. International cooperation is a necessity. We need to pursue our objectives both through multilateral cooperation in international organisations and through partnerships with key actors.

Acting together, the European Union and the United States can be a formidable force for good in the world.

The transatlantic relationship is irreplaceable. Acting together, the European Union and the United States can be a formidable force for good in the world. Our aim should be an effective and balanced partnership with the USA. This is an additional reason for the EU to build up further its capabilities and increase its coherence.

We should continue to work for closer relations with Russia, a major factor in our security and prosperity. Respect for common values will reinforce progress towards a strategic partnership.

Our history, geography and cultural ties give us links with every part of the world: our neighbours in the Middle East, our partners in Africa, in Latin America, and in Asia. These relationships are an important asset to build on. In particular we should look to develop strategic partnerships, with Japan, China, Canada and India as well as with all those who share our goals and values, and are prepared to act in their support.

Conclusion

This is a world of new dangers but also of new opportunities. The European Union has the potential to make a major contribution, both in dealing with the threats and in helping realise the opportunities. An active and capable European Union would make an impact on a global scale. In doing so, it would contribute to an effective multilateral system leading to a fairer, safer and more united world.

Annex 2

COUNCIL OF THE EUROPEAN UNION

Council Conclusions on a Policy framework for Security sector reform

(2736th GENERAL AFFAIRS Council meeting - Luxembourg, 12 June 2006)

The Council adopted the following conclusions:

1. The Council welcomes the release of the European Commission Communication "A Concept for European Community Support for Security Sector Reform". This concept complements the Concept for ESDP support to Security Sector Reform, adopted in November 2005. Together the two concepts constitute a policy framework for EU engagement in Security Sector Reform, stressing the importance for the EU to take a comprehensive and cross-pillar approach to SSR recognizing the fact that SSR is a holistic, multi-sector, and long-term process encompassing the overall functioning of the security system as part of governance reforms.

2. This EU policy framework for SSR is an important contribution to EU's external action. Preventing and resolving violent conflict and addressing fragile states are part of the EU's efforts to reduce insecurity and eradicate poverty through strengthening good governance and the rule of law in third countries; finding solutions to existing problems; thus helping to achieve the commitments of the Millennium Declaration and the Millennium Development Goals, sustainable development and global security and to implement the EU's Development Policy Statement "The European Consensus on Development", including the security objectives of the EU as set out in the European Security Strategy.

3. The EU action on SSR should be based on the following principles, drawing on the OECD-DAC definition on SSR:

- nationally/regionally owned participatory reform processes designed to strengthen good governance, democratic norms, the rule of law and the respect and promotion of human rights, in line with internationally agreed norms;

- addressing the core requirements of a well functioning security system, including the development of a nationally owned concept of security, well defined policies and good governance of security institutions;

- addressing diverse security challenges facing states and their populations, based on a gender-sensitive multi-sector approach to the provision of security and access to justice, and targeting reform needs in different key sectors. This includes separating tasks between different services and institutions and taking into account the role of civil society and other non-state structures of governance;

- accountability and transparency standards should be the same that apply across the public sector, in particular improved governance through greater civilian and parliamentary oversight of security processes;

- political dialogue with each partner country, addressing human rights, development and security concerns, and be carried out in synergy with other instruments.

4. The EU has a broad range of civilian and military instruments which are able to support SSR activities. A case-by-case analysis based on a situation specific approach is always needed to assess whether any proposed activities are most appropriately carried out through ESDP or Community action or a combination of both with the objective of ensuring effective and coherent EU external action in this area. The Council and the Commission will ensure consistency between their activities in accordance with Article 3 of the TEU.

5. The Council agrees to take forward work during the Finnish Presidency with the Commission to develop an EU approach to contribute to Disarmament, Demobilisation and Reintegration (DDR) as part of broader SSR support and consistent with the EU policy framework for SSR.

6. The Council invites future Presidencies and the Commission to progressively translate this policy framework for EU engagement in SSR into operational actions by the European Community and in the framework of ESDP, in order to provide effective, coherent and sustainable support to EU partner countries and regions. "

Annex 3

COUNCIL OF THE EUROPEAN UNION

Brussels, 13 October 2005
12566/4/05
REV 4
LIMITE
ESDP/PESD
COSDP 613
PESC 784

NOTE

from : Secretariat

to : Political and Security Committee

Subject : EU Concept for ESDP support to Security Sector Reform (SSR)

In accordance with the PSC tasking of 19 July, the Council General Secretariat, in close consultation with the Commission, has drafted the attached EU Concept for ESDP Support to SSR.

The Commission intends to present in due course a draft Community concept on SSR.

Table of contents

Reference documents:

A. European Security Strategy: A secure Europe in a better world

B. OECD/Development Assistance Committee: DAC Guidelines and Reference series "Security System Reform and Governance"

C. Initial elements for an EU Security Sector Reform (SSR) concept (Council doc. 11241/05 dated 15 July 2005)

D. Comprehensive EU concept for missions in the field of Rule of Law in crisis management (Council doc. 9792/03 dated 26 May 2003)

E. EU Concept for Crisis management missions in the field of Civilian Administration (Council doc. 15311/03 dated 25 November 2003)

A. INTRODUCTION

1. Support to Security Sector Reform (SSR) in partner countries is one of the core areas for EU action identified in the European Security Strategy (ESS). Security sector reform will contribute to an accountable, effective and efficient security system, operating under civilian control consistent with democratic norms and principles of good governance, transparency and the rule of law, and acting according to international standards and respecting human rights, which can be a force for peace and stability, fostering democracy and promoting local and regional stability.

2. EU support to SSR will be based, inter -alia, on the following principles:;

- democratic norms and internationally accepted human rights principles and the rule of law, and where applicable international humanitarian law;

- respect for local ownership; and

- coherence with other areas of EU external action.

3. EU action should build on national ownership and partnership. EU action will be defined in the political dialogue and in close consultation with the partner government, and adapted to the specific country situation. In the absence of a partner government in a crisis situation or in the immediate aftermath of a conflict, the early stages of EU support should pave the way for long-term country-owned SSR reforms based on a participatory and democratic process. The EU will take a coherent and consistent approach, where complementarity of actions undertaken in the framework of ESDP and by the European Community is vital, both in the area of SSR, and in relation to Community activities in other areas in a given country.

4. The OECD/Development Assistance Committee[1] has developed guidelines on "Security System Reform and Governance", which were endorsed by Ministers and Agency Heads on 16 April 2004.[2] Although they do not reflect the specificities of the EU, nor those security aspects that fall under ESDP, an EU Concept for ESDP support to SSR should take due account of their key elements.

5. In order to contribute to sustainable development, SSR has to be locally owned. Thus, national development plans, such as Poverty Reduction Strategies, should be taken into account. Support to SSR may also be part of broader multilateral frameworks.

6. The purpose of this paper is to provide a concept for ESDP support to Security Sector Reform in partner countries. The EU has a broad range of civilian and military instruments which are able to support SSR activities. A case-by-case analysis will always need to be undertaken to assess whether any proposed activities are most appropriately carried out through CFSP/ESDP or Community action or indeed a combination of both. This concept is deliberately broad in order not to constrain future CFSP/ESDP or Community activities but in any situation, the Council General Secretariat and the Commission will need to work in close co-operation both to ensure a clear, functional division of responsibilities and to ensure maximum coherence and effectiveness of overall EU effort. It is foreseen that the paper on a Community concept on SSR will build on the same premise.

1 The following EU Member States are member of OECD Development Assistance Committee (DAC): Austria, Belgium, Denmark, Finland, France, Germany, Greece, Ireland, Italy, Luxembourg, the Netherlands, Portugal, Spain, Sweden, and the United Kingdom. The Commission is also a member of this Committee.

2 Commission Representatives have also participated in developing the OECD/DAC guidelines.

B. BACKGROUND

7. SSR plays an important role in serving the EU's strategic objectives as outlined in the ESS, as well as contributing to the prevention of violent conflict. Consequently, the European Security Strategy points out that *"as we increase capabilities in different areas, we should think in terms of a wider spectrum of missions. This might include joint disarmament operations, support for third countries in combating terrorism and security sector reform. The last of these would be part of broader institution building"*.

8. In addition to a willingness within the EU to do more in this regard, it is considered that a more active EU contribution in this field would be welcomed by the International Community. It is assessed that the EU can expect further requests for assistance from third States and/or from the UN, Regional or Sub Regional Organisations.

9. On 19 July 2005, the PSC discussed "Initial elements for an EU Security Sector Reform (SSR) concept" (Ref. B.) developed by the GSC, in close co-operation with the Commission. Subsequently the PSC invited the Secretariat to develop, in close co-operation with the Commission, a draft EU Concept for ESDP support to Security Sector Reform (SSR). It was noted that the Commission will develop, in close co-operation with the Council Secretariat, an EC concept for SSR covering first pillar activities. At a later stage, consideration should be given to bringing these two strands closer together. This would complete an overall SSR concept.

C. AIM AND SCOPE

10. The purpose of this paper is to provide a concept for ESDP support to Security Sector Reform in a partner state. This concept should focus on principles, key elements, and modalities; it should be flexible enough to be drawn on and adapted for the needs of each specific action in this field on a case-by-case basis. This paper aims to spell out the contribution of ESDP in supporting SSR. With its dimensions of both civilian and military crisis management, including an emphasis on the prevention of conflict, ESDP can offer an integrated as well as focussed approach to SSR. The EU aims at a coherent approach to SSR in which complementarity between action undertaken in the framework of ESDP and those undertaken by the Commission is vital. Furthermore, this concept is without prejudice to activities undertaken under the first pillar. It intends to complement existing concepts such as the *"Comprehensive EU concept for missions in the field of Rule of Law in crisis management"* (Council doc. 9792/03 dated 26 May 2003) or the *"EU Concept for Crisis management missions in the field of Civilian Administration"* (Council doc. 15311/03 dated 25 November 2003).

11. ESDP support to SSR in a partner state will apply to an ESDP action which usually will take the form of advice and assistance to the local authorities (executive, legislature and judiciary) in reform issues in the Security Sector, in a manner consistent with democratic norms and sound principles of good governance, human rights, transparency and the rule of law.

12. It has been noted that Disarmament, Demobilisation and Reintegration (DDR) can constitute a significant pillar of SSR and is regarded as central to conflict resolution and internal stability. In such cases, SSR will call for DDR-type activities. However, SSR goes well beyond DDR and should be considered as the primary concept; DDR should be addressed separately, but consistently with this SSR concept, noting that the Commission is particularly active in the field of Reintegration.

13. This document aims to provide:

- A definition of the Security Sector;

- An overview of the breadth and scope of potential ESDP support to Security Sector Reform (SSR);
- A proposal for integration of civilian and military SSR initiatives within ESDP, co-ordination with SSR activities in other pillars, and co-operation with other partners;
- Modalities on how to plan and conduct SSR activities within ESDP.

D. THE SECURITY SECTOR

14. Taking as a basis the OECD Guidelines, the security sector can be defined as a system which includes:

- **The core security actors:** armed forces; police; gendarmeries; paramilitary forces; presidential guards, intelligence and security services (both military and civilian); coast guards; border guards; customs authorities; reserve or local security units (civil defence forces, national guards, militias).
- **Security management and oversight bodies:** the Executive; national security advisory bodies; legislature and legislative select committee; ministries of defence, internal affairs, foreign affairs; customary and traditional authorities; financial management bodies (finance ministries, budget offices, financial audit and planning units) and civil society organisations (civilian review boards and public complaints commissions).
- **Justice and law enforcement institutions:** judiciary; justice ministries; prisons; criminal investigation and prosecution services; human rights commissions and ombudsmen; customary and traditional justice systems.
- **Non-statutory security forces, with whom donors rarely engage:** liberation armies; guerrilla armies; private bodyguard units; private security companies; political party militias.

15. Following the OECD guidelines there is a need to take a broad approach, engaging all these actors in reform efforts. Rather than focussing on a limited number of key sectors, a holistic, multi-sectoral approach is advocated. This approach includes the need to develop a clear institutional framework for providing security, strengthening of governance and political oversight of the security institutions, effective civilian control, as well as the need to build a capacity throughout the security system both accountable to civil authorities and capable of carrying out the required operational tasks. The relevant aspects of this approach should be reflected in an ESDP concept.

E. SECURITY SECTOR REFORM

16. SSR can be a useful instrument to prevent conflict in fragile states. It is also a core task in countries emerging from conflict, and is a central element of the broader institution-building and reform efforts in countries in a more stable environment. Depending on whether a state faces a post-conflict situation or is reforming its institutions in a more stable environment, a broad spectrum of different SSR requirements might need to be addressed.

17. Security sector reform seeks to increase the ability of a state to meet the range of both internal and external security needs in a manner consistent with democratic norms and sound principles of good governance, human rights, transparency and the rule of law. It concerns not only state stability and regime security of nations but also the safety and well-being of their people. SSR involves addressing issues of how the security system is struc-

tured, regulated, managed, resourced and controlled. It is also important to take into account external security in relation to the neighbourhood and regional stability.

18. SSR activities may target an individual agency or institution, as part of a broader SSR framework and part of a broad co-operation between different donors.

19. In many cases, SSR activities are long term issues necessitating support for a considerable period of time. These activities should be submitted to periodical comprehensive evaluations in order to assess regularly the efficiency of the support given. Consideration could also be given to complementarity between actors/donors in relation to timing.

20. SSR activities are locally owned and based on democratic norms and human rights principles[3] and the rule of law.

21. SSR activities are generally undertaken in close co-operation with the work of other International Community actors, including third States, the United Nations and other International Organisations as well as Non-Governmental Organisations (NGOs). The role of the UN's future Peace-Building Commission will be particularly relevant, as are the activities currently undertaken by UN missions mandated by the Security Council.

F. ESDP SUPPORT TO SSR

22. Durable stability and development need a well organised and controlled security system that is managed in accordance with democratic norms and principles of accountability, transparency and good governance. The EU is able to bring together a wide range of instruments needed both for stability and development. It has the capacity to take a holistic approach in supporting security sector reform in a partner state, by using the economical, political, diplomatic, civilian and military means suitable to provide advice and assistance to the authorities of the state concerned. The EU is uniquely placed to bring together a wide range of civilian and/or military activities needed in the framework of SSR.

23. In the context of crisis management operations, the EU can undertake military operations, civilian operations, as well as integrated actions comprising both civilian and military elements. This integrated approach is to be taken also for ESDP actions in support of SSR, which are a conflict prevention and crisis management tool.

24. Concepts for civilian activities in support of strengthening/reorganising particular agencies or institutions (e.g. strengthening/reorganising civilian administration or rule of law) have already been developed in the ESDP framework and can contribute to the objectives of SSR.

25. ESDP actions in support of SSR contribute to the ultimate goal which is to reach a situation where the security system is organised in a way which ensures an effective Security Sector, the protection of individuals as well as of sustainable state institutions through ensured democratic oversight, transparency and accountability in accordance with internationally recognised values and standards.

26. Although these standards might not be fully applied by the partner state concerned at the

3 Notably as set out in the International Covenant on Civil and Political Rights, the International Covenant on Economic, Social and Cultural Rights and, for gender and children's issues, UNSCR 1325 on Women, Peace and Security and UNSCR 1539 on Children in Armed Conflict, the Convention on the Rights of the Child, the EU Guidelines on Children and Armed Conflict (doc. 15634/03) as well as the OSCE Code of Conduct on politico-military aspects of security.

time when the EU is considering to bring support, a commitment to fully apply them should be sought by the EU.

G. PRINCIPLES FOR AN ESDP ACTION IN SUPPORT OF SSR

27. **Local ownership**. SSR will be conducted under local ownership. The EU will bring support to this reform. This local ownership is defined as the appropriation by the local authorities of the commonly agreed objectives and principles. This includes the commitment of the local authorities to actions on the ground, including their active support of the implementation of the SSR mission's mandate; implementation and sustainability of Security Sector Reform are their responsibility. The clear affirmation by the EU of its values, principles and objectives as well as consultation with local authorities at all stages should make local ownership possible. ESDP support of SSR will be defined in dialogue with the partner government and adapted to the specific country situation. In the absence of a partner government in crisis situations or in the immediate aftermath of a conflict, early stages of EU support for SSR should pave the way for later long-term country owned SSR reforms based on a participatory and democratic process. In this case, the aim would be to strengthen gradually and steadily this local ownership with the involvement of the civil society.

28. **Measuring progress**. Continued support for SSR should be linked to the progress achieved against mutually pre-defined and agreed benchmarks. PSC will be kept informed on this progress by regular reporting and assessments.

29. **Holistic approach**. SSR should take a broad, coherent and integrated approach that addresses wider governance and security concerns of the people. This multifaceted approach should be managed in a coherent way, ensuring that all the lines of action, such as good governance, democratic norms and rule of law, respect for human rights and long term institution building, personnel management, training and provision of equipment are mutually reinforcing.

30. **Tailored approach**. SSR activities need to be tailored to the specific needs of an individual state and its people as well as to its political environment both nationally and regionally. The state's perspective to become member of an International/Regional/Sub-regional Organisation has also to be taken into account.

31. **Co-ordinated approach**. Close co-ordination between the Council, Member States and the Commission and co-operation with other IC actors is crucial in order to avoid duplication and ensure coherence of efforts between all actors/donors. In order to ensure complementarity and avoid duplication between ESDP actions in support of SSR and other assistance activities managed by the Commission, co-ordination with the Commission is necessary from the early steps of planning, both in Brussels and at the level of EC Delegations. Co-ordination is also to be ensured with those Member States which might engage, on a bilateral basis, in SSR activities in the same states, as well as the UN, other international organisations, donors and NGOs. Good co-operation between ESDP SSR missions and with these actors should be ensured to the maximum extent possible, also with a view to ensuring synergy with them and to avoiding unnecessary duplication. In this context, lessons learned should be shared with other IC actors.

H. POSSIBLE SCENARIOS FOR ESDP ACTIONS IN SUPPORT OF SSR ACTIVITIES

Recognising that SSR can also be a useful instrument to prevent conflict in fragile states, possible scenarios where ESDP could be involved in SSR activities are set out below:

32. **In an immediate post conflict situation** where the military of the state concerned is likely to be deeply involved both in politics and in the whole security sector, the early steps of reform of the security sector is likely to require disarmament and demobilisation and subsequently reintegration of ex-combatants, for which community instruments are already available. SSR in this context may also be part of, and contribute to an exit strategy for, a more complex crisis management operation. Security would likely be ensured by an external military or police presence and political authority might be exercised by an external actor for a limited period of time.

33. **In a transition and stabilisation phase**. Local political authorities would be in place at least on a temporary basis. ESDP actions in support of SSR activities would then be undertaken in a more stable environment and in the spirit of preventing a return to violence. In this case, support for SSR could be a mission of its own tying in with already existing crisis management operations and/or community activities. Local ownership by the political authorities can be expected to a larger degree than in an immediate post-conflict situation.

34. **In an environment that is assessed as stable and where no return to significant conflict is to be expected**, ESDP actions in support of SSR could assist the on-going development of democratic institutions. Such actions would need to tie in closely with other governance reforms conducted by the state concerned, and would be complementary with Community assistance and those provided by other actors/donors in that respect.

I. RELEVANT AREAS OF ACTIVITIES RELATED TO SSR

35. The EU could give support to SSR in military and civilian areas. It should be noted that, on a case-by-case basis, sharing of civilian activities with the Commission would be necessary to ensure complementarity and avoid duplication. The assignment will be primarily based on the added value which could be brought by each of the two pillars, thereby taking into account the specifics of ESDP action.

36. Whereas Crisis Management missions may have specific mandates that include SSR activity, SSR is a horizontal concept that may cover a broader spectrum than tasks encompassed by Crisis Management missions only.

37. **Support in Reforming the Defence Sector, the armed forces, including if needed the relevant non-statutory bodies. The EU could, inter-alia, provide assistance in:**

- defining a defence policy, a clear delineation of tasks between armed forces and police;
- organising defence structures, including political control (civilian and/or adequate parliamentary control), oversight/budget control, administration, transparency;
- defining military planning procedures;
- training the armed forces, including Chiefs of Defence, chiefs of armed forces or military, including in the democratic principles of modern armed forces, regarding human rights, international law, international humanitarian law, gender issues, etc;
- reorganisation of the armed forces, which could include demobilisation, aspects related to conscription; aspects relating to ethnic integration of previously segregated armed forces units;
- military governance issues;

- co-locating experts to the national Ministry of Defence to monitor, mentor and advise local authorities in issues related to defence policy and SSR;
- the process of equipping the armed forces, establishing a mechanism for procurement, maintenance, as well as budgetary or financial regulations, etc.

38. **Support in Reforming the Police Sector, including the relevant non-statutory bodies. The EU could, inter-alia, provide assistance in the following domains:**

- assessment of policing needs;
- defining the objectives of a comprehensive policing policy and strategy, fully integrated with the objectives of the Justice/Rule of Law sector;
- developing a methodology for achieving such objectives, including critical and success factors and their measurement;
- organising the police sector, including oversight/budget control, administration, transparency and accountability, as well as political control;
- educating the police sector in the principles of modern policing and police management, including respect for human rights, international law, gender issues;
- guiding and accompanying the police force in their daily tasks during a transitional period;
- co-locating experts to the national ministry of home affairs to monitor, mentor and advise local authorities in issues related to home affairs policy and SSR;
- launching public awareness campaigns in order to secure the trust and co-operation of the community.

39. **Support in Strengthening Justice/Rule of Law elements in Security Sector Reform.** EU activities could support SSR by contributing to strengthen or reorganize justice and other rule of law structures. The principles and modalities to be applied are, among other international standards, those contained in the "*Comprehensive EU concept for missions in the field of Rule of Law in crisis management*" (Council doc. 9792/03 dated 26 May 2003) and in the Civilian Headline Goal 2008. Depending on the concept, the EU could, inter-alia, provide assistance in:

- identifying the needs of the judiciary, prosecution service and penitentiary system and support in developing a comprehensive development strategy;
- identifying administrative, human and material recourses required for the judiciary, prosecution service and penitentiary system;
- reviewing the legislative needs and assisting in planning and drafting the legislation;
- organising vetting procedures and if necessary promote or improve the training system for judicial and other personnel in the fields of rule of law;
- co-locating experts to the national ministry of justice to monitor, mentor and advise local authorities in issues related to justice policy and SSR;
- working with international organisations, NGOs, Member States and third

states to help to ensure that the rule of law sector have equipment and temporary facilities for their work;

- the development of emergency rule of law mechanisms and transitional justice institutions such as special tribunals and truth/reconciliation commissions;

- promoting the right of victims throughout the criminal justice process and improving witness protection from any intimidation and harassment;

- launching of public awareness campaigns in order to reach the confidence of the public.

40. **Support in strengthening the border and customs sector**. The EU could provide assistance in assessing needs, defining policies, objectives and rules related to border and customs services. It could also support in organising the border and customs sector, in training the border guards and customs officers, including respect for human rights, international law and gender issues. The EU could inter-alia give assistance in the following domains:

- establishing and implementing an overall strategy and policies for the management of border control and customs, including political control;

- co-locating experts to the national ministries/agencies responsible for border control and customs to monitor, mentor and advise local authorities in issues related to border and customs policy, especially in relation with SSR.

41. **Support in reforming the financial and budgetary aspects of the Security Sector**. The EU could provide advice and support, while promoting the principles of transparency, efficiency, accountability and democratic control by parliament, in the domain of co-locating experts to the national ministry of finance to monitor, mentor and advise local authorities in issues related to finance policy and SSR.

42. **General support**. In the framework of a holistic approach, the EU could also contribute to give assistance in establishing and ensuring the efficient functioning of government and division of responsibilities on all levels of public administration. Although not fully part of the Security Sector, these aspects could need consideration in the framework of an ESDP action in support of SSR. Support in re-organising the structure/working methodologies/linkage with the Security Services/Intelligence agencies of a state is often essential to the reform process.

43. **Support in DDR**: The EU, in the context of ESDP, can also bring support to DDR which can constitute a significant pillar of SSR. This specific issue, which needs specific means and expertise, will be addressed separately, but consistently with this SSR concept. Special attention will be paid to the capacities of the Commission, in particular in the field of Reintegration.

J. CORE REQUIREMENTS AND MODALITIES

44. **Legal basis.** The legal basis for an EU action should be either a UNSCR or an invitation by a host partner state or International/Regional/Sub-Regional Organisation, bearing in mind that proposals for EU action in support of SSR in a partner state can be initiated by EU Member States or the Commission, in the framework of the Treaty.

45. **Legal framework**. As a general rule, a Joint Action, under article 14 TEU, would be the legal instrument for such action. Privileges and immunities and other relevant provisions for the

international personnel of the ESDP Action in support of SSR should be set out in a SOFA/SOMA.

46. **General framework**. An ESDP action for support to SSR in a partner state would be set up under the political control and strategic direction of the PSC. A general concept describing the EU's approach to the management of a specific EU action in support of SSR in a partner state should be developed[4]. It should address the full range of activities envisaged and is an important tool to ensure coherence and comprehensiveness of possible ESDP actions. This general concept should in particular:

- set out clear objectives and tasking, including definition of the desired end state and of benchmarks; the objectives for the ESDP Action (Mission Statement) should be defined in such a way that they are possible to fulfil;
- be specific and coherent with other SSR actions supported by the European Community and other international actors;
- be goal-oriented and include an evaluation mechanism based on the objectives set;
- be time-limited and set out a clear exit strategy; these time-limited mandates could be reviewed after comprehensive evaluation; clear criteria for the termination of ESDP support should be established which would be subject to review in the course of the ESDP action;
- include flexibility in the tasking, to enable the HoM to fulfil the mandate taking into account new needs on the ground, reporting to the PSC as necessary.

47. **EUSR**. When an ESDP action in support of SSR occurs in an area where an EUSR is in place, the EUSR should ensure the overall political co-ordination of EU's actions on the ground.

48. **Security**. An ESDP action in support of SSR can be implemented only where a basic degree of security and order exists in the state concerned. This level of security could also be ensured by an international military or police presence.

49. **Resources**. Well-trained and well-equipped personnel are needed (e.g. the Action Plan for ESDP support for peace and security in Africa (doc. 10538/3/04) provides for plans for gathering and training teams of military and civilian experts to be made available by Member States on a voluntary basis. This approach could be applied to other regions). Consideration should be given to ensuring that EU personnel have the correct professional and when necessary the region-specific knowledge. ESDC courses and other courses offered through the EU training programme should be taken into account. Appropriate personnel and equipment (operational kits, including inter-alia vehicles, CIS, secure communications) are required in time to provide personal security, to be available for an early and quick deployment and to allow the timely establishment and accomplishment of the mission. To this end, logistics, effective planning capability and financial procurement mechanisms are needed.

50. **General Support to ESDP Action**. Support given by the partner state is to be ensured by a firm commitment. Support from the local Commission delegation, when existing, should also be considered and taken into account during the planning phase of the mission in order to ensure complementarity. The HoM should be able to count on the support of the

4 The general concept corresponds to the development of the Crisis Management Concept in the Crisis Management Procedures.

local diplomatic missions of Member States, in particular the Presidency and, as appropriate, the EC delegations.

51. **Standard Operating Procedures/Guiding principles**. Standards Operation Procedures (SOPs) for ESDP Actions in support of SSR and/or guiding principles for HoMs should be developed.

52. **Public Information strategy**. Support to a Public Information policy of the government for the SSR reform to which the ESDP action contributes should be fully considered.

K. PREPARATION/PLANNING

53. **Fact-finding Mission**. On the basis of a risk assessment and, when possible in consultation with the partner government, a fact-finding mission would be launched with the aim of collecting all the pertinent facts as preparation for the establishment of a SSR mission. Whenever possible and appropriate the potential HoM should participate in this FFM. Whenever possible, fact-finding missions should be carried out in association with the Commission.

54. **General concept**. On the basis of these findings, the general concept for an ESDP action will need to be developed. It will set out the general framework in which action will be taken and civilian and military operations integrated. This general concept will be approved by the Council. The concept should allow for the deployment of an advance party, in order to assess needs and prepare the deployment of the complete SSR team.

55. **Civilian-military integration**. Throughout this whole process, integration of civilian and military aspects should be ensured in a comprehensive way[5]. Initial contacts with the potential Heads of Mission and the potential contributors should be established well in advance, as well as the necessary political dialogue with the partner state authorities concerned. The Civ-Mil Cell's expertise in managing the civ-mil interface should contribute to promoting this integration.

56. **Operation Plan for ESDP Action in Support of SSR**. The HoM will then be responsible for developing this plan, on the basis of the general concept and, when appropriate, a concept of operations (CONOPS). This plan will be approved by the Council.

L. CHAIN OF COMMAND

57. According to the key principles, the mission would be conducted respecting local ownership. Nevertheless, a clear chain of command/reporting chain should be established, in accordance with the specific nature of the mission, to ensure situational awareness, political control and strategic direction exercised by the PSC.

58. The Head of Mission will report to the PSC. As part of SOPs, standard reporting procedures and a format for reporting on ESDP actions in support of SSR should be developed, taking into account the possible presence of an EUSR. A method for assessing the quality of the support offered by the partner state should also be developed.

59. In accordance with the specific nature of the mission, EUMC as well as CIVCOM will be involved to allow them to provide advice within their respective competences.

60. During the preparation, planning and conduct of the EU action by the appropriate Council bodies, the comprehensive integration of civilian and military aspects will, as appropriate,

5 A comprehensive planning concept is under development.

need to be ensured. In this field, the Civ-Mil Cell can provide an important contribution, given its expertise in managing the civ-mil interface.

M. PARTICIPATION OF THIRD STATES

61. Third States participation in any civilian or military action undertaken in support of SSR will have to be determined on a case-by-case basis. The following elements would need to be considered:

- The possible inclusion of countries of the region and/or States with a specific interest/added value for the mission.

- The possible inclusion of States contributing bilaterally to SSR in the state concerned.

62. The Joint Action should provide necessary indications on third States invited and modalities of their participation. Personnel from Third States (either seconded or contracted) should be covered by the SOFA/SOMA applicable to the mission. Conditions under which a third State would participate in the ESDP action in support of SSR will be provided for within a particular agreement to be concluded between the EU and the State.

N. FURTHER STEPS

63. **Equipment and procurement**. The envisaged DGE IX/CION joint paper on procurement could serve as a basis for equipment for ESDP actions in support of SSR. Arrangements with the Commission should be sought in relation to possible support by local Commission delegations.

64. **Standard Operating Procedures/Guiding principles**. Standard operating procedures and/or guiding principles for HoMs for ESDP Actions in support of SSR should be developed, including standard reporting procedures.

65. **Financial arrangements**. ESDP support to SSR will have an impact on resources. Due consideration should be given to matching future commitments and resources. This work should be undertaken as soon as possible by the competent bodies.

66. **DDR**. Support to DDR in a partner state within the framework of SSR should be addressed separately but consistently with this SSR concept.

67. **Overall SSR concept**. The Commission is expected to develop, in close co-operation with the Council Secretariat, an EC Concept for SSR covering first pillar activities. At a later stage, due consideration should be given to joining these two strands within the framework of an overarching EU concept for SSR.

Annex 4

COMMISSION OF THE EUROPEAN COMMUNITIES

Brussels, 24.5.2006
COM(2006) 253 final

COMMUNICATION FROM THE COMMISSION TO THE COUNCIL AND THE EUROPEAN PARLIAMENT

A Concept for European Community Support for Security Sector Reform

{SEC(2006) 658}

COMMUNICATION FROM THE COMMISSION TO THE COUNCIL AND THE EUROPEAN PARLIAMENT

A Concept for European Community Support for Security Sector Reform

1. INTRODUCTION

The European Union's external action underlines its identity as a global player and partner working to promote its common values, namely respect for human rights, fundamental freedoms, peace, democracy, good governance, gender equality, the rule of law, and solidarity and justice, including in the area of security sector reform.[1] Preventing and resolving violent conflict, combating terrorism and addressing state fragility are part of the EU's efforts to reduce insecurity and eradicate poverty, thus helping to achieve the Millennium Development Goals, sustainable development and global security.

Today there is greater recognition in the international community and within the EU that security sector reform, or security system reform as it is also referred to, reflecting the multi-sector nature of the security system, is an important part of conflict prevention, peace building and democratisation and contributes to sustainable development. SSR concerns reform of both the bodies which provide security to citizens and the state institutions responsible for management and oversight of those bodies. Thus, security system reform goes beyond the notion of effectiveness of individual services (including the military, the police, the justice institutions, etc.) and instead focuses on the overall functioning of the security system as part of a governance reform policy and strategy of the public sector. In other words, SSR should be seen as a holistic process, strengthening security for all citizens as well as addressing governance deficits. This is to ensure that the security sector is not placed or treated out-

1 As reflected in key policy documents like the European Union's Development Policy Statement, "The European Consensus" on development, adopted by the Council on 22 November 2005, published in Official Journal No C 46 of 24/02/2006, and in the European Security Strategy (ESS) adopted by the European Council in December 2003.

side the overall public sector, but seen as an integral but balanced part of public resource allocations and the institutional framework of the state. Although some aspects of SSR can be short-term, the overall SSR process needs to be long-term and be based on strong national ownership.

SSR is not a new area of engagement for the European Union. It has been an integral part of EU integration, enlargement and external assistance for many years. Through Community instruments the EU has supported reform processes in partner countries and regions in different parts of the world and under a wide range of policy areas. These include policies and instruments which fall under Development Cooperation, Enlargement, the Stabilisation and Association Process, the European Neighbourhood Policy, Conflict Prevention and Crisis Management, Democracy and Human Rights, and the External Dimension of the area of Freedom, Security and Justice.

In recent years the EU has developed additional capacity to support SSR under its Common Foreign and Security Policy (CFSP), as reflected in the European Security Strategy.[2] In this way European Security and Defence Policy (ESDP) missions and Community action in the area of SSR can complement each other, especially in countries in crisis or post-crisis situations. Some EU Member States are also very active in supporting security sector reform processes on a bilateral basis. The need for a more coherent and common EU concept on SSR across the three pillars has, therefore, been raised by Member States and the Commission in order to contribute to more effective EU external action in this area. This concept paper is the European Commission's contribution to a clearer and integrated EU policy framework for engaging in security system reform.

2. RATIONALE AND OVERALL AIM

The paper sets out principles and norms for the European Community's engagement in SSR, based on current support in different countries and regional settings, the relevant policy frameworks under which the EC supports SSR, and the rationale for SSR as an important part of Community support. In this way the policy framework will help to ensure more coordinated and strategic approaches to Community activities falling under the different policy instruments, recognising that SSR needs to be treated as a cross-cutting issue, spanning the various strands of EC external assistance. In addition, the concept seeks to define the Community's role in the wider framework of EU external action in the area of SSR in order to ensure complementarity between EC activities and those undertaken by the EU as part of CFSP/ESDP and by Member States bilaterally. The aim is that this concept and the EU Concept for ESDP support for Security Sector Reform (SSR), which was agreed under the UK Presidency,[3] will complement each other and be joined within the framework of an overarching EU concept for SSR.

3. THE SECURITY SYSTEM AND ITS REFORM

3.1. The need for security sector reform

For the EC, security is not limited to the territorial security of the state or to the security of a particular regime; it includes both the external and internal security of a state and its people. Thus, it focuses on human security (freedom from want, freedom from fear and freedom to take action on one's own behalf),[4] putting the security of citizens at the centre and thus complementing state security. Citizens should be able to expect the state to be capable of maintaining peace and guaranteeing the strategic security interests of the country, as well as ensuring that their lives, property, and political, economic and social rights are safeguarded. The State has to be able to protect citizens from the threats of insecurity, including violent conflict and terrorism, while protecting rights and institutions from being undermined by these threats. This concept paper focuses on those aspects which are designed to contribute to peace, the protection of life and limb, and to ensure the upholding of the law and oversight through the justice system and democratic institutions of the relevant executive bodies.

Oversized and underpaid regular forces, irregular forces and security firms operating outside the law, lack of judicial independence, status and resources, lack of capacity, legal competence and

2..Ibid.

3 Council Conclusions, General Affairs and External Relations Council, 21-22 November 2005

4 *Human Security Now*, the final Report of the Commission on Human Security (2003) and the Commission Communication on Governance and Development, COM(2003) 615 final.

sometimes political will by parliaments to ensure accountability of security services, human rights abuses by police and defence forces, a culture of state impunity and the inability to protect the population against terrorist acts; these are some of the challenges faced by EU partner countries, hampering common efforts to achieve sustainable development. Citizens' rights are most vulnerable to abuse by state agents in states where there is no space for civil society to be effective and democracy is weak or non-existent as a result. These challenges also have an impact on the stability of regions and on the international community as a whole.. The military is only one instrument for providing security for the population. The police and gendarmerie, the courts and the prison system provide security by upholding law and order within the state. By guarding against abuse of powers and ensuring that policies are implemented according to mandates granted, democratic oversight bodies (parliaments, ombudsmen, etc.) and the judicial system also contribute to security. Oversight may also be provided by civil society institutions (civilian review boards, public complaints commissions), as well as informally through NGO lobbying, investigative media, etc.

3.2. The security system and its reform

Based on the OECD-DAC definition,[5] **the security system** can be defined as all state institutions and other entities with a role in ensuring the security of the state *and* its people.

Core security actors including law enforcement institutions: armed forces; police; gendarmeries; paramilitary forces; presidential guards; intelligence services; coast guards; border guards; customs authorities; reserve or local security units.
Security management and oversight bodies: parliament/legislature; government/the executive, including ministries of defence, internal affairs, foreign affairs; national security advisory bodies; customary and traditional authorities; financial management bodies; and civil society, including the media, academia and NGOs.
Justice institutions: justice ministries; prisons; criminal investigation and prosecution services; the judiciary (courts and tribunals), implementation justice services (bailiffs and ushers), other customary and traditional justice systems; human rights commissions and ombudsmen; etc.
Non-statutory security forces: liberation armies; guerrilla armies; private bodyguard units; private security companies; etc.

Security system reform means transforming the security system, which includes all these actors, their roles, responsibilities and actions, working together to manage and operate the system in a manner that is consistent with democratic norms and sound principles of good governance, and thus contributing to a well functioning security framework. For the EC, the objective is to contribute explicitly to strengthening of good governance, democracy, the rule of law, the protection of human rights and the efficient use of public resources. In this respect, civilian control and Parliamentary oversight are key aspects of SSR.

4. EUROPEAN COMMUNITY SUPPORT FOR SSR

4.1. Areas of engagement

The European Community (EC) is engaged in SSR-related support in over 70 countries, through both geographical and thematic programmes.[6] This includes SSR support for Eastern Europe, North and South Caucasus and Central Asia, Western Balkans, Africa, Caribbean and the Pacific, South Mediterranean and the Middle East, Latin America and Asia.

The EC has supported SSR in countries and regions in relatively stable environments, in countries undergoing transition and long-term democratisation processes as well as in countries in immediate post-conflict and in longer-term postconflict peace building and reconstruction processes.[7] This includes support for the reform of law enforcement institutions, justice institutions,

5 Security System Reform and Governance, Policy and Practice, DAC Guidelines and Reference Series (Paris: OECD 2004)..

6 See annex 2 - Areas of EC support for SSR – Regional and Country examples.

7 Ibid.

and state institutions dealing with management and oversight of the security system. There are also a large number of activities designed to strengthen civilian control and democratic governance of the public sector in general and to guarantee the respect for human rights which also encompass the security sector and thus indirectly contribute to security sector reform. Linked to this is the EC support for capacity building of regional and sub-regional organisations concerning security-sector related activities and reforms in the area of peace and security to contribute to regional aspects of SSR. This can also have a positive impact on SSR efforts at national level.

A number of policies and strategies are relevant to support in this area. Although principles guiding support for SSR should be the same for all forms of Community support for SSR, approaches and methods of implementation may vary depending on policy frameworks and country contexts.[8] Within the OECD/DAC, EU Member States and the EC have helped to development guidelines for support for SSR, *Security System Reform and Governance,*[9] which provide an important basis for EC engagement in this area, in terms of norms, principles and operational guidance.

Extension of Official Development Assistance (ODA) eligibility to the area of security, as agreed at the OECD/DAC High-Level Meeting in March 2005, means that a wider spectrum of SSR activities can be financed by development cooperation funds than before. This encompasses all civilian aspects of SSR, as well as activities in relation to democratic and civilian control of the military parts of SSR, including financial and administrative management of defence issues.[10]

EC support is provided in close cooperation with national, regional and international actors, including the UN, the Council of Europe and the OSCE, to ensure sustainable and nationally owned processes of change. Political buy-in by national stakeholders is of central importance to ensure a sustainable reform process. National ownership of the overall reform process should therefore always be ensured, together with engagement by the different national and regional stakeholders. Political dialogue with third countries is an important instrument for helping the EU and partner countries to agree on common objectives and priorities for action. In addition, implementation of the OECD/DAC principles for good international engagement in fragile states,[11] by both the Community and the Member States, could further help to consolidate an enabling framework for support for SSR in such country situations.

4.2. Principles guiding EC support for SSR[12]

Security system reform processes should be:

- nationally/regionally owned reform processes designed to strengthen good governance, democratic norms, the rule of law and the respect for human rights, in line with internationally agreed norms;[13]
- addressing the core requirements of a well functioning security system, including the development of a nationally owned concept of security, well defined policies and good governance of security institutions, while ensuring that any develop-

8 See annex 1 - EC Policy frameworks - and annex 3 concerning the programming cycle.

9 *Security System Reform and Governance, Policy and Practice,* DAC Guidelines and Reference Series (2004)

10 Technical cooperation provided to parliament, government ministries, law enforcement agencies and the judiciary to assist, review and reform the security system and thus improve democratic governance and civilian control; technical cooperation provided to governments to improve civilian oversight and democratic control of budgeting, management, accountability and auditing of security expenditure, including military budgets, as part of a public expenditure management programme; assistance to civil society to enhance its competence and capacity to scrutinise the security system so that it is managed in accordance with democratic norms and principles of accountability, transparency and good governance. Direct support for the military and non-statutory security forces is not included.

11 The OECD/DAC High-Level Meeting of Development Ministers and Heads of Agencies agreed on 3 March 2005 that the principles drafted by the OECD/DAC Fragile States Group on "good international engagement in fragile states," by both development and security stakeholders, should be piloted in 9 fragile states until the end of 2006 and be considered for adoption by the HLM in 2007.

12 These are based on the principles outlined in the OECD/DAC Guidelines: Security System Reform and Governance, Policy and Practice, DAC Guidelines and Reference Series (Paris: OECD 2004).

13 See annex 4

ment of professional security forces leads them to be both accountable to the civil authorities and capable of carrying out the operational tasks assigned to them;

- seen as a framework for addressing diverse security challenges facing states and their populations, based on a gender-sensitive multi-sector approach, and targeting reform needs in different key sectors. This includes separating tasks between different services and institutions and taking into account the role of civil society and other non-state structures of governance, for example, traditional justice systems in some societies, in the development and implementation of national SSR;
- based on the same principles of accountability and transparency that apply across the public sector, in particular improved governance through greater civilian and parliamentary oversight of security processes;
- based on political dialogue with each partner country, addressing human rights, development and security concerns, and be carried out in synergy with other instruments.

4.3. The particular role and strength of EC support for SSR

The EC aims to provide added value in support of SSR on the basis of the following factors:

- The Commission's supranational nature and its experience in promoting democracy, human rights and nation-building, including in very difficult situations, provides it with the ability to conduct activities which might not be possible for other actors, including bilateral donors.
- The global reach of the EC enables the Commission to act in almost any region of the world, if considered necessary, and to respond to a wide variety of situations.
- Long-term presence on the ground, through the EC Delegations, means that the EC can lend long-term support to both the national dialogue on SSR and to different aspects of the SSR process.
- The commitment to policy coherence for development, in particular where EC policies have a significant impact on developing countries. A coherent approach to SSR, taking into account the close inter-linkages between security, development and governance, including democratic principles, rule of law, human rights and institutional capacity building, is crucial for successful reform and effective use of scarce financial resources, not only at Community and Member States level, but also at partner country level.
- The vast array of instruments – EC support for SSR forms part of its regular external assistance and EU political dialogue. The potential to coordinate EC action through its spectrum of policy instruments and financial instruments is a critical advantage in security system reform.
- The EC can draw on the wide variety of experiences of SSR among Member States. In most of the new Member States, there has been comprehensive reform of the security sector in the context of regime change and the establishment of democratic institutions and the rule of law.
- The potential to coordinate and to facilitate harmonisation of EC actions in transitional situations by promoting linkages after a crisis to recovery and longterm development, by addressing root causes of conflict and by ensuring coordination and complementarity with action carried out by the EU in the framework of the CFSP/ESDP, by Member States, by other regional and multilateral organisations and by local civil society, is a critical advantage in security system reform. This can reinforce the reform process in post-conflict situations and should be guided by integrated transition strategies, including clear links between SSR support and support in the area of Disarmament, Demobilisation and Reintegration of former combatants (DDR).

5. EU SUPPORT FOR SSR IN THE FUTURE

5.1. EC perspectives on how to strengthen the overall EU support for SSR

Security sector reform is an integral part of EU enlargement, as regards pre-accession countries, and is an important part of development cooperation and external assistance to third countries. The new instruments for external assistance, which are all relevant to EC SSR support, will enable the Community to increase its support still further.[14] The Community needs to focus more clearly on the governance aspects of SSR, including the strengthening of parliamentary oversight, judicial independence and media freedom, and take a more holistic approach to SSR by engaging in coordinated support for the different sectors of the SSR process. This will contribute to better implementation of EC support in this area and result in more coordinated and comprehensive support from the EU as a whole. In order to achieve this, SSR needs to be more clearly integrated into Country and Regional Strategy Papers and action plans as well as into other forms of cooperation with partner countries.

While the EU's medium to long-term engagement in SSR needs to be ensured through Community programmes and Member State bilateral support, more short to medium-term engagement can kick-start and complement long-term instruments. The Stability Instrument will boost the capacity of the Community to respond rapidly and engage more flexibly in the short term in different parts of the world. ESDP missions are often involved in supporting the early stages of SSR in crisis or post-crisis situations and in initiating new areas of EU support, especially in areas such as core military and intelligence reform. To consolidate EU support for SSR, the EU needs to ensure greater synergy between ongoing Community and Member State bilateral support, on the one hand, and more effective coordination between missions undertaken in the framework of ESDP and Community and Member State action, on the other.

It is important for the EU as a whole to take a comprehensive and pragmatic approach to the reform process in order to provide timely, well coordinated and relevant support throughout the overall process and its different parts. Joint strategic analyses and needs assessments[15] of the overall process and comprehensive planning, where applicable, will ensure more coherent and coordinated action. Effective support needs exchanges of expertise and a broader base of experts in the Member States who can be deployed in the different aspects of SSR.

Based on political dialogue with the partner country, the EU needs to ensure that its support matches the needs and wishes of national stakeholders and is provided within the political context of the overall reform process. Civil society action, without the prior agreement of governments, can also contribute to improvements in oversight of the security sector. In addition, an analysis should be made concerning what EU action would be most appropriate for any given context, complementing existing programmes and adding value in terms of international support for SSR. Comprehensive implementation guidelines would be an important next step.

EU action also needs to be coordinated with the work of other external actors. Implementation frameworks for SSR in the OECD/DAC, with the active participation of the Commission, Member States and other donors (e.g. Canada, US, Japan, Norway and Switzerland), could improve donor coordination and enable donors to complement each others' support. In promoting effective multilateralism, close coordination and cooperation with the UN and other international organisations should always be sought, including with regional and sub-regional organisations, such as the OSCE and the African Union, and with civil society. This reflects the fact that they are important partners and stakeholders for the EU in the development and implementation of SSR approaches and programmes. Capacity building at regional and sub-regional level will therefore also be an important focus in the future for SSR support.

14 For example, the European Neighbourhood and Partnership Instrument offers new approaches to crossborder cooperation and the capacity to support a wide range of SSR activities. Under the Instrument for Pre-accession Assistance, beneficiary countries will be supported in their efforts to undertake reforms, in particular concerning their legal systems, police, prosecution, judiciary and penitentiary systems, customs and border controls. Cross-border cooperation will also help to prevent and combat common security threats in border areas.

15 EC, CFSP/ESDP and MS

5.2. Recommendation to strengthen the EC contribution to overall EU support for SSR

Strengthening policy and programming dialogue

- Ensuring a more effective and holistic policy and programming dialogue with stakeholders in partner countries by bringing international standards on SSR[16] and the principles of EC support to the policy dialogue and agreeing on objectives, priorities and follow-up mechanisms with governments and Non-State Actors, in an effort to address the capacity and performance of public institutions more effectively. EC assistance may be agreed in countries where the quality of security sector governance is deteriorating.

Integrating SSR in Country (CSP) and Regional (RSP) Strategy Papers, Action Plans and programming tools

- Integrating SSR in CSPs, RSPs and Action Plans, based on governance and conflict analyses and specific security sector analyses. This will make it easier for the EC to take a holistic approach to SSR. At the same time, flexibility needs to be ensured to enable the EC to adjust its programming to circumstances on the ground. Coordination between EC and Member States bilateral CSPs can enhance the planning of overall EU efforts in this area.

Ensuring coordinated planning

- A coordinated planning approach across the three-pillar structure, when applicable, will ensure better coherence of all EU actions.
- Needs assessments and the use of assessment and planning teams to carry out factfinding missions can assist in the planning of (additional) EC activities and wider EU action. Joint missions with the Council Secretariat and/or Member States should also be considered.

Strengthening overall implementation of EU support

- Work towards strengthening coordination and complementarity between EU actions by the EC, the EU in the framework of CFSP/ESDP and Member States' bilateral programmes at headquarters and field level.
- Work towards enabling more joint implementation between the Community, the Member States and EU action undertaken in the framework of CFSP/ESDP.

Developing tools for planning and implementation

- Developing tools for comprehensive SSR analyses as well as operational guidelines for implementing SSR as a follow-up to this concept can assist in the overall assessment, programming and implementation of EU/EC support in the field.

Expanding the expertise and pool of experts for field missions and programmes

- Contributing to the development of institutional cooperation between the relevant institutions in the Member States and the Commission to respond to the need to

16 See annex 4. EN 11 EN

deploy numerous and qualified experts for short, medium and long-term activities and to ensure coherence in profiles, training and equipment for such experts due to be seconded abroad, within the framework of specific SSR programmes. Appropriate modalities for effective mobilisation of human resources need to be identified.

Developing SSR-specific training for the mainstreaming of SSR

- For the EU to take a more holistic and comprehensive approach to SSR, specific training should be developed for SSR to help mainstream SSR into programming and to broaden expertise across EU and Member States institutions.

Prioritising SSR under the new Financial Instruments

- Support for SSR should, where relevant, be prioritised under the new Financial Instruments by taking a comprehensive and holistic approach to SSR, including the instruments for Pre-Accession Assistance, European Neighbourhood and Partnership, Development Cooperation and Economic Cooperation, and Stability. The Stability Instrument could have an important role in ensuring rapid and flexible support for critical phases of the reform process, and complementing both long-term assistance programmes and other short-term instruments.

Strengthening cooperation with international partners

- Strengthening cooperation with regional and multilateral organisations, including the UN, OECD, Council of Europe, OSCE and AU, in training, information sharing on best practice and more coordinated planning and implementation of SSR support. Cooperation should also be strengthened with civil society organisations and other donors at field level with a view to improve the efficiency of EU support in the area of SSR.

Annex 5

COMMISSION OF THE EUROPEAN COMMUNITIES

Brussels, 24.5.2006
SEC(2006) 658

COMMISSION STAFF WORKING DOCUMENT

Annexes to the Communication from the Commission to the Council and the European Parliament

"A Concept for European Community Support for Security Sector Reform"

{COM(2006) 253 final}

I. ANNEX 1 - EC POLICY FRAMEWORKS RELEVANT FOR SUPPORT IN THE AREA OF SSR

A number of policies and strategies are relevant for support in this area. Although principles guiding the support to SSR should be the same for all forms of Community support in this area, approaches and implementation modalities may vary depending on policy frameworks and country contexts.

a) The EU Development Policy

The promotion of human rights, democracy, the rule of law and good governance are seen as integral parts of EU's development cooperation and constitute an area where the Community will be particularly active, as stated in "the European Consensus" on development. It recognises that security and development are important and complementary aspects of EU relations with third countries. Furthermore, it states that the EU will improve its response to difficult partnerships and fragile states, and strengthen its efforts in conflict prevention and will support the prevention of state fragility through for example governance reform, rule of law, and the building of viable state institutions.

Community action under the new EU Africa Strategy: "*The EU and Africa: Towards a strategic partnership*" will in the area of governance, peace and security particularly focus on enhanced support to post conflict reconstruction, the new UN Peace building Commission; the strengthening of fragile states; DDR and SSR programmes in African States; promotion of human rights, good governance and support to African efforts to improve governance including support to the Africa Peer Review Mechanism and to African Parliaments. In taking this strategy forward the EC will not only engage at national and regional level[1] but also at Pan-African level.[2]

The Commission Communication on Governance and Development[3] underlines the fact that security system reform is an integral component of good governance. "Effective management, transparency and accountability of the security system are necessary conditions for the creation of a security environment that upholds democratic principles and human rights. Reform of core security actors such as the military, paramilitary, police as well as its civilian oversight structures are of fundamental importance to create safe security environments and to keep the security sector permanently subject to the same governance norms as other parts of the public sector and military forces under the political control of a civilian authority".

b) Human rights and democracy policy

This is also a cross-cutting policy integrated into development cooperation, the ENP, Association agreements etc. While these objectives were already set under Article 177 of the EC Treaty on development cooperation[4], and subsequently included under Article 181 a, a further step in integrating human rights and democratic principles into the policies of the European Union was taken with the entry into force of the Treaty on European Union (TEU) on 1 November 1993. The treaty also includes as one of the objectives of the Common Foreign and Security Policy of the European Union the development and consolidation of "*democracy and the rule of law, and respect for human rights and fundamental freedoms*". Human rights clauses are now routinely included in EC bilateral agreements and democracy and human rights are mainstreamed in all development policy instruments (see (a) above). The European Initiative on Democracy and Human Rights is the main tool for EU support to civil society initiatives in this field and will be succeeded by a new thematic programme 2007-13.

c) The Enlargement Policy and the Stabilisation and Association Process

The enlargement process is an important tool for bringing about SSR in Central and Eastern

1 Through CSPs/National indicative programmes (NIPs) and RSPs/Regional Indicative Programmes (RIPs)
2 The EU and Africa: Towards a Strategic Partnership, Council of the European Union, (doc. 15702/1/05 Rev 1) adopted by the European Council 15-16 December 200
3 COM(2003)615 final
4 "Community policy in this area shall contribute to the general objective of developing and consolidating democracy and the rule of law and to that of respecting human rights and fundamental freedoms".

Europe. It has also inspired significant reforms in Turkey, Croatia and Western Balkans, which are all candidates or potential candidates for EU membership. In the latter case, SSR support is an integral part of the Stabilisation and Association Process (SAP).

The reform of the security sector in candidate or potential candidate countries is partly covered under the political Copenhagen criteria (guaranteeing democracy, the rule of law, human rights, respect and protection of minorities) for EU membership. The prospect of EU membership also carries with it a series of very specific obligations in the areas of border controls, migration, asylum and visa, police cooperation, or judicial co-operation in criminal or civil matters, which falls under the *EU policy of freedom, security and justice*. Fulfilling membership requirements in these areas is not only about transposing in national legislation the related EU acquis under Chapter 24 of accession negotiations. The countries must also demonstrate their capacity to successfully implement this *acquis*, and more generally align the rest of the related legislation and practice of their services in line with commonly accepted EU standards and best practices.

At the Thessaloniki summit (June 2003), the SAP was enriched by including European partnerships, identifying short and medium-term priorities which the countries need to address, in order to help them with their reforms and preparations for future membership. As of 1 January 2007, candidate countries, as well as potential candidate countries, will be covered by the Instrument for Pre-accession Assistance IPA, which will help beneficiary countries to progressively align with the standards and policies of the European Union, including where appropriate the *acquis communautaire*.

d) The European Neighbourhood Policy (ENP)

Through the ENP launched in May 2004 through a Communication from the Commission[5], the EU is notably seeking to promote good governance and economic development in its own immediate vicinity. Security-sector reform and cooperation on common security threats as well as on justice and security matters are among the priorities identified in the action plans already adopted with seven partner countries (Israel, Jordan, Moldova, Morocco, the Palestinian Authority, Tunisia and Ukraine) or currently in preparation with Armenia, Azerbaijan, Egypt, Georgia and Lebanon. To support their implementation, the Commission has proposed a new European Neighbourhood and Partnership Instrument[6] (ENPI) which will offer a new approach to cross-border cooperation and the capacity for the Community to support a wider range of activities than is possible under the existing financial instruments (MEDA and TACIS).

e) Conflict Prevention and Crisis Management

In the EC Communication on Conflict Prevention[7] it was emphasized that more targeted action needs to be undertaken in the areas of:

- **Democracy the rule of law and civil society**, with emphasis on electoral processes, parliamentary activities and the administration of justice
- **Reform of the security sector**, underlying that the Commission intends to play an increasingly active role
- Specific post-conflict measures such as demobilisation, disarmament and reintegration, identifying DDR as one important dimension of SSR.

In addition, the EC engaged in civilian crisis management activities in situations of crisis and immediate post-crisis. *The Rapid Reaction Mechanism*[8] (RRM), set up in 2001 has proven to be an important mechanism for enhancing the European capacity to intervene quickly and effectively in crisis or potential crisis situations. Although short term in nature it has been proved useful in kick-

5 European Neighbourhood Policy, Communication from the Commission (2004) 373

6 Implementing and Promoting the European Neighbourhood Policy, Communication to the Commission SEC (2005) 1521

7 The European Community Communication on Conflict Prevention (COM 2001 211)

8 Council Regulation (EC) No 381/2001

starting support also in the area of SSR that is then followed up by more long term assistance through regional budget lines, ensuring that EC engagement is not short term but has a long term perspective, reflecting the fact that SSR is a long term process requiring long-term commitment both in pre- and post-conflict settings. The proposed Stability Instrument which should replace the RRM in 2007, would provide short-term funding and enable the Community to act rapidly and more flexibly with support to the early stages of the reform process, paving the way for more long-term EC support.

f) External dimension of the area of freedom, security and justice.

The external dimension of the area of freedom, security and justice concerns all third countries with whom the EU has relations, both those partners which aspire to EU membership and thereby have the obligation to align with the *acquis* or EU best practices as well as other countries which can benefit from EU experience and models. Freedom, security and justice policies increasingly form an important part of relations with third countries through Stabilisation and Association Agreements; Partnership or Association Agreements. Sharing the values of freedom, security and justice with third countries contribute to advancing the EU's external relations objectives by promoting the rule of law, democratic values and sound institutions. Practical examples of cooperation with third countries in the JLS area cover areas such as border management; migration and asylum as well as readmission agreements; the fight against corruption and organised crime, including trafficking in human beings and drugs as well as money laundering; police and law enforcement, judicial cooperation as well as justice issues; counter-terrorism. Community assistance is offered under various external strategies and programmes in these areas, covering, for example, institutions and capacity building. In December, the Council adopted a strategy for the external dimension of justice and home affairs which highlights as key thematic priorities that the Union must respond to the security threats of terrorism and organised crime and to the challenge of managing migration flows for the mutual benefit of partner countries and EU.

II. ANNEX 2 – AREAS OF EUROPEAN COMMUNITY SUPPORT TO SSR

The Community is supporting SSR related activities in over seventy countries. In addition, many programmes are carried out within a regional framework to enhance regional cooperation. EC support can be divided into the following seven broad categories (with programmes often spanning over more than one category):

The EC has primarily been engaged in the following areas of SSR support:

1. *Civil Management Bodies* (including support to. executive branches of government concerning planning and execution, security policy development and personnel management of SSR bodies)

2. *Civil Oversight Mechanisms* (including support to the legislature to exercise democratic and civilian control and to civil society capacity building and watchdog functions)

3. *Justice reform* (including support to justice ministries, prosecution, judiciary, prison system, human rights commissions, ombudsman functions etc)

4. *Law enforcement* (including support to police or other law enforcement agencies such as border guards, customs etc)

5. *Armed Forces (limited support in the areas of training and aspects of army integration)*

6. *Support to Disarmament, Demobilisation and Reintegration* of former combatants and efforts to tackle Small Arms and Light Weapons

7. *Regional Capacity Building*

A comprehensive reform process is most easily achieved in stable partnerships where the country is undergoing a process of transition towards good governance, rule of law, respect of democratic principles and human rights. South Africa and Ukraine are good examples of this where the EC has given substantial support to the SSR process in such a context. In post-conflict situations where national stakeholders show an interest in engaging in reform, there can also be ample opportunities for the Community to engage in SSR. Concretely, Peace agreements can offer the opportunity to begin restructuring the security sector, including demobilising, disarming and reintegrating former combatants (DDR) and integrating rebel forces into a new national army.

In difficult partnerships and fragile states, including many countries in ongoing violent conflict or early post-conflict it can be more difficult to carry out SSR activities. For this reason linking SSR activities with DDR and Peace Support Operations (PSO) such as, for example those conducted in the framework of the African Peace Facility (APF) can be important. EC is involved in support to SSR in fragile states and in countries in crisis, either in conjunction with ESDP missions or on its own, as part of the implementation of the EC country and/or regional strategy or through specific policy objectives of crosscutting issues such as human rights, governance and conflict prevention.

Africa, Caribbean and Pacific

In relation to the ACP region the EC is involved in SSR both in relation to countries in conflict, countries in post-conflict and countries in more stable environments.

At least the following countries receive SSR related support:

Angola, Benin, Burkina Faso, Burundi, Cameroon, Comoros, Dominican Republic, Democratic Republic of Congo, Eritrea, Fiji, Guinea Bissau, Equatorial Guinea, Guinea Conakry, Haiti, Ivory Coast, Jamaica, Kenya, Liberia, Madagascar, Malawi, Mauritius, Mozambique, Niger, Nigeria,

Republic of Congo, Rwanda, Seychelles, Sierra Leone, Solomon Islands, South Africa, Sudan, Somalia, Chad, Togo, Vanuatu and Uganda.

The majority of support is in the area of **Justice Reform, Law Enforcement and Civil Management**, especially in the area of rule of law. This often includes capacity building of law enforcement agencies, key ministries, legal reforms and access to justice for the population, by strengthening and modernising legal institutions that are primarily responsible for the administration of justice. It often also includes human rights components. The support is often aimed at strengthening key ministries, law commissions, university law faculties, anticorruption bureaus etc. The support has also been aimed at strengthening individual services including police, courts, and prison services, concerning capacity building and human rights.

Support to democratic governance programmes cover SSR related support to **Civil Oversight Mechanisms**, including national assemblies and commissions for the human rights etc. as in the case of Kenya. Chad is another example, having received support in the area of good governance, including the national assembly, ministry of justice and the Supreme Court, to enhance capacity and transparency in decision making in relation to the justice system. In Fiji transforming communities through good governance support, involves key stakeholders in capacity building on rule of law and good governance issues and is provided to institutions and civil society.

Public Financial Management Reforms, including capacity building in budget management, which can have an impact to SSR. Support in that area is the objective of many projects in ACP countries.

In the case of DRC the community instruments have also supported **Military Aspects** of SSR, through support to the Centres de Brassage for Army Integration, in this way also complementing Operation EUSEC assisting the government in defence reform.

Disarmament, Demobilisation and Reintegration is another area with relatively substantial EC support. Through the Multi-donor Demobilization and Reintegration Programme for the greater Great Lakes region, the EC is providing funding and participating actively in the coordination of the MDRP. In, addition complementary support is given to some of the seven countries covered by the MDRP, including DRC, Republic of Congo, Burundi and Angola.

In addition the EC has given DDR support to countries like Liberia, Sierra Leone, Eritrea, Somalia, and Guinea Bissau in the ACP region. Support is also provided to countries in the region in the area of addressing the destabilizing accumulation and spread of small arms and light weapons.

Country example – South Africa

The EC has been engaged in SSR support to South Africa for many years, especially in relation to justice reform and police reform. This has included support to transforming the justice system working on capacity building with the Department for Justice, Safety and Security.

In the area of policing, the focus has been on reforming the police at the federal and provincial level. This includes working on capacity building and institutional development of the South African Police Service and the Department for Justice, Safety and Security. At the provincial level the support includes support to the police in the Eastern Cape Province, working with the Ministry of Safety and Security in the Eastern Cape.

Through the *Conflict and Governance Facility*, EC supports the promotion of informed decisions on issues related to governance and conflict involving the National Treasury, the Office of the President, a number of line departments and civil society.

The aim is to improve:

- policy analysis as a better informed policy making and implementation,
- capacity and joint-research in and between research institutions, in order to enhance transfer of knowledge and skills
- the policy debate, enhancing the involvement and quality of debate on security related issues in South Africa.

In addition, he Institute for Security Studies has received specific support for strengthening their capacity and research in relation to fighting crime, arms trafficking etc

Regional initiatives, includes the MDRP for DDR in the greater Great Lakes region and Regional Palop (Pays Africains de langue Officielle Portugaise) in the area of justice reform.

Western Balkans

Beneficiary countries: Albania, Bosnia-Herzegovina, Croatia, Serbia and Montenegro including Kosovo (under UNSCR 1244) and the former Yugoslav Republic of Macedonia.

The European Community has given support in the areas of **Civilian Management** supporting capacity building for example in the Ministry of Security through the establishment of the National Security Authority.

In the area of **Justice Reform and Internal Security** substantial support has been granted to all CARDS beneficiary countries, including the creation of independent justice Commissions, as well as support to new criminal legislation, training of prosecutors, and capacity building of judicial and prosecutorial institutions, ministries of justice, and training centers etc. Further assistance has been granted to achieve more effective and modern operation of the court system, legal aid, and support to judicial and law faculties, to ensure transparent and integral diffusion of court rulings to the legal community and the general public. Support has been provided to High Courts and inspectorates, the establishment of judicial system in juvenile matters as well as support to training of court administrators, renovation of courts, prison construction and training of prison officers etc. Support to Dayton-established human rights institutions has also been granted. At regional level, support has focused on enhancing judicial cooperation.

In the area of **Police Reform**, substantial support has been given to all the beneficiary countries, including capacity building in the areas of resource management, analysis, general logistics and technical support, support to a functional reviews for police reform, upgrading of police operational centres, police training and equipment etc. At regional level, support has focused on enhancing police cooperation. This has included not only general policing but also support to specialized police forces (e.g. organized crime, money laundering etc.), border police, border guards and migration authorities, other law enforcement agencies such as customs, financial intelligence units etc.

Particular attention was given to regional co-operation under the CARDS programme, including in the area of strengthening national capacities for the gathering and sharing international police and judicial information, including the enhancement of the Interpol network.

Support has also been given to improve **Border** as well as **Migration Management**.

Last but not least, as part of the comprehensive approach towards improving Financial Management and Control, **Financial Management of SSR related expenditure** has been supported throughout the region. This comprehensive reform includes capacity building of the Ministry of Finance and Treasury in introducing decentralized implementation systems, as well as in the areas of economic policy planning and research, public procurement and audit systems, human resource management etc. This has included support in the area of public internal financial control, public administration reform, including salary reform and training and reform in the area of public procurement. It has also included support to the Supreme Audit Institution and upgrading of Ministry of Finance district offices.

Country example – Albania

Through the CARDS programme, the EC has provided significant support to SSR-related activities in Albania. This has aimed primarily at strengthening the administrative capacities of the relevant institutions (Ministries of Justice and Interior, as well as customs, police, judicial and penitentiary administrations). Albania has benefited from both national and regional programmes, aiming respectively at consolidating the rule of law and enhancing regional cooperation.

Significant progress on SSR-related areas has been achieved through the Customs Assistance Mission in Albania (CAM-A), the Police Assistance Mission of the European Community to Albania (PAMECA), the European Assistance Mission to the Albanian Judicial System (EURALIUS), as well as other complementary actions.

The CAM-A programme has aimed initially at assisting the Albanian Customs Service to restore its ability to collect revenue and improve the customs revenue yield. Subsequently, it has provided specialised advice and assistance based on the EU Customs Blueprints, to assist the Albanian effort to create an efficient and self-sustaining Customs service (incl. the computerisation of the customs service through the provision of the ASYCUDA system).

The EC also supported the efforts of the Albanian customs and police services to fight organised trafficking through an ad hoc initiative (the Organised Crime Initiative, managed by CAM-A) which involved the deployment of an operational team consisting of both customs and police officers.

PAMECA has aimed to assist the Albanian authorities in establishing a more effective police force in Albania, able to professionally and accountably investigate and counter criminal activities and ensure public order, in cooperation with the judiciary.

EURALIUS has aimed at supporting the development of a more independent, impartial, efficient, professional, transparent and modern justice system, restoring people's confidence in their institutions, and the consolidation of democracy and rule of law.

Eastern Europe and Central Asia

EC support to the region includes activities in at least the following countries:

Armenia, Azerbaijan, Belarus, Moldova, Georgia, Kazakhstan, Kyrgyzstan, Russia, Tajikistan, Ukraine and Uzbekistan.

EC support includes activities within the area of **Justice Reform and Law Enforcement** including institution building, equipment and training, customs administration, combating human trafficking as part of support to improve border as well as migration management. There are a number of activities supported in this area in relation to Belarus, Moldova, Ukraine and Central Asia, many times in the framework of a regional approach.

Justice reform includes support to institutional capacity building to enhance transparency and efficiency of key ministries and institutions, including capacity building of the ministry of interior and justice and advice to the ministries of justice on strategic and organizational issues.

This also includes support to courts, legal advice centres, prison services, training of judges, bailiffs and other legal professionals etc. In the area of police reform, support has been given to strengthen respect for human rights and rule of law in the case of Kyrgyzstan, as well as support to assess needs of broader police sector reform programme.

In the case of Azerbaijan support has also been provided in the area of broader administrative and legal reform, including support to the Ministry of Finance in relation to National Account Standards etc. This has also been the case in Russia, as part of the Public Sector Institutional Reform. In the case of Kazakhstan the focus has been on rationalizing and restructuring the public administration, to improve public governance and assist in implementing sound public expenditure management.

In the area of **Civilian Oversight** and Civilian **Management** it includes support to national Assemblies in relation to legislative capacity building and for strengthening the democratic control on government spending by developing an independent audit chamber.

Through the European Initiative for Democracy and Human Rights (EIDHR), activities have been supported in the areas of improving access to justice, human rights monitoring, improving rule of law and legal protection of human rights, defending minority rights and support campaigns against the use of torture.

Country example - SSR related assistance to Ukraine

Through the TACIS programme, the EC has provided significant support to many of the SSRrelated areas in Ukraine. This support has mainly focused on institution- and capacity-building efforts to relevant services, including investment in infrastructure at border crossing points and specialised equipment for police, customs and other services.

In 2001 the EC started to cooperate closely with the State Border Guard Service in order to support their reform efforts with the long-term objective to approximate their standards towards the EU. This cooperation has resulted in several TACIS-funded capacity building projects including the provision of training and equipment, both under the national and regional TACIS programmes.

In the area of Customs, the State Customs Service of Ukraine has, among other things, received support in reviewing the Ukrainian Customs Code, in capacity building through training and in receiving special equipment for border controls.

In the area of asylum and migration management, the regional TACIS programme has supported the Söderköping Process, which promotes cross border cooperation between the Western NIS and the EU. The EC has also supported Ukraine in its reform efforts both in the area of illegal and legal migration, as well as asylum.

Under the regional TACIS programme, the Belarus-Ukraine-Moldova Anti-Drug-programme (BUMAD) has provided support to the three countries in fighting drug-trafficking in the context of a broader approach, addressing organised and cross-border crime in the region.

In the area of money laundering, the EC has equally provided support under the TACIS programme. This support has focused on the introduction of new legislation and its implementation as well as provision of specialised IT systems and related equipment.

In addition to the above, the European Commission has foreseen to carry out a comprehensive JLS assessment mission, in close cooperation with the Ukrainian authorities. The aim of the assessment mission is to evaluate the state of play in this area and to provide recommendations for short-, medium and long-term priorities to be addressed, possibly under the TACIS programme and the future ENPI instrument.

South and East Mediterranean and the Middle East

In relation to the MEDA region, the EC is providing support to at least the following countries: Algeria, Egypt, Jordan, Morocco, Tunisia, the Palestinian Authorities and Yemen.

Justice and Law Enforcement and **Civilian Management** are the areas where the EC has been especially active in the region. This includes support for the modernisation and reform of the justice system, working with key ministries and institutions, in Morocco, Algeria, Tunisia, Yemen and the Palestinian Authorities. It includes institution building, equipment and training for interior and justice ministries, courts and other institutions, access to justice and public information. In the area of penal reform the EC has supported capacity building and reforms, including non-custodial measures. In the case of the Palestinian Authorities, EC support has addressed the urgent needs of reforming the judiciary following the enactment of key legislation.

Police Reform has been supported, modernising the police and providing training in the areas of rule of law and democratic principles as well as regarding confidence building between the forces and the public. Support has also included the creation of a national research institute for criminology.

Support has been given to promote regional cooperation among the Mediterranean countries in the area of police and judicial cooperation.

Support has also been given to improve **Border** as well as **Migration Management**. In the areas of **Civilian Oversight and Civilian Capacity Building**, support has been provided to Algeria, Morocco, the Palestinian Authorities, Egypt and Jordan. This includes support to national centres and functions for human rights, civil society capacity building in the area of democracy and human rights and support to media work in the area of public dialogue on good governance and human rights. Regional support has been given in the area of human rights.

Example – SSR related support to the Palestinian Authorities

Activities of the EC in the Judiciary/Rule of Law sector[9]

1. *Bilateral Programme "Empowering the Palestinian Judicial System"*

This programme addresses the most urgent needs of the Judiciary following the enactment of key legislation (Basic Law and Judicial Authority Law). It also responds to several of the priorities for the reform process in the sector in line with the PA Reform Plan. It foresees three components following an integrated approach: institutional support, development of permanent professional training system and provision of equipment and refurbishment of judicial locations. The programme is raising high expectations from the PA, and currently constitutes the major programme in the sector. With this programme, in addition to the coordination of the Reform Support group, the EC is becoming a major player in the sector.

2. *Regional Programme on Good Governance and the Rule of Law*

This is a three-fold programme (Migration, Justice and Police). It aims at enabling regional co-operation between Europe and its Mediterranean Partners to be implemented in several areas of judicial reform; fight against drug trafficking, organised crime, and terrorism; and migration related issues. This programme is seen as good complement to the EC's bilateral programme. Police component is the most advanced. Justice and Migration components are just starting.

3. *Regional Programme on the Promotion of International Arbitration*

The programme focuses on promoting the use of International Arbitration and ADR in the MEDA countries/partners.

4. *Coordination of the Reform Support Group on Judiciary/Rule of Law*

The EU (EC/NL) is the chair of the RSG. It reflects the European current lead role as major donor in the judicial sector. The group is composed of more than 20 different donors and international agencies. Besides monitoring the reforms, this group ensures donors coordination in the sector.

Asia

EC is supporting SSR reforms in at least the following countries in Asia: Afghanistan, Indonesia, Laos, Nepal, the Philippines and Vietnam.

In the areas of **Civilian Oversight**, support has been provided in the area of strengthening the capacity of national assemblies to enhance democratic control and transparency. This includes training for parliamentarians and administrative staff, but also for line ministries and other state institutions. This includes procedures for legislation, relations with the electorates, budget issues as well as implications for implementation of laws. The EC is also supporting efforts to strengthen the role of the Office of the Ombudsman in preventing corruption and to enhance the cooperation with civil society and line ministries. In addition, support has been given in relation to enhancing the capacity of civil society, including media awareness campaigns and human rights training.

9 This is only for EC institution-building activities in the sector, and does not include activities with human rights NGOs.

In the area of **Civilian Management** and **Justice and Law Enforcement,** EC provides support in the areas of judicial reform as in the case of the Philippines, Indonesia, Afghanistan and Vietnam. This includes capacity building and institutional development of line ministries, including payment of civil servant salaries. It also includes nation wide payments of police staff, non-lethal equipment and rehabilitation of facilities. Support has also been directed towards training of judges and courts staff and to increase the transparency of courts and the accountability of judges and public access to justice.

In the area of **Border Management**, as in the Border Management Programme in the Philippines, support has been provided to enhance border security and management in accordance with international norms and protocols.

Country example – SSR related support to Afghanistan

In Afghanistan, the EC contributed to the Law and Order Trust Fund (LOTFA) for 2003-2006 (€95.5 million). Financial support under this project goes to the restructuring of the law enforcement system in the country (salaries, equipment, premises and training), with reference to all law enforcement activities. The objective of LOTFA is to support the national police force to ensure security throughout Afghanistan. The main focus has been on supporting police salaries, which is vital since the Government has little in the way of central budget to support public sector salaries.

In future programmes, the EC will be focusing on rural development programmes in key provinces and work to strengthen the rule of law in the different provinces. For the latter, support to the Afghan police will continue through the multi-donor Law and Order Trust Fund. Moreover, the EC will aim to assist in the extension of the new Criminal Justice Task Force to the provinces, specifically targeting narcotics-related crimes. Related to this, the EC will also build on its earlier support in the justice sector, increasing local access to justice through provision of district level courts.

Country example – DDR in a cross-pillar approach – Aceh/Indonesia

In the Indonesian province of Aceh, the Commission-funded mediation was crucial to find a negotiated settlement between the Indonesian government and the former rebel movement GAM. It led to a Memorandum of Understanding (MoU) providing for the disarmament and the demobilisation of former combatants, and to the withdrawal of excessive army and police forces. The Commission addresses the reintegration of fighters in a longer perspective. Under an ESDP mandate, the Council deployed a monitoring mission (AMM), which monitors the implementation of the provisions of the MoU. The Commission is further supporting the peace process with a series of measures, including capacity building of police and justice bodies and with funding for the organisation of local elections.

Latin America

EC supports SSR reform activities at least in the following Latin American countries:
Colombia, El Salvador, Guatemala, Mexico, Nicaragua, Panama and Uruguay.

As in other regions the dominant areas of support are **Justice Reform**, **Law Enforcement** and **Civilian Management**. This includes support for judicial reform in the areas of capacity building, training and equipment. The beneficiaries are presidency offices, key government ministries, supreme courts, public prosecution functions, Attorney General's Offices etc. as in the case of

Colombia, Guatemala, Panama, Nicaragua, Mexico and Uruguay. In the case of Colombia an important part of the reform concerns the need to address impunity. Support has also been given in the area of penal reform, concerning prison conditions, rehabilitation and family support, as well as in the areas of access to justice, new codes of criminal procedures capacity building of public institutions etc.

In the area of **Police Reform** the EC has been involved in capacity building, with a focus on creating a police force under democratic control and adhering to the human rights of the population. Support has also been provided in the area of strengthening **Civilian Oversight** through support to national parliamentary assemblies in relation to strengthening legislation and budget control. The EC is also providing support to modernisation and decentralisation of the public administration. Substantive support has been given in the area of civil society capacity building enhancing the role of civil society in relation to peace and security issues.

Country example – Support to the Judiciary/Rule of Law sector in Colombia[10]

Bilateral Programme for the strengthening of the legal sector in order to reduce impunity

The objective of the programme is to contribute to the consolidation of the Rule of Law and a reduction of impunity, through the improvement of the response capacity of the judicial system. Activities entail:

1. Training and capacity building of judges, ombudsmen, prosecutors to the new penal system;
2. Modernisation of the legal documentation centre;
3. Creation of the virtual campus of the Law school;
4. Creation of an investigation unit for the public defence;
5. Start international cooperation and coordination strategies in the justice field and in the fight against impunity and serious human rights violations;
6. Preparation of the local judges to tackle minor penal conflicts;
7. Widening of the coordination between the National Legal System and the Indigenous authorities;
8. Development of alternative conflict resolution mechanisms.

Component of the bilateral programme "Peace Laboratory I"

The focus is on strengthening the institution of the ombudsman's office in the Magdalena Medio region.

Support to the activities of the UN high Commissioner for Human Rights

3.1. Prison conditions in Colombia : institutional strengthening of the Prosecutor General's office, the Ombudsman's office and the Minsitry of Justice
The aim of this projects is twofold : 1. to strengthen the Colombian penitentiary system at a national level; 2. to promote and defend the rights of detainees and prisoners.
3.2. Institutional strengthening of the State Public Prosecutor's office
The aim of this project is to strengthen the judicial system, its efficiency and to train the State Prosecutor's office on human rights issues
3.3. Support to the creation of municipal development plans including the human right dimension.
The objective is to strengthen and develop the work of municipal ombudsmen for the protection of human rights. In total, 900 of them will be trained through 45 sessions.

10 This does not include EC support to human rights organisations in Colombia

III. ANNEX 3 – THE EUROPEAN COMMISSION PROGRAMMING CYCLE

Programming cycle for national and Regional Programmes

The multi-annual programming documents are part of the strategic framework with a partner country or region. A Country or Regional Strategy Paper (CSP/RSP) is drafted on the basis of dialogue with the partner country/region and should be based on the partner countries' priorities. It covers a specified period of time, for example 2007-2013. The strategy as defined in the CSP/RSP is translated into National or Regional Indicative Programmes (NIP/RIP) in partnership with Partner Governments. The NIPs/RIPs are a management tool and covers a period of 3-5 years. It identifies and defines the appropriate measures and actions for attaining established strategy objectives and should be fully consistent with the analysis made in the CSP/RSP.

Identification

During the identification phase, project and programme areas for cooperation are identified and relevance and feasibility of these are assessed. These project/programme areas identified have to be based on partner country priorities, as described in the relevant CSP/RSP and NIP/RIP.

This stage includes the preparation of an Identification Fiche per priority area and the documents are evaluated by a Quality Support Group who gives recommendations for further work and improvements.

Formulation

During this stage, the relevance and feasibility of the project ideas as proposed in the Identification fiche are verified and a detailed project/programme proposal is prepared. This phase ends with the preparation of a Financing Proposal for funding the activities proposed.

The whole set of documents are evaluated a second time in the Quality Support Group. After approval, the Financing Proposal is sent to Member States, discussed and adopted in the relevant Member State Committee and thereafter the Commission decides on financing the activities. When the Commission Decision is taken, a separate Financing Agreement is prepared with the country/region and a financial commitment taken to fund the activities decided upon.

Implementation

The purpose of this stage is to:

- Achieve the purpose and contribute effectively to the overall objective of the project/programme;
- Manage the available resources efficiently;
- Monitor and report on progress.

Within the framework of its standard procurement rules[11], in the area of SSR the EC primarily relies on the expertise of International Organisations, EU Member States institutions, government agencies and NGOs to a large extent.

Consortia with a combination of, for example, International Organisations and EU Member States institutions and government agencies, have also proved to have an added value in cases where the different actors are mandated with complimentary tasks.

As a way ahead, the use of Member states' expertise, combined with that of other actors, seems to be one of the most appropriate implementation models. The institutional nature of these implementing partners has been largely appreciated by the partner countries, who have considered the secondment of officials from corresponding national institutions (Experts who are civil servants in national institutions of EU member states), an important source of expertise.

11 See http://europa.eu.int/comm/europeaid/index_en.htm.

Evaluation

The purpose of an evaluation is to make a systematic and objective assessment of an ongoing or completed project or programme, its design, implementation and results. The aim is to determine the relevance and fulfilment of objectives, efficiency, effectiveness, impact and sustainability. The evaluation should provide information enabling the incorporation of lessons learned into policy development and future programming.

Audit

The purpose of the audit is to assess an activity that is the responsibility of another party against identified criteria and to express a conclusion that provides the user with a level of assurance. This conclusion should include:

- The legality and regularity of project expenditure and income, compliance with laws and regulations and with applicable contractual rules and criteria;
- Whether project funds have been used efficiently and economically, i.e. in accordance with sound financial management;
- Whether project funds have been used effectively, i.e. for the purpose intended.

Programming cycle for thematic programmes

The programming cycle for thematic programmes based on the proposed simplified regulatory structure for 2007-13 will be similar to past practice. On the basis of the relevant Commission Communication for a thematic programme, the multi-annual programming will be defined in the Thematic Strategy Paper. This document sets out the EU's objectives in the thematic area over a period of 3-4 years, an analysis of the theme at global level, an overview of previously financed activities including lessons learned and the response strategy with possible links to national and regional programming identifying specific objectives, actions and performance indicators. In the case of the proposed thematic programme for Democracy and Human Rights as in the past for the European Initiative for Democracy and Human Rights (EIDHR) under which activities of relevance to security sector reform have been financed, no prior agreement from the government in the country targeted is required. Activities are implemented mainly by organisations in civil society or by international organisations with a particular mandate in the area covered by the programmes. Following informal consultations on the priorities for the thematic programme with civil society, the Thematic Strategy Paper is drawn up and adopted by the Commission in accordance with comitology procedures.

The objectives defined in the Thematic Strategy Paper are translated into an Annual Action Programme, also adopted in accordance with comitology procedures. The Annual Action Programme is a management tool that includes a breakdown of the multi-annual strategy paper into annual activities. The action programme will include information about planned calls for proposals to select projects for grant support and cooperation with international organisations. Both documents are reviewed by a Quality Support Group. The Annual Action Programme also serves as a financing decision in all cases where a sufficient level of detail is known about the activities that will be financed.

Identification and formulation

During the identification and formulation phase, guidelines for calls for proposals, calls for tenders and selection criteria for contracts to be awarded without a call for proposals will be elaborated. All project proposals will be screened to assess the capacity of the applicant, the relevance and methodology of the project proposed in relation to the programme objectives in the area the project addresses as well as sustainability of the action and the cost effectiveness. Guidelines for calls for proposals are reviewed by a Quality Support Group.

Implementation

The purpose of this stage is to:

- Contribute effectively to the overall objective of the project/programme;

- Manage the available resources efficiently;
- Monitor and report on progress.

Thematic programmes often are implemented in partnership with organisations in civil society and emphasis is put on dialogue with the partner organisations both at headquarters level and in the countries as carried out by EC delegations. This is of particular importance to explore any possible synergies between civil society initiatives and bilateral cooperation programmes as well as to keep a flow of formal and informal information about trends and ongoing initiatives.

Evaluation

The purpose of an evaluation is to make a systematic and objective assessment of an ongoing or completed project or programme, its design, implementation and results. The aim is to determine the relevance and fulfilment of objectives, efficiency, effectiveness, impact and sustainability. The evaluation should provide information enabling the incorporation of lessons learned into policy development and future programming. Projects financed under thematic programmes are evaluated both at project and programme level and are also included in sector or country evaluations.

Audit

The purpose of the audit is to assess an activity that is the responsibility of another party against identified criteria and to express a conclusion that provides the user with a level of assurance. This assessment should include:

- The legality and regularity of project expenditure and income, compliance with laws and regulations and with applicable contractual rules and criteria;
- Whether project funds have been used efficiently and economically, i.e. in accordance with sound financial management.

The Rapid Reaction Mechanism (RRM)

The RRM programme is designed as a tool enabling the Commission to urgently provide short-term support in crisis situations (maximum 6 months duration). Thus, the RRM programmes and actions are identified on a case-by-case basis to respond to immediate needs either as self-standing interventions or as an enabling tool "kick-starting" urgent actions later followed-up under the geographical instruments or by other bilateral or multilateral donors. In this light it is obvious that the identification and development step demands a very close coordination with relevant EU institutions (in the Commission, EC Delegations, the Council Secretariat, etc.) as well as other donors and International Organisations both in Brussels and on the ground. The RRM projects are either implemented directly by DG RELEX or (increasingly) de-concentrated to the relevant Delegations when appropriate. Also this programme relies on expertise from International Organisations, the EUMS and NGOs.

The RRM programme comes too an end in December 2006 and it is the intention to replace this programme, from 2007, by funding under the Stability Instrument.

IV. ANNEX 4 – EXAMPLES OF INTERNATIONAL STANDARDS RELEVANT FOR SUPPORT IN THE AREA OF SSR

Democracy

Conclusions of the CSCE Copenhagen Meeting 1990

Inter-American Democratic Charter 2001

Council of Europe Parliamentary Assembly Resolution 800 (1983) on the principles of democracy

Code of Good Practice on Electoral Matters, Opinion 190/2002 of the Venice Commission

IPU 1997 Universal Declaration on Democracy

Human rights

Universal Declaration of Human Rights

International Covenant on Civil and Political Rights

International Covenant on Economic, Social and Cultural Rights

International Convention on the Elimination of All Forms of Racial Discrimination

Convention on the Elimination of All Forms of Discrimination against Women

Convention against Torture and Other Cruel, Inhuman or Degrading Treatment or Punishment

Convention on the Rights of the Child

Rule of law

UN Basic Principles on the Independence of the Judiciary

UN Guidelines on the Role of Prosecutors

UN Code of Conduct for Law Enforcement Officials

Basic Principles on the Role of Lawyers

Annex 6

COUNCIL OF THE EUROPEAN UNION

Brussels, 6 December 2006
16387/06

LIMITE

COSDP 1018
DEVGEN 316
PESC 1236
CIVCOM 564

"I/A" ITEM NOTE

From : Secretariat

To : Permanent Representatives' Committee/Council

No. prev. doc. : 13727/4/06 REV 4 COSDP 787 DEVGEN 249

Subject : Draft EU Concept for Support to Disarmament, Demobilisation and Reintegration (DDR)

1. At its meeting on 1 December 2006, having taken note of the advice of the CIVCOM and the EUMC, the Political and Security Committee agreed to forward the draft EU concept for support to disarmament, demobilisation and reintegration (DDR) (doc. 13727/4/06 REV 4) via COREPER to the Council for approval.

2. The COREPER is invited to recommend that the Council approve the draft EU Concept for Support to Disarmament, Demobilisation and Reintegration (DDR), as set out in the Annex.

EU CONCEPT FOR SUPPORT TO DISARMAMENT, DEMOBILISATION AND REINTEGRATION (DDR)

Draft jointly developed by the Council General Secretariat and the European Commission

TABLE OF CONTENTS

G. Principles for EU support of DDR

H. Measures to strengthen EU's support to DDR in the future

REFERENCE DOCUMENTS

1. European Security Strategy: A secure Europe in a better world, adopted by the European Council in December 2003
2. European Union's Development Policy Statement, "the European Consensus" on development, adopted by the Council on 22 November 2005, published in the Official Journal n° C 46 of 24/02/2006
3. The EU strategy 'The EU and Africa: Towards a strategic partnership' (doc. 15702/1/05 REV 1)
4. Cotonou Agreement, 2000
5. EU Concept for ESDP support to Security Sector Reform (SSR) (Council doc. 12566/4/05)
6. Commission's Communication A Concept for European Community Support for Security Sector Reform SEC(2006) 658
7. Communication from the Commission to the European Council of June 2006, Europe in the World – Some Practical Proposals for Greater Coherence, Effectiveness and Visibility
8. EU Guidelines on Children and Armed Conflict (2003)
9. EU Checklist for the Integration of the Protection of Children Affected by Armed Conflict into ESDP Operations (2006)
10. EU Checklist to Ensure the Implementation of UNSCR 1325 in the Context of ESDP Operations (2005)
11. European Union's Strategy to combat illicit accumulation and trafficking of small arms and light weapons (SALW) and their ammunition, adopted by the European Council in December 2005.

A. INTRODUCTION

1. Disarmament, Demobilisation and Reintegration (DDR) of former combatants has been identified as a key area for the European Union's engagement in post-conflict peace building. This has been highlighted, inter alia, in the Union's Development Policy Statement, "The European Consensus on development", in the European Security Strategy and in the EU Strategy for Africa.

2. DDR processes need to contribute to immediate security needs and be part of the foundations for longer term stability and development in a country or region. While DDR in the past was seen as a purely military and technical issue, there is increased recognition today that DDR needs to be part of the political and social developments and will be most successful when properly linked to an overall peace process, democratic governance issues, transitional justice and long-term development criteria.

3. DDR refers to a set of interventions in a process of demilitarising official and unofficial armed groups by disarming and disbanding non-state groups and, possibly, downsizing armed forces. DDR is often more successful when part of a broader Security Sector Reform (SSR).

The ultimate objective of DDR processes is the social and economic reintegration of former combatants in order to contribute to sustainable peace, reconciliation of society, stability and long-term development. The aim is to help ex-combatants moving away from the roles and positions that defined them during the conflict to identifying themselves as citizens and members of the local communities. This includes providing alternatives for combatants and their dependents in terms of access to the political process, viable livelihoods and social and economic prospects for the future. Depending on the context, the focus may also need to gradually shift from the combatant to the needs of the wider community in this process. Reintegration into civilian life can only be sustained in the long term if a sound and sustained economic prospect, functioning State institutions capable of providing basic services, a legal framework and close coordination with civil society exist, not least to ensure that former fighters find viable livelihoods, in terms of food, shelter/housing, education, a job or a pension and a new purpose in life.

4. The EU has been active for a long time in supporting DDR processes all over the world, especially through Community programmes and policies and Member states' bilateral support. In the case of the European Community it includes support to around 20 DDR processes in Africa since the early 1990s, as well as support in Latin America and Asia. In 2005, the EU launched an ESDP civilian operation, the Aceh Monitoring Mission (AMM), aimed, inter alia, at monitoring and supervising disarmament operations in Aceh.

5. DDR is often included as an explicit part of the mandate of United Nations (UN) peacekeeping operations and is also undertaken under specific DDR programmes by the United Nations Development Programme (UNDP), the United Nations Children's Fund (UNICEF) and other parts of the UN system, the World Bank or other international actors. The EU brings added value in the field of DDR by being able to bring together a wide range of instruments for security, stability, development, democratic governance and the promotion of human rights. It also possesses a whole bandwidth of capabilities in order to support the assessment, conception, planning, implementation and funding of DDR programmes and can thus effectively contribute to multi-lateral efforts or undertake bilateral support in relation to third countries.

6. The Council agreed in June 2006 a policy framework for EU support to SSR. It states that *'support to DDR in a partner state within the framework of SSR should be addressed separately but consistently with this SSR concept'*. The mandate for the Presidency includes a commitment *'to take forward work on security sector reform (SSR), including through region/country specific approaches, and to develop an EU approach to contribute to disarmament, demobilisation and reintegration (DDR).'* An expert seminar "The EU and DDR: Supporting Security and Development", held in Brussels on 13 July 2006, contributed to the further development of this work.

B. RATIONALE AND OVERALL AIM

7. The objective of this concept is to set out the EU approach to DDR for future engagements, based on previous experiences and lessons learned within the international Community. It aims at ensuring a common understanding with potential partners. It includes clear principles for EU support and measures for strengthening the Union's work in the future in this area.

8. A great deal of work has already been undertaken to strengthen policies and methods for implementing DDR, especially in the UN, which should be taken into account in developing an EU approach. International efforts on DDR have been developed in the framework of the *Stockholm initiative on Disarmament, Demobilisation and Reintegration (SIDDR)*, through the UN based *Inter-Agency Working Group on DDR*, which has collected the knowledge, best practice and guidance from 15 UN agencies in the *Integrated DDR standards (IDDRS)*. The newly created *UN Peacebuilding Commission (PBC)* is also expected to play a role in this field. The EU should make the best use, where appropriate, of the guidance provided in this work when engaging in support to DDR. The EU concept should be based on the experiences and lessons learned by the International Community and by the Union itself in supporting DDR processes in different parts of the world, through Community instruments, Member States bilateral programmes and more recently ESDP operations and actions.

9. Given the close link between DDR and Security Sector Reform (SSR) in the country specific and regional context, this concept aims to complement the Policy Framework for EU support to SSR adopted by the Council in June 2006. It will also draw on and complement other EU policies and commitments at Reference.

10. Actions in support to DDR can be undertaken by Member states bilaterally or by European Community (EC) under its external action instruments or also under the Common Foreign and Security Policy (CFSP) including European Security and Defence Policy (ESDP). This concept also outlines steps to enhance coordination and complementarity between EU activities, including civilian and military aspects. This includes better coherence between EC and CFSP/ESDP instruments for those cases where both the EC and CFSP/ESDP actions to support DDR are envisaged in the same location.

C. DEFINITIONS

11. The UN has adopted the following definitions, which will also be the basis for the EU approach[1]:

Disarmament is the collection, documentation, control and disposal of small arms, ammunition, explosives and light and heavy weapons of combatants and often also of the civilian population. Disarmament also includes the development of responsible arms management programmes[2].

Demobilisation is the formal and controlled discharge of active combatants from armed forces or other armed groups. The first stage of demobilisation may extend from the processing of individual combatants in temporary centres to the massing of troops in camps designated for this purpose (cantonment sites, encampments, assembly areas or barracks). The second stage of demobilisation encompasses the support package provided to the demobilised, which is called reinsertion[3].

Reintegration is the process by which ex-combatants acquire civilian status and gain sustainable employment and income. Reintegration is essentially a social and economic process, primarily taking place in communities at the local level. It is part of the general development of a country and a national responsibility, and often necessitates long-term external assistance.

Children

12. The Optional Protocol to the Convention on the Rights of the Child establishes eighteen as the minimum age for compulsory recruitment by States, and for any recruitment or use in hostilities by non-governmental armed groups, and also establishes that States shall take all feasible measures to ensure that members of their armed forces who have not attained the age of 18 years do not take a direct part in hostilities.

13. This document recognises that children eligible for release, reintegration and development programmes include those associated with any kind of regular or irregular armed force or armed group in any capacity, including but not limited to cooks, porters, messengers, and those accompanying such groups, other than purely as family members. Thus, this concept does not only refer to children who are carrying or have carried arms.

14. During the DDR process, a special attention must be paid to girls recruited for sexual purposes and forced marriage and those recruited, abducted or forced into domestic labour.

1 These definitions are drawn from the Report of the UN Secretary General to the General Assembly on Disarmament, demobilisation and reintegration (Doc. number A/60/705 dated 2 March 2006).

2 This is not mandatory. It should be noted that Disarmament is often linked to civilian voluntary surrender programmes.

3 The UN also uses the term "reinsertion" to define this short-term transitional package between demobilisation and reintegration processes. Reinsertion is defined as the assistance offered to ex-combatants during demobilisation but prior to the longer-term process of reintegration. Reinsertion is a form of transitional assistance to help cover the basic needs of ex-combatants and their families and can include transitional safety allowances, food, clothes, shelter, medical services, short-term education, training, employment and tools. While reintegration is a long-term, continuous social and economic process of development increasingly focusing on the need of communities rather than on individual combatants, reinsertion is a short-term material and/or financial assistance to meet immediate needs, and can last up to one year.

D. CHALLENGES, LESSONS AND KEY REQUIREMENTS

15. Who is an ex-combatant and who should qualify for the DDR process?

The international experiences and those of the EU to date illustrate the enormous challenges of implementing DDR; in terms of the number of former combatants which can range from a few thousand to over 150 000[4]; and in terms of identifying who is an ex-combatant and who is not and who should be qualifying for DDR support and thus managing expectations. A great challenge is also associated to the fact that, most of the time, numbers are derived from commander's lists, are often overestimated and consequently need to be verified by other means. The eligibility criteria need to be tightly defined and expectations need to be carefully manages from the outset. While there is a general recognition in the international community that the needs of war affected communities and especially vulnerable groups should be met, there is increased understanding that the DDR process as such should focus on the ex-combatants. This needs to include not only those carrying a weapon, but also non-fighters associated with armed groups. Early identification of the eligibility of women and children to this process is necessary.

16. Gender issues

In conflicts both sexes and both adults and children are associated with armed forces and groups: they can be fighters or accompany regular or irregular forces as cooks, porters, messengers or perform other tasks. Women and girls are often recruited for sexual purposes and forced marriages. Sometimes men and boys are also abused sexually. Defining "combatant" as someone carrying a weapon has often resulted in women and girls being excluded from DDR processes. In many cases, women and girls associated with fighting forces also face particular difficulties in reintegrating back into societies where they are stigmatised and subject to traditional views of the role of women in society. A further difficulty is related to the psychological and physical health problems that many woman and girls have as result of having been abducted and raped and to the fact that they often have children as a result. Based on the EU's policies, and in line with the social and economic influence of DDR processes, an equalised gender approach should be added to DDR programmes. It should therefore offer equal benefits to men and women ex-combatants, and prevent eligible women being ignored or not registered for the programmes in the first place.

17. Children

Efforts must be made to prevent the recruitment of children to armed forces and armed groups in violation of applicable international law[5] and, where they are already recruited, they should be removed from armed forces and armed groups as early as possible in particular to avoid that they become a bargaining tool in the political process. Measures should also be taken to prevent their reinvolvement in violent activities. Particular attention should be paid to separate effectively the children from the armed groups and demobilised chain of command.

Immediate support should be offered to children to reintegrate into society, through community-based approaches. The focus should also be to ensure that the special needs of children associated with fighting forces are taken into account in a child-focused release process, including family reunification whenever possible, education, including life skills courses, psychological and physical rehabilitation and trauma-healing. One size-fits-all approaches should be avoided as children need to benefit from programmes specifically designed to address these particular needs.

4 And as many as 450 000, as in the case of the regional DDR process in the Great Lakes Region.

5 Such as the UN Convention on the Rights of the Child (General Assembly resolution 44/25 of 20 November 1989), the Worst Forms of Child Labour Convention 1999 (N° 182) and the UN Optional protocol to the Convention on the Rights of the Child on the involvement of children in armed conflict (General Assembly resolution A/RES/54/263 of 25 May 2000). In addition, the Rome Statute of the ICC provides that conscripting or enlisting children under 15 is a war crime.

18. Funding

DDR is most often funded through assessed contributions to UN peacekeeping operations and through voluntary contributions as part of an overall post-conflict recovery package, funded via Trust Fund Mechanisms or through regular development programmes. Children's DDR should start before formal mechanisms are in place for the overall DDR process and is therefore often funded through humanitarian assistance. Providing sufficient funds for reintegration has many times been a problem as often not enough money has been earmarked for this part of the process and reintegration phases have not always been complemented by other programmes, like more extensive, follow-on community development activities. The international donor community needs to make long-term commitments and sequence support in such a way that it can ensure that sufficient funds are allocated to the entire process before it starts, including the costs for reintegration, and ensure that no gap occur between funding to disarmament, as part of peace support operations and the developmental aspects of demobilisation and reintegration. One of the recommendations that came out of the Stockholm Initiative on DDR, was that serious consideration should be given to channelling DDR funding through a multi-donor Trust Fund Mechanism with pre-committed financing. In this context, it was proposed to have two different windows for different components of the DDR process, one for long-term reintegration of ex-combatants and one for support to affected communities.

19. From past experiences in the international community, including EU's own experiences, some important lessons and requirements have been identified.

- DDR should be context-driven and be addressed in the framework of a peace process or political agreement. It should also be noted that a DDR process cannot alone bring solutions to every problem and might not be, in specific contexts, an appropriate solution. Most of the time, to be successful, DDR has to be conducted in conjunction with other activities, for example in the framework of Security Sector reform.
- DDR pre-supposes that a certain degree of trust has been established between the parties to the conflict. That they are committed to ending hostilities, are ready to engage in a process of disarmament and demobilisation and that a peace agreement or at least a ceasefire has been agreed between them. Many times it is difficult to keep the political momentum for the process and to deal with spoilers and those who do not have confidence in the success of the political process or are marginalised by it. Confidence-building between the parties needs to be ongoing and progressing for DDR to succeed.
- The local, national and regional political context of DDR underlines the importance of local and national ownership of the process, which involves a broad range of stakeholders. When appropriate, regional organisations should also be involved. This requires extensive consultation and participatory approaches that enables consensus building, prior to starting the process. One challenge of DDR processes is to manage expectations as these are often very high. For DDR to be successful, both the target group and potential host communities need to know exactly what the process involves, what is to be achieved, what is expected from them.
- DDR needs to take place within a comprehensive framework of peace building and long-term development conducive to democratic governance and be based on dialogue and a comprehensive analysis to assess the conditions for DDR. This should be linked to the strengthening or the establishment of sustainable and accountable state institutions; of a viable and enforceable legal framework; and of a functioning economy. It should be considered an aspect of Security Sector Reform and take its point of departure from an assessment of future needs and structures of the overall security system, recognising at the same time that parts of DDR go outside SSR. DDR processes also have to be linked to efforts addressing the spread of small arms and light weapons (SALW), as this phenomenon can jeopardise stability and disarmament efforts by increasing insecurity, and efforts in the area of Reconciliation and Transitional justice.

- DDR programmes need to be well targeted focusing on ex-combatants and their dependants as appropriate over a certain period of time. So while reintegration processes will continue over many years, specific and time limited reintegration programmes will come to an end. Instead long-term reintegration efforts should be integrated into broader development programmes. Thus, development programmes in this context should take into account the reintegration needs of former combatants without necessarily labelling them as such.
- The reintegration of ex-combatants is especially challenging and is considered to be one of the more difficult phases of DDR. Thus, reintegration needs to be clearly linked to disarmament and demobilisation from the outset. Reintegration into civilian life is clearly linked to the wider socio-economic development of the country, which will determine to what extent it can offer jobs to the demobilised persons, a job that will give them sufficient resources to take care of their families and dependants.. In many cases, unemployment can be quite endemic and lack of livelihood might have been one of the sources of the conflict. A great deal depends on sustained external support that can be brought by the International Community to complement and reinforce national efforts. It is especially important to focus on the local communities and their ability to provide jobs and alternative livelihoods through specific projects and programmes. In addition, budget and sector support should take into account the needs of former combatants. At the same time, consideration must be given to ensure balance support between demobilised ex-combatants and other citizens.
- Components of DDR processes do not necessarily follow one after another in a fixed order, nor do these components necessarily happen at the same time throughout a country or region. All elements should be assessed and planned as part of one overall DDR process. Their implementation would have to be considered in the context of local circumstances and needs.
- DDR cannot be implemented in the absence of security for the population, the disarming parties and international personnel. It is therefore essential that security is provided by national civilian or military security forces, if feasible, or international forces before new national security structures are in place.
- Most DDR programmes have clear regional dimensions and implications and should be carried out in a way which is sensitive to regional issues, in close cooperation and proper involvement of the relevant regional organisations. This is particularly important when dealing with recruitment and trafficking in children, with combatants and excombatants crossing borders to engage in neighbouring conflicts, and weapons floating regionally. There are also examples of regional DDR processes as in the case of the Multi-country Demobilisation and Reintegration Programme for the Great Lakes Region.

E. DDR IN THE UN AND OTHER INTERNATIONAL EXPERIENCES

20. The UN has been involved in DDR programmes for more than 15 years. Since 2000, the UN has launched six peacekeeping operations having included disarmament, demobilisation and reintegration as part of their mandate[6].

21. The UN has also been more engaged in countries where peacekeeping operations have not been

6 These are: the United Nations Organization Mission in the Democratic Republic of the Congo (MONUC); the United Nations Mission in Liberia (UNMIL); the United Nations Operation in Côte d'Ivoire (UNOCI); the United Nations Operation in Burundi (ONUB); the United Nations Stabilization Mission in Haiti (MINUSTAH); and the United Nations Mission in the Sudan (UNMIS).

deployed by the Organisation[7], especially through UNDP and UNICEF but also through other agencies, funds, departments and programmes of the UN system that have played a key role in supporting the development of disarmament, demobilisation and reintegration programmes and strategies, such as the United Nations High Commissioner for Refugees (UNHCR) or the Office of United Nations High Commissioner for Human Rights (OHCHR). DDR programmes have most often been implemented in concert with programmes of Return of refugees and Rehabilitation/reconstruction of destroyed habitats and livelihoods.

22. The World Bank is another very active actor in supporting DDR[8], providing governments with financial, technical and capacity-building support but also promoting community-based recovery efforts.

23. DDR is sometimes implemented by Sub-regional organisations, by States through bilateral support or by specialised NGOs and civil society actors. These actors are present in countries where the EU is supporting DDR and are sometimes also implementing EU support. Civil society and NGOs' activities therefore need to be considered, where appropriate, in EU assessment and planning.

24. Given the challenges experienced in the past by the UN and other international organisations as well as local, national and regional actors, the international community is making efforts to address the shortcomings and systematically take into account lessons learned.

25. The UN has recently developed a new approach to enhance coordination between UN agencies, which sees the sustainable reintegration of ex-combatants as a key objective of DDR, rather than an afterthought, which has sometimes been the case in the past. Consequently, the UN has developed IDDRS which set the framework for a more coherentand efficient cooperation of all UN agencies. The World Bank has also drawn importantlessons learned from its engagement in DDR and other international agencies such as the International Organization for Migration (IOM) have also conducted DDR activities and have identified important lessons while implementing DDR activities.

26. To avoid duplication of efforts, and taking account of the many aspects that need to be considered in a DDR process, it is expected from the different UN agencies, international, regional and local organisations, to attain a high level of coordination. In each situation, a shared overall framework would contribute to the success of the process.

27. The UN and the World Bank remain the key actors in international efforts to manage and deliver DDR programmes.

28. On a political level, DDR could be one of the thematic priorities of the new UN Peacebuilding Commission (PBC). It is expected to play a key role in bringing together all relevant actors to marshal resources and to advise on and propose integrated strategies for peace building. The EU should push the issue of DDR forward on the agenda of the UN Peacebuilding Commission.

29. The Stockholm Initiative on DDR was launched to review current practices and has come up with a number of recommendations in relation to political aspects and the role of DDR in a peace process and transition, on reintegration issues and on the financing of DDR programmes.

30. Many international legal instruments[9] set up child protection standards and focus on children associated with fighting forces. UNSCR 1612, establishing a monitoring mechanism for children affected by armed conflict, is of particular importance in this context. The work of the Special Representative of the Secretary General on Children in Armed conflict is also to be considered.

7 such as Afghanistan, the Central African Republic, Indonesia (Aceh), the Niger, the Congo, Somalia, Solomon Islands, Sri Lanka and Uganda.

8 Especially in the Great Lakes region, where the Multi-Country Demobilisation and Reintegration Programme for the Great Lakes is being implemented. The Bank has also worked in Ethiopia and Côte d'Ivoire among others. In addition, the World Bank has been very active in Sierra Leone.

9 See footnote 5.

31. Although not being a legal instrument, the Cape Town Principles of 1997[10] deal with the prevention of recruitment of children into the armed forces and demobilisation and social reintegration of children in Africa. On the basis of this work, current legal standards[11] and lessons learned from previous child DDR processes, new guidelines on prevention of recruitment, demobilisation and social reintegration of child soldiers, are currently being drafted through a joint effort of a larger range of institutions and governments. The aim is to achieve a global reach and not limit the efforts to Africa.

32. UNSCR 1325 reaffirms the important role of women in the prevention and resolution of conflicts, peace negotiations, peace-building, peacekeeping, humanitarian response and in post-conflict reconstruction and stresses the importance of their equal participation and full involvement in all efforts for the maintenance and promotion of peace and security. The Resolution urges all actors to increase the participation of women and incorporate gender perspectives in all United Nations peace and security efforts, including DDR.

33. The extension of Official Development Assistance (ODA) eligibility in the area of security, decided by the OECD DAC High Level Meetings in 2004 and 2005, means that a clearer definition has been established concerning DDR. This included technical co-operation provided to government, and assistance to civil society organisations, to support and apply legislation designed to prevent the recruitment of child soldiers. Demobilisation and reintegration of former combatants was already eligible for ODA as was disarmament, as part of a post-conflict peace-building phase of United Nations mandated peace operations.

F. THE EU SUPPORT TO DDR

34. The EU has been involved for a long time in supporting DDR programmes in many partner countries, mainly through Community activities. In the case of Central America, this has included European Community support to DDR processes in Guatemala and El Salvador and in South America the EC has recently supported Children's DDR in Colombia and is in the process of designing assistance to communities receiving demobilised combatants. In Africa, the EC has been engaged in supporting DDR in 16 countries since the early 1990s. In Southern Africa, this includes support to Mozambique and Namibia. In the Great Lakes region, in the current Multi-Country Demobilisation and Reintegration Process involving seven countries, the Commission is playing an active role in the overall donor coordination. In West Africa, the EC has supported the DDR processes in Sierra Leone, Guinea, Ivory Coast and Liberia. In East Africa it has included support to Ethiopia, Somalia and Djibouti. In Asia EC support has been granted to reintegration in Aceh, in coordination with the ESDP Aceh Monitoring Mission (AMM) and more recently DDR related support is being prepared in support of the Mindanao Peace Process in the Philippines.

35. This includes support to the overall DDR process, in terms of strategic planning and setting up the national coordination mechanisms as well as giving support to the demobilisation and reintegration phases. In some cases it has also included disarmament aspects. The bulk of the support has been channelled through geographical programmes financed, especially, by the European Development Fund (EDF). In addition, substantive support has also come through humanitarian assistance, especially in relation to children's DDR and through the Rapid Reaction Mechanism and the Aid to Uprooted people budget line.

36. The European Community, in the framework of its external action, is able to support all the DDR phases with a focus on demobilisation and reintegration, through short term humanitarian assist-

10 The Cape Town Principles of 1997 were adopted by the participants in the Symposium on the Prevention of Recruitment of Children into the Armed Forces and Demobilisation and Social Reintegration of Child Soldiers in Africa, organized by UNICEF in cooperation with the NGO Sub-group of the NGO Working Group on the Convention on the Rights of the Child, Cape Town, 30 April 1997. They represent a landmark in dealing with the prevention of recruitment of children into the armed forces and demobilisation and social reintegration of children in Africa.

11 See footnote 5.

ance, under certain conditions, rapid response through the Stability Instrument and through long-term external support of the overall DDR process. EC support is also provided to the wider recovery and development efforts, notably by applying conflict sensitive approaches, which can contribute to long term reintegration needs, including support to democratic governance processes and institution building, respect for human rights, consolidation of the social and economic development of the country including health and education programs.

37. In the framework of ESDP and in line with the European Security Strategy, the EU has launched a civilian operation in support of disarmament, the Aceh Monitoring Mission (AMM) in Indonesia. The operation started in September 2005, immediately after conclusion of the peace agreement between the former resistance movement (GAM)and the Indonesian government. It is part of a broader DDR programme, which in turn forms part of the broader peace process. It specifically monitors disarmament of members of the GAM and withdrawal of government troops, in a phased manner. Demobilisation and Reintegration monitoring is part of the AMM mandate, however their completion will require more time. For the first time, human rights monitors took part in an ESDP mission. The Aceh case shows the ability of the ESDP and EC to reinforce and complement each other, based on good coordination at head quarters and field level from the fact-finding phase through to the planning and the implementation of the operation and activities on the ground. The deployment of AMM was preceded by the successful mediation efforts of President Ahtisaari funded by the EC's Rapid Reaction Mechanism and then accompanied by and followed up with EC programmes on reintegration support to ex-combatants and local communities.

38. ESDP support to DDR in a partner state will usually take the form of support to the local authorities, through a military, civilian or military/civilian operation. It is envisaged that modalities for preparing, planning and conducting ESDP missions in support of DDR would often be the same as the ones used for supporting SSR. In immediate post-crisis situations, military means/expertise might be necessary, especially in the area of disarmament. Contribution to DDR could also be included as a supporting task in the mandate of an ESDP operation. When and if there are both ESDP and EC actions, coordination and a smooth continuum needs to be ensured. This should be taken into account when defining the mandate and the end state of an ESDP operation and be reflected in the Council's Joint Action.

39. In addition, the EU SALW Strategy adopted by the European Council in December 2005, develops an integrated approach and a comprehensive plan of action to combat illicit accumulation and trade of SALW and their ammunitions, which refers to the Union's action, particularly in Africa, within civilian and military crisis management, and *"supports approaches to promote an increased role for peacekeeping missions authorised by the UNSC in the area of SALW and their ammunitions"*. Furthermore, it recommends as an effective response to the problems posed by the availability of existing SALW stocks, to *"continue the financial assistance provided by the EU since 1993 under DDR operations, while improving effectiveness through the direct participation of European experts in those programmes and ensure consistency and complementarity between Council decisions in the CFSP framework and actions implemented by the Commission in the field of development aid in order to promote a consistent approach for all EU activities in the SALW area"*. Thus, efforts in this area, such as SALW collection ad destruction activities, could facilitate DDR processes and ensure a comprehensive EU approach in relation to crisis situations.

40. The involvement of the EU in DDR programmes will vary considerably according to context. The EU's role as both a donor and a political actor can be of great significance also when the UN and/or World Bank are the key actors for management and delivery of DDR programmes. At the same time, The EU's involvement in supporting DDR is mainly linked to the added value that can be brought by the EU in comparison to other actors, and the EU may, in some situations, be asked to take on a specific task in the area of DDR, as in the case of Aceh.

41. The EU is also able to provide support to local and regional organisations involved in DDR. This was the case with AMM where the EU worked closely together with ASEAN nations in the early phases of the DDR process. Another instance of such support is the EU's cooperation in this domain with the African Union. For example, DDR is one of the issues for dialogue in the EU-AU Joint Task Force established in 2005.

42. The EU intends to use all instruments at its disposal to ensure that its action in support of DDR is efficient and coherent. The delineation of tasks between the two pillars will be made on the basis of a case-by-case analysis and assessment, bearing in mind the possibility that EC and ESDP actions would be undertaken together as an integrated approach to DDR either deploying simultaneously or in a sequenced fashion depending on the situation or singly. It is especially important for the EU to use its existing presence on the ground, including EC delegations, EUSRs and member states' embassies as well as ongoing programmes and missions when engaging in a DDR process. Close coordination, e.g. through early sharing of information and joint assessments, are also necessary to ensure that the EU action is coherent. Parameters setup in the framework of Civil-Military Co-ordination (CMCO) for the coordination of civilian and military ESDP activities are also particularly relevant.

43. The EU support to DDR, through EC and CFSP/ESDP instruments can be provided in each phase of a DDR program:

- *Overall preparation and setting up of a DDR process*: the EU can give support for the overall process, by engaging early in the process, by integrating DDR aspects in the political dialogue with the country, by providing advice and support to enable proper planning and analysis as well as support to the establishment of regional, national and local structures for carrying out the different stages of the process. This also includes active participation in the overall donor coordination and steering of trust funds and programmes.
- *Disarmament*: the EU engagement in supporting DDR in this phase can, for example, range from giving advice to the local authorities to sending monitors to oversee the disarmament phase or to sending a military or civilian operation to undertake the disarmament phase, or parts of the disarmament phase of the programme and to ensuring a safe and secure environment, normally as a specific task within a peace support operation.

  EU involvement in disarmament could also include support to State and non-State actors. In this broad range of possible activities are included the sending of military and/or civilian experts to give advice to any actor on weapons, ammunition and explosives collection, registration, transportation, and storage or destruction, the sending of a monitoring or evaluation team and the providing of financial support for capacity building.
- *Demobilisation*: in this phase, the EU can undertake to monitor and give support to the reception, screening, registration, discharge of ex-combatants, building or maintaining and/or managing a cantonment sites, assembly area or barracks as well as sensitisation (AIDS awareness etc) and provide assistance in terms of clothing, food, psychosocial, medical and immediate physical assistance.
- *Reintegration*: in the phases of reinsertion and reintegration, the EU can give support to ex-combatants, their dependents and receiving communities including shelter, food, vocational training, education, tools, micro-credits, employment opportunities, and addressing psychosocial and physical needs. Support can be provided either as part of broader development programmes or through specific projects, including institution building. Essential in this phase is the involvement of local communities and to provide sufficient financial support to the local communities which can play a key role in providing social integration, jobs and livelihoods for the ex combatants. The works and initiatives implemented "together" will have an important impact in terms of reconciliation, involving not only ex-combatants but also the wider war affected community.

G. PRINCIPLES FOR EU SUPPORT TO DDR

The principles below, elaborated on the basis of the above definitions and lessons learned, should apply for EU support to DDR.

44. *The EU should aim at strengthening local, national and regional ownership of DDR processes*

The EU should fully respect local, national and regional ownership of DDR processes, which is key to success. However, in some exceptional situations, the International Community, including the EU, may need to assume the role of acting local authority and consequently start a DDR process, without a recognised partner government, basing its approach on dialogue and working closely with local, national and international actors, including civil society. In such cases, the EU should aim at strengthening local, national and regional ownership of DDR processes, which means in particular strengthening leadership and accountability.

45. *EU support should be carried out within a broad peace-building strategy.*

EU support to DDR should be carried out within a broad peace-building, recovery and development strategy, including institution building, and should be closely linked to aspects such as security sector reform, democratic governance, reconciliation and transitional justice, community based programmes and socio-economic development.

46. *The EU should ensure respect for Human Rights and carry out DDR support in relation to efforts in the area of reconciliation and transitional justice*

The EU should continue to promote the ratification and implementation of the key UN Human Rights Instruments and their Optional Protocols[12]. Human rights of all, both victims and offenders, should be ensured at all stages of the process and at all times. This requires ending the culture of impunity, such as granting a role to war criminals in a national army or political bodies. All war crimes, crimes against humanity and other offences must be duly and timely investigated and the perpetrators brought into a fair trial. Sufficient support should be given to the International Criminal Court (ICC), International Criminal Tribunal for Rwanda (ICTR), International Criminal tribunal for Yugoslavia (ICTY), Special Court for Sierra Leone (SCSL) and other similar structures. Children recruited or used by armed forces and groups, in violation of applicable international law, should be considered primarily as victims of violence, not perpetrators. All children should be protected from disproportionate and excessive use of force and treated in accordance with international law in a framework of restorative justice and social rehabilitation.

47. *EU support should be carried out in the context of the political dialogue.*

DDR should be carried out in the context of the EU's political dialogue with each partner country, in relation to democratic principles, rule of law, human rights, development and security issues. The political dialogue should be seen as a guiding element throughout the process.

48. *Gender-sensitive approaches should be applied to EU support*

Particular attention should be given to the complexities of gender issues, addressing the special needs and roles of women, men, girl and boy ex-combatants, non fighters and their dependants. A gender-sensitive approach should be adopted from the early planning stage to the implementation, monitoring and evaluation of DDR. The EU efforts to ensure the implementation of UNSCR 1325 in the context of ESDP Operations, as set out inter alia in a checklist (doc. 12068/06) and in document 11932/2/05, are particularly relevant in this field.

49. *EU support should effectively address issues related to children and armed conflict*

The EU should ensure that children's DDR processes are dissociated from adult ones and not linked to the political process. They should start as early as possible. Immediate support should be offered to children to reintegrate into society, through community-based approaches. Reunification with

12 Such as the International Covenant on Civil and Political Rights (ICCPR) 1966, the International Covenant on Economic, Social and Cultural Rights (ICESCR) 1966, The Convention on the Elimination of All Forms of Discrimination against Women (CEDAW) 1999, The Convention on the Rights of the Child (CRC) 1989, the Convention against Torture and Other Cruel, Inhuman or Degrading Treatment or Punishment (CAT) 1985, the International Convention on the Elimination of All Forms of Racial Discrimination (ICERD) 1965 and all their optional protocols.

the family should be a priority, avoiding institutional approaches, if possible. The EU Guidelines on Children and Armed Conflict, recent strategies towards the implementation of these guidelines (doc. 8285/06 REV 1) and the Checklist for the Integration of the Protection of Children affected by Armed Conflict into ESDP Operations (doc. 9767/06) are particularly relevant here.

50. *The EU should ensure a coherent and coordinated approach*

The EU should ensure that its DDR support is carried out in a coherent and integrated way, ensuring complementarity between activities supported under different instruments. As DDR in most cases requires long-term involvement, various EU activities should be timed carefully taking into account the particular circumstances on the ground in the country and region in question. All actions initiated should build on already existing activities of the Member states, the EC and CFSP/ESDP.

51. *The EU should seek for an early engagement*

As one of the most important donors and political actors, in order to ensure that any DDR programme is starting on a sound basis, the EU should be involved at the earliest stages of peace or cease-fire negotiations, in close coordination and cooperation with other actors such as the UN Peacebuilding Commission, as well as in supporting the assessment and early planning phases of DDR programmes. This could facilitate the definition of its future involvement and enhance budgetary planning.

52. *The EU should apply conflict sensitive approaches*

The EU support to DDR should take into account root causes of conflict and not undertake activities that could perpetuate or aggravate real and perceived grievances in society. Particular attention should be paid to historic, geographical, ethnic, religious characteristics of the country and should lead to community targeted programs.

53. *The EU should pay particular attention to co-operation with other actors*

The UN and other international actors in DDR activities, like the World Bank should remain key channels for EU support. The role of and support to local, national and regional actors is especially important given the principle of local, national and regional ownership. In most cases Non-Governmental Organisations are very active in this area, including in terms of implementing EU support. The private sector is a key player in post-conflict circumstances in income generation, sustainable job creation and recruitment as well as improving vocational training. Consequently, co-ordination and co-operation, involving all stakeholders, including national governments, local authorities, civil society, NGOs, the private sector, international and regional organisations, Member States and other participants, are essential.

H. MEASURES TO STRENGHTEN EU'S SUPPORT TO DDR IN THE FUTURE

The EU is able to bring together a bandwidth of capacities to conduct a full range of actions needed to support DDR, ranging from crisis management and peace building to support to democratic governance processes, the rule of law and human rights, and long-term development. Efforts should be made to mainstream DDR into the various EU activities in a partner country.

In order to improve the coherence and efficiency of EU engagement in supporting DDR, further consideration should be given to the following aspects.

54. *Political dialogue*

DDR considerations should more systematically be integrated into the political dialogue with relevant partner country, in relation to democratic principles, rule of law, human rights, end of impunity, reconciliation, development and security issues.

55. *Coordination including joint assessments*

Appropriate ways to ensure enhanced coordination between all EU actors should be considered. Early exchange of information as well as joint security assessment and joint assessments regarding DDR needs in the partner country should also be sought. Any joint assessments on the democratic governance situation where available should also be taken into account.

56. *Measuring impact and evaluation*

Impact assessments, monitoring and evaluation should systematically be built into DDR programmes and missions to enable an accurate assessment of their effectiveness. Although success of disarmament and demobilisation is key for the next phase, final appreciation of DDR processes should be linked to the success of their reintegration component. Since reintegration needs to happen in the communities, DDR programmes should be planned and delivered within the framework of community level development and include communities in all stages of the process. Appropriate methods should be defined in order to assess regularly the success of the DDR process and the efficiency of the support given by the EU.

57. *Integration and mainstreaming*

In countries where DDR processes are being implemented, international standards on DDR should be brought to the policy dialogue with partner countries in the preparation of Action Plans and Country Strategy Papers, as appropriate, and with other relevant partners in order to agree on objectives, priorities for action and follow-up mechanisms. Conflict sensitive approaches taking into account the long-term reintegration needs of excombatants should be integrated in relevant development programmes, including in sector programmes dealing with health, education, rural/urban development, Rule of Law and security.

58. *Lessons and experiences*

Lessons learned on DDR should be gathered in a systematic manner in order for the EU, including the institutions and Member states, to draw lessons from previous experiences when preparing and implementing DDR activities.

59. *More effectively address the issue of children affected by armed conflict*

The European Union should support the setting up of the Monitoring and Reporting Mechanism provided for in UNSCR 1612. It should also prioritise efforts to prevent the recruitment of children in the first place, in accordance with the international human rights treaties, conventions and optional protocols, through support to awareness-raising, training and the creation of child protection units and focal points for children within law enforcement institutions. In addition, it should intensify its efforts to implement the 2003 EU Guidelines on Children and Armed Conflicts.

60. *Ensuring a gender perspective*

Gender aspects must be accounted for during the whole DDR process. The European Union must reinforce its action along the lines of the documents "Implementation of UNSCR 1325 in the context of ESDP" and the "Checklist to ensure gender mainstreaming and the implementation of UNSCR 1325 in the planning and conduct of ESDP operations" as well as Council conclusions on promoting gender equality and gender mainstreaming in crisis management[13], when implementing UNSCR 1325 and the relevant international human rights treaties and conventions.

61. *Establishing a pool of experts*

There is a need to strengthen institutional cooperation between the relevant institutions in the Member States, the Commission and Council Secretariat to respond to the need to deploy qualified experts for short, medium and long-term activities and to ensure coherence in profiles, training and equipment for such experts due to be seconded abroad, within the framework of specific DDR pro-

13 Adopted by the Council on 13 November 2006.

grammes. Lessons learned from the Technical Assistance Information Exchange Programme (TAIEX), Twinning and Election monitoring pool of experts, the Civilian Headline Goals 2008 process and the creation of ESDP Civilian Response Teams and EC Assessment and Planning teams, should be taken into account.

62. *Developing DDR-specific training for the mainstreaming of DDR*

For the EU to take a more holistic and comprehensive approach to DDR, specific training should be developed for DDR to help mainstream DDR into programming and to broaden expertise across EU and Member States institutions. National, European Security and Defence College courses and other courses offered through the EU training programme as well as EC training courses should be taken into account.

63. *Funding*

DDR processes demand considerable and sustained human and financial resources to be planned, implemented and monitored and it is important that the EU as a whole is able to prioritise support to DDR and ensure sufficient resources to the process. The EU can use rapid and flexible EC instruments such as the Stability Instrument and, under specific conditions, the Humanitarian Aid instrument. Financing under short term instruments will need to be closely linked to any Member States' bi-lateral funding, and longer-term financing under the Community's geographic and, when appropriate, thematic programmes. From as early a stage as possible funding for DDR needs to be linked with national development plans and the PRSP process, where it is in place.

The EU should continue to use multi-donor trust funds, when applicable and considered the best option, when providing support to DDR, in order to ensure that the whole process is sufficiently funded. ESDP support to DDR would be financed in accordance with Art 28 of the Treaty on the European Union. Concerning all those activities that are not eligible for ODA (Official Development Assistance), for example when disarmament efforts are carried out outside an UN –mandated operation, the EU needs to examine, on the basis of existing treaties and related financial instruments and in cooperation with partner countries and regions, the possibility to finance such activities.

COUNCIL OF THE EUROPEAN UNION

Brussels, 7 December 2006

16387/06
COR 1

LIMITE

COSDP 1018
DEVGEN 316
PESC 1236
CIVCOM 564

CORRIGENDUM TO THE "I/A" ITEM NOTE

From : Secretariat

To : Permanent Representatives' Committee

No. prev. doc. : 13727/4/06 REV 4 COSDP 787 DEVGEN 249

Subject : Draft EU Concept for Support to Disarmament, Demobilisation and Reintegration (DDR)

First paragraph on page 1 should read as follows:

'1. At its meeting on 10 November 2006, CODEV reached an agreement on the content of the draft EU concept for support to disarmament, demobilisation and reintegration (DDR) (doc. 13727/2/06 REV 2) and at its meeting on 1 December 2006, having taken note of the advice of the CIVCOM and the EUMC, the Political and Security Committee agreed to forward the draft EU concept for support to disarmament, demobilisation and reintegration (DDR) (doc. 13727/4/06 REV 4) via COREPER to the Council for approval.'

INDEX

Note: the annexes are not indexed